THE ARCHAEOLOGY OF CHINA

This book explores the roles of agricultural development and advancing social complexity in the processes of state formation in China. Over a period of about 10,000 years, it follows evolutionary trajectories of society from the last Paleolithic hunting-gathering groups, through Neolithic farming villages, and on to the Bronze Age Shang dynasty in the latter half of the second millennium BC. Li Liu and Xingcan Chen demonstrate that sociopolitical evolution was multicentric and shaped by interpolity factionalism and competition, as well as by the many material technologies introduced from other parts of the world. The book illustrates how ancient Chinese societies were transformed during this period from simple to complex, tribal to urban, and preliterate to literate.

Li Liu is Sir Robert Ho Tung Professor in Chinese Archaeology in the Department of East Asian Languages and Cultures at Stanford University. She is the author of two books, *The Chinese Neolithic: Trajectories to Early States* and (with Xingcan Chen) *State Formation in Early China*, as well as more than seventy journal articles in both English and Chinese.

Xingcan Chen is Senior Fellow and Deputy Director of the Institute of Archaeology at the Chinese Academy of Social Sciences as well as Professor in the Department of Archaeology, Graduate School, Chinese Academy of Social Sciences. He is the author of numerous articles and books, including *The History of Chinese Prehistoric Archaeology (1895–1949), Essays on Archaeology*, and (with Li Liu) *State Formation in Early China*.

CAMBRIDGE WORLD ARCHAEOLOGY

SERIES EDITOR
NORMAN YOFFEE, *University of Nevada, Las Vegas*

EDITORIAL BOARD
SUSAN ALCOCK, *Brown University*
TOM DILLEHAY, *Vanderbilt University*
STEPHEN SHENNAN, *University College, London*
CARLA SINOPOLI, *University of Michigan*
DAVID WENGROW, *University College, London*

The Cambridge World Archaeology series is addressed to students and professional archaeologists, and to academics in related disciplines. Most volumes present a survey of the archaeology of a region of the world, providing an up-to-date account of research and integrating recent findings with new concerns of interpretation. While the focus is on a specific region, broader cultural trends are discussed and the implications of regional findings for cross-cultural interpretations considered. The authors also bring anthropological and historical expertise to bear on archaeological problems and show how both new data and changing intellectual trends in archaeology shape inferences about the past. More recently, the series has expanded to include thematic volumes.

RECENT BOOKS IN THE SERIES
STEPHEN D. HOUSTON AND TAKESHI INOMATA, *The Classic Maya*
PHILIP L. KOHL, *The Making of Bronze Age Eurasia*
LAWRENCE BARHAM AND PETER MITCHELL, *The First Africans*
ROBIN DENNELL, *The Palaeolithic Settlement of Asia*
CHRISTOPHER POOL, *Olmec Archaeology and Early Mesoamerica*
SAMUEL M. WILSON, *The Archaeology of the Caribbean*
RICHARD BRADLEY, *The Prehistory of Britain*
LUDMILA KORYAKOVA AND ANDREJ EPIMAKHOV, *The Urals and Western Siberia in the Bronze and Iron Ages*
DAVID WENGROW, *The Archaeology of Early Egypt*
PAUL RAINBIRD, *The Archaeology of Micronesia*
PETER M. M. G. AKKERMANSA AND GLENN M. SCHWARTZ, *The Archaeology of Syria*
TIMOTHY INSOLL, *The Archaeology of Islam in Sub-Saharan Africa*

CAMBRIDGE WORLD ARCHAEOLOGY

THE ARCHAEOLOGY OF CHINA

From the Late Paleolithic to the Early Bronze Age

LI LIU

Stanford University

XINGCAN CHEN

Chinese Academy of Social Sciences

CAMBRIDGE
UNIVERSITY PRESS

CAMBRIDGE
UNIVERSITY PRESS

32 Avenue of the Americas, New York NY 10013-2473, USA

Cambridge University Press is part of the University of Cambridge.

It furthers the University's mission by disseminating knowledge in the pursuit of education, learning and research at the highest international levels of excellence.

www.cambridge.org
Information on this title: www.cambridge.org/9780521644327

First published 2012

A catalogue record for this publication is available from the British Library

Library of Congress Cataloguing in Publication data

Liu, Li, 1953 December 12–
The archaeology of China : from the late paleolithic to the early bronze age / Li Liu,
Xingcan Chen.
   pages cm. (Cambridge world archaeology)
Includes bibliographical references and index.
ISBN 978-0-521-64310-8 (hardback)
1. Prehistoric peoples – China.   2. Archaeology – China – History – 20th century.
3. Antiquities, Prehistoric – China. I. Chen, Xingcan. II. Title.
GN855.C6L64   2012
931–dc23   2011052557

ISBN 978-0-521-64310-8 Hardback
ISBN 978-0-521-64432-7 Paperback

Dedicated to

Professor Kwang-chih Chang

If we have been able to see further, it was only because we stood on the shoulders of giants.

CONTENTS

ILLUSTRATIONS

TABLES

PREFACE

The development of early Chinese civilization occupies a unique position in world history, and new archaeological discoveries from China in recent decades have made Chinese archaeology a fascinating topic for both academic circles and the general public. Nevertheless, because of the linguistic, cultural, and social obstacles that have historically existed between China and the Western world, comprehensive studies of Chinese archaeology published in English for Western readers have been lacking.

The most widely used book on Chinese archaeology in English has so far been *The Archaeology of Ancient China* by the late Professor Kwang-chih Chang. It covers periods from the Paleolithic to early dynasties and was continuously revised during the course of twenty-three years, published in four editions in 1963, 1967, 1977, and 1986. It is a rich sourcebook for scholars and students interested in Chinese archaeology, but its last edition was published twenty-five years ago, and much of the information available then should be updated. As former students of K.-c. Chang, we are responsible for carrying on the mission to which he devoted much of his professional life.

Evidently, there has long been a great need for a book that would cover a longer period of early Chinese history and embrace broader topics commonly treated in the study of world archaeology. Such a book not only should provide basic and up-to-date information on Chinese archaeology, but it should also address some fundamental issues that concern the development of ancient civilization in China and are also relevant to the understanding of social evolution worldwide. This book, therefore, is intended to fulfill this need.

As the title of the book implies, the major theoretical topics covered in it are the roles of agricultural development and state formation in the processes of advancing social complexity within the area defined by modern China. It focuses on a period of about 10,000 years of ancient history, with a brief background of preceding cultural developments up to ca. 24,000 cal. BP. It involves evolutionary trajectories from the last Paleolithic hunting-gathering groups, through Neolithic farming villages, to the Bronze Age Shang dynasty. The book illustrates how ancient societies during this period were transformed from simple to complex, tribal to urban, "uncivilized" to "civilized," and preliterate to literate.

In Chapter 1 we review the history of Chinese archaeology and provide a sociopolitical background for the development of this discipline since the early twentieth century. Chapter 2 introduces the natural environment of China and the relationship between ever-changing ecosystems and human responses and adaptations. Chapter 3 focuses on the transitional period from Pleistocene to Holocene, emphasizing the early Holocene when the last foragers began to intensively exploit plant foodstuffs under conditions of reduced mobility, a subsistence strategy that eventually led to sedentary agriculture. Unlike a recent trend in some archaeological literature that classifies this period as the early Neolithic in China, on the basis of the presence of pottery, we use the term "Epi-paleolithic" to describe those early Holocene sites lacking clear evidence of domestication. A Neolithic revolution, based on current data, appeared around 7000 BC. Chapter 4 is devoted to the origins of animal husbandry and plant domestication; whereas some species were domesticated locally, others were introduced from outside China. Nevertheless, they all became economically significant and contributed to the development of complex society. Chapters 5, 6, and 7 cover the early, middle, and late Neolithic periods, respectively, lasting about five thousand years (ca. 7000–2000 BC). During this period, social stratification emerged, early complex societies rose and fell, populations increased and declined, and fortified settlements were built and collapsed. This turbulent era nevertheless formed the foundation for the development of early states in China. Chapter 8 discusses formation of the first states, Erlitou and Erligang. Social transformations took place not only within the states' core area in the Central Plain, but were also manifested through intensive interactions between the center and periphery, as the state rapidly expanded to the surrounding regions, to control key resources. In Chapter 9 we extend our scope to the Bronze Age cultures in the northern frontiers and beyond, which were contemporary with the Erlitou and Erligang states. This approach helps us to understand social and cultural changes that occurred over a broader region, and how these changes may have influenced the core area of early Chinese states. Chapter 10 is concerned with the late Shang dynasty, the first historical state. At this stage of the narrative, our study is facilitated by the increase in available types of materials to work with, including writing. Because the wealth of information from the late Shang period cannot be fully discussed in this chapter, we focus on the political landscape and regional interactions between Shang and its neighbors, as an overview of this extremely complex dynasty. We end this book, in Chapter 11, with a discussion on some particular characteristics of Chinese civilization, or Chineseness, without attempting to generalize.

In this volume we frequently use the concept "archaeological culture," such as Yangshao culture and Longshan culture. The term has been widely used in Chinese archaeological literature to describe material remains, a concept similar to complexities and horizons in archaeological literature in the West. It refers to a material assemblage with shared characteristics, found in archaeological contexts at multiple sites and distributed through a region. A culture is normally named after the location from which such a material assemblage was first identified (Xia, N. 1959). It is notable that, following Soviet practice introduced in the 1950s, an archaeological culture is often considered in China to correspond with a distinct ethnic entity (Xia, N. 2000). The term "culture" (as used in this book), however, is aligned with the conventional description of archaeological assemblages in time and space, and bears no implication as to the ethnic identity of the people who used these material items.

This book does not cover most of the Paleolithic period, because that subject deserves an independent volume and is beyond our present scope. We conclude the book with the late Shang period because there are already a number of publications devoted to archaeology of the Western Zhou and Eastern Zhou periods during the first millennium BC (Falkenhausen 2006; Hsu and Linduff 1988; Li, F. 2006, 2008; Shelach 2009a). Our primary objective is to present the developmental processes of prehistoric complex societies, which are best manifested by the evolutionary paths from first villages to first states.

To provide the most updated archaeological information, we draw primarily on findings reported in the Chinese literature. Because this book is written for English readers, we have also made efforts to use English sources as much as possible. As for carbon 14 dates, BP is used for uncalibrated dates before the "present" (i.e., 1950), cal. BP for calendar/calibrated dates before the "present" (1950), and BC for calibrated dates before the Common Era. We follow the custom in China for writing Chinese people's names, placing the surname before the given name (e.g., Tong Enzheng), when using references published in Chinese, but use the Western order of names (e.g., Kwang-chih Chang) if the original publication is in English.

We express our sincere gratitude to many individuals and institutions for their support of this project. Many ideas discussed in this book have been inspired by communications over the years with numerous outstanding scholars, who are, to name a few, Henry Wright, Norman Yoffee, David Keightley, Peter Bellwood, Richard Meadow, Ajita Patel, Gary Crawford, Tim Murray, Arlene Rosen, John Webb, Judith Field, Richard Fullagar, Gyoung-Ah Lee, Yun Kuen Lee, Han Wei, Wang Wenjian, Zhao Zhijun, Zhang Juzhong, Jin Zhengyao, Jiang Leping, Jing Zhichun, Tang Jigen, Xu Hong, Liu Guoxiang, Jiao Tianlong, Yang Dongya, Ma Xiaolin, Li Xinwei, Qiao Yu, Dai Xiangming, Sun Zhouyong, Sun Guoping, Zheng Yunfei, Shi Jinming, Song Yanhua, Jiang Zhilong, Min Rui, Fang Hui, Luan Fengshi, Jia Weiming, Ge Wei, Sheahan Bestel, and Duncan Jones. Thomas Bartlett and Victoria Bartlett painstakingly edited the manuscript, and Thomas Bartlett also provided many constructive comments. Wei Ming, Qiao Yu, Zheng Hongli, and Fu Yongxu helped create illustrations. Wang Tao and Qi Chen helped compile the glossary. Research related to this book project was generously supported by the Australian Research Council, the Chiang Ching-kuo Foundation, La Trobe University, Stanford University, and the Institute of Archaeology at the Chinese Academy of Social Sciences.

CHAPTER 1

CHINESE ARCHAEOLOGY: PAST, PRESENT, AND FUTURE

The archaeological materials recovered from the Anyang excavations . . . in the period between 1928 and 1937 . . . have laid a new foundation for the study of ancient China.

(Li, C. 1977: ix)

When inscribed oracle bones and enormous material remains were found through scientific excavation in Anyang in 1928, the historicity of the Shang dynasty was confirmed beyond dispute for the first time (Li, C. 1977: ix–xi). This excavation thus marked the beginning of a modern Chinese archaeology endowed with great potential to reveal much of China's ancient history. Half a century later, Chinese archaeology had made many unprecedented discoveries that surprised the world, leading Glyn Daniel to believe that "a new awareness of the importance of China will be a key development in archaeology in the decades ahead" (Daniel 1981: 211). This enthusiasm was soon shared by the Chinese archaeologists when Su Bingqi announced that "the Golden Age of Chinese archaeology is arriving" (Su, B. 1994: 139–40). In recent decades, archaeology has continuously prospered, becoming one of the most rapidly developing fields of social science in China.

As suggested by Bruce Trigger (Trigger 1984), three basic types of archaeology are practiced worldwide: nationalist, colonialist, and imperialist. China's archaeology clearly falls into the first category. Archaeology in China is defined as a discipline within the study of history that deals with material remains of the past and aims to reveal the laws of historical evolution, based on historical materialism (Xia and Wang 1986: 1–3). This definition, to some extent, summarizes the practice of archaeology in China since the early twentieth century. It consists of two important components: Archaeology is a means to discover the evidence for reconstructing China's national history, on the one hand, and its goal is to verify the Marxist theoretical framework, on the other. The former, in particular, has been the essential objective throughout the development of Chinese archaeology (Chang 1999).

THE FORMATIVE PERIOD (1920s–1940s)

The beginning of modern archaeology can be traced back to 1928, when the Institute of History and Philology, Academia Sinica, launched the excavation of Yinxu (The Waste of Yin), a capital city of the late Shang dynasty, at Xiaotun in Anyang, Henan province. This excavation was the first state-sponsored archaeological project in China. Fifteen seasons of excavation took place between 1928 and 1937, and were ended at the outbreak of the Sino-Japanese War. This series of excavations at Anyang was not a random occurrence, but was preceded by several lines of cultural, political, and technological development that served as the foundation for the establishment of archaeology as a new discipline.

The Historical Context of Chinese Archaeology

There has been a tradition of interest in antiquarianism throughout Chinese history. Many antiquities were thought to possess a divine nature, and some bronze vessels were regarded as symbols of power and authority. This tradition encouraged the collecting and recording of ancient artifacts and, at the end of the nineteenth century, led directly to the discovery and decipherment of oracle bone inscriptions of the Shang dynasty. The discovery of the original source of the oracle bones at Xiaotun in Anyang further facilitated the identification of the late Shang capital city Yinxu at that site (Li, C. 1977).

The emergence of nationalism around the turn of the twentieth century was a significant political stimulus to the development of modern archaeology. Toward the end of the Qing dynasty, many revolutionary intellectuals were discontent and sensed that China under the Manchus was politically and militarily inferior to foreign countries. This discontent led to awakening nationalism. Liang Qichao, a Confucian reformer, was the first to heighten the Chinese national consciousness, particularly in response to Japanese aggression. Writing in a journalistic context, Liang argued in 1900 that people in China had failed to give a consistent name to their own country through history, and had always referred to themselves as people of the current ruling dynasty, which was in some cases not established by Han Chinese. Thus, the name "China" (*Zhongguo*), Liang noted, "is what people of other races call us. It is not a name which the people of this country have selected for themselves" (Liang, Q. 1992: 67–8).

In the early twentieth century, the concept of nationalism was ethnically centered on the Han Chinese, and minority groups were largely neglected (Dikotter 1992: 123–5; Townsend 1996). This ethnocentric nationalism was explicitly addressed by Sun Yat-sen when he said, "China, since the Qin and Han dynasties, has been developing a single state out of a single race" (Sun, Y. 1943: 6). According to Sun, although the Chinese people were distinct from all other "races" of the world, the boundaries of the race were drawn along the borders of the Chinese state, and no comparable ethnic distinctions were made within China itself. Minority peoples were thus expected to adjust their beliefs and behavior if they wished to be counted among the "Chinese people" (Fitzgerald 1996: 69). Within this broad political climate that emphasized China as a whole entity, many Chinese intellectuals constantly endeavored to promote broader consciousness of national identity, and the search for Chinese cultural origins became an important part of their intellectual agenda. The initial impetus for archaeological research was closely tied to this issue.

It should be noted that, after the 1911 revolution, as the revolutionaries gained power and controlled the country, the Chinese nationalism moved away from its racialist/ethnocentric orientation to one of a state-based political entity. In time, the Nationalist government prescribed an elaborate cultural regimen to assist the people of Tibet, Mongolia, Manchuria, and the Xinjiang and Han regions to achieve a thorough comprehension of their common national identity as joint members within a republic of five ethnic peoples (*wuzu gonghe*), and to "recover" the sentiment of "central loyalty" toward the state (Chiang, K.-s. 1947: 10–13). This new concept of multiethnic nationalism, however, seems to have been practiced more in the political arena than in the cultural domain, with the dominant ideology in China remaining centered on the cultural superiority of the Han race. The legendary sage-ruler known to the Chinese as *Huangdi* (often translated as "Yellow Emperor") was progressively elevated to the status of the founding ancestor of the Han Chinese, as a symbol of national identity (Leibold 2006; Liu, L. 1999). It was only after the 1950s, under the rule of Communism, that multiethnic nationalism began to affect archaeology. This is evident in the shift of emphasis from the Central Plain (*Zhongyuan*) to a focus on multiregional development (see later in this chapter). It is not surprising, therefore, that the choice of locations for early excavations done by Chinese archaeologists was based on the primary concern to search for the indigenous cultural origins of the Han Chinese. Moreover, influenced by the May Fourth Movement of 1919, the traditional Confucian ways of learning were criticized, while western science and field methodology became influential (Li, C. 1977: 34–5; Xia, N. 1979). A group of young historians, referred to as "Doubters of Antiquity" (*yigupai*), led by Gu Jiegang (1893–1980), developed a skeptical view of textual accounts of Chinese history. Their mission was to search for scientific evidence by which to reconstruct Chinese history (Schneider 1971). Archaeology, therefore, was endorsed by the *yigupai* as a scientifically based discipline to achieve this goal.

In the early twentieth century, modern archaeological fieldwork methods were introduced into China by Western scholars, who were not, however, necessarily archaeologists. The major investigations by foreigners included surveys of Paleolithic sites in Ningxia, Inner Mongolia, and northern Shaanxi by E. Lecent and P. Teilhard de Chardin; excavations of *Homo erectus* remains at Zhoukoudian near Beijing by O. Zdansky, D. Black, and J. F. Weidenreich; and excavations of a Neolithic site at Yangshao in Henan by J. G. Andersson (Chen, X. 1997; Li, C. 1977).

Zhoukoudian is located at a cluster of limestone hills in Fangshan County, 48 km southwest of Beijing. It became world famous after some of the earliest human fossils were discovered there in limestone caves. The site with abundant fossil remains – referred to as dragon bones (*longgu*) by the locals – was first discovered in 1918, with large-scale excavations following in 1927 under the leadership of the Geological Survey of China. During the first year of excavation (1927) an extremely well-preserved hominid lower molar was discovered, and was named *Sinanthropus pekinensis*, or "Peking Man" (now classified as *Homo erectus pekinensis*), by the Canadian anatomist Davidson Black. In 1929 the Chinese scientist Pei Wenzhong (Pei Wen-chung) discovered the first complete skullcap of Peking Man. Until the excavations were interrupted by World War II in 1937, a large workforce essentially "mined" the deposits at the cave site, removing more than half a million tons of material in the quest for fossils (Jia, L. and Huang 1990; Wu, R. and Lin 1983). At this time in the 1930s, when national unity and ethnic identity were major concerns, the discovery of Peking Man led some academics and government officials to argue that these fossils showed evidence of an indigenous genesis of Chinese ethnicity (Leibold 2006).

The hominid fossils found before World War II and subsequently lost in the confusion of wartime were studied by the German paleontologist J. F. Weidenreich. On the basis of twelve morphological features present in both Peking Man and modern peoples in East Asia, he concluded that some of the genes of Peking Man were transmitted into the modern Mongoloid populations who inhabit the same region of the world (Weidenreich 1943). This view, although controversial, was later adopted by many Chinese archaeologists to support the multiregional development theory of human evolution (Wu, R. and Olsen 1985; Wu, X. 2004).

An equally important discovery around this time was the Yangshao culture found by Johan Gunnar Andersson, a Swedish geologist. He was employed by the Chinese government in 1914 to conduct geological surveys, but it turned out that his achievements in archaeology surpassed those in geology. Andersson first participated in the early expeditions at Zhoukoudian. What made him famous, however, was not Zhoukoudian, but Yangshao village in Henan, where he found and undertook the first excavation of a Neolithic site in China. The name of this village was then used to designate the first recognized Neolithic material assemblage in the region: the Yangshao culture. Andersson asserted that the Yangshao material remains belonged to the ancestors of the Han Chinese, but suggested that the Yangshao pottery was probably transmitted from the West, as the stylistic patterns of Yangshao painted pottery looked similar to those from the Anau culture in Central Asia and the Tripolje culture in southern Russia (Andersson 1923). As a result, Andersson's diffusion hypothesis initiated a decades-long debate on the origins of Chinese culture and civilization (Chen, X. 1997; Fiskesjö and Chen 2004).

It should be noticed that not all foreign expeditions in China were for the purpose of scientific archaeological fieldwork. After the Opium War in 1840, China was forced to open its doors to the world. China soon became a hunting ground for foreign imperial powers, as well as for adventurers from Europe, North America, and Japan – such as Aurel Stein, Sven Hedin, D. Klementz, and P. Pelliot – who were in search of exotic antiquities in the Far East, especially in the northwestern part of China (Chen, X. 1997: 42–51; Hopkerk 1980). These activities began when the government was weak and local officials were corrupt. The treasure hunters were able to carry away large quantities of artifacts from China to their own countries without significant hindrance.

The behavior of these treasure hunters in China was humiliating to Chinese who had a strong nationalist consciousness, especially historians and archaeologists (Brysac 1997). These activities, which were later stopped by the Chinese government, have had a long-term impact on state policies regarding the handling of cultural relics and excavations in China. These policies include the prevention of the export of antiquities from China and prohibitions on foreigners unilaterally conducting archaeological work in China.

The Beginning of Modern Chinese Archaeology

Although the scientific field methods used by Western archaeologists were enlightening to Chinese scholars, their general research orientations were not considered satisfactory. Paleolithic and Neolithic remains were thought by some Chinese scholars to be too remote to be connected directly to early Chinese history (Chen, X. 2009: 109–27; Li, C. 1990 [orig. 1968]), especially the Three Dynasties. Andersson's proposal, which traced the origins of the Yangshao painted pottery to the Near East, was even less appealing. As Fu Sinian (Fu, S. 1996: 187) complained, "the foreign archaeologists in China do not pay any attention to the material which represents indigenous Chinese culture, but are only interested in the remains which indicate cultural connections between China and the West."

Excavations in Anyang

It was in the 1920s that a group of Chinese scholars, who had received training in modern archaeology from Western universities, returned to their homeland with a high spirit of nationalism to build a strong country with science and technology. The first was Li Chi, a PhD trained in physical anthropology at Harvard, who, with others, launched a series of archaeological research projects beginning in 1926. Excavations in Anyang from 1928 through 1937, organized by Li Chi in his position at the Institute of History and Philology, Academia Sinica, were the first attempts to search for indigenous Chinese cultural origins through archaeology.

The excavations in Anyang yielded numerous material remains, including hundreds of bronze objects, nearly 25,000 pieces of inscribed oracle bones, bronze workshops, palace and temple foundations, and large royal tombs. These discoveries proved the site to be a capital city of the late Shang dynasty, and for the first time provided archaeological evidence confirming the existence of ancient indigenous Chinese culture (Li, C. 1977).

The excavations in Anyang not only marked the beginning of modern field archaeology conducted by Chinese scholars in China, but also became a field station where many leading Chinese archaeologists were trained. Most associates of Li Chi who worked in Anyang (such as Tung Tso-pin, Liang Siyong, Kao Ch'ü-hsun, Shih Chang-ju, Guo Baojun, Yin Da, and Xia Nai) became the first generation of Chinese archaeologists who dominated the field for decades on the two sides of the Taiwan Strait (Chang 1981b, 1986a).

Despite the success of the archaeological work at Anyang, there was still a gap in the evidence of material cultures between the historical Shang dynasty and the Neolithic Yangshao, as the latter was then regarded to be a cultural diffusion from the Near East. Chinese scholars were still dissatisfied with the general notion that predynastic cultures in China were derived from ripples of influence extending from the West. Fu Sinian (Fu, S. 1934) made the objection that the study of Chinese history by foreigners was mainly focused on Sino-foreign relationships, which was only a "semi-Chinese" (ban Han) endeavor. He continued, however, that the more important issues to be studied were those "completely Chinese" (quan Han), that is, concerned with building the basic structure of Chinese history.

Discovery of the Longshan Culture

The evident cultural disconnect between Yangshao and Anyang prompted archaeologists to search for a direct progenitor of the Shang, and the general consensus among archaeologists and historians was that the most likely area was in eastern China. After work at Anyang was halted around 1930 due to the civil war, the excavation team moved its operations to Chengziya in Longshan township, Shandong, where Wu Jinding's (Wu Chin-ting) previous preliminary surveys revealed promising discoveries (Fu, S. 1934; Li, C. 1990 [orig. 1934]; Wu, C.-t. 1938).

The excavations at Chengziya were more fruitful than the excavators had expected. Distinctively different from the Yangshao painted pottery, the black pottery from Chengziya was similar to the Neolithic remains found at Hougang in Anyang, which were found directly beneath the Shang cultural remains.

Uninscribed oracle bones found at Chengziya provided an even more direct link between the Longshan and the Shang cultures. The Longshan culture of black pottery in the east (representing indigenous Chinese culture) thus came to be viewed as a system independent from the Yangshao culture of painted pottery in the west (thought to be a result of foreign diffusion). Chinese archaeologists hoped that "if we can trace back the distribution and development of the black pottery culture at Chengziya, most problems in the formative period of Chinese history would be resolved" (Li, C. 1990 [orig. 1934]: 193). Therefore, as Li Chi further pointed out, this discovery not only identified a homeland for a part of the Shang culture but also made a major contribution to knowledge about the origins of Chinese civilization (Chen, X. 2009).

Excavations at Doujitai in Shaanxi

While the Academia Sinica headed by Li Chi was working in Henan and Shandong, the National Beiping Academy, led by Xu Xusheng, carried out excavations at Doujitai in Shaanxi province in 1934–7. The intention of this project was to search for the prehistoric origins of the Zhou dynasty. Su Bingqi, who later became the paramount senior archaeologist in China, participated in this project, which established his first research achievement in ceramic typology, focusing on changing forms of the *li* vessels (Falkenhausen 1999a; Su, B. 1948). Su regarded *li* as a vessel form of diagnostic value for distinguishing ethnic affiliations and Chinese civilization. His approach has served as a model of archaeological methodology for several generations of Chinese students.

Western Origin, Dual Origins, and Indigenous Origin of Chinese Civilization

Identifying the origins of Chinese culture has been one of the most sensitive issues in Chinese archaeology. Upon his discovery of the Yangshao culture, Andersson determined to find the route of the eastward cultural diffusion in northwestern China. On the basis of his findings in the Gansu region, Andersson established a sequence of ceramic cultures that perfectly supported his hypothesis. According to this sequence, the Yangshao culture was preceded by the indigenous Qijia culture in far western China, so that, by extension, an even more remote Western origin of the Yangshao pottery seemed plausible. Discovery of the Longshan culture in the 1930s, however, changed the paradigm that proposed a solely Western origin for Chinese civilization, as inferred from the Yangshao painted pottery. The Longshan culture, characterized by black pottery, was thought to represent the indigenous Chinese culture that arose in eastern China concurrently with, but independently of, the Yangshao culture in western China. As a result, a new concept about the dual origins of Chinese civilization was put forward: Whereas the Yangshao culture diffused from west to east, the Longshan culture moved from east to west. The two traditions were thought to have encountered one another and mixed, later becoming the progenitor of the Shang civilization (Chen, X. 1997: 217–27). This proposition dominated in archaeological circles until the 1950s (Chen, X. 2009: 69–74).

During the Sino-Japanese War (1937–45) and the subsequent civil war (1945–9), major archaeological projects were halted, although some fieldwork was still occasionally carried out in peripheral regions. Xia Nai participated in Academia Sinica's expedition in the northwest, where his excavations yielded stratigraphic evidence indicating that the Qijia culture was in fact later than the Yangshao culture (Xia, N. 2000 [orig. 1946]). This conclusion challenged Andersson's sequence of prehistoric cultures in western China and therefore subverted his theory on the Western origin of the Yangshao culture. Xia Nai's victory over Andersson on this issue became a legend, which has inspired Chinese archaeologists for decades.

During this formative period of the discipline, Chinese archaeologists struggled to achieve two primary objectives: (1) to defend their belief in the indigenous origins of Chinese culture against foreign diffusionism, and (2) to reconstruct a reliable cultural history based on material remains, to resolve awkward uncertainties found in textual records, which had been highlighted by radical historical revisionists known as "Doubters of Antiquity." These objectives, in turn, determined the nature of archaeology as an enterprise closely aligned with the ethnic nationalism centered on the Han Chinese.

DEVELOPMENT OF ARCHAEOLOGY IN THE PEOPLE'S REPUBLIC OF CHINA (1950–PRESENT)

When the Communist Party took over China in 1949, the archaeologists in the Institute of History and Philology at the Academia Sinica divided into two groups. Li Chi and several of his colleagues moved to Taiwan, and Xia Nai and Liang Siyong stayed in the mainland. Xia Nai was the one who eventually gained the most international recognition in the discipline (Chang 1986b; Falkenhausen 1999b). Since the 1950s, archaeological fieldwork, research, and training developed rapidly, but dramatic fluctuations occurred in accord with the vicissitudes of varying political tides. Archaeological activities can be divided into three periods: before, during, and after the Cultural Revolution.

Archaeology Before the Cultural Revolution (1950–65)

Soon after the founding of the People's Republic of China, in the 1950s and early 1960s, archaeology was in high demand by the state, as the country undertook groundbreaking construction projects on a tremendous scale. In 1950, the Institute of Archaeology, led primarily by Xia Nai, was established under the Chinese Academy of Sciences (or Academia Sinica), which changed its name to the Chinese Academy of Social Sciences in 1977. Then, in 1952, Peking University's Archaeology Program, headed by Su Bingqi, was set up under the Department of History. These two newly created organizations were the leading forces in conducting archaeological research and in training young archaeologists at that time. Many provinces also set up an archaeological institute or a Management Bureau of Cultural Relics, which was primarily involved in salvage archaeology. In addition to Peking University, two other universities (Northwest and Sichuan) started archaeology programs to train students. The number of professional archaeologists multiplied from a mere handful before 1949 to more than two hundred by 1965. Moreover, the first radiocarbon laboratory was set up in 1965 at the Institute of Archaeology, Chinese Academy of Sciences, soon followed by a second one at Peking University. Three major archaeological journals – the so-called Three Great Journals, including *Kaogu Xuebao* (Acta Archaeologica Sinica), which resumed its previously interrupted publication under a new name, as well as *Kaogu* (Archaeology) and *Wenwu* (Cultural Relics) – were established in Beijing.

Paleolithic Archaeology

Paleolithic archaeology was carried out by the Institute of Vertebrate Paleontology and Paleoanthropology, Chinese Academy of Sciences. Excavations at Zhoukoudian were resumed after the 1950s. This site has so far yielded hominid fossils of more than 40 individuals dating from 550,000 to 250,000 years ago, more than 100,000 stone artifacts, and a large number of mammalian fossils. In addition, cranial remains of *Homo erectus* dating to 700,000 years ago were discovered in Lantian, Shaanxi province, and two incisors of *Homo erectus* dating to 1.7 million years ago were found in Yuanmou, Yunnan province. Hominid fossils and stone implements belonging to archaic *Homo sapiens* and *Homo sapiens sapiens* were found in many locations over northern and southern China (Liu, Q. 2010; Lü, Z. 2004b; Wu, R. and Olsen 1985).

Neolithic Archaeology

Most fieldwork projects in the 1950s were carried out in the Yellow River Valley in connection with hydraulic construction projects in the region. The excavations at Miaodigou in Shanxian County, Henan province, were a breakthrough that completely changed the proposition of dual origins for Chinese civilization. Archaeologists identified a ceramic assemblage, which they named Miaodigou Phase II, representing a transitional culture between Yangshao and Longshan (Zhongguo Kexueyuan 1959). This discovery confirmed the relationship between the Yangshao and Longshan cultures as being successive, rather than contemporaneous. Chinese civilization, therefore, seems to have derived from a single source – the Yangshao culture, which originated in the Central Plain region (Chang 1963; Chen, X. 2009: 69–74).

It should be noted that the first attempt to interpret ancient Chinese history by using a Marxist model can be traced back to Guo Moruo's (Guo, M. 1930) *A study of ancient Chinese society* (*Zhongguo Gudai Shehui Yanjiu*). In this publication, Guo introduced the Morgan-Engels evolutionary theory described in Engels's (1972 [orig. 1884]) *The Origin of the Family, Private Property and the State*; accordingly, Guo applied concepts such as matrilineal and patrilineal society to Chinese prehistory. These two extremely influential books have shaped archaeological and prehistoric research in China for decades. Under the Communist regime, implementing the Marxist interpretation of Chinese history was seen as a new mission for the discipline, in addition to the search for Chinese cultural origins. The first application of this evolutionary scheme in archaeology was the analysis of a Yangshao site at Banpo near Xi'an. The excavations, led by Shi Xingbang, revealed a large portion of a Yangshao settlement. Based on burials and residential patterns, the Banpo Neolithic village was described as a matrilineal society in which women enjoyed high social status and in which "pairing marriage" was practiced (Zhongguo Kexueyuan 1963). Such statements soon became standard phrases adopted in many interpretations of Neolithic sites dating to the Yangshao period. Although some criticisms demonstrated faults in both theory and applications (Pearson 1988; Tong, E. 1998: 262–72; Wang, N. 1983, 1987), the classic evolutionary model was commonly accepted among Chinese archaeologists then, and has continued to be influential, but to a lesser extent, today (e.g., Zhongguo Shehui Kexueyuan 2010: 204, 413, 652–3).

Archaeology of the Three Dynasties

After 1949, Shang archaeology remained a focus of research, and Anyang resumed its importance as a center of archaeological excavations that yielded royal tombs, sacrificial pits, craft workshops, and inscribed oracle bones. These finds provided enriched understanding of the spatial organization of the site (Zhongguo Shehui Kexueyuan 1994b). In the early 1950s, Shang material remains datable to a period earlier than Anyang were first recognized at Erligang, near Zhengzhou, Henan. A fortified Shang city belonging to the Erligang phase was then found at Zhengzhou. The enormous size of the rammed earth enclosure (300 ha in area) and the abundance of remains found at the site (craft workshops, palace foundations, and elite burials) indicate that it may have predated Anyang as a capital city (Henansheng Wenhuaju 1959). This discovery encouraged archaeologists to search for the earliest remains of the Xia and Shang dynasties. Endeavors devoted to such a search proved fruitful, as the subsequent survey in Yanshi County, western Henan, by Xu Xusheng revealed an even earlier large site, known as Erlitou, which was thought to have been an early dynastic capital city (Xu, X. 1959).

The discovery of Erligang and Erlitou generated considerable debate on many critical issues, such as whether Erlitou was a capital city of the Xia or Shang, which phases of the Erlitou culture belong to the Xia or Shang cultures, and to which capital cities named in ancient texts Erligang and Erlitou correspond. Most such arguments were made on the basis of textual records that were written a thousand or more years after the existence of the putative Xia and documented Shang dynasties, and were reinterpreted by many individuals afterward. As people use different textual sources, which frequently contradict one another, to support their opinions, these debates have continued for decades without reaching consensus (see Chapter 8).

The Central Plain Focus

Archaeological research during the pre–Cultural Revolution period primarily focused on the Central Plain of the Yellow River Valley, where a clear sequence of cultural development could be traced from Yangshao through Longshan to the Three Dynasties. Many Neolithic sites in southern China were also found and excavated, such as Beiyinyangying near Nanjing, Qianshanyang in Zhejiang, and Qujialing in Hubei. These sites, however, yielded neither a material assemblage as old as the Yangshao culture, which was viewed as the earliest Neolithic culture, nor a continued sequence illustrating a regional cultural development. They were regarded as the peripheries of the Central Plain with minor significance for Chinese civilization proper. Such a paradigm of ancient Chinese cultural development was accepted by archaeologists in China and abroad, not only because of the limitations of archaeological findings, but also because the traditional view of Chinese civilization's origins was focused on the Central Plain (Chang 1963, 1977).

Archaeology During the Cultural Revolution (1966–77)

Similar to other disciplines in academic institutions, archaeology was stalled during the early part of the Cultural Revolution. Research and teaching were replaced by insurrection, as most junior members of archaeological institutes and students in universities were busy criticizing the senior archaeologists and professors. Excavations never completely ceased, however, as continuing construction projects always required salvage archaeology. It was also soon recognized by the leadership of the Cultural Revolution that archaeology could serve as an instrument of propaganda for political purposes. Sending museum exhibitions of archaeological findings to foreign countries was considered useful to improve China's international relationships and promote China's image as a great civilization; evidence of a highly developed material culture recovered from ancient times could reconfirm Chinese people's national pride; and the wealth discovered from elite burials could be used for mass socialist education, in terms of class consciousness. Cultural relics unearthed in the People's

Republic of China were displayed for the first time in Paris and London in 1973 to demonstrate the glory of Chinese civilization and the achievements of archaeology in New China (Xia, N. 1973). Elaborately constructed ancient architecture, burials, and artifacts were interpreted as testimony of class oppression and exploitation of the poor by the rich.

To meet these new demands, the three major archaeological publications – *Kaogu, Kaogu Xuebao,* and *Wenwu* – were resumed in 1972, after being discontinued in 1966. *Wenwu* became a popular magazine, as most journals with intellectual content in the social sciences ceased publication. Between 1972 and 1977, eight new archaeology programs were established in universities (Shanxi, Jilin, Nanjing, Xiamen, Shandong, Zhengzhou, Zhongshan, and Wuhan), to train much needed archaeologists for the rapidly expanding discipline.

Excavations of Neolithic sites were carried out in many regions, such as Dawenkou in Shandong, Cishan in Hebei, Jiangzhai in Shaanxi, Liuwan in Qinghai, Daxi in Sichuan, Honghuatao in Hubei, Caoxieshan in Jiangsu, Hemudu in Zhejiang, Sanyuangong in Hunan, and Shixia in Guangdong. These sites provided rich information for the understanding of prehistoric development in different regions. In addition, by 1977 the Radiocarbon Laboratories at the Institute of Archaeology and Peking University had published four sets of ^{14}C dates, providing some early absolute dates from Neolithic sites outside the Central Plain, which revolutionized archaeological research (Xia, N. 1977).

The discoveries of several Neolithic sites in southern China were especially important. The Hemudu site in the lower Yangzi River Valley yielded the earliest evidence of rice cultivation in China, as radiocarbon dates pointed to a period as early as the Yangshao culture. The Hemudu culture seems to have been succeeded by a series of Neolithic assemblages, referred to as Majiabang, Songze, and Liangzhu, which formed a continued cultural sequence in the region. These new data seriously challenged the traditional view that regarded the Central Plain as the only center of the developmental process of Chinese civilization, as for the first time it was realized that the notion of a single origin of Chinese Neolithic culture needed to be reconsidered (Xia, N. 1977) and that southeast China, meaning primarily the lower Yangzi River Valley and environs, may have played an important role in the development of Chinese civilization (Su, B. 1978a; Xia, N. 1977).

Most discoveries that made newspaper headlines during the Cultural Revolution were elite tombs that had been discovered accidentally. In 1976, for example, archaeologists excavated a well-preserved, late Shang royal burial, Tomb no. 5, in Anyang. Based on bronze inscriptions found in the burial, the tomb was determined to have belonged to Fuhao, who was referred to as a consort of King Wuding in oracle-bone inscriptions. In addition to a large amount of bronze and jade artifacts unearthed from the tomb, this discovery served a more significant function: For the first time, a named individual in the oracle-bone inscriptions was identifiable in an archaeological context (Zhongguo Shehui Kexueyuan 1980).

Despite numerous new discoveries, theoretical interpretations were dry and dogmatic. This situation was inevitably affected by the political climate of the era. Restrictive policies regarding foreign relations blocked exchange of information between China and Western countries, and the only theoretical frameworks applicable at the time were those of Marxism and Maoism. Mortuary and settlement data obtained from many Neolithic sites were commonly used to support Morgan-Engels or Marx-Lenin style propositions regarding the emergence of private property, class differentiation, the practice of matrilineal or patrilineal social organizations, and state formation as the result of class conflict. In some publications, which were purely data descriptions, Marxist and Maoist slogans were formulaically inserted into the contents but appeared superficial and far-fetched. Lack of fresh theoretical approaches prevented archaeologists from engaging in critical discussion, and rapid accumulation of archaeological data also forced scholars into preoccupation with articulating the relevant sequences of material culture, leaving no time for theoretical thinking. Chinese archaeology, therefore, remained a discipline largely defined by efforts to correlate dual traditions of artifact-oriented typology and textually based historiography (Chang 1981b).

Archaeology in the Post-Cultural Revolution Era (1978–Present)

After the Cultural Revolution, the relatively relaxed political atmosphere and the implementation of economic reform promoted new developments on all fronts of Chinese archaeology. Salvage excavations conducted by regional archaeological institutes have been in extremely high demand, as a decentralized economic system has stimulated construction projects across the country. Provincial institutes have become financially dependent on salvage archaeology. Many more universities have developed archaeology programs, training hundreds of archaeologists each year. These new graduates soon become the key staff of local archaeological institutes. The number of archaeological periodicals multiplied from a few (mainly the Three Great Journals) before the Cultural Revolution to a list (by 1991) of some 140 periodicals on archaeology-related subjects, most of which are published at local venues (Falkenhausen 1992). As a result, provincial archaeological institutions have become increasingly independent of the Institute of Archaeology in Beijing with regard to administrative, academic, and financial matters (Falkenhausen 1995).

Economic reform has also opened China's doors to the world more broadly. As a result, scholarly exchange between China and Western countries has been actively encouraged, and Western archaeological methods and theories have been introduced. Archaeology in China has found itself facing new challenges from the outside world. During the 1980s and 1990s, as Deng Xiaoping was seeking a route for China to become a Chinese-style socialist country, archaeologists were struggling to define and formulate an archaeology with Chinese characteristics. Nationalist feelings have recently increased among Chinese intellectuals in various fields, partially as a reaction to rapidly changed relationships between China and the rest of the world. Therefore, archaeology in this era has also been influenced by the new concept of multiethnic nationalism.

As large quantities of archaeological data from all periods have been accumulated during recent decades, three major topics have become the focal points of Chinese archaeological research on ancient China: the origins of early humans, the origins of agriculture, and the origins of civilization.

In China to date, approximately 1,000 Paleolithic sites have been located and more than 100 excavated (Lü, Z. 2004a). As world Paleolithic archaeology has been engaged in the debate between the "out-of-Africa" (single-place origin) and "multiregional development" schools regarding the origin of modern humans, evidence from China has become crucial. Whereas some scientists are favorable to the "out-of-Africa" theory on the basis of genetic evidence (e.g., Jin, L. and Su 2000; Ke, Y. et al. 2001), the majority of Chinese archaeologists and paleontologists supports the multiregional development model, proposing a hypothesis of regional continuity with hybridization between immigrants and indigenous populations in the evolution from *H. erectus* to *H. sapiens* in East Asia (e.g., Gao, X. 2010; Gao, X. and Wang 2010; Wu, X. 1997, 2004). This argument is primarily based on two factors. First, in accordance with Weidenreich's observations published in 1943, paleontologists continue to find morphological characteristics that are shared by East Asian hominid fossils and modern populations in the same region; the continuous evolution of a series of inherited characteristics indicates that no major population replacement occurred in China (cf. Jin, C. et al. 2009; Shang, H. et al. 2007; Wu, X. 1997, 1999). Second, after decades of fieldwork, archaeologists have gradually defined regional lithic traditions throughout the Paleolithic period in China, which show strong local continuities and are evidently distinct from those in Africa and Europe (Gao, X. and Hou 2002; Wang, Y. 2005; Zhang, S. 1990). Apparently, archaeological data show continuous human activities in the region with no evidence for a large-scale interruption of evolution (Gao, X. 2010).

The Peking Man site at Zhoukoudian has continued to play an important role in the reconstruction of early Chinese history. Lewis Binford and Chuan Kun Ho challenged the long-established conclusions that Peking Man controlled fire and that the Zhoukoudian cave was the home of Peking Man (Binford and Ho 1985). Many Chinese archaeologists were outraged, and Jia Lanpo, one of the excavators of Zhoukoudian, defended the original understanding of Peking Man's unique status with great passion (Jia, L. 1991). The strong reaction from the Chinese archaeological community is understandable if the issue is placed in the context of rising nationalist sentiment in China. Within the framework of the regional evolutionary model, Peking Man appears to have been one of the direct, albeit remote, ancestors of the nation.

The origins of food production and civilization are the topics that have drawn the most attention from Chinese archaeologists, and they will be discussed in detail in the following chapters.

During recent decades, numerous archaeological discoveries have been made, mostly in areas outside the Central Plain. In southern China, new evidence indicates that this region not only had its own indigenous origins of Neolithic traditions (earliest rice and pottery), and evolved into complex societies at the same time as, if not earlier than, the Central Plain, but also developed high-level, Bronze Age cultures with characteristics distinct from those of the Central Plain. Several Neolithic walled settlements have been found in the Yangzi River Valley, and the one found at Bashidang in Hunan (ca. 7000–5800 BC) marks the earliest example of walled settlements in China. In the lower Yangzi River Valley, distinctive elite tombs filled with large quantities of jade objects first occurred in the Songze culture (Dongshancun in Zhangjiagang City, Jiangsu) (ca. 3800 BC) (Zhou, R. et al. 2010) and then became prevalent in the Liangzhu culture (ca. 3200–2000 BC). The high level of craftsmanship, reflected in jade manufacture and construction of large burial mounds, has led some archaeologists to argue for the existence of early states in the Liangzhu culture. In the upper Yangzi River Valley, sacrificial pits containing large numbers of bronze figurines – life-size or bigger – have been discovered at Sanxingdui in Sichuan, revealing a previously unknown kingdom with a highly developed bronze culture contemporary with the earliest dynasties in the Central Plain.

In northeastern China, the Neolithic tradition now can be traced back to the Xinglongwa culture (ca. 6200–5200 BC) in Liaoning and Inner Mongolia. Complex societies seem to have evolved around 3500 BC in this region, indicated by the construction of large public architecture and elite burials in the late Hongshan culture, especially at the Niuheliang site. These astonishing discoveries completely changed the traditional view, which regarded peoples outside the Central Plain as barbaric and uncivilized.

In eastern China, including Shandong and northern Jiangsu, archaeologists discovered the earliest Neolithic assemblage at Houli in Shandong (ca. 6200–5600 BC), which was followed by the Beixin, Dawenkou, and Longshan cultures, forming another regional tradition of cultural development. Many elaborately furnished elite burials and more than a dozen walled settlements dated to the Dawenkou and Longshan periods (ca. 4100–2000 BC) have also been found, generating more claims for the emergence of state-level societies in the Neolithic period in this region.

In the Central Plain, primarily including the middle Yellow River, the Fen River, and the Wei River Valleys, and traditionally regarded as the center of

Chinese civilization, archaeological findings seem to demonstrate a cultural tradition that may not have been much more advanced than those in the "peripheries" during the Neolithic period. Similar to the antiquity of other locally developed regional cultures, the Neolithic traditions of the Central Plain can be traced to the Peiligang culture of 7000 BC, which was followed by continuing development through the Yangshao and Longshan cultures. Although Yangshao elite burials associated with jades and large houses used for ritual purposes occurred by 3500 BC in the middle Yellow River region (Wei, X. and Li 2003; Zhongguo Shehui Kexueyuan and Henansheng 2010), these features are not unique among, and certainly not earlier than, comparable remains in other regions.

Diversified regional cultural traditions are easily observable based on these new data, which have encouraged new interpretations concerning the origins of civilization in China.

INTERPRETATIONS

Interpretations of archaeological findings have been primarily concerned with two major topics: reconstruction of spatiotemporal framework of material remains and reconstruction of national history.

Multiregional Development of Civilization in China

A research model known as "regional systems and local cultural series," *quxi leixing*, was first proposed by Su Bingqi in the early 1980s (Su, B. and Yin 1981; Wang, T. 1997). It is based mainly on ceramic assemblages, with an emphasis on the independent development of, and interaction between, different regional cultural traditions. The *quxi leixing* concept was intended to provide a methodological framework for the reconstruction of Chinese prehistory, as it shifted away from the center-periphery model toward a multiregional approach to the development of Chinese civilization. As stated by Su Bingqi (1991), after 10,000 BP six relatively stable regional divisions (*quxi*) had formed within the area much later embraced by historical China. The six regional cultures are further divided into a number of local phases (*leixing*). Each of these regions, according to Su, had its own cultural origins and developments, and interacted with the others in the developmental processes of Chinese civilization. Yan Wenming (Yan, W. 1987) also suggested a similar model for "the unity and variability of Chinese prehistoric culture," seeing the Central Plain as the center of a flower and cultural traditions in the surrounding areas as layers of petals. Instead of giving equal weight to all regional cultures, as implied in Su's hypothesis, Yan's model emphasizes the leading role of the Central Plain in the processes toward civilization, while acknowledging the existence of elements of civilization in the peripheries during prehistory.

The general trend, of a shift from monocentered to multicentered development of Chinese civilization, which Falkenhausen (1995: 198–9) observed, is also reflected in the four editions of *Archaeology of Ancient China* by K. C. Chang, which have been the most comprehensive and authoritative reference sources on Chinese archaeology in English for decades. In the first three editions, published in 1963, 1968, and 1977, the Central Plain was seen as the nucleus within which complex society and dynastic civilization rose. In the fourth edition published in 1986, this view was replaced by the concept of "Chinese interaction sphere," covering a geographic dimension much broader than the Central Plain, and providing an enlarged foundation for the development of the Three Dynasties (Chang 1986a: 234–42).

Such a change of paradigm in Chinese archaeology seems to integrate well with a new perspective in the reconstruction of national history.

National History and the Origins of Civilization

Ever since the day of its birth in the Anyang excavation of 1928, Chinese archaeology has had one clear objective: to reconstruct the national history. The concepts of nation, and thus also of the national history, however, have changed over time. These reconstruction tasks have been inevitably affected by new perspectives on national history.

As the state has attempted to bring China's multiethnic population into a viable political entity since the 1950s, the concept of the Chinese nation has become equivalent to that of the state, best described by Fei Xiaotong (Fei 1989) as a "single entity with multiple components" (*duoyuan yiti*). As argued by Fei, China as a nation (a substance without self-consciousness) has gradually come into existence through thousands of years. This formative process was amalgamative, with a dominant core constituted by the Huaxia, and then by the Han people. The cultural interaction between the Huaxia-Han and other groups, however, was not a matter of one-way diffusion, but of mutual influence. This national entity now, according to Fei, includes all ethnicities (more than fifty) residing within the entire territory of modern China. It seems that this new concept of national identity fits relatively well with the archaeological *quxi leixing* paradigm and, in particular, with the "unity and variability" hypothesis. Evidently the archaeological and sociological models mutually support each other in constructing the national history.

With increased knowledge of regional archaeological cultures, scholars have developed a strong willingness to construct cultural history based on archaeological material remains in conjunction with the historical record. There has been a tendency to identify archaeological cultures, phases, sites, and even artifacts directly with specific ancient groups of people or places named in legendary or historical literature. The continuous debates on textual identification of several Bronze Age cities – such as Erlitou, Erligang, the Yanshi

Shang city near Yanshi, and Xiaoshuangqiao near Zhengzhou – best exemplify this attempt (see Chapter 8). By doing so, archaeological assemblages (mainly defined by pottery types) become historically meaningful, although the logical connections between the two sets of information – ceramic typology and ethnic affiliation – have not been made explicit.

The phrase "five-thousand-year history of civilization" has been commonly used in China to summarize the national history, and the archaeology profession is committed to tracing its origins and to demonstrating the processes of this history. Because dynastic history, as recorded retrospectively in late antiquity, is said to have begun no earlier than ca. 2070 BC (Xia Shang Zhou 2000), much effort has been made to connect regional Neolithic cultural developments with the putative activities of predynastic legendary kings and sages, such as the so-called Wudi (often dubiously translated as "Five Emperors"), to fill the time gap of a thousand years. Attempts have also been made to link certain cultural achievements with the dawn of civilization, such as the manufacture of jade objects and the construction of large ceremonial monuments, which are traceable to the Neolithic period. As a consequence, not only are legends read as reliable history and used to interpret Neolithic archaeology, but also the origins of Chinese civilization are pushed back 1,000 or more years to match counterparts in Mesopotamia and Egypt (Su, B. 1988, 1997). In the early twentieth century when the *yigupai* questioned traditional texts, they hoped that archaeologists would uncover reliable ancient history from the field. For many archaeologists today, these legendary accounts are seen as blueprints for reconstructing prehistory, and the *yigupai* has become the target of criticism (e.g., Li, X. 1997b).

A state-directed project in the 1990s pushed this endeavor to its peak. In his visit to Egypt, State Councilor Song Jian was introduced to a detailed chronological record of dynastic Egypt that started from 3100 BC. Dissatisfied with the Chinese dynastic chronology, which not only begins 1,000 years later but also is less precise than that of Egypt, Song Jian called for a project to reconstruct an accurate chronology of the Three Dynasties, so that Chinese civilization would be comparable to that of Egypt. This project, known as the Xia-Shang-Zhou Chronology Project, was officially launched in 1996. For nearly four years, more than 200 experts in history, archaeology, paleography, astronomy, and radiocarbon dating technology were involved in the project, focusing on nine primary research topics, which were further divided into 44 subtopics. The project has achieved four of its originally prescribed objectives: (1) to provide accurate dates for a time period from the conquest of the Shang by the Zhou to the beginning of recorded chronology in 841 BC; (2) to determine relatively accurate chronology for the late Shang period; (3) to define a relatively detailed time frame for the early Shang period; and (4) to outline a basic time frame for the Xia dynasty. By completion of the project, the chronology of the Three Dynasties has indeed become more precise and detailed than before (Lee, Y. 2002; Xia Shang Zhou 2000). The project, however, has not made Chinese civilization temporally comparable with some older civilizations in other parts of the world, but instead has generated much debate on its goals, methods, and results (e.g., Jiang, Z. 2002; Liu, Q. 2003; Liu, X. 2001; Shaughnessy 2008).

Regardless of the ongoing debate on details of the project results, the Xia-Shang-Zhou Chronology Project has inspired a series of programs under a new research scheme, known as the Searching for the Origins of Chinese Civilization Project. By using multidisciplinary methods, this project aims to determine dynastic ancestries and the earliest civilizations in Neolithic times (Wang, W. and Zhao 2010; Yuan, J. and Campbell 2008).

INTERNATIONAL COLLABORATIVE RESEARCH IN CHINA

Since the 1980s, scholarly exchange between China and foreign countries has increased dramatically. It has also evolved from exchanging ideas at international conferences to jointly conducting field research. In 1991, the Chinese National Bureau of Cultural Relics released a document on policies for Sino-foreign collaborative research in archaeology (Guojia 1992), which, after more than forty years, reopened the door for foreign archaeologists to work on China's soil. Many collaborative projects have been carried out in recent years in regions across the country. International scholarly exchange has also introduced Western theories to China, which have to some extent enriched research orientations and interpretations. New methods and technologies introduced in fieldwork and laboratory analyses include systematic use of the flotation method in recovering macrofaunal and macrofloral remains; full-coverage regional survey methods, incorporation of regional survey with geoarchaeology, geographic information system (GIS) applications, and remote sensing in the study of settlement patterns; mineralogical studies of archaic jade; development of interdisciplinary approaches such as zooarchaeology, archaeobotany, and environmental archaeology; and application of advanced laboratory technology such as the Accelerator Mass Spectrometry dating method, genetic studies, and analyses of phytoliths, starch, isotopes, and stone tool use-wears. The introduction of these methods and techniques has brought Chinese archaeological research to a higher level of sophistication.

A new generation of Chinese archaeologists who received PhDs from foreign universities in North America, Europe, Australia, and Japan since the 1990s has either returned to China or worked in archaeological institutions outside China. With their up-to-date knowledge of Western archaeological method and theory, they have also been making important contributions, by introducing new ideas and using new methods and techniques in collaborative research projects. The discipline has become more internationalized than ever in this Golden Age of Chinese archaeology.

Interestingly, the research orientations of these Sino-foreign collaborative projects seem to follow some traditional patterns. Most projects initiated by Western archaeologists have primarily focused on Paleolithic and Neolithic sites or on cultures in peripheral areas, which appeal to internationally oriented research topics, whereas projects designed by overseas Chinese archaeologists tend to focus on the Central Plain in search of the developmental processes of Chinese civilization (Liu, L. and Chen 2001c).

CONCLUSIONS

The birth of modern Chinese archaeology in the early twentieth century was a product of the introduction of Western scientific methods, the rise of nationalism, and the search for the cultural origins of the nation. These three factors have had a continuing influence on the development of this discipline, with the consequence that archaeology in China has been firmly placed in the general field of history. Its research orientations and interpretations have been significantly affected by different political agendas of the nation – especially the ever-changing concept of nationalism in particular eras (Chang 1998).

Archaeologists have worked hard to overcome all kinds of economic, social, and political difficulties during turbulent eras, and have made extraordinary contributions to the field. Our understanding of ancient China has been markedly improved because of these archaeological achievements. In many cases, archaeology has been driven by the contemporary trend toward a more multiethnic concept of nationalism and used as an instrument to support, rather than to evaluate, particular theoretical themes or political agendas. In other situations, it has provided independent data for creating new paradigms, which changed traditional perspectives toward Chinese national history. State-promoted nationalism has indeed played an important role in shaping the discipline. For many individual archaeologists, participating in the construction of national history confers dignity and pride as Chinese citizens.

The emergence and development of an interest in archaeology cannot be understood apart from contextualization within the prevailing local sociopolitical framework. In many countries, nationalism has shaped the assumptions, methods, and practices of the discipline of archaeology, and archaeological inquiry and achievements have also influenced ideals concerned with the building of national identity (e.g., Diaz-Andreu 2001; Kohl and Fawcett 1995; Smith A. 2001; Trigger 1984). Nationalist archaeology, as Trigger (1984: 360) observed, tends to become strongest among peoples who feel politically threatened, insecure, or deprived of their collective rights by more powerful nations. This was certainly the case when archaeology was first established in China. Today, although China has become much more secure and prosperous economically, the need for building national identity seems to have not diminished. Therefore, despite growing influences from Western ideology and technology during recent decades, which in many cases are positive, the general objective for the mainstream of Chinese archaeology has not changed significantly – the discipline is committed to the reconstruction of national history. This mission will probably continue (Su, B. 1991). It is also notable, however, that more varied research approaches have emerged in recent years. Whereas some archaeologists continue to pursue regional historical issues, others have become engaged in theory building and cross-cultural comparative studies, which have endowed the discipline with a more international outlook.

Chinese archaeology has made enormous contributions to our understanding of world history, and its Golden Age is likely to continue for many years to come.

CHAPTER 2

ENVIRONMENT AND ECOLOGY

> In all their settlements, the bodily capacities of the people are sure to be according to the sky and earthly influences, as cold or hot, dry or moist. Where the valleys are wide and the rivers large, the ground was differently laid out; and the people born in them had different customs.
>
> Chapter, "Royal Regulations" in *Book of Rites* (written in 475–221 BC); translated by James Legge (1960b)
>
> 凡居民材, 必因天地寒暖燥湿, 广谷大川异制, 民生其间者异俗。《礼记·王制》

Situated between latitudes 20° and 54°N and between longitudes 30° and 75°E, China has a vast territory, measuring approximately 9,600,000 km² in area. The current administrative districts include 22 provinces, five Autonomou Regions, and four municipalities, in addition to Taiwan (Figure 2.1), comprising 56 ethnic groups. China is characterized by geographic, climatic, cultural, and ethnic diversities.

GEOGRAPHY

Viewed within a broad geographical perspective, China is surrounded by a series of natural barriers: boreal, desert, and high mountains stretch along its northern, western, and southwestern borders, and oceans embrace its eastern and southeastern shores. It has long been recognized that, under such circumscribed physical conditions, China's prehistoric culture developed without significant direct interactions with other major Old World civilizations (Murphey 1972; Yan, W. 1987). It is notable, however, that China's northern frontiers are open, as the mountain chain from the northeast to northwest leaves many wide gaps, through which pathways formed that have facilitated contacts between China and its neighbors since antiquity. Therefore, Chinese civilization was far from evolving in isolation. Such interactions started long before the dramatic expansion, some 2,000 years ago, of cross-continental trade

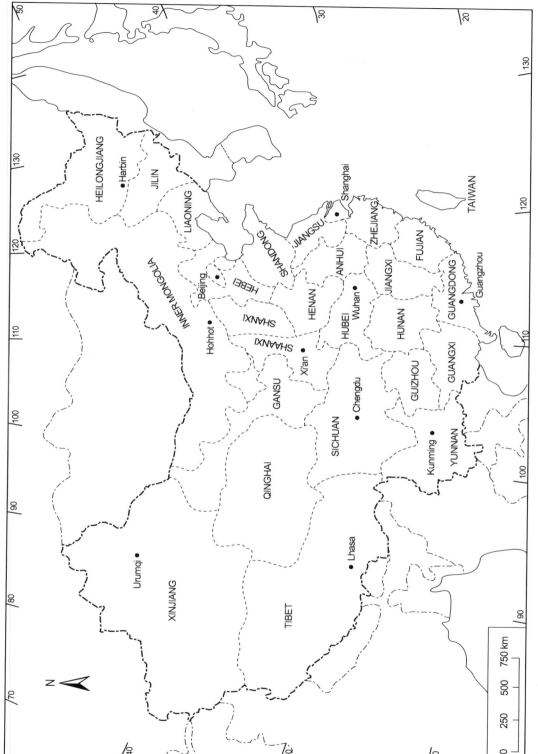

Figure 2.1. Administrative divisions of China.

along routes (known since the nineteenth century as the "Silk Road") that connected ancient Chinese dynastic capitals with the Roman Empire.

China can be topographically described, in brief, as highlands in the western part and lowlands in the eastern, and the entire country can also be divided into seven ecological zones, on the basis of natural conditions, agricultural potential, and current provincial units. These zones are (1) North China, in the middle and lower Yellow River Basin; (2) humid, temperate Northeast China; (3) arid Northwest China, including most of Inner Mongolia; (4) Central China, in the middle and lower Yangzi River Basin; (5) humid subtropical and tropical South China; (6) humid subtropical and tropical Southwest China; and (7) the Tibetan Plateau, in China's far west (Figure 2.2) (Zhao, S. 1994). These zones are each characterized by particular geomorphological features (Figure 2.3).

All of western, together with part of southwestern, China consists of great upland subregions, separated from each other by massive mountain systems. The most dramatic part of the western landscape is the Tibetan Plateau, which averages well over 3,500 m in altitude and is surrounded by mountains, including the Karakoram, Pamir, Kunlun, and Himalayan ranges. Most of Tibet is a dry and cold alpine desert, unsuitable for farming except in a few lowland pockets (Tregear 1965, 1980).

The most northwesterly subregion is Xinjiang. In southern Xinjiang the Tarim Basin, with a general altitude of 1,000 m, is hemmed in by great mountain ranges: the Pamirs on the west, the Tian on the north, and the Kunlun on the south. The basin is dominated by the Taklamakan desert in the center and is sparsely watered by glacier-fed streams that originate in the surrounding heights, supporting many oases that fringe the northern and southern edges of the desert. To the northeast of the Tarim Basin is the Turpan Basin, which is 154 m below sea level and well known for its extremely dry climate. Further to the north lies the triangular Dzungarian Basin, where the lowest point is 300 m above sea level. Its sides are bordered by mountain ranges: the Tian on the south, the Altai on the northeast, and the Tarbagatai on the northwest; the three corners are relatively open to access (Tregear 1965, 1980). Through the oases scattered in these basins lie ancient trade routes, the Silk Road. After the Han dynasty extended its rule through the Hexi corridor (or Gansu corridor) around 2,100 years ago, the Yellow River heartland of China became directly linked to these ancient trade routes and thus distantly connected with remote regions in Central Asia and beyond. The arid climate in Xinjiang has helped to preserve enormous numbers of artifacts and human burials, providing unique opportunities for archaeologists to study ancient ways of life there.

East of Xinjiang lies the vast Mongolian steppe, divided by the Gobi desert into Inner Mongolia to the south and the independent republic now called simply Mongolia, to the north. Much of Inner Mongolia is a long-grass steppeland ideally suited to grazing, and has served historically as the basis for pastoral and,

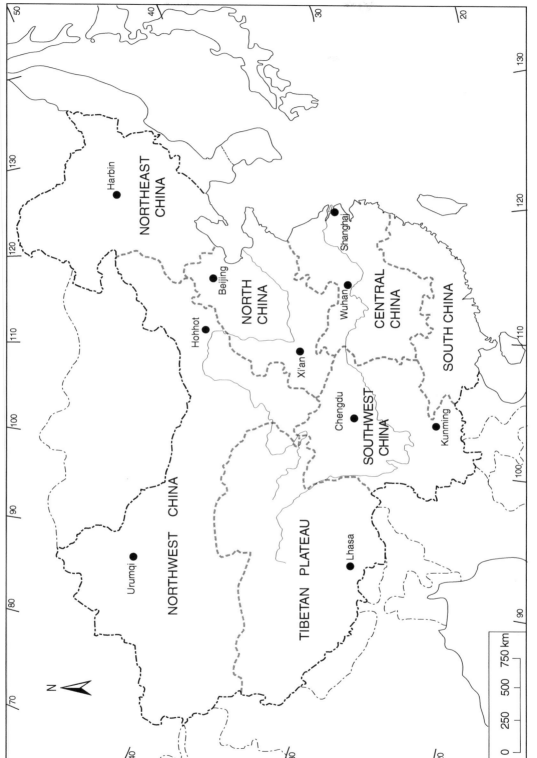

Figure 2.2. Ecological zones of China.

later, pastoral-nomadic economies (Tregear 1965, 1980). The developmental process of pastoralist adaptations in the steppe has included complex and contradictory interactions with agriculturalists to the south, including both trade and warfare. Walls to separate the pastoral and agricultural domains were first built by several feudal states in north China during the pre-imperial late Eastern Zhou period. Under unified imperial rule of the Qin and Han dynasties, when abiding patterns of Sino-barbarian relations took form, remaining early northern walls were consolidated and extended to form the Great Wall, made of tamped earth. Repeatedly rebuilt in later centuries, and finally of stone in the sixteenth century, it manifests the long-term recurrence of hostile relations between the sedentary and nomadic societies.

East of Inner Mongolia lies the Northeast Plain, also known as Manchuria. It is bounded by the Greater Xing'an Mountains on the west, the Lesser Xing'an Mountains on the north, and the Changbai Mountains on the east, separating China from Korea. The northern part of the Northeast Plain, which is bitterly cold in winter, is marginal for farming, whereas the southern part, especially the Liao River valley, is milder (Tregear 1965, 1980). Some early Neolithic villages have been found in the Liao River region, marking it as one of the earliest sites of sedentary communities in China.

The heartland of China proper is generally described as composed of three great river valleys, with their adjacent plains: The Yellow (Huang) River in north China, the Yangzi River (Changjiang) occupying most of central China, and the Pearl (Zhu) River in the far south. The Huai River and Qinling Mountains demarcate North from Central China, and the Nanling Mountains separate Central from South China. In addition to this geographically accurate three-part division, another influential two-part distinction is often cited, by which subtropical south China and temperate north China are divided along an east-west axis formed by the Huai River and the Qinling Mountains (Figure 2.3). This demarcation marks general ecological and cultural differences between south and north, which can be traced back to early historical times (Gong, S. 1994; Wang, Y. 1988; Yu, W. 2010). In this book both of these systems of geographical division are used, as both have been adopted by researchers in various contexts. To avoid confusion, in the following chapters "north China" and "south China" will refer to the two parts of China proper, as described earlier in this section, whereas "North China," "Northeast China," and "South China" are used in reference to two of the seven ecological zones defined at the start of this chapter.

RIVER SYSTEMS

Three major river systems in China formed great alluvial plains, where agriculture was most productive and water transport was possible. It is in these river valleys and flood plains that the major centers of early Chinese civilization were formed.

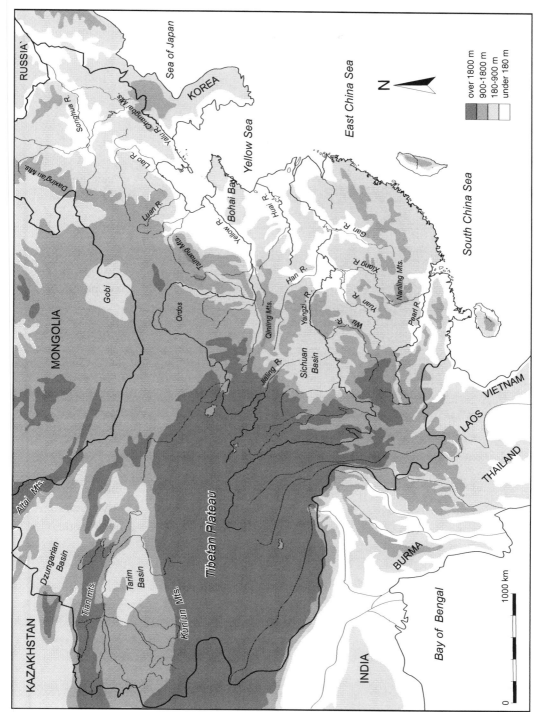

Figure 2.3. Geomorphology of China.

The Yellow River rises on the eastern slopes of the Tibetan plateau, running northeast in a great loop through the steppe-desert area, into the Ordos and the North Shaanxi and Shanxi Loess Plateau, before turning east across the great North China Plain and the Shandong peninsula, and finally emptying into the sea.

The fertile, yellow type of soil called loess (derived from a German word meaning "loose") dominates a large part of the upper and middle Yellow River Valley, reaching a thickness of up to 400 m in some areas. It is easily eroded by wind and water, even on gentle slopes, and agricultural activities accelerate soil erosion dramatically in the Loess Plateau region (Jing, K. et al. 1997; Quine et al. 1999). As a result, the Yellow River has a high silt content, received from tributaries that pass through the Loess Plateau (often reaching 40% or more at present). When the river's course enters the plains of central Henan, it becomes broader and its water flows more slowly, depositing gravel and sand in the riverbed thus gradually raising the riverbeds. This situation has led to instability of the river's course and to frequent floods. Throughout prehistoric and historic times, the Yellow River has repeatedly changed course, switching back and forth between the north and the south of the Shandong peninsula in its passage to the sea (Murphey 1972; Wang, Q. 1993). Before dikes were built in the fourth century BC along the lower Yellow River to regulate its course, the lower reaches of the river had followed several paths (Tan, Q. 1981; Zou, Y. 1990). This unstable situation is attested to by the scarcity of settlements, prior to the second century BC, in a large region north of the Yellow River in the Hebei Plain (Guojia 1991). Throughout prehistory and history, flooding of the Yellow River occurred every few years on varying scales, causing disastrous damage to nearby lowland villages (Luo, C. and Le 1996: 137–82; Zou, Y. 1990). One of the most devastating floods recorded during the past 100 years occurred in 1933, with more than 50 burstings of the dikes. The floods inundated 853,000 ha of land in the middle and lower Yellow River regions, destroying 1,690,000 houses, causing 12,700 deaths, and leaving 3,640,000 people homeless (Luo, C. and Le 1996: 157–60). In sharp contrast to the life-giving Nile River in Egypt, the Yellow River's floods have been a source of disasters, earning it the sobriquet "China's sorrow."

The advantage of the loess soil, in contrast, is its loose structure, which allows fresh nutrients to be brought continually to the surface, making its fertility virtually inexhaustible. The loess thus offered an easy base for early dry land farming, testified to by the presence of domesticated millet remains at several early Neolithic sites (see Chapter 4). It was in this region that the earliest Chinese dynasties developed, and people inhabiting this yellow loess land have been referred to as "Children of the Yellow Earth" (Andersson 1973 [orig. 1934]).

The accumulation of the loess layer and the opposite process of soil erosion have also affected the practice of archaeology in this region, as the loess deposits containing buried ancient sites are highly susceptible to changes of depth. For example, in the Yiluo region of western Henan, many Neolithic burial sites, which were originally implanted several meters below ground level, have become exposed on the surface, due to soil erosion or intensive agricultural activities. Such geomorphological distortions cause great difficulties for archaeologists who attempt to determine the distribution of ancient settlements (Liu, L. et al. 2002–4).

The Yangzi River, also originating in the Tibetan plateau, flows eastward through the Red Basin of Sichuan, over flood plains drained by the Han, Yuan, Xiang, and Gan Rivers, and finally reaches its delta, before emptying into the East China Sea. With fertile land and abundant water resources from rivers and lakes, the Yangzi River Valley was the homeland of the earliest rice cultivation.

The Yangzi contains less silt than the Yellow River, but it has not been immune to disastrous flooding; due to high precipitation, the water flow of the Yangzi increases dramatically during summer. At Wuhan in Hubei, for example, the average difference between summer and winter water levels in the Yangzi is approximately 14 m (Tregear 1965: 240). Floods recorded throughout the historical period have occurred in different parts of the river at different times but with particular concentration in the months of June and July (Luo, C. and Le 1996: 237–95). In the 1931 case, more than 350 dikes burst along the Yangzi River channel, causing 3,773,000 ha of land to be inundated, with 145,400 deaths and 1,780,000 houses destroyed; the city of Wuhan (previously Wuchang and Hankou) was flooded for some 100 days (Luo, C. and Le 1996: 259–62). Floods certainly occurred in ancient times, as implied by the building of many Neolithic settlements on high ground with walled enclosures, most probably as a strategy for flood control (Wang, H. 2003).

The Pearl River, rising from the Yunnan plateau in Southwest China, follows an eastward course. It is a much lesser stream, and its watershed is restricted by the high-relief contours characteristic of South China's landscape, so its plains and delta are much less extensive than those of the Yellow and the Yangzi. This region, as the southern frontier of China, played an important role in cultural contacts with people in South and Southeast Asia (see Chapters 6 and 7).

All three great rivers flow from west to east, forming major transportation routes that facilitated west–east cultural interactions. In addition, several rivers run along the north–south axis, such as the Nu, Lancang, and Hong in the southwest. These water channels promoted interactions between China and Southeast Asian regions, manifested in the development of the Southwest Silk Road.

ECOLOGICAL DIVISIONS

China is also described as divided into two primary cultural-ecological regions. On the one hand, there is Inner China, or China Proper, characterized by densely populated fertile lands suitable for agriculture. On the other hand,

there is Outer China, which forms the northern and western frontiers; it is
much less densely populated and is predominantly desert, mountain ranges,
and steppelands (Figure 2.3). These two ecological zones conditioned two
types of ecological adaptations over time: agricultural and pastoral (Murphey
1972). The demarcation between these two zones gradually arose during the
Neolithic and Bronze Age periods, and appears to have shifted back and
forth throughout Chinese history, primarily affected by climatic fluctuations.
The cultural traditions that developed in these two regions have interacted
in various and even contradictory modes: both raiding and trading, ethnic
conflict as well as intermarriage, and not only political incorporation but also
independent self-rule (Di Cosmo 1999; Tong, E. 1990; Yan, W. 1987).

PALEOCLIMATE, PALEOENVIRONMENT, AND HUMAN ADAPTATIONS

Coupled with China's geomorphic variety is the great diversity of climate in
this vast land, ranging from extremely hot and dry conditions in the Tarim
Basin to temperate continental climate in the northeast, and from perennial
snow on the high western mountains in the Tibetan plateau to warm and
humid tropics along the southern coast. China today can be divided into three
distinct climatic, edaphic, and vegetational sectors: arid steppe, in the northwest
and north–central regions; grasslands, in the east–central and southwestern part
of the country; and forests, in the eastern coastal plain, southeast, and south.
Types of arboreal growth found in eastern China range from Arctic conifers
in the extreme northeast to tropical rainforests in the southeast (Winkler and
Wang 1993) (Figure 2.4D).

Many studies in recent years have focused on paleoenvironmental changes
since the last glacial maximum. Winkler and Wang (1993) have summarized
a general pattern of long-term climate fluctuations in the subcontinental area
that comprises modern China, as follows: At 18,000 BP, most of this vast land
mass was cold and dry. Sea level was 120 m below the present level, spruce and
fir forests expanded, and frozen steppe covered large sections of the northern
part. At 12,000 BP, moisture increased in the north, the northeast, and parts
of the center; warm-temperate forests grew in the south; and lake levels rose
(Figure 2.4A). These changes were probably affected by weakened continental
air masses from the north and stronger East Asian monsoons from the ocean.
Glacial conditions had ended in most parts of the subcontinent by 9000 BP:
Temperatures were generally warmer than at present, perhaps by 1–3°C; the
monsoonal climate was strengthened; lake levels were higher than before; and
the vegetation shifted from sparse, arid, or cold-climate associations to more
thermophilic and mesophytic communities in the west, south, and northeast
(Figure 2.4B). The interval of peak warmth and moisture, known as the mid-
Holocene optimum, occurred between ca. 8000 and 3000 BP throughout

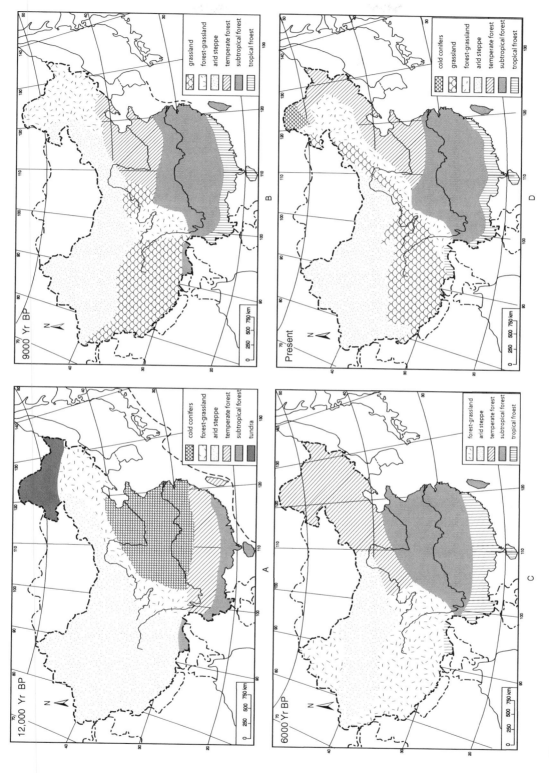

Figure 2.4. Reconstruction of vegetation zones, dating to (A) 12,000 BP, (B) 9000 BP, (C) 6000 BP, and (D) contemporary China, showing fluctuations through time. (Redrawn from figure 10.11 of Winkler and Wang 1993.)

the subcontinent. During that time, seasonal contrasts waned, whereas plant and animal ranges expanded (Figure 2.4C), and human settlements spread over much broader regions. After 3000 BP, the climate cooled in the entire subcontinental area.

The outline just presented provides a general indication of trends in climatic change but, due to the somewhat unrefined resolution of analytical intervals (3,000 years) and the uncalibrated BP dates, the data are insufficient for making archaeological comparisons. Apparently we need more detailed analysis of climatic fluctuations in fine-grained time scale, based on calibrated radiocarbon dates from each region. In the discussion that follows, we calibrate the BP dates whenever necessary by using the CalPal online program with 68 percent probability. When standard deviation is not available for the dates in original reports, we use ±80 years to facilitate the calibration process.

Variation of the Monsoon System

A number of factors may lead to climatic variations, including topography, latitude, altitude, and proximity to the sea, but one basic element of causation is the monsoon rhythm arising from the huge land mass of Asia. The Asian monsoon system has three relatively independent subsystems: the Indian monsoon, the East Asian monsoon, and the Plateau monsoon. The Plateau monsoon (or the winter monsoon) is a cold air mass that gathers in Siberia and Mongolia around November each year, before moving southeast to drive the winter season into China. The Indian and East Asian monsoons (the summer monsoons), in contrast, are formed in the Indian and Pacific oceans, respectively, before moving northward and bringing the summer season (Tregear 1980: 14–18; Winkler and Wang 1993: 249–54).

The East Asian monsoon reaches the coast of southeast China by May and spreads across a broad swath covering the eastern part of the northwestern, the entire northern, and most of northeastern ecological zones of China. Interaction of the monsoon front with a northern mass of cooler air produces a rainfall belt that migrates with the monsoon's frontal system, leading to asynchronous onsets of precipitation in different areas, as the front advances. Throughout the Holocene, the East Asian monsoon varied systematically in response to changes of solar insolation caused by alterations of the Earth's orbital parameters. The monsoon's variations are also conditioned by many other factors, such as differing configurations of sea and land, the uplift of the Tibetan Plateau, the distribution of high-latitude and high-altitude ice and snow, and the sea's surface temperature. The strength of the East Asian monsoon is a principal determinant of the level of precipitation, and therefore has been one of the most important factors affecting lake levels, vegetation, river flooding, and the ecological adaptations undertaken by human inhabitants of central and eastern China (An, Z. et al. 2000; Tregear 1980: 5–36).

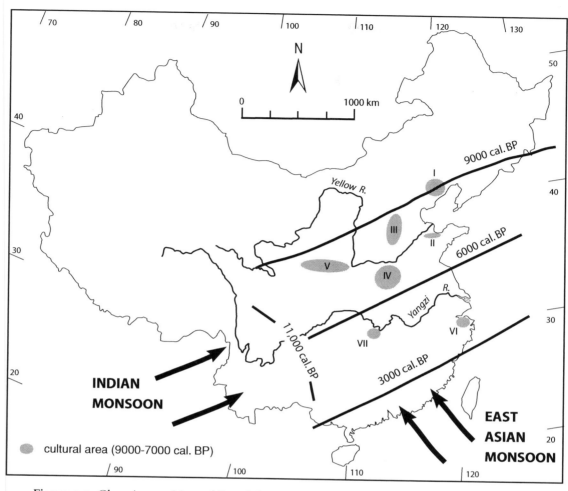

Figure 2.5. Changing position of East Asian monsoon maximum in China around 9000, 6000, and 3000 cal. BP (redrawn from figure 13 of An et al. 2000), in relation to the earliest Neolithic cultures. I: Xinglongwa; II. Houli; III: Cishan; IV. Peiligang; V: Laoguantai and Dadiwan; VI: Xiaohuangshan and Kuahuqiao; VII: Pengtoushan.

A precipitation peak appeared in the southwest of the Chinese subcontinent ca. 12,000 cal. BP, probably associated with the strengthened tropical Indian monsoon. Around 11,000–10,000 cal. BP, the northernmost frontal zone of the East Asian monsoon's rainfall advanced northward into regions that are arid and semiarid at present. As a result of the strengthened East Asian monsoon, precipitation in most parts of eastern China continued to grow until it reached a maximum ca. 9000 cal. BP. About 6000 cal. BP, the weakening of the summer monsoon caused the frontal zone to retreat southward, and the belt of maximum precipitation lay in the middle and lower reaches of the Yangzi River. By about 3000 cal. BP, the regional precipitation peak had shifted to southern China (An, Z. et al. 2000) (Figure 2.5).

This variation of the monsoon systems had a profound impact on human adaptation in the region. The widespread monsoon maximum in north China ca. 9000 cal. BP provided favorable conditions for the flourishing of early Neolithic villages along the Liao and the middle and lower Yellow River Valleys, as expressed in the Xinglongwa, Houli, Peiligang, Cishan, Laoguantai, and Dadiwan archaeological cultures (Figure 2.5). Moreover, the monsoon frontal zone retreated southward to the Yangzi River region during 6000–3000 cal. BP, a period corresponding to the growth of cool and dry conditions in the north and northwest and to wet episodes in the south. These changes may have forced Neolithic peoples to take various measures in response to the environmental deterioration. In some regions, settlements were abandoned and the population shrank, exemplified by the collapse of the Hongshan culture in the Liao River Valley around 5000 cal. BP, whereas in other regions walled enclosures were constructed around settlements for flood control, as revealed in the Daxi, Qujialing, Shijiahe, and Liangzhu cultures (ca. 6000–4000 cal. BP) in the Yangzi River Valley (Chapters 6 and 7). The collapse is defined as an event when a society displays a rapid, significant loss of an established level of sociopolitical complexity (Tainter 1988: 4).

Sea Level Fluctuation

China has a long coastline stretching from the border with Vietnam on the South China Sea to the border with Korea at the mouth of the Yalu River by the Liaodong peninsula. Since the last glacial maximum, sea level fluctuations have changed the landscape of the coastal areas and have profoundly affected human adaptations.

First, there was fluctuation in the elevation of the East China Sea during the postglacial period (Figure 2.6); this fluctuation changed the landscape of the coastal areas. To the north, around the Bohai Gulf area, the coastline in 8000–7500 BP more or less resembled that of modern times; the highest sea level occurred during the period between 7000 and 6000/5500 BP, reaching 3–5 m higher than at present; and the coastline also moved westward about 30–100 km inland. During the period 6000–5000 BP, the sea level was about 1–3 m higher than at present; after 5000 BP, although it tended to decrease in general, an instance of maximum sea level occurred again around 4000 BP. Sea level fluctuations like those around the Bohai Gulf have also been found along other parts of China's coastal lines (Zhao, X. 1996: 44–83). As a result of these changes, landscapes along the coasts altered dramatically, as land became ocean and vice versa, triggering movements of populations in these regions (Stanley et al. 1999; Stanley and Chen 1996; Wang, Q. and Li 1992; Wu, J. 1990; Zhao, X. 1984: 178–94; Zhao, X. 1993; Zhao, X. 1996: 44–100) (Figure 2.7). The rise and fall of several Neolithic cultures around the Hangzhou Bay

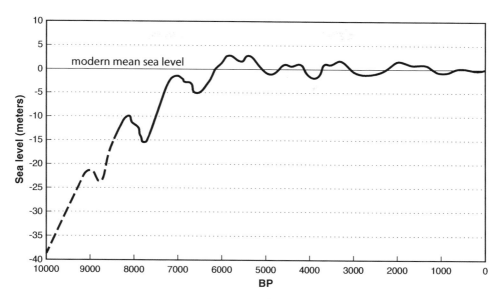

Figure 2.6. General curve of Holocene sea level changes along coastal areas in China. (Redrawn from Zhao 1993: 39.)

area, such as Kuahuqiao and Hemudu, appear to have been closely associated with sea level changes (see Chapters 5 and 6).

The sea level in southeast China and Taiwan also shows a similarly changing pattern. It rose rapidly around 7500 BP, reaching a maximum stand ca. 6000–4500 BP (Chen, Y. and Liu 1996; Winkler and Wang 1993; Zheng, Z. and Li 2000). The fluctuation of sea level directly affected population migrations from the Mainland to the islands in the Pacific. A Paleolithic population appears to have crossed the Taiwan Strait on foot in the late Pleistocene, when the sea level was 120 m lower than at present; in contrast, the Neolithic people who migrated from the Mainland to Taiwan in the fifth millennium BC must have been familiar with seafaring techniques (Chang and Goodenough 1996; Rolett et al. 2002).

Postglacial Abrupt Climate Changes

The global Holocene climate was punctuated by a series of millennial-scale shifts, expressed as abrupt cooling/drying events (Bond et al. 1997). Recent paleoclimatic studies suggest that there have been four major abrupt climatic changes on a world-wide scale during the postglacial era, at 12,800, 8200, 5200, and 4200 cal. BP. Each of these cold/dry episodes lasted for a few hundred years or longer and had a profound impact on human societies, leading to social change of many kinds (Weiss 2000; Weiss and Raymond 2001). In China, several Holocene climatic fluctuations have also been recorded, but these events, which have been documented in different regions, vary considerably

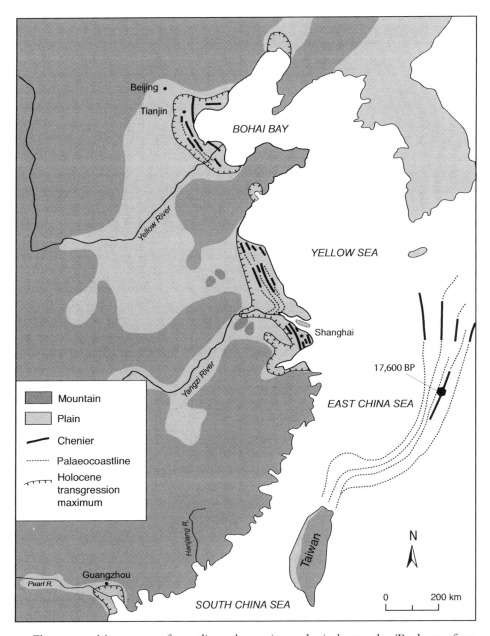

Figure 2.7. Movement of coastlines shown in geological records. (Redrawn from Zhao 1993: 93.)

in the temporal dimension (Figure 2.8). For example, Shi et al., drawing on data from all of China, argued that the climatic fluctuations occurred at 8700–8500, 7300, 5500, and 4000 BP during the Holocene climatic optimum (Shi, Y. et al. 1992). Kong et al. detected seven cold/dry events in north China during the Holocene, at 9800, 8300, 7200, 4800, 3400, 2000, and 700 BP (Kong, Z. et al. 1992). Zhou et al. suggest that the continental glaciers

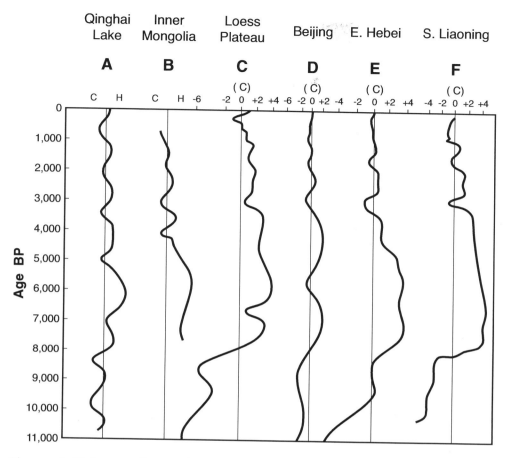

Figure 2.8. Holocene climatic changes recorded at several locations in northern China. (Redrawn from figure 2 of Shi et al. 1992.)

advanced at about 8300, 5700, 4000, and 400 BP in western China (Zhou, S. et al. 1991). Zhang et al. presented a series of climatic deteriorations during the interval 8500–3000 cal. BP, including cooling events at 6380–5950, 5340–5290, 5070–4670, 4300–3740, and 3410–3230 cal. BP in the desert-loess transition belt of north China (Zhang, H. et al. 2000). In addition, Yi et al. reported that cooling events occurred from 4500 to 2700 cal. BP, and then from 2300 to 1700 cal. BP in the Yellow River delta region (Yi, S. et al. 2003a). Such variation and even contradiction of dates presented in different reports have caused enormous frustration for scholars who attempt to comprehend the relationship between environmental change and cultural transformation. Given China's great regional variability of geomorphology and the related differing susceptibility to effects of the monsoon frontal belt, it is likely that these climatic changes observed within different parts of the Chinese subcontinent resulted from a combination of geographic and climatic factors that were active on both regional and global levels. The relative weight of regional and global dynamics in this putative interaction is not clear, however. Nevertheless, some of these events in China do appear to be comparable in character to global climatic fluctuations, which have also, to some extent, been correlated with social-cultural transformations in other parts of the world (Wu, W. and Liu 2004).

The first abrupt climate change, the Younger Dryas interval at 12,900–11,600 cal. BP, or 11,000–10,000 BP (Rind et al. 1986), triggered the transition from hunting-gathering subsistence to the domestication of cereals in western Asia (Bar-Yosef 2002; Weiss and Raymond 2001). In China a cooling/drying spell comparable to the Younger Dryas was recorded at ca. 12,830–10,500 BP in south China (Jiang, Q. and Piperno 1999), ca. 11,200–10,000 BP in central north China (Li, Xiaoqiang et al. 2003), and ca. 11,400–11,000 BP in north and northeast China (Liu, K. 1988). Whether this event also had a significant effect on the origins of rice and millet cultivation in the Yangzi and Yellow River regions, respectively, in China remains to be investigated.

The second postglacial climatic shock, dated to ca. 8200 cal. BP (6400–6000 BC), generated abrupt aridification and cooling in the North Atlantic and in North America, Africa, and Asia. In the Middle East, for example, a two-hundred-year drought led to the abandonment of agricultural settlements in the Levant and in northern Mesopotamia, and the subsequent return to warm/wet conditions may have encouraged early irrigation agriculture in southern Mesopotamia (Weiss 2000; Weiss and Raymond 2001). This cold spell also may have been widespread in China, comparable to the fluctuation dated to ca. 7300 BP (ca. 8039–8201 cal. BP as calibrated with CalPal), identified by Shi et al. (Shi, Y. et al. 1992). This climatic change may be supported by the fact that few Neolithic sites datable to before 8000 cal. BP have been found in the most optimum areas, such as Xinglonggou in the Liao River Valley, early Peiligang culture sites on the Huanghuai Plain, and Xiaohuangshan and Pengtoushan culture sites in the Yangzi River Valley. After this event, the subsequent warm and moist conditions returned, and the East Asian monsoon reached its highest strength, as mentioned earlier in this chapter. This improved climate condition correlates to the flourishing of early Neolithic cultures across north and south China (see Chapter 5).

The third major global postglacial climatic deterioration occurred at ca. 5200 cal. BP (3200–3000 BC), correlating with some complex social-cultural changes. In Mesopotamia, such events include the terminal Uruk period urbanization in southern Mesopotamia and the nucleation of settlements in northern Mesopotamia (Weiss 2000: 77; Weiss and Raymond 2001). This event may be comparable to the cooling/drying intervals at 5340–5290 and 5070–4670 cal. BP documented at Midiwan in north China (Li, X. 2008). The archaeological record also shows marked social transformations in north and northeast China around 5000 cal. BP; the highly developed Hongshan culture in the Liao River Valley, characterized by its elaborate jades and monumental ritual sites, collapsed (Li, X. 2008; Nelson 1995). The Yangshao culture in the Yellow River region declined and was replaced by the Longshan culture, which was characterized by intensive intergroup conflict and warfare (Liu, L. 1996b; Underhill 1994).

The fourth abrupt climate change ca. 4200 cal. BP (2200–1900 BC) has drawn the most scholarly attention worldwide because it coincided with the fall of major civilizations in Egypt, Mesopotamia, and the Indus valley (Weiss 2000; Weiss and Raymond 2001). An interval of climatic fluctuation at ca. 4000 cal. BP has also been documented in many regions in China. It was accompanied by the weakened monsoon system's retreat southward and was expressed as drought in the west and northeast of China and as flooding and waterlogging in the Central Plain and the Yangzi River region (Wu, W. and Liu 2004). Many studies demonstrate that some major social changes took place at the end of Neolithic China around 4000 cal. BP, testified by the collapse of the Liangzhu and Shijiahe cultures in the middle and lower Yangzi River regions (Stanley et al. 1999; Zhang, C. 2003: 224–9), the decline of the Longshan culture in the Yellow River Valley (Liu, L. 1996b, 2000b), the shift of subsistence from agriculture to agropastoralism in western China (Li, F. et al. 1993; Shui, T. 2001a, b) and, shortly after this event, the rise of the first state-level society, the Erlitou culture, in the Central Plain (Liu, L. and Chen 2003).

The mid-Holocene optimum ended around 4000–3000 cal. BP as documented in different regions in China, and the climate became generally cooler and drier (Feng, Z.-D. et al. 2004; Feng, Z.-D. et al. 2006; Winkler and Wang 1993). This event coincided with the flourishing of the late Shang and early Western Zhou dynasties in the Central Plain and the development of pastoralism in the northern and western frontiers due to progressively more arid conditions. In northwestern China, these conditions accelerated the pastoralist adaptations associated with the domestication of grazing animals, revealed in the archaeological record as the development of small, scattered, and increasingly mobile groups in the Siwa, Shajing, and Kayue cultures (Li, F. et al. 1993; Shui, T. 2001a, b). In Inner Mongolia and northeast China, this cooling/drying event seems to have had a rather severe impact. In the Daihai region of southern Inner Mongolia, for example, the collapse of the agricultural communities of the Zhukaigou culture was followed by a period of nearly a thousand years with a scarcity of material culture (ca. 3500–2600 cal. BP) before the rise of a pastoralist adaptation, the Maoqinggou type, characterized by the Ordos bronzes (Tian, G. and Tang 2001). Similarly, in the Chifeng region of northeast China, the transition from the agricultural Lower Xiajiadian culture (ca. 4200–3600 cal. BP) to Upper Xiajiadian culture with strong pastoralist components (ca. 3100–2600 cal. BP) is marked by a time gap of 500 years (Shelach 2001b). Such changes in ecological adaptations facilitated the development of complex relationships between the agriculturalists in China proper and the growing numbers of pastoralists in the northern and western frontiers. This sociopolitical theme later dominated Chinese history for some two thousand years (Di Cosmo 1999; Wang, M.-k. 2001).

Human-Induced Environmental Deteriorations

China's landscapes have been altered dramatically due to a long history of intensive agriculture, and deterioration of the ecosystem may have started in the middle Neolithic period. Recent studies on the mapping of Holocene pollen data and vegetation in China have revealed marked changes in vegetation during the Holocene. For a large southeastern part of the region north of the Yangzi River, arboreal taxa and forest biomes generally expanded until 6000–4000 cal. BP, then shrank during the late Holocene. The forest decline first started in the southeastern Loess Plateau, the southern Taihang Mountains, and the western North China Plain, then spread out from there. These regions were the most densely populated by agricultural settlements during this time period, and were home to the Yangshao and Longshan cultures. This pattern suggests that the deforestation was most likely related to intensified agricultural activities (Ren, G. and Beug 2002). Deforestation seems also to have occurred later in other regions. In the Yellow River delta, for example, pollen profiles show a significant reduction in percentage of deciduous broad-leaf plants (*Quercus*) in the arboreal total, followed shortly thereafter by an increase in conifer representation (*Pinus*) at ca. 4000 cal. BP, together with the first appearance of buckwheat pollen (*Fagopyrum*) at 1300 cal. BP. These changes probably signal human impacts, including deforestation and widespread cultivation in the lower Yellow River region (Yi, S. et al. 2003a). Forest clearance by humans throughout prehistory and history has accelerated soil erosion and led to frequent floods, particularly in the Yellow River region (Quine et al. 1999; Zou, Y. 1990).

All these natural and social factors have had a significant impact on the ecosystem, and human societies have responded variously to the ever-changing environment. How different human societies evolved in particular geographical and environmental conditions is an intriguing topic for archaeologists to pursue.

Communications in Geographical Contexts

The development of ancient culture and civilization in China has unquestionably been affected by geographical contexts. Although mountain ranges may have functioned as natural barriers forming circumscribed regional cultural variants, the complex systems of rivers and lakes on the alluvial plains facilitated water transportation, making interregional communications possible. These conditions perhaps encouraged the development of navigating technology during the early Neolithic period in both north and south China. This development is exemplified by 8,000-year-old canoes unearthed at Kuahuqiao in Zhejiang (Jiang, L. and Liu 2005); a paddle and a rudder of the Daxi culture (ca. 7000–5300 cal. BP), discovered at Chengtoushan in Hunan (Hunansheng 2007: 486); and a boat-shaped pottery object from Beishouling in Shaanxi (ca. 6800–6100 cal. BP) (Zhongguo Shehui Kexueyuan 1983: plate II.1). These discoveries suggest that many Neolithic communities were probably connected with one another by boat via water channels. The interregional communication between south and north China also largely depended on river systems throughout history; many of these routes have been recorded in ancient texts (e.g., Chen, G. 1995; Wang, W. 1996; Wang, Z. 1994), and some can be reconstructed archaeologically (Liu, L. and Chen 2003: 50–4).

CONCLUSIONS

Ancient China was characterized by its variability in geography, climate, and ecology, as well as by humans' adaptation to their environments. Throughout prehistory and history both natural and human forces have dramatically altered China's landscape, and human responses to the ever-changing environment have helped to form diverse cultural traditions.

Although China's topography appears to form geographically circumscribed conditions, Chinese civilization did not develop in isolation. Interactions between the peoples in China and in other parts of the world, and the technologies introduced to China through these interactions, have played dynamic roles in the development of complex society and the formation of early states in China. These arguments will be demonstrated in detail in the following chapters.

CHAPTER 3

FORAGERS AND COLLECTORS IN THE PLEISTOCENE-HOLOCENE TRANSITION (24,000–9000 CAL. BP)

> Anciently birds and beasts were numerous, and men were few, so that they lived in nests in order to avoid the animals. In the daytime they gathered acorns and chestnuts, and in the night they roosted on the trees; and on account of this they are called the people of the Nest-builder (youchaoshi).
>
> Chapter "Daozhi" in *Zhuangzi* (the fourth century BC), translated by James Legge (1891)
>
> 古者禽兽多而人民少、于是民皆巢居以避之。昼拾橡栗、暮栖木上，故命之曰有巢氏之民。〈〈庄子 · 盗跖〉〉

The transition from Pleistocene to Holocene (ca. 10,000 BP or 11,700 cal. BP) corresponds with many changes in climate, environment, landscape, material technology, settlement patterns, food acquisition strategies, ideology, and social relations. In Chinese archaeology, this transitional phase also reveals some developmental trends similar to those that occurred in other parts of the world, including an increase of sedentary lifestyle, the origins of pottery, the flourishing of microliths, the emergence of polished stone technology, intensified exploitation of plant foods, and the initial stages of cereal cultivation. These phenomena need to be explained from both local and global perspectives. In this chapter we will first provide an overview of environmental conditions and important archaeological findings, then discuss major issues relating to this transitional process. Figure 3.1 shows the locations of major sites mentioned in this chapter.

ENVIRONMENTAL CONDITIONS AND HUMAN ADAPTATIONS

It has been well established that the late Pleistocene and early Holocene witnessed conspicuous climatic and environmental changes on a global scale, characterized by closure of the Last Glacial Maximum (LGM) toward the terminal Pleistocene and the start of a warm episode in the early Holocene. In China the LGM had a severe impact on vegetation and landscape, through lower

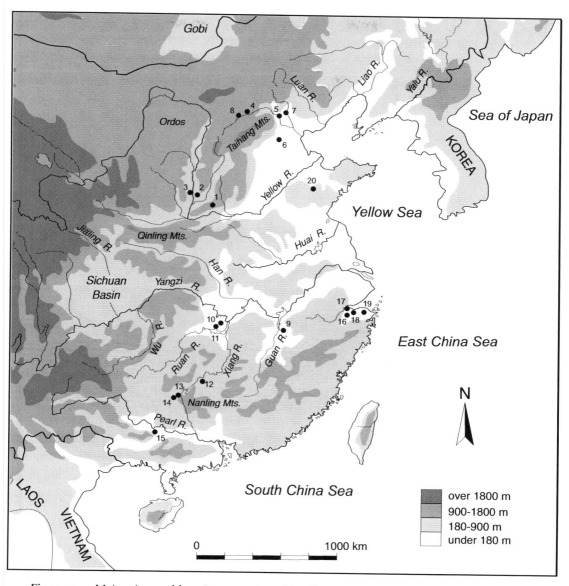

Figure 3.1. Major sites and locations mentioned in Chapter 3. 1: Xiachuan; 2: Shizitan; 3: Longwangchan; 4: Hutouliang; 5: Donghulin; 6: Nanzhuangtou; 7: Zhuannian; 8: Yujiagou; 9: Xianrendong, Diaotonghuan; 10: Bashidang; 11: Pengtoushan; 12: Yuchanyan; 13: Zengpiyan, Miaoyan; 14: Dayan; 15: Dingsishan; 16: Shangshan; 17: Kuahuqiao; 18: Xiaohuangshan; 19: Hemudu; 20: Bianbiandong.

temperatures and reduced precipitation. Deciduous trees retreated southward, and grasses dominated many landscapes. Compared to present times, the average annual temperature in north China was about 6–9°C lower, and in the Yangzi River region was 4–5°C lower. The sea level was about 130–155 m below the present level. After the LGM climatic conditions generally became warmer and wetter, but fluctuated through time (for a summary, see Lu, T. 1999, 2006).

Pollen profiles from Shizitan in the middle Yellow River Valley show that herbaceous taxa were generally predominant from 35,000 to 9400 BP. From 17,000 BP onward this area entered the last deglaciation, characterized by mild and arid or semiarid steppe environmental conditions, with herbs accounting for 79.2–100 percent and trees for 0–24.3 percent of taxa present in the pollen assemblages. A dry and cold glacial episode occurred from 11,000 to 10,500 BP, when deciduous and broadleaf species were rare. The climate during the early Holocene (10,500–9400 BP) in this region became warm and was characterized by a temperate steppe environment. In the later phase of this period, tree pollen concentration was high with increased deciduous and broadleaf species, such as *Betula, Quercus*, and *Acer*. Herbs accounted for 76.4–90.4 percent of taxa, predominantly *Artemisia*, and followed by Chenopodiaceae and Poaceae. Temperate steppe species also included Fabaceae (previously Leguminosae), among others (Xia, Z. et al. 2002). In the Yellow River delta region, pollen profiles indicate a short-term climatic deterioration at 12,000 cal. BP and a transition to warmer conditions around 11,000–9800 cal. BP (Yi, S. et al. 2003a). In the Yangzi River region, pollen profiles also reveal a similar pattern. A cool and dry episode occurred during 12,900–10,300 cal. BP, which was followed by wet and warm conditions around 10,300–9000 cal. BP (Yi, S. et al. 2003b). The cool and dry change around 12,000 cal. BP is comparable to the Younger Dryas, and the subsequent warm and wet period was consistent with the improved global climatic conditions of the early Holocene.

These changes affected human adaptations in profound ways, which are observable in the archaeological record. Settlement patterns, tool types, and faunal and floral remains all point to a mobile hunting-gathering way of life, relying on hunting medium-sized, fast running animals as major sources of food, supplemented by collecting locally available plant foods (Lu, T. 1999). This innovative subsistence economy provided a basis for further growth of sedentism and intensified the exploitation of plant foods during the early Holocene, leading finally to food production in the Neolithic period.

RESEARCH QUESTIONS AND TERMINOLOGY

Because the shift from food foraging to food production occurred in many places across the globe, archaeologists have attempted to provide theoretical models to explain these human behaviors generally, and many studies have focused on subsistence strategies. As Bettinger (2001) summarized, in many parts of the world this change is represented by two different hunting-gathering strategies, temporarily divided by the Pleistocene-Holocene boundary. In terms of cultural ecology, under the conditions of rapid climatic changes during the late Pleistocene, hunter-gathers responded more to temporal than to spatial variability of their environment. This response resulted in a foraging strategy of highly mobile "niche chasers," moving rapidly across the landscape to keep pace with abrupt changes in climate. In contrast, hunter–gatherers of the early Holocene, living in environments that provided abundant and stable resources, developed more diverse and specialized tactics and strategies to procure more localized and diverse resources, and depended more on plants. This proposition helps to provide a starting point for our discussion here, but further fine-grained analysis, articulating scattered archaeological data, is required to describe the transitional process in strategies for food procurement.

The forager–collector model proposed by Binford (1980) is helpful for investigating adaptive strategies of hunter–gatherers from the perspective of ecological anthropology. Based on this model, if resources are available in reasonable quantities year round, the hunter–gatherers tend to move their residential base frequently, to cope with resource exhaustion at one location; that is the simpler *forager strategy*. This strategy is characterized by high residential mobility, non-intensive resource procurement, relatively simple and generalized procurement technology, and lack of storage facilities. In contrast, if resources are highly seasonal and at times scarce or unavailable, hunter–gatherers will adopt a more complex strategy by sending out small, organized task groups to collect food resources, which are brought back to residential areas and stored there for the lean season. This is the more complex *collector strategy*, characterized by relatively stable residential bases, logistical procurement of food from nonresidential settlements, more complex and specialized procurement technology, and the presence of food storage facilities. The forager and collector strategies, according to Binford (1980: 12), are not two polar types of subsistence-settlement systems, but a graded series from simple to complex. This model has been found to be constructive for research in East Asian archaeology (Habu 2004; Lu, T. 1999: 124–6). In this chapter we will use the forager-collector model to conceptualize the cultural-ecological variation in relation to different temporal and spatial conditions in China, particularly in reference to the causal factors behind the emergence of sedentism and pottery use.

The study of this transitional phase correlates with an expansion of disciplinary approaches used in Chinese archaeological research, as warranted by the shift of emphasis from Paleolithic to Neolithic. Thus, we must refer to a set of terms and concepts that has been used to describe and interpret the differing material remains. A few decades ago, a clear temporal gap of several thousand years was seen in the archaeological record, between the Upper Paleolithic assemblages of the late Pleistocene on the one hand, and the early Neolithic cultures of the middle Holocene on the other. The former type is characterized by chipped stone and/or microlithic technologies and highly mobile settlement patterns, whereas the Neolithic cultures appear to have comprised a subsistence package, including sedentary villages, domesticated plants and animals, pottery, and polished stone tools. This gap in the record has been gradually filled in recent years, however, thanks to new discoveries of a number of sites dating to the transitional phase itself; these sites are primarily Paleolithic in nature but also contain some Neolithic elements, such as pottery, polished stone tools, and grinding stones. The presence of these material assemblages have challenged the traditional understanding of the concept of Neolithic. Although some researchers have adopted the term "Epipaleolithic" to describe these assemblages (e.g., MacNeish and Libby 1995), a recent tendency in archaeological literature refers to "Neolithization" as a feature already evident in the terminal Pleistocene in China and particularly hallmarked by the appearance of pottery vessels (Kuzmin 2003a; Wu, X. and Zhao 2003) that date to as early as 18,000 cal. BP (Boaretto et al. 2009).

Appropriate use of terminology will help us to present relevant data in conceptual renderings that facilitate fruitful comparisons with other cultural regions of the world. The term "Neolithic" is a concept, used in Old World archaeology – particularly for the Near East, Europe, and Africa – which has in the past conventionally designated certain material features including, among others, polished stone tools, pottery, domesticated plants and animals, and sedentary habitation. It is always dangerous, however, to formalistically reduce a complex concept to a mere list of specific cultural traits, as if they were sufficient collectively to define a given case as being Neolithic, because no common set of traits can be universally applicable to all regions. Thus, a newer use of Neolithic, as used in a global context, often gives more attention to economic processes, indicating food production, than to specific technological innovations (e.g., Karega-Munene 2003; Thomas 1999). Following this current application of the term, we here define "Neolithic" in China to mean an economic transformation in which people exploited food differently from hunting-gathering communities, including particularly the domestication of plants and animals. This new economic mode is interrelated with a range of changes in tool technology, settlement patterns, and social organization. The transitional phase we discuss in this chapter is characterized predominantly by hunting-gathering subsistence, with little evidence of domesticated plants and animals as dietary staples; therefore, we adopt the term Epipaleolithic to describe material assemblages dating to the Pleistocene-Holocene transition in China.

TERMINAL PLEISTOCENE FORAGERS IN NORTH CHINA

The terminal Pleistocene cultures in north China can be exemplified by four sites/site clusters: Xiachuan, Shizitan, Longwangchan, and Hutouliang (or Yujiagou), all located on river terraces in mountainous basins (Figure 3.1). Each site cluster comprises a dozen or more small seasonal campsites, reflecting a highly mobile subsistence strategy. Unlike many other Upper Paleolithic sites the toolkits of which are predominantly flakes with a few heavy-duty tools excluding microblades, these four site clusters represent the emergence and flourishing of a new technological complex, dominated by a tripartite repertory of microblades, flakes, and heavy-duty stone tools. These sites also show an increase in activities relating to collecting and processing plant foods, such as nuts and wild cereals, as indicated by the presence of grinding slabs and handstones (Lu, T. 1999: 60–1).

Xiachuan

One example suggesting the emergence of a new subsistence strategy directed at increased exploitation of plant foods is the Xiachuan complex, which refers to a characteristic material assemblage found in the upper strata (23,900–16,400 BP) of some sixteen site localities scattered in the Xiachuan Basin (about 93 km² in area), Shanxi province (Figure 3.2). The Xiachuan lithic complex reflects a typical tripartite tradition: predominantly flaked blades (77.7%) but also including microblades (19.8%) and heavy-duty tools (2.4%) (Figure 3.2). The flaked blades include points, arrowheads, scrapers, burins, blades, perforators, and denticulates. A preliminary use-wear analysis indicates that some flakes were used for reaping grass panicles (Lu, T. 2006: 135). The second largest category of tools is microblades, which were inserted into cleft handles made of soft materials to form the cutting edges of composite tools. Microblades were effective foraging tools commonly seen in North and East Asia. In China, the earliest example of such tools with blades still inserted in the tool is a microblade knife with a bone handle, unearthed from Donghulin and dating to 11,000–9000 cal. BP (see later in text). The heavy-duty stone tools were made of large flakes and pebbles, including axes, adzes, and grinding tools, which are among the earliest grinding slabs and handstones found in China to date (Chen, Z. 1996; Lu, T. 1999: 28–31; Wang, J. et al. 1978). According to Lu's (1999: 28–32) observation, the use-wear on these grinding implements can be classified into four patterns, resulting from different pounding and grinding movements. One of the use-wear patterns, appearing as a long, shallow groove, is similar to those on some grindstones found in Australia that were used for wet-grinding of seeds with soft husks. Some stone flakes from Xiachuan, suggested by Lu, also show "sickle gloss" on the cutting edges, perhaps used for reaping grass panicles. It is therefore proposed that seed processing was a part of Xiachuan subsistence, although it is difficult to quantify the proportion of cereals in the diet.

Longwangchan

Contemporaneous with Xiachuan is the Longwangchan site (20,000–15,000 BP), located at a foothill on the western bank of the Yellow River in Yichuan County, Shaanxi province. The excavation area of 40 m² has revealed some

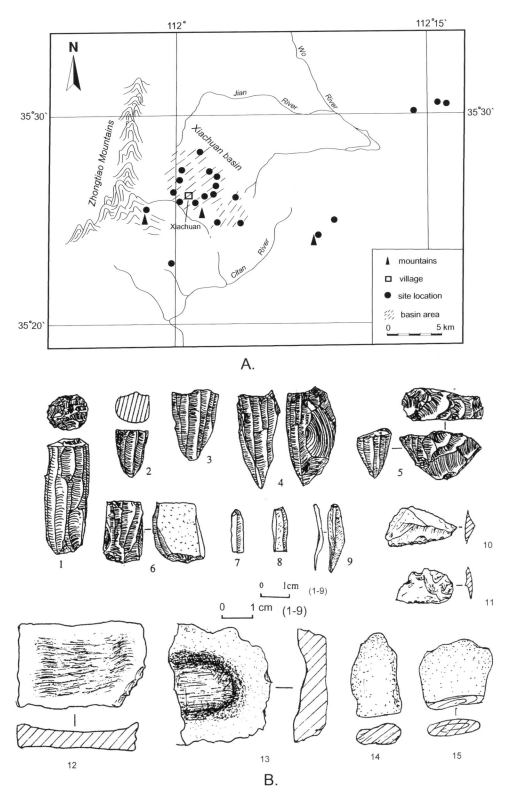

Figure 3.2. The Xiachuan site cluster and artifacts unearthed. (**A**) Paleolithic site locations in the Xiachuan Basin. (**B**) Partial tool assemblage from Xiachuan. 1–6: microcores; 7–9: microblades; 10 and 11: flake sickles; 12 and 13: grinding slabs; 14 and 15: handstones (modified from figures 4-2, 4-4, and 4-5 of Lu 1999) (10–15 not to scale).

Figure 3.3. Late Paleolithic site at Shizitan and artifacts unearthed, middle Yellow River region. 1: Location of Shizitan Locality 9, Shanxi (Shi and Song 2010: plate 1); 2 and 3: edge-ground spadelike implement (12.7 cm in length, 9.2 cm in width, and 0.8 cm in thickness) and a shell ornament (3.7 cm in length and 1.6 cm in width) from Longwangchan, Shaanxi (after Yin and Wang 2007: plate 2.4 and 2.5); 4 and 5: grinding slab and handstone from Shizitan, Shanxi (after Shi and Song 2010: plate 2).

20 hearths, more than 20,000 lithic artifacts, and some fragmentary animal bones. The lithic assemblage consists of a large number of microblades and microcores mostly made of quartz and chert, and the large tools include points, chopping tools, hammer stones, anvils, whetstones, and grinding slabs. The site also yielded one of the earliest ground-edge stone tools in China: a spadelike implement made of shale with a polished cutting edge. Some shell ornaments also unearthed here are rare finds in Paleolithic China (Figure 3.3).

This site is identified as a stone-tool production locale, as indicated by clusters of anvils, waste products, and abundant lithic debitage associated with hearths. Longwangchan, together with nineteen other Paleolithic sites distributed along the banks of the Huiluogou River (Yin, S. and Wang 2007), form a system of settlements occupied by mobile hunting-gathering groups. Longwangchan was likely a seasonal campsite, specialized for making stone tools. The grinding slabs and partially polished spade may indicate the exploitation of plant food. As the analyses of artifacts and soil samples are ongoing, it remains to be seen whether cereals, such as wild millet, were part of the diet.

Shizitan

On the eastern side of the Yellow River, about 20 km from Longwangchan, is the Shizitan site cluster (21,000–8500 cal. BP). It consists of more than twenty-five site locales within a distance of about 15 km along the Qingshui River in Jixian, Shanxi. These sites were largely contemporaneous and share some similarities in material culture with Longwangchan and Xiachuan. Hearths, burnt animal bone fragments, and large quantities of microblades were found, and a small number of grinding stones was also uncovered (Figure 3.3). The grinding stones, consisting of slabs and elongate handstones, referred to as *mopan* and *mobang*, became more regular in shape and larger in size through time, suggesting their importance in subsistence economy. The faunal remains are fragmentary, and substantial amounts were burnt. The identifiable species include antelope, wild pig, deer, ox, and rat. Some of the site localities appear to have been occupied for only short periods of time, as indicated by the distributional pattern of ash and artifacts (Guojia 2004a; Shi, J. and Song 2010; Xie, X. et al. 1989). Like the two site clusters described earlier in text, Shizitan clearly points to a mobile hunting-gathering subsistence strategy supplemented, to a certain degree, by exploitation of plant food.

Residue and use-wear analyses of grinding stones from Shizitan Locality 9 indicate that a wide range of plant foodstuffs were processed, including acorns (*Quercus* sp.), grasses (Panicoideae and Pooideae), beans (cf. *Vigna* sp.), and tubers (*Dioscorea* sp.) during the Pleistocene-Holocene transitional period (ca. 12,700–11,600 cal. BP) (Liu, L. et al. 2011). These residues suggest that various plants of value for subsistence, perhaps including the wild ancestors of foxtail and broomcorn millets, had been exploited by hunter-gatherers for thousands of years before their domestication took place.

Hutouliang

Hutouliang (16,300–14,700 cal. BP; GrA-10460, dated from potsherd) (Yasuda 2002: 127) comprises a group of ten site localities with middens at corresponding stratigraphic levels and with similar material contents. These localities are

Foragers and Collectors in the Pleistocene-Holocene Transition   51

distributed on the second level terrace of the Sanggan River, at the Nihe-wan Basin in northwestern Hebei province. The lithic assemblage consists of microblades, flakes, and heavy-duty tools, and the animal remains include species from fox, ostrich, mouse, wolf, wild horse and onager, deer, ox, gazelle, and wild boar. This faunal assemblage indicates a temperate steppe ecosystem in a cool, dry environment. The pollen profile is dominated by herbaceous plants and shrubs (78–98%), indicating dry grassland vegetation in a cold and arid climate. People made and used specialized tools, such as pointed and adze-shaped tools, to adapt to the changing climatic environ-ment. The occupants of the Hutouliang site cluster were apparently mobile hunting-gathering groups, as suggested by pronounced intersite variability. Archaeologists have determined various functions associated with different site localities, as inferred from the artifactual remains, ranging from campsite, and tool-manufacturing site, to butchering site (Guo, R. and Li 2002; Lu, T. 1999: 34).

Recent excavations have revealed several potsherds, identified as the earli-est pottery discovered to date in north China. The pottery is porous, sand-tempered, and fired at low temperatures. The vessels are pot-shaped with flat bases, and lack any traces of burning on exterior surfaces (Guo, R. and Li 2002). It is clear that, in north China, pottery first appeared within a mobile hunting-gathering context, as also occurred at many places in other parts of the world (Rice 1999: 28–9).

The Pleistocene hunting-gathering communities in north China were highly mobile "niche chasers" (Bettinger, R. 2001) and apparently adapted to the LGM environment affected by abrupt changes in climate. They used mainly the simpler forager strategy (Binford's term; Binford, L. R. 1980), moving their residential base frequently to replenish resources exhausted at an established location; however, Binford's collector strategy also may have been practiced to some extent. That is, foragers in the Xiachuan, Shizitan, and Hutouliang areas may have adopted a mobility pattern typical of the logistic food and resource collector endowed with increased residential stability, as indicated by evidence for exploitation of seasonally available wild plants, man-ufacture of pottery, and principal focus on a residential campsite, with other working stations being reserved for special tasks (Lu, T. 1999: 124–6). There is no evidence of storage facilities or residential structures in any of these sites, however.

EARLY HOLOCENE COLLECTORS IN NORTH CHINA

Five sites dating to the beginning of the Holocene have been found in north China, including Donghulin and Zhuannian near Beijing, Nanzhuangtou in Hebei, Lijiagou in Xinmi, Henan (Wang, Y. et al. 2011), and a cave site at Bian-biandong in Yiyuan, Shandong (Sun, B. and Cui 2008) (Figure 3.1). These early Holocene sites, like their Pleistocene predecessors, manifested a predominantly hunting–gathering tradition; however, several changes are notable: intensified collection of plant foods, more frequent occurrences of pottery production, and a clear tendency toward increased degrees of sedentism.

Donghulin and Zhuannian

Donghulin (11,000–9000 cal. BP) in Mentougou (Zhao, Chaohong 2006; Zhou, G. and You 1972) and Zhuannian (ca. 10,000 BP) in Huairou (Yu, J. et al. 1998) are similar in terms of settlement location and material assemblage. Both sites are located on river terraces in mountainous basins. Pollen profiles from Donghulin show that during the early Holocene (ca. 10,000–8200 BP) arboreal plants accounted for a considerable percentage (up to 55%) of the pollen assemblage, which consisted of a mix of conifer and broadleaf trees, the latter category being predominantly oak (*Quercus*) and walnut (*Juglans*). Grass plants were predominantly *Artemisia*, Chenopodiaceae, *Cyperaceae*, and Leguminosae, and Poaceae increased proportionately toward the later part of this time period. Study of terrestrial snail numbers and diversity also indicates that the early Holocene was characterized by warm and wet conditions, with intermittent dry and cool phases. In general, the Donghulin site was situated in a region characterized by mixed vegetation typical of forests and grassland, with an annual temperature 2–3°C higher than at present (Hao, S. et al. 2002). This ecological environment provided humans with new types of plant foods, particularly nuts.

Donghulin has been excavated several times since the 1960s. The site was found on the third-level terrace on the northern bank of the Qingshui River, in the mountainous region that forms the transition between the North China Plain and the Loess Plateau (Figure 3.4). The remains of the site measure about 3,000 m² in size and are situated 25 m above the Qingshui River today; however, in antiquity the river course was much higher in elevation and closer to the site. Excavations have revealed human burials, hearths and ash pits, along with a large quantity of material remnants, including artifacts made of stone, bone and shell, as well as animal and plant remains (Figure 3.4).

Some burials show no clear traces of grave structure, whereas others were constructed as vertical pits and are among the earliest examples of such mortuary features found in China. The skeletons show signs of either single interment or multiple secondary interments. Some were buried with offerings, such as small ground-stone axes and ornaments made of snails and shells. Hearths were round pits, about 0.5–1 m in diameter and 0.2–0.3 m in depth, and were filled with burnt rocks of various sizes, burnt animal bones, and ash. On the lower level of the hearth the rocks were arranged in a circle, but on the upper level rocks were placed in disorderly array (Figure 3.4). The excavators suggest that these hearths were abandoned after being used seasonally (Zhao,

Figure 3.4. The Donghulin site and major finds. 1: Excavation at Donghulin; 2: burial;
3: hearth; 4: bone knife inserted with microblades; 5: grinding slab and handstone;
6: potsherd; 7: polished stone tool (1: Li Liu's photo; 2–7: Zhao, C. 2006: plates 1
and 2).

Chaohong 2006; Zhou, G. and You 1972). Some pits have been found, but it is unclear if these were used as storage.

The lithic assemblage consists mainly of chipped stone tools, as well as microblades and grinding stones (slabs and handstones in various forms), plus a small number of polished axes and adzes. One particular composite tool is a type of knife with a handle made of animal bone, decorated in a carved geometric pattern, and with a microblade still embedded in the handle's groove (Figure 3.4). The grinding stones account for a significant proportion of the tool assemblage, and starch and use-wear analyses indicate that they were primarily used for processing plant foods, including acorns and siliceous plants (Liu, L. et al. 2010b), which were abundant in the early Holocene in this area, as indicated by the pollen record. Ceramics appear to have been flat-bottomed basins, jars, and bowls. The potsherds are particularly noteworthy; these are the fragments from some sixty pottery vessels. They are porous, brown in color, and sand tempered, and they were fired at low temperatures. The vessels were made by coiling and slab techniques, and some were decorated with impressed or relief patterns (Figure 3.4). The faunal remains are reportedly predominated by deer, followed by pigs and badgers, and freshwater shells are also abundant (Zhao, Chaohong 2006; Zhou, G. and You 1972). Two species of hackberry seeds (*Celtis bungeana Bl.* and *C.* cf. *koraiensis* Nakai) have been uncovered from a burial (Hao, S. et al. 2008). The pollen and archaeological data indicate that various types of nuts and probably some edible grass seeds were locally abundant and as such may have been collected for food.

Donghulin indicates the emergence of a new type of settlement and subsistence strategy, which differs from the Pleistocene counterpart. The site is larger in size and was occupied for a longer interval of time. The occurrence of formal burials, in particular the practice of multiple secondary burials, implies that the site was a relatively permanent settlement to which the dead were brought back for ritual burial, as suggested by many ethnographic studies (for more examples, see Watanabe 1986). The presence of various forms of sand-tempered, thick-walled pottery vessels (basins, jars, and bowls) indicates that pottery making was more advanced than the initial stage of this technology, as exemplified by those from Yuchanyan (see later in text). The relatively complex structure of the hearths indicates that an enhanced expenditure of energy was invested in their construction, suggesting a distinctive intention to stay at this location for a longer duration of time. Grinding slabs and handstones point to intensive exploitation of wild plant foods, such as nuts and cereals, among others, which are particularly abundant in autumn. The polished stone axes and adzes are hypothetically woodworking tools, presumably used to build shelters, although evidence of dwellings is still lacking in the archaeological record.

The archaeological remains suggest that the site was perhaps particularly used for gathering shellfish, hunting deer, and collecting plant foods. Such

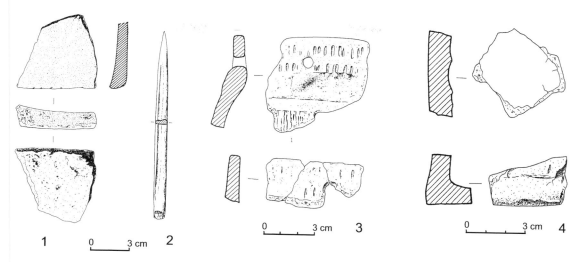

Figure 3.5. Artifacts from Nanzhuangtou in Hebei. 1: Grinding slab; 2: bone awl; 3: pottery rim sherds; 4: pottery body and base sherds (after figures 16-4, 16-7, 17-8, 17-11, 18-1, and 20-1 of Li, J. et al. 2010).

a broad-spectrum subsistence strategy, in the context of decreased residential mobility, is consistent with the initial transition to a sedentary way of life, and its features are comparable to components of the more complex collector strategy adopted by Holocene hunter-gatherers in many other parts of the world.

Nanzhuangtou

The Nanzhuangtou site (ca. 10,510–9690 BP; or 12,408–11,018 cal. BP as calibrated by CalPal) (Yuan, S. *et al.* 1992), measuring 2 ha in area, is located in Xushui County, Hebei province, some 35 km west of Lake Baiyangdian and 15 km east of the Taihang Mountains. Among the contemporary sites in north China discovered to date, it is the first one found on alluvial plains rather than in mountainous terrain. Pollen profiles are dominated by herbaceous plants (above 70% on average), whereas arboreal plants comprise less than 20 percent. Among the broadleaf trees, oak is the most numerous type (Li, Y. et al. 2000).

Three seasons of excavation in the 1980s and 1990s revealed gullies, ditches, ash pits, and hearths. Several concentrated deposits of wood ash and decayed wood have been found, in association with scattered broken animal bones, antlers, rocks, and artifacts. Artifacts unearthed from the site include potsherds, grinding slabs, handstones, stone flakes, bone awls and arrowheads, and cut antlers (Figure 3.5). Different from other early Holocene sites in north China, the Nanzhuangtou lithic assemblage does not consist of microliths (Guo, R. and Li 2002; Li, J. et al. 2010; Xu, H. et al. 1992).

Most potsherds can be identified as deriving from vessels, including flat-bottomed pots and bowls. They are porous, gray or yellowish-brown in color, and tempered with shell fragments or quartz. Some are decorated with simple designs, such as relief patterns, on the neck. Many sherds show traces of fire and smoke, and some have carbonized substances on the internal side of the vessel wall (Guo, R. and Li 2002), suggesting that some pottery was used as cooking vessels.

Identifiable species from the faunal remains include chicken, bird, rabbit, wolf, dog, pig, buffalo, many types of deer, turtle, fish, and shellfish (Yuan, J. and Li 2010; Zhou, B. 1992). Among these animals, dog has been recently identified as domesticated (Yuan, J. and Li 2010), marking the first evidence of animal domestication in China. Unfortunately, the flotation method was not used in the excavations, so plant remains are missing from the archaeological record.

Evidence from Nanzhuangtou also indicates relatively lengthy durations of intermittent occupation, as implied by the thickness of the burnt clay forming the hearths and by the presence of various types of pottery vessel. Although no evidence of house structures has been identified archaeologically, some decayed wooden poles found here could have been used for constructing simple dwellings. The presence here of grinding implements and pottery vessels, as at Donghulin and Zhuannian, is a good indicator of plant food exploitation. The function of the ash pits is unclear; future research may clarify whether these were used as storage facilities. The material remains from Nanzhuangtou, consistent with those from Donghulin, show a hunting–gathering way of life that used a pronounced collector strategy, with more intensified plant exploitation and a decreased degree of residential mobility.

Lijiagou and Bianbiandong

These two sites are newly discovered and have not been fully reported. The Lijiagou site is situated on the second terrace of the Chunban River (upper reach of the Zhen River) in Xinmi County, central Henan, dating to 10,500–8600 cal. BP. The cultural deposits show a continuous development of microlithic assemblages, with pottery sherds and grinding slabs occurring in the upper strata. The pottery vessels are mainly cylindrical in shape, and are decorated with cord marks and incised patterns. Material remains tend to cluster in concentrations, consisting of rocks, grinding slabs, anvils, burnt rock fragments, pottery sherds, and animal bones. Such a cluster may be remnants of relatively stable residence (Wang, Y. et al. 2011). Xinmi is also the heartland of the early Neolithic Peiligang culture (ca. 9000/8500–7000 cal. PB), which developed subsequently to the period of the Lijiagou site (see Chapter 5). The

Figure 3.6. Landscape of Yuchanyan and artifacts from Yuchanyan and Zengpiyan. 1: Yuchanyan cave site; 2: hoe-shaped stone implement, Yuchanyan; 3: pottery vessel (31 cm in rim diameter and 29 cm in height), Yuchanyan (after figures 1, 3, and 7 of Yuan 2002); 4: pottery vessel, Zengpiyan (after figure 27 of Zhongguo Shehui Kexueyuan 2003).

Rice, likely wild species, was collected but probably did not play any important role in the diet.

Several clusters of small fragments of potsherds were found in the cultural deposits. These are dated to 18,300–15,430 cal. BP, among the earliest pottery vessels in the world (Boaretto et al. 2009). The clay was tempered with charcoal and coarse sand, and the potsherds are crumbly; they were roughly made, with uneven walls up to 2 cm thick. From these sherds, two vessels were reconstructed, one of which is a pot shaped with a pointed bottom and decorated with a cord-mark pattern (Figure 3.6) (Yuan, Jiarong 2002). Because the pottery is associated with rice remains in several Pleistocene cave sites, it has been suggested that cooking of wild rice may have led to the origins of pottery (Higham and Lu 1998; Lu, T. 1999: 124).

Zengpiyan

Zengpiyan is a cave located in the limestone mass of Mt. Du, some 9 km south of Guilin in Guangxi. The entire site is about 240 m² in area, of which 100 m² has been excavated in several stages since the 1970s, revealing cultural deposits up to 3.2 m thick and containing burials, hearths, ash pits, and numerous artifactual, faunal, and floral remains. The chronology of the deposits embraces five phases, of which Phases I–IV (12,000–8000 cal. BP) show characteristics of a transitional process from the Paleolithic to the Neolithic. From the deposits of Phase I (12,000–11,000 cal. BP) archaeologists found pottery and tools made of stone, bone, and shell. The stone industry is predominantly of the chopping tool tradition prevalent in late Paleolithic South China. The lithic assemblage includes large numbers of cobbles, blanks, flakes, and lithic debitage; some flakes can be rejoined, suggesting that tools were manufactured on site. Raw materials were largely obtained from the nearby Lijiang River. A ceramic vessel discovered here is a porous, round-bottomed pot, fired at a temperature of no more than 250°C (Figure 3.6). The paste is tempered with course quartz, the vessel was hand-pitched and roughly made, and a large part of its surface is undecorated. Throughout Phases II–IV the chopping-tool tradition continued, and ground stone tools, such as axes and adzes, emerged and increased in proportion. Pottery forms were predominantly large jars, tempered with crushed calcite, manufactured mainly with slab technology, and decorated with cord-marked, incised, and impressed patterns (Zhongguo Shehui Kexueyuan 2003a).

Large quantities of faunal remains were uncovered, including fish, shellfish, birds, and mammals. Of these, snails (*Cipangopaludina*) are particularly abundant, and mammalian species are, predominantly, several varieties of deer, wild pig, and water buffalo. Few plant remains were found, and rice is absent. Tubers appear to have been important in the diet, as suggested by the presence of carbonized tuber remains in flotation samples and residues of taro starch on cutting edges of stone and bone tools. The Zengpiyan people apparently practiced a broad-spectrum subsistence economy, including hunting animals and collecting shellfish, tubers, and other plants. Zengpiyan human teeth appear to be heavily worn, perhaps due to the intensive consumption of snails, which contained much sand. As the best way of extracting meat from shellfish is by boiling, the pottery vessels were probably used for cooking shellfish, among other foods (Zhongguo Shehui Kexueyuan 2003a).

Yuchanyan and Zengpiyan were likely seasonal campsites, but the duration of residential occupation may have been relatively long, given that the process of making pottery required extended habitation. These Epipaleolithic sites were probably occupied by hunter-gatherers who had become more logistically organized for food procurement, with reduced mobility in their residential patterns (see more discussion on sedentism later in this chapter).

HOLOCENE COLLECTORS IN CENTRAL CHINA

Although some Pleistocene cave sites mentioned earlier in text contained early Holocene deposits, they do not reflect the whole picture of settlement patterns during the transitional period, because open air sites have been absent from the archaeological record until the last few years. Fortunately, recent excavations at Shangshan (ca. 11,000–9000 cal. BP) in Pujiang, Zhejiang, have revealed a settlement on an alluvial plain, providing much new information about residential-subsistence strategies during the early Holocene in the lower Yangzi River Basin.

Shangshan

The Shangshan site (2 ha) is located on a small basin of the upper Puyang River, surrounded by low mountains (Figure 3.7). The site is situated on two small tablelands about 3–5 m above the surrounding plain, separated by a modern irrigation canal. A total of 1,800 m² has been excavated (Jiang, L. 2007; Jiang, L. and Liu 2006). Geological profiles from Shangshan indicate that the site experienced a series of dry and wet cycles in antiquity (Mao, L. et al. 2008), which may have compromised the long-term survival of organic remains, as indicated by the absence of pollen in soil samples from the site and by the lack there of residues from human or animal bones.

The lower Yangzi River region lies in the northern portion of the subtropical zone. Regional weather patterns are largely influenced by the summer and winter monsoon systems, showing clear seasonal changes (Winkler and Wang 1993). This region experienced a period of relatively dry and cold climate from 13,000 to 11,670 cal. BP, corresponding to the Younger Dryas (Yi, S. and Saito 2004). This phase was followed by a wet and warm period during the early and middle Holocene, interspersed with some cooler and dryer episodes, but climatic fluctuations did not change the general subtropical conditions here. Vegetation was dominated by broadleaved evergreen and deciduous trees, such as *Quercus, Cyclobalanopsis, Castanopsis, Lithocarpus, Corylus, Ostrya*, and *Lepidobalanus*, many of them being nut-bearing trees. A range of nonarboreal and wetland herbs were also present in lower frequencies; among them Poaceae, Cyperaceae, and Typha were most common (Atahan et al. 2008; Yi, S. et al. 2003b; Zong, Y. et al. 2007). The flourishing, in this region, of nut-bearing trees and a variety of other economically valuable plants coincided with the emergence of the Shangshan settlement and with the subsequent development of Neolithic villages during the early and middle Holocene.

At Shangshan, eight strata have been recorded. The oldest horizons (Strata 5–8) span the early Holocene period, which is alternatively known as the Shangshan period and dates to 11,400–8600 cal. BP (Jiang, L. 2007). Preliminary analyses of flotation samples from Shangshan period deposits have

Figure 3.7. Features and artifacts discovered at Shangshan, Zhejiang. 1: Location of Shangshan; 2: excavation area at Shangshan; 3: storage pits; 4: cache H121 containing seven ceramic vessels; 5: pottery basin with a ring-shaped loop; 6: stone tools; 7: grinding stones (slabs and handstone); 8: perforated pottery pedestal plate, late Shangshan phase (1–6: courtesy Jiang Leping; 7 and 8: Li Liu's photos).

uncovered some organic remains, including a rice grain, a few small fragments of carbonized nutshells, and as yet unanalyzed animal bones.

The lithic assemblage is dominated by flaked stone tools, with some grinding stones (more than 400 slabs and handstones). A small number of polished axes and adzes were also identified. The handstones vary in form, including round, square, and rectangular, and appear to have been used for both grinding and pounding. An overwhelming majority (around 80%) of pottery vessels are large, flat-bottomed basins, with jars, plates, and bowls also occurring. Some vessels from later phases are rendered with a perforated pedestal; such vessel forms were apparently not designed for mobility, implying increased sedentism (Jiang, L. 2007) (Figure 3.7).

The pits at Shangshan can be classified into three types: (1) those containing purposefully arranged caches of complete pottery vessels stored for future use, suggesting a mobile and intermittent residential mode, with anticipation of return; (2) vertical shafts, square or round in shape and more than 70 cm deep, originally used for food storage before ultimately being abandoned (Figure 3.7C, D); and (3) Deposits of secondary refuse, documenting efforts to manage domestic waste from sedentary settlements. In contrast to Type 1, pits of Types 2 and 3 show a tendency toward long durations of residence. The different types of pits suggest a mixed pattern of occupation: both intermittent residence, with seasonal or annual mobility, and extended habitation by relatively stable sedentary communities, although the duration of sedentary occupation is unclear.

Postholes were generally irregular in distribution, but a group of them, arranged in three rows of 10–11 holes each, and altogether delimiting a space of 14 m by 6 m, has been found in the upper stratum of Shangshan's southern section. The postholes are probably remnants of a pile-dwelling structure (Jiang, L. 2007), a feature indicating increased sedentism (more discussion on the theory of sedentism in Chapter 5).

Starch and phytolith analyses of residue samples collected from grinding stone tools suggest that these implements are unlikely to have been used for dehusking rice, but rather for processing acorns (*Quercus* sp.) and, to a lesser extent, other wild starchy foodstuffs, such as Job's tears (*Coix lacryma-jobi*), tubers (probably yam, *Dioscorea* sp.), and possibly water caltrop (*Trapa* sp.). They may also have been used to process fiber additives for making pottery vessels (Liu, L. et al. 2010c). This botanic assemblage, determined from starch residues, is paralleled by plant remains unearthed from waterlogged Neolithic sites in the region, such as Kuahuqiao (Zhejiangsheng and Xiaoshan 2004: 270–7). The discovery of acorn starch is also consistent with pollen records, which document that several genera of oak were common in the lower Yangzi River region during the early Holocene.

The dominant pottery form is a flat-bottomed basin, with rim diameter of 30–50 cm, height of 9.5–12.5 cm, and base diameter of 10.5–24 cm; a ring-shaped loop is sometimes attached to the middle of the vessel's exterior wall (Figure 3.7E). The pottery appears to have been fired at low temperature, the walls are thick (in some cases more than 2 cm), and the exterior and interior surfaces are covered with red slip. The slab-modeling technique was used, and most vessels on the lower strata are fiber-tempered, but the proportion of sand-tempered pottery increased with time. None of the ceramics can be identified as cooking vessels, due to the lack of soot on the surface. Given that many small, broken rocks have been found at the site, it is possible that some of the large fiber-tempered basins were used for stone-boiling, although further research is needed to test this proposition (Liu, Li 2006). This cooking method has been well documented in the North American ethnographical and archaeological records (Sassaman 1993) and among some ethnic groups in China, such as the Hezhe, Ewenke, and Elunchun in the Northeast (Ling, C. 1934: 65; Song, Z. 1998).

Shangshan is the earliest example of a settlement in Holocene China in which dwellings, permanent storage facilities, possible burials, pottery, ground stone tools, and the consumption of considerable quantities of plant foodstuffs occurred all together. Some of these features, particularly dwellings and storage, are often seen in ethnographical (Hitchcock 1987) and archaeological literature as indicators of increased sedentism. Evidently, Shangshan was a sedentary village, and its people were logistic collectors, but we are uncertain whether the occupation was year-round or nearly year-round.

SUMMARY

Pleistocene mobile hunter-gatherers in Central and South China exploited a wide range of faunal and floral resources. Their residential patterns on the regional level remain unclear, due to the dearth of known contemporary open-air sites. Nevertheless, people may have occupied the cave sites for relatively long durations during the year, at least long enough to produce pottery.

Not until the early Holocene did a high degree of sedentism develop in the Yangzi River region, as exemplified by Shangshan. This site was occupied by hunter-gatherers, who used a complex collector strategy to maximize their capability for food procurement. They used many types of plants, including rice, in duplicate roles, both as food and as pottery-making material. We know little, however, about how their strategy of logistic mobility was carried out, due to a lack of studies on regional settlement-subsistence patterns.

ORIGINS OF POTTERY IN CHINA

Pottery making was one of the important techno-economic innovations that characterized the Pleistocene-Holocene transition in China. Pottery first appeared as early as 18,300–14,000 cal. BP during the LGM in both south and north China (Yuchanyan and Hutouliang), but it is unclear what impact this technology may have had on the predominant hunting-gathering subsistence mode of that time. During the early Holocene period, pottery became more widespread (Figure 3.8) (see also Lu, T. 2010 for a summary of early pottery). It formed an important component of adaptation strategies, which show reduced residential mobility and increased reliance on collecting fish/shellfish and plant foods, including nuts, cereals, and tubers.

Early ceramic remains unearthed in China show characteristics of the initial development of this technology, such as low firing temperatures, thick walls,

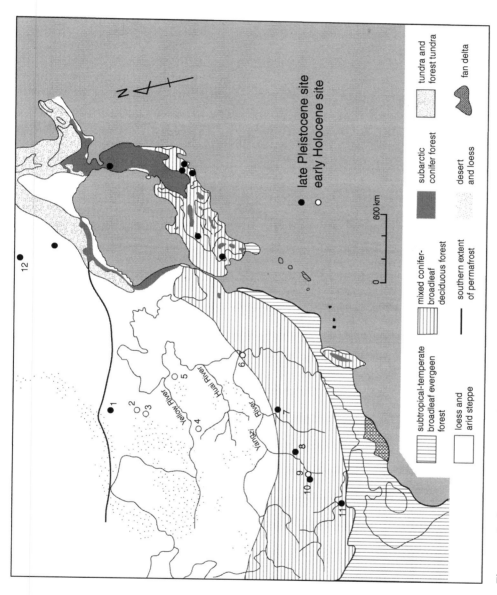

Figure 3.8. A reconstruction of the East Asian coastline and phytogeographic zones of the Last Glacial Maximum, 21,000–15,000 BP, and the distribution of early pottery sites in China, Japan, and the Far East. 1: Hutouliang; 2: Zhuannian, Donghulin; 3: Nanzhuangtou; 4: Lijiagou; 5: Bianbiandong; 6: Shangshan; 7: Xianrendong; 8: Yuchanyan; 9: Zengpiyan; 10: Miaoyan; 11: Dingsishan; 12: Gasya (the location for pottery sites in Japan and the Far East based on figure 7 of Tsutsumi 2002; map redrawn from figure 1 of Cohen 2002).

65

and simple forms and techniques. Many scholars have pointed out that the major function of early pottery vessels was for cooking (Lu, T. 1999: 124, 2010; Wu, X. and Zhao 2003). As discussed earlier in text, foods available in abundance during the transitional period were small game animals, fish, shell-fish, nuts, tubers, and cereals, and many of them required boiling before being consumed, particularly acorns, cereals, and shellfish. It is possible that the origin of pottery sprang from the new opportunity to intensively exploit specific foods; within that context, certain ways of cooking may have required particular forms of vessels. Some regional variation existed among early ceramic products, regarding form of the vessel, additive material used in the paste, and the presence or absence of soot on the vessel's surface. Because potters may have intentionally designed certain forms and selected certain types of tempering material to improve performance during use, the differences of form and paste may have been closely related to the vessel's function (Schiffer and Skibo 1987; Skibo et al. 1989).

In north China, the majority of vessels dating to the early Holocene are pots with a cylindrical shape and a flat bottom, often referred to as *yuxingqi* in archaeological literature. They are mostly sand-tempered, but in some cases crushed shells were also used as temper. These vessels were most likely heated directly, as shown by the soot often found on the exterior surface. These cylinder-shaped cooking pots, as a regional tradition, continued to be used during the early Neolithic period at sites distributed over the North China Plain and Shandong region (see Chapter 5).

In the lower Yangzi River area, Shangshan revealed the earliest example of ceramics. The predominant form is a fiber-tempered basin with flaring walls, finished with red slip and, in some cases, fitted with an attached loop. No soot is observable on the surface of any Shangshan ceramics; nevertheless, presumably some of these vessels were in fact cooking utensils to which heat was applied internally, by insertion of heated stones into water, leaving no external traces.

Based on their experimental study of the technical effects of different ceramic pastes, Skibo et al. (1989) suggested that fiber-tempered pottery technology prioritizes ease of manufacture and portability, with diminished heat transfer. Fiber-tempered vessels are much lighter than sand-tempered ones; they are also better insulators than conductors of heat, and this effect is enhanced if the vessels are coated. These characteristics make fiber-tempered pottery most suitable for boiling food by inserting heated stones, as would plausibly be favored in a society that was mainly hunter-gatherer in its subsistence base and semisedentary in its residential pattern. Based on Reid's (1989: 173–5) research, the design characteristics of a vessel well suited for stone-boiling should include: use of a thick, porous fabric that will retain rather than conduct heat; a watertight interior; an overthickened, flat, stable base that can absorb radiant heat and impact energy from the inserted hot stones; and straight or flaring walls with a wide mouth to facilitate skimming of surface liquid or extraction of food contents. In view of these observations, it may not be only coincidental that the Shangshan pottery basins show all the prescribed characteristics of vessels used for stone-boiling.

It is also worth noting that, among some Native Americans in California, acorns, which were eaten as a staple food, were ground to meal with grinding stones, and cooked by the stone-boiling method (Driver 1961: 68–9; Fagan 2000: 209). Thus, it is possible that some of Shangshan's fiber-tempered pottery basins were used for stone-boiling acorn meal.

In the lower Yangzi River region, following development of all components of the Neolithic cultural mix, fiber-tempered pottery was eventually replaced by mineral-tempered varieties. The shift in ceramic ingredients seems not to have led immediately to change in vessel form, however. At Xiaohuangshan (ca. 9000–8000 cal. BP), some 80 km northeast of Shangshan, flaring-walled basins similar in form to those from Shangshan constitute a major part of the pottery assemblage, but all of these basins were sand-tempered (Zhang, H. and Wang 2005). This distinction may indicate that food preparation methods, like stone-boiling, continued unaltered despite the technical change in ceramic composition. The use of fiber-tempered ceramics also declined gradually; they continue to appear in pottery assemblages from the Kuahuqiao and Hemudu sites (ca. 8000–6000 cal. BP), but have not been found among later remains. The replacement of fiber-tempered by mineral-tempered ceramics in the Yangzi River region is correlated with increased dietary reliance on cultivated rice. This situation seems to parallel the case implied by archaeological data from southeastern North America, where change in ceramic technology, particularly from fiber tempered to mineral tempered, was closely related to the transition in subsistence technology, meaning that, in the latter situation, foods consumed and their cooking methods were related to cultivation of cereals (Schiffer and Skibo 1987: 602).

In the middle Yangzi River region and South China, potsherds have been found at several late Pleistocene and early Holocene sites, including Yuchanyan, Xianrendong, Zengpiyan, Dingsishan, and Dayan. The reconstructed vessels have pointed or round bottoms and are tempered with sand or crushed calcite or quartz; some show soot on the surface (e.g., Dayan). Archaeologists have suggested that these vessels were used to cook foods, such as rice and shellfish (Lu, T. 1999: 124, 2010; Zhongguo Shehui Kexueyuan 2003a: 452).

Exploitation of nuts, cereals, and shellfish existed before the use of pottery; therefore, these foods must have been cooked by other means for many thousands of years before pottery was invented. In this view, the innovation of pottery in China can be seen as an improvement of cooking method within a continuous subsistence system in the late Pleistocene. In general, the regional variability in ceramic form and technology may have been linked to vessel function. To understand, however, which types of food were involved, we cannot rely only on the technofunctional principle; rather, residue analysis will need to be performed, to test hypotheses about the function of early pottery.

Various theories have been proposed concerning the origins of pottery within a global framework. The first is the architectural hypothesis, which sees the development of pottery making as parallel to that of early building construction; the second is the culinary hypothesis, which states that pottery was invented as kitchen-based containers; and the third is the resource intensification hypothesis, which explains the origin of pottery as part of an adaptive subsistence strategy, in response to changing environment and food resources during the late Pleistocene-early Holocene transition (see summary by Rice 1999). Pottery remains observed in the archaeological record from China seem to support the second and third hypotheses.

ORIGINS OF POTTERY IN THE REGIONAL CONTEXT OF EAST ASIA

The origins of pottery in China were a part of sociotechnological changes within a much broader geographic scope in East Asia, including China, Japan, and the Russian Far East. During the LGM, the sea level was as much as 140 m lower than at present, and the Japanese archipelago was a single landmass connected with continental Asia in the north (through Sakhalin to Siberia) and probably also in the south (via the Korean peninsula) (Aikens and Akazawa 1996; figure 1 of Cohen 2002; Ikawa-Smith 1986: 203). Across this greater East Asian landmass, the movements of mobile hunting-gathering populations, along with their technologies, would have been rather fluent, and interregional interactions would have been frequent. It is within this context that the earliest pottery technology emerged in several regions of East Asia, all dating to ca. 16,000 cal. BP or earlier (Figure 3.8).

The occurrence of the earliest pottery in Japan marks the transition from Paleolithic to the Incipient Jomon (12,800–10,500 BP). These earliest pottery remains are small fragments that have been found only in cave sites, such as Odai Yamamoto I in Aomori Prefecture, northern Honshu (ca. 16,500 cal. BP), and Fukui on the southern island of Kyushu (Habu 2004: 26–32; Tsutsumi 2002). The oldest pottery is mostly plain ware, and some have fiber tempering. Although in most cases the vessels' forms cannot be clearly reconstructed, some evidently have flat bases (Keally et al. 2003: 5; Kidder 1957: 7). It is commonly held that the oldest pottery in Japan was used for boiling food (by externally applied heat, evidently), given the discovery of soot attached to undecorated pottery and of pots containing the remains of carbonized foodstuffs (Kobayashi 2004: 19–20; Tsutsumi 2002: 249).

Those early pottery fragments were found in association with stone tools belonging to the Mikoshiba-type industries, characterized by edge-ground axes and large points, which originated in and around the Russian Far East and Siberia (Habu 2004: 26–32; Tsutsumi 2002). Some settlements dated to the Incipient Jomon show characteristics of a sedentary way of life, such as the construction of stable pit dwellings, hearths formed with stones, food storage, fire pits, and stone clusters, all of which are evidence of residential facilities used for an extended period of time. The stone tool assemblage of the Incipient Jomon consists of chipped stone points, scrapers, semilunar tools, and spearheads; chipped and polished axes, perhaps for woodworking; and grinding stones for processing plant and animal foods (Habu 2004: 57–78; Kobayashi 2004: 7–17). These material assemblages are largely comparable with those from terminal Pleistocene sites in China.

The Jomon people relied on a variety of food resources in a warm, temperate, and rich environment, with increased exploitation of inland water fishery and nuts, such as chestnuts, walnuts, and acorns (Kobayashi 2004; Tsutsumi 2002). The degrees of sedentism vary significantly in time and space; whereas some may have developed full sedentism, others appear to have had seasonal sedentary bases (Habu 2004: 79–134; Pearson 2006). Despite increased scholarly recognition of a significant role of food production among Jomon populations (Crawford 2008), in general, Jomon subsistence is believed to have been characterized by developed logistical mobility and the exploitation of various resources in the ecosystem. This situation indicates that the Jomon was close to the collector end of the forager–collector spectrum (Habu 2004: 63). The subsistence-settlement strategies of the Jomon can also find parallels in early Holocene China.

In the Russian Far East, the earliest pottery remains were unearthed from the lower Amur River region, represented by Gasya and Khummy, dating to around 16,500–14,500 cal. BP (Kuzmin 2003b: 22; Kuzmin and Orlova 2000: 359). The ceramic samples are fragile and weak, and the estimated firing temperature was not more than 600°C. The early ceramics are flat-bottomed vessels and are made of two types of pastes: natural clay without temper and clay with plant fiber temper (Zhushchikhovskaya 1997). They were made by packing clay into or onto a plaited basketry container used as a mold (Zhushchikhovskaya 2005: 23).

The lithic assemblage associated with the earliest pottery is characterized by the Mesolithic tradition. The pollen data from Gasya suggest that the environment during the period when the earliest pottery developed was rather cold, and the predominant vegetation was light pine and larch forest with large open spaces filled by grassy meadows. The origin of the earliest pottery in this region was probably associated with the consumption of nuts and the intensification of fishing (Kuzmin 2003b). The presence of residue on the surface of some ceramic samples from Gasya supports the argument for cooking function (Zhushchikhovskaya 2005: 29). It has also been suggested that the earliest pottery was coupled with the emergence of sedentism, as remains of a dwelling were found at Khummy (Kuzmin 2003b), and the sites in this general region during the Pleistocene-Holocene transitional period show evidence of long occupation in one place (Zhushchikhovskaya 2005: 28).

These data suggest that the people who made the earliest pottery in the Russian Far East practiced a subsistence economy primarily relying on hunting, fishing, and gathering strategies in an environment with a wide range of food resources available. The communities may have spent a fair amount of time at seasonal campsites, long enough for pottery making. This situation was probably similar to that of Hutouliang, where the earliest pottery in north China has been found.

In the Russian Far East, not only was the earliest pottery made by basketry molds, but the surface decorations on vessels in subsequent Neolithic ceramics also show imitations of basket patterns (Zhushchikhovskaya 2005: 62–71). It is worth noting that the rim sherds in the earliest pottery assemblages from Donghulin and Nanzhuangtou in north China also show cornice-like decorations imitative of braided artifacts (Figures 3.4 and 3.5). This phenomenon points to correspondences between these two types of containers – similarity of technological designs and concepts, and certain functional congruence – which together support the proposition that cooking by stone-boiling was associated both with baskets and early pottery vessels. More important is that, as Zhushchikhovskaya (2005: 71) has noticed, early potters in East Asia, including the Russian Far East, north China, the Korean peninsula, and the Japanese Archipelago, all copied the form and design of plaited artifacts. Nevertheless, at this point it is uncertain to what extent such similarities resulted from interregional interactions or from coincidentally independent development.

THE EMERGENCE OF SEDENTISM IN CHINA

The developmental process of sedentism in China has not been studied systematically, and few attempts have been made to understand the degree of sedentism among foraging communities in south China. Lü (1999: 97) argued, based on the presence of wild rice and deer antlers with skull fragments at the Xianrendong cave site, that it was probably occupied from autumn to the next spring. In contrast, Yasuda (2002) inferred from the appearance of pottery that the "sedentary revolution" occurred in East Asia at the end of the LGM and expanded widely around 16,500 cal. BP; however, he did not specify what degree of sedentism may have been practiced. Based on current data, high degrees of sedentism may have emerged in some regions by the early Holocene, exemplified by Shangshan.

Shangshan was situated in a subtropical environment rich in natural resources, although their availability was highly seasonal: Food was abundant during summer and autumn but scarce in winter. Compared to late

Palaeolithic times (Lu, T. 1999), population density at Shangshan in the early Holocene was considerably higher, as indicated by larger settlement sizes. The archaeological assemblages from these sites suggest a mixed residential mode characterized by a combination of both seasonal/yearly mobility, likely related to the logistical collector strategy (cf. Binford 1980), and gradually increased sedentism. Plant foodstuffs, particularly acorns, were exploited.

Acorns have been exploited as a staple food by people in many parts of the world (Mason 1992, 1996). The acorn contains a considerable concentration of tannins: 2.21 to 22.74 percent as determined from fifteen species of *Quercus* (Jia, H. and Zhou 1991); 2.21 to 15.75 percent from four species of *Cyclobalanopsis* (Duanmu 1995); and 0.63 to 3.31 percent from eight species of *Lithocarpus* (Duanmu 1997). Acorns have to be rendered edible before human consumption, by an acid removal process (including grinding and leaching), which can be complicated and time consuming (Bettinger et al. 1997; Mason 1992, 1996). In China today, acorn is mainly used for fodder, alcohol, and industrial starch (Jia, H. and Zhou 1991; Yang, P. et al. 2005), but it is also consumed by people, particularly in times of famine. Processing methods vary from region to region, but the essential procedures include soaking, grinding, shelling, sieving, leaching, and drying, with the entire process involving several days' work (e.g., Bai, K. et al. 2000; Jia, H. and Zhou 1991). Because acorns have to be ground as part of the process to make them edible, the large numbers of grinding stones uncovered at early Holocene sites and the associated residues suggest that acorn is likely to have been an important staple in people's diet during the early Holocene.

A close connection between intensive storage and sedentism in hunting-gathering societies has long been recognized (e.g., Testart 1982), but not all types of storage led to sedentism (Soffer 1989). Whereas mobile hunting-gathering groups may store foods that have a short use-life (such as frozen, dry, or salted animal products), sedentary hunting-gathering communities store foods with long shelf or social use-life (such as nuts and cereals). Therefore, the nature of the stored resources is the most important variable motivating the rise of sedentism and its ultimate intensification via food production (Hitchcock 1987; Soffer 1989). Acorns can easily be collected in large quantities in the autumn and stored for long periods of time. Traditional methods of acorn storage in China include piling up inside houses, caching in pits, and packing in baskets submerged in running water (Anonymous 1975).

Due to its known instability of yield from year to year, acorn is a potentially unreliable food resource (Gardner 1997). If a population depended heavily on acorns as a staple, the community may have had to move to another richer resource patch when food resources became depleted locally. Such movements would have occurred in cycles ranging from seasonal to multiannual, and this variety would explain the mixture of caches with more permanent residential features at Shangshan.

Taken together, the factors required for collecting and processing acorns – such as optimally abundant seasonal productivity and long-term storability, followed by high processing costs of time and energy – all allowed and encouraged a stable residential mode, at least among a part of the population in a community. At the same time, cyclic variability in the productivity of oak trees also may have ensured residential mobility, which appears to have occurred at Shangshan. Further research is needed to investigate regional settlement distribution, population densities, and foraging behavior involved with the procurement of acorn and other food resources, to better understand changing settlement-subsistence patterns in this region.

Bruce Smith (1995: 212) has predicted that the predecessors of the rice-farming communities in the Yangzi River region would have been affluent sedentary societies dependent on aquatic resources and wild rice. The current data suggest that sedentism in the lower Yangzi River region emerged in a resource-rich environment (cf. Smith 1995); nevertheless, instead of wild rice, the main staple may have been other starch-rich plants, particularly the locally abundant nuts, like acorns. The factors of intensive acorn exploitation, the development of grinding technology for processing starchy foods, and the construction of facilities in which to store these highly preservable foods all combined to underpin increased sedentism prior to the appearance of intensive rice agriculture.

Both wild and cultivated types of rachis on rice spikelet are present at Shangshan (Liu, L. et al. 2007b; Zheng, Y. and Jiang 2007), and we can probably infer that abundant wild rice was available around the site and that people may have attempted to cultivate it. From an ecological perspective, the storability of rice certainly made it an ideal alternate source of food for the lean season. From a social point of view, rice has been an important food in feasting and ritual events in many traditional rice-producing groups (Hayden 2003), and the oldest fermented beverages in China that we know of were made of rice (McGovern et al. 2004, 2005). Therefore, rice may have functioned as a luxury food and may have played a significant role in ritual activities. These properties of rice would have encouraged its domestication. Nevertheless, Shangshan's subsistence economy was most likely characterized by a hunting-gathering way of life, with limited emphasis on rice collection and, perhaps, cultivation.

Putting all these lines of evidence together, we may conclude that the Shangshan subsistence economy was characterized by the broad-spectrum strategy, relying on fishing, hunting, and collecting wild plants. On the continuum of forager-collector strategies, Shangshan can be placed at the end of the collector side. That is, the hunting-gathering community settled in a perhaps semisedentary or almost fully sedentary village. The rich and diverse food resources in the region encouraged logistic mobility, meaning that small task groups traveled to different locations far away from the residential base to procure specific foods. Seasonal differences in resource availability would cause food shortages during the period of winter and early spring, leading to the need for food storage. If nuts, especially acorns, were abundant in this region, they would be the most desirable foods for storage, due to their long shelf life. The complex and time-consuming process of acid removal, required in preparation for eating the nuts, also would have encouraged a higher degree of sedentism. Evolving the necessary type of food processing and perfecting the conditions for extended storability of the nuts are activities involving not only environmental provisions but also technological inventions and may have been prerequisites for emergence of the logistic sedentary lifestyle evident at Shangshan. The lightweight, fiber-tempered pottery basin may have been designed partially for these logistically organized collectors.

Many characteristics apparent at the Shangshan site parallel those of Jomon, in terms of subsistence adaptation. Both culture groups made chipped and ground stone tools, rendered pottery, practiced logistic mobility, adopted intensive storage, and exploited a wide range of faunal and floral resources in a rich natural environment. These resemblances may be attributable to the similar ecosystems that existed in the two regions. We would also expect that some cultural interactions, by land bridge or by boat, may have occurred between these two regions during upper Paleolithic times (Ikawa-Smith 1986). It is entirely possible that some ancient settlements earlier than Shangshan were distributed over the landscape between these two regions but that they are now under the East China Sea (Figure 3.8). Such putative sites might provide missing links that would articulate the chronological record of broad-scale cultural development in East Asia. In this view, the uniqueness of the Shangshan material assemblage in the lower Yangzi River region may signify predominant affiliations with a cultural tradition that has otherwise disappeared under the ocean and was largely different from other cultures found at inland locales.

TRANSITIONS IN OTHER REGIONS OF CHINA

It needs to be pointed out that not all regions in China show evidence of a changing subsistence strategy during the Pleistocene-Holocene transition. Some groups apparently continued the Epipaleolithic tradition well into the Holocene, continuously relying on hunting, fishing, and gathering. These hunting-gathering communities have been found in the arid and semiarid areas of north China (Bettinger et al. 1994), in the high altitude regions of Northwest and Southwest China (Bettinger et al. 1994; Huang, W. and Hou 1998; Madsen et al. 1996; Rhode et al. 2007), at some cave sites in South China (e.g., Zengpiyan), and in tropical areas of southeast and Taiwan (Zhang, S. 2000). The lag of subsistence-settlement change in those regions seems to suggest that the temperate ecosystem, with seasonally abundant natural resources, may have been a necessary environmental condition for technological and social transformation during the Pleistocene-Holocene transition in China.

CONCLUSIONS

The Pleistocene-Holocene transition in China is characterized by various regional trajectories that shared some similarities with one another but that also show distinctive local traditions in material culture. In the Yellow River and Yangzi River regions, several major technological innovations and social developments occurred, including the invention of pottery, the production of ground stone tools, the increasing exploitation of plant foods, and the use of storage facilities, which together led to the emergence of a sedentary way of life and to notable population growth.

These developments need to be understood from the perspective of a subsistence-settlement system, with reference to the environmental and ecological backgrounds. The transitional period witnessed a general trend away from more forager-oriented human groups during the late Pleistocene to more collector-oriented communities during the early Holocene. As foragers, people moved their residential bases constantly to the locations where food was available, as exemplified in the site clusters found at Xiachuan, Shizitan, and Hutouliang in North China. As collectors, people formed logistically organized task groups to procure foods far from their residential bases, stored relatively imperishable foods, and extended the sedentary duration in their residential bases. This situation is best manifested in Shangshan, but is also observable, to a lesser extent, in Donghulin, Nanzhuangtou, and Lijiagou. Three factors appear to have formed the necessary conditions for this transition to occur: (1) a warm temperate and subtropical environment, which provided a wide variety of food resources with seasonal rhythms of abundance and scarcity; (2) the availability of storable foods, particularly nuts and cereals, which made the sedentary lifestyle possible; and (3) technological improvements in the utilization of certain foods, by cooking them in ceramics, which allowed people to adapt to the changing environment. As a result, sedentism, population increase, and, possibly, the initial cultivation of cereals all emerged from the transitional period, leading to further socioeconomic development in the Neolithic period from 9000 cal. BP onward, which will be discussed in the next chapter.

Youchaoshi, the nest-building people mentioned in the classical text quoted at the start of this chapter, may be understood as a mythological expression of an ancient memory of remotely early dwellers who initiated a more sedentary way of life while still relying on a hunting-gathering economy.

CHAPTER 4

DOMESTICATION OF PLANTS AND ANIMALS

> To the rulers people are the most important, and to people food is the most important.
>
> > Chapter "Li Yiji Biography" in *Hanshu*, by Ban Gu (AD 32–92)
> > (Ban, 1962: 2108)

"王者以民为天，而民以食为天。"〈〈汉书·郦食其传〉〉班固

China is one of the few primary loci of plant and animal domestication and of emergent agriculture in the world (Bellwood 2005; Smith 1998). Chinese society has been predominantly agrarian since antiquity, and, as in other parts of the world, agriculture formed the economic foundation for the rise of civilization in China. Among the most important crops and animals known in early China (rice, millet, soybean, pigs, dogs, and perhaps chickens) were domesticated indigenously, whereas wheat, barley, sheep, goats, and horses were introduced, already domesticated, from elsewhere. The origins of domesticated cattle and water buffalo are unclear at present; these species were surely domesticated separately in time and place, but exactly where and when those transformations occurred remain moot. Unlike other chapters in this book that present archaeological information in a temporospatial order, in this chapter, we focus on the domestication of each species just mentioned. The purpose of this arrangement is to provide a database for easy discussion in the following chapters.

DOMESTICATION OF PLANTS

Before systematic flotation methods were used in Chinese archaeology (Zhao, Z. 2004d), floral remains visible to the naked eye were collected unsystematically in excavations, with only occasional use of flotation methods. The study of plant remains was mainly focused on taxonomic identification, conducted by botanists. In recent years archaeobotanic research has developed rapidly; more projects have used flotation methods and quantitative analysis, and the results from these studies have significantly improved our understanding of plant domestication in China. In this section we mainly discuss the current understanding of domestication processes related to major crops in ancient China – rice, millet, soybeans, wheat, barley, and oats. Among these domesticates, rice has received the most attention from researchers.

Rice

Asian domesticated rice (*Oryza sativa*) consists of two subspecies: *O. sativa indica* and *O. sativa japonica*, and it is generally agreed that *O. sativa* was derived from common wild rice (*Oryza rufipogon*). When, where, and how people first domesticated rice have been long discussed and debated. Figure 4.1 shows the sites associated with rice discussed in this section.

Where? It was first proposed that rice was domesticated in the Himalayan foothills, including an area from northeast India's Assam-Meghalaya region to mountain ranges in mainland Southeast Asia and Southwest China (Chang, T. 1976), but the evidence for this argument is limited and unreliable. In particular, archaeological data indicate that rice remains from Southeast Asia and Southwest China date to much later times than do those of the Yangzi River region. In the 1970s, with the discovery of several rice-producing Neolithic sites dated to ca. 7000 cal. BP, such as Hemudu, Luojiajiao, and Caoxieshan, Yan (1982) suggested that the lower Yangzi River Valley was the major center of rice domestication. In the 1980–90s, new finds of early rice remains reportedly dated to 8000 cal. BP or earlier from Yuchanyan, Xianrendong, Pengtoushan, and Bashidang in Hunan led archaeologists to switch their attentions to the middle Yangzi River region for the origins of rice domestication (MacNeish et al. 1998; Pei, 1998; Yuan, Jiarong 2002; Zhao, Z. 1998). In the 2000s, three sites, Shangshan (Jiang, L. and Liu 2006), Xiaohuangshan (Zhang, H. and Wang 2005), and Kuahuqiao (Zhejiangsheng and Xiaoshan 2004), all in the lower Yangzi River region, have revealed rice remains dating to 11,000–7000 cal. BP. These findings regenerated discussion about the origins of rice domestication. There is now a general consensus among scholars that rice was first domesticated along the middle and lower Yangzi River region (Bellwood 2005; Crawford 2006; Crawford and Shen 1998; Higham and Lu 1998; Yan, W. 2002), although some believe that the upper Huai River was also a part of the region where rice domestication took place (Zhang, J. et al. 1996). The findings of wild rice remains from Pleistocene deposits at Xianrendong and Diaotonghuan in Jiangxi (Zhao, Z. 1998) and from a number of Epipaleolithic and early Neolithic sites in Zhejiang (Zheng, Y. et al. 2007; Zheng, Y. and Jiang 2007) confirm that the Yangzi River region was a natural habitation of wild rice, making the original area of rice domestication more plausible.

When? The question regarding when rice was first domesticated is still a matter of debate, largely attributable to the use of different methods and criteria by scholars to distinguish between wild and domesticated rice. Three methods

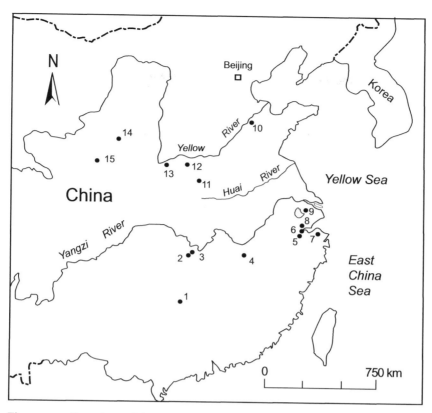

Figure 4.1. Location of sites associated with rice remains mentioned in Chapter 4. 1: Yuchanyan; 2: Pengtoushan; 3: Bashidang; 4: Xianrendong-Diaotonghuan; 5: Shangshan; 6: Kuahuqiao; 7: Hemudu, Tianluoshan; 8: Luojiajiao; 9: Caoxieshan; 10: Yuezhuang; 11: Jiahu; 12: Huizui; 13: Nanjiaokou; 14: Qingyang; 15: Xishanping.

have been frequently used in China. The first one addresses the morphology of grain shape, by measuring the length/width ratio to differentiate wild (L/W > 3.2) and domesticated varieties, *indica* (L/W = 2.3–3.2) and *japonica* (L/W = 1.6–2.3). On the basis of primarily this method, some argue that the initial human intervention in the life cycle of rice had emerged in the late Pleistocene, as exemplified at cave sites such as Yuchanyan (Yuan, Jiarong 2002). Some believe that rice agriculture was already in effect by 9000 cal. BP, as indicated by the remains of rice from Pengtoushan, Bashidang, and Jiahu, although it may not have played a dominant role in the subsistence economy (Pei, A. 2002; Zhang, J. and Wang 1998). Nevertheless, many people are cautious about the antiquity of Yuchanyan rice, which has not been directly dated. Crawford and Shen (1998: 864–5) have pointed out that, without knowing the presence/absence of a brittle rachis, the domesticity of Bashidang rice is inconclusive.

The length/width ratio method may not work in practice, because the great variation of size and proportions among domesticated and wild rice species today makes it difficult to assign ancient rice grains to any given population (Fuller et al. 2007). This method also seems to be based on a presumption that division into the subspecies *japonica* and *indica* occurred after domestication was achieved; therefore, it has been held, the occurrences of these two forms in a rice assemblage would imply a domesticated status. This presumption seems questionable, however. On the basis of nuclear DNA restriction fragment length polymorphism analysis of common wild rice, Sun et al. (1997) pointed out that common wild rice is genetically diverse in China: There is a primitive type, an *indica*-like type, and a *japonica*-like type. According to the results of DNA analyses, Sato (2002) has argued that the *indica-japonica* differentiation occurred before domestication had begun in the group of *sativa* varieties, and his examination of twenty-eight seeds from archaeological assemblages in China shows that all of them have genetic features of *japonica*. In an experimental cultivation of wild rice conducted by Oka and Morishima (1971), a hybrid population of *perennis* and *sativa* grown in bulk (rather than in pedigrees) showed rapid development of domesticated features. Historically, such populations are most likely to have been secondary products that appeared after the inception of rice cultivation. In the early stage of cultivation, rice populations would have included elements variously undergoing primary and secondary processes of domestication, and thus might have contained a large degree of genetic variation (Oka and Morishima 1971). In view of these observations, the great morphological variety of grain shape found in early rice assemblages probably reflects a mixture of wild, initially domesticated, and hybrid forms.

The second method for determining rice domestication is phytolith research, but the conclusions from different researchers vary significantly. Zhao Zhijun (1998) analyzed double-peaked glume cells in rice phytoliths from the Diaotonghuan cave in Jiangxi, and the results show evidence of wild rice collection during the late Pleistocene (12,000/11,000 BP), followed by a mix of collected wild rice with harvested early domestic rice during 10,000–8000 BP, and finally primary use of domesticated rice about 7000 BP. Zhang Wenxu (2002) compared the bipeak tubercle in rice phytoliths from ancient and modern rice remains, and suggested that an initial phase of rice cultivation can be traced back to the late Pleistocene/early Holocene period. The study by Zheng et al. (2007) of phytoliths from motor cells indicates that the phytolith morphology of Shangshan rice (11,000–9000 cal. BP) is similar to that of tropical *japonica*, indicating the beginning of rice cultivation in early Holocene. On the contrary, Fuller et al. (2007) analyzed bulliform phytoliths in rice remains from the lower Yangzi River region and argued that domesticated rice did not occur until the Songze and Liangzhu phases (after 6000 cal. BP).

The third method for identifying domesticated rice focuses on the morphology of panicle rachis. The spikelets of wild cereals/rice have a brittle rachis, which allows the seed to be shed naturally upon maturity. On the contrary, the spikelets of domesticated cereals/rice have a strong rachis, which prevents natural shedding and thereby facilitates planned harvesting. Thus, domestic rice spikelets, when shattered by humans, often retain a tell-tale fragment of the rachis (Hillman and Davies 1999; Sato 2002). A study of Shangshan rice remains (ca. 11,000–9000 cal. BP) also suggests an early date of possible rice cultivation. Microscopic observations on panicle rachis of rice spikelets show that characteristics of both wild and domestic varieties are present, and the latter appear to resemble *japonica* (Zheng, Y. and Jiang 2007).

According to a study by Zheng et al. (2007), among 120 spikelets from Kuahuqiao, 42 percent show fragments of panicle rachis, resembling domesticated *japonica*, whereas 58 percent of samples show a smooth scar on the rachis, a characteristic of wild rice. Among 451 spikelets from Luojiajiao and Tianluoshan, both contemporary with Hemudu, 51 percent show a tough rachis of the cultigen type, and 49 percent have a brittle rachis like wild rice. When comparing the Kuahuqiao rice with Luojiajiao–Tianluoshan assemblages, the proportion of cultigen type changes from 42 to 51 percent, accounting for a 9 percent increase in 500 years from 8000 to 7500 cal. BP. If this figure is regarded as an average domestication rate, the initial domestication would have occurred before 10,000 cal. BP (Zheng, Y. et al. 2007). This account also suggests that, hypothetically, the transition from the beginning of rice cultivation (near 0% cultigen type) to full domestication (near 100% cultigen type) would have taken more than 5,000 years. The argument made by Zheng et al. still needs to be tested with larger sample sizes from more sites. For example, a more recent examination of the morphology of rice panicle rachis from Tianluoshan suggests that the proportion of nonshattering domesticated rice spikelet bases increased over a period of 300 years (6900–6600 cal. BP) from 27 to 39 percent (Fuller et al. 2009), a considerably lower result than previous measurements. In any event, the overall data indicate that, during a long period of time between the initial cultivation/human intervention and the full domestication, rice populations may have shown morphological characteristics of a mix composed of wild, domesticated, and hybrid types (Liu, L. et al. 2007b). Rice domestication was a continuum, and we may never be able to draw a clear demarcation between cultivated wild rice and cultivated domesticated rice in the archaeological record.

In summary, rice remains from late Pleistocene Yuchanyan and Diaotonghuan possibly represent a stage of wild rice collection, and those from Shangshan in the early Holocene should be a focus of research seeking evidence of early rice cultivation. In north China, by 9000 cal. BP, rice, most likely a mix of wild and domesticated, became more habitually used than previously, as evidenced in Jiahu in the Huai River region (Henansheng Wenwu Kaogu 1999a; Zhao, Z. and Zhang 2009). By 8000 cal. BP, rice reached north to the lower Yellow River region, as seen in Yuezhuang in Shandong (Crawford et al. 2006). Rice dispersed to the middle Yellow River region by 6000–5500 cal. BP, as exemplified by Nanjiaokou (Wei, X. et al. 2000) and Huizui in Henan (Lee,

G. and Bestel 2007; Lee, G. et al. 2007), and then spread further to the upper Yellow River Valley by 5500–5000 cal. BP, as seen at Qingyang (Zhang, W. 2000) and Xishanping in Tianshui (Li, X. et al. 2007), both in Gansu (Figure 4.1). Rice domestication had developed by 9000–8000 cal. BP in both south and north China, exemplified by Jiahu and Kuahuqiao (Liu, L. et al. 2007b).

There is little consensus among archaeologists as to when rice became a staple food. Some believe that, at Hemudu, rice was produced in large quantities and that hoe-agriculture based on rice was already underway (e.g., Huang, W. 1998; Yan, W. 1982), whereas others consider the importance, in the Yangzi Basin, of wild rice and other wild plants in addition to rice cultivation (e.g., Crawford 2006; Crawford and Shen 1998). In particular, K. C. Chang (1981a) argued that people of the Hemudu and Majiabang cultures were affluent foragers who explored the abundant wild faunal and floral resources, as well as cultivating rice. Cai (2006) questioned the inference, drawn from the discovery of a large number of bone spades at Hemudu, that hoe-agriculture existed there. He pointed out that these bone spades were more likely used to dig storage pits and postholes than to work in rice paddies, as evidenced by the digging marks left on pits, which match the width of these spades. He further argues that, based on the material remains, hunting-gathering made up the major components of subsistence, whereas domesticating rice played only a minor role in the Hemudu economy. A similar view is also held by other researchers (e.g., Fuller et al. 2007). These different views regarding the function of bone spades need to be evaluated by use-wear analysis of the tools. Nevertheless, the existing data suggest a long and gradual progress of several thousand years toward the establishment of rice-based agriculture in southern China.

How? What are the major factors involved in the process of evolutionary selection that led from wild rice collection to full domestication? As with the analogous transformations of wheat and barley (Hillman and Davies 1999), several conditions are required for the transition to rice cultivation, as summarized by Higham (1995). First, whereas collectors of wild rice simply beat the mature seeds into boats or containers, early cultivators of domestic rice had to harvest the plant by cutting the stalks, then growing new generations of it in a field. Such laborious processes, repeated over time, would promote selection favoring mature spikelets with a tough rachis. Second, the group taking up the destructive, manipulative, and regenerative activities of cutting, selecting, planting, and burning must regard those new practices as acceptably compatible with their religious and cultural values. Third, sedentism would need to be already well established, and only then could cultivation be adopted as a fundamental economic strategy; in turn, this strategy, once adopted, would further reinforce the commitment to sedentism, to protect the considerable new investment being made in cultivation. To identify the existence of these conditions in the archaeological record is not a simple and straightforward matter, however.

On the basis of their experimental study, Oka and Morishima (1971) showed that, by using knives in harvesting and planting rice seeds in a field, after only five generations, the resulting sample showed an increase in weight and spikelet number and a reduction in the rate of seed shedding, due to selection for non-shedding genes. Similar observations have been made through an experimental study on wheat and barley cultivation by Hillman and Davies (1999). These studies suggest that, in such controlled conditions, the morphology of cereals (including rice) can change fairly rapidly under so-called cultivation pressure. In reality, however, rice domestication may have taken a much longer time than the experiments suggested, considering that many conditions in the initial process of cultivation remain unknown to us.

How rice was harvested during the terminal Pleistocene in the Yangzi River region is unclear. Based on Lu's study, the perforated small shells with a sharp cutting edge, found at Yuchanyan in Hunan, may have served as cutting tools, and the glossed edge seen on a few small blades made from chert, unearthed at Diaotonghuan (or Wangdong), may have resulted from cutting cereals; these observations are inconclusive, however (Lu, T. 1999: 87, 94). According to Zhao's phytolith analysis of soil samples from Diaodonghuan, *Oryza* leaf phytoliths are few, but *Oryza* glume cells from grains are abundant, suggesting that the grains were mainly brought into the site (Zhao, Z. 1998: 891–2), probably without the stalks being cut.

In south China the earliest evidence for harvesting rice with the stalks may be traced back to the Shangshan site, where abundant rice husks and leaves are found in burnt clays and as tempers in pottery. We are not sure whether the stalks were cut by tools or pulled by hands, however. Cutting tools, such as stone knives, are also present, although use-wear analysis has not yet been carried out to determine their function (Jiang, L. 2007). The middle stratum at Kuahuqiao (ca. 7700–7300 cal. BP) revealed a dozen rice stalks with spikelets still attached (Zhejiangsheng and Xiaoshan 2004: 325), and the absence of roots suggests that rice was collected by cutting the stalks. No sickle or knife, however, has been unearthed from Kuahuqiao. In north China, Jiahu has revealed the earliest evidence of harvesting tools. A considerable number ($N = 45$) of polished stone sickles has been unearthed, accounting for 16 percent of the total polished stone implements. It has been commonly assumed that some sickles, particularly those with a denticulate cutting edge, were used for harvesting rice (Henansheng Wenwu Kaogu 1999a). Again, however, the function of these tools needs to be determined by use-wear analysis. In view of these observations, at present we do not have hard evidence to show exactly when people began to intervene, intentionally or unintentionally, in the life cycle of rice, a moment which eventually led to domestication.

Management of rice fields may have been rather labor intensive even in the early stages of cultivation. Early rice paddies and associated irrigation systems have been excavated at Tianluoshan in Zhejiang (5000–2500 BC) (Zheng, Y. et al. 2009), Chengtoushan in Hunan (4500–4300 BC) (He, J. 1999), and Caoxieshan in Jiangsu (ca. 4000 BC) (Zou, H. et al. 2000), suggesting that rice production had become more intensified by 7,000 years ago in the Yangzi River region. Burning during the dry season may have been a common method of field management in early agriculture, to clear the rice fields, as evidenced by the markedly abundant microcharcoals found in the deposits of rice fields at Tianluoshan (Fuller and Qin 2009; Zheng, Y. et al. 2009).

A laboratory analysis of pollen, algal, fungal spore, and microcharcoal material taken from sediments at Kuahuqiao suggests that by 7700 cal. BP the Neolithic people in the Kuahuqiao area appear to have adopted several methods to establish their settlement and undertake rice cultivation. Thus, it is argued, they cleared land by fire, cultivated rice in lowland swamps, and maintained paddy fields by managing seasonal flooding and by burning and manuring, thus enhancing yields from rice cultivation (Zong, Y. et al. 2007). This interpretation has been challenged, however, by the Kuahuqiao excavator, who pointed out that the samples used in the study just mentioned were in fact taken from within the settlement area; therefore, the deposits sampled reflect residential refuse and are not definitive traits of the rice field (Jiang, L. 2008).

The process of rice domestication is an ongoing research topic, and there are more questions than answers at the present (see a summary by Crawford 2011). Most researchers would now agree, however, that, if it took several thousand years from the onset of wild rice exploitation in the terminal Pleistocene to the occurrence of fully domesticated rice in the early-middle Holocene, the selection pressure was apparently not intensive, and rice played only a minor role in the broad-spectrum subsistence economy during the transitional period (e.g., Zhao, Z. and Zhang 2009).

Millets

Two species of millet are believed to have been domesticated in China: foxtail millet (*Setaria italica*) and broomcorn millet (*Panicum miliaceum*), referred to as *su* and *shu* in Chinese, respectively. The wild progenitor of foxtail millet is green foxtail (*Setaria viridis*), which is an annual grass widely distributed over a large part of China. The wild progenitor for broomcorn millet, however, is uncertain (Gao, M. and Chen 1988; Lu, T. 1999).

Where and when? Collection of wild plants including cereals became a part of the broad-spectrum subsistence economy during the terminal Pleistocene, based on residue and use-wear on stone tools from Xiachuan (ca. 23,900–16,400 BP) and Shizitan Locality 9 (ca. 12,700–11,600 cal. BP) in Shanxi

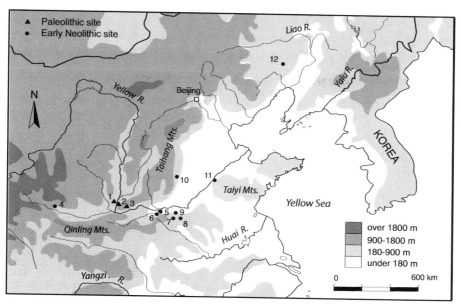

Figure 4.2. Location of sites related to the discussion on the millet domestication process. Late Paleolithic sites: 1: Longwangchan; 2: Shizitan; 3: Xiachuan. Early Neolithic sites: 4: Dadiwan; 5: Wuluoxipo; 6: Fudian; 7: Egou; 8: Peiligang; 9: Shawoli; 10: Cishan; 11: Yuezhuang; 12: Xinglonggou.

(Liu, L. et al. 2011; Lu, T. 1999: 28–32) (see also Chapter 3). These results indicate that humans began to collect and process wild grasses, some of which may have been the wild ancestors of millets, along with other plant foods, more than 20,000 years ago in north China.

Research is lacking on the transition between the wild and domesticated varieties of millet. The earliest phase of domesticated millet, dated between 8,200 and 7,000 years ago, appears widely in the archaeological record, stretching across north China from the Liao River Valley in the northeast to the upper Yellow River in the northwest. The earliest examples of domesticated millet remains were discovered at Xinglonggou in Chifeng, Inner Mongolia (8200–7500 cal. BP) (Zhao, Z. 2004a); at Yuezhuang in Shandong (ca. 8000 cal. BP) (Crawford et al. 2006); at Dadiwan in Qin'an, Gansu (7800–7350 cal. BP) (Liu, C. 2006); at Cishan in Wu'an, Hebei (7400–7200 cal. BP) (Sun, D. et al. 1981); and at several Peiligang sites in Henan (8000–7000 cal. BP), including at Fudian and Wuluoxipo in Gongyi (Lee, G. et al. 2007), and at Peiligang and Shawoli in Xinzheng (Wang, J. 1983; Zheng, N. 1984). A recent study has indicated the presence of millet starch in residues found on several grinding stones from a Peiligang culture site at Egou in Henan, supporting previous macrobotanic findings (Liu, L. et al. 2010a) (Figure 4.2). The millet grains unearthed from Xinglonggou, Yuezhuang, and Dadiwan are predominantly broomcorn. The Xinglonggou millet is said to be intermediate in size between modern domesticated and wild *Panicum*, and rounder and fuller in shape than the wild form, representing an early stage of domestication (Zhao, Z. 2004a). Because the progenitor of *Panicum miliaceum* is unknown, it is difficult to demonstrate how the domesticated form evolved from its wild ancestor. In general, two trends are observable in the millet assemblages from several sites in the Liao River (Zhao, Z. 2004a) and Yellow River regions (Crawford et al. 2006; Lee, G. et al. 2007; Liu, C. 2006). First, millet grains show a gradual increase in size over time (Figure 4.3). Second, in proportionate terms, foxtail millet seems to have increased and broomcorn millet to have decreased from the Neolithic to the early Bronze Age.

The Cishan site has been interpreted as an example of intensified millet production, as suggested by the reported eighty storage pits containing thick layers of millet remains (Sun, D. et al. 1981), estimated to be some 50,000 kg in volume (Tong, W. 1984). No carbonized millet has been preserved, however, and the evidence for the existence of millet there is from phytolith and starch analyses (Huang, Q. 1982; Lu, H. et al. 2009; Yang, X. et al. 2012). In addition, some pits contained pig and dog skeletons below the "millet layers," a condition not suitable for millet storage. Therefore, the nature of these "millet storage pits" and the quantity of millet remains at Cishan have long been unsolved questions (for more details, see Chapter 5).

Recent phytolith analysis of soil samples, from five pits at the site, suggests that the earliest domesticated millet at Cishan was broomcorn millet (*Panicum miliaceum*), dating to 10,300 cal. BP; foxtail millet (*Setaria italica*) appeared after 8700 cal. BP (Lu, H. et al. 2009). This study is the most systematic to date, and it enables us to distinguish two types of domesticated millet from wild millet grasses, through phytolith analysis. This important finding, however, has been questioned by Chinese archaeologists for the extremely early dates assigned to domesticated millet and the methods of sampling. The soil samples analyzed were collected from pits without systematic survey or excavation, and the accelerator mass spectrometry (AMS) dates were not derived from carbonized seeds. Further investigations and excavations will help to provide a more complete picture of this settlement.

The proportion of millet consumed appears to have been rather minor in the diet of these early Neolithic people. At the Xinglonggou site, for instance, millet grains from deposits of the Xinglongwa period account for only 15 percent of all seeds recovered by flotation, as opposed to 99 percent of all seeds taken from the Lower Xiajiadian deposits of the Bronze Age (4000–3500 cal. BP) at the same site (Zhao, Z. 2004a). Residue analysis on grinding stones from Egou also shows a low proportion of starch grains belonging to millet (Liu, L. et al. 2010a). In the Yellow River Valley, a millet-based subsistence economy appears to have been established during the Yangshao period. Staple isotopic analysis of human and animal bones shows that types of millet comprised 75–85 percent of the human diet at Jiangzhai and Shijia in the Shaanxi

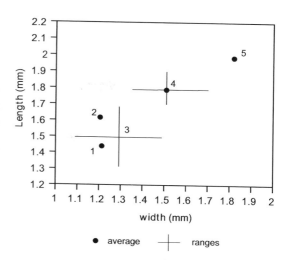

Figure 4.3. Increase in size of broomcorn millet from the early Neolithic to the Bronze Age. 1: Dadiwan; 2: Xinglonggou (7000–5000 BC); 3: late Yangshao at Dadiwan (3500–3000 BC); 4: early Longshan at Bancun (3000–2500 BC); 5: Lower Xiajiadian at Xinglonggou (2000–1500 BC).

(6900–6000 cal. BP), and nearly 90 percent of the diet of pigs and dogs at Xipo in Henan (6000–5500 cal. BP) (Pechenkina, E. et al. 2005) (Figure 4.1). Millet remains in the floral assemblages become predominant in the Yiluo region by the late Yangshao period (ca. 5500–5000 cal. BP) (Lee, G. et al. 2007).

How? It is unclear how millet was first cultivated. Through her experiments on millet cultivation and harvesting, Lu (1998, 2002) has demonstrated that green foxtail, the progenitor of domestic foxtail millet, can grow well without human attention, so people did not have to tend the field after sowing. The yields of green foxtail are low, and it would be impossible for communities to rely on this cereal alone. These observations indicate, according to Lu, that the first farmers were mobile foragers who may have cultivated this cereal intentionally, but the early cultivation would have led to little change in their subsistence strategy (Lu, T. 1998, 2002).

A relatively low level of millet production would have not required much effort in terms of field management. Therefore, we would not expect pronounced changes in the material assemblages, and thus the cultivation activities would be difficult to detect in the archaeological record. We also do not know to what extent the initial cultivation may have changed the morphology of seeds, making the identification of early millet cultivation difficult. Systematic and rigorous methods of data collection, such as flotation, use–wear study, and residue analyses, have to be used more regularly in Chinese archaeology, particularly at late Paleolithic and Epipaleolithic sites, to trace the origins of millet cultivation.

Soybeans

The soybean (*Glycine max* subsp. *max*) is one of the most widely grown crops in the world today, but its geographical and temporal origins have been a matter of debate. Domesticated soybean probably arose from wild soybean (*Glycine max* subsp. *soja*), which has been found in large parts of mainland China (except for Qinghai, Xinjiang, and Hainan), Taiwan, Korea, Japan, and the Russian Far East (Guo, W. 2004; Hymowitz 1970; Hymowitz and Singh 1986). Wild and domestic soybeans are interfertile and have similar morphologies, distributions, isozyme banding patterns, and DNA polymorphisms (Hancock 1992: 231). These factors make it difficult to distinguish the domestic and wild varieties (Lee, G. et al. 2011).

Researchers in different disciplines, such as botany, history, and archaeology, have attempted to study the origins of this crop, and five hypotheses have been proposed: (1) Northeast China origins, (2) Yellow River origins, (3) Yellow River and Northeast as two original centers, (4) southern China origins; and (5) multicentered origins within and beyond China (Choi 2004; Zhao, T. and Gai 2004). Such diversity of opinion implies some general problems in the investigative approaches used. A number of studies infer the origin of domestic soybean on the basis of identifying centers of genetic diversity for modern wild and/or cultivated soybeans. These modern centers of genetic diversity, however, may not correlate with the original centers, and are most likely to reflect current conditions, rather than the origins, of these plants (Zhao, T. and Gai 2004: 958). More importantly, most botanic and genetic studies do not take into account recent archaeological discoveries.

To understand the origins of soybean domestication we need to incorporate multiple lines of evidence from ethnohistory, archaeology, and biology.

Ethnohistorical evidence: The earliest text recording the soybean is *Shijing* (*Book of Songs*), dated to ca. 1000–600 BC (Loewe 1993). Soybean, referred to as *shu* and *renshu*, is repetitively mentioned in several poems concerned with various social activities related to this plant. Two different verbs, *cai* and *huo*, are used in reference to collecting soybean. Some scholars believe that the former indicates gathering the wild plant and the latter refers to harvesting the domesticated form (Guo, W. 1996).

The word for soybean, *shu*, also appears in the text "Xiaxiaozheng," a section of the classic *Dadai Liji* (Riegel 1993). Xiaxiaozheng is believed to contain an agricultural and ritual calendar, said to have originated in the Xia dynasty (traditionally dated to ca. 2100–1600 BC); it was later compiled into *Dadai Liji* during the first century BC. In this text, *shu* occurs together with references to millet, indicating that both were sown during the fifth month in the Xia calendar (Zhu, Y. 2003), which is equivalent to the early part of the sixth month in the current Chinese lunar calendar (Wang, A. 2006) or to early July in the solar Gregorian calendar. This passage seems to indicate that the summer soybean was already cultivated during the late third and early second millennium BC in the middle Yellow River region, where, as traditionally believed, the Xia people originated.

The chapter "Wanghuijie" in *Yi Zhou Shu*, dated to the third through the first centuries BC (Shaughnessy 1993), contains the first mention of soybean in

Northeast China. The text describes that, after the Western Zhou conquered Shang (ca. 1046 BC), the Zhou king convened lords from many regions. Among the tributary items brought by those local lords, there was *rongshu* (the soybean of the Rong) presented by the Shanrong (the Mountain Rong). The name Shanrong is believed to refer to a people resident in the northeastern part of China (Guo, W. 1996). Ping-ti Ho (1975: 77–81) has suggested that this account points to the geographic origin and affiliated ethnic (proto-Tungusic) background of the domesticated soybean. If soybean *shu* already existed in the Yellow River Valley by 1000 BC, as mentioned in Xiaxiaozheng, then *rongshu* may be better understood simply as a different variety of soybean introduced to the Zhou court.

The term *rongshu* also appears in the chapter "Jiepian" of *Guanzi*, a statecraft classic that was progressively compiled during the fifth through the first centuries BC (Rickett 1993). This text records that Duke Huan of the Qi state (685–643 BC), in the Shandong region, attacked the Shanrong people to the north, and brought back *rongshu* as a trophy; afterward, *rongshu* was dispersed to "all lands under Heaven" or *tianxia*, in the characteristic wording of the time. This account seems to imply that a variety of soybean, which originated in the northeast, spread widely to other unspecified parts of China after the seventh century BC.

Archaeological evidence: The domestication of beans, in general, illustrates three characteristics: (1) an indehiscent pod in maturity; (2) a thinner seed coat (testa); and (3) an increasing seed size (Butler 1989). The first two traits are not easily recognizable in archaeological contexts, so the only feature accessible to archaeologists is seed size. Size should not be considered the sole distinguishing trait of cultigen soybeans (Crawford and Lee 2003); however, increases in seed size consistently over time in the archaeological record would be a good indicator of cultivation/domestication (Lee, G. et al. 2011).

Soybean remains have been found at more than thirty sites in China, dating from the Peiligang culture to the Han dynasty (7000 BC–AD 220) (Figure 4.4). In north China, the earliest remains identified as wild soybean have been uncovered from Jiahu (7000–5500 BC) (Zhao, Z. and Zhang 2009) and Bancun (ca. 5500 BC) (Kong, Z. et al. 1999b), both in Henan, and from Yuezhuang in Shandong (ca. 6000 BC) (Crawford et al. 2006). At Jiahu, soybean seeds ($N = 581$) account for 14 percent of the total seed remains. They are uniform in size (3.28 mm ± 0.47 in length; 2.33 mm ± 0.35 in width), but smaller than modern wild soybean samples from Anhui (3.81 mm ± 0.49 in length; 2.77 mm ± 0.33 in width). Given the large number of soybeans unearthed at Jiahu, they were certainly anthropogenic plants collected for food (Zhao, Z. and Zhang 2009). The only find of soybeans seeds (*Glycine max* subsp. *soja*) from Neolithic and Bronze Age southern China is reported from Bashidang (ca. 7000–5800 BC) in Hunan (Hunansheng 2006: 525), making it unlikely to have been a center of origin for this plant.

Soybean remains dating to the late Yangshao period (ca. 3500–3000 BC) have been uncovered from several sites in the Yellow River Valley; the largest assemblage is from Dahecun in Zhengzhou, Henan (Figure 4.4) (Lee, G. et al. 2011; Liu, L. et al. 2012). The Dahecun seed remains, originally misidentified as sorghum (Li, F. 2001), were stored in a pottery jar, which was discovered on a house floor (F2) during excavation (Zhengzhoushi 2001: 169–70). This assemblage represents the earliest evidence that Neolithic people collected and stored significant amounts of soybean, although the plant's domesticity is unclear.

Compared to finds from the Yangshao period, soybean seeds are more numerous at late Neolithic Longshan culture sites and are distributed over a much broader region through the middle and lower Yellow River Valley, including Shandong, Henan, and Shaanxi. The seeds unearthed from Zhuanglixi (Shandong) are small and are identified as wild species (Kong, Z. et al. 1999a), whereas those from other sites are generally larger than wild ones but still smaller than modern domesticates (Crawford et al. 2005; Zhao, Z. 2004b; Zhao, Z. and Xu 2004). Jiaochangpu (Shandong) has revealed the most abundant soybean remains, amounting to nearly 10,000 grains in 270 flotation samples (Zhao, Z. 2004b). The embryonic stems and hila of soybean seeds from the Yiluo Basin are identical to those of the modern domesticates (Lee, G. et al. 2007).

The size ranges of soybean seeds from Longshan sites are quite variable. Crawford et al. (2005) point out that seeds from the late Longshan site at Liangchengzhen in Shandong are significantly smaller than the earliest known domesticated soybeans found in the middle Mumum site at Daundong (760–600 BC), South Korea (Crawford and Lee 2003). Therefore, it is likely that those small soybeans found at Yellow River Neolithic sites were still wild (Crawford 2006: 81). In contrast, Zhao Zhijun argues that, although small as compared with the modern domesticated form, soybeans from several late Longshan sites are rather uniform in shape and size, which may be seen as characteristic of a cultivated type. In addition, the large quantity of soybeans found at Jiaochangpu suggests that this food was important in the human diet of the Longshan culture, and may have already undergone some degree of human intervention (tending or cultivation) (Zhao, Z. 2004b; Zhao, Z. and Xu 2004). Specimens from the Yiluo Basin, however, show great variation of size (Lee, G. et al. 2007); this fact contradicts Zhao's observations. These conflicting data probably suggest the existence of a wide variety of soybean types in different regions, perhaps including both wild and domestic forms.

More than a dozen sites associated with bean/soybean remains from the early Bronze Age (ca. 2000–1000 BC) have been found, not only along the middle and lower Yellow River Valley but also in the Liao River region of Northeast China (Figure 4.4). The soybean remains found in the Lower Xiajiadian culture

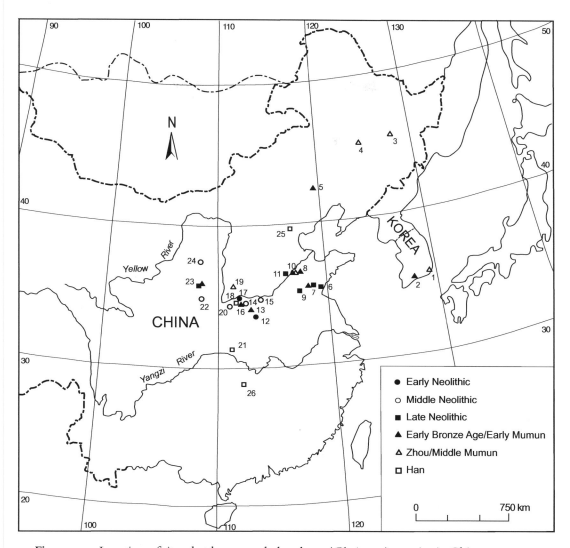

Figure 4.4. Location of sites that have revealed soybean (*Glycine* sp.) remains in China and Korea mentioned in the text. 1: Daundong; 2: Nam River sites; 3: Damudan-tun and Niuchang; 4: Dahaimeng and Wulajie; 5: Xinglonggou; 6: Liangchengzhen; 7: two Longshan sites and three Yueshi sites in Luxian; 8: Ma'an; 9: Zhuanglixi; 10: Daxinzhuang and Tangye; 11: Jiaochangpu; 12: Jiahu; 13: Xinzhai; 14: Huizui; 15: Dahecun; 16: Zaojiaoshu; 17: Bancun; 18: Luoyang Xijiao; 19: Niucun Gucheng; 20: Xipo; 21: Fenghuangshan; 22: Yangguanzhai; 23: Wangjiazui; 24: Wuzhuangguoliang; 25: Laoshan; 26: Mawangdui.

deposits (ca. 2000–1500 BC) at Xinglonggou are the earliest examples of this cultigen in Northeast China. This general region was later referred to as the homeland of the textually identified Shanrong people, who are said to have cultivated the *rongshu* soybean. The Xinglonggou site has revealed a profile of agricultural development covering 4,500 years; although only millets were uncovered from the early Neolithic strata (ca. 6000–5500 BC), both millets and soybean occurred in the Bronze Age deposits (Zhao, Z. 2004a).

In the Yiluo region, soybean seeds from several Erlitou culture sites (Lee, G.-A. et al. 2007; Luoyangshi 2002) are clearly larger in size than the Neolithic specimens; some overlap with the smaller sized examples of domesticated soybean from early historical sites in Korea (Lee, G. et al. 2011). In Shandong, both wild and domesticated soybeans, as determined by their sizes, have been reported from the Shang site at Daxinzhuang. Those seeds identified as domesticates are few in number ($N = 7$; 0.1% of the total seeds); they are similar in size (4.91 × 3.21 × 2.36 mm on average) to those from Longshan and Erlitou sites in the Yellow River region, but are smaller than the normal modern domesticated type (Chen, X. and Fang 2008).

Soybean remains from the Zhou period (1045–221 BC) have been found at six sites in the middle and lower Yellow River Valley and Northeast China (Figure 4.4). Among these findings, the assemblage from Dahaimeng in Jilin (5.81 × 4.38 mm) (2655 ± 120 cal. BP, or ca. 700 BC) appears to resemble the modern small domesticated type, and is also similar to, but slightly smaller than, the soybean grains (6–7 × 3–4.5 mm; 6.52 × 5.02 mm) unearthed from Han tombs at Laoshan in Beijing and Mawangdui in Hunan, respectively (Kong et al. 2011; Liu, S. et al. 1987). The general lack of soybean remains in the Yellow River region during this period is probably due to the predominant focus on excavation of large burials rather than of residential areas, as well as to the deficiency of archaeobotanical study in Zhou archaeology.

The Qin-Han period (221 BC–AD 220) witnessed the greatest geographical expansion of this plant over both northern and southern China. Soybean became a regular component of offerings used in funeral rituals during the Han dynasty, as indicated by inscriptions on pottery vessels from burials (Chen, J. and Ye 1963) and by soybean remains found in waterlogged tombs, such as Mawangdui in Hunan (Chen, W. 1994: 55–6) and Fenghuangshan in Hubei (Jinancheng 1975). The soybean sample from Mawangdui Tomb 1 shows the largest example of grain size among those reported from China so far, and is as large as the modern domesticated variety.

When and Where? Archaeological evidence discussed earlier in text indicates that wild soybean, characterized by small seeds, was first exploited by ca. 7000 BC in China. The entire middle and lower Yellow River region was the area of this plant's early dispersal during the Neolithic period. The degree of soybean domesticity attained in the Yellow River region during the late Neolithic is still an open question, due to the small seed sizes. Considering that soybean samples of various sizes have been rather commonly uncovered from Erlitou culture sites around the Yiluo region, dated to early second millennium BC, and that it was referred to in *Xiaxiaozheng* as a crop of the Xia people, who are supposed to have originated in the middle Yellow River area (including the Yiluo region) around the same time, it is possible that a small variety of domesticated soybean appeared then (Lee, G. et al. 2011).

The earliest soybean remains uncovered from Northeast China date to the Lower Xiajiadian culture (ca. 2000–1500 BC), but their sizes have not been published. The earliest known large-size domesticated soybean from Northeast is dated around 700 BC. This evidence seems to be parallel with that from Korea.

The earliest botanically identified soybean seeds in Korea, dating to the early Mumum (1400–800 BC), show wide ranges of length and width. By the middle Mumum (800–400 BC), soybean had become a dominant crop with high density at some sites, exemplified by Daundong, indicating its economic importance in the subsistence economy (Lee, G. 2003). Examples of the earliest domesticated soybeans from Northeast China and Korea resemble the modern small variety of soybean in size, and are clearly larger than their domesticated counterparts in the Yellow River Valley. In Japan, wild soybean was exploited by humans as early as 5000 BC, and large seeded soybean, indicating human selection, appeared by 3000 BC. These phenomena suggest that soybean was, most likely, independently domesticated in multiple centers, including the Yellow River region, Korea, and Japan (Lee, G. et al. 2011).

The northeastern soybean's putative, but as yet archaeologically undocumented, dispersal into other parts of China, during the late Eastern Zhou and Western Han periods, is indicated by the report in *Guanzi*, which speaks of *rongshu* being introduced from the north into the Shandong area in the seventh century, and spreading widely thereafter. Ongoing dispersal of this larger soybean through south China was apparently facilitated by expansion of the Han dynasty's administrative and economic power and by rapid demographic growth in the south due to migration. Therefore, it is remarkable that soybean seeds found in early Han tombs at Mawangdui in Hunan are similar in size to the large variety from the distant northeast. Thus, the archaeological evidence seems to be clearly in accord with the textual tradition in this case. An important remaining question is the following: Was the indigenous small soybean variety, which existed in the Yellow River region for several thousand years, replaced by the larger type introduced from the northeast? At present there is a lack of morphological data for soybean remains from the Yellow River region dating to this crucial period (700 BC–AD 200); therefore, this question remains open.

Tubers

Traditional root crops in China include Chinese yam (*shanyao; Dioscorea opposita*), taro (*yu; Colocasia esculenta*), lotus roots (*lian'ou;* rhizomes of *Nelumbo nucifera*), Chinese arrowhead (*cigu; Sagittaria sagittifolia* L.) (Zhao, Z. 2005a), and kudzu vine root (*gegen;* root of *Pueraria lobata*). The exploitation of some of these tubers can be traced back to late Paleolithic times.

Starch grains identifiable as *Dioscorea* sp., some probably belonging to *D. opposita* yam, have been found on grinding slabs from Shizitan Locality 9 in Shanxi (12,700–11,600 cal. BP) (Liu, L. et al. 2011), Shangshan in Zhejiang (11,000–9000 cal. BP) (Liu, L. et al. 2010c), Egou in Henan (8500–7000 cal. BP) (Liu, L. et al. 2010a), as well as on pottery from a Western Zhou period site at Xishan in Lixian, Gansu (Ge, W. 2010). It is unclear, at present, however, when yam was first cultivated.

Archaeobotanical investigations at Zengpiyan in Guilin have revealed remains of tubers in flotation samples and starch grains of taro on stone tools, dating to all phases of the site. Based on an experimental study of wild rice harvesting near Zengpiyan, foraging tubers is evidently much more efficient than collecting wild rice, and the Guilin region is suitable for taro growing (Zhongguo Shehui Kexueyuan 2003a: 341–3). It is likely that people in South China already had knowledge of rice cultivation by interacting with their neighboring communities in the Yangzi River Valley, but they continued to rely mainly on tubers for starchy food. Given that tubers are relatively easy to cultivate compared to cereals, it is also possible that the intensive exploitation of tubers may have eventually led to the production of root crops in South China (Zhao, Z. 2005a). Further research is warranted to understand when and how tubers were domesticated. Several sites in Guilin, such as Xiaojin and Dingsishan, show no sign of rice in archaeological contexts before 4000 BC, suggesting that tubers were probably the staple starchy food. Rice agriculture is most likely to have been introduced to South China from the Yangzi River region some 6,000 years ago.

These finds indicate a long history of widespread use of tubers in ancient China from the late Pleistocene through the entire Holocene. Tubers are rarely found preserved in archaeological settings; therefore, starch analysis is the most effective method to recover tuber remains. Further residue analyses on ancient artifacts will certainly improve our understanding of the exploitation of tubers.

Wheat, Barley, and Oats

There is no evidence for the process of domestication of wheat, barley, and oats in China, based on the archaeological record; therefore, these three crops are most likely to have been introduced from elsewhere. Wheat (*Triticum* sp.) first appeared in the Yellow River region by the middle of the third millennium BC (Jin, G. 2007). The earliest wheat-bearing sites, dating to before 1700 BC, are found in at least six locales, spreading from Gansu to Shandong. The sites include Xishanping in Tianshui, Gansu (ca. 1700 BC) (Li, X. et al. 2007), Zhouyuan in Shaanxi (Zhao, Z. and Xu 2004), Xijincheng (ca. 2300 BC) (Chen, Xuexiang et al. 2010) and Wadian in Henan (Liu, C. and Fang 2010),

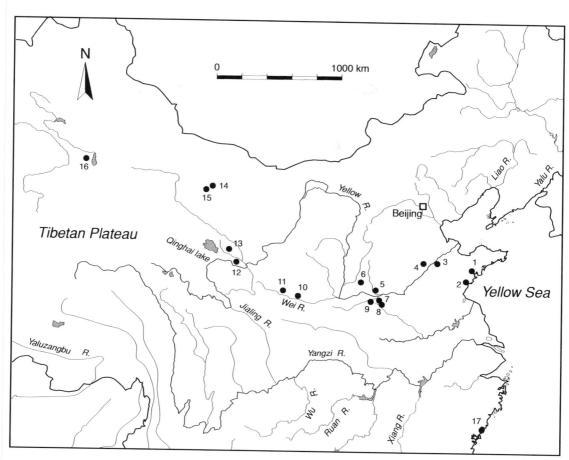

Figure 4.5. Major sites, in North China, associated with early wheat, barley, and oats, dating to the third and second millennia BC. 1: Zhaojiazhuang; 2: Liangchengzhen; 3: Daxinzhuang; 4: Jiaochangpu; 5: Xijincheng; 6: Taosi; 7: Tianposhuiku, Fengzhai; 8: Wadian; 9: Zaojiaoshu; 10: Zhouyuan; 11: Xishanping; 12: Donghuishan; 13: Fengtai; 14: Huoshiliang; 15: Ganggangwa; 16: Gumugou; 17: Huangguashan.

and Liangchengzhen, Jiaochangpu, and Zhaojiazhuang, all in Shandong (2600–1900 BC) (Crawford et al. 2005; Jin, G. 2007). By the end of the third or early second millennium BC, wheat farming reached the southeast coastal region, as indicated by the wheat grains and phytoliths recovered at the Huangguoshu site (2480/2200–1880/1620 BC) in Xiapu, Fujian (Jiao 2007) (Figure 4.5).

Wheat remains become more broadly distributed and are more frequently encountered in archaeological contexts dating to the second millennium BC, as revealed in sites stretching from Xinjiang (Gumugou or Qäwrighul) and Tibet (Changguogou) in the far west to Shandong in the eastern extremity (Jin, G. 2007). In the Central Plain, wheat remains have been found at many Erlitou culture sites in Henan (Beijing Daxue and Henanshang 2007; Lee, G. and Bestel 2007; Lee, G. et al. 2007). In the Yiluo region wheat became a significant crop, together with millet and rice, by the Erligang culture period (1600–1300 BC) (Lee, G. et al. 2007). At Zhouyuan in Shaanxi, wheat grains account for nearly 8 percent of the total seeds in the proto-Zhou period (Zhao, Z. and Xu 2004).

The earliest barley (*Hordeum vulgare*) has been unearthed from Xishanping (ca. 2600 BC) (Li, X. et al. 2007) and Taosi in Shanxi (2500–1900 BC) (Zhao, Z. 2005b). Often coexisting with wheat, barley remains continue to appear at sites dating to the second millennium BC, distributed from Qinghai (Fengtai in Huzhu) and Gansu (Donghuishan in Minle) to Henan (Zaojiaoshu in Luoyang) (Jin, G. 2007). Barley was particularly favored by people who lived in the northwestern high-altitude region. Barley remains (1487 grains) from Fengtai (a Kayue culture site) account for 92 percent of the cereal seeds in the flotation samples (Zhao, Z. 2004c). Together with wheat, barley grains were also found at Huangguashan in Fujian (Jiao 2007). The presence of these two crops in the southeast coastal area appears to be an isolated occurrence in this time period, and may be explained as being due to transport from overseas.

The earliest oat (*Avena* sp.) remains, together with wheat and barley, have been found only in northwestern China. One find is from Xishanping in Gansu, AMS dating to 5070 cal. BP (Li, X. et al. 2007), and the other is from Fengtai in Qinghai (1600–700 BC). Because oats often occur as weeds in agricultural fields, it is unclear whether these oats were intentionally cultivated (Zhao, Z. 2004c). Barley and oats seem to occur only in small quantities in the eastern part of China.

Archaeological finds to date do not provide enough information for discussion as to how wheat, barley, and oats were introduced into China, because these crops seem to have appeared almost simultaneously over a broad region in the north. Many scholars have speculated that wheat was brought into China through Xinjiang and the Hexi corridor (Figure 4.5), which later functioned as a major trade route connecting East and West, known since the late nineteenth century as the "Silk Road." The earliest wheat remains in Xinjiang from Gumugou (Qäwrighul) in Lopnur, however, date to 2000–1500 BC (Wang, B. 2001b: 35, 42) – later than other wheat finds in the Yellow River region. These crops may have been introduced to China from multiple routes. The Eurasian steppe in the north would be a likely candidate for the origins of those crops, as agropastoralism (cultivating barley and wheat, while also raising goats and sheep) was established in western Central Asia by 6000 BC (Harris 2010: 73–91). It has been suggested that people of the Northern Zone cultures who were distributed along the regions where the Great Wall stretches from east to west (referred to as the northern frontiers) may have helped to facilitate the diffusion of these crops from Bronze Age cultures in the Eurasian steppe to the Yellow River Valley (Zhao, Z. 2009a). (There is more discussion on the Northern Zone culture in Chapter 9.)

Development of the Multicropping Agricultural System

People exploited wild indigenous plants, such as rice, millets, soybean, and various tubers, in late Paleolithic times, and domestication of these plants was a long process. Farming did not become a major component of the subsistence economy until the middle Neolithic period (ca. 5000–3000 BC) or even later in some regions. Based on current data, the middle and lower Yangzi River regions witnessed the process of rice domestication, and rice gradually became a major staple crop there. The Liao and Yellow River regions were the original centers of millet domestication, and millets were the major crops for several thousand years before wheat took over. Areas between the Yangzi and Yellow Rivers seem to have been characterized by a mix of millet and rice production (Zhao, Z. 2006). In South China, tubers were the staple starch food for many millennia before rice was introduced around 4000 BC (Zhao, Z. 2005a), as exemplified by Zengpiyan (Zhongguo Shehui Kexueyuan 2003a). The Yellow River Valley during the third and second millennia BC experienced a dynamic process of cultural and economic amalgamation. Some nonindigenous cereals, mainly wheat and barley, had become well integrated into local multicropping systems. Of these domesticates, foxtail and broomcorn millets, rice, wheat, and soybean are often mentioned in ancient texts as the "Five Grains" of the traditional cropping system.

Diachronic change in cropping systems is clearly documented in the Yiluo region, Henan (Liu, L. et al. 2002–4). The earliest domesticated plant found there is foxtail millet, dating to the late Peiligang period (ca. 6000–5000 BC); this crop remained predominant among the cereal staples there during the entire investigated period of 6,000 years. Rice was introduced to the region by the late Yangshao period (3500–3000 BC), followed by wheat and barley during the Erlitou period (1900–1500 BC). Soybean first appeared in late Yangshao deposits, and remained as a minor component in the plant assemblages. By the Erligang period (1600–1300 BC) the proportion of wheat was second only to that of foxtail millet, both being more suitable for the dry-land agriculture of this region (Lee, G. and Bestel 2007; Lee, G. et al. 2007). A similar trend of development in multicropping agriculture has also been found in the Central Plain (Zhao, Z. 2009b).

The continuing spread of crops to ever broader regions may be attributable to multiple factors, including climatic change, population movement, interactions between human groups, and political needs. At Xishanping in Tianshui, Gansu, for example, wheat, barley, and oats (all introduced from the west or the north), together with rice (introduced from the east), millet, and soybean (indigenous to the region), were gradually adopted during the course of site occupation (3300–2350 BC), and especially flourished around 2700–2350 BC. This development coincides with an episode of warm and wet climatic conditions suggested by the disappearance of conifers and expansion of chestnut trees around 2650 BC. In this case, optimum climatic conditions and cultural/population interactions may have played important roles in the introduction of new crops (Li, X. et al. 2007). In contrast, the Yiluo region witnessed an episode of drier and cooler climate during the Erlitou period (1900–1500 BC), coinciding with a period of unprecedented social change, the formation of early states. The introduction of wheat and barley to the Erlitou culture region may be explained as an economic strategy to adapt to the drier environment, but the continuous rice cultivation was probably partially needed to meet the demand for elite food (Lee, G. and Bestel 2007; Lee, G. et al. 2007; Rosen 2007a), such as making alcoholic beverages for ritual feasting.

DOMESTICATION OF ANIMALS

The study of animal remains in Chinese archaeology since the 1950s can be divided into two phases. The initial period (1950s–70s) is characterized by an emphasis on taxonomic identification and on identifying the climatic conditions reflected in faunal assemblages, whereas the formative period (1980s–present) has experienced the introduction and use of zooarchaeological methods and principles developed in the West (Yuan, Jing 2002). Research on animal domestication clearly reflects this change, as testified in recent years by a rapid growth of publications using systematic analytical methods to record and interpret faunal remains. This shift in research orientation also means that the quality of previous zooarchaeological reports varies significantly, in terms of recording methods used and osteometric information reported. As a result, in many cases it is difficult to conduct systematic and statistical analyses or to make cross-regional comparisons. The available data on which we rely still provide some insight to our questions, although we have to overcome problems arising from the uneven quality of databases.

The domestic animals most frequently discussed in archaeological reports of the Neolithic and Bronze Age include dogs, pigs, sheep, goats, cattle, water buffalo, horses, and chickens. Figure 4.6 shows the major sites associated with the faunal remains discussed in this chapter.

Dogs

The dog, used as an aid for hunting, was the earliest domesticated animal, with multiple maternal origins worldwide (Vila et al. 1997). In other parts of the Old World, such as Belgium and Siberia, evidence of dog domestication can be traced back to more than 30,000 years ago (Germonpré et al. 2009; Ovodov et al. 2011). In China the course of canine transformation is one of the least understood among comparable processes there. It is generally agreed that the

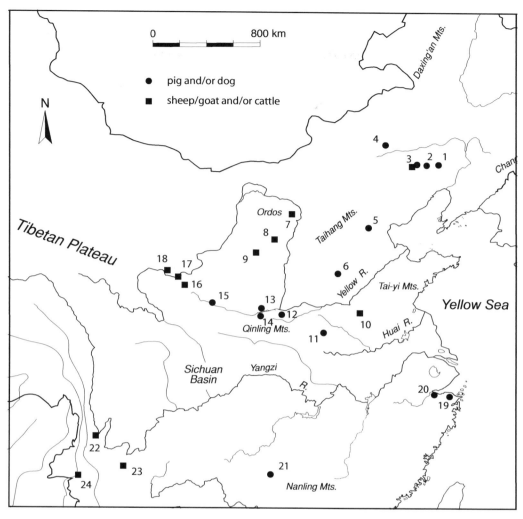

Figure 4.6. Distribution of sites associated with domesticated dogs, pigs, sheep/goats, and cattle mentioned in Chapter 4. 1: Xinglongwa, Xinglonggou; 2: Zhaobaogou; 3: Hongshanhou, Dadianzi; 4: Baiyinchanghan; 5: Nanzhuangtou; 6: Cishan; 7: Zhukaigou; 8: Huoshiliang: 9: Wuzhuangguoliang; 10: Shantaisi; 11: Jiahu; 12: Xipo; 13: Kangjia; 14: Jiangzhai; 15: Dadiwan; 16: Majiayao; 17: Majiawan; 18: Donghuishan; 19: Hemudu; 20: Kuahuqiao; 21: Zengpiyan; 22: Haimenkou; 23: Shizhaishan; 24: Cangyuan.

Chinese dog (*Canis familiaris*) originated from the Chinese wolf (*Canis lupus chanco*) (Olsen and Olsen 1977), but when this process occurred is unclear. The earliest domestic dog has been reported as present at Nanzhuangtou in Hebei (ca. 10,000 cal. BP), based on shortened dental length in a mandible identified as canine by comparison to known examples of wolf. It has been suggested that the initial process of dog domestication in China may have happened much earlier than this case (Yuan, J. and Li 2010).

More evidence for the early domestic dog comes from Jiahu in Henan (ca. 7000 BC) (Henansheng Wenwu Kaogu 1999a), Cishan in Hebei (ca. 6000 BC) (Sun, D. et al. 1981), and Dadiwan in Gansu (ca. 6000 BC) (Qi, G. et al. 2006). Complete dog skeletons were intentionally buried in cemeteries or near houses at Jiahu, and on the bottom of some pits at Cishan. In these Neolithic villages, hunting was still an important component of the subsistence strategies, as indicated by finds of abundant hunting tools; ritual burial of dogs at these sites seems to suggest their close relationship with humans, perhaps as aids for hunting.

Dog remains are present at many Neolithic sites, and in most cases this animal seems to have been consumed as a source of protein. This situation is suggested by the frequent discovery of dog bones in domestic refuse, mixed with other animal bones. Traces of burning on canine bones are recorded at Dadiwan (Qi, G. et al. 2006), and dog remains are represented, at Kangjia, in the fragmented bones evidently consumed (Liu, L. et al. 2001). Dogs appear to have been used as sacrificial offerings associated with human burials during the late Neolithic period, particularly in the lower Yellow River region, and dogs were later more routinely sacrificed in Shang ritual ceremonies (Gao, G. and Shao 1986; Yuan, J. and Flad 2005).

There is still a considerable gap in the record, between ancestral canids in the Paleolithic and fully domesticated dogs in the Neolithic. More research on canid remains from the terminal Pleistocene and early Holocene can probably reveal evidence for the origins of dog domestication in future studies.

Pigs

The origin of domesticated pigs (*Sus domesticus*) has been the major focus of multidisciplinary studies in China. Recent genetic studies indicate that pigs were domesticated in multiple areas across Eurasia, including at least once in China (Larson et al. 2005). Pig remains have been found in many Paleolithic sites, and it is one of the most frequently encountered species at Neolithic sites (Luo, Y. 2007). Wild pigs (*Sus scrofa*) are also widely distributed in China today, identifiable to ten local forms (Feng, Z. et al. 1986: 160–5; Luo, Y. 2007: 3–4; Zhongguo Zhupinzhongzhi 1986: 7–8). Paleontologists have long recognized the similarities between Pleistocene fossil *Sus* and modern boars, and suspected that, in different regions of the world, domestic pigs were derived from local boars (Olsen and Olsen 1980). Recent studies on morphology, chromosome, serum protein, and DNA of modern pigs also suggest multiple origins of domestic pigs in China (see a summary in Luo, Y. 2007). Despite all these efforts, it is still unclear when and where, exactly, the first events of domestication took place. Archaeology may hold a key to answering these questions.

In Chinese archaeology the determination of pig domestication primarily relies on the following six criteria:

(1) Morphological change, as indicated both by reduced dental size (a value of 40 mm for the length of third molar on mandible (M_3) has sometimes been used to distinguish the wild from domesticated varieties) and by distorted alignment of teeth (the observed distortion of tooth alignment is considered to be caused by decreased length of the mandible, but tooth size did not decrease proportionately during the early phase of pig domestication);
(2) Age-related culling, as most pigs were slaughtered at 1–2 years of age;
(3) A high percentage of pig bones in a given faunal assemblage;
(4) Cultural factors, such as pig skeletons found in association with human burials (Zhongguo Shehui Kexueyuan 2003a: 337–41);
(5) Pathological evidence, such as high frequency of linear enamel hypoplasia (LEH) on pig tooth crowns, which has been proven in other parts of the world to be a result of domestication (Dobney et al. 2006); and
(6) Stable isotope data showing a closely related food web between humans and pigs in settlements.

Based on these criteria, the earliest examples of domesticated pigs have been identified from Jiahu in Henan, Cishan in Hebei, Dadiwan in Gansu, and Kuahuqiao in Zhejiang, dating to ca. 7000–5000 BC (see summary in Luo, Y. 2007).

The Yellow and Huai River region: Several lines of evidence suggest that the pig was already domesticated by 7000 BC in the Huai River Valley, as exemplified by Jiahu. Three pig specimens from this site show distorted teeth alignment, the range of M_3 length overlaps with both wild and domesticated forms (36.39–46.66 mm) (Figure 4.7), some 27 percent of meat consumed is from pigs, about 80 percent of pigs were killed before reaching three years of age, pig bones were associated with human burials, and the LEH frequency is higher than that of wild pig populations (Figure 4.8). Moreover, stable isotope analysis indicates that a majority of pig samples examined shows a diet closely related to the local human diet, implying domestication, whereas a small number of samples is completely separate on the isotope distribution chart, probably from wild pigs (see summary in Luo, Y. 2007).

As at Jiahu, most Dadiwan pigs (ca. 5800–2800 BC) died before reaching three years of age, including those from the site's earliest phase; the sizes of pig M_3 fall into the ranges of both wild and domesticated types (30.8–46 mm) (Qi, G. et al. 2006); and pig mandibles were associated with human burials (Gansusheng 2006). Isotope analysis of pig bones from Dadiwan Phase I shows, however, that all pigs were wild, eating predominantly C3 plants (plants whose carbon-fixation products have three carbon atoms per molecule; e.g., nuts,

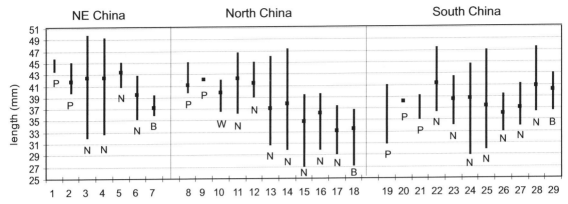

P = Paleolithic; N = Neolithic; W = modern wild boar; B = Bronze Age

■ average or single measurement reported;   ——— range

Figure 4.7. Comparison of sizes of M$_3$ from Paleolithic, Neolithic, Bronze Age, and modern wild pig assemblages in different regions, showing changes of body size influenced by environmental temperature or domestication. 1: Yanjiagang; 2: Jinniushan; 3: Xinglonggou; 4: Xinglongwa; 5: Zhaobaogou; 6: Shihushan I; 7: Dadianzi; 8: Zhoukoudian Locality I; 9: Zhoukoudian Upper Cave; 10: Modern boar in Henan; 11: Jiahu; 12: Cishan; 13: Dadiwan; 14: Xishuipo; 15: Xipo; 16: Yuchisi; 17: Shantaisi; 18: Erlitou; 19: Yanjinggou; 20: Dalongtan; 21: Guilongyan; 22: Zengpiyan; 23: Kuahuqiao; 24: Shazui; 25: Saidun; 26: Diaolongbei III; 27: Sanxingcun; 28: Weidun; 29: Maqiao (data based on appendices 1 and 2 of Luo 2007).

tuber, soybean, and rice), which is presumably different from a human diet (Barton et al. 2009). This conclusion contradicts the faunal analysis, probably due to the small sample size of the pig bones ($N = 4$) and to the lack of human bones for comparison in the isotope analysis.

The evidence for pig domestication at Cishan is apparently mixed, being mainly based on circumstantial phenomena, as several complete skeletons of young pigs were found at the bottom of ash pits, although the M$_3$ size range (39.2–45 mm) is more like a wild form (Yuan, J. and Flad 2002; Zhou, B. 1981).

Yangzi River and South China: The earliest evidence for the Yangzi River region is from Kuahuqiao. Three pig mandibles show distorted alignment of teeth, and M$_3$ also show a general trend of reduction in size from early to late phases. The distribution of M$_3$ sizes (34.29–42.37 mm), similar to Jiahu and Dadiwan, falls into both wild and domesticated ranges (Yuan, J. and Yang 2004).

The domesticity of pigs from Zengpiyan in Guilin has been long debated (Li, Y. and Han 1978; Yuan, J. and Yang 2003), and the frequency of LEH on pig teeth (Figure 4.8) seems to support the view favoring domestication (Dobney et al. 2006). It is notable that the Zengpiyan occupation lasted for some 5,000 years (ca. 10,000–5000 BC), and that most pig remains were unearthed from

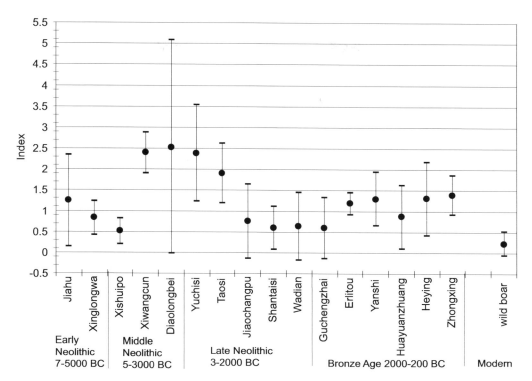

Figure 4.8. Comparison of LEH frequency on pig tooth crowns from archaeological assemblages and modern wild pig population (modified from figure 2-7-2 of Luo 2007).

early excavations in the 1970s and were grouped together for analysis without further chronological division. The pig assemblage also shows great variations in size (36.57–47.46 mm for M_3), falling into both wild and domesticated ranges (Figure 4.7). It is entirely possible that this assemblage consists of wild and domestic populations, but we are unable to pinpoint exactly when the domesticated ones first occurred.

Northeast China: Pig remains have been uncovered from several Xinglongwa culture sites (6200–5200 BC), including Xinglongwa, Xinglonggou, and Baiyinchanghan, all in the Liao River Valley (Luo, Y. 2007). Morphologically, the pig bodies from these early Neolithic settlements are generally large in size (judging by teeth measurements), and this morphology has been seen as an indicator of a wild form (Tang, Z. et al. 2004b). The lower range of M_3 length from Xinglongwa, however, also overlaps with that of the characteristic domesticated variety (Figure 4.7), and the frequency of LEH is higher than is typical of wild pig (Figure 4.9). Both factors indicate domestication (Luo, Y. 2007). As with pig assemblages from Jiahu and Dadiwan, those from the Xinglongwa culture also may consist of both wild and domestic populations.

Some cultural factors also suggest that domestication may have indeed been underway. At Xinglongwa, for instance, two complete adult pig skeletons, a male and a female, were found in a human burial. The animal's legs appear to have been bound together before it was placed in the tomb (Yang, H. and Liu 1997). This is the earliest example of complete pigs being included in human burials, a phenomenon that later become widespread during the Neolithic period in north China and is referred to as animal sacrifice. Different interpretations have been proposed concerning this joint human–porcine burial; some believe that wild pig was worshipped as a totem (Yang, H. and Liu 1997), whereas others argue that it reflects a special relationship between pig and human that distinguished the pig from other wild animals (Luo, Y. 2007; Yuan, J. and Yang in press).

Multiple centers of pig domestication: Archaeological data seem to support the theory of multicentered pig domestication. At the least, Jiahu and Kuahuqiao pigs may represent two separate, early domestication events in North and Central China, respectively (Luo, Y. 2007). Northeast China may have been another center of pig domestication. The large size of Xinglongwa pigs may reflect a local form, because pig remains from later periods in the Liao River region also tend to be larger than contemporary counterparts in the Yellow River region. The Zhaobaogou pigs (ca. 5200–4500 BC) from Aohan, for example, are larger (M_3 length 41–45 mm) than the early Yangshao pigs. Likewise, the Dadianzi pigs (ca. 2000–1500 BC) from Chifeng are bigger than the pigs from several Erlitou culture sites (Luo, Y. 2007) (Figure 4.7).

Size variation of pig bones can be affected by age, sex, and individual variation (Payne and Bull 1988). Environmental temperature also influences the body size of some mammals; as demonstrated by Davis (1987: 70–1), boars tend to become larger in colder regions. This factor may have caused the appearance of large pigs, both wild and domesticated, in Northeast China, where the climate is colder than in the Yellow and Yangzi River regions. When comparing M_3 length in pig populations from northern and southern China, including Pleistocene, Neolithic, and modern wild varieties (Figure 4.7), three phenomena are observable. First, compared to Pleistocene pigs, the smaller body size of modern wild populations is the result of the warmer Holocene climate, whereas the smaller body size of Neolithic pigs is the result of domestication. Second, the Pleistocene pigs from Zhoukoudian in Beijing and Yanjiagang in Heilongjiang are much larger than those from Yanjinggou in Sichuan, suggesting a range of body sizes among wild pigs, as influenced by differing climatic conditions of north and south. Third, the body size of individual pigs in Neolithic assemblages of Northeast China, whether wild or domesticated, tends to be larger than that of most of their southern counterparts, also affected by environmental temperature level. These observations support the proposition that pigs from Northeast China were domesticated from local wild boars independently of parallel events in North and Central China.

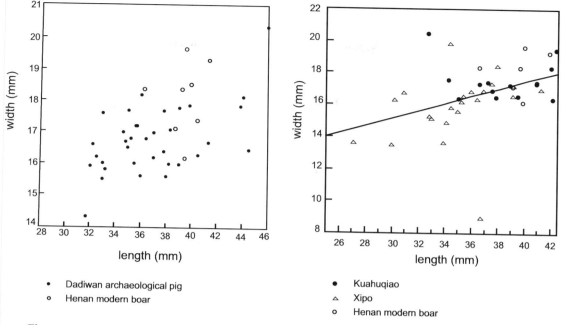

Figure 4.9. Comparison of pig mandibular M₃ from Kuanhuqiao, Dadiwan, Xipo, and modern boars, showing greater variation in the archaeological assemblages (data based on Ma 2005; Qi et al. 2006: 884; Yuan and Yang 2004).

The processes of pig domestication: Animal domestication is a continuum, and the terms "domestic" and "wild" merely describe the extremes of a spectrum defined as follows. Domestic populations are characterized by complete human control of survival, reproduction, and nutrition. Archaeologically observed pig populations, however, often consist of wild, domestic, feral, and genetically hybrid varieties. This may have especially been the case during early stages of domestication, when control of animal populations may have been loose, and genotypic and phenotypic changes in pigs were still minimal (Albarella et al. 2006; Hongo and Meadow 1998). Therefore, it is difficult to determine domestication for the pig.

Wild pigs have been identified together with domesticated ones in several Neolithic faunal assemblages, such as Jiahu (Henansheng Wenwu Kaogu 1999a) and Hemudu (Wei, F. et al. 1990). This complex situation seems also to have existed in other Neolithic sites. Figure 4.9 compares pig M₃ measurements from an early stage of pig domestication (Kuahuqiao and Dadiwan) with those from a mature stage of domestication (Xipo; ca. 4000–3500 BC), and with those for modern boars from Henan. Both of the archaeological assemblages show partial overlap with modern wild boars, but most of the archaeological specimens are smaller than the wild ones. Comparing the coefficients of variation (CV; the standard deviation as a percentage of the mean) is a method

TABLE 4.1. *Comparison of CV values of M₃ length in pig assemblages from modern boar populations and archaeological assemblages from the Neolithic*

	Turkey boar[a]	Henan boar[b]	Kuahuqiao	Xinglongwa	Xipo
Mean	41.1	39.82	38.24	42.32	34.97
Std Dev	1.3	1.53	3.11	3.447	3.42
Min	39.7	36.65	32.78	32.87	27
Max	42.8	41.87	42.37	49.27	41.25
N	5	8	13	74	22
CV	3	3.8	8.1	8.1	9.8

[a] Data from Payne and Bull 1988.
[b] Data from Ma, Xiaolin, personal communication.
Std Dev: Standard deviation.

of testing for the existence of mixed pig populations (Payne and Bull 1988). When comparing the CV values of M₃ length shown among two populations of wild boars from Turkey and China with the values from three archaeological assemblages, the Neolithic groups show much greater variation (8.1–9.8) than do the modern boar populations (3 and 3.8) (Table 4.1), suggesting that each archaeological assemblage contains more than one population.

Three implications may be drawn from these phenomena. First, these remains include both wild and domestic populations, as people hunted wild boars while keeping domesticated ones in their settlements. Second, some of the pig populations at early Neolithic sites were in early stages of domestication, and therefore show more resemblances to wild morphology. Third, some of the specimens may represent hybrid forms.

The development of pig husbandry is not synchronous cross-regionally in China (Luo, Y. 2007). In the Central Plain, for example, pig became increasingly important in the subsistence economy by the fifth millennium BC. In the Xipo faunal assemblage, 84 percent of identifiable animal bones dating to the middle Yangshao period (4000–3500 BC) belong to pigs, predominantly domesticated. Pig rearing may have been largely intended to supply the ritual feasting that facilitated competition for power and prestige among social groups. The importance of this function in turn encouraged more intensive pig husbandry (Ma, X. 2005). It is worthwhile to note, however, that increased dependence on domesticated pigs was not an unbroken trend cross-regionally. Faunal assemblages from several sites in the lower Wei River region have revealed a proportional decrease of pig bones during the Neolithic and an increase of wild animal bones, as exemplified by Jiangzhai and Kangjia (Liu, L. et al. 2001; Qi, G. 1988). Moreover, pig husbandry decreased during the Bronze Age in areas where grazing animals were introduced and pastoralism flourished (Luo, Y. 2007).

Sheep and Goats

Recent phylogenetic analyses, on an international scale, of domestic sheep (*Ovis* sp.) and goats (*Capra* sp.) have identified multiple distinct domestic lineages in each species, suggesting that they were domesticated several times in different civilizational zones. Genetic research indicates that the initial domestication event for both animals occurred in the Fertile Crescent. This conclusion is consistent with archaeological evidence (Zeder et al. 2006). The introduction of sheep and goats to China seems to parallel, at least to some extent, the eastward dispersal of wheat and barley, but exactly when and through which routes the diffusion took place is unclear.

Mitochondrial DNA (mtDNA) analysis indicates that modern Chinese breeds of sheep are composed mainly of lineages A and B, with a small fraction of lineage C. Among them, lineage B has a Near Eastern origin (Guo, J. et al. 2005). Ancient mtDNA tests performed on twenty-two sheep bone samples from four archaeological sites in northern China (ca. 2500–1500 BC) show that lineage A was predominant, reaching a frequency of 95.5 percent, whereas lineage B was present in only one sample. When compared with all sheep mtDNA lineages from different regions across Eurasia, lineage A has the highest frequency in East Asia. This sheep population may have derived from a now extinct ancient lineage the geographic origin of which is unclear. The presence of lineage B in ancient north China suggests the introduction of sheep from a Near Eastern origin, and lineage A seems to hold the key to understanding the origin of domesticated Chinese sheep (Cai, D. et al. 2007; Cai, D. et al. 2011).

Phylogenetic analyses have identified four mtDNA lineages (A–D) in Chinese goats, with lineage A predominant, suggesting multiple maternal origins of domestic goats (Chen, S. et al. 2005). No ancient DNA testing has been used on archaeological goat remains, however, so we know little about the origins of this animal in China.

Sheep/goat bones from the Neolithic period have been found, but specimens from early Neolithic sites, once thought to be domesticates, now appear more likely to come from wild species. The earliest remains of domestic sheep (*Ovis* sp.), dating to the fourth millennium BC, have been reportedly found in areas to the west and north of the Central Plain, including Hongshanhou in Chifeng, Inner Mongolia, and Majiawan in Yongjing and Majiayao in Lintao, both in Gansu province (Zhou B. 1984). Sheep and goats (*Capra hircus*) began to appear in the middle and lower Yellow River Valley during the early Longshan period, and became more widely dispersed during the late Longshan period and the Bronze Age (for a summary, see Flad et al. 2007; Liu, L. 2004: 59).

The introduction of sheep/goats appears to be associated with the post-Mid-Holocene Climatic Optimum, when north China became generally colder and drier, a condition more favorable to pastoralism, especially in the northwest. Increased interaction between pastoralists in the Eurasian steppe and early Chinese agriculturalists (see Chapter 9) also may have contributed to the appearance in China of new animals and plants, added to the existing subsistence economy as supplementary food sources. This situation is clearly exemplified at the Donghuishan site, in Minle, Qinghai (ca. 2000–1500 BC), where the faunal assemblage is dominated by pig and deer bones, accompanied by remains of sheep and dogs, in lesser proportions (Qi, G. 1998), and of various crops, including millet, wheat, barley, and rye, as discussed earlier in text (Gansusheng 1998: 140). In contrast, primary reliance on sheep/goats (59.22%) is evident in the faunal assemblage (1,111 number of identified specimens [NISP]) at the Huoshiliang site (ca. 2150–1900 BC) in Yulin, northern Shaanxi, supplemented here by pigs (12.62%), cattle (8.74%), and some wild animals (19.42%) (Hu, S. et al. 2008). These finds suggest that, by the end of the third millennium BC, a mature agropastoral economy emphasizing grazing animals became established in the Ordos region. By the early second millennium BC, at the latest, an agropastoralist subsistence strategy had already emerged in north China, producing both indigenous and introduced crops and animals.

In the Central Plain, sheep sacrifice, as an addition to the traditional pig sacrifice, first became a part of ritual usage at Yanshi Shang City in Henan (ca. 1600–1300 BC). This practice became more frequently performed at Yinxu, the capital of the late Shang in Anyang (Yuan, J. and Flad 2005).

Cattle

The two species of cattle, humpless taurine (*Bos taurus*) and humped zebu (*Bos indicus*) are believed to have been domesticated independently. Based on archaeological and genetic evidence, the domestic origin of taurine cattle has been traced back to the eighth millennium BC in the Near East, whereas the domestication of indicine cattle occurred as early as 7000 BC in the Indus Valley (Bradley and Magee 2006). Modern Chinese cattle have been divided into three major groups on the basis of their geographic distribution, morphological characteristics, and sex chromosome polymorphisms: the northern group in northern China, the central group in the middle and lower areas of the Yellow River, and the southern group in southern China. Phylogenetic analysis suggests that the southern breeds are dominated by zebu mtDNA, whereas the northern breeds are dominated by taurine mtDNA. Cattle breeds from the central area of China reveal a geographical zone of taurine-zebu hybrids (Cai, X. et al. 2007). These data strongly suggest that cattle were introduced to China from north and south through different routes.

Bos primigenius, the ancestral species of domestic cattle, was widely distributed during the Pleistocene in China, and *Bos* remains, which have been thought to represent a domesticated species, have been reported from many Neolithic sites. Many attributions of domestic status to cattle remains surely dating to early and middle Neolithic have been questioned, however (Flad et al. 2007; Huang, Y. 2003), and no evidence shows that a process of cattle domestication took place in China. No systematic study attempting to distinguish wild from domesticated *Bos* remains has been done in Chinese archaeology.

A preliminary survey of *Bos* remains dating to the Neolithic period recently has been undertaken by Lü Peng (Lü, P. 2010), who demonstrates changes in bone morphology, body size, and kill-off pattern through time. Based on this study, only some five sites in North China have revealed wild cattle bones dating before 5000 BC in the Holocene. The number of sites associated with cattle bones increases to around twenty during the period 5000–3000 BC, and the largest assemblage is from Jiangzhai in Shaanxi (84 NISP); these remains are most likely still wild species, based on the large sizes of bones. About thirty sites have yielded cattle remains, dating to the third millennium BC, particularly from the late Longshan and Qijia cultures (ca. 2500–1900 BC) (Figure 4.10). By this time, the cattle assemblages show characteristics of domestication, such as reduced body size and evidence of being slaughtered at a young age, making them identifiable as domestic cattle (*Bos domestica*). There is also a marked increase in NISP at several sites, exemplified by Shantaisi in Zhecheng (790) and Guchengzhai in Xinmi (183), both sites in Henan (Lü, P. 2010). At Shantaisi, a sacrificial pit containing nine articulated cattle skeletons has been found. It is viewed as the origin of the cattle sacrifice, a ritual practice that later became commonly used during the Shang period (Murowchick and Cohen 2001; Yuan, J. and Flad 2005).

Taken as a whole, the domesticated cattle of northern China, perhaps related to *Bos taurus*, do not appear in the region's archaeological record until the late part of the third millennium BC. They are distributed along the entire Yellow River region, and often coexisted with sheep/goats as part of pastoralist assemblages, especially in the Ordos region and upper Yellow River region, suggesting a probable derivation from the Eurasian steppe.

We know little about the first archaeological occurrence of domestic zebu in south China. Bovine remains have been unearthed from Neolithic and Bronze Age deposits at Haimenkou (3300–500 BC) in Jianchuan, Yunnan, but detailed identification has yet to be completed (Min, R. 2009). Bronze sculptures found at Shizhaishan in Yunnan (third century BC through first century AD) depict zebu in scenes of ritual, sacrifice, and husbandry, most of which seem to show domestic animals (Zhang, Z. 1998) (Figure 4.11A). In the rock art found in Congyuan in Yunnan (first through fifth centuries AD), images of zebu (and possibly also of buffalo, the two species being distinguishable by the presence/absence of the zebu's hump) show some individuals as prey hunted by humans, suggesting a wild nature, and others tied with ropes and led by humans, indicating domestication (Wang, N. 1985) (Figure 4.11B). Based on

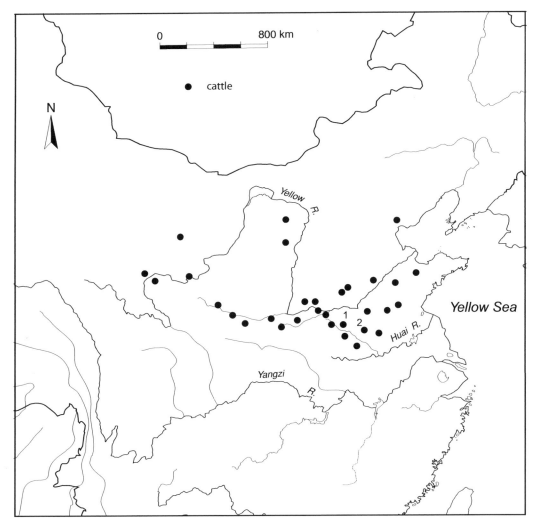

Figure 4.10. Distribution of sites associated with domesticated cattle in north China. The sites of Guchengzhai (1) and Shantaisi (2) yielded the highest NISP (modified from figure 4 of Lü 2010).

representations in art, therefore, we may infer that zebu was introduced to southwest China no later than the third century BC.

Water Buffalo

The modern domestic water buffalo (*Bubalus bubalis*) can be broadly classified into two major categories based on phenotype, behavior, and karyotype: One is the river buffalo, found in the Indian subcontinent, the Middle East, and Eastern Europe; the other is the swamp buffalo, distributed in China, Bangladesh, Southeast Asia, and the northeastern states of India (Cockrill 1981). A recent study of mtDNA from modern buffalo in India suggests that

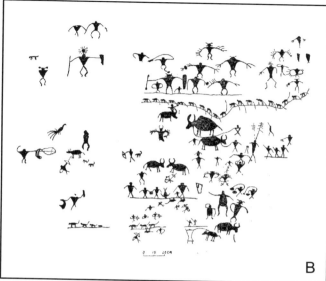

Figure 4.11. Art presentation of animals from Yunnan. **(A)** Bronze shell container from Shizhaishan, with zebus and man riding horse. **(B)** Cangyuan rock art showing images of wild and domesticated zebu and buffalo (after Zhang, Z. 1998: color plate 31; figure 14 of Wang, N. 1985).

these two types were domesticated independently, from separate groups of a common wild progenitor (*Bubalus arnee*) (Kumar et al. 2007). Morphological studies of ancient buffalo remains from South Asia have demonstrated that water buffalo (most likely the river type of buffalo) was first domesticated in northwestern South Asia some time before the Harappa civilization (3300–1300 BC) (Patel 1997; Patel and Meadow 1998). In contrast, in Southeast Asia wild buffalo remains have been found in the Paleolithic context (Mudar and Anderson 2007), but it is unclear whether they were the swamp type. DNA sequences for wild buffalo are currently unavailable.

All indigenous buffalo remains in China have been identified as the swamp type. Whereas eight species have been found in Pleistocene deposits, only one species (*Bubalus mephistopheles*) has been dated to the Holocene (Xue, X. and Li 2000). It was previously thought that water buffalo was first domesticated in the Yangzi River region during the Neolithic period, based on buffalo remains found at the rice-farming site of Hemudu in Zhejiang, dated to about 5000 BC (Bellwood 2005: 125; Chang 1986a: 211; Chen, Y. and Li 1989; Han, D. 1988). Because *B. mephistopheles* is the only buffalo species found in Neolithic China, the assumption has been that the modern swamp type of buffalo in China was first domesticated from indigenous *B. mephistopheles*. Tests of mtDNA, however, have revealed that the modern buffalo in China is identical to the swamp type distributed in Southeast Asia (*B. bubalis*)

(Lei, C. et al. 2007); therefore, these populations are unlikely to have derived from the indigenous wild buffalo in China.

Recent zooarchaeological studies of *B. mephistopheles* remains (based on body size and kill-off patterns) from Neolithic and Bronze Age sites in China indicate that no evidence for a domestication process can be found in Chinese indigenous buffalo remains (Liu, L. et al. 2004, 2006). An ancient DNA study of buffalo remains identifiable to *B. mephistopheles* and dating to 6000–1600 BC from several sites in the Wei River Valley shows a clear separation between this ancient bovine and modern domestic swamp buffalo, strongly pointing to the possibility that the indigenous Chinese buffalo (*B. mephistopheles*) is unlikely to have been involved in the process of swamp buffalo domestication (Yang, D. et al. 2008). This finding challenges the accepted view that buffalo domestication was closely related to rice cultivation in the Neolithic Yangzi River region.

The domesticated variety of swamp buffalo would, plausibly, have first appeared in the distribution area of the wild type of swamp buffalo (*B. arnee*), presumably in Southeast Asia. In Thailand, the earliest *B. arnee* remains have been uncovered from the Lang Rongrien Rockshelter, Krabi, dating to the Pleistocene (Mudar and Anderson 2007), whereas domesticated buffalo remains have been identified at Ban Chiang, dating to 300 BC (Higham et al. 1981). In Yunnan, Southwest China, buffalo bones have been uncovered from at least two early and middle Holocene sites (Zhang, X. 1987), with one skull from Pupiao in Baoshan (ca. 6000 BC) identified as *B. mephistopheles* (Zong, G. and Huang 1985). No *B. arnee* remains have been reported archaeologically from China, however. To date, the earliest evidence for domestic buffalo in south China is from representations in art. Some bovine images in the Cangyuan rock art (first through fifth centuries AD), Yunnan, have been interpreted as buffalo, configured in both hunted (i.e., wild) and domesticated forms (Wang, N. 1985) (Figure 4.11B). The buffalo images in the Cangyuan rock art resemble *B. bubalis* or its wild ancestor, *B. arnee*, and are different from *B. mephistopheles* regarding shape of the horn, suggesting that Yunnan may have been part of a distribution area of the wild ancestor of *B. bubalis*. The images in this rock art are schematic, however, so they cannot be used as reliable evidence. Other artistic portrayals of domesticated buffalo are seen in sculptures cast on bronze drums and in clay models from tombs, all dating to the second century AD or later (Liu, L. et al. 2006).

Unfortunately, it is still too early to determine where and when the swamp type of buffalo (*B. bubalis*) was first domesticated. Human exploitation of buffalo, from wild to domesticated forms, has a long history in Yunnan, but whether Yunnan was part of a region in which buffalo domestication took place is currently uncertain. A better understanding of the timing and the locations of this animal's domestication must rely on more discovery and zooarchaeological analysis of buffalo remains in China, as well as on DNA tests of archaeological buffalo remains from Southwest China and its bordering regions.

Horses

The origin of the domestic horse (*Equus caballus*) has been a focus of multi-disciplinary research for decades, but conclusions are controversial. Osteoar-chaeological data point to a restricted area in Central Asia as the locale of the earliest horse domestication some 5,000 years ago (Levine et al. 2003; Mashkour 2006). Most archaeologists and historians believe that horses were introduced from the steppe region to China around the late part of the second millennium BC (Flad et al. 2007; Linduff 2003; Mair 2003; Yuan, J. and Flad 2003, 2006).

Genetic studies, however, have demonstrated a more complex picture. A 2,800-year-old domesticated stallion from Siberia showed that the male-inherited Y chromosome was diverse, but modern domestic horses world-wide display no sequence diversity on Y chromosome due to domestication processes (Lippold et al. 2011). In contrast, domestic horses display abun-dant genetic diversity within female-inherited mtDNA (Jansen et al. 2002; McGahern et al. 2006; Vila et al. 2001), including both modern and ancient horses from China (Cai, D. 2009; Lei, C. et al. 2009). The mtDNA results can be explained as mares from multiple separate lineages contributing to the modern genetic pool. Levine (2006) has pointed out that, as the orig-inal domesticated population expanded, horses from wild populations were occasionally introduced into the domestic herds. The question is, does any archaeological evidence from China indicate either domestication of indige-nous wild horses or introduction of wild mares to domesticated horse herds there? To address this issue, we need to start with the distribution of indigenous wild horses in China.

At least seven species of *Equus* have been reported from thirty-three Pleis-tocene sites, mostly in north China, but the most frequently occurring species during the late Pleistocene was *Equus przewalskii* (Olsen 1988; Qi, G. 1989). This animal lived in the wild throughout the Holocene until some 100 years ago, before it disappeared due to hunting and environmental deterioration, with few surviving in zoos around the world. Since 1985 some of the *E. prze-walskii* surviving in captivity have been reintroduced to the Dzungarian Basin, an area in which they were last seen a century ago (Ryder 1993).

About a dozen Upper Palaeolithic sites contain *E. przewalskii* remains (Qi, G. 1989); among them Shiyu in Shuoxian, northern Shanxi, has revealed the most abundant quantity (120 minimum number of individuals [MNI]) (Jia, L. et al. 1972). Horse bones also have been widely found at Neolithic and early Bronze Age sites across north China, spreading from the Liaodong peninsula in the east to Qinghai in the west (Linduff 2003) (Figure 4.12). Attempts have been made to identify the particular species of horse bones from five sites, which are the following: Guantaoyuan (late Yangshao and Western Zhou) and Banpo (Yangshao) in Shaanxi, Miaozigou and Dabagou in Inner Mongolia (late Yangshao), and Yinxu in Henan (late Shang). In all five cases, the remains were assigned to *E. przewalskii* (Appendix).

It is important to note the similarity of morphological proportions between the skeletons of wild and domesticated horses. The similarity is particularly apparent in the early stages of domestication; thus, distinguishing domesticated horses from their wild ancestors is not a straightforward task, and researchers often have to rely on multiple lines of evidence (Olsen, Sandra 2006, Olsen, Stanly 1988). As Stanley Olsen (1988: 162) has pointed out, unless horse remains are found together with artifacts exclusively associated with the domestic type, it is difficult to satisfactorily determine whether the animal remains represent wild, tame, or domesticated varieties. Indeed researchers working on horse remains in the Iranian central plateau have found it challenging to distinguish between *E. przewalskii* and domestic horses and have thus resorted to citing the low proportion of Przewalski horse remains, among all recovered fauna, as a rationale for classifying this equine material as wild (Mashkour 2003).

Yangshao culture sites bearing horse remains have all revealed an agricultural economy supplemented by hunting, with no domesticated grazing animals. Horse bones are scarce among the faunal material, and almost certainly belong to wild species. Thus, horse bones from Miaodigou appear to have been chopped and burned, indicating that the animals were hunted for food (Huang, Y. 2003). Beginning at sites from the late Longshan and Qijia periods (ca. 2500–1800 BC), horse bones have often been unearthed together with sheep/goats and cattle. At Dahezhuang in Gansu, for example, three horse mandibles were found in human burials as sacrificial offerings, ritual practices that were also applied to pig and sheep mandibles at the site (Zhongguo Shehui Kexueyuan 1974) (Appendix 1). Remains of these horses are widely found in the archaeological record, but in proportionately small amounts among faunal material at any single site, giving rise to controversy over their domesticity. Many researchers argue for their wild status, based on their relative scarcity at any given site (Linduff 2003), whereas others favor the possibility of domestication, arguing from their frequency of incidence in the archaeological record (Yuan, J. and Flad 2006). Current data provide no hard evidence by which to determine their domesticity. Nevertheless, as Linduff (2003) has noticed, the archaeological contexts of horse remains from the northwest region point to limited human utilization, primarily dietary and burial purposes, which are rather different from circumstances found in the Central Plain during the Shang dynasty.

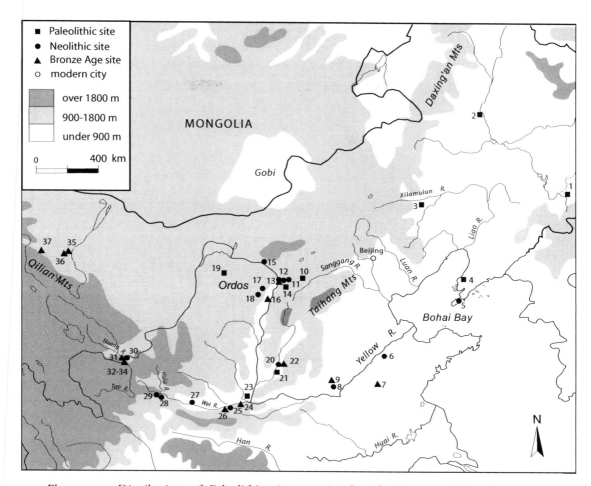

Figure 4.12. Distribution of Paleolithic sites associated with *E. przewalskii* and Neolithic and Bronze Age sites associated with horse remains, showing the Ordos region's highest concentration of horse-bearing sites. 1: Antu; 2: Qingshantou; 3: Wuerji; 4: Xiaogushan; 5: Beiwutun; 6: Chengziya; 7: Qianzhangda; 8: Baiying; 9: Anyang; 10: Xujiayao; 11: Miaozigou; 12: Dabagou; 13: Xicha; 14: Shiyu; 15: Zhuan-longzang; 16: Lijiaya; 17: Huoshiliang and Yuanxihaizi (in Shaanxi); 18: Wuzhuang-guoliang; 19: Salawusu; 20: Gaodui; 21: Dingcun; 22: Qiaobei; 23: Dali; 24: Nan-shacun; 25: Banpo; 26: Laoniupo; 27: Guantaoyuan; 28: Shizhaocun; 29: Xishanping; 30: Majiawan; 31: Jijiachuan; 32: Dahezhuang; 33: Zhangjiazui; 34: Qinweijia; 35: Huoshiliang (in Gansu); 36: Ganggangwa; 37: Huoshaogou.

More horse-bearing sites date to the late Shang period. Equine remains have been found in two types of deposits. One type is ceremonial, in which horses were used as sacrificial offerings, often together with chariots, in mortuary contexts. This situation occurs almost always in large political centers, such as Yinxu, Laoniupo, Qiaobei, and Qianzhangda (Appendix). It is commonly agreed that those sacrificial horses were domesticated and introduced from elsewhere. At Yinxu, a capital city of the Shang dynasty, large numbers of horses, often together with chariots, appear as prestigious sacrificial items within the royal cemeteries and close to temple/palace structures (Figure 10.9.4), but are nearly absent from ash pits in residential areas evidently because the animals were precious tribute gifts brought to the Shang kings from elsewhere (Shih, C. 1953). No systematic analysis on osteological morphology of horse remains at Yinxu has been carried out. The only available measurements, from two teeth, show rather small sizes, leading Teilhard de Chardin and Young (1936: 19) to suggest that the small Yinxu horse represents a domesticated form probably derived from the Przewalski horse. It is unknown whether other horses from Yinxu also belonged to a domesticated form of *E. przewalskii*, but at least some of the Yinxu horses were probably from this species.

The second type of horse deposits during the late Shang period is domestic, found in residential contexts, where horse remains were a part of household refuse. Sites belonging to this category have been found mainly in the Ordos region, such as Lijiaya and Xicha (Figure 4.12 and Appendix). This type of sites may hold the key for resolving the problem of horse domestication in China. The Xicha site in Qingshuihe, central-south Inner Mongolia, was occupied from Yangshao to the late Shang-Zhou period, and horse remains have been found in the Longshan and Shang-Zhou deposits. The Longshan faunal remains are small in sample size (37 NISP), and horse bones (4 NISP) account for 10.8 percent of the total assemblage. The late Shang-Zhou phase of this site expands to an area of 120 ha, containing rich residential features. Horse bones account for 9.1 percent of the total faunal assemblage (531 of 5835 NISP), which consists predominantly of pigs, sheep/goats, cattle, and a small proportion of wild animals. All the faunal remains were recovered, as scattered bones, from residential contexts. Many horse bones were used as material for making tools, and some were covered with red pigment, suggesting ritual functions (Yang, C. 2007). Apparently, horses, which may have been consumed as food and used as sacrificial items, played an important role in the local agropastoralist economy. This kind of human-equine relationship is consistent with the tradition found in the Qijia culture and the Eurasian steppe.

Although identification of species has not been made for the horse remains from Xicha, the relatively high representation of horses in the fauna, particularly from the late Shang-Zhou period, is in sharp contrast to sites in other areas, where horse remains are extremely sparse. Such intensive exploitation of horses is likely to have been the result of domestication. The key question, however, is: Were indigenous wild horses domesticated locally?

Taken as a whole, almost all the Palaeolithic *E. przewalskii* remains have been uncovered from sites in northeast and northwest regions (Qi, G. 1989), coinciding with the distribution of most Neolithic and early Bronze Age horses. Whenever taxonomical identification has been attempted, the Neolithic and Shang samples have been assigned to *E. przewalskii*. The highest concentration of recorded horse-bearing sites from the Neolithic and Bronze Age falls in the vicinity of the Ordos region. These include one microlithic, three late Yang-shao, three late Longshan, and two late Shang sites (Appendix 1). Notably, the Shiyu site, which has yielded the largest Paleolithic *E. przewalskii* assemblage, is also located in the Ordos (Figure 4.12).

The Ordos region, where vegetation has alternated between forest-steppe and semiarid steppe throughout history (Tang, Z. et al. 2004a), witnessed the longest continuing presence of horses in all of China, from the wild form to the domesticated one. Olsen (1988: 161) has suggested that people had close contact with horses over a long period of time in north China, so early taming and eventual domestication in China is highly probable. Another possible scenario is that, when seminomadic people in the Eurasian steppe spread toward Eastern Asia with their domesticated grazing animals, including horses, the Przewalski mares may have been introduced to a putatively domesticated horse population in north China. It is notable that researchers have found that modern Przewalski displays DNA haplotypes not present in domestic horses (modern and ancient), thus it is unclear if the former was ancestral to the latter (Cai et al. 2009; Lippold et al. 2011). Modern Przewalski, however, may not be genetically same as ancient one because this species underwent a severe genetic bottleneck that may have reduced its genetic variation. A large-scale analysis of the ancient Przewalski DNA is needed in future to detect potential extinct lineages (Cai et al. 2009). Indeed, bronze sculptures of the domestic form of Przewalski horses have been found in north Shaanxi, dating to the late Shang period (see Chapter 9). More taxonomic and ancient DNA studies are needed to clarify the relationships between the indigenous wild horse and the Neolithic and Bronze Age horse in north China.

Chickens

The most probable wild progenitor of the domestic chicken (*Gallus gallus domesticus*) was the red jungle fowl (*Gallus gallus*); however, the location of its domestication remains controversial. An mtDNA analysis has been conducted on 834 domestic chickens across Eurasia as well as 66 red jungle fowls from Southeast Asia and China. The results suggest that chickens have multiple maternal origins and that domestications occurred in at least three regions of South and Southeast Asia, including Yunnan, south and southwest

China and/or surrounding areas, and the Indian subcontinent (Liu, Y.-P. et al. 2006).

Archaeologically, we know little about the timing and location of the chicken's original domestication in China. Many Neolithic sites have revealed chicken remains, reported as domesticated species. The earliest citation of such remains is from Cishan in Hebei, dating to around 6000 BC (Zhou, B. 1981). This claim, however, has not been accepted by many archaeologists. Chicken bones similar in size to modern domestic ones have been identified at Kangjia in Shaanxi (ca. 2500–2000 BC) (Liu, L. et al. 2001). Clay chickens, along with other types of clay animals used in ritual contexts, have been unearthed from some Shijiahe culture sites (ca. 2500–2000 BC), and are also particularly abundant at the Dengjiawan site in Hubei. They are individually distinguishable as chicks, hens, or roosters (Shijiahe 2003) (Figure 7.15:2). It is possible that chickens were domesticated by the later part of the third millennium BC, but zooarchaeological studies differentiating wild from domestic chickens are currently lacking in the Neolithic context.

Secondary Products in Animal Domestication

As in other parts of the Old World, domesticated livestock in China was first used largely for meat; the exploitation of milk, wool, riding, vehicle pulling, plowing, and pack transport, which are described as "secondary products" by Sherratt (1981), develop much later.

A few studies based on zooarchaeological data from China have touched on issues of animal secondary products. According to a recent study by Brunson (2008) on faunal remains from a late Longshan culture site at Taosi in Shanxi (2500–1900 BC), the kill-off patterns for sheep may indicate that they were being used for wool production. In Xinjiang, where artifacts have been well preserved, sheep and cattle pastoralism was an important part of the economy, and the exploitation of milk and wool are evident in the second millennium BC (see Chapter 9).

Where agriculture was predominant in China, secondary products may have been mainly associated with the muscle power of bovines. Although zooarchaeological information is scarce, many discussions based on textual information have been put forward by historians. A main question is the following: When and where did bovine-traction/plow technology develop in ancient China? Some people believe that buffalo-plow technology was already used during the Neolithic period, as particularly exemplified by stone plow-shaped artifacts unearthed from several sites of the Songze and Liangzhu cultures, such as Zhuangqiaofen in Pinghu, Zhejiang (Xu, X. and Cheng 2005). Evidence for domestication of buffalo, however, is absent in faunal assemblages from these cultures (Liu, L. et al. 2006). A preliminary use-wear analysis of several plow-shaped tools from a Songze culture site at Pishan in Zhejiang (4000–3300 BC) suggests that these tools are multifunctional implements, but none of them shows use-wear traces resembling a plow (Liu and Chen 2011). More use-wear analysis needs to be done on these Neolithic implements to determine their functions.

Many scholars agree that the earliest bovine-plow complex did not appear until the Eastern Zhou period in the Yellow River region, and that it resulted from the development of iron production for making agricultural implements (Chen, W. 1991: 131; Yang, Z. 1995). Thus, in the classical text "Discourses of the States" (*Guoyu*), compiled in the fifth and fourth centuries BC, part 9 of the chapter "Discourses of Jin" ("Jinyu, jiu") records that, in the state of Jin, situated in the middle Yellow River Valley, "the animal [cattle] which was formerly used as a sacrificial offering in ancestral temples is now used as a productive force in the field." This statement on the ritual function of cattle can be supported by copious finds of sacrificial cattle remains at Yanshi Shang City and Anyang, dating to 1600–1046 BC (Yuan, J. and Flad 2005).

There is a lack of zooarchaeological evidence for animal secondary products mainly because archaeological excavations of late Bronze Age sites have been focused on burials, which normally do not contain animal remains. Therefore, we can rely only on other lines of evidence to trace the earliest bovine-plow technology, including physical remains of iron plows and artistic representations of plowing scenes on artifacts. Based on available information, the iron plow-cattle complex was evidently developed during the Warring States period (475–221 BC) and became widely applied to dry-land farming in north China, especially in the Yellow River region, during the Han dynasty (206 BC–220 AD) (Chen, W. 1991: 190–5; Qian, X. 2002a, b).

Art representations of buffalo suggest that this animal was used both as carrier and as traction (for sledge and cart), exemplified by sculptures of buffalo on the bronze drums and mortuary clay models in South and Southwest China, dating to no earlier than the second century AD. There is also no hard evidence for the presence of the buffalo-plow complex until much later. Bovine-plow technology was probably brought to South China by people migrating from the north, but it is still unclear exactly when it first occurred (Liu, L. et al. 2006).

Summary

The earliest evidence for domestication of dogs can be traced back to 8000 BC (Nanzhuangtou), and pigs to 7000 BC (Jiahu), but the first attempts to domesticate these animals may have been much earlier. Sheep, goats, and cattle were introduced to China by the second half of the third millennium BC. Horses became common when sheep, goats, and cattle were introduced to northwest China, and these grazing animals tend to co-occur at some sites, suggesting that they were introduced together as a part of pastoralist economy. The horses may have belonged to a domesticated species, despite their being usually underrepresented in the faunal remains. By the late part of the second millennium BC, domesticated horses were widespread in north China, and also became a part of elite culture. How these animals were brought into China has been a matter of debate. Because of its geographical position, Xinjiang has been seen as an area with potential for manifesting East-West interactions; however, regarding domesticated animals, the earliest dates for cattle, sheep, and horses in Xinjiang are no earlier than those from the Yellow River Valley. Thus, these domesticated grazing animals were likely diffused during multiple events and through various routes from the Eurasian steppe to a broad region in north China. These routes may have included those precursors of the historical lines of communication, such as the Silk Road in the west and many routes connecting north China and Mongolia in the north.

The domestication processes of buffalo and zebu are likely to have been related to interregional interactions between Southwest China and its neighboring areas. The development of the so-called Southwest Silk Road, which connected Southwest China with Burma and India during the Han dynasty, likely encouraged trade between different regions and promoted the dispersal of domestic bovines. Such interactions may have existed long before the Han dynasty, and future research may reveal earlier evidence for the origins of these bovines.

DYNAMICS OF DOMESTICATION

There are two competing theories regarding the underlying dynamics of food-producing economies. One theory takes a cultural-ecological view, which in general emphasizes the emergence of farming in environmentally marginal areas, where severe climatic change forced human populations to find new food sources (Watson 1995). This model has been used to explain rice domestication in China. The Yangzi River Valley during the terminal Pleistocene was a temperate to cool-temperate zone with clear differentiation of seasons; therefore, wild rice was not abundant and food shortages may have occurred during winter. Scarcity of wild rice may have provoked a desire to increase its availability by cultivation (Higham 1995; Lu, T. 1999: 139–40). Thus, environmental change, as well as the marginal character of wild cereal distribution in the Yangzi River region, may have been among the major factors responsible for the origins of rice cultivation in that area (Lu, T. 1999: 139–40; Yan, W. 1992). Based on currently available data, however, it is questionable whether rice was used as a major staple food during the late Pleistocene. Accordingly, it is difficult to argue that rice cultivation was adopted to solve the problems of food shortage and population pressure. Rather, in the absence of clear evidence, the earliest rice cultivation may also be thought to have happened during the early Holocene, when the climate was much improved and rice was only one of the abundant natural resources. In brief, the cultural-ecological approach still leaves room for further explanation regarding rice domestication.

Similarly, animal domestication also has been interpreted as a solution for food shortage. Yuan and Flad proposed four preconditions for pig domestication: (1) a need for acquiring new sources of protein due to insufficiency of meat gathered by traditional hunting; (2) availability of wild pigs near human settlements; (3) the successful cultivation of certain cereals, which encouraged people to further pursue domestication of certain animal species; and (4) a surplus from cereal farming, allowing the feeding of animals with the by-products of cereals (Yuan, J. and Flad 2002). These conditions, however, do not fit archaeological findings from those sites that have yielded domestic pig remains, such as Kuahuqiao, Jiahu, and Xinglongwa. All these sites reveal conditions with abundant natural resources; evidently the people relied on a broad-spectrum subsistence economy, with farming as a minor component. At present, no evidence from these sites implies a shortage of meat in the human diet, nor does any such evidence show that pigs primarily depended on cereal by-products. More research is needed to understand the process of early animal domestication.

A second theory offering a dynamic explanation for the origins of domestication involves a sociopolitical approach that follows Bender's (1978) original argument – that competition between neighboring groups to achieve local dominance through community feasting was the driving force behind food production. This motivation required increased subsistence resources and therefore intensified the process of food production. This view has gained increasing support in recent years. Several archaeologists have drawn evidence from different regions around the world to show that purposeful accumulation of domesticates was linked with prestige seeking by the aggrandizers rather than with subsistence needs of the populace (Clark and Blake 1994; Hayden 1995, 2003). Hayden (1995) has argued that in many areas the first domesticate was a nonedible plant or specialty food, such as hemp, bottle gourd, chile pepper, and cardamom and other condiments. These situations, therefore, suggest that early domesticated edible plants were prestige goods or luxury foods rather than subsistence material and that competitive feasting was the driving force behind the transition to farming. According to Hayden, domestication occurs when status distinctions and socioeconomic inequalities first appear within societies. "It is only when people begin to 'fight with food' for power, wealth, and status that labor-intensive foods begin to be developed as prestige components" (Hayden 1995: 282). In this view, domestication, feasting, and social inequality are intertwined factors. On the basis of ethno-graphic information derived from some tribal groups in Southeast Asia, Hay-den (2003, 2011) has argued that rice was first domesticated as a luxury food, particularly for feasting, as it is still used by these tribes today.

This approach, often referred to as the socioeconomic competition model or food-fight theory, is by no means accepted by all archaeologists. The problems are that, first, it is not difficult to find many domesticates that, indeed, are subsistence food items, both before and after being domesticated, such as millets, barley, beans, buffalo, cattle, pigs, and so forth. Second, there is simply no well-documented correlation anywhere in the world between the initial emergence of social inequality and the first appearance of domesticates (Smith 2001b).

Nevertheless, Hayden's argument, that rice was first domesticated in China as a luxury food, is well worth further study. Although ethnographic data on rice cultivation and consumption from tribal groups in Southeast Asia may not represent the situation in the early Holocene Yangzi River region, that still does not say that rice was not used as a luxury food for feasting or that rice domestication was unrelated to political motivations during the early phase of cultivation. For instance, as Hayden (2011) also noticed, Jiahu has revealed both the early rice remains and evidence for the emergence of incipient social differentiation (Henansheng Wenwu Kaogu 1999a); chemical analysis of ancient organic substances absorbed into pottery vessels indicates that Jiahu rice was used for brewing fermented beverages that may have played an essential role in ceremonies that confirmed social hierarchies (McGovern et al. 2004). Thus, it is possible that early rice, at least in some cases, was used for luxury consumption by some aggrandizers engaged in negotiation for power. Nevertheless, because the initial phase of rice domestication is still unclear, as discussed earlier in text, Jiahua rice's association with ritual use may not represent the motivation for the first rice domestication.

Likewise, if pigs were first domesticated in areas with abundant food resources, we cannot rule out the possibility that pork was favored over other animal flesh, as a delicacy at competitive feasts, at least occasionally. This situ-ation also may have reinforced the incentive for pig domestication.

Each of these two theoretical models is useful, to some degree, for explain-ing the human and natural dynamics underlying early food production, but each also displays biases influenced by a particular theoretical framework (pro-cessual vs. post-processual approaches). In contrast, rather than seeing plant domestication as a corrective resolution of environmental stress, an alterna-tive view explains it as the natural fruition of a benignly selective relation-ship between people and plants (Rindos 1980, 1984, 1989). Indeed, many recent studies have revealed that agriculture was often initiated in areas of relatively abundant resources (Price and Gebauer 1995). It is not difficult to see that all the sites in China associated with early domesticates were situated in rich environmental surroundings and that these domesticates, however small their role in the overall subsistence economy, nevertheless formed a stable part of the local human diet for a long period of time before intensified farming was undertaken. During this extended process, these domesticates were probably used both as routine staples and as luxuries for conspicuous consumption, so the dynamics of domestication were both ecological and social.

CONCLUSIONS

As in many parts of the world, foraging peoples in China initiated domestication, intentionally or unintentionally, through the routine and necessary daily tasks of locating, hunting, harvesting, processing, and consuming foodstuffs. These first domesticates, including rice, millets, soybean, dogs, and pigs, played rather minor roles for a few millennia before becoming dominant staples or major sources of protein in the subsistence system, during the middle Neolithic (ca. 5000–3000 BC) or even later.

Several new domesticates were introduced to north China during the third and second millennia BC, including wheat, barley, oats, cattle, sheep, goats, and horses. The appearance of these domesticates in China is likely to have resulted from a combination of dynamics. For example, changing environmental conditions after the Mid-Holocene Climatic Optimum made north China more suitable for pastoralism, and movement of populations from the Eurasian steppe to north China may have promoted the spread of economically valuable technologies.

Various species of tubers (taro and yams) seem to have played an important role in the human diet of both north and south China since the Paleolithic, but the relevant domestication processes are difficult to trace due to a lack of archaeological data. Starch analysis appears to hold great potential for the recovery of tuber remains, but the application of this method is still at an early stage in Chinese archaeological research.

The late dates for the first known evidence of domestic buffalo and zebu in south China are probably affected by currently insufficient zooarchaeological investigation in this region. In any event, intensified cultural interactions between Southwest China and Southeast and South Asia during the Han dynasty may have contributed to more frequent use of these two animals, as depicted in art forms of that time.

Domestic animals and plants not only played crucial roles in the subsistence economy but were also used as ritual offerings at various ceremonial events, facilitating negotiations for power. While indigenous domesticates formed the economic basis for the emergence of complex societies in the Neolithic, introduced domesticates contributed to accelerated sociopolitical changes in the early Bronze Age, leading to the formation of early states/civilization in north China. Social and economic innovations during the Bronze Age, which were supported by enhanced levels of plant cultivation and animal husbandry, include multicropping, new sources of protein for growing populations, and elaborate ritual sacrifices and ceremonies. These topics will be revisited repeatedly in the following chapters.

CHAPTER 5

NEOLITHIZATION: SEDENTISM AND FOOD PRODUCTION IN THE EARLY NEOLITHIC (7000–5000 BC)

> On the death of Baoxi, there arose Shennong (in his place). He fashioned wood to form the hoe, and bent or straightened wood to make the hoe-handle. The advantages of tilling and weeding were then taught to all under heaven.
>
> Chapter, "The Great Treatise II," in *Book of Changes* (ca. the ninth century BC), translated by James Legge (1879), modified
>
> "包牺氏没, 神农氏作, 斫木为耜, 揉木为耒, 耒耨之利, 以教天下,..."
> 《《周易 · 系辞下》》

The development of Neolithic cultures in China coincided with the arrival of the Mid-Holocene Climatic Optimum. The warm and wet climatic conditions enabled the flourishing of small villages in major river valleys, from the northeast to south China. These settlements' archaeological remains are characterized by dwellings, storage pits, burials, and, sometimes, by ditched or walled enclosures. Domestication of plants and animals is clearly evident, and ritual activities are reflected in burials and on artifacts. Pottery vessels are prevalent. Polished stone tools increase in proportion, but chipped stones and microliths continue to be found. Grinding stones (slabs, handstones, mortars, and pestles) are common in toolkits. The *mopan* slabs and *mobang* elongate handstones, often occurring together in the archaeological context, now became a diagnostic tool complex in the toolkits, particularly in North and Northeast China.

It has been widely accepted in Chinese archaeology that the sedentary village, agriculture, pottery, and ground/polished stone tools were interrelated elements of the Neolithic cultures in 7000–5000 BC. This interpretation is primarily based on the contextual presence of residential features, domesticated cereal remains, and certain tool types with presumed agricultural function (An, Z. 1989; Chang 1981a, 1986a: 87–95; Shi, X. 1992). Although some scholars are cautious about overemphasizing the role of agriculture during this period (Shi, X. 1992; Wu, J. 1989), the term "agriculture" has been used loosely, referring to archaeological cultures that show any material trait of food

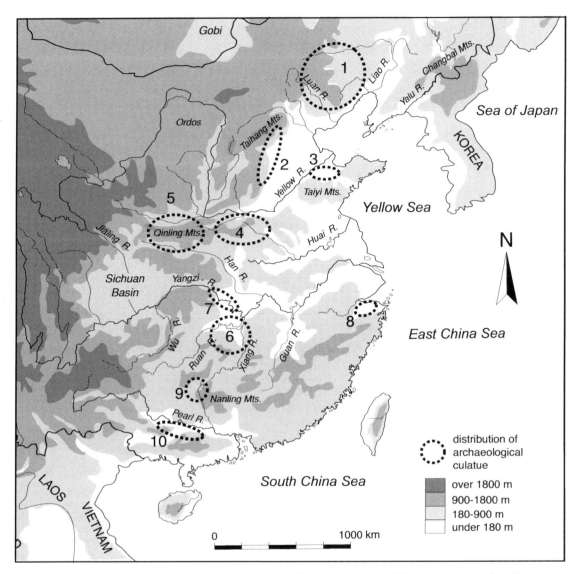

Figure 5.1. Distribution of early Neolithic cultures in China mentioned in Chapter 5. 1: Xinglongwa; 2: Cishan-Beifudi; 3: Houli; 4: Peiligang; 5: Baijia-Dadiwan; 6: Pengtoushan-Lower Zaoshi; 7: Chengbeixi; 8: Xiaohuangshan-Kuahuqiao; 9: cave sites in north Guangxi; 10: Dingsishan shell middens.

production and in which research on the level of food-producing activity is lacking. The level of sedentism during the early Neolithic has also not been sufficiently studied.

From a perspective of world prehistory, all the traits conventionally attributed to the Neolithic appear to have developed independently from each other and to have been interrelated with varying combinations of factors in different regions (Marshall 2006), and China is no exception, as discussed in Chapter 3. The transition from hunting and gathering to agriculture is a continuum with

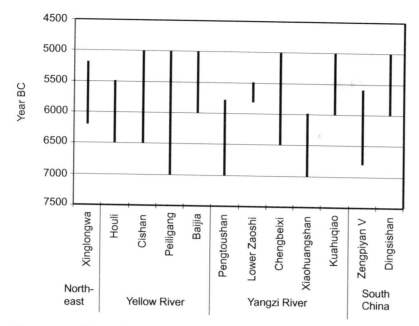

Figure 5.2. Chronology of early Neolithic cultures in China.

a boundary zone characterized as "low-level food production," and agriculture may be defined as a condition in which 30 to 50 percent of annual caloric intake in human diet is derived from domesticates (Smith 2001a: 17–18). Apparently, an economy both sedentary and agricultural did not develop overnight; the emergence of sedentism and the transition to agriculture are not necessarily connected, and both of these developmental processes need to be quantified, if possible. Our goal in this chapter is to investigate forms of settlement-subsistence systems during some 2000 years of the early Neolithic period. Because it is a matter of investigation to establish the levels of caloric intake contributed from domesticates in the human diet, we will use the term "food production" instead of "agriculture" in this chapter. We will focus on the variability of sedentism and food production cross-regionally, and also examine interrelationships between different variables that characterized early Neolithic cultures.

This chapter covers major archaeological cultures dating to the period of 7000–5000 BC in China, and discusses them as three regional groups. The first group is north China, consisting of the Liao, Yellow, Huai, and upper Han River Valleys; the second is the Yangzi River Valley (excluding the upper Han River Valley, which was culturally similar to the Wei River region), the principal drainage basin of Central China; and the third is South China, mainly referring to the Pearl River, or Zhu Jiang, region. Figure 5.1 shows the distribution of archaeological cultures, and Figure 5.2 provides basic chronology. We will first briefly discuss the criteria for sedentism and the data for determining subsistence modes, then demonstrate the variability of residential-subsistence systems cross-regionally. In addition, we will investigate the development of social complexity, which often manifested in ritual activities.

DETERMINING SEDENTISM AND SUBSISTENCE STRATEGIES

Kelly's (1992: 49) definition of sedentism refers to settlement systems in which at least part of the population remains at the same location throughout the entire year; this definition is adopted for the purposes of this book. It has been challenging to identify sedentism in the archaeological record, as no single universal model applies to all cases. Nevertheless, common elements, which may be seen as indicators of sedentism, recur in the archaeological record from many parts of the world.

The most frequently cited archaeological evidence for sedentism is listed as follows: (1) High levels of investment in architectural construction; (2) heavy-duty material culture, especially smooth-worn stone tools used for intensive grinding; (3) storage pits; (4) cemeteries; (5) high frequencies of human commensals, specifically house mice, house sparrows, and rats; (6) indications of year-round hunting; (7) thickness and density of archaeological deposits as indications of occupational duration and population density (see summary in Belfer-Cohen and Bar-Yosef 2000; Boyd 2006; Marshall 2006); (8) high frequencies of domesticates (Rosenswig 2006); (9) increased frequency of functionally specific vessels, designed with less concern for portability than customarily shown by mobile communities (Rosenswig 2006), whose pottery vessels are multipurposed, durable, and transportable in form (Arnold 1999); and (10) high frequencies of secondary refuse, resulting from increased efforts at refuse disposal to meet the requirements of long-term sedentary living, as opposed to high levels of primary refuse and caches in residential areas, which are indicators of short-term residential stays and anticipated return (Hardy-Smith and Edwards 2004).

Sedentism, as an analytic concept, implies a dynamic process that appears with great variability in the archaeological record of different regions. The presence of any of these variable elements is not necessarily a definitive indicator of sedentism, in any given case. In Chinese archaeology, not all the criteria just listed are applicable, because certain types of data required (e.g., human commensals and hunting seasonality) have not yet become available through zooarchaeological research. In addition, some variables, such as pottery, polished stone tools, and grinding stones, had already occurred in mobile hunting-gathering communities during the terminal Pleistocene in China (see Chapter 3). Evidently, sedentism can also be developed independently of food production.

Therefore, we are not trying to determine the presence/absence of sedentism, but to investigate levels of sedentism, the different ways human groups moved around, and various relationships between the character of human communities and their use of the landscape. Based on the nature of our data, the following criteria for sedentism will be used in this chapter, although not all of them can be quantified:

(1) higher levels of investment in architectural construction, such as larger buildings and well-finished walls and floors;
(2) higher frequencies of storage pits;
(3) increasingly well-arranged spatial plan of a settlement, such as regular layout of cemeteries and dwellings, and fortification around the village;
(4) increased thickness and density of archaeological deposits;
(5) higher frequencies of domesticates, particularly pig and cereals;
(6) increased use of functionally specific vessels with less concern for their portability; and
(7) a contrast between higher frequencies of primary refuse inside dwellings and de facto refuse (particularly caches) in activity areas, indicating the mobile tradition, and higher frequencies of secondary refuse in designated residential areas (e.g., refuse pits near houses), indicating increased sedentism.

The subsistence strategy will be investigated through many lines of evidence. Settlement distribution in relation to availability of natural resources, as well as faunal and floral remains at settlement sites, can offer great insight into the modes of food procurement; pathological and isotopic analyses of human remains can provide invaluable information about economic behavior and diet; the composition of toolkits may indicate kinds of subsistence activities involved; and residue and use-wear analyses of artifacts can reveal the function of tools as well as types of food consumed in ancient times.

NORTHEAST AND NORTH CHINA

China's northeast and north-central regions began to experience a warm-wet event at around 9000 cal. BP (An, Z. et al. 2000). This condition led to the appearance of warm-temperate deciduous forests in these previously semiarid regions. Several hundred early Neolithic sites have been identified; they are normally small in size, ranging from a few thousand square meters to a few hectares. Most sites are situated in mountainous basins or floodplains near hills or at the base of mountains. These site distributions are referred to as the Xinglongwa culture in the Liao River, the Cishan-Beifudi culture to the east of the Taihang Mountains, the Houli culture to the north of the Taiyi Mountain ranges, the Peiligang culture in central and western Henan, and the Baijia-Dadiwan culture along the Wei and Han River Valleys (Figure 5.1).

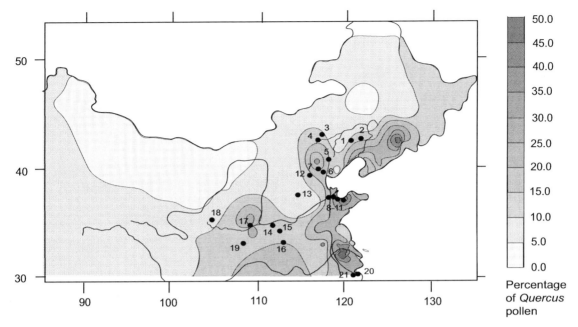

Figure 5.3. Location of major early Neolithic sites (ca. 9000–7000 cal. BP) in rela-tion to the distribution of high concentrations of *Quercus* (ca. 8000–6000 BP or 8871–6847 cal. BP) (pollen map modified from figure 10 of Ren and Beug 2002). *Xin-glongwa culture*: 1: Xinglongwa, Xinglonggou; 2: Chahai; 3: Baiyinchanghan; 4: Nan-taizi; 5: Xizhai, Dongzhai; 6: Menggezhuang; 7: Shangzhai, Beiniantou. *Houli culture*: 8–11: total of 12 sites on the north of the Taiyi Mountains. *Cishan-Beifudi culture*: 12: Beifudi; 13: Cishan. *Peiligang culture*: 14: Tieshenggou; 15: Peiligang; 16: Jiahu. *Baijia-Dadiwan culture*: 17: Baijia; 18: Dadiwan; 19: Lijiacun. *Lower Yangzi River*: 20: Xiaohuangshan; 21: Kuahuqiao.

The preference for situating settlements in such environments has been interpreted as typically motivated by concern for close proximity to natural resources and to land for cereal cultivation. It is notable that the appearance of warm, temperate, deciduous forests in northern China is particularly associated with an increase of *Quercus* species (oaks) around the mountainous regions (Ren, G. and Beug 2002) where Neolithic settlements were distributed in concentration (Figure 5.3). This pattern of settlement location suggests that acorn, a plant with high levels of starch and oil, may have been one of the major resources exploited by these early Neolithic populations. This proposition is supported by the results of several starch and use-wear analyses on grinding stones from several early Neolithic sites, suggesting that these tools were used to process various starchy plants, including acorns, beans, tubers, and millet, among which acorn appears significant in quantity (Liu, L. et al. 2010a; Yang, X. et al. 2009). Taking this situation into consideration, it is important to investigate the whole range of resources exploited and the levels of food-productive activity involved in these regions.

Figure 5.4. The settlement layout of the Xinglongwa site (after Yang H. and Liu 1997: plate 1).

The Xinglongwa Culture (ca. 6200–5200 BC)

The Xinglongwa culture represents the early stage of the Neolithic development in Northeast China. About 100 sites of the Xinglongwa culture have been found, distributed mostly in the hilly Liaoxi region (west of Liaoning), in today's southeastern Inner Mongolia, western Liaoning, and northern Hebei. Some ten settlements have been excavated to date, and the most well-known sites are Xinglonggou and Xinglongwa in Aohan Banner, Baiyinchanghan in Linxi County, and Chahai in Fuxin (Li, X. 2008). Xinglongwa sites are characterized by rectangular subterranean houses arranged in rows, and some settlements appear to have been surrounded by ditches (Figure 5.4). Most houses are 50–80 m² in size, with some as large as 100 m². Storage pits occur both inside and outside houses, and human burials have been occasionally found underneath the house floors. Abundant debris was often left on the house floors, including tools, ceramic vessels, pottery sherds, and occasional human bones. The ceramic vessels are simple in form and dominated by bucket-shaped pots. They are sand tempered, brownish in color, and made with the coiling method. The tool assemblage includes chipped stone hoes, spades, and knives; grinding stones, such as *mopan* slabs, *mobang* handstones, mortars, and pestles; and ground stone axes and adzes. There are also large numbers of microliths, used as blades for notched bone knives and fish spears (Li, X. 2008) (Figure 5.5).

The type-site Xinglongwa (3 ha), for example, was a moated settlement. It is situated near low hills, about 20 m above the surrounding land. The site is close to a natural spring and 1.5 km from a river course. Excavations have revealed 170 houses throughout the entire occupation period, which can be divided into three phases. During Phase I, houses were built in eight rows, more than ten in each row, and a moat, about 2 m in width and 1 m in depth, was also constructed. Most houses were 50–80 m² in size, with the two largest ones (140 m²) located in the center of the settlement. The majority of these houses appear to have been residential dwellings, but some may have been used for ritual purposes, as indicated by animal skulls (mainly deer and pig); some were perforated, arranged in clusters, and placed on the floor. Storage pits were normally located outside houses, and ten burials have been found inside houses. Among these indoor burials, Tomb M118 revealed the most unusual mortuary offerings. The tomb occupant was an adult male, who was buried with two pigs (see also Chapter 4) and numerous artifacts made of ceramic, lithic, bone, shell, and jade. The most predominant lithic tool type is microblade ($N = 715$). Indoor burial was not a common practice in the Xinglongwa culture, as only few such features have been found. Therefore, those individuals who received this mortuary custom may have had special status in the community. On the whole, however, there are no significant differences among houses and burials that would indicate social stratification (Liu, G. 2001; Yang, H. and Liu 1997; Yang, H. and Zhu 1985).

Most of the material assemblages on house floors appear to have resulted from abandonment rituals (Li, X. 2008), and so provide convenient access for our understanding of household activities. Grinding stones constitute an important part of the tool assemblages in many houses. A physical anthropological study of human skeletons from Xinglongwa suggests that young females show deformed knees, probably resulting from prolonged kneeling while using grinding stones to process food (Smith B. L. 2005).

It has been suggested by some archaeologists that grinding tools are likely to have been used to process wild plants (Liu, G. 2004). Residue analyses of grinding stones from Baiyinchanghan and Xinglonggou have revealed that these tools were indeed used for processing various plants, identifiable as yams (*Dioscorea* sp.), acorn (*Quercus* sp.), and many types of grass (Paniceae and Triticeae tribes), including domesticated millet. Most of these foods processed are likely wild (Liu, L. et al. in preparation; Tao, et al. 2011). Carbonized wild walnuts also have been recovered at Xinglongwa (Kong, Z. and Du 1985).

Although no harvesting tool has been identified from the lithic assemblage at Xinglongwa (Wang, X. 2008), domestic millets were apparently a part of the human diet. The remains of foxtail and broomcorn millets have been uncovered at Xinglonggou, although they account for only a small percentage of the plant remains (Zhao, Z. 2004a). Isotope analysis of human bone ($N = 7$) from Xinglongwa shows that 85 percent of the human diet consisted of C4 food (plants

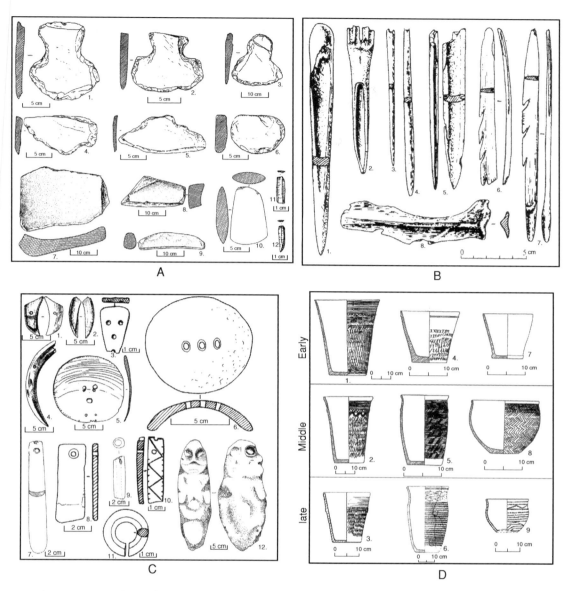

Figure 5.5. Artifacts of the Xinglongwa culture (after figures 3.2–3.5 of Li, X. 2008). A: Stone tools: 1–3: shouldered-hoe; 4 and 5: knives; 6: plate-shaped tool; 7: grinding slab; 8: grinding stone; 9: handstone; 10: axe; 11 and 12: microlithic blades (all from Xinglongwa). B: Bone tools: 1 and 2: awls; 3 and 4: needles; 5: notched knife with microlithic blades; 6 and 7: notched fish spears with microlithic blades; 8: knife (all from Xinglongwa). C: Ornaments and figurine: 1, 2, and 4: tusk pendants; 3: stone human face; 5 and 10: mussel shell ornaments; 6: holed human cranium ornament; 7: jade ornament; 8: stone ornament; 9: jade tube; 11: jade earring; 12: human figurine (1–5, 10–11 from Xinglongwa; 6 and 8 from Nantaizi; 7 and 9 from Chahai; 12 from Baiyingchanghan). D: Pottery: 1–6: pots; 7–9: bowls (1, 2, 4, 5, 7, and 8 from Xinglongwa; 3 and 9 from Baiyinchanghan; 6: from Chahai).

whose carbon-fixation products have four carbon atoms per molecule; e.g., millet, maize, and sorghum), which may be partially attributable to domestic millets (Zhang, X. et al. 2003). Pig husbandry was already underway (see Chapter 4), and many species of wild animals were hunted, including various species of deer, bovid, horse, and wild pig, as demonstrated in the faunal assemblage from Baiyinchanghan (Tang, Z. et al. 2004b). A study of Xinglongwa human skeleton remains suggests that old men tend to show degenerative joint disease in the knee and ankle, perhaps reflecting their habitual engagement in long-distance foraging and hunting (Smith, B. L. 2005). Taken all together, the available data point to a broad-spectrum subsistence strategy, with great emphasis on a hunting and gathering way of life, with minor components of food production.

The Xinglongwa culture also witnessed the first development, in this region, of ritual activities using figurations. Arrays of artifacts with symbolic significance have been unearthed from household deposits and burials at Xinglonggou and Baiyinchanghan. These artifacts include clay and stone human figurines, clearly depicting female bodies; jade and stone ornaments in the shape of cicada and bear; and face masks made of shell, stone, and human skullcap (Figure 5.5C). For example, a clay figurine (5.2 cm in height), unearthed from an ash pit at Xinglonggou, depicts three squatting female human figures hugging each other. A stone female human figurine (35.5 cm in height) was discovered in situ having been inserted into a house floor near the hearth at Baiyinchanghan (Figure 5.5C.12). The figurines, including female figurations, face masks, and naturalist images of animals, appear to have been specifically associated with domestic features (Liu, L. 2007).

It is unclear how the sedentary way of life first developed in the Liaoxi region because of the apparent lack of a transitional phase from the microlithic cultures that predate the Xinglongwa assemblages in the archaeological record. Given the considerable changes involved in the transition from small mobile hunting-gathering groups to rather large sedentary communities, the Xinglongwa people must have experienced enormous social, political, and economic challenges. These challenges may have included rivalries for assertion of territorial control, competition for resources, as well as conflicted inter- and intracommunity relationships. These fundamental changes seem to be reflected in the household remains. In these early villages, households seem to have been the central focus of subsistence consumption and ritual activity, as suggested by indoor storage facilities and indoor burials, as well as by figurations placed within houses (Liu, L. 2007). The anthropomorphic figurations and ornaments, found inside or near residential structures, were probably used as paraphernalia in household rituals (Li, X. 2008). It is also noteworthy that the earliest iconographies in this region are associated with ritual power derived from female human fertility, but we are not sure whether these figurations represent deities, ancestors, or both. In any event, such ritual activities centered on the household may have been a social response to scalar and economic stresses at the time.

The Cishan-Beifudi Culture (ca. 6500–5000 BC)

A few dozen sites, found on river terraces near mountain ranges on the eastern piedmont of the Taihang Mountains, are known as the Cishan and Beifudi cultures in the archaeological record. Here we discuss them together for convenience (Figure 5.1). Material remains at these sites show clear links with the early Holocene cultural traditions in this region (Donghulin and Nanzhuang-tou), as exemplified by the continuous presence of microliths, grinding stones, and flat-bottomed pottery vessels (see Chapter 3). In contrast, many new cultural elements also emerged at these sites. For instance, ceramics are mostly sand-tempered, and predominant forms are flat-bottomed *yu* pot and *zhijia* (or *zhijiao*) support, which were used in combination as cooking utensils. Lithic assemblages consist of increased proportions of polished stone tools (Figure 5.6). Both wild and domesticated animals and plants are present in the archaeological record. Among these sites, Cishan in Wu'an and Beifudi in Yixian, both in Hebei province (Figure 5.3), provide the best examples for investigating the changes in subsistence economy.

Cishan: This site is located on a terrace extending north to the Ming River and south to the piedmont of the Gu Mountains. It is now 25 m above the riverbank, but the river course was likely much higher 8,000 years ago. The site size has not been reported, but excavation of a 2,579 m² area revealed a settlement containing 474 pits, 2 house foundations, and some 2,000 artifacts, as well as abundant faunal and floral remains. The ceramic assemblage is dominated by the flat-bottomed *yu* pot and *zhijia* support, with small numbers of jars, plates, cups, and tripods. The toolkit consists of many types of tools made of stone, bone, and shell for woodworking (axe, adze, and chisel), digging soil (spade), hunting and fishing (arrowhead, harpoon, etc.), and perhaps harvesting cereals (sickle). Some 110 grinding *mopan* slabs and *mobang* handstones (Figure 5.6.1) were uncovered, accounting for 12.5 percent of total stone tools ($N = 880$) (Sun, D. et al. 1981).

The Cishan site has long been interpreted as an example of intensified millet production, as suggested by the reported eighty storage pits containing thick layers of millet remains (Tong, W. 1984), although this interpretation is controversial. Recent phytolith analysis of soil samples from Cishan, suggesting even earlier dates of millet domestication, has stimulated new interest in this site (Lu, H. et al. 2009). This analytic test result has been questioned, however, and further investigations are needed (see Chapter 4).

The Cishan subsistence economy should be reconstructed from a more holistic view of the archaeological record. The extremely small number of sickles ($N = 6$, or 0.6 percent of the total stone tools), which may have been used for harvesting cereals, identifiable in the lithic assemblage makes the claim for intensive millet production questionable. It is important to point out that nut remains have been found from several pits at Cishan and identified as including wild walnuts (*Juglans regia*), hazelnuts (*Corylus heterophylla*), and hackberry (*Celtis bungeana*) (Sun, D. et al. 1981). The large number of grinding stones uncovered from the site seems to support a scenario of nut consumption. These *mopan-mobang* grinding stones are often found associated with flat-bottomed cooking vessels and ceramic supports, sometimes also with axes and spades. A total of forty-five groups of such tool assemblages were found, forming several clusters in open areas. Within each cluster, the number of such tool groups ranges from three to about a dozen (Sun, D. et al. 1981). Studies of Australian aboriginal cultures have recognized the task of grinding wild plants, with slabs and handstones, as women's work normally carried out in a sociable communal setting (Pedley 1992: 39). These formations at Cishan may be viewed as a collective activity of processing foods, perhaps including nuts and cereals.

The considerable proportion of fishing-hunting implements in the tool assemblages is paralleled by corresponding faunal remains. Twenty-three species of animals were identified, including six species of deer, carnivores, pig, dog, chicken, fish, and shellfish. Only pig and dog have been identified with confidence as domesticated (Zhou, B. 1981).

Several phenomena at Cishan point to a high level of sedentism. These phenomena include a large number of pits, many of which may have been used for storage; abundant ceramics, grinding stones, and polished tools; and domestication of pigs and dogs. The ceramic tripods, which are few in number, reflect an emergent design suitable only for a stable residential mode, as the legs would be an obstacle to mobility. In contrast, duplex cooking utensils, formed of *yu* pots joined with separate *zhijia* supports, seem emphatically portable when disassembled. This modular design continued an established Paleolithic tradition (the flat-bottomed pot), improved by a Neolithic innovation (*zhijia* supports). Cishan appears to have been a sedentary village, perhaps year-round, the people of which practiced a broad-spectrum subsistence economy, including hunting, fishing, nut collecting, animal husbandry, and millet cultivation. Such a subsistence mode would have required part of the population to engage in food procurement, such as hunting and nut collection, entailing certain degrees of logistic mobility.

Beifudi: This site is located on the terrace of a small valley formed by the Zhongyishui River and surrounded by low hills and mountains (Figure 5.7). The remaining site is about 3,000 m² in area, and some 2,000 m² has been excavated. Only the last two seasons of excavation (1,200 m²) have been reported in detail, providing information for the discussion later in text. The cultural deposits are divided into three phases, and Phase I dates to 6000–5000 BC (Duan, H. 2007).

Figure 5.6. Artifacts from the Cishan–Beifudi culture (1 and 2 Cishan; 3–6 Beifudi). 1: Slab and handstone; 2: *yu* pot and *zhijiao* supports; 3 and 4: stone tools and pottery vessels unearthed from plaza at Beifudi; 5: ceramics and stone tools *in situ* in the plaza, Beifudi; 6: pottery mask (1 and 2 author's photo; 3–6 from Duan 2007: color plates 6, 10, 12).

Excavations have exposed two areas, Section I and Section II. Section I appears to have been a residential area, consisting of fourteen subterranean house foundations and thirty-four pits. Houses are mostly square or rectangular in shape, measuring about 6.5–15 m² in size; the soil deposits on the floor are rather thick, often containing abundant artifacts, ranging from a few dozen to a few thousand (Table 5.1). Among these artifacts, river pebbles and lithic waste products predominate, followed by lithic tools, ceramic fragments, and remains of nuts. Several houses revealed broken pieces of ceramic face masks; their sizes are suitable for human use, and the eye slits are carved out, enabling the wearer to see through (Figure 5.6.6); thus, they may have been used

Figure 5.7. Landscape of the Beifudi site (after Duan 2007: color plate 1).

for household ritual activities. Material remains revealed in pits are similar in kind to those from house deposits, all rather fragmentary. The toolkit is dominated by axes, spades, and grinding stones (Duan, H. 2007). Few tools can be morphologically identified as being designed for hunting or fishing (e.g., arrowheads or harpoons).

Section II was an open plaza, about 90 m² in size. It has revealed nine small shallow pits and one large pit. These pits were associated with eleven clusters of artifacts, consisting of grinding stones, axes, spades, pottery vessels, and ornaments. Most artifacts were found at ground level, but some on the bottom, or in the fill, of small pits. In contrast to the fragmentary condition of artifacts from the residential area, most tools and pottery vessels from the plaza are complete. Pottery vessels are predominantly pots with thick, vertical walls. Although abundant remains of wild walnuts and acorns have been uncovered, no animal bones or seeds were present at the site (Duan, H. 2007).

Material remains from Beifudi can be classified into three categories on the basis of their depositional contexts, adapting Schiffer's model for abandonment patterns, namely, *primary, secondary,* and *de facto refuses* (Schiffer 1976: 30–3). Most of the remains from house floors can be classified as primary refuse, which refers to the deliberate disposal of items at or near the end of their use-life and in their location of use. Artifacts recovered from pits near houses

TABLE 5.1. *Inventory of material remains uncovered from house floor deposits at Beifudi, Hebei*

House	Estimated floor area	Total artifacts	Potsherds	Pebbles	Lithic wasters	Lithic products, most broken	Microliths	Floral remains
F1	15 m²	2801	374 13.3%	1503 53.4%	562 20%	110 3.9%	247 8.8%	Wild walnuts
F2	15 m²	1246	193 15.5%	44 3.5%	906 72.7%	71 5.6%	31 2.5%	Wild walnuts
F3	7 m²	49	2 4%	17 34.6%	21 42.9%	8 16.3%	1 2%	
F7	8 m²	169	100 59.1%	4 2.4%	64 37.9%	1 0.6%	–	
F8	6.5 m²	72	17 23.6%	4 5.5%	48 66.6%	3 4.1%	–	
F10	8 m²	78	23 29.5%	14 17.9%	41 52.6%	–	–	
F12	14.6 m²	778	219 28.1%	63 8.1%	476 61.2%	8 1%	10 1.3%	Wild walnuts
F15	11 m²	74	15 20.2%	9 12.1%	48 64.9%	2 2.7%	–	
F16	10 m²	308	73 23.7%	11 0.3%	212 68.8%	9 2.9%	–	

can be seen as secondary refuse, which contains unwanted items intentionally discarded in areas other than where they were used. In contrast, de facto refuse refers to cultural materials, still usable and intentionally left within the area of their normal activity. This third case applies to the artifactual clusters found in shallow pits at the open plaza of Beifudi. The artifacts showed a pattern of orderly distribution into type-defined groups, and of concentrated location within small pits, suggesting that the plaza at Beifudi was, most likely, a locale where people processed foods collectively and that the tools were cached in the pits when not in use. The composition of these remains corresponds to that of comparable tools found in pits at the Cishan site, as discussed earlier in text, and suggests that a similar situation may have occurred at Cishan.

Cross-cultural comparison of the Middle East and other areas of the world, based on Schiffer's model of abandonment patterns, has articulated further correspondences to varying levels of sedentism (Hardy-Smith and Edwards 2004). Thus, primary refuse is particularly linked with mobile hunter-gatherers and short-term residential stays, and abundant primary refuse in dwellings implies that the population had not adjusted their household sanitation practices to the needs of long-term sedentary living. High levels of de facto refuse, including numerous cached items, may have resulted from planned abandonment and anticipated return.

Secondary refuse tends to be associated with an intention of longer residential duration (Hardy-Smith and Edwards 2004). At Beifudi, the presence of secondary refuse in pits points to intended long sedentary duration, but many other lines of evidence there are also consistent with mobility. The abundant primary refuse inside houses suggests that the residents practiced a tradition similar to that of mobile hunter-gatherer populations, and the high level of de facto refuse, as cached items, also suggests an anticipated return, which is a characteristic of mobile populations.

The mobile residential strategy is also reflected in the pottery types, which are small, simply designed pots, probably with multiple functions for cooking, storage, and serving. Ceramic supports, manufactured as separate pieces attachable to a cooking vessel when used, were apparently designed for portability. The absence of animal remains or domestic cereals and the presence of abundant walnuts and acorns together indicate strongly that this site was occupied specifically for collecting nuts. Grinding *mopan* slabs, *mobang* handstones, mortars, and pestles ($N = 37$) account for 11.1 percent of the total number of stone tools, further suggesting that processing nuts was an important component of the subsistence activities there. These findings are consistent with the hypothesized scenario that the open plaza was a communal activity area for nut processing. Beifudi, therefore, may have been a seasonal campsite, visited intermittently by certain communities for exploiting nuts, which were abundant in the surrounding area.

Summary: Cishan and Beifudi represent two types of settlement in this region, one a full sedentary village and the other a seasonal camp site, which coexisted during the early Neolithic period. Different subsistence strategies manifested in these sites may be seen as components of an overall subsistence-settlement system. Part of the Cishan population may have visited their campsites seasonally, whereas other parts of the community stayed in the permanent settlement. The Beifudi population may have come from a larger village to collect certain kinds of food on a seasonal basis. The variation in levels of sedentism and food procurement strategies was evidently conditioned by differing environmental settings and local availability of resources.

The Houli Culture (ca. 6500–5500 BC)

About a dozen Houli culture sites have been found on the floodplains along the northern piedmont of the Taiyi Mountains in Shandong (Figure 5.1). Among these sites, Houli in Linzi, Xiaojingshan and Xihe in Zhangqiu, Qianbuxia in Weifang, and Yuezhuang in Jinan have been excavated (Shandongsheng 2005). Major archaeological features from these sites include dwellings, pits, kilns, and burials. Settlements tend to be large in size, as at Xiaojingshan and Xihe, each of which measures more than 10 ha. The occupational area at any one time, however, was probably much smaller than the full extent of the site as observed archaeologically. This inference is drawn from the evident division of

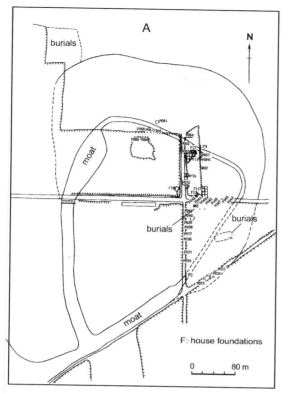
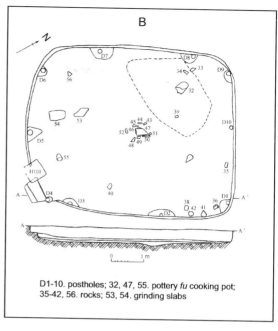

D1-10. postholes; 32, 47, 55. pottery *fu* cooking pot; 35-42, 56. rocks; 53, 54. grinding slabs

Figure 5.8. Settlement and dwelling of the Xiaojingshan site, Houli culture. A: Xiaojingshan site; B: dwelling from Xiaojingshan (after figures 2 and 7 of Wang, S. and Ning 2003).

cultural deposits at most sites into diachronically distinct occupations, situated in different sectors of the site, without later features intruding into earlier ones (Sun, B. 2006).

Among these sites, Xiaojingshan is the only one surrounded by ditches, measuring 12 ha in area. At least forty house foundations have been identified, and some thirty tombs, clustered into three groups, have been found inside and outside the ditches (Wang, S. and Ning 2003) (Figure 5.8A). In general, houses varied in size and abundant artifacts were sometimes left on floors. At Xihe, for example, excavations revealed two types of dwellings among nineteen houses. Large dwellings (normally 25–50 m²) are well built with finished walls and floors and furnished with multiple hearths, and many complete pottery vessels and tools were left on the floors (Figure 5.8B). Small dwellings (mostly 10–20 m²) had unfinished walls and floors, and some contained abundant potsherds, rocks, and flakes left on the floor (Liu, Y. et al. 2000). The settlement layout seems to suggest an intention of long-term occupation, but the abundant primary refuse on house floors indicates a tendency toward mobility. Such a combination may be seen as an early stage of transition to increased degrees of sedentism, a situation similar to the Cishan-Beifudi culture.

TABLE 5.2. *Frequency and percentage of grinding stones in lithic assemblages from two Houli culture sites*

Site	Slab	Handstone	Other types of grinding stone	Whetstone	Ball	Axe	Adze	Hammer	Others	Total
Yuezhuang	67	69	0	15	11	5	3	1	6	177
	38%	39%	0%	8%	6%	3%	2%	1%	3%	
	Grinding stones 77%			Other tool types 23%						
Xiaojingshan	22	7	17	1	0	15	2	3	13	79
	28%	9%	20%	1%	0%	19%	3%	4%	16%	
	Grinding stones 57%			Other tool types 43%						

Note: Excluding *zhijia* supports.

Lithic assemblages at some sites are dominated by grinding stones, primarily *mopan* slabs and *mobang* handstones (Figure 5.9). At Yuezhuang and Xiaojingshan, grinding stones account for 77 percent ($N = 136$) and 57 percent ($N = 46$) of the total stone tool assemblage, respectively (Table 5.2). Stone woodworking tools (axe and adze) and hunting-fishing tools made of bone (arrowhead and harpoon) are present, and a few tools may be morphologically identified as partially agricultural in function (such as sickle) at some sites (Figure 5.9) (Ning, Y. and Wang 1994; Wang, J. et al. 2006; Wang, S. and Ning 1996).

Ceramic assemblages are characterized by round- or flat-bottomed vessels, classified as cauldrons, jars, pots, bowls, basins, lids, and supports (Luan 1997) (Figure 5.9). No vessel can be categorized as a tripod. Similar to the Cishan-Beifudi culture, supports (*zhijiao*, mostly made of stone) are used together with pots for cooking. Concern for mobility seems implicit in the general design of the ceramic forms.

It is particularly interesting to note that carbonized millet and rice grains have been uncovered from Yuezhuang. A few rice grains, which are the earliest such remains found in the Yellow River region, appear no different morphologically from domestic rice in the later period of this region (Crawford et al. 2006). Stable isotope analysis of human bones from Xiaojingshan shows that millet (as a C4 plant) contributed only about 25 percent of diet (Hu, Y. et al. 2006). Given that agricultural implements are lacking in the toolkit, millet and rice farming could not have played an important role in the economy of the Houli culture.

Summary: Houli culture sites share considerable similarities with Cishan-Beifudi sites in that they are all located on mountain piedmont, pottery forms are predominantly round- or flat-bottomed pots, there is a large proportion of grinding stones in toolkits, and domesticates are present at some sites.

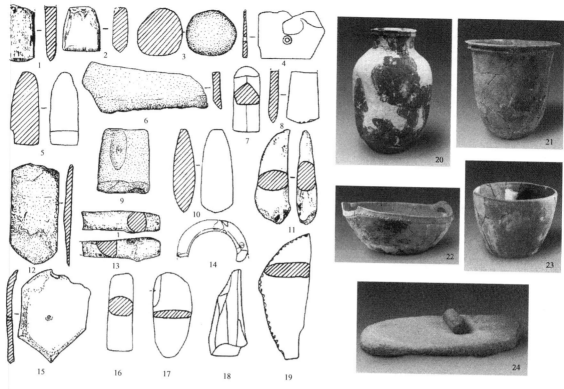

Figure 5.9. Artifacts from the Houli culture (1–19, 24 lithics; 20–23 pottery). 1 and 2: Jade chisels; 3: ball; 4 and 17: slabs; 5 and 7: grinding tools; 6: sickle; 8 and 10: axes; 9: hammer; 11, 18, and 19: *zhijiao* supports; 12: spade; 13 and 16: handstones; 14: ornament; 15: plough-shaped object; 20: *hu* jar; 21: *fu* caldron; 22: *Yi* basin; 23: *guan* pot; 24: grinding slab and handstone (after figure 21; color plates 2 and 3 of Shandongsheng 2005).

These commonalities likely reflect a comparable mode of adaptation to similar environmental settings, characterized by hunting, fishing, gathering, and low-level food production. Compared to the Cishan–Beifudi tool assemblages, Houli culture sites have revealed much higher proportions of grinding stones, probably suggesting a higher level of nut consumption. This phenomenon is consistent with the distribution of *Quercus* pollen, which indicates a much higher percentage of oak forest in the Taiyi Mountains than in the Taihang Mountains. It is likely that high degrees of sedentism were present in the Houli culture, but that logistic residential mobility (as required by collecting strategies) was also practiced.

The Peiligang Culture (ca. 7000–5000 BC)

Peiligang culture sites are distributed over a large area of the middle Yellow River Valley in Henan (Figure 5.1). More than 120 sites have been identified,

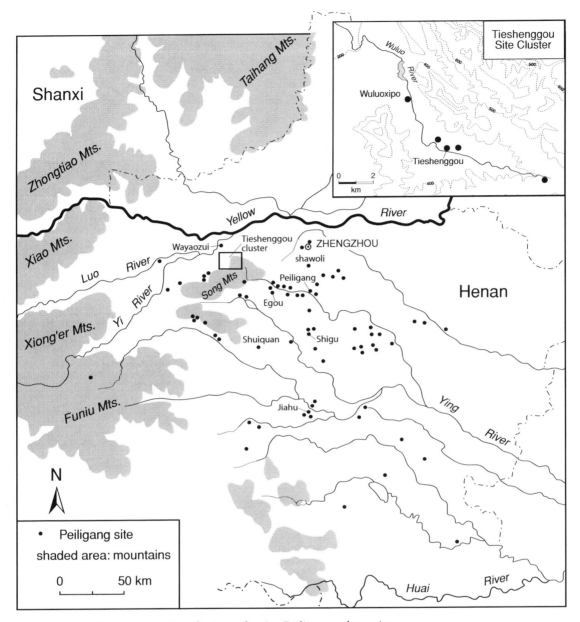

Figure 5.10. Distribution of major Peiligang culture sites.

mostly distributed on the hilly lowlands near rivers. These sites are generally small, ranging from a few thousand square meters to a few hectares. On the floodplains, some relatively large settlements with thick cultural deposits, such as Jiahu in Wuyang (5 ha) (Henansheng Wenwu Kaogu 1999a) and Tanghu in Xinzheng (30 ha) (Zhang, S. et al. 2008), are likely to have been occupied all year round (Figure 5.10). Pottery is characterized by various functional types, distinguishable as cooking, serving, and/or storage vessels, many of which

TABLE 5.3. *Stone tool assemblages and plant remains from major Peiligang culture sites in Henan*

Site	Grinding stone, N (%)	Sickle, N (%)	Total stone tools	Wild Cultigen	plants	Reference[a]
Jiahu	186 (18%)	45 (4%)	1031	Rice	Wild rice, acorn (*Quercus* sp.), water caltrop, tubers, lotus root, walnut, wild grape, soybean	KG 2009.8
Peiligang	88 (26%)	23 (7%)	337	Possible foxtail millet	Walnut, plum, jujube	KG 1978.2 KG 1979.3 KGXB 1984.1
Shawoli	8 (10%)	7 (8%)	83	Possible millet	Walnut, jujube	KG 1983.12
Egou	27 (20%)	6 (5%)	133		Acorn (*Q. acutissima*), walnut, jujube	KGXJK 1981
Shigu	11 (14%)	3 (4%)	78		Hazelnut, walnut, jujube, elm fruit	HXKG 1987.1
Shuiquan	62 (27%)	15 (7%)	230		Acorn (cf. *Q. variabilis*), walnut (*Juglans mandshurica*), jujube (*Zizyphus jujube*)	KGXB 1995.1
Tieshenggou	61 (39%)	7 (4%)	156		Fruits and nuts	HWTX 1980.2 WW 1980.5 KG 1986.3
Wuluo Xipo				Foxtail millet	Nuts, foxtail grass, panic/manna	
Fudian				Foxtail millet		

[a] KG = *Kaogu*; KGXJK = *Kaoguxue Jikan*; HXKG = *Huaxia Kaogu*; HWTX = *Henan Wenbo Tongxun*; WW = *Wenwu*.

are customarily referred to as tripods because of their three-legged design. Lithic implements include both chipped and ground tools, and the latter are morphologically classified into axes, adzes, chisels, spades, sickles, and knives. Microliths also have been found at sites near mountains (e.g., Tieshenggou). *Mopan-mobang* grinding stones often have been uncovered from female burials (Figure 5.11).

Denticulate sickles and grinding stones have been commonly found in Peiligang culture sites, and grinding stones account for considerably high proportions in the toolkits (14–39%) (Table 5.3). They often have been identified as tools for harvesting and processing cereals, which indicates agriculture (An, Z. 1989: 648; Chang 1986a: 91; Smith 1998: 134–5). According to recent

---

research, however, these tools were multifunctional. Use-wear and residue analyses on denticulate sickles from Jiahu and Shigu show that they are likely to have been used for cutting reeds and grasses (perhaps including millet), as well as for collecting fruits and/or nuts from trees (Fullagar, R. et al. in preparation; Bestel, et al. 2011). Starch and use-wear analyses of grinding stones from Egou indicate that they were mainly used for processing acorns and, to a lesser extent, beans, tubers, and millet (Liu, L. et al. 2010a). These results are consistent with the residue analyses on early Holocene grinding stones from Shangshan, Donghulin, and Shizitan, which have also revealed multifunctional usage of grinding stones, with acorn starches as an important component in the residue samples (Liu, L. et al. 2010b,c, 2011) (see also Chapter 3). Evidently there was a widespread and long-lasting adaptation to a nut-based economy in northern China during the early and middle Holocene.

Floral remains recovered from Peiligang sites are also more heavily weighted toward wild plants (soybean, acorns, walnuts, hazelnuts, jujube, plums, and water caltrops) than toward cultigens (rice and millet) (Table 5.3), although this observed balance may be affected by the various remains' relative degree of preservation and by the fact that the flotation method was not used in most excavations. Dogs and pigs (see Chapter 4) were the domesticated animals, whereas a wide range of wild animal species were hunted (Henansheng Wenwu Kaogu 1999a). Peiligang culture has long been regarded as having achieved a considerable level of agriculture, but the archaeological record shows that the people actually practiced broad-spectrum subsistence strategies, in which food production was only a minor component of the economic system.

Peiligang sites can be classified into two types in terms of their environmental settings: those on the alluvial plains and those in hilly areas. The former tend to be larger in size, with thicker deposits and more elaborate material assemblages. In contrast, the latter appear to be smaller in size, with thinner deposits, less variety among artifacts, and pottery vessels of simpler form, made more crudely. These contrasting traits may reflect different subsistence-residential strategies and various levels of social complexity. We argue that the sites on alluvial plains may have had higher levels of sedentism and more complex social organization, and some of those in hilly areas are likely to have been seasonal campsites or small villages. Next we illustrate this point with two examples: Jiahu in the floodplain of the Hui River Valley and the Tieshenggou site cluster in the Song Mountain ranges.

Jiahu in Wuyang is bounded by a lake and two rivers, and is situated on the alluvial plain. The cultural deposits can be divided into three phases, dating to ca. 7000–5500 BC. Excavations of an area of 2,359 m² revealed 45 house foundations, 370 pits, 349 burials, and 9 kilns. Features were closely spaced, and early houses and burials were often intruded upon or disturbed by later features, indicating high population density and long period of occupation (Figure 5.11.1). The houses associated with burials and pits tend to be grouped into

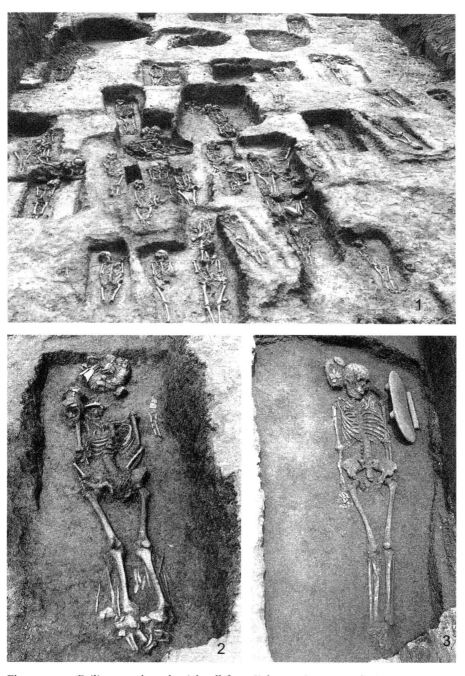

Figure 5.11. Peiligang culture burials, all from Jiahu. 1: Cemetery during excavation; 2: Tomb M344 containing a male occupant with missing head, replaced by a group of turtle shells, two flutes on the right side, and many hunting tools near the legs; 3: Tomb M371 containing a female occupant, associated with a set of grinding stones (after color plates 2–2, 7–32, and 7–3 of Henansheng Wenwu Kaogu 1999a).

several clusters, showing increasing regularity of residential planning through time. Houses vary in size, ranging from 2 to 40 m², most (69%) measuring 10 m² or smaller. A majority of houses are round and semisubterranean, and house floors are often formed by thick layers of soil deposits containing rich material remains. Most items from the floor deposits belong to primary refuse, including potsherds, tools, and faunal and floral remains. House F17 (24 m² in size), for example, yielded 1,884 potsherds (39 kg), various types of stone and bone tools, lithic blanks and flakes, turtle shells, animal teeth, antlers, and rice grains. Similar types of material have been found in pits near houses, as secondary refuse (Henansheng Wenwu Kaogu 1999a). The different methods used in the treatment of household refuse imply a combination of old traditions followed by mobile people with new efforts made to adapt to a sedentary way of life, a situation resembling the Beifudi site.

Jiahu's toolkit consists of various forms of stone, bone, and ceramic implements, classifiable into more than thirty tool types, which were used for construction, farming, hunting, fishing, and domestic maintenance. An analysis of the typological composition of production tools shows that farming tools (stone spades, sickles, knives, and bone hoes) account for 6.8 percent of the toolkit in Phase I, 11.4 percent in Phase II, and 53.4 percent in Phase III. These changes suggest that food production was rather minor in the early period but increased gradually through the 1,500 years of Jiahu occupation (Henansheng Wenwu Kaogu 1999a; Lai, Y. et al. 2009). Recent excavations at Jiahu have revealed three contemporary cemeteries consisting of ninety-six tombs in total, with each cemetery tending to be associated with particular types of burial offerings. One cemetery yielded mainly farming implements, whereas the other two were associated with hunting-fishing tools (Zhang, J. and Pan 2002). It is unclear whether these phenomena imply economic specialization among different social groups, but we can at least argue that the procurement of wild food played a significant role in Jiahu's subsistence economy.

Ceramics appear to have been functionally specific, represented by many forms of cooking, serving, storage, and drinking vessels (Henansheng Wenwu Kaogu 1999a). Some *ding* tripods, used as cooking vessels, have rather slender legs, a design not suited to a mobile way of life.

Jiahu has been subjected to a number of multidisciplinary studies. Macrobotanical remains uncovered by the flotation method include a wide range of plants, such as rice, soybeans, beans, tubers, acorns, walnuts, and so forth. Rice, which has been identified as domesticated, contributed only 10 percent of the plant remains, suggesting that Jiahu people primarily relied on wild plants (Zhao, Z. and Zhang 2009). Stable isotopic analysis of human bones shows that the main dietary sources at Jiahu were predominantly C3 plants and C3-feeding animals (Hu, Y. et al. 2006). Rice and nuts (e.g., acorns), which are C3 plants, may have been the main staples of the Jiahu population's diet.

Chemical analyses of residues on Jiahu pottery jars have revealed that a mixed fermented beverage of rice, honey, and fruit was produced (McGovern et al. 2004). A study of Jiahu human remains suggests that young individuals (16–35 years of age), especially males, tended to have degenerative joint disease in their wrists and ankles, which may have been partly caused by tilling fields with a heavy spade-shaped stone tool. The general health conditions of the Jiahu population, however, as measured by life span and rates of dental caries, anemia, and periosteal reactions, are worse than for the Xinglongwa population, but are better than in the fully developed agricultural community of the Yangshao culture at Shijia (ca. 4300–4000 BC) (Smith B. L. 2005).

Jiahu is likely to have been a fully sedentary village, with a noticeable proportion of economic activity devoted to food production, whereas a large part of the population still conducted hunting and gathering activities. The diminished conditions of the population's physical health indicate selective pressures introduced by their increased farming and sedentary way of life.

Jiahu has revealed a remarkably sophisticated material culture. It is well known for the discovery there of several elaborate burials associated with turtle shells and containing small pebbles and flutes made from ulnae of the red-crowned crane. The turtle shells may have been used as rattles, and the flutes rank as the earliest playable multinote instruments ever found. These turtle shells and flutes were probably musical instruments used in ritual activities, at which the occupants of these tombs were ceremonial practitioners (Chen, X. and Lee 2004; Zhang, J. et al. 2004). Some turtle shells are incised with signs, and several signs anticipate later inscriptions on oracle bones in the late Shang dynasty, although these symbols do not represent a true writing system (Li, Xueqin et al. 2003) (Figure 5.12).

Division of labor in subsistence activities is reflected in mortuary offerings; accordingly, large quantities of hunting-fishing tools normally occur in male burials, whereas grinding stones are always associated with female burials (Figure 5.11.3) (Zhang, Z. 2009). The tombs containing ritual objects (turtle shells and flutes) are generally large in size and rich in burial offerings (Figure 5.11.2), suggesting special degrees of social status assumed by some ritual practitioners. In general, though, the mortuary remains from the entire site show a low level of variability. The Jiahu society therefore is likely to have been egalitarian in nature, but some individuals appear to have achieved higher social prestige because of their special abilities (Liu, L. 2004: 126–8). Jiahu represents one of the most complex sedentary communities known to be datable to the early Neolithic. Its optimum location, with abundant and diverse natural resources, provided ideal conditions for development of sedentism, domestication of plants and animals, and social complexity.

The Tieshenggou site cluster is situated along the upper stream of the Wuluo River, which is a tributary of the Yiluo River in western Henan. Originating in the Song Mountains, the Wuluo River is embraced by hilly ranges, and the river valley is narrow, with little flat land suitable for farming, particularly in its upper reach. A full-coverage regional survey located five late Peiligang sites (ca. 5500–5000 BC), stretching about 16 km along the river valley. All sites are small in size and have a thin depth of deposits, the largest ones being those at Tieshenggou and Wuluoxipo, which measure 1 ha and 2 ha, respectively. Stone tools include polished axes, spades, sickles, *mopan-mobang* grinding stones, and microliths. Animal bones, unidentified fruit remains, and nut shells were unearthed from pits and houses. Pottery is mostly reddish in color and crumbly, apparently fired at low temperatures. The vessels are small in size, including globe-shaped jars, bowls, and tripods. The ceramic paste's consistency is so weak that the vessels were found in fragmented conditions, with few complete examples recovered. At Tieshenggou, one small subterranean house (6.6 m^2) and four pits have been uncovered, and more than fifty *mopan* slabs and *mobang* handstones, mostly in fragmented condition, have been found (Fu, Y. 1980; Li, Y. 1980; Liu, L. et al. 2002–2004; Zhao, Y. 1992; Zheng, N. 1986). Foxtail millet grains have been recovered from Wuluoxipo with flotation methods, although in extremely low densities (Lee, G. et al. 2007).

On the whole, remains from these Peiligang sites by the Wuluo River show a subsistence strategy composed of hunting-gathering and millet farming. The extreme fragility of the pottery suggests that the vessels were not intended for long-term use. Some of them, such as the small and globe-shaped water jars, show forms well suited for portability.

The Tieshenggou site cluster in the mountainous area shows characteristics of residential mobility. Some of the sites may have been occupied seasonally for exploiting specific food resources, such as cereals, fruits, nuts, and animals. A part of the Wuluoxipo site was situated on a floodplain, most likely occupied during a relatively dry season, when streams were not flooding. All these sites date to the late Peiligang phase; each site probably represents a place of intermittent seasonal occupations, used repetitively by the same community over time (Liu, L. et al. 2002–2004).

Contrary to the Tieshenggou cluster, the Wayaozui site on the Yiluo River floodplains, some 20 km northwest of Tieshenggou (Figure 5.10), revealed a rather different material assemblage. It lacked grinding stones and microliths, but yielded various types of high-quality ceramics, including some unusually thin black ware fired at high temperatures (Liao, Y. and Liu 1997). Such sharp contrast between contemporary sites within a small region indicates that site function varied significantly in different ecological settings.

Summary: The settlement-subsistence systems of the Peiligang culture show great variability in time and space. Jiahu and the Tieshenggou site cluster represent two extreme types on a continuum of possible adaptations. On the one hand, some villages in floodplains developed a high level of sedentism, rather complex material culture, and sophisticated ritual practice; on the other

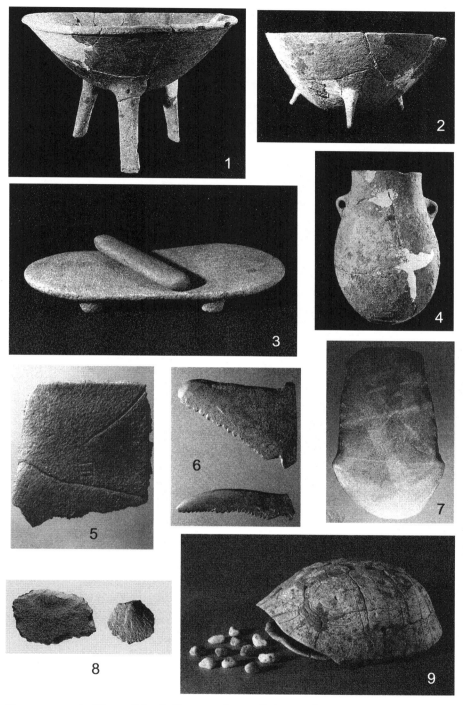

Figure 5.12. Artifacts of the Peiligang culture, all from Jiahu. 1: Pottery *ding* tripod; 2: pottery *bo* tripod bowl; 3: grinding slab and handstone; 4: pottery *hu* jar; 5: turtle shell with inscription; 6: stone sickles; 7: stone spade; 8: chipped stone scrapers; 9: turtle shells with pebbles (not to scale) (after plates 52–2, 108–6, 18–5, 60–3, 158–7,8; color plates 18–1, 2, 3, 43–1, and 48–5 of Henansheng Wenwu Kaogu 1999a).

hand, some small settlements in mountainous regions are likely to have been small villages or to have been used by specific task groups possessing high levels of mobility. In all Peiligang sites, regardless of the level of sedentism and the size of settlement, cereal domestication is evident in the archaeological record, but food production appears to have constituted a minor component in the subsistence system, compared to hunting and gathering activities.

The Baijia-Dadiwan Culture (ca. 6000–5000 BC)

A number of early Neolithic sites distributed along the Wei and upper Han Rivers are referred to as the Baijia–Dadiwan culture (Figure 5.1). Some forty sites have been identified, mostly concentrated in the lower Wei River Valley (Gansusheng 2006; Guojia 1999), whereas those found in the Han River Valley are often designated as the Lijiacun type (Shaanxisheng and Shaanxisheng 1994). These sites have revealed small subterranean houses, pits, and burials. The most common ceramic forms are *bo* bowls, *guan* jars, *weng* urns, and *bei* cups. Some bowls, jars, and urns are rendered with three small feet (Figure 5.13). The sites reported in greatest detail are Baijia in Lintong, Shaanxi, and Dadiwan in Tianshui, Gansu.

Baijia is located on the northern terrace of the Wei River. The site was estimated as 12 ha in size, and an area of 1,366 m² has been excavated, revealing 2 house foundations, 49 pits, 36 burials, abundant potsherds, some 200 tools made of stool, shell, and bone, as well as many animal bones. The lithic assemblage (92 tools) consists of chipped tools (34%; predominantly choppers and scrapers), polished tools (44%; mainly spades and axes), and grinding stones (22%; slabs, handstones, and pestles). Sixteen shell sickles with a denticulate edge were unearthed (Figure 5.13), and may have been used for harvesting cereals, although no floral trace was reported. Among twelve animal species identified in the faunal assemblage, the pigs and dogs were domesticated, and pig bones are the most numerous in NISP (number of identified specimens) (35%). Wild buffalo bones, identified as *Bubalus mephistopheles* (Yang, D. et al. 2008), are the second most numerous in NISP (23%), followed by those from two species of deer. It is worth mentioning that many *bo* bowls are painted, showing a red band along the rim. These bowls are the earliest known examples of painted pottery in north China (Zhongguo Shehui Kexueyuan 1994a). The material assemblages in Baijia show adaptation to mixed subsistence, featuring both hunting-gathering and farming activities. The community may have practiced a high level of sedentism, as indicated by the presence of domesticated pigs, but the level of food production was probably not high.

Dadiwan is a multicomponent site located on the second terrace of the Qingshui River, a tributary of the Wei River. Its entire deposits date from the early Neolithic to the Bronze Age, and the lowest layer, Phase I, dates to 5800–5300 BC. The occupation area of Phase I is small (0.8 ha), and cultural

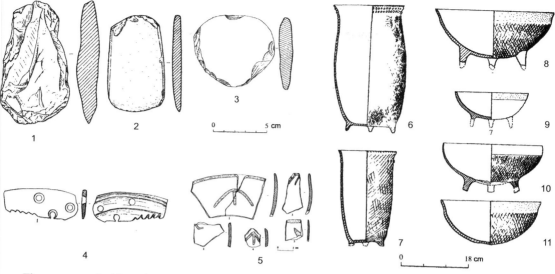

Figure 5.13. Artifacts from the Baijia-Dadiwan culture (1–3: lithics; 4: shell; 5–11: pottery). 1: Axe; 2: spade; 3: chopper; 4: sickle; 5: pottery marks; 6 and 7: *guan* tripods; 8–10: *bo* tripods; 11: *bo* bowl (all from Dadiwan except the shell sickle) (after figures 31, 50, 53 of Gansusheng 2006 and figure 19 of Zhongguo Shehui Kexueyuan 1994a).

deposits are thin (0.15–0.25 m). Excavations have revealed 4 small subterranean house foundations (no larger than 6.6 m² in area), 17 pits, 15 burials, and 403 artifacts (Gansusheng 2006).

Pottery types are similar to those from other contemporary sites along the Wei River. One or another of thirteen different geometric figures, painted in red or white pigment, appears individually on twenty-three potsherds, in some cases near the rim of the vessel (Figure 5.13). The forms of some of these signs, such as those shaped like a cross or an arrow, anticipate potter's marks carved on the rims of ceramic vessels from the Yangshao culture in this region (see Chapter 6). Stone tools (forty-seven pieces) are predominantly chipped, but some are edge-polished, such as the knife, axe, and spade. Choppers, knives, and scrapers are the most numerous tools in the lithic assemblage (Figure 5.13) (Gansusheng 2006).

Remains of broomcorn millet (*Panicum miliaceum*) and coleseed (*Brassica*) were uncovered from the bottom of a pit (Gansusheng 2006: 60; Liu, C. 2006), suggesting that farming was part of the subsistence strategy. Fourteen animal species/genera were identified in the faunal assemblage (748 in minimum number of individuals [MNI]). The most numerous animals (based on MNI) are several species of deer (47%), followed by pig (21%), including wild and domestic (Qi, G. et al. 2006) (see also Chapter 4). Pig mandibles were used as burial offerings, initiating a mortuary practice that later became prevalent in Neolithic north China.

TABLE 5.4. *Components of the lithic toolkits from three Baijia-Dadiwan culture sites*

Site	Chipped (chopper, scraper, etc.) N (%)	Polished, semipolished, and tool blank (spade, knife, axe, adze, chisel, etc.) N (%)	Grinding stones (slab, handstone, mortar, pestle, etc.) N (%)	Total
Lijiacun	117 (47.6%)	106 (43.1%)	23 (9.5%)	246
Baijia	31 (33.7%)	41 (45.7%)	20 (21.7%)	92
Guantaoyuan	55 (74.3%)	10 (13.5%)	9 (12%)	74
Dadiwan	36 (76.6)	9 (19%)	1 (2 %)	47

Summary: Early Neolithic sites in the Wei and Han River regions exhibit great similarities to their counterparts in other regions. The settlements show strong components of sedentism, as exemplified by the presence of many permanent residential features, mortuary practice with a certain level of regulation, well-made ceramics, and domestication of millet and pig. Nevertheless, the material remains seem to point to a subsistence strategy still heavily reliant on hunting and gathering, rather than on food production. This inference is supported by lithic assemblages from several sites, in which chipped stone tools account for large proportions of the toolkits (Table 5.4). Grinding stones, likely used for processing mostly wild plants, also occurred in significant numbers at sites in the lower Wei and Han River Valleys, a region with a high percentage of *Quercus* pollens (Figure 5.3).

THE YANGZI RIVER REGION

The Yangzi River region lies at the northern portion of the subtropical zone and is endowed with abundant floral and faunal resources. Geographically, this region is characterized by diverse landscapes, ranging from flat alluvial plains to mountain ranges. Early Neolithic sites are distributed in various environments, and subsistence strategies vary significantly. Some communities adapted to rice farming to some extent, whereas others persisted in a hunting-gathering way of life for millennia.

The Middle Yangzi River Region

The earliest Neolithic remains in the middle Yangzi River are defined by the Pengtoushan culture (ca. 7000–5800 BC), primarily distributed in the area around Lake Dongting, Hunan. Some fifteen sites have been found, concentrated in the floodplain north of the Lishui River. They are located on either low mounts or the plain, as represented by Pengtoushan and Bashidang in Lixian, respectively (Hunansheng 2006). The Pengtoushan culture was followed by the Lower Zaoshi culture (ca. 5800–5500 BC), which was also

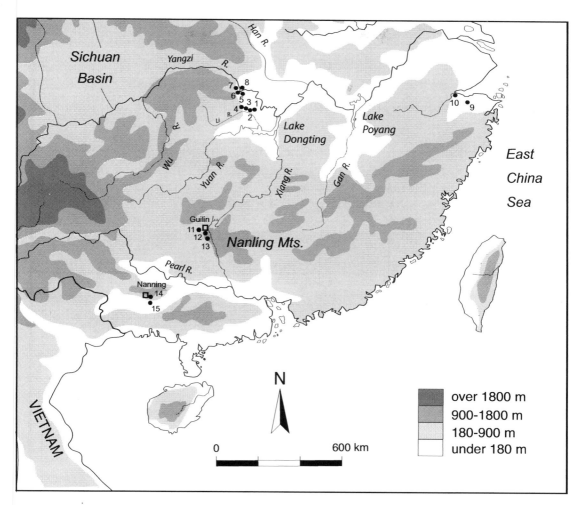

Figure 5.14. Location of major early Neolithic sites in the Yangzi River region and South China. 1: Bashidang; 2: Pengtoushan; 3: Hujiawuchang; 4: Zaoshi; 5: Jinzishan; 6: Zhichengbei; 7: Chengbeixi; 8: Qinglongshan; 9: Xiaohuangshan; 10: Kuahuqiao; 11: Dayan; 12: Zengpiyan; 13: Miaoyan; 14: Baozitou; 15: Dingsishan.

centered in the area around Lake Dongting, but spread over a much large region. More than thirty sites have been found, and the most reported one is Hujiawuchang in Linli. In addition, some ten sites distributed along the middle Yangzi River are known as the Chengbeixi culture (ca. 6500–5000 BC) (Pei, A. 1996; Yang, Q. 1991) (Figures 5.1 and 5.14).

Pengtoushan (3 ha) is situated on a small mount, some 8 m higher than the surrounding land. An excavation area of 400 m² has revealed six houses (ground level and subsubterranean), fifteen pits, and twenty-one burials. The distribution of these features, however, shows little deliberate spatial planning. Pengtoushan is well known for showing carbonized rice grains in its fiber-tempered pottery, but few organic remains have survived at the site because of the acidic soil conditions (Hunansheng 2006).

Bashidang (3.7 ha) was surrounded by a river on the west and north sides and by earth walls and ditches on the east and south. The remaining walls were less than 1 m high and no more than 6 m wide at the base; the ditches varied in depth and width, with the deepest part measuring 1.7 m in Ditch 8 (G8) and 5.7 m at the widest part of Ditch 9 (G9). The walls were not rammed, but simply piled up by accumulation of soil removed from the ditches. The wall-ditch enclosures were constructed over a long period and changed in size through time, as they were rebuilt many times. These structures show little effectiveness for defense, and were most likely made for flood control. Within an excavation area of 1,200 m², archaeologists have uncovered twenty-four dwellings, mainly pile structures and ground-level houses, ninety-eight secondary burials, and eighty pits. Thanks to the waterlogged conditions, Bashidang has revealed abundant organic remains made of wood, reed, bamboo, cane, or hemp. Some sixty-seven species of plant have been identified. In addition to nearly 10,000 rice grains, large amounts of wild plants have been unearthed, including water caltrop (*Trapa* sp.), Gorgon fruit (*Euryale ferox*), legume, and many types of fruits and vegetables. Seven genera or species have been identified in the faunal assemblage, including birds, buffalo, pig, deer, and fish. None of the mammals can be confirmed as domesticated (Hunansheng 2006). Rice grains have been identified as a domesticated form, although this claim is not based on characteristics of the rachis; further study on the morphology of Bashidang rice husks is warranted (Crawford and Shen 1998). In any event, the botanic remains from the site suggest that the Bashidang people exploited a variety of wild plants and animals and that rice is unlikely to have been the main staple food at that time.

Ceramics from Pengtoushan and Bashidang are simple in form, predominantly globe-shaped *guan* jars, *bo* bowls, *pan* plates, and *zhizuo* supports (Figure 5.15). The technology appears to be rather crude; vessels are mainly made by slab-mold techniques, walls are uneven in thickness, and the pastes are mostly fiber-tempered. These ceramic designs seem to be consistent with the makers' presumed concern for portability. Lithic toolkits from these two sites are dominated by choppers made of river pebbles (70.8%), followed by chert (21%), and only 1.4 percent are polished tools (Hunansheng 2006) (Figure 5.16). This lithic assemblage shows a clear continuity with the regional chopping tool tradition of the late Paleolithic (Pei, A. 1996; Wang, Y. 1997). The ceramic and lithic technologies, together with faunal and floral assemblages, reflect a society primarily based on a hunting-gathering economy, with low levels of food production in an environment offering abundant edible resources. The wall-ditch enclosure constructed at Bashidang represents the earliest currently known fortification in ancient China. Such a communally built structure indicates not only a high level of sedentism, but also a strong social response to natural challenges, such as floods caused by monsoonal rainfalls.

Figure 5.15. Pottery vessels from the Pengtoushan (1–5), Lower Zaoshi (6–8), and Chengbeixi (9–12) cultures. 1: *Guan* jar with loops; 2: *guan* jar; 3 and 4: supports; 5: plate; 6: ring-based plate; 7: lid, 8: *guan* jar; 9: *guan* jar; 10: ring-based plate; 11: tripod; 12: support (after Hunansheng 1999: 21, 2006: color plates 4–1, 8–1, 3, 5, and 25–4; Hubeisheng 2001b: color plates 4–2, 7–2, and 8–2, plate 33–4).

The Lower Zaoshi culture: Dwellings, burials, and pits have been found at several sites. At Hujiawuchang the house floors appear to have been finished with layers of burnt clays, sand, and fragments of lithics and pottery. Compared to those of the Pengtoushan period, ceramic assemblages of the Lower Zaoshi culture consist of various types. Some plates were rendered with a ring-shaped high stand and decorated with elaborated engraved designs. Whereas most ceramics are still fiber-tempered and made of slab-mold techniques, some vessels have thin walls, are finished with white slip, or made of white ware (Figure 5.15). Lithic assemblages are still dominated by chopping tools (70% and 90% at Zaoshi and Hujiawuchang, respectively) with small proportions of polished stone tools, mainly woodworking implements. Carbonized rice grains have been found at several sites, and Hujiawuchang has also revealed remains of lotus root, plum, mountain peach, cherry, and persimmon. The faunal remains from Hujiawuchang indicate that people exploited many species of mammal, bird, fish, and shellfish, and also raised domesticated pigs (Wang, W. and Zhang 1993; Yin, J. 1996).

The Chengbeixi culture sites are small in size, located in the Xiajiang area of western Hubei (Figures 5.1 and 5.14). This section of the Yangzi River is bounded by high mountains, and arable land is limited. The sites are situated in different geographic configurations; some are found close to the Yangzi River at low altitude, such as Chengbeixi and Zhichengbei, and are normally inundated during the rainy season. A few dwelling remains have been identified, and associated faunal remains include buffalo, deer, and many types of fish and shellfish. These sites are likely to have been seasonal camps, used for exploiting aquatic and other resources when the Yangzi River level was low. Other sites are located on hills, some 15–20 m above the surrounding land. These sites, represented by Qinglongshan and Jinzishan, were probably occupied during the flooding seasons (Hubeisheng 2001b; Yang, Q. 1991).

Chengbeixi ceramics are dominated by globe-shaped jars, supports, bowls, and plates during the early phases; the jars were multifunctional, used for both cooking and storage. More variations of vessel forms occurred during the late phases, including ring-based plates, painted pottery, and polished black wares (Figure 5.15). Vessels are formed with slab-mold techniques, and pastes are tempered with sand, shells, and grasses, including rice. Lithics are primarily chipped tools made of river pebbles (axe, adze, chisel, scraper, fish-sinker, chopper, ball, etc.), some with polished edges. The tool types suggest that they were generally used for woodworking, hunting, and fishing (Yang, Q. 1991). These artifactual types seem to be consistent with the settlement patterns of mobile communities. Chengbeixi culture sites show strong characteristics of a subsistence strategy principally focused on hunting and gathering, with some components of mobility as logistic collectors. Although rice remains were present in pottery pastes here, these vessels could have been obtained from farming communities elsewhere, as Yan Wenming (2001) has pointed out.

Summary: The early Neolithic cultures of the middle Yangzi River share several material elements. They all consist of large proportions of chipped stone tools and fiber-tempered pottery, *guan* jars and *zhizuo* supports used together as compound cooking utensils in the early phases, and vessels with a ring-shaped stand in the later phases. Although all these communities appear to have practiced a broad-spectrum subsistence strategy, marked regional variations in settlement-subsistence adaptations are observable. Whereas people in the alluvial plain of the Lake Dongting region cultivated rice and built permanent villages, residents of the mountainous Xiajiang area continued the hunting-gathering way of life and many were seasonally mobile.

Several archaeologists have pointed out that material influences from the Pengtoushan and Lower Zaoshi cultures can be found at many sites in the surrounding regions (Yin, J. 1999). For example, Jiahu in the Huai River

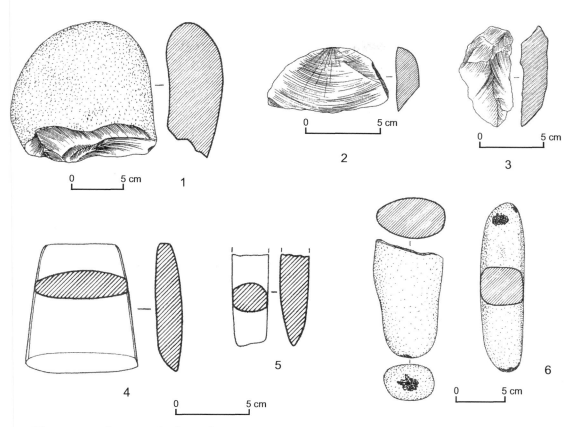

Figure 5.16. Stone tools from the Pengtoushan culture. 1: Chopper; 2: scraper; 3: burin; 4: axe; 5: adze; 6: pestles (modified from figures 74–1, 77–5, 78–9, 99–1, 11, 72–1, 3 of Hunansheng 2006).

Valley shares many similarities with Pengtoushan, such as burial patterns (globe-shaped jars as grave offerings) and ceramic technology (slab-mold and fiber-tempered pottery) (Henansheng Wenwu Kaogu 1999a: 532–3). Ceramics resembling the Lower Zaoshi styles can also be seen at Kuahuqiao in the lower Yangzi River Valley (Jiao 2006). The eastward diffusion of the Lower Zaoshi's influence has been interpreted as due to demographic expansion resulting from the development of rice agriculture (Jiao 2006). Based on the increase of site numbers and expansion of the site location in the archaeological record, it is plausible that a marked population growth occurred during the sixth millennium BC in the middle Yangzi region, leading to population dispersal. The causes of population growth, nevertheless, may have more to do with the development of sedentism, which was based on broad-spectrum subsistence strategy, than with rice cultivation. Nevertheless, rice cultivation, one of the economic technologies that was spread with human migration and progressively intensified over time, unquestionably contributed to further population growth in the new lands of colonization.

The Lower Yangzi River Region

For many years, we had little knowledge about early Neolithic development in the lower Yangzi River Valley before the Hemudu culture (ca. 5000–3000 BC). Thanks to archaeologists working in Zhejiang, a series of discoveries has been made in recent years, revealing important material assemblages dating to the early Neolithic period, including two early Neolithic sites, at Xiaohuangshan and Kuahuqiao (ca. 7000–5000 BC) (Figures 5.1 and 5.14).

Xiaohuangshan (ca. 7000–6000 BC) in Shengzhou is located in a small basin surrounded by low mountains, and few organic remains have been preserved in the archaeological record because of acidic soil conditions. The cultural deposits can be divided into three phases; the material remains from Phase I share many similarities with Shangshan (see Chapter 3), whereas those from Phases II and III show much more variety of lithic and ceramic types, some resembling those from Kuahuqiao. Storage pits are abundant in number and regular in shape (square and round); the lithic assemblage is dominated by grinding stones (slabs and handstones) with low proportions of hammer stones, tools bearing perforations (of unknown function), balls, and polished woodworking tools. Ceramics are characterized by large basins with flared walls, round-bottomed jars, and plates. Rice is present in the soil deposits (Zhang, H. and Wang 2005). Starch analysis on grinding stones suggests that the Xiaohuangshan people exploited a wide range of wild plants, including Job's tears, beans, chestnuts, acorns, tubers, and rice (Liu, L. et al. 2010c; Yao, L. 2009).

Kuahuqiao (ca. 6000–5000 BC) is located in Xiaoshan near Hangzhou city. The site, about 1 m below sea level, is now situated on the southern bank of the Qiantang River's mouth, facing Hangzhou Bay. When it was inhabited, the site was bounded by mountains in the northwest and fresh water bodies in the southeast. Above the settlement deposits is a layer of sediment 3–4 m thick, belonging to the supralittoral and eulittoral zones. These deposits suggest that the site was abandoned because of rising sea level and marine transgression. Since 1990 archaeologists have conducted three seasons of excavation there, covering a total area of 1,080 m² (Zhejiangsheng and Xiaoshan 2004) (Figure 5.17).

Thanks to the waterlogged conditions, the site revealed abundant artifacts and organic remains. The residences were pile dwellings, as indicated by the remains of wooden structures and supporting earth walls. Some timbers show traces of tenon and mortise joinery techniques, whereas others were cut into ladder-shaped forms, apparently used for climbing up to the pile dwellings. Some storage pits were constructed with wooden frames and filled with acorns (Figure 5.18). The pottery forms are distinctive, including *fu* cauldron, *guan* pot, *pan* plate, *dou* stand, and *bo* bowl, as well as a large quantity of painted wares. Many vessels have thin walls of uniform thickness, and were elaborately made (Figure 5.17). The ceramic technology reached an unparalleled level among all

Figure 5.17. The Kuahuqiao site and artifacts unearthed. 1: Excavation at Kuahuqiao; 2: black pottery jar; 3: pottery jar with painted design; 4: *dou* pedestal plate; 5: wooden handle (probably attached with bone spade); 6: bone spade; 7: stone adze; 8: wooden handle (probably attached with adze); 9: dugout canoe; 10: paddle (courtesy Jiang Leping).

the contemporary archaeological cultures in China. Interestingly, 58 percent of the ceramics, mostly noncooking vessels, are made of fiber-tempered clay, a tradition that had already declined in the Xiaohuangshan pottery assemblage (Zhejiangsheng and Xiaoshan 2004). The presence of fiber-tempered pottery at Kuahuqiao may be explained as a result of population migration from the Lower Zaoshi culture in the middle Yangzi River (Jiao 2006), where such technology was commonly used then.

More than 5,000 animal bones were unearthed, identifiable to thirty-two species, including crab, turtle, alligator, swan, crane, dolphin, dog, badger, raccoon dog, pig, tiger, leopard cat, rhinoceros, sika, antelope, and water buffalo. Among these animals, pig and dog appear to have been domesticated, but they are underrepresented there, as compared to the wild mammals found (deer and buffalo). The botanic remains are mostly wild species, including water caltrop, acorn, chestnut, and fox nut. Excavations yielded more than 1,000 grains of rice, which show characteristics of both domestic and wild forms (see also Chapter 4). A spade made of animal scapula was probably attached to a wooden handle for tilling fields (Figure 5.17) (Zhejiangsheng and Xiaoshan 2004; Zheng, Y. and Jiang 2007). Evidently, the Kuahuqiao subsistence economy was predominantly one of hunting and gathering, and rice cultivation already had been established. The people there appear to have adapted to a full sedentary way of life.

Another important discovery at Kuahuqiao is an incomplete dugout canoe, made of pine and dated to 6000 BC. The canoe is 560 cm long and 2.5 cm thick, in its extant form. Three paddles were unearthed at the site. Whetstones, stone adzes, wooden adze handles, and flakes chipped off from adzes have been found near the canoe (Figure 5.18). All these remains suggest that the site was a village associated with a workshop for making or repairing canoes. The Kuahuqiao canoe is rather narrow and shallow, probably only suitable for navigating rivers and lakes, rather than for seafaring. This canoe, however, may represent the earliest watercraft technology developed in southeast China (Jiang, L. and Liu 2005).

The geographic contours of the lower Yangzi River region were unstable during the early part of the Holocene, being particularly affected by the fluctuation of sea level. The Kuahuqiao people settled at the site during an episode of low sea level, and the settlement was ultimately destroyed by marine transgressions (Zhejiangsheng and Xiaoshan 2004). There may have been more sites contemporary with Kuahuqiao in this region but distributed in areas today inundated by the Hangzhou Bay.

SOUTH CHINA

Pollen data from Dahu Swamp in the Nanling Mountains area have revealed a warm and wet period (10,400–6000 cal. BP) during the early and middle

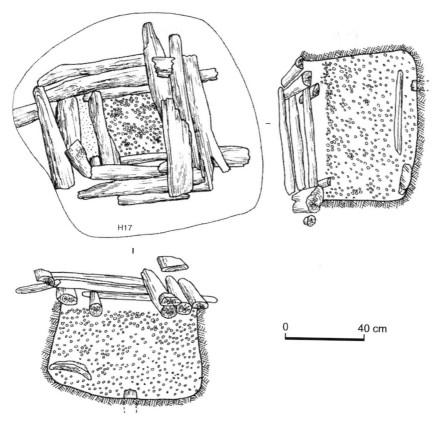

Figure 5.18. Storage of acorns, Kuahuqiao (after figure 16 of Zhejiangsheng and Xiaoshan 2004).

Holocene in this tropical forest zone of South China. There is a proportional increase of *Castanopsis/Lithocarpus* to a maximum of 30 percent, and herb pollen is low (<10%). The average precipitation was around 1,800 mm, and average temperature was about 1–2°C above the present (Zhou, W. et al. 2004).

The early Neolithic cultures in South China (ca. 6000–5000 BC) are characterized by two types of settlements – shell middens and cave sites – but many are not well dated. Several better reported sites are from Guangxi province. In the Nanning area of southern Guangxi, the sites are shell middens, known as the Dingsishan culture, exemplified by Dingsishan in Yongning (Fu, X. et al. 1998) and Baozitou in Nanning (Zhang, L. 2003). These sites are located on the first terraces of the Zuo, You, and Yong Rivers near the mountain ranges (Figures 5.1 and 5.14). People there made simple-form pottery, mostly sand tempered and round-bottomed jars. Many tools are made of shells. Chipped stone tools include choppers and perforated stones, and polished stone tools consist of axes and adzes. The dead were buried in various positions, such as flexed or squatting, or were dismembered (Figure 5.19). Faunal remains consist of bovine, deer, pig, and various species of shellfish, suggesting that the people mainly relied on hunting and shellfish collecting.

More than forty cave sites, many of which were continuously occupied from the late Paleolithic to the Neolithic times, have been located in the limestone areas of Guangxi and Guangdong provinces. These caves normally face south, with a large expanse of open land in the front, and are situated near a river. The cultural deposits often consist of abundant remains of shellfish (Jiao 1994). Several sites in northern Guangxi, such as Zengpiyan and Miaoyan in Guilin and Dayan in Lingui, have revealed long cultural sequences and abundant material remains. The people manufactured pottery with a variety of forms and decorations, made both chipped and polished stone tools, collected wild plants and shellfish, and hunted animals. It is interesting to note that caves were no longer in use after 5000 BC in South China, signifying some fundamental changes in subsistence–settlement strategy in the region, which are yet to be investigated (Chen, Y. 2003; Fu, X. et al. 2001; Zhongguo Shehui Kexueyuan 2003a).

None of the early Neolithic sites in South China has revealed any evidence for rice cultivation. Instead, remains of tubers and starch granules of taro have been uncovered from Zengpiyan (Zhongguo Shehui Kexueyuan 2003a). The early Neolithic people in South China may have already known about rice cultivation from neighboring communities in the Yangzi River Valley, but they continued the hunting-gathering way of life, relying mainly on tubers, fish, shellfish, and wild animals as staple foodstuffs. The high-level availability and long-term exploitation of tubers may have led to the domestication of root crops in South China (Zhao, Z. 2005a). The level of sedentism associated with these shell middens and cave sites is unclear because of a lack of study.

DISCUSSION

Our survey of early Neolithic cultures in north and south China illustrates wide varieties of settlement pattern, subsistence adaptation, and social complexity in time and space. Although a general tendency toward increased degrees of sedentism and greater emphasis on food production is evident over time, hunting-gathering adaptations persisted in various ways throughout all regions. This situation is particularly manifested in the logistical collector strategy (foraging for seasonally available food resources in particular locations away from the permanent residences; see Chapter 3 for more explanation), in that seasonally available foods (such as nuts, tubers, fish, and shellfish) continued to form the major components of staple foodstuffs. Next we summarize the main viewpoints from our discussion.

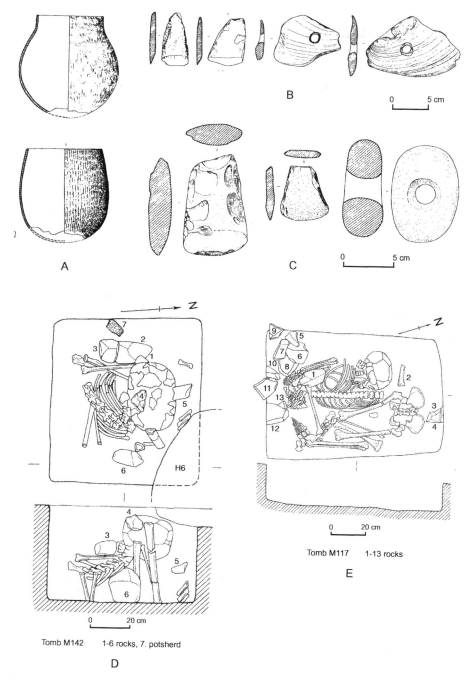

Figure 5.19. Artifacts and burials from Dingsishan, Yongning, and Guangxi. **A:** *Guan* jars; **B:** bone adzes and shell knives; **C:** stone axes and perforated stone; **D:** squatting burial; **E:** dismembered burial (modified from figures 13–15, 20, 21, and 26 of Fu, X. et al. 1998).

Variability in Settlement Pattern, Site Function, and Subsistence Strategy

Tool assemblages, together with faunal and floral remains, provide crucial information on the subsistence economy. Macrobotanic remains and residues on stone tools all point to the exploitation of a wide range of wild foodstuffs, including nuts, beans, cereals, and tubers. The high proportions of grinding stones in the tool assemblages in the Liao, Yellow, and lower Yangzi Rivers during the early Neolithic period suggest intensive exploitation of wild plants over broad geographical regions. These regions, belonging to warm temperate forest and subtropical forest zones, are characterized by clear seasonal changes in climate. This means that the natural environments provided abundant plants and animals during summer and autumn, whereas food resources diminished dramatically during the winter and early spring. If food shortage was a condition during part of the year, then to overcome environmental challenges collecting and storing starchy foods would have been the best solution. The presence of storage pits at all early Neolithic sites also lends further support to this proposition.

Significant development of food production is indicated by the presence of domesticated cereals at many sites in the Liao, Yellow, and Yangzi River regions (see also Chapter 4). Contemporary populations in areas with little arable land tended to maintain hunting-gathering ways of life, as demonstrated by Chengbeixi sites in the Xiajiang region. It is also notable that some sites located on piedmonts, such as Beifudi near the Taihang Mountains, perhaps represent specialized seasonal camps used for intensified nut collection.

Variability in Sedentism

Level of sedentism is not directly correlated to degree of food production in China. At a time when food production often shows low levels of development, sedentism seems to have been already well established in most regions, and is closely associated with technology used in processing and storing starchy foodstuffs, such as nuts, cereals, and tubers.

Examining the data against the criteria for sedentism listed at the beginning of this chapter, we see that the development of sedentism was a long process showing great temporal and spatial variation in China. The levels of investment in architectural construction vary from building small semisubterranean dwellings, less than 10 m² in area, to constructing large houses more than 100 m² in area (e.g., Xinglongwa). Not every settlement shows clear signs of spatial planning, but for those surrounded by ditches or walled enclosures (e.g., Xinglongwa, Xiaojingshan, Jiahu, Bashidang) it is unquestionable that significant expenditure of human energy was directed to a long-term residential strategy. Ash pits are commonly found in archaeological contexts, and many may have once been used as storage facilities. Burials are frequently present at sites, and some appear to be intentionally arranged in close proximity to the residential area (e.g., Jiahu), suggesting that mortuary practice was affected by regulations that defined lines of descent. Cultural deposits at many sites are rather thick, although some sites, such as Beifudi, may not have been occupied year-round.

Pigs and dogs were the domesticated animals. Pig husbandry, in particular, is most likely the best indicator of a sedentary lifestyle. Domesticated millet and rice were widely spread over a broad swathe, extending from the Liao River southward to the northern side of the Nanling Mountains, and tubers may have also undergone degrees of domestication, given that taro, yam, and other root plants were regularly exploited in both south and north China since the late Pleistocene (see Chapter 4).

Ceramic assemblages show a clear trend toward growing proportions of functionally specific vessels designed without particular concern for portability. This change is best exemplified by the shift, over time, from early predominance of round- and flat-bottomed vessel forms with thick walls, to later increased frequency of tripods with slender legs (in the north) and tall, ring-based vessels (in the south).

Many sites, such as Beifudi and Jiahu, showed high frequencies of primary refuse and de facto refuse (particularly caches), a condition that may be regarded as indicating residential mobility. The same sites, however, particularly at Jiahu, also revealed high frequencies of secondary refuse in designated residential areas, (e.g., refuse pits near houses), which may signify increased sedentism. Such mixed residential features may be interpreted as characteristic of a transitional period, when the Palaeolithic traditions still persisted, but the new residential-subsistence system, with its attendant sanitation regime suited to long-term occupation, gradually affected the people's way of life.

All these phenomena point to a complex situation. Although many villages may have been occupied year-round, part of the population in some communities still practiced a logistical collector strategy. This strategy is best exemplified by Chengbeixi sites near the Yangzi River, Beifudi near the Taihang Mountains, and the Tieshenggou site cluster in the Song Mountains.

Variability in the Development of Food Production

Zhao Zhijun has convincingly argued that the origins of agriculture in China are manifested by three patterns, used in different regions. The first pattern is dry land farming in northern China, focusing on millets. The second pattern is rice cultivation in a region south of the Huai River and north of the Nanling Mountains. The third pattern is root crops, mainly distributed in the middle and lower Pearl River Valley south of the Nanling Mountains (Zhao, Z. 2005a). These patterns are not geographically distinct, mixed production of rice and millet occurred in the region south of the Yellow River and north of the

Yangzi River (Zhao, Z. 2006), and tubers were also used in North China. Similarly, people in the lower Yangzi River region and the Huang-Huai plain also exploited rice, tubers, and aquatic starchy food.

The development of cereal agriculture has been intensively studied by researchers in recent years, and few disagree that rice and millet domestication had emerged by early Neolithic times. The domestication of root crops, however, is a new topic raised only recently, particularly since the excavation of Zengpiyan in South China (Zhao, Z. 2005a; Zhongguo Shehui Kexueyuan 2003a). These data suggest that subsistence systems in South China were rather different from those in north China, and apparently shared many traits with contemporary systems of Southeast Asia and New Guinea, where a range of tubers and fruits were also exploited (see Bellwood 2005: 134–45).

It is uncertain whether any of the early Neolithic cultures can be categorized as an agricultural society (defined as consuming 30–50% domesticated food), considering the predominant presence of wild species in the faunal and floral remains, as well as the contrasting makeup of tool assemblages, with high percentages of grinding stones (used for processing various wild plants) and low proportions of sickles (used for harvesting cereals and other plants that were not necessary all domesticates) (Table 5.3).

The Role of Nut Collection and Arboriculture

We now understand better the intensification of nut collection in many areas of the Yellow and lower Yangzi River Valleys during this period. In accordance with the warm and wet climatic trend of the Holocene, nut-bearing trees, particularly oaks, flourished in both north and south China. As a result, people in many regions took advantage of these nutritious plants and gradually intensified their nut economy. This new adaptation explains why most early Holocene sites have been found near rivers in piedmont areas. In addition to many food resources (including cereals) available in the piedmont environments, it is important to note that the most productive nut trees are normally distributed on the edge of forests and open areas (Crawford 1997; Gardner 1997), and running water is needed for processing acorns. It is logistically reasonable for people to locate their settlements near rivers and mountains, to gain easy access to those crucial resources. Within a broader East Asian context, this subsistence mode corresponds to that of sedentary hunter-gatherers in the Jomon period of Japan (Habu 2004; Kobayashi 2004; Pearson 2006).

This phenomenon leads to new questions: Had Neolithic people begun to manage tree crops, leading to the emergence of arboriculture? Did they simply exploit wild resources? It has been well documented in ethnographic and archaeological accounts that management of tree crops was a form of plant-food intensification in many parts of the world. Examples include transplanting oaks in southern California (Shipek 1989), raising oaks and other nut-bearing trees in Mediterranean Europe (Harrison 1996), domesticating several types of indigenous trees in New Guinea (Denham 2004), and selecting chestnut trees to grow near villages in the Jomon period of Japan (Kobayashi 2004: 85–6). In early Neolithic China, grinding stones for nut processing are present at sites in different ecosystems, either by a hillside, such as Baiyinchanghan abd Beifudi, or on a floodplain, such as many Peiligang sites in the Huanghuai plain. It is possible that, whereas wild nut-bearing trees in particular mountainous regions were targeted by communities, a certain level of arboriculture was developed by people in the alluvial regions to raise the productivity of these trees. If this were the case, we would need to reassess the level of food production during early Neolithic times. This proposition needs to be tested in future studies.

Variability in Ritual Activity and Social Complexity

Early Neolithic populations must have experienced significant social, political, and economic changes that may have involved contests for territorial control, competition for resources, and dynamics of inter- and intra-community relationships. In this regard, two types of ritual practice are observable in the archaeological record. One is represented by the Xinglongwa culture, wherein households seem to have been the focus of ritual activities, as suggested by indoor burials and figurations placed inside houses (Li, X. 2008: 50). Such household-oriented ritual activities may have been a social response to scalar and economic stresses at the time. The zoomorphic masks unearthed in residential contexts at Beifudi also show affinities with the household ritual model.

The second type of ritual practice is focused on mortuary ceremony, as revealed at Jiahu. A small number of individuals appear to have received more elaborate burial offerings (ritual paraphernalia) than other members of the community. This mortuary pattern manifests the social status of individuals who may have possessed special ritual abilities and enjoyed a high degree of prestige (Liu, L. 2004: 127–8). The early Neolithic cultures appear to have been relatively egalitarian in nature, but there were differences among community members, based on individual achievements.

CONCLUSIONS

Shi Xingbang (1992) has suggested that the transition from late Paleolithic to Neolithic in the Yellow River Valley can be described as three developmental phases: (1) the mountain forest culture, characterized by food foraging, which is represented by Xiachuan in southern Shanxi; (2) the piedmont culture, with origins of food production; and (3) the river valley culture, with initial establishment of food production, represented by the pre-Yangshao cultures of

The Archaeology of China

the early Neolithic. Shi is correct to point out the general trend in settlement-subsistence modes through time, but our analysis suggests that the transition was not unilineal in the Yellow River region, and the diversity was even greater cross-regionally.

The early Neolithic cultures are characterized by a broad-spectrum subsistence strategy with low-level food production, consisting of foraging for wild resources and domesticating animals (pig and dog) and plants (millet and rice). Sedentism was practiced to varying degrees in different areas, ranging from year-round full sedentary villages to seasonal camps. The emergence of sedentism is attributable to the development of technologies for resource management and food storage, with particular emphasis on starch-rich foodstuffs (nuts, tubers, aquatic plants, and cereals). Regional differences in material culture, such as ceramic forms, tool types, and settlement patterns, are closely related to the variety of food resources in different areas and to correspondingly various methods of food acquisition adopted by local populations.

As demonstrated in the next chapter, not until the middle Neolithic period did agriculture become intensified in many regions of China. The remaining question for future research is the following: How and why was low-level food production, which appears to have been a successful mechanism, transformed to intensified agriculture in China?

CHAPTER 6

EMERGENCE OF SOCIAL INEQUALITY – THE MIDDLE NEOLITHIC (5000–3000 BC)

When the ancients buried their dead, they covered the body thickly with pieces of wood, having laid it in the open country. They raised no mound over it, nor planted trees around; nor had they any fixed period for mourning. In subsequent ages the sages substituted for these practices the inner and outer coffins.

> Chapter, "The Great Treatise II," in *Book of Changes* (ca. the ninth century BC), translated by James Legge (1879)

"古之葬者, 厚衣之以薪, 葬之中野, 不封不树, 丧期无数。后世圣人易之以棺椁 . . ."
〈〈周易 · 系辞下〉〉

During the fifth and much of the fourth millennia BC, fully developed Neolithic communities flourished in most of China. Settlements increased dramatically in number, and spread to ever broader and more varied geographic regions, suggesting a rapid growth in population. These developments coincided with a period of warm and wet climatic conditions known as the Mid-Holocene Climatic Optimum, during which some large-scale centennial warming was accompanied by increased precipitation, due to the expansion of monsoon circulation. The deviation of annual mean temperature from today's is estimated at $1°C$ in South China, $2°C$ in the Yangzi Valley, and $3°C$ in North and Northeast China (Shi, Y. et al. 1993). It appears that the northwest of China experienced the strongest warming, as the mean temperature was $3-4°C$ higher than today near the Tenggeli (Tengger) Desert around 7290–6380 cal. BP (Zhang, H. C. et al. 2000). The duration and amplitude of the Optimum period, as well as the times of its start and end, differed in different parts of China, however, and a cooling/drying event that followed the Optimum was also asynchronous (An, C.-B. et al. 2006; An, Z. et al. 2000; He, Y. et al., 2004). A number of studies show that this episode of climatic deterioration seems to have occurred around 5000 cal. BP in many parts of north China (An, C.-B. et al. 2006; Li, Xiaoqiang et al. 2003; Schettler et al. 2006).

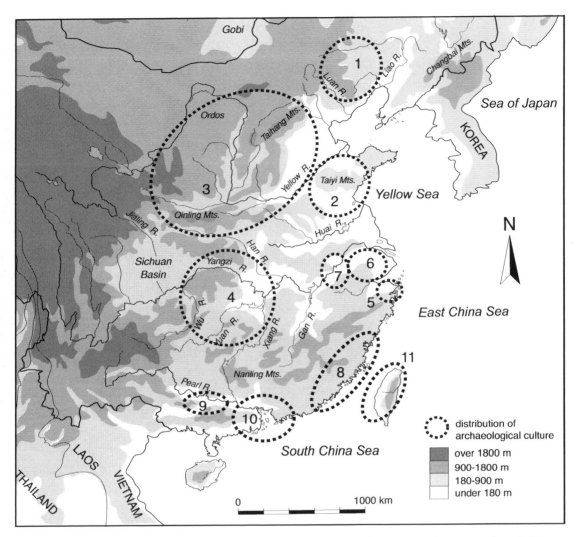

Figure 6.1. Distribution of middle Neolithic cultures in China mentioned in Chapter 6. 1: Zhaobaogou–Hongshan; 2: Beixin–Dawenkou; 3: Yangshao; 4: Daxi; 5: Hemudu; 6: Majiabang–Songze; 7: Lingjiatan–Beiyinyangying–Xuejiagang; 8: Keqiutou; 9: Dingsishan IV; 10: Xiantouling; 11: Dabenkeng.

These conditions are the environmental backdrop underlying the economic and social decisions made by the Neolithic communities.

Some important social changes took place during this time period. First, under favorable climatic conditions farming became a primary source of food supply in both North and South China, leading to a steady growth in population, an increase in village size, and thus the development of more complex social organizations. Second, population pressure on established agricultural areas led to the expansion of farming communities into arable lands in marginal regions, resulting in ever broader distribution of Neolithic assemblages in China. Third, the first remarkable signs of social hierarchy began to appear in some regions during the fourth millennium BC. Walled settlements were built

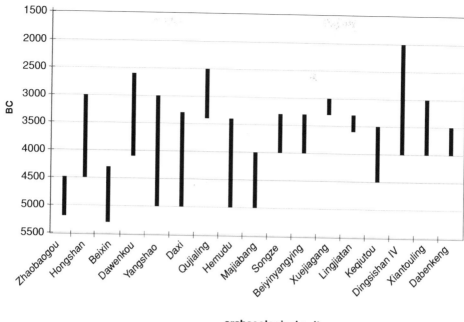

Figure 6.2. Chronology of major cultures of the middle Neolithic period.

in both north and south China, large ceremonial edifices were constructed in forms clearly distinguishable from the structures of ordinary villages, and elites were buried in elaborate tombs with finely made jades and/or other rich furnishings. Fourth, the change in social structure was represented in different forms from region to region, but one element common to all was the emergence of social elites whose status was undoubtedly related to the ritual power that they had acquired. Fifth, the rise of these early complex societies was directly associated with a wave of cultural interactions among these regions. It is during the later part of this period that the so-called Longshanoid horizon took form, through the great expansion of certain styles of artifact (Chang 1986a: 234–42). Sixth, toward the end of this period, overexploitation of the environment by agricultural activities, such as deforestation, coupled with climatic fluctuation, led to deterioration of the ecosystem, forcing people to adjust their socioeconomic strategies. In some cases, more hierarchical social organizations emerged, whereas in other cases social systems collapsed.

In this chapter, we first describe the material remains of several regional cultures that flourished along the major river systems, including the Liao River, the Yellow River, the Yangzi River, and corresponding waterways in South China (Zhongguo Shehui Kexueyuan 1984, 2010). Then we discuss some major issues of concern, including the development of sociopolitical complexity, regional interaction, the role of ideology, and population expansion. Figure 6.1 shows the distribution of the major cultures discussed in this chapter, and the basic chronology for this period is shown in Figure 6.2.

THE LIAO RIVER VALLEY

In Northeast China, the early Neolithic Xinglongwa culture was succeeded by the Zhaobaogou (ca. 5200–4500 BC) and Hongshan (ca. 4500–3000 BC) cultures, distributed over a broad region in the Liao River system (Figures 6.1 and 6.3). Nearly 100 Zhaobaogou sites and more than 500 Hongshan sites have been reported, but only a few dozen have been excavated. Results from several regional survey projects show that the population grew steadily from Xinglongwa to Zhaobaogou, then increased rapidly during the Hongshan period before it declined sharply by the Xiaoheyan culture (ca. 3000–2200 BC) (Chifeng 2002; Li, X. 2008; Liu, G. 2006; The Chifeng 2003).

There is a clear continuation of material culture from Xinglongwa to Zhaobaogou in terms of pottery and lithic styles, but the Zhaobaogou people made some rather elaborate ceramics and manufactured more ground stone tools. The subsistence economy of the Zhaobaogou period was a mixture of hunting, gathering, and, to a lesser degree, food production (Li, X. 2008; Linduff et al. 2002–2004; Shelach 2006). A use-wear analysis of microblades from Zhaobaogou has revealed the evidence of harvesting domesticated cereals (Wang, X. 2008), although typical agricultural harvesting tools, such as knives or sickles, are still lacking. Ritual practice, in general, seems to have continued regional traditions involving animal and female fertility cults, particularly shown in clay sculptures/figurines, jade artifacts, and pottery decorations (Li, X. 2008; Liu, L. 2007; Nelson 1995; Shen, J. 1994) (Figure 6.4). Intracommunity-level hierarchy had emerged, as indicated by evidence that only a few households were associated with more elaborate pottery and/or involved in communal ritual feasting and the long-distance exchange of prestige items. The Zhaobaogou culture also manifests the first occurrences of monumental public structures for community-level practice of ritual, as indicated by a stone altar near Zhaobaogou. This new type of structure marks a significant change in ritual practice, which was then further developed in the Hongshan culture (Li, X. 2008: 51–71).

The subsequent Hongshan culture was the first complex society to develop in Northeast China, revealing the astonishing construction of public architecture for ritual performances and the emergence of elites whose social status while living was expressed posthumously by the presence of jades in their tombs. Thanks to many new discoveries made since the 1970s, this culture has become one of the major focal points of recent studies of the origins of complex society in China. The Hongshan culture displays some marked changes in settlement patterns and material assemblages. First, there is a dramatic increase in the number of sites, reaching more than five times that of the Zhaobaogou culture. Second, pottery types and decorations changed considerably. Although local traditions were maintained, many new pottery types suddenly emerged, some resembling vessel forms and painted pottery found in the Yellow River

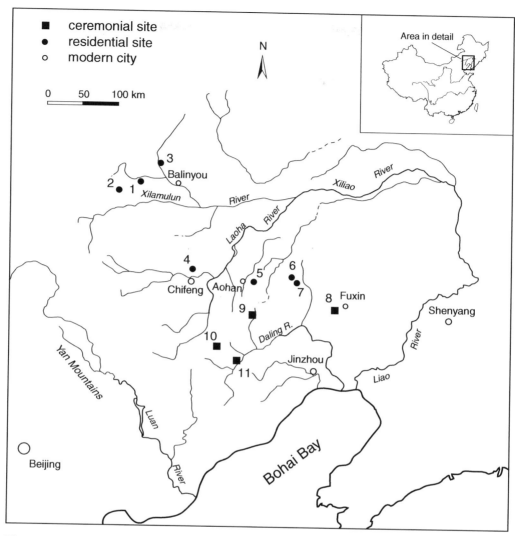

Figure 6.3. Distribution of major Zhaobaogou and Hongshan sites discussed in Chapter 6. 1: Baiyinchanghan; 2: Nantaizi; 3: Erdaoliang; 4: Xishuiquan; 5: Zhaobaogou; 6: Xinglonggou; 7: Xinglongwa; 8: Hutougou; 9: ritual structures in Laohushan River; 10: Niuheliang; 11: Dongshanzui.

Valley. Third, although most traditional stone implements were still in fashion, two important changes appeared: an increased variety in types of spades, and the initial occurrence of leaf-shaped and rectangular stone knives (Figure 6.5), often thought to have been used for harvesting cereals. Fourth, residential houses were semi-subterranean, in most cases with a gateway in the wall facing the hearth, a type similar to that of the Yangshao culture in the Yellow River region. Evidence of continuous local cultural development abounds, but many changes also point to some significant influences from neighboring cultures in the Yellow River region (Li, X. 2008: 73–82).

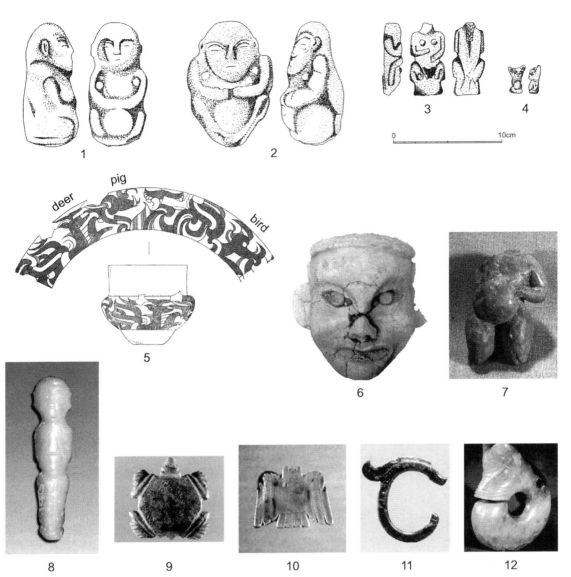

Figure 6.4. Art representations from the Liao River region (1–5: Zhaobaogou culture; 6–12: Hongshan culture, not to scale). 1–4: Human figurines representing a sequence of pregnancy, giving birth, and infant (Houtaizi); 5: animal motifs on a *zun* vessel (Xiaoshan); 6: "Goddess" face (Niuheliang); 7: female figurine (Dongshanzui); 8–12: jade human, turtle, bird, and pig-dragons (Niuheliang) (1–4: after figure 13 of Shen, J. 1994; 5: after figure 4.17 of Li, X. 2008; 8: after Guojia 2004b: 21; 6, 7, 9–12: after color plates 2, 4, 28, 39, 71, and 88 of Liaoningsheng 1997).

Hongshan Subsistence Economy

The consensus of archaeologists is that the Hongshan people were agriculturalists. This view is based on the following factors: (1) the fact that the high density of Hongshan settlements could be supported only by intensified agricultural

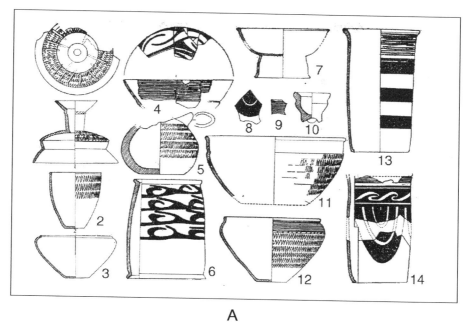

A

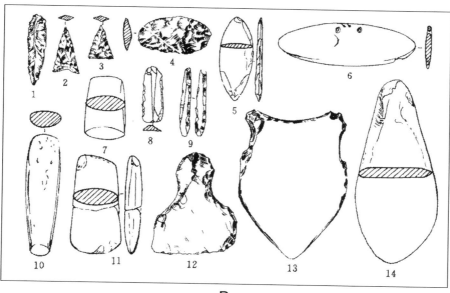

B

Figure 6.5. Pottery types and stone tools of the Hongshan culture (modified from figures 5.2 and 5.5 of Li, X. 2008). (A) Pottery in late Hongshan phase: 1: lid; 2 and 12: pots; 3: bowl; 4 and 11: basins; 5: kettle; 6, 13, and 14: cylinders; 7: *dou* pedestal plate; 8 and 9: painted pottery sherds; 10: tripod cup. (B) Tool assemblage: 1: awl; 2 and 3: arrowheads; 4: scraper; 5 and 6: knives; 7 and 11: axes; 8 and 9: blades; 10: chisel; 12–14: spades.

TABLE 6.1. *Lithic assemblages from seven Hongshan sites*

Site	Total lithic tools	Microliths N (%)	Chip and ground tools	Grinding stones N (%) of total tools, excluding microliths	Knives N (%) of total tools, excluding microliths	Reference[a]
Baiyinchanghan	134	62 (46%)	72	41 (57%)	4 (6%)	*Baiyin Changhan* 2004
Nantaizi	31	13 (42%)	18	5 (28%)	0	*NWKW* (2)1997: 53–77
Xishuiquan	278	221 (79%)	57	3 (5%)	13 (23%)	*KGXB* 1982.2: 183–98
Gacha	24	2 (8%)	22	4 (18%)	1 (5%)	*KG* 2002.8: 91–6
Niuheliang	387	377 (97%)	10	4 (40%)	0	*KG* 2001.8: 15–30
Shuiquan	36	20 (56%)	16	7 (44%)	2 (13%)	*KG* 2005.11: 19–29
Erdaoliang	67	14 (21%)	53	18 (34%)	5 (9%)	*NWKW* (1) 1994: 96–113

[a] *NWKW = Neimenggu Wenwu Kaogu Wenji; KGXB = Kaogu Xuebao; KG = Kaogu.*

production; (2) the presence of domesticated pigs and millets at several Hongshan sites; (3) the presence of leaf-shaped and rectangular stone knives, commonly regarded as evidence for cereal harvesting; (4) an apparent increase of communication with traditional agricultural areas in the Yellow River region, as exemplified by noticeable similarities of house structures and pottery styles between the Hongshan and known agricultural cultures in the Yellow River Valley; and (5) the fact that a new ideology seems to have been established, based on a cosmology originating in the agricultural peoples and focused on assuring abundant harvests of cereals (see later in this chapter) (Li, X. 2008: 76–82).

There is no doubt that farming activities increased in the Hongshan subsistence economy. It is unclear, however, whether agricultural products were the main staples in the subsistence economy, and the archaeological data show a mixed picture. Quantitative analysis of flotation samples from the Hongshan culture deposits at Xinglonggou indicates that the floral assemblage is dominated by nuts and fruits, including acorns (*Quercus* sp.), hazelnuts (*Corylus heterophylla*), and Manchurian walnuts (*Juglans mandshurica*) (Zhao, Z. 2004a). Like the older Xinglongwa and Zhaobaogou sites, Hongshan culture sites have also yielded significant numbers of microliths, indicating the continuing importance of a hunting-gathering way of life. Grinding stones are often present, but their proportion within Hongshan tool assemblages (excluding microliths) ranges widely among seven sites, from 5 percent (Xishuiquan in Chifeng) to 57 percent (Baiyinchanghan in Linxi) (Table 6.1). If the presence of these grinding tools indicates that wild plants (e.g., nuts, tubers, and, to a lesser extent, cereals) were the main objects of processing, as demonstrated in Chapters 3 and 5, then variability among sites, regarding level of tool usage, may suggest diversity of subsistence adaptation among settlement communities. Interestingly, Xishuiquan, the site with lowest proportion of grinding stones, shows the highest percentage of leaf-shaped and similar reaping knives (23%). In contrast, Baiyinchanghan, with the highest proportion of grinding stones, shows one of the lowest percentages of such reaping knives (6%) (Table 6.1). This clear contrast of tool usage could indicate that some Hongshan settlements developed more intensive agriculture, where others continued to rely on a traditional hunting-gathering way of life.

Staple isotopic analyses of human bones ($N = 7$) from the Xinglongwa site show that, on average, 14.7 percent of those people's diet during the early Neolithic Xinglongwa period consisted of C_3 plants (such as nuts and tubers; see definition in Chapter 4), some of which could have been derived from eating nuts or animals that had consumed C_3 plants. In contrast, C_3 foods in the human diet, as briefly sampled from two later periods at the same Xinglongwa site, declined to 0 percent in both the middle Neolithic Hongshan period sample ($N = 1$) and the Bronze Age Lower Xiajiadian samples ($N = 2$), suggesting a general trend toward an increase of C_4 food (such as millet; see definition in Chapter 4) intake resulting from millet agriculture (Zhang, X. et al. 2003). These sample sizes from the Hongshan and Lower Xiajiadian periods are small, however; therefore, the results from this one site, Xinglongwa, may not fully reflect the putative variability of human diet within the entire Liao River region, on either the intrasettlement or intersettlement level. Finally, taking into further consideration the evident variety among tool assemblages and the high proportions of wild plants in floral remains seen at other Hongshan period sites, we may infer that the Hongshan culture's subsistence adaptations were not uniformly homogeneous.

The Hongshan people are likely to have relied on broad-spectrum subsistence strategies, although with agriculture playing a much more important role than ever before in this region. It is also possible that there were variations in subsistence economies among different Hongshan settlements. Whether these differences were affected by ecological conditions or social factors should be a topic for investigation in the future. Further research based on residue analyses of artifacts and human teeth, in conjunction with flotation and isotope analysis of human bones with larger sample sizes from different sites in various ecological environments, should reveal more details for understanding the Hongshan subsistence economies.

Hongshan Settlement Patterns and Ritual Landscape

The Hongshan culture is characterized by two types of sites: One is ceremonial centers composed of various types of public architecture, and the other is ordinary villages. The ceremonial sites have been found in only four locations within the Daling River system, whereas numerous residential sites are scattered over several river valleys in the Liao River region (Figure 6.3) (Li, X. 2008: 82–94).

We have only limited knowledge about the settlement patterns of ordinary villages in the Hongshan culture, due to lack of excavation at residential sites. In general, small Hongshan villages are characterized by orderly rows of semi-subterranean houses arranged sometimes in groups within the rows. Cemeteries have been found near the villages, and only small numbers of burials show stone slab construction or jade contents. During the past few decades, archaeological excavations have primarily focused on Hongshan monumental ritual architectures, represented by altars, cairns, stone platforms, and elite tombs. Four sites or site clusters containing such features have been identified at Niuheliang, Dongshanzui, Hutougou, and at least seven locations in the upper Laohushan River Valley (Figure 6.3). All these sites are located in mountainous areas along the Daling River system; each spreads over an expansive landscape, with several ritual complexes placed in a core area primarily designated for ceremonial activities (Barnes and Guo 1996; Li, X. 2008). Among them, Niuheliang in Jianping County and Dongshanzui in Kazuo County, Liaoning province, provide the best information.

Niuheliang refers to a cluster of sixteen major ritual sites, each composed of cairns, altars, or other monumental architecture, spread over a mountainous area of 50 km². It is the largest ritual complex discovered to date. These sites were constructed during the late Hongshan period (ca. 3650–3150 BC), and form a spectacular ritual landscape. The cairns were built in round and square shapes, many containing elite tombs (Figure 6.6), which have yielded a large number of jade objects, including human and animal figurines. Small clay human figurines, some showing female characteristics, have been found in burials and pits near the ritual structures. The best known site is the Goddess Temple; situated on a mountaintop at the center of the Niuheliang area, it is composed of two semi-subterranean structures, one large (18.4 m long and 6.9 m wide) and one small. Multiple broken parts of clay sculptures, evidently from human and animal figures, were found in these two structures. The human fragments – from hand, ear, shoulder, arm, breast, and other body parts – belong to seven individuals; only female characteristics (such as breasts) can be identified, so all the human figures have been regarded as representations of females, resulting in the name "Goddess Temple." The human sculptures were made in various scales, as suggested by the three sizes of ears found, which range from life-size to three times life-size. A life-sized clay human face with green jade balls inserted into the eye sockets is an unprecedented discovery (Figure 6.4.6). Animal figures include bird claws and fragments of hybrid pig-dragons, including a jaw and a head connected to part of a body (Fang, D. and Wei 1986; Liaoningsheng 1997; Liu, L. 2007).

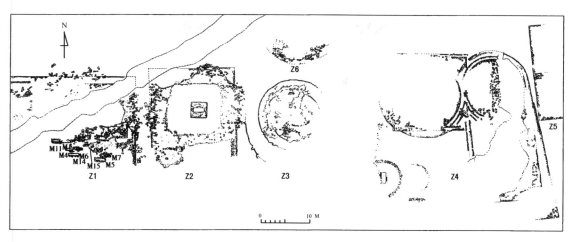

Figure 6.6. Altars with elite burials at Locality II at Niuheliang, Hongshan culture (after figure 18 of Guo, D. 1997).

Dongshanzui is a late Hongshan site (5485 ± 110 cal. BP) situated on a terrace near the Daling River, surrounded by loess tablelands on three sides. This site was occupied for a long period of time. During the early phase, it probably had only a burial and a house; later, stone structures were gradually built, likely used as altars for ritual purposes. Excavation yielded a cluster of stone structures within an area of 2,400 m². At the center of the cluster are two stone structures, one round and one rectangular in shape; on two sides are stonewalls and stone foundations arranged in symmetrical patterns. More than twenty fragments of clay human figurines and sculptures, some identifiable as pregnant females (Figure 6.4.7), were found near the round central structure (Guo, D. and Zhang 1984; Yan, W. 1984).

The landscape of this ritual core area in the Daling River Valley is dominated by high mountains and small hills with limited arable land, and the Niuheliang complex appears to have assumed the highest position in the ritual world of the Hongshan people. Its ceremonial significance is also manifested by the observation that no residential site has been found within an area of 100 km² around the Niuheliang complex (Guo, D. 1997). In other words, this area was a sacred zone designated exclusively for the ritual life of the Hongshan seople.

Hongshan Jades

The Hongshan culture is famous for its jade artifacts, and numerous studies have been devoted to this subject (e.g., Xi, Y. and Liu 2006: 247–502). These jades were primarily associated with elite tombs in stone altars at ceremonial locations. More than 250 jade objects have been excavated or collected from nearly 30 sites; in addition, more than 100 are kept in museums and in personal collections all over the world. The major types include animal (dragon, pig-dragon, turtle, bird) and human figurines, *bi* discs, axes, adzes, awls, *jue* earrings, hook-cloud ornaments, small tubes, and beads (Cui 2006; Li, X. 2008: 74, 79). A jade human figurine (18.5 cm in height) with three interconnecting holes on the back, likely used as a pendant, has been found near the pelvic area of a human skeleton in the largest tomb at Locality XVI (Guojia 2004b) (Figure 6.4). The figurine is portrayed in a standing position with arms folded in toward the chest, a posture that seems to hold some ritual significance, as it recurs in jade figurines found at the Lingjiatan site more than 1,000 km to the south (see later in this chapter on Lingjiatan).

Manufacture of jade objects was a highly specialized industry, and the Hongshan culture underwent a dramatic increase in the quantity and quality of jade production. The provenance of Hongshan jade (nephrite) has been a matter of debate for decades, but recent research demonstrates that most Hongshan jade objects are similar, in terms of texture, color, and gloss, to jade specimens from the Xiuyan jade mines in the Liaodong Peninsula. Xiuyan is approximately 300 km east of Niuheliang, and Xiuyan jade resources appear to have been used since the early Neolithic period, so that products made of this material are distributed through many Neolithic cultures over a broad region in Northeast China and Shandong (Wang, S. et al. 2007). These findings suggest that Hongshan craftsmen may have obtained jade raw material from regional exchange systems. Considering the rarity of jade resources and the special techniques required for processing, jade production may have been controlled by specialists. The large number and high quality of the jade objects found indicate a significant degree of specialization in the jade industry of the Hongshan culture. Small chert tools such as drills and scrapers, likely used for manufacturing jade objects, have been found in cairns (Guojia 2004b) and pits near the ritual structure in Niuheliang (Fang, D. and Wei 1986: 14–15), suggesting that elites may have been involved, to certain extent, in the production of these jade artifacts (Liu, L. 2003), although more evidence is needed to test this proposition.

Social Complexity of the Hongshan Culture

The social complexity of Hongshan society can be seen in several aspects. First, hierarchy among settlements is indicated by the growth of some large sites as central locations within river valleys, surrounded by many small villages, but no evidence suggests the existence of a centralized political entity embracing the entire Liao River region. Second, clear segregation of functions at different sites is seen in the emergence of ritual complexes, such as are represented by Niuheliang and Dongshanzui (Chen, X. 1990). This change suggests increased significance given to ritual activities in Hongshan society, a trend that became particularly accelerated during the late Hongshan period. Third, large monumental architectures, such as cairns, altars, the Goddess Temple, and so forth,

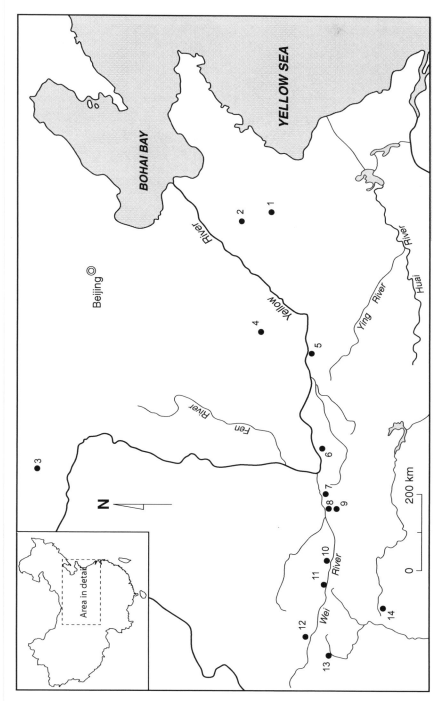

Figure 6.7. Locations of major middle Neolithic sites in the Yellow River Valley. 1: Beixin; 2: Dawenkou; 3: Shihushan; 4: Xishuipo; 5: Xishan; 6: Xipo; 7: Shijia; 8: Jiangzhai; 9: Banpo; 10: Anban; 11: Beishouling; 12: Dadiwan; 13: Gaositou; 14: Longgangsi.

were built. Construction of these edifices was apparently labor-intensive and required managerial activity exerted beyond the community level. Fourth, craft specialization in the manufacture of ritual goods, particularly jade carving, reached a high degree. The production process involved procurement of raw materials from distant sources, manufacture of objects with specified standard forms, and distribution of finished products among elite groups. All these activities required considerable heightening of managerial leadership, including control of knowledge and technology, so the production-distribution processes are likely to have been managed by elites, at least to some significant extent. Fifth, some traditional ritual paraphernalia grew in physical size and social context. Animal and female human figurations and face masks were unique cultural/ritual traditions of this region. Such objects from the early Neolithic Xinglongwa and Zhaobaogou cultures are small in size and associated only with domestic locales. In contrast, corresponding examples from the Hongshan period are dramatically larger, and have become important components of public ritual structures. These changes suggest that the context of ritual performances was broadened from households to a regionally integrated scale (Chen, X. 1990; Li, X. 2008: 83–91; Shelach 1999).

These social and religious features together define the uniqueness of Hongshan complex society, which was unparalleled in China during the fourth millennium BC. It is unclear, however, what forms of regional level sociopolitical organization may have been involved in the construction of ritual landscapes on such a magnificently extensive scale.

The Collapse of Hongshan Complex Society

The Hongshan culture reached its heyday in the late part of the fourth millennium BC and finally collapsed at approximately 3000 BC. How rapidly the collapse took place is unclear, but the archaeological record shows that the succeeding Xiaoheyan culture (ca. 3000–2600 BC) exhibits lower levels of social complexity in many respects: The population declined dramatically, agriculture was replaced to a great extent by pastoralism, the residential mode became more mobile, all the great ritual sites were abandoned, no public architecture was built, and few manufactured jades were produced (Li, X. 2008).

The collapse of Hongshan coincided with an episode of climatic deterioration due to decreased precipitation, when summer monsoons weakened at approximately 3000 BC (An, Z. et al. 2000). In northeast China, summer monsoon rainfall reached a minimum at ca. 2950 BC, as recorded in the sediments of Lake Sihailongwan (Schettler et al. 2006). A prolonged dry-cold episode in the early part of the third millennium BC has also been apparent in other locations in northeast China, and many researchers have linked the Hongshan collapse with this drought event (e.g., Jin, G. 2004; Li, X. 2008).

In addition, Song Yuqin (2002) suggests that excessive farming may have caused desertification in this fragile landscape, contributing to decline in agricultural productivity. As Hongshan subsistence was increasingly reliant on millet farming, prolonged drought would have led to agricultural failure. If nuts were still an important food resource of the Hongshan population, the climatic change may have also affected yields of oak and other nut-bearing trees. Li Xinwei (2008) has also pointed out that the sociopolitical collapse of the Hongshan culture is partially attributable to the way in which elite groups responded to environmental pressures. Based on Li's research, dry and warm conditions had already developed during the late phase of the Hongshan period, challenging the subsistence economy. Instead of developing technology to improve agricultural production, the elites appear to have turned to religion. This situation is clearly reflected by their emphasis on construction of public architecture for rituals and by their obsession with making and using jade ritual objects (Li, X. 2008: 119–132). Taken together, the collapse of Hongshan complex society may have been related to multiple factors, including climatic fluctuation, overexploitation of land, and social responses to external challenges. Thus, the third factor implies that material achievements often regarded as indicators of civilization, such as increased quantities of monumental architectures and jade artifacts, were in fact desperate measures taken against environmental uncertainties, signaling the eve of Hongshan complex society's final collapse.

THE YELLOW RIVER REGION

Our present understanding of the middle Neolithic period in the Yellow River Valley is defined by assemblages manifesting an increased sedentary and agricultural way of life, found at Beixin and Dawenkou culture sites in the lower reaches and at Yangshao culture sites in the middle reaches. In contrast, nonagricultural populations, associated with microlithic technology, occupied the upper Yellow River region through much of the Holocene until the Neolithic Majiayao culture assemblages appeared toward the end of the fourth millennium BC (Rhode, et al. 2007). In this section we focus on the lower and middle reaches of the Yellow River.

In the lower Yellow River Valley, Neolithic remains after the Houli culture are represented by the Beixin (ca. 5300–4300 BC) and Dawenkou (ca. 4300–2600 BC) cultures. Whereas Beixin sites are distributed in only a part of Shandong, Dawenkou sites appear to have spread over a much broader region (Figure 6.1). The Dawenkou culture also showed continued development for some 1,700 years, while exhibiting much higher levels of social complexity in its late phase than in earlier phases. In this chapter, we will discuss only the early and middle Dawenkou periods (ca. 4300–3000 BC), which are comparable with contemporary cultures in other regions.

The Beixin Culture

Since the discovery, in the 1960s, of the type site Beixin in Tengxian, Shandong (Figure 6.7), nearly one hundred Beixin culture sites have been found, mostly located in the floodplains of the piedmont regions to the north and northwest of the Taiyi Mountains. About a dozen sites have been excavated. Most settlements appear to have been sedentary villages (up to 10 ha in area), with small dwellings, ash pits, kilns, and burials (Shandongsheng 2005: 84–125).

Chipped stone tools were still in use, but ground tools (including spades, knives, sickles, axes, adzes, and chisels) were more common; *mopan-mobang* grinding stones also were found at many sites. Some tools (including awl, chisel, spear, arrowhead, and sickle) were made of bone, antler, and shell. Ceramics are mostly yellowish brown in color, and the main types include *ding* tripod, *fu* cauldron, *guan* jar, *pen* basin, *bo* bowl, and *zhijia* support. *Ding* and *fu* were cooking vessels, and *fu* cauldrons were used together with *zhijia* supports; this usage continued a tradition, widespread in the lower Yellow River region during the early Neolithic, which perhaps represented a logistical collector strategy (foraging for seasonally available food resources in particular locations away from the permanent residences), as argued in Chapter 5. The knives and sickles found at Beixin sites were probably used for cereal harvesting (Figure 6.8), and remains of millet have been identified; domesticated animals include pigs and dogs (Shandongsheng 2005: 84–125). Grinding stones have been found from at least seventeen sites; use-wear and preliminary starch analyses tentatively indicate that these tools were used mainly for processing nuts and cereals (Wang, Q. 2008). Few burials have been found; male skeletons tend to be associated with arrowheads, spears, or other tools, and females with pottery or bone awls (Shandongsheng 2005: 123–4). The Beixin culture's people apparently practiced broad-spectrum subsistence strategies, in which hunting-gathering activities were combined with domestication of animals and cereals. There is no evidence to indicate that a clear social hierarchy existed in the society, and the division of labor was primarily gender based.

The Dawenkou Culture

Compared with the Beixin culture, the Dawenkou culture manifested a much more rapid development of social complexity. Early Dawenkou sites were centered around the Taiyi Mountains, but in later periods they gradually spread to a broad region, including Shandong, northern Jiangsu, northern Anhui, and eastern Henan, suggesting a marked increase of population through time and with particular rapidity in some regions during the late Dawenkou phase (ca. 3000–2600 BC). In Shandong some 550 Dawenkou sites have been found, and more than twenty have been excavated (Shandongsheng 2005: 132–3; Underhill et al. 2008).

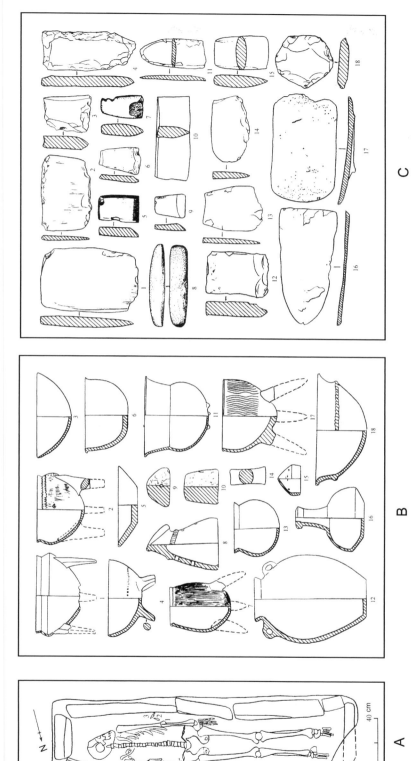

Figure 6.8. Examples of burial, pottery, and stone tools from the Beixin culture (adapted from figures 34, 38, and 40 of Shandongsheng 2005). (A) Tomb M1011 from Dawenkou. 1–3: tooth arrowheads. (B) Major pottery types. 1, 2, 7, and 17: *ding* tripods; 3 and 4: *bo* bowl; 5: *pan* plate; 6: *yu* vessel; 8–10 and 14: *zhijiao* supports; 11 and 13: *fu* cauldron; 12: *guan* jar; 15: pointed object; 16: *hu* jar; 18: *pen* basin. (C) Major stone tool types. 1–4 and 13: spades; 5 and 9: adzes; 6, 7, 12, and 15: axes; 8: grinding handstone; 10 and 14: knives; 11: spear; 16 and 17: grinding slabs; 18: chopper.

Agriculture seems to have been well established during this period, as indicated by higher frequencies of knives and sickles, used for harvesting, in tool assemblages (Figure 6.9) and by remains of millet, rice, and soybeans in archaeological deposits. Domesticated animals mainly included pigs and dogs, and pig heads and mandibles were often used as mortuary offerings (Shandongsheng 2005: 182–9). Grinding stones, which are likely to have been used mainly for processing nuts and cereals, have been found in at least twenty-one sites, which are primarily shell middens in the Jiaodong peninsula and sites near the Taiyi Mountains (Wang, Q. 2008: figure 4.3). These data suggest that nut collecting was still part of the subsistence strategy in some hilly areas, and agriculture had become predominant where arable land was available.

Most excavated Dawenkou sites are cemeteries; therefore, archaeological research has primarily focused on mortuary patterns. In many Dawenkou cemeteries, tombs appear to be arranged in rows and grouped into clusters, probably representing different kin-groups. At its type-site, Dawenkou in Tai'an (Figure 6.7), tombs dating to the early phase are small in size and associated with few grave goods; social hierarchy begins to show in burial patterns from late phases, when a small number of tombs (including those of juveniles) were, compared to others, constructed larger in size and furnished with more elaborate grave goods. Many large tombs contained 100–200 grave goods, whereas small ones had only few. Items that may be related to high social status or ritual functions – including turtle shells, carved cylinders made of ivory or bone, jade, black pottery goblets, and pig mandibles – were found to be primarily associated with rich tombs (Figure 6.9). Throughout the Dawenkou period, there was an overall increase in the number of graves with markers of status, and the late Dawenkou phase shows an increase in the diversity of labor intensive or presumed prestige goods. In general, men enjoyed a higher social status than women at that time, with a few exceptions. Social stratification, inferred from varying burial treatment among different burial groups within a common cemetery, is observable. The development of mortuary stratification was closely associated with the emergence of social hierarchy within kin-based communities in the Dawenkou culture (Fung, C. 2000; Liu, L. 2004: 138–41; Underhill 2000).

The Dawenkou culture assemblages indicate the existence of complex societies, characterized by the emergence of social hierarchy among whole kin groups as well as among individuals within a kin group. Mortuary patterns show elaborate funerary ceremonies that were often directed primarily toward individual ancestors, especially male ancestors. Such ritual practices may have in turn stimulated the development of social hierarchy and enhanced the social status of some individuals and kin groups. Such individually oriented ritual activities contrast the Yangshao culture in the middle Yellow River region, as discussed next.

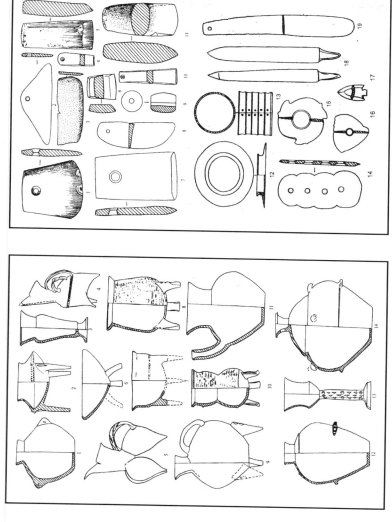

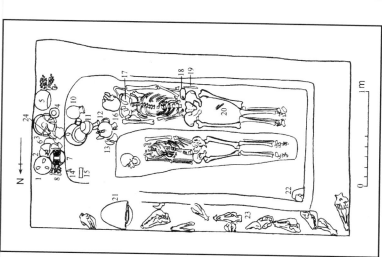

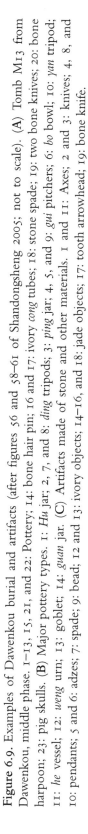

Figure 6.9. Examples of Dawenkou burial and artifacts (after figures 56 and 58–61 of Shandongsheng 2005; not to scale). (A) Tomb M13 from Dawenkou, middle phase. 1–13, 15, 21, and 22: Pottery; 14: bone hair pin; 16 and 17: ivory *cong* tubes; 18: stone spade; 19: two bone knives; 20: bone harpoon; 23: pig skulls. (B) Major pottery types. 1: *Hu* jar; 2, 7, and 8: *ding* tripods; 3: *ping* jar; 4, 5, and 9: *gui* pitchers; 6: *bo* bowl; 10: *yan* tripod; 11: *he* vessel; 12: *weng* urn; 13: goblet; 14: *guan* jar. (C) Artifacts made of stone and other materials. 1 and 11: Axes; 2 and 3: knives; 4, 8, and 10: pendants; 5 and 6: adzes; 7: spade; 9: bead; 12 and 13: ivory objects; 14–16, and 18: jade objects; 17: tooth arrowhead; 19: bone knife.

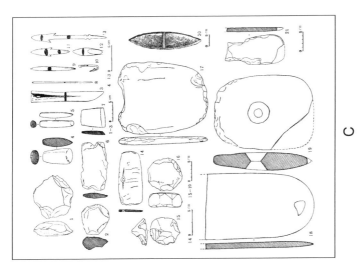

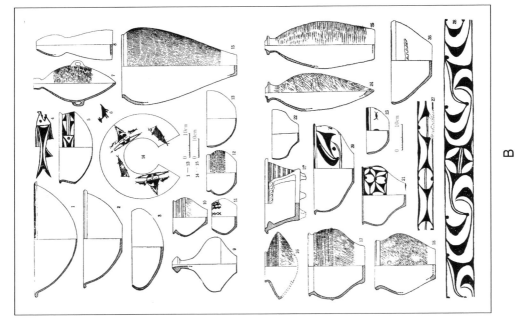

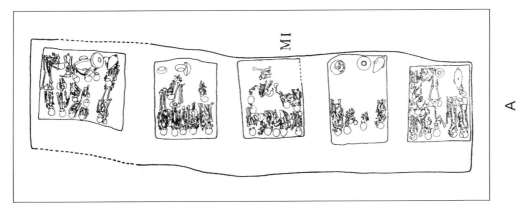

188

The Yangshao Culture

The Yangshao culture (ca. 5000–3000 BC) represents the flourishing of Neolithic farming villages in the middle Yellow River Valley. Compared to the previous period, when early Neolithic sites are few in number, small in size, and scattered mainly in the piedmont areas of the Central Plain and the Wei River Valley, Yangshao sites show some new patterns. The number of sites increases dramatically, the distribution of sites expands northward to the Loess Plateau and Inner Mongolia, and the sizes of settlements vary significantly, ranging from a few hundred square meters to more than 100 ha in area. By the end of the 1990s, more than 5,000 Yangshao sites had been identified and some 100 sites excavated (Ren, S. and Wu 1999), covering a region including today's Hebei, Henan, Shanxi, Shaanxi, and part of Inner Mongolia (Figures 6.1 and 6.7). Sedentary farming societies were well established, indicated by frequent discoveries of remains from domesticated plants (millet and rice) and animals (pigs and dogs). Semisubterranean or ground-level dwellings with wattle-and-daub walls were built in various shapes, and sometimes multiroom compounds were built. Adults were often buried in well-arranged cemeteries, and primary and secondary burials were practiced at different times and in various areas. Pottery vessels are diverse in form, mostly red in color, and often painted in geometrical or animal patterns. Pottery marks have been found at several sites, although their exact meanings are still a matter of speculation. Lithic assemblages are predominantly polished stone tools, and stone and pottery knives were the most common tools used for harvesting cereals (Figure 6.10) (Yan, W. 1989c). Few grinding stones have been found, suggesting much less reliance on nut collecting, compared with the previous period. High proportions of grinding stones in lithic assemblages occur at several sites (e.g., Shihushan) in the Daihai region, Inner Mongolia (Yang, Z. 2001), where the natural habitat was largely intact when the Yangshao population expanded there. Yangshao settlement patterns and social organizations show great variability in time and

Figure 6.10. Examples of Yangshao burials and artifacts (after figures 12 and 17–19 of Zhongguo Shehui Kexueyuan 1984). (A) Secondary burials, Tomb M1, from Hengzhen in Shaanxi, early Yangshao phase. (B) Pottery of Banpo (1–15) and Miaodigou (16–28) phases. 1, 2, and 5: *Pen* basins; 3 and 13: *bo* bowls; 4, 6, and 14: animals and human motifs; 7: *jiandiping* pointed-bottom vessel; 8 and 9: *hu* jars; 10–12, 17, and 18: *guan* jars; 15: *weng* urn; 16: *fu* cauldron; 19: *zao* stove; 20, 21, and 26: *pen* basins; 22 and 23: *wan* bowl; 24 and 25: *ping* vessels; 27 and 28: geometric motifs. (C) Tools. 1: Chopper; 2: scraper; 3: bone knife; 4 and 19: axes; 5: adze; 6 and 14: knives; 7: chisel; 8: bone needle; 9, 11, and 12: bone arrowheads; 10: fish hook; 13: harpoon; 15 and 16: discoids; 17, 18, and 21: spades; 20: pottery file. (D) Pottery marks from Banpo (1) and Jiangzhai (2).

space, reflecting the broad temporal and spatial expanse within which this archaeological culture developed.

Early Yangshao period (ca. 5000–4000 BC): Settlements dating to the early Yangshao period, often referred to as the Banpo phase, tend to be moderate in size; for example, several well-investigated sites in the Wei River region all measure 5–6 ha. Extensively excavated sites include Jiangzhai in Lintong (Xi'an et al. 1988), Banpo in Xi'an (Zhongguo Kexueyuan 1963), Beishouling in Baoji (Zhongguo Shehui Kexueyuan 1983), and Dadiwan in Qin'an (Zhao, J. 2003) (Figure 6.7). The Yangshao community appears to have been highly self-sufficient, unprecedentedly producing a majority of its subsistence needs from domesticated sources, such as cereals, pigs, and dogs, while also continuing long-established activities, such as hunting several species of deer, birds, and other wild animals; fishing for freshwater fish and shellfish; collecting wild plants; and manufacturing pottery and stone tools. These sites share remarkable similarities in spatial pattern and cultural elements, which are best exemplified by the Jiangzhai site.

Jiangzhai is located on terrace land, near the Lin River on the piedmont of the Li Mountains. Phase I of the site, which covers an area of 5 ha, dates to the early Yangshao period. The center of the settlement was a plaza, and a circle of houses was built on the periphery, with all the doors facing the central plaza. The entire residential area, measuring about 2 ha, was surrounded by ditches, outside of which burials were clustered in a few groups. The houses were partitioned into five groups or residential sectors, and each group included several small and medium-sized houses and one large house (Figure 6.11). Dead children were buried in pottery urns near houses, and deceased adults were buried in cemeteries outside the ditches. The burials may have been organized based on descendant regulations, as each cemetery appears to be spatially correlated with a residential cluster inside the ditches. Grave goods were predominantly utilitarian ceramic utensils and tools, with no obvious difference between graves, suggesting a relatively egalitarian society (Xi'an et al. 1988). The Jiangzhai population is estimated at 75–125 persons based on settlement data and 85–100 persons based on burial data (Zhao C. 1995, 1998); these estimates account for an average population range of 80–112.5 persons, at a mean population density of 53.5 persons per hectare.

Chinese scholars have previously interpreted the Jiangzhai society as a matrilineal social system that practiced pairing marriage. It was inferred that small and medium-sized houses were used for the members of matrilineal clans, and that the large houses were the residences of either chiefs or secret social groups (Xi'an et al. 1988: 352–7; Yan, W. 1989b). On the basis of a spatial analysis of the Jiangzhai settlement pattern, however, Lee (1993) has suggested that the spatially separated residential sectors were the primary segments of the community; thus, it is argued, the organizational principle of the Jiangzhai community was hierarchical nesting, sequenced from nuclear family,

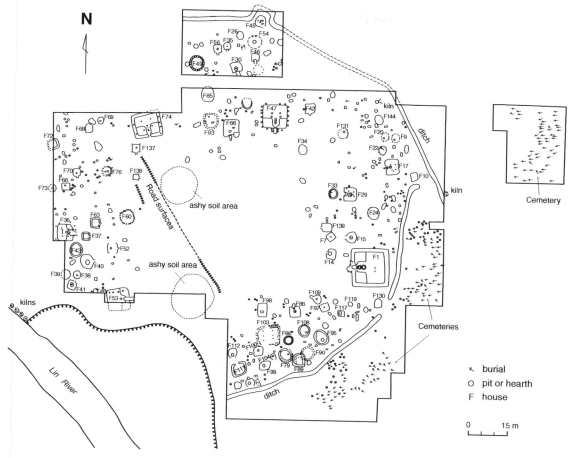

Figure 6.11. Layout of the Jiangzhai site in Lintong, Shaanxi; early Yangshao period (redrawn from figure 6 of Xi'an Banpo Bowuguan et al. 1988).

household, household clusters (lineages or clans), to village community. Such a settlement layout reflects the segmentary organizational principles, commonly observed in tribal societies, that seem to underlie many early Yangshao settlements distributed along the Wei River Valley in the fifth millennium BC (Lee, Y. 1993).

Middle Yangshao period (ca. 4000–3500 BC): This period is also referred to as the Miaodigou phase, during which Yangshao settlements expanded in all directions, so that many marginal areas in the north and the west, previously occupied by microlithic culture populations, came to support Yangshao settlements (Dai, X. 1998). Yangshao ceramic styles appear to have influenced the surrounding cultures, such as Hongshan and Dawenkou, although the social implications of such influence are unclear. The archaeological record also shows the development of regional settlement hierarchy.

Archaeological surveys and excavations in Lingbao, western Henan, have revealed unmistakable evidence of social change (Ma, X. et al. 1999; Wei, X.

and Li 2003; Wei, X. et al. 2002). A clear tendency toward settlement nucle-ation, growing numbers of sites, and increased levels of site hierarchy is dis-cernible from the early to middle Yangshao period. In Zhudingyuan, a sys-tematically surveyed area, some large settlements (40–90 ha) are identifiable as central places, and regional settlement patterns show a three-tiered system. All these patterns suggest that the population increased rapidly and societies became more integrated on a regional level (Ma, X. 2005: 11–28).

Xipo (40 ha) was one of the central places in Zhudingyuan. Its layout is remarkably different from those of the early Yangshao settlements. Although still enclosed by ditches, its large size indicates a much larger population. Near the center of the site was found a cluster of several medium and large buildings, which were constructed over thick subterranean layers of rammed-earth foun-dations. Each building had a long and narrow entrance; some were plastered with red pigment (cinnabar) on the floor, and some contained grinding stones for processing cinnabar, which had an important function in mortuary practice (Ma, X. 2005: 29–50).

The faunal remains from domestic refuse near medium-sized buildings (measured 75–106 m² in occupation area) are predominantly domestic pig bones. Intensive pig husbandry appears to have been practiced in the village; a large number of pigs were slaughtered, and many of them were consumed near these houses. This impressive level of pig husbandry was likely intended to supply the ritual feasting that evidently took place near the medium-sized buildings. The households that occupied these medium-sized buildings may have engaged in producing ritual items and hosting competitive feasts; they were probably the emergent elite families who were competing with one another for prestige and status (Ma, X. 2005: 74–99).

The largest building (F105) measures 204 m² in room area and 516 m² in occupation area, with an entrance 8.75 m long. Its construction is estimated to have required a considerable labor force, probably assembled from several villages, and its function was more likely for holding ritual ceremonies than for domestic purposes (Ma, X. 2005: 34–7). Because this building was set on top of the medium-sized houses, its construction may manifest the dom-inance of some elite groups, resulting from factional competition within this community.

A cemetery has been found outside the ditches, and thirty-four burials have been excavated to date. All burials have a similar structure – a rectangular earth pit with second-tier platforms (*ercengtai*) along two long sides – but differ in size and grave offerings. Pottery, jade, stone, and bone objects were found in burials as grave offerings. There are two forms of jade objects, *yue* axe and *huan* ring, unearthed from male, female, and child burials. The size of the tomb does not always correlate with the quantity and quality of its grave goods. The two largest burials (M27, M29), for example, contained no jade or ivory objects, whereas the burial with the most jades (M11; three jade *yue* axes) belonged to a child. In general, however, larger tombs tend to hold more grave offerings, and small ones usually have none (Zhongguo Shehui Kexueyuan and Henansheng 2010).

Both residential and mortuary patterns at Xipo apparently imply that social hierarchy emerged there, representing the first complex society in the Yangshao culture. Further excavation will help us to gain better knowledge about the social organization of this community.

Late Yangshao period (ca. 3500–3000 BC): In contrast to the middle Yangshao period, when hierarchically organized settlement patterns appeared only in isolated areas, in the late Yangshao period complex regional systems flourished in many parts of the Yellow River Valley. This development is indicated by the emergence of two types of settlement systems. The first type is seen in several large regional centers (up to 100 ha) distributed along the Wei River Valley, including Dadiwan and Gaotousi in Gansu and Anban in Shaanxi. Each site, with a large public building occupying the central location of the settlement, functioned as the regional center for its adjacent settlement system (Lang, S. 1986; Lang, S. et al. 1983; Xibei 2000; Zhao, J. 1990). The second type is represented by the Xishan site in central Henan, a settlement surrounded by rammed–earth walls (Zhang, Y. et al. 1999) (Figure 6.7). The best example of these large regional centers in the Wei River Valley is Dadiwan in Qin'an, Gansu.

Dadiwan: Situated on a hillside near the Qingshui River, the site was first occupied ca. 5800 BC as a small village. It gradually expanded in size, reaching 50 ha in area during the late Yangshao period. Many houses have been found here, which have been classified into three ranks based on size and structure. Three large houses are located in the center of the settlement, with medium and small houses apparently clustered into separate groups in the surrounding areas. The largest house (F901) was a multiroomed structure covering an area of 290 m² (420 m² including affiliated structures) (Figure 6.12). Its plan comprises a major room in the center and several small rooms on the two sides and at the back. Two rows of postholes and one row of stone pillar bases, in front of the building, may indicate that a large porchlike structure existed there. No other contemporary house remains, but pressed soil layers exist within an area of about 1,000 m² in front of this foundation, indicating that this area was probably used as a large public plaza for communal activities. Ceramic remains found in structure F901 include storage urns, some ceramic scoops or vessels of regularly graduated sizes, presumed to be used for measuring grain, and piled-up bowls. A large hearth (2.51–2.67 m in diameter) was located in the center of the major room. The F901 location may have functioned as a central place for activities of regional communities (Gansusheng 2006), probably including feasting and redistribution. Judging from the settlement patterns described earlier in this chapter, it is likely that these societies were regionally integrated, that their leaderships developed a supracommunal dimension, and that leadership strategies were focused on intra- and inter-group cooperation (Liu, L. 2004: 85–8).

The second type of social development during the late Yangshao period, in contrast to the one found in the Wei River Valley, is a settlement system characterized by interpolity conflict. This settlement system is found in the Zhengzhou area in Henan, where several medium-sized central places were distributed equidistantly. One of these sites is the walled settlement at Xishan (25 ha), located on a terraced area, near a river. Violence seems to have afflicted this settlement, as some ash pits also contained adult human skeletons in postures of struggle, mixed with animal bones. Some ceramic utensils found at Xishan are stylistically nonnative to the Central Plain but relatable to the Dawenkou culture in Shandong and Qujialing culture in Hubei. The appearance of these nonlocal cultural elements may have resulted from migration of populations from other places (Zhang, Y. et al. 1999). These external influences occurred simultaneously with the construction of the rammed-earth enclosure, suggesting that intergroup conflict played an important role in the development of this settlement pattern (Liu, L. 2004: 166–8).

Chinese archaeologists have viewed the emergence of walled settlements in China's prehistory as a significant milestone in cultural evolution. It implies the achievement of a certain level of technology, social organization, and leadership. Fortification later became an important component of urban planning in ancient China. Walled sites occurred in this period only in isolated instances, however. Not until the late Longshan culture did the erection of fortifications become widely prevalent.

Ritual Power

Reconstructions of ritual activities and belief systems have primarily relied on mortuary patterns and artistic symbols, and the ritual practices of Neolithic cultures in the Yellow River region show great variations in time and space. Many researchers have suggested that major religious forms in the Neolithic period probably included ancestor worship and shamanism (or *wu*, in the traditional Chinese conception) (Chang 1995; Keightley 1985; Liu, L. 2000a), although in some cases it is difficult to separate the two forms of practice based only on archaeological evidence.

Ancestral cults are observable from mortuary rituals. During the early Yangshao period, the deceased members of a community were normally buried in single or collective burials in cemeteries, and both primary and secondary interments were practiced. The dead appear to have been worshipped in groups, and no apparent economic differentiation is archaeologically visible in grave furnishing. This pattern is exemplified by the Longgangsi site of the early Yangshao culture in south Shaanxi, where the entire cemetery was surrounded by sacrificial pits, and no particular individual was ritually treated differently

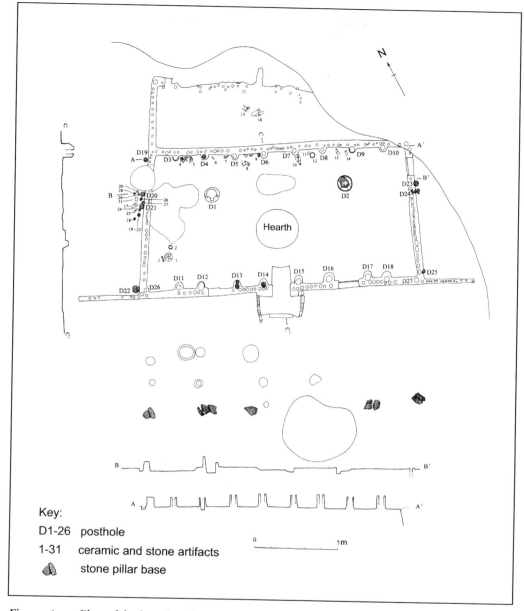

Figure 6.12. Plan of the large building F901 at Dadiwan in Qin'an, Gansu; late Yangshao period (redrawn from figure 2 of Lang, S. 1986).

from others. This pattern indicates the ongoing existence of group-oriented ancestral cults, focused on the interests of the entire community, which had been continuously practiced from the early Neolithic period on, as exemplified by the Shuiquan site of the Peiligang culture (Lee, Y. and Zhu 2002; Liu, L. 2000a).

Group-oriented ancestral cults are also seen in many middle Yangshao culture cemeteries, where secondary collective burial was practiced (Figure 6.10).

The Shijia site in Shaanxi, for example, revealed that deceased persons with consanguineal relationships were interred together in the same grave, ranging from family to lineage in a patrilocal community. The sex ratio among skeletons is heavily biased, however, against females, particularly in the middle-aged and older groups, meaning that many females were excluded from the death ritual because they married into other communities (Gao, Q. and Lee 1993). Although the dead were still venerated in groups, it appears that fewer females became ancestors, probably because they held little importance economically and politically in their natal kin communities. This phenomenon signifies a starting point in the archaeological record, when people began to treat some of their dead forebears differently in ancestral cult rituals, even though their societies were still egalitarian in nature (Liu, L. 2000a).

In contrast to the group-oriented ancestral cults, which were widespread over large regions of the Yangshao culture, Xipo burials reveal a different type of ancestral veneration, more oriented toward individuals. This mortuary pattern also shares some similarities with the Dawenkou burials, which show rather developed hierarchical features.

Religious practice characteristic of shamans, or *wu*, is believed to be revealed in Burial M45 at Xishuipo in Puyang, Henan. A male adult skeleton (1.84 m tall) found in this burial is said to be the physical remains of a Yangshao religious practitioner. This burial also contains three groups of large-scale mosaic images, made from mollusk shells, which are identified as dragon, tiger, deer, spider, bird, and a person riding a dragon (Ding, Q. and Zhang 1989; Sun, D. et al. 1988) (Figure 6.13). The human skeleton, oriented southward, rests in the center of three mosaic images: a dragon to the east, a tiger to the west, and the Big Dipper (formed with human tibias and shells) to the north (Figure 6.13A). This arrangement has been interpreted as an early form of the lunar mansions, probably indicating that Burial M45's occupant possessed some important astronomical knowledge (Feng, S. 1990). This man is also believed to have been a *wu*, shaman, and the associated images are understood to represent animal helpers that assisted the shaman to communicate with the supernatural world (Chang 1988). These two interpretations, one protoscientific and one magical or religious, are nevertheless not contradictory, because *wu* were supposed to be rationally knowledgeable about the supernatural world where they traveled in their ecstatic state. It is notable, however, that, although the burial was elaborate and complex in form, it did not contain any personal wealth or items representing economic privilege. This mortuary practice suggests that the individual who controlled ritual power had not, while living, assumed special economic status in his community that could be expressed posthumously.

Both the Dawenkou and Yangshao cultures show emergent social inequality. Whereas the Dawenkou people seem to have developed more elaborate

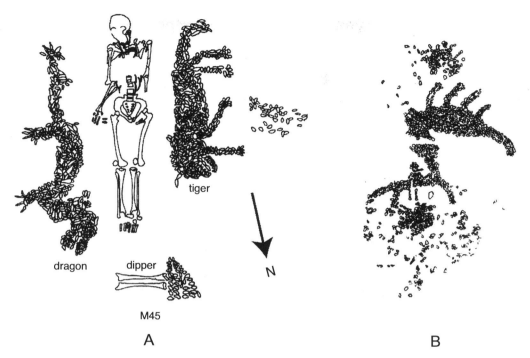

tiger

dragon   dipper

N

M45

A   B

Figure 6.13. Human burial accompanied by shell mosaics from Xishuipo, Henan; Yangshao culture. **(A)** M45: A male skeleton accompanied by dragon, tiger, and the Big Dipper. **(B)** A person riding on a dragon accompanied by a bird and a tiger, among other creatures (after figure 5 of Sun, D. et al., 1988 and figure 4 of Ding and Zhang 1989).

mortuary rituals to express their social differentiations, most Yangshao communities tended to practice rather moderate burial ceremonies and emphasize less the economic wealth of individuals. These general differences between the two regions continued to some extent during the late Neolithic period.

THE YANGZI RIVER REGION

The Yangzi River region also witnessed the full growth of Neolithic farming communities and a rapid increase in population density. Rice agriculture was well established, indicated by findings of rice paddy fields and abundant rice remains. Pigs and dogs were the main domesticated animals. Meanwhile, the abundant wild plants and animals available in this subtropical region continuously formed a large part of the people's diet. Well-preserved archaeological remains have been uncovered from several water-logged sites and provide great opportunities for understanding the socioeconomic development of the middle and lower Yangzi River Valley. Figure 6.14 shows the location of major sites discussed in this section.

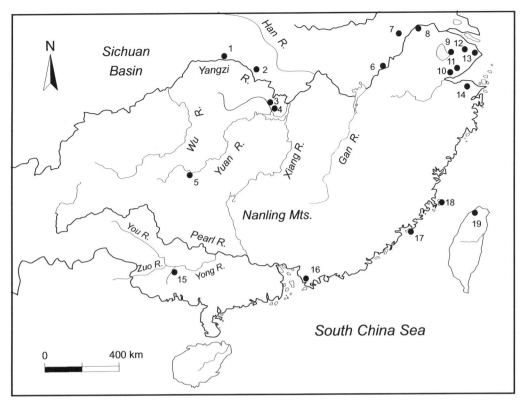

Figure 6.14. Middle Neolithic sites in south China mentioned in Chapter 6. 1: Daxi; 2: Guanmiaoshan; 3: Chengtoushan; 4: Tangjiagang; 5: Gaomiao; 6: Beiyinyangying; 7: Lingjiatan; 8: Xuejiagang; 9: Chenghu, Caoxieshan; 10: Majiabang; 11: Luojiajiao; 12: Chuodun; 13: Songze; 14: Hemudu, Tianluoshan; 15: Dingsishan; 16: Xiantouling; 17: Fuguodun, Jinguishan; 18: Keqiutou; 19: Dabenkeng.

The Middle Yangzi River

Archaeological remains in the middle Yangzi River region are designated as the Daxi culture (ca. 5000–3300), named after the type-site, discovered at Daxi in Wushan, near Chongqing. This culture covers a broad region including the Three Gorges, Jianghan plains and Lake Dongting, and has been further divided into several regional variants, such as the Guanmiaoshan in the north, and the Tangjiagang in the south, which were closely related to previous local cultural traditions (Figures 6.1 and 6.14). Several hundred Daxi sites have been identified, of which many measure 5–15 ha in size. The lithic assemblages are predominantly ground tools, with a few chipped stones, such as choppers and scrapers. Ceramics are mostly red in color, some with painted patterns, and are often tempered with fibers or sand. The proportion of black pottery increased over time, and some elaborate white pottery vessels have been found at Tangjiagang and Gaomiao in Hunan (Figure 6.15). Some settlements were

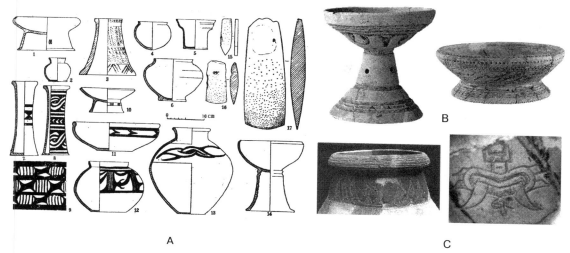

Figure 6.15. Daxi culture ceramics. (A) Major pottery types from Daxi. (B) White pottery vessels from Tangjiagang. (C) Motifs on white pottery from Gaomiao (after figure 41 of Zhongguo Shehui Kexueyuan 1984 and Hunansheng 1999: 22, 28).

surrounded by moats, a tradition continued from the previous Bashidang site (see Chapter 5) (Zhang, C. 2003: 39–47; Zhongguo Shehui Kexueyuan 2010: 414–18).

The Liyang Plain in Hunan is one of the areas where Neolithic sites flourished. This region was covered by many river courses; forty-six sites dating to the Daxi culture have been located, compared to seventeen sites belonging to the previous Lower Zaoshi culture in the same area. Settlements show a clear increase in site number and site size, indicating rapid population growth (Pei, A. 2004). Among these sites, Chengtoushan in Lixian (Figure 6.14) has been excavated extensively.

Chengtoushan is located on a flat mound, about 2 m higher than the adjacent land (Figure 6.16). When it was first occupied, ca. 4500 BC, people had begun to build a moat around the settlement, and then constructed a walled enclosure and ditches, measuring about 8 ha in area, ca. 4000 BC. The walls and ditches were subsequently rebuilt many times during the Daxi and Qujialing periods. The ditches were connected with a river to the east of the site, evidently for water transport, an inference supported by discovery of a wooden paddle at the site. Rice paddies and associated irrigation systems were found in the early Daxi deposits, dating to ca. 4500 BC. Abundant organic remains were unearthed from the waterlogged deposits, particularly in the ditches. Within the enclosure, many houses, burials, and kilns were uncovered. A sacrificial altar, about 200 m² in size and made of clean yellow soil, was found in the eastern part of the settlement inside the enclosure. Many pits were distributed over the altar and adjacent areas, and contained human skeletons, burnt clays, ash, pottery, animal bones, or rice. Although most burials yielded no grave offerings and only small numbers of ceramics, one tomb (M678), of which the main occupant was an adult male, was scattered with cinnabar and associated with two jade ornaments, twenty-seven pottery vessels, and a child's skull (Hunansheng 2007). The Chengtoushan people apparently practiced sophisticated ritual ceremonies, and social differentiation had probably emerged. The walled enclosure may have been multifunctional – used as a defensive facility as well as for flood control.

Chengtoushan has revealed one of the earliest rice paddy fields in China, dating to as early as the Tangjiagang culture (ca. 4600 BC) (Figure 6.16). The floral remains are identifiable to seventy-five species. Besides rice, which occurred most frequently in samples, many other edible plants were found, such as water caltrop, Job's tears, gorgon fruit, purple perilla, winter melon, chestnut, peach, plum, and so forth. It is uncertain how many of these plants were domesticated, but it seems that a great variety of food was available to the Chengtoushan people. Faunal remains consist of nearly twenty species/genera of animals, among which pig was definitely domesticated. The wild animals include elephant, water buffalo, and Large Indian Civet, indicating an environment with abundant water and forest resources in the region (Hunansheng and Guoji 2007). Chengtoushan was certainly a sedentary farming community, although people's diet seems to have been composed of many types of wild foods.

The population density of Daxi culture settlements in the middle Yangzi River region was rather high, as judged by the profusion of sites distributed on the Liyang Plain (Pei, A. 2004). Local population growth, resulting from sedentary lifestyle and rice agriculture, may have led to migration southward. Some archaeologists have argued that the concurrence around the Pearl River delta region (also including Hong Kong, Macao, and other islands) of painted and white ceramics similar to Daxi types and also datable to the fourth millennium BC, is attributable to diffusion from the Daxi culture. Likely routes of this putative transfer were probably multiple, such as one which passes through the Yuan River to the Xi River and leads on to the lower course of the Pearl River (He, J. 1996; Tang, C. 2007), or another going through the Xiang River and across the Nanling Mountains into the Lingnan region (Bu, G. 1999).

The Lower Yangzi River

Archaeological cultures in this region are represented by Hemudu (ca. 5500–3300 BC) in the Ningshao Plain, Majiabang (ca. 5000–4000 BC) and Songze (ca. 4000–3300 BC) around the Lake Tai region, and Beiyinyangying (ca. 4000–3300 BC) and Xuejiagang (ca. ?–3300 BC) in the western part of the lower Yangzi River area (Figure 6.1). Rice agriculture was well underway, as indicated by the large quantities of rice grain/chaff remains found at waterlogged sites (e.g., Hemudu, Tianluoshan, and Luojiajiao, all in Zhejiang), the identification

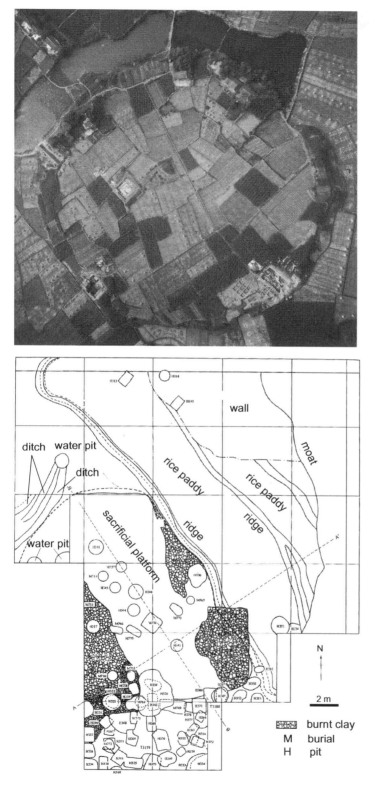

Figure 6.16. Chengtoushan walled site and remains of ancient rice paddies (after color plate 1 and figure 109 of Hunansheng 2007).

of morphologically domesticated rachis on rice spikelet (Zheng, Y. et al. 2007), and rice paddy fields found at four sites. The earliest rice field has been found at Tianluoshan (5000–4500 BC), determined by the presence, in the field deposits, of many husk fragments and spikelet bases of rice, dense bulliform phytoliths derived from motor cells of rice, and a high percentage of grass pollen larger than 38 mm in diameter. High microcharcoal content was also present in the paddy, implying that people used fire in managing these fields (Zheng, Y. et al. 2009). Three other sites include Caoxieshan in Wuxian, Chenghu in Suzhou, and Chuodun in Kunshan, all in Jiangsu province, dating to ca. 4000–3200 BC (Figure 6.14). The paddies vary in size and shape, and often were situated near ponds and wells, from which water was channeled by irrigation systems, such as ditches (Ding, J. and Zhang 2004; Li, C. et al. 2007; Zou, H. et al. 2000).

Craft specialization was highly developed and was exemplified by elaborate jade objects found in many sites. Jade ritual paraphernalia is often associated with the small number of well-furnished large burials, suggesting elite control of ritual power. Among these archaeological discoveries, the Hemudu culture and the Lingjiatan site provide the best examples for understanding the overall development of this region.

Hemudu culture sites are mainly distributed in the east coastal area, and are particularly concentrated along the Yao River. Two waterlogged sites, Hemudu and Tianluoshan in Yuyao, have been excavated extensively (Figure 6.17). They are located on both sides of the Yao River, 7 km apart, and their occupations were partially contemporaneous. Dwellings were made of wooden pile-structures, in which the timbers show clear traces of mortise-tenon techniques. Thick layers of archaeological deposits contained large quantities of faunal, floral, and human remains. Ceramics are predominantly black and gray, tempered with fiber and/or sand; some are decorated with plant and animal designs. Several wooden paddles have been uncovered, testifying to the long history of water transport in the Yangzi River region. Some spades, made of scapular bones of large animals, are believed to indicate the development of field-tilling technology. Abundant rice remains have been uncovered, identified as both wild and domesticated forms (see Chapter 4). Although rice was consumed as an important staple food, many wild plants were also exploited by the Hemudu people, as indicated by the remains of acorn, water caltrop, wild jujube, gorgon fruit, and Job's tears, among others (Sun, G. and Huang 2007; Zhejiangsheng 2003). The most numerous faunal remains are aquatic animals, particularly fish, shellfish, and turtle; some of these animals were evidently captured from the sea. Among many types of bones from terrestrial animals, those of several species of deer are dominant in quantity. Domesticated animals include pig and dog (Wei, F. et al. 1990). The water buffalo (*Bubalus mephistopheles*) found at Hemudu was once believed to have been domesticated, but recent research, based on zooarchaeological and ancient DNA analyses,

Figure 6.17. Hemudu culture in Zhejiang. 1: Landscape of the Tianluoshan site; 2: excavation at Tianluoshan; 3: pottery decorated with pig image (Hemudu); 4: bone spade (Hemudu); 5: wooden paddle (Tianluoshan) (1: courtesy Sun Guoping; 2: author's photo; 3 and 4: color plates 14–2 and 26–1 of Zhejiangsheng 2003; 5: figure 17 of Sun, G. and Huang 2007).

suggests otherwise (see Chapter 4) (Liu, L. et al. 2004; Yang, D. et al. 2008). It is more likely that people relied primarily on wild food resources, even though domestication of plants and animals was already well established. This situation resembles that in the contemporary middle Yangzi River region.

The Hemudu culture seems to have been rather egalitarian in nature, with little evidence of social stratification in material remains. Recent excavation, however, of a Songze culture site at Dongshancun (ca. 3800 BC) in Zhangjiagang city, Jiangsu province, has revealed clear evidence of social differences in mortuary practice. At this site, the residential area is situated in the center, with two cemeteries located to the east and west. The cemetery to the east contained 27 small tombs associated with a total of 140 grave goods, and the one to the west consisted of nine large tombs, each revealing more than thirty grave items. The largest tomb (M90) had sixty-seven items of grave offerings, including jade, ceramic, and stone artifacts. Such a segregated mortuary arrangement at Dongshancun provides the earliest known evidence for the emergence of social stratification in Neolithic China (Zhou, R. et al. 2010).

Early Hemudu (ca. 5000–3900 BC) deposits have been found at only four sites along the Yao River Valley, but the late Hemudu period (ca. 3900–2900 BC) is represented in nearly forty sites distributed over a much larger region. These changes suggest rapid population growth during the fourth millennium BC, a dynamic also linked with the dispersal of Hemudu material culture to some islands along the southeast coast, exemplified by finds from the Keqiutou site in Pingtan Island, Fujian (Figure 6.14). Several factors may be responsible for the migration of the Hemudu population. First, the rise of sea level around 4000 BC led to ecological degradation, which may have forced the Hemudu people to find new resources elsewhere. Second, the longstanding traditions of constructing inland watercraft and exploiting freshwater aquatic resources may have encouraged the Hemudu people to migrate across the sea. This migration may have been the initial population movement, through seafaring, which later gave birth to the Austronesian expansion (Wang, H. and Liu 2005) (see later in this chapter in the section on South China).

Lingjiatan (ca. 3600–3300 BC) is located in Hanshan County, Anhui province. The 160 ha site, measuring about 5 km long north to south and 200 m wide east to west, lies in low mountainous terrain, which is an extension of the Taihu Mountains to the north, and the Yuxi River runs west to east to the south of the mount. At the central part of the site, on the highest spot, is a burial complex consisting of a large platform (1,200 m²) made of layers of soil and pebbles, several round or rectangular stone altars, sacrificial pits containing pottery vessels, and many burials. More than fifty tombs have been excavated, revealing large numbers of jade and stone objects; but little organic material has survived due the acidic soil conditions. In Tomb 07M23, for example, a total of 330 items of grave offerings were unearthed, including 200 jade objects (Figure 6.18) (Anhuisheng 2006; Zhang, J. 2008).

The burials appear to have been arranged in several groups, associated with grave offerings varying in quality and quantity, suggesting pronounced mortuary stratification. Some jade-bearing tombs have also revealed evidence of jade making, including a sandstone drill and numerous jade wasters, indicating that elite individuals were involved in jade manufacturing. Burials containing the most elaborate and the largest quantities of grave goods (likely the high elite) tend to be grouped in the southern part of the cemetery; those with the most jade wasters (probably representing craftsmen) appear to be concentrated in the northwestern part, and tombs in the north yielded few grave goods (these tombs were perhaps those of lower status individuals). The jade manufacturing area at Lingjiatan has not been excavated, but jade production there was specialized. The manufacturing techniques are astonishing: One of the holes drilled on a human figurine measures only 0.17 mm in diameter, and many artifacts show traces of manufacture by use of emery wheels. The production

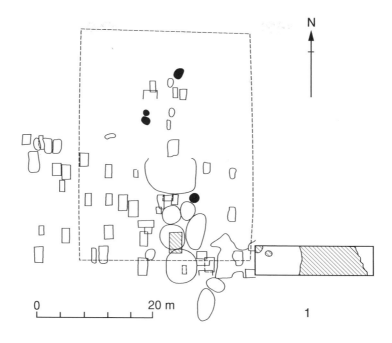

Figure 6.18. Lingjiatan cemetery and jade artifacts unearthed. 1: Distribution of burials at Lingjiatan; 2: human figurine; 3: dragon; 4: plaque; 5: bird with pig-head wings; 6: turtle shells (after color plates 20–1, 21–1, 157–2, 199–2, 201 of Anhuisheng 2006).

was probably also intensive, as suggested by the discovery of 111 jade cores, the debris from coring holes on jade objects, at Tomb 98M20 (Anhuisheng 2006).

Lingjiatan jade/stone objects are rendered in various forms, including *yue* axes, *bi* discs, *huang* pendants, and *jue* earrings, as well as a small number of human and animal figurines. Six jade human figurines (7.7–9.9 cm high) are depicted in either standing or sitting positions with their arms folded upward on the chest. A jade bird, with an octagonal star (probably representing the sun) carved on its chest, is portrayed with open wings (8.4 cm wide), with the heads of pigs emerging from the tips of the wings. A jade dragon is shown with the head biting the tail, so the body forms a circular shape with a hole in the center, and the mane runs along the entire back of the body (4.4 × 3.9 cm in diameter). A turtle, made of two pieces of jade (9.4 cm long), has a jade plaque (11 cm long) inserted between its shells. The plaque, convex in shape, is incised with a complex geometrical design showing an octagonal star in the center. Three jade tubes with oval-shaped cross sections, each containing one or two jade sticks, are thought to imitate turtles and used for divination. Animal forms depicted on other jade items include bird, cicada, rabbit, pig, and tiger; most are portrayed in schematic styles (Figure 6.18) (Anhuisheng 2000, 2006; Zhang, J. 2008).

Numerous publications have attempted to interpret the meanings of the jade objects from Lingjiatan (e.g., Anhuisheng 2000; Zhang, J. 2006). Most scholars believe that some animal figurines and the geometric patterns on some jades held cosmological significance: Thus, the jade turtlelike tubes containing sticks are divination devices, and the jade human figurines depict images of religious practitioners. Many studies have focused on the jade turtle–plaque set. For example, Li Xinwei (2004) has argued that the convex-shaped plaque probably symbolized the domed heaven, and the design on the plaque, including an octagonal star (symbolizing the sun or polestar), may represent the universe, as conceived by Neolithic people. These jade objects were most likely used by elite individuals as ritual paraphernalia, a situation resembling that observed in the contemporary Hongshan culture of the Liao River region (see summary in Liu, L. 2007).

The pottery assemblage from Lingjiatan seems rather unique; although it shares some common elements with other sites, it cannot be likened stylistically to the ceramics of any contemporary cultures in the surrounding areas. In contrast, some jade ornaments similar to *huang* pendants and *jue* earrings from Lingjiatan have been frequently found in the archaeological record of the Yangzi River Valley (Anhuisheng 2006). Therefore, it is possible that some Lingjiatan jades were exported to other communities, probably through exchange networks.

Lingjiatan evidently assumed a special status in the region: It was a center of jade manufacturing and ritual ceremony, the elite may have held unique ritual power suited for communicating with supernatural realms, and jade was apparently the crucial medium through which that power was enabled to reach the required destinations. Nevertheless, as excavations to date have focused only on the cemetery, we know little about the residential area of the Lingjiatan site or the settlement patterns of the region, which are crucial factors for understanding the social organization of the Lingjiatan settlement and of the larger region.

Ritual Power

As most explicitly expressed at the Lingjiatan burial site, ritual activities and the related artifacts, often manifesting a cosmological awareness, may have been closely related to the development of agriculture, which required close observation of celestial phenomena and an understanding of astronomy. The Hongshan and Yangshao cultures also show similar traits.

Several features of jade figurines were shared by cultures in both the lower Yangzi and Liao River Valleys: The posture of the standing Lingjiatan human figurines is remarkably similar to that of their Niuheliang counterpart (standing with arms folded on the chest); jade birds (many are owls) and turtles are common to both regions; and a cosmological concept, round heaven and square earth, was expressed in the stone cairns and altars at the Hongshan ritual sites, and in the jade turtle and plaque from Lingjiatan (Li, X. 2004).

These phenomena suggest that some cultural contacts, direct or indirect, between these two regions occurred during the late fourth millennium BC. These contacts and their material manifestations served as vehicles for the diffusion of both cosmological knowledge and certain forms of elite behavior in prehistoric China.

SOUTH CHINA

In South China, Neolithic cultures are characterized by several regional developments, referred to as Dingsishan Phase IV in Nanjing, Guangxi, Keqiutou in the coastal region of Fujian, Xiantouling in the Pearl River delta, and Dabenkeng in Taiwan (Zhongguo Shehui Kexueyuan 2010: 497–505) (Figure 6.14).

Neolithic remains identified as Dingsishan Phase IV are distributed in Guangxi province, a region where early Neolithic settlements were predominantly shell middens and cave shelters, representing a hunting–gathering and fishing way of life (see Chapter 5). Only a few sites dating to ca. 4000–2000 BC have been found in this region, located on hill slopes, river terraces, and caves, where they appear to have been occupied by people who adopted rice agriculture. This change in subsistence economy is indicated by the disappearance of shell middens and the presence of a wide range of tools, including agricultural implements, and ceramic vessel types such as white pottery (Zhongguo Shehui Kexueyuan 2010: 500–2). Phytolith remains from Dingsishan also show that domesticated rice certainly occurred at the site around 4000 BC, signifying the beginning of agriculture in this region (Zhao, Z. et al. 2005). The shift from hunting-gathering to agriculture appears to have been provoked by the introduction of rice farming from elsewhere, rather than by local development. The ceramics show similarities with both the Daxi culture in the middle Yangzi River and the Xiantouling culture in the Pearl River delta region, suggesting cultural interactions on a broad regional level. Although it is still unclear whether this shift in subsistence strategy was due to the introduction of new population or new technology, we cannot rule out the possibility that it was partially a result of the migration of rice-farming communities from the middle Yangzi River region, where population pressure was building up during the Daxi period.

The Keqiutou culture sites (4500–3000 BC) are distributed on off-shore islands, represented by shell middens at Keqiutou in Pingtan, Fuguodun and Jinguishan in Jinmen. These sites show well-developed Neolithic traits, such as pottery and ground stone tools, which had no local origins. Keqiutou (ca. 4500–3000 BC) pottery is handmade, with low temperature firing. The major vessel forms are jars, plates, and bowls, with small numbers of pedestal cups. Shell impressions, dot impressions, incision, and cord marking are the most common types of decoration. The lithic industry is characterized by flake tools and small stone adzes with polished edges. On the basis of stylistic comparison of artifacts, archaeologists have argued that Keqiutou was an immigrant culture of Hemudu (Jiao 2007; Wang, H. and Liu 2005). The ceramics from Fuguodun are decorated with wavy lines, dotted lines, and shell impressions. Fuguodun's early date (ca. 4700–4000 BC) and the similarities of its pottery with that of the Dabenkeng culture in Taiwan have led some archaeologists to believe that the two cultures were related (Hung 2008; Jiao 2007).

The Xiantouling culture (ca. 4000–3000 BC) was named after the discovery of the type-site at Xiantouling in Shenzhen in the 1980s (Peng, Q. et al. 1990). Subsequent archaeological work has revealed a number of sites in the Pearl River delta region, including Hong Kong and Macao, which share similar material traits with Xiantouling. These sites are either sand dunes or shell middens, and were probably occupied as seasonal camps. The toolkit consists of both chipped and ground stone tools. The pottery is mostly handmade, low-temperature fired, and sand-tempered *fu* caldrons and *guan* jars, with small proportions of basins, plates, and pedestal cups. Pottery decorations include red painting, cord markings, incisions, and shell impressions. There are also some white pottery vessels, which, together with the painted pottery, are seen as an influence of the middle Yangzi region (Figure 6.19) (Zhongguo Shehui Kexueyuan 2010: 497–500).

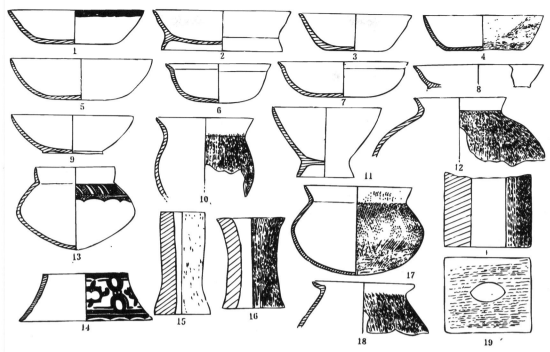

Figure 6.19. Pottery assemblage from Xiantouling, Shenzhen. 1, 2, 4, 5, and 7: *Pan* plates; 3, 8, and 9: bowls; 6: basin; 10 and 18: *guan* jars; 11: *dou* pedestal cup; 12, 13, and 17: *fu* cauldrons; 14: ring-foot plate (foot with open work and painted in red); 15, 16, and 19: stands (after figure 9 of Peng, Q. et al. 1990).

Neolithic cultures in the southeast coastal regions show strong maritime subsistence orientation and apparently well-developed seafaring capabilities. It has long been argued that the earliest Neolithic assemblages in Taiwan, known as the Dabenkeng culture (ca. 4000–2500 BC) (Figure 6.1), originated in the southeast coastal areas of mainland China, including the Fujian and Guangdong regions (e.g., Chang 1964; Jiao 2007; Tsang 2005). This argument has been continuously supported by archaeological evidence that shows that similar cultural traits occurred on both sides of the Taiwan Strait. These traits include cord-marked pottery with comb and shell-edge patterns on the rims, pecked pebbles, polished adzes, projectile points with holes in the center, grooved beating sticks for making bark cloth, perforated shark teeth used as ornaments, the custom of tooth extraction, and sand dunes and shell middens as locales of settlement (Figure 6.20) (Chang and Goodenough 1996; Hung 2008; Tsang 1992). Most scholars have reached consensus that the Neolithic peoples from the southeast coastal regions were the ancestors of the Austronesian speakers, who first migrated to Taiwan and then eventually colonized the Pacific region, known as the expansion of Austronesians (Bellwood 1995; Goodenough 1996). The origins of this population expansion may be traced back to the southward population movement from the middle and lower Yangzi River Valleys during the fourth millennium BC.

CONCLUSIONS

More than twenty years ago, Chang observed two developmental trends during the fourth millennium BC. The first is that all regional cultures became more extensively distributed, and interaction among them was intensified; the second is that each region's Neolithic culture became increasingly complex, leading to the foundation of a distinct civilization in each region. He described such an interlinked regional cultural development as "the Chinese Interaction Sphere," or "the Longshanoid Horizon," which is particularly characterized by the wide distribution of two types of vessels, *ding* tripods and *dou* pedestal cups. These pottery forms appear to have spread from the Yellow River Valley to the south in the archaeological record (Chang 1986a: 234–42).

Two decades later, as more archaeological data have become available to us, we are now able to draw further insights into social changes during the fifth and fourth millennia BC. The three most important issues relating to this period are (1) the emergent elite authority expressed in ritual power, (2) the formation of ideological systems on an interregional scale, and (3) population expansion as the result of the long development of sedentary agriculture.

Kin-based and economically self-contained villages were the basic social unit, although communities were interrelated by the exchange of utilitarian goods, such as stone tools. During the fifth millennium BC, most of these farming communities were egalitarian in nature, but this situation gradually changed in the following millennium. Some individuals may have acquired certain political roles and possessed special social status, because of their knowledge of astronomy, medicine, and agriculture or their ability in performing rituals. Social stratification appears to have emerged in some areas, as indicated by hierarchically organized settlement patterns, the construction of large public buildings, social differentiation in mortuary practice, and elite control over production and distribution of prestige goods, such as jades.

The arts, including painted or carved images and other types of ritual paraphernalia, were closely related to matters of ideological concern, such as cosmological knowledge, ancestor worship, fertility cults, and supernatural powers of animals. Although each region appears to have developed its own belief system, certain elements were shared by communities cross-regionally in ritual contexts, such as images of dragonlike creatures, turtles, birds, circles and square shapes, and so forth. The exchange of artistic items or ritual paraphernalia associated with certain ideological dimensions appears to have been one of the most important forms of regional interaction at this time. Elite individuals may have controlled both ritual knowledge and the production and

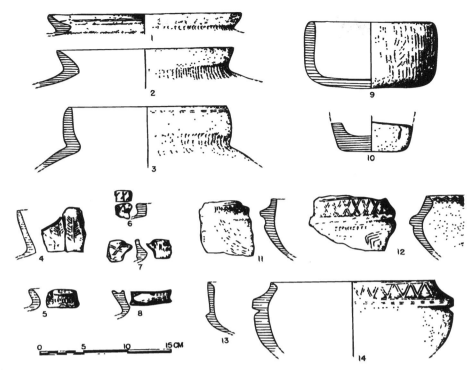

Figure 6.20. Cord marked and incised pottery from Dabenkeng, Taiwan (after figure 82 of Chang 1969).

distribution of ritual paraphernalia, particularly jade objects. They also may have been responsible for the exchange of ritual knowledge on an interregional basis, leading to the formation of some common beliefs over a vast area, as shown in the archaeological record (Li, X. 2004).

Population dispersion was a common phenomenon in both north and south China. Whereas the Yangshao culture first spread northward to Inner Mongolia and later westward to the upper Yellow River regions, the Daxi and Hemudu cultures expanded southward to the Pearl River and the southeast coastal regions. These Neolithic farmers apparently moved to new territories in search of arable land, bringing their technology and knowledge of agriculture, but they seem to have inevitably adapted to the local environment in their new homelands. This fact is well illustrated by the strong hunting–gathering components in the Yangshao culture sites in Daihai, Inner Mongolia, and the hunting–fishing economy in the southeast coastal sites, which may have had ancestral links with the agricultural population in the Yangzi River regions. It is unclear, however, to what extent, in each case, such subsistence changes were the result of the migrants' adaptation to a new ecological system or were due to influences received from the preexisting indigenous peoples in these regions, no matter how small these populations may have been.

The material similarities in the archaeological record, such as pottery types, ornamental motifs, decorations, and jade forms, resulted from various modes of human interaction, direct and indirect. This trend of development continued during the third millennium BC, which will be discussed in the next chapter.

CHAPTER 7

RISE AND FALL OF EARLY COMPLEX SOCIETIES: THE LATE NEOLITHIC (3000–2000 BC)

When Yu assembled the States on mount Tu, there were 10,000 States whose princes bore their symbols of jade and offerings of silk.

Chapter, "Duke Ai, 7th Year" (489 BC), in *The Zuo Zhuan* (compiled 475–221 BC), translated by James Legge (1960a)

禹会诸侯于涂山，执玉帛者万国。〈〈左传·哀公七年〉〉

During the third millennium BC, intensive farming became widespread along the Yellow and Yangzi River regions, where we also see the highest population densities and the most developed complex societies in the archaeological record. In contrast, hunting-gathering communities, sometimes incorporating low-level food production, appear to have continuously dominated the landscapes in many other areas, such as the Northeast, Xinjiang, most areas in the Tibetan Plateau, and some parts of South China.

In the highly populated regions, some major social changes took place. Most of these societies were hierarchically organized, exchange of prestige goods was a common practice among elite individuals, and intergroup warfare intensified. Political control, ritual power, and material wealth were closely related and concentrated in small groups of elites. Regional centers were frequently built with walled enclosures, and some developed early forms of urbanism with political, religious, and economic functions. In ancient Chinese texts the polities in the Yellow River region have been referred to as "myriad (literally, 'ten thousand') states" prior to the first dynasty, the Xia.

Compared to the previous periods, there are much greater amounts of data available for the late Neolithic, and it is impossible to describe archaeological findings in detail for each region. In this chapter, we will provide an overview of archaeological information, with emphasis on those regions that show greater social changes. The distribution of late Neolithic cultures and major sites are shown in Figures 7.1 and 7.2, and the chronology in Table 7.1.

The major issues concerning this period include the impact of ecological changes, settlement patterns, population movement and growth, warfare,

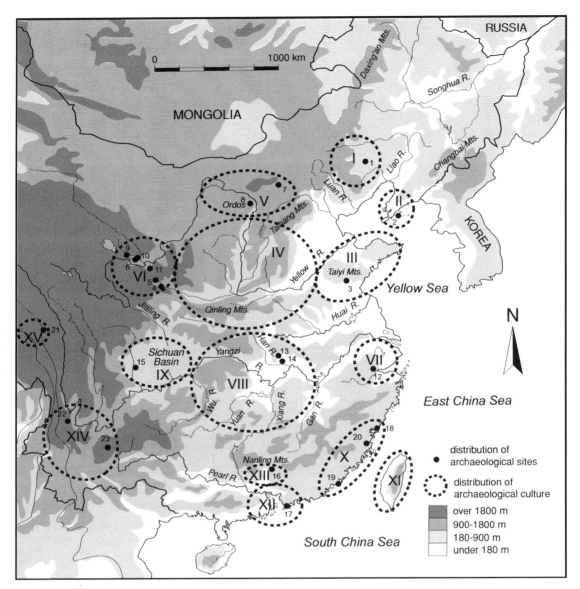

Figure 7.1. Distribution of late Neolithic cultures. I: Xiaoheyan; II: Upper Xiaozhushan; III: Late Dawenkou-Shandong Longshan; IV: Longshan; V: Laohushan; VI:
Majiayao; VII: Liangzhu; VIII: Qujialing-Shijiahe; IX: Baodun; X: Tanshisan; XI:
Yuanshan; XII: Yonglang; XIII: Shixia; XIV: various Neolithic assemblages in Yunnan; XV: Karuo. Distribution of archaeological sites. 1: Xiaoheyan; 2: Xiaozhushan;
3: Dawenkou; 4: Shilingxia; 5: Majiayao; 6: Machang; 7: Laohushan; 8: Dakou;
9: Liuwan; 10: Yangshan; 11: Banshan; 12: Liangzhu; 13: Qujialing; 14: Shijiahe;
15: Baodun; 16: Shixia; 17: Yonglang; 18: Huangguashan; 19: Damaoshan; 20: Tanshishan; 21: Karuo; 22: Haimenkou; 23: Shizhaishan.

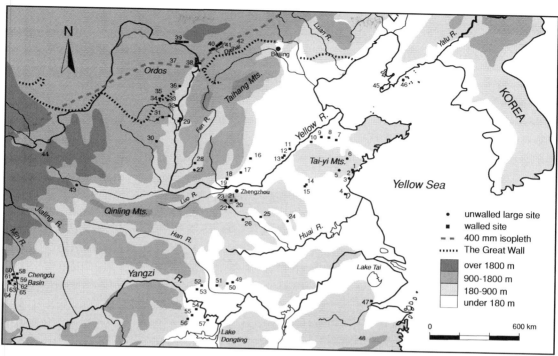

Figure 7.2. Distribution of major sites and walled settlements mentioned in the text, the third millennium BC. The Yellow River and Liaodong: 1: Dantu; 2: Liangchengzhen; 3: Yaowangcheng; 4: Tenghualuo; 5: Lingyanghe; 6: Chengzi; 7: Bianxianwang; 8: Tonglin-Tianwang; 9: Dinggong; 10: Chenziya; 11: Jiaochangpu; 12: Wangzhuang; 13: Jingyanggang; 14: Xuegucheng; 15: Xikangliu; 16: Hougang; 17: Mengzhuang; 18: Xijincheng; 19: Xubaocun; 20: Guchengzhai; 21: Xinzhai; 22: Wadian; 23: Wangchenggang; 24: Yuchisi; 25: Pingliangtai; 26: Haojiatai; 27: Zhouji-azhuang; 28: Taosi; 29: Houzhaizimao, Guanhugada; 30: Lushanmao; 31: walled sites in the Dali River Valley; 32: Shilouloushan; 33: Shimao; 34: Huoshiliang; 35: Xinhua; 36: Zhaimao; 37: Zhukaigou; 38: walled sites in the Qingshui River Valley; 39: walled sites south of the Daqing Mountains; 40: walled sites in the Daihai Lake region; 41: Shihushan; 42: Miaozigou; 43: Shizhaocun, Xishanping; 44: Dongxiang; 45: Guojia-cun; 46: Xiaozhushan, Wujiacun. The Yangzi River: 47: Mojiaoshan; 48: Haochuan; 49: Menbanwan; 50: Taojiahu; 51: Shijiahe; 52: Majiayuan; 53: Yinxiangcheng; 54: Jimingcheng; 55: Jijiaocheng; 56: Chengtoushan; 57: Zoumaling; 58: Gucheng; 59: Yufucheng; 60: Mangcheng; 61: Shuanghe; 62: Zizhucun; 63: Baodun; 64: Yandian; 65: Gaoshan.

TABLE 7.1. *Chronology of the late Neolithic cultures in China*

Region	Culture	Chronology (BC)
Liao River	Xiaoheyan	3000–2600?
Liaodong Peninsula	Upper Xiaozhushan	2200–2000
Lower Yellow River	Late Dawenkou	3000–2600
	Shandong Longshan	2600–1900
Middle Yellow River	Early Longshan	3000–2500
	Late Longshan	2500–2000/1900
Upper Yellow River	Shilingxia	3980–3264
	Majiayao	3300–2500
	Banshan	2500–2300
	Machang	2300–2000
Daihai-Ordos region	Laohushan	2500–2300
	Dakou I	ca. 2000
Lower Yangzi River	Liangzhu	3300–2000
Middle Yangzi River	Qujialing	3400–2500
	Shijiahe	2600–2000
Upper Yangzi River	Baodun	2800–2000
	West Xiajiang	ca. 2000
Tibet	Karuo	3300–2300
South China	Shixia, Guangdong	3000–2000
	Yonglang, Pearl R. Delta	3000–2000
	Tanshishan, Fujian	3000–2000

exchange system, religion and ritual practice, technology, and status symbols and social hierarchy. We will also address factors that may have caused the development and decline of some complex societies. In recent years, many archaeologists have focused on the nature of late Neolithic cultures, namely, whether these societies were early states. This issue deserves some extended discussion, which will be presented in Chapter 8.

THE YELLOW RIVER VALLEY

The Yellow River Valley has long been a focus of the research of late Neolithic cultures, primarily because this region witnessed the rise of the first dynasties of China, known as the Xia, Shang, and Zhou. Archaeological cultural developments can be divided into three general areas: (1) the late Dawenkou-Shandong Longshan culture in the lower Yellow River, (2) the Longshan culture in the middle Yellow River, and (3) Majiayao-Banshan-Machang in the upper Yellow River (Figure 7.1).

The lower Yellow River Region

The lower Yellow River region is often referred to as the Haidai region, where the Dawenkou culture (late phase, 3000–2600 BC) and subsequent Longshan culture (2600–1900 BC) are distributed in Shandong, eastern Henan, northern Anhui, and northern Jiangsu (Luan 1997; Shandongsheng 2005: 126–274).

Settlement patterns: Population growth from middle Neolithic to late Neolithic is clearly indicated by a general trend of increase in number of sites from the Dawenkou culture (547 sites) to the Longshan culture (1,492 sites) in Shandong (Guojia 2007). This growth is particularly rapid during the late Dawenkou and Longshan period. Some twenty walled sites have been reported, but only seven have been confirmed by excavation (Figure 7.2). The earliest one, Dantu in Wulian, was built in the late Dawenkou and continued to be used until the mid-Longshan. Others were constructed during the Longshan period, and some lasted until the Yushi period (1900–1500 BC) (Luan 2006). Regional centers, some of which were walled, were often distributed at regular distances (ca. 30–50 km) from each other. The settlement patterns, together with archaeological evidence of increased warfare and violence against humans, indicate a competitive relationship between regional polities (Liu, L. 2004: 192–207; Underhill 1994; Underhill et al. 2008).

Recent full-coverage regional surveys in southeastern Shandong provide detailed and systematic information for understanding changing settlement patterns. Population growth is clearly shown in the number of sites, which increase from 2 for the Beixin period to 27 for the late Dawenkou, and then to 463 for the Longshan. Settlement distribution for the Longshan period also shows processes of nucleation of sites centered in two large settlements, Liangchengzhen (272.5 ha) and Yaowangcheng (367.5 ha), representing two coexisting polities. Each is characterized by a four-level settlement hierarchy, but there are different patterns of settlement around the large centers: The settlement system centered in Liangchengzhen is more nucleated than that in Yaowangcheng. This pattern may represent diverse strategies of elite control in the two polities (Underhill et al. 2008).

Some regional centers appear to have been locales for craft production, making both utilitarian and prestige goods. Recent excavations at Liangchengzhen, for instance, have shown compelling evidence for stone tool production (Bennett 2001; Cunnar 2007). Prestige objects, such as jade and eggshell pottery, may also have been manufactured at the site (for references, see Liu, L. 2004: 108). These phenomena suggest that the nucleation of population toward large centers was partially attributable to the development of craft specialization and production at these locations.

Recent studies have shown that salt making near the Bohai Bay can be traced back to Neolithic times. There are rich deposits of underground brine along the coastline in the southwestern part of the Bohai Bay, and this region was a major salt production area in antiquity. Some fifteen Dawenkou sites were distributed along the coastline dating to 4500–3000 BC. This area has poor soil and is not suitable for agriculture. Archaeological remains indicate that some structures, such as pits filled with ash and showing traces of burning, appear to have been used as salt-making facilities. Stone/jade objects and painted pottery artifacts unearthed from some sites (e.g., Wucun in Guangrao County) were evidently obtained from elsewhere. These remains indicate that salt making was already a specialized production and salt was an exchange item in the Dawenkou period. During the Longshan period, a dozen small sites were distributed in the lowland area along the coastline, coinciding with the distribution of underground brine. Four walled sites – Chengziya, Dinggong, Tonglin, and Bianxianwang – spaced equidistantly, were located on the inland alluvial plains to the north of the Taiyi Mountains. The coastal sites are rather small (1–2 ha) in size, and may have been seasonally occupied for making salt and affiliated with the inland regional centers (Wang, Q. 2006b). Therefore, the competitive relationships between these walled centers may have related to the control of natural resources (such as salt) for trade.

Mortuary patterns: The Dawenkou culture is well known for its burials with many elaborate grave goods, including such items as jades, ivory objects, fine pottery vessels, pig mandibles, deer tusks, and so forth (Gao, G. 2000; Shao, W. 1984). Drinking and serving vessels often assume large proportions of the grave goods. At the Lingyanghe burial site, 663 drinking goblets were found in 45 tombs, accounting for 45 percent of the entire amount of grave goods. In Tomb M25, for example, more than thirty goblets among seventy-three vessels were associated with a male occupant (Figure 7.3) (Wang, S. 1987). The burial patterns manifest a particular cultural tradition, in which feasting was an important part of mortuary practice, and social stratification was explicitly expressed in mortuary display (Fung, C. 2000; Keightley 1985; Underhill 2000, 2002).

This mortuary tradition continued in the Longshan period, as suggested by the rich assemblages of grave goods associated with elite tombs, with drinking and serving vessels accounting for significant proportions of the grave-goods assemblages. Typical prestige items in mortuary contexts include finely made black eggshell pottery goblets, jades, alligator drums, pig skulls/mandibles, and so forth. At several burial sites, such as Chengzi in Zhucheng (Du, Z. 1980), archaeological remains show nonrandom patterns as evidence of ancestral renovation in mortuary activities: Offerings were continuously made to certain tombs from the time of burial onward. Ancestral worship ritual also became intertwined with hierarchical social systems: The ancestors were individuals who both held ascribed high social status and enjoyed political, religious, and economic prestige in certain families and lineages. Ancestral cult ritual became a part of the political institutions and reinforced the stratified, but still kinship-based, social system (Liu, L. 2000a).

Residential patterns: Excavations at Yuchisi (2800–2600 BC) in Mengcheng, Anhui, have revealed a well-preserved late Dawenkou village (Zhang, L. and Wang 2004; Zhongguo Shehui Kexueyuan 2001). Several houses yielded excessive numbers of ceramic vessels, which probably indicate

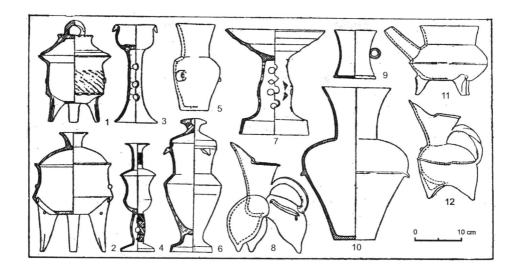

A

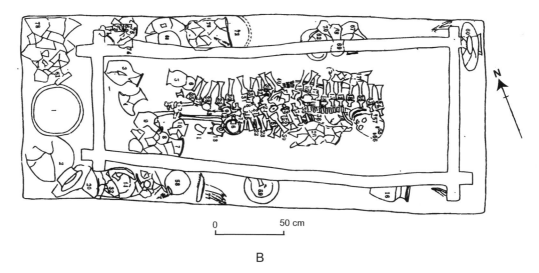

B

Figure 7.3. Late Dawenkou mortuary goods and burial custom. (**A**) Ceramic types. 1 and 2: *ding* tripods; 3 and 4: *gaobingbei* goblets; 5: *hu* jar; 6: *ping* jar; 7: *dou* pedestal plate; 8 and 12: *gui* vessels; 9: *bei* cup; 10: *hu* jar; 11: *he* vessel (after Shao, W. 1984: 90). (**B**) Burial M25 from Lingyanghe, showing abundant grave goods, including more than thirty goblets, mostly placed on top of the skeleton (after Wang, S. 1987: 71).

frequent feasts conducted by these households (Liu, L. 2004: 96–100). It has been observed in many complex societies in the world that feasting is a part of competitive emulation behavior adopted by ambitious individuals to gain and maintain power and prestige (Dietler and Hayden 2001). Such behavior seems to be most clearly manifested in both mortuary and residential data of the Dawenkou culture.

Signs and symbols: More than twenty pictographs, identifiable to eight types, have been found on *dakouzun* urns dating to the late Dawenkou period. *Dakouzun* is a type of large vessel, sometimes containing animal bones and usually found in burials and houses, and its function may have been related to certain ritual activities. In addition, pottery sherds carved with multiple characters have been uncovered from Dinggong in Zouping (Shandong) and Longqiuzhuang in Gaoyou (Jiangsu) (Figure 7.4), all dating to around 2000 BC. The nature of these inscriptions on pottery is a controversial issue. As for the pictographs on *dakouzun* urns, some scholars have insisted that these are writing and comparable to characters and clan emblems on oracle-bone and bronze inscriptions, but others believe that these are only signs or marks with specific meanings. Some scholars have attempted to decipher the scripts from Dinggong but have reached no consensus as to their meaning (Feng, S. 1994; Keightley 2006; figure 323 of Longqiuzhuang 1999; Shandongsheng 2005: 201–4, 278; Yang, X. 2000: 68–72).

Decline: The Longshan culture in the Haidai region declined around 2000 BC, as indicated by a marked drop in the number of settlements and the disappearance of most regional centers, suggesting a decrease of population density and political complexity. The reduction of population began during the late Longshan phase in some areas (e.g., Liangchengzhen in southeastern Shandong), whereas regional centers continued to function throughout the subsequent Yueshi culture in other regions (e.g., Chengziya in northern Shandong). There is also evidence for the Dawenkou population moving toward the west, as many late Dawenkou sites appeared in northeast Anhui and central Henan during the early part of the third millennium BC (Chen, H. 2007; Liu, L. 2004: 185–8). The exact causes for these changes are still unclear. They could be both natural and human-induced disasters, which are unlikely to have been a single catastrophic event.

The Middle Yellow River Valley

This broad region has great diversity in topography and vegetation coverage. It includes Henan, southern Hebei, southern Shanxi, and central Shaanxi provinces (Figure 7.1). The archaeological culture is generally divided into early (or Miaodigou II) and late Longshan periods. More than ten regional variations based on ceramic typology have been classified, and are often referred to as different *leixing*, meaning "types" or "variants."

There was a dramatic increase in population density. The results from a nationwide survey project show that the numbers of sites in Henan, Shanxi, and Shaanxi provinces increased from 800, 716, and 2,040 for the Yangshao period (total of 3,556) to 1,000, 1,102 and 2,200 for the Longshan period (total of 4,302), respectively (Guojia 1991, 1999, 2006) (Figure 7.5). Considering that the Yangshao culture lasted twice as long as the Longshan culture, the actual

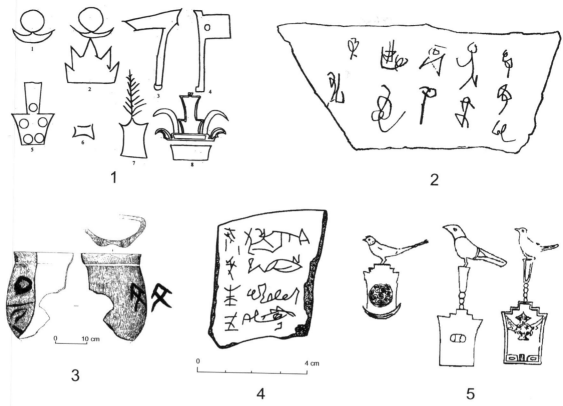

Figure 7.4. Signs and symbols found on pottery and jade objects, late Neolithic. 1: Symbols on Dawenkou *dakouzun* urns; 2: inscription on a potsherd from Dinggong, Shandong; 3: characters on a pottery from Taosi, Shanxi; 4: inscription on a potsherd from Longqiuzhuang, Jiangsu; 5: pictograms on Liangzhu jade objects (1: after figure 75 of Shandongsheng 2005; 2: after figure 1 of Feng 1994; 3: after figure 1 of Feng 2008; 4: after figure 323 of Longqiuzhuang 1999; 5: after Ren 1996: 327).

rate of population growth from Yangshao to Longshan should have been much greater than the numbers shown here.

Settlement patterns show three tiers of site hierarchy in most areas, and at least nine fortified regional centers have been found, all in Henan and southern Shanxi (Figure 7.2) (Liu, L. 2004: 159–91). In the Central Plain, regional centers are normally no more than 50 ha in size and distributed in a nearly equidistant pattern over the landscape, suggesting competitive relationships among the polities. One of the examples is Wangchenggang in Dengfeng, Henan. In the more environmentally circumscribed region, such as the Linfen Basin in Shanxi, the Taosi site emerged as a large regional center, which may have dominated the entire basin for several hundred years. These sites are situated in the region where the earliest dynasties emerged subsequently; therefore, archaeologists are particularly interested in the development and historical affiliations of the large walled sites discovered there.

Wangchenggang is located on a terraced area in the floodplain of central Henan. The site has a long occupational history, from the early Neolithic to the Bronze Age. During the Longshan period, this region was characterized by a multicentered competitive settlement system, in which some centers were enclosed by rammed-earth fortifications. Wangchenggang (ca. 2200–1835 BC) was such an enclosed site, and served as the settlement center for twenty-two unwalled sites distributed in the upper Ying River Valley. At Wangchenggang two connected small rammed-earth enclosures (ca. 1 ha each) were built around 2200 BC, and a large enclosure (35 ha) was constructed by ca. 2100–2050 BC. Many ash pits, some containing human sacrifices, were unearthed at the site. This site was also a craft-production center, to judge by stone drills and blanks, uncovered there, for making spades, axes, knives, and sickles (Beijing and Henanshang 2007; Henansheng Wenwu Yanjiusuo 1992).

Some scholars have argued that Wangchenggang's location coincides with Yangcheng, the capital city said to have been established by Yu the Great, who founded the Xia dynasty, according to textual accounts. Since the discovery in 1977 of small internal enclosures, suggesting a segregated ruling elite, Wangchenggang often has been regarded as the ancestral place of the Xia dynasty (Henansheng Wenwu Yanjiusuo 1992). The recent discovery of the large urban enclosure has promoted a new interpretation – that the small enclosures were built by Gun, the legendary father of Yu the Great, and the large town walls by Yu himself (Beijing and Henanshang 2007: 789–91). Nevertheless, such an attribution fails to explain a gap of some 100 years between the two constructions at Wangchenggang.

Taosi (2600–2000 BC) represents the most complex regional center in the middle Yellow River Valley. It is situated on sloping land to the north of the Chong (Ta'er) Mountains in the middle of the Linfen Basin, which is bounded by mountain ranges on all sides. Taosi (300 ha) was a major center during the late Longshan period, surrounded by a number of smaller sites, together forming a three-tiered settlement hierarchy (Liu, L. 1996b). The occupation can be divided into three phases: early, middle, and late, each lasting about 200 years. A rammed-earth enclosure (56 ha) was built during the early phase, and a much larger enclosure (289 ha) was constructed in the middle phase (Figure 7.6). Social stratification is clearly visible in the archaeological record. More than 1,000 excavated burials can be classified into three ranks. The majority were small tombs that had few or no grave goods; in contrast, the large tombs (<1%) were associated with hundreds of items, including elaborate pottery, jade, alligator drums, stone and wooden artifacts, and exotic ritual goods for ceremonial purposes (Figure 7.7). Among jade items, *cong* tubes and *bi* discs share designs similar to those from many other regions, as far as the Liangzhu culture in the lower Yangzi River Valley (see later in text). The elite families lived in palatial structures that were separated, by walled enclosures, from the

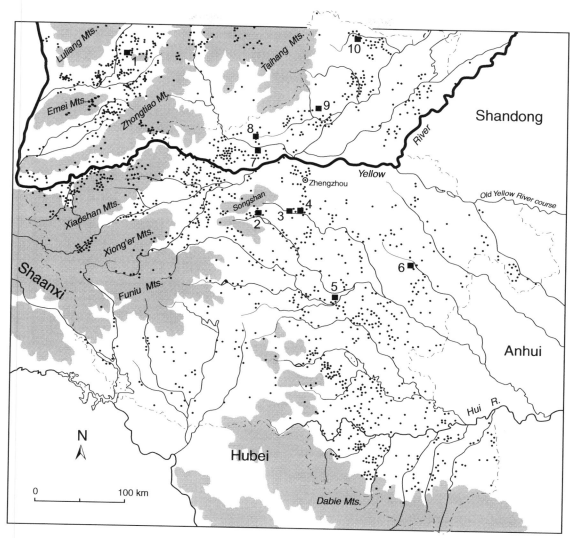

Figure 7.5. Distribution of Longshan sites in Henan, southern Shanxi and western Shandong. Walled sites: 1: Taosi; 2: Wangchenggang; 3: Xinzhai; 4: Guchengzhai; 5: Haojiatai; 6: Pingliangtai; 7: Xubao; 8: Xijincheng; 9: Mengzhuang; 10: Hougang; 11: Jingyanggang.

commoners who dwelt in semisubterranean houses and earthen shelters (Liu, L. 1996a, 2004; Yan, Z. and He 2005).

Several other discoveries at Taosi also make this site unique. A group of rammed-earth terraces and square-shaped columns (IIFJT1) has been found in the small enclosure, dating to the mid-Taosi phase (Figure 7.6). The rammed-earth structures formed a semicircular plan in correlation with a circular central point also made of rammed earth (Figure 7.7). Standing at the central point, one can observe the sunrise from the Chong Mountains in the southeast

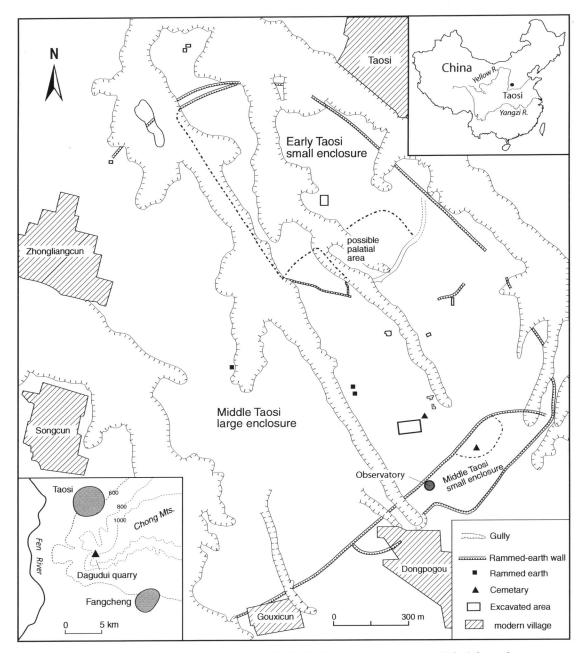

Figure 7.6. The Taosi site, late Neolithic Longshan culture (modified from figure 1 of Yan, Z. and He, N. 2005).

through the narrow gaps between rammed-earth columns, and some gaps appear to correspond to the positions of sunrise in certain calendrical cycles. The entire construction measures about 1 ha in area, and has been identified as an astronomical observatory for defining seasonal changes (He, N. 2007a). This interpretation has been strongly supported by astronomers (Liu, C. 2009;

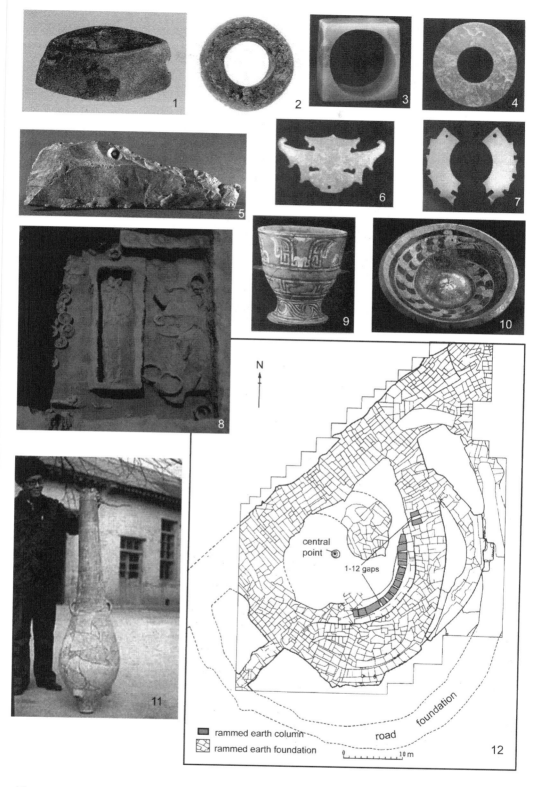

Figure 7.7. Artifacts and features unearthed from Taosi, late Longshan period. 1: Copper bell; 2: bronze object attached to a jade disc; 3: jade *cong* tube; 4: jade *bi* disc; 5: chime stone; 6 and 7: jade ornaments; 8: elite burial; 9 and 10: polychrome ceramics; 11: ritual object (function unknown); 12: plan of the Observatory (after and modified from color plates in Xie, X. 2007; Guojia 2002: 27; and figure 7 of He, N. 2007a).

Wu, J. et al. 2008), although some archaeologists are skeptical. A recent discovery of a lacquer pole (180 cm in length) from a large tomb (IM22) has been identified as gnomon shadow template used to measure the solar shadow of spring equinox, autumn equinox, and winter solstice during the middle Taosi period (2100–2000 BC) (He, N. 2009), further suggesting that the Taosi elite is likely to have been involved in astronomical observations. If these conclusions are reliable, this structure is the earliest observatory in China. As seasonal changes were crucial moments for Neolithic farming societies, by which to schedule their agricultural activities, the Taosi elite may have held great ritual power by possessing astronomical knowledge needed to determine the calendar. Therefore, the importance of this site was also attributable to its ritual function.

Taosi is one of the Neolithic sites at which the earliest copper/bronze objects have been found in China. A copper bell, probably made of piece-mold techniques, was unearthed from a small tomb (Zhang, D. 1984), a gear-shaped arsenic bronze object attached to a jade *yuan* disc was discovered in a medium-sized burial (Guojia 2002: 27), and a fragment of rim probably from a basin was uncovered from a palatial foundation (He, N. et al. 2008); all date to the late Taosi phase. It is unclear, however, whether these metal objects were locally made or obtained through exchange. It is also notable that at this time metal was not a part of the regular inventory of prestige goods revealed in elite burials. The practice of using bronze objects as the most important status symbols did not develop until several hundred years later in the Erlitou culture (Allan, S. 2007). Two glyphs painted in red pigment were found on a pottery vessel (Figure 7.4). A number of interpretations have been proposed for these glyphs. He Nu suggests that one of the characters is Yao, who is a legendary predynastic king (He, N. 2007b), and Feng Shi identifies the two characters for *wen yi* and believes that they refer to the name of a capital of the Xia Dynasty (Feng, S. 2008).

Taosi was also a stone tool-manufacturing site, where a large number of tool blanks and manufacturing tools (e.g., hammer-stone) have been unearthed. A quarry also has been found at Mount Dagudui, 7 km south of Taosi (Figure 7.6). The tool types identified at the Dagudui quarry clearly resemble those found at Taosi, including both utilitarian tools (spade, axe, wedge, chisel, large knife, and so forth) and ritual objects (chime stone) (Tao, F. 1991; Wang, X. et al. 1987). The Taosi elite may have controlled access to the raw material at Dagudui; the lithic manufacturing appears to have been carried out by many households in this walled settlement, and the products were used for exchange with surrounding communities (Zhai, S. 2011).

All these discoveries at Taosi indicate that the site was the most important economic, political, and religious center of the region, engaged in craft production and witnessing the emergence of elite groups. It shows characteristics of early urbanism, but its political domination was probably limited to the area within the Linfen Basin, circumscribed by mountain ranges. To the south of the Linfen Basin, the Yuncheng Basin also witnessed rapid settlement nucleation and the rise of a large center at Zhoujiazhuang in Jiangxian during the Longshan period. This site, measuring more than 200 ha in area, was fortified by ditches and surrounded by many smaller settlements. Contemporaneous with Taosi, Zhoujiazhuang appears to have been another regional center in southern Shanxi (Dai, X. et al. 2009; Drennan and Dai 2010).

Taosi seems to have experienced some political turmoil during its late phase. The large, rammed-earth enclosure was destroyed; the palatial area of the early phase became a craft production area, for the making of stone and bone artifacts, particularly bone arrowheads; many human skeletal remains near the palatial area show evidence of violence; finally, some elite burials were broken into and disturbed (Liu, L. 2004: 109–13; Yan, Z. and He 2005). These changes coincided with the emergence of another large site at Fangcheng (230 ha) in the south of the Chong Mountains (Figure 7.6), suggesting the intensification of intergroup conflict in the basin (Liu, L. 1996b). It is unclear, however, what the social organization was at this settlement during the late Taosi phase. None of the large burials is dated to this phase, but the settlement appears to have been densely populated and stone tool production continued.

By the beginning of the second millennium BC Taosi was abandoned and the regional settlement system disappeared from the archaeological record. The process and cause of the collapse of this urban settlement are unclear, but some scholars have suggested that the Taosi site was destroyed by floods around 2000 BC (Xia, Z. and Yang 2003). It remains to be investigated whether Taosi experienced a gradual decline during its late phase or suddenly ended with a catastrophic event some 4,000 years ago.

Some Chinese archaeologists have attempted to link Taosi with prehistoric kings, such as Yao and Shun, two of the legendary so-called Five Emperors (*Wudi*), whose activities were recorded to have been in the southern Shanxi region, according to ancient texts (see Xie, X. 2007). The observatory identified at Taosi has been said to reflect Yao's achievement in astronomy, also mentioned in ancient texts (He, N. 2004). In our view, these legendary accounts were recorded more than a thousand years later than the Taosi culture, and therefore should not be used to determine Taosi's historical affiliation.

Social organization: Longshan regional centers apparently show different levels of social complexity. One interesting phenomenon is the variability in settlement and mortuary patterns between Taosi and Wangchenggang. The Taosi site, on the one hand, represents a society where social hierarchy and individual status were clearly expressed in mortuary practice. The Wangchengang site, on the other hand, is a good example of many walled settlements in the Henan region, where no evidence for elaborate elite burials has been found. Such a striking contrast should not be dismissed simply as a result of insufficient archaeological work; it may be related to different leadership strategies used by the Longshan elite (see discussion in Liu, L. 2004: 249–51).

The Northern Zone

The Northern Zone includes northern Shanxi, northern Shaanxi, and central-southern Inner Mongolia; and much of the region is referred to as the Ordos Plateau (Figure 7.1). There are also several regional cultural variants, as defined by ceramic typology, and archaeological remains dating to the late Longshan period are generally referred to as the Laohushan (2500–2300 BC) and Dakou (ca. 2000 BC) cultures. This region consists of various geological configurations, including the Loess Plateau, mountain ranges, lakes, desert, and alluvial plain in the bend of the Yellow River. It is a transitional area between arid north and warm-temperate south, and has been environmentally sensitive and ecologically fragile regarding climatic change. Several episodes of climatic fluctuation during the Holocene have been recorded (Guo, L. et al. 2007; Xiao, J. et al. 2006), and these changes often coincide with the rise and fall of human populations in the region (Tian, G. and Guo 2004).

Subsistence economy: The earliest agricultural population appearing in this region was from the fifth millennium BC when the Mid-Holocene Climatic Optimum arrived. This situation is likely to have been a result of the northward expansion of the Yangshao culture from the densely populated Central Plain. The rich natural habitation there may have been a great attraction to the Yangshao culture migrants, and agricultural villages soon spread over the region. The archaeological record shows over time a general trend toward a decline of wild animals, but domestic animals, particularly grazing animals, increased in proportion and taxon. In central-southern Inner Mongolia, for example, faunal remains from Shihushan (ca. 4500 BC) near the Daihai Lake have revealed fifteen wild species, including water buffalo. Domestic pig and dog account for only 10 percent of the total faunal NISP (number of identified specimens) (Huang, Y. 2001). After 1,000 years in the same region, the faunal assemblage from Miaozigou in Huangqihai (3500–3000 BC) contains only seven wild species, while domestic pig and dog increased in proportion to 23 percent of the total NISP (Huang, Y. 2003). In the Ordos region, faunal assemblage from Huoshiliang (ca. 2150–1900 BC) in Yulin, northern Shaanxi, has revealed nineteen species, with wild animals accounting for only 19 percent of NISP. Domesticated animals (81% of NISP) are mainly sheep/goats (59.22%), followed by pigs (12.62%) and cattle (8.74%) (Hu, S. et al. 2008). Huoshiliang is the first site indicating the rise of pastoralism in the region. This pattern continued at Zhukaigou (2000–1500 BC) in Yijinhuoluo Banner; where the faunal assemblage consists of only six wild species (8%), while sheep/goats (41%) and cattle (24%) outnumber pigs and dogs (28%) in the total NISP (Figure 7.8).

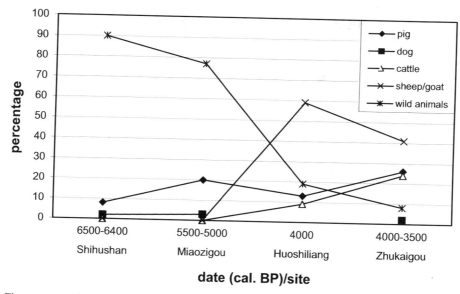

Figure 7.8. Changing ratio between wild and domestic animals in faunal assemblages in the Northern Zone during the Neolithic and early Bronze periods.

Other artifacts also show interesting changes in this region. In central-southern Inner Mongolia, ceramic cooking vessels were characterized by flat-bottomed pots during the Yangshao period; but this tradition completely changed during the Longshan period when *jia* and *yan* tripods became the cooking utensils (Tian, G. 1991a,b). This change not only may reflect a cultural influence from the Central Plain, but it may also imply a change in the kinds of staple food being consumed. In addition, grinding stones (the *mopan-mobang* complex) were common at most sites dating to the fourth and third millennia BC. At Shihushan I in Liangcheng (early Yangshao period), for example, grinding stones (55) account for 35 percent of the total tools (157), and acorn (*Quercus* sp.) remains have been identified (Tian, G. and Akiyama 2001: 71–5). In contrast, during the Longshan period, the *mopan-mobang* grinding stone complex markedly declined in number, but several sites have revealed earthen mortars on house floors, which presumably were used together with wooden pestles (Tian, G. and Guo 2004). Although no use–wear or residue analyses have been applied to these tools, this pattern of decline in grinding stones seems parallel to the situation in the Central Plain. As demonstrated in several studies, the *mopan-mobang* complex appears to have been used mainly for processing acorn in other regions (e.g., Liu, L. et al. 2010a,b,c; Yang, X. et al. 2009). In contrast, ethnographic data show that the mortar–pestle complex is an effective tool for dehusking cereals (Yin, S. 1996). One possible explanation for the change in toolkits in the Northern Zone is that the nut-collecting economy was gradually replaced by cereal farming there. Further functional studies on pottery and tools are warranted to understand these shifts in material culture.

All these changes indicate a general trend toward intensive agriculture and pastoralism in the Northern Zone during the third millennium BC. This situation probably resulted from multiple causes, such as overexploitation of natural resources by humans, reduction of natural habitation of wild animals due to hunting and intensive farming, human population growth, and climatic deterioration toward the end of the Mid-Holocene Climatic Optimum.

Fortifications: During the Longshan period, some sites became fortified with stone walls. There are four areas where the fortifications were concentrated (Figure 7.2). First, more than twenty fortified sites have been found in northern Shaanxi, spread over an area including the modern counties of Wubu, Hengshan, Zizhou, Shenmu, and Jiaxian. The earliest examples date to the late Yangshao period and the latest ones to the Shang dynasty, but the majority belongs to the Longshan period. These sites are usually located on hilltops near rivers, and stone walls were constructed on the top of natural cliffs to protect the settlements (Figure 7.9). The walled sites were often surrounded by smaller nonwalled sites, suggesting that these fortifications probably offered protection to the population in the adjacent areas. Discovered only in recent years, these sites have not been fully reported, and it is expected that more of such fortifications will be found (Shaanxisheng 2005; Wang, W. and Ma 2006). The second cluster consists of five fortifications together with at least six nonwalled sites, dating to the early Longshan period, in the Qingshui River area, at the northeast bend of the Yellow River. The third concentration of walled settlements, dating to the early Longshan period, is distributed along the southern foothill of the Daqing Mountains to the north of the Yellow River. At least thirteen fortified sites in five groups (2–4 sites in each group) were built in a linear pattern, about 5 km from each other. The fourth group consists of ten sites around the Daihai region, dating to the late Longshan period. Seven fortifications have been found on the southern side of the Man-han Mountains, west of the Daihai Lake (Han, J. 2003; Tian, G. 1993; Wei, J. and Cao 1999) (Figure 7.2).

These fortifications are distributed roughly along the 400 mm precipitation isopleth, which divides China into two parts: the southeast monsoon region and the northwest inland region. Interestingly, these sites are also situated in the region of the Great Wall, which was built in the historical period and demarked the two ecological zones, agricultural and pastoralist (Figure 7.2). The changing strength of the summer monsoon would have had a significant effect on temperature and precipitation. The Daihai region experienced a cold-dry period during 2450–2150 BC (Xiao, J. et al. 2006), an event which coincided with the presence of the stone fortifications in the Laohushan culture there. The construction of these fortifications may have been the result of intergroup conflict, which was at least partially caused by climatic fluctuation and deterioration of the ecosystem, coupled with population pressure.

A　　　　　　　　　　　　　　B

Figure 7.9. Stone fortifications in northern Shaanxi. (**A**) Landscape (bottom right) and the stone wall of the Jinshanzhai site in Hengshan, early Longshan period. (**B**) Landscape of the Guanhugada site in Wubu, middle-late Longshan period (after Shaanxisheng 2005).

Social organization and prestige goods: We do not have enough data for a discussion of social organization in this region; but, given that building stone fortifications and intergroup warfare would have required management and leadership, there may have been well-developed social stratification in some of the communities there. A further indication of the existence of a high level of social complexity is the large numbers of jade objects (many are nephrite) found at several sites in northern Shaanxi, such as Lushanmao in Yan'an city and Shimao and Xinhua in Shenmu County. The major forms include axes, knives, *yazhang* blades, *cong* tubes, *bi* discs, and various pendants (Yang, Y. 2001). Most jade objects were accidentally found by the locals rather than excavated by archaeologists, but the recent excavation at Xinhua in Shenmu provides a rare opportunity to understand the function of jade objects there. At the Xinhua site, thirty-two pieces of jade (mostly actinolite, tremolite, and serpentine) were uncovered from cache 99K1, including *yue* axes, *chan* spades, *dao* knives, *fu* axes, *huan* rings, *huang* pendants, and *zhang* blades. In the middle of the cache were also found some bird bones. Many jade items are thin, some only 2–3 mm in thickness, and without a sharp cutting edge, indicating their nonutilitarian function. This cache was surrounded by a dozen burials, suggesting that these jade objects were probably used in a ritual event associated with the burials (Shaanxisheng and Yulinshi 2005). No jade source has been identified in northern Shaanxi, and the geology in this region does not provide conditions for forming nephrite (Huang, C. and Ye 2006). Therefore, it is unclear where the jade raw material came from and where the artifacts were made.

Some jade items are similar in form to those from other parts of China, such as *cong* tubes, *bi* discs, and *yazhang* blades, suggesting that some specific knowledge and belief systems associated with these ritual objects were shared among elite individuals cross-regionally. The Northern Zone was apparently part of a much larger system of regional interactions.

The Upper Yellow River

Much of the upper Yellow River region was occupied by the Majiayao culture (3300–2000 BC), distributed in Gansu, Ningxia, Qinghai, and part of Sichuan (Figure 7.1). This culture, characterized by its painted pottery, was first discovered by Andersson in the 1920s and identified as the Yangshao culture in Gansu. It was then thought to have been the result of cultural diffusion from the west and to have given rise to the painted pottery of the Yangshao culture in the Central Plain (Andersson 1925). Subsequent archaeological investigations later indicated, on the contrary, that the Majiayao culture was a regional development of the Yangshao culture originating in North China and particularly related to the Miaodigou variant, through the intermediate Shilingxia phase (See Chapter 1). To date, more than 1,400 Majiayao culture sites have been identified, and some 20 have been excavated. The Majiayao culture is often divided into three phases: Majiayao, Banshan, and Machang. The distribution of Shilingxia and Majiayao sites shows a trend toward settlements spreading from east to west through time, reflecting a gradual expansion of population toward the west (Xie, D. 1986; Zhongguo Shehui Kexueyuan 2010). The development of the Majiayao culture may have been partially the result of population pressure in the Yangshao culture heartland during the Mid-Holocene Climatic Optimum, leading to the exploitation of new farming land in the surrounding, less populated regions.

The subsistence of the Majiayao culture is characterized by agriculture and hunting-gathering. At Linjia in Dongxiang, Gansu (ca. 2900–2700 BC), for example, stone and pottery knives, similar to those from the Yangshao culture, were numerous; but bone knives inserted with microblades, which are normally associated with hunting-gathering activities, were also found. Large quantities of broomcorn millet and hemp seeds were unearthed from storage pits, and domesticated animals included pigs and dogs. Many species of wild animals were hunted, including deer, wild pig, antelope, and beaver (Guo, D. and Meng 1984). Remains of cattle and sheep/goats also have been uncovered from several sites, sometimes as burial offerings, reported as domesticates (Gesangben 1979; Qinghaisheng Wenwu Guanlichu 1978), but these claims have not been confirmed.

The agricultural activities seen in the Majiayao culture were apparently a continuation of the Yangshao cultural tradition, but the Majiayao culture's strong hunting-gathering components and possible practice of pastoralism are likely to have been an adaptation to the dryer and colder environment there. Similar to the situations in the Northern Zone and Liao River Valley, farming and pastoralism have dominated northwestern China alternatively throughout history.

Most sites excavated are burial sites, which have often yielded large quantities of pottery vessels as mortuary offerings (Figure 7.10A). Although most burials were associated with grave goods, there seems to have been a tendency toward increased inequality through time, in terms of differences in quantity and types of grave goods in burials. At Liuwan in Ledu, Qinghai, for example, more than 11,000 vessels were unearthed from 872 burials of the Machang phase. The wealthiest tomb was M564, which contained an adult male and ninety-five pots, mostly *hu* jars painted with various geometric patterns (Qinghaisheng and Zhongguo 1984). At Yangshan in Minhe, Qinghai, the rich burials contained not only pottery vessels but also objects indicating ritual power or high social status, such as pottery drums, large stone axes, and marble tubes and beads (Qinghaisheng Wenwu Kaogu 1990).

At the Yangshan cemetery, twelve sacrificial pits were found, some containing animal bones, pottery sherds, or rocks of different sizes, and some also showing traces of burning. Most of the pits (10 of 12) are placed in close proximity to two elite burials, which contained ritual paraphernalia (pottery drums). Some of the sacrificial pits date up to 200–300 years later than these burials (Qinghaisheng Wenwu Kaogu 1990). These data indicate that sacrificial offerings were made especially for the two elite tombs and that ritual observances may have been continuously conducted from the time when the drum-bearing tombs were constructed until a period after the cemetery ceased to be active as a burial site. It is conceivable that the individuals in the tombs surrounded by sacrificial pits represent chieftainly figures of the community, who were remembered and venerated as ancestors by the descendants (Liu, L. 2000a).

Large quantities of elaborately painted pottery of the Majiayao culture are intriguing, and interpretations have been proposed from various aspects, ranging from subsistence economy to human mentality. Li Shuicheng (1998), for instance, links the development of painted pottery with the distribution of early agricultural populations. Allard (2001) believes that the painted *hu* jars from burials were symbolic storage vessels used in funerary occasions for status competition. Keightley (1987) groups all the pottery types from northwest China, including the Majiayao culture, into one category of less articulated shape or function, as compared with more elaborate and refined types from eastern China. The characteristics of these cruder types of pottery from northwest China, according to Keightley, suggest less developed social differentiation among people.

Artistic representations on pottery provide tantalizing information for exploring ancient belief systems. A pottery jar from Liuwan portrays a human figure with both female breasts and a male genital. A pottery basin from Banshan in Guanghe (Chang 1995) and a jar from Shizhaocun in Tianshui (Zhongguo Shehui Kexueyuan 1999a), both in Gansu and dating to the Banshan phase, are decorated with human figures, the bodies of which were drawn in the X-ray style (Figure 7.10B,C). These forms of images have been interpreted as shamanistic representations (Chang 1995).

The upper Yellow River region is also characterized by its function as a trade route connecting the East with the West, known as the Hexi Corridor, which later formed a part of the Silk Road. It witnessed cultural influence from all directions in antiquity. At Xishanping in Tianshui, Gansu, for example, six species of domesticated cereals have been uncovered. Based on accelerator mass spectrometry (AMS) dates from carbonized seeds, rice, foxtail millet, broomcorn millet, and oats appear to have been cultivated around 3000 BC, and wheat and barley cultivation occurred by 4600 BC (Li, X. et al. 2007). These crops, except for the millet, originated outside this region – rice from the Yangzi River Valley and wheat, barley, and oats from West Asia. This finding at Xishanping marks the earliest occurrence of West Asian cereals in China, and it is also the first time that we see such various crops appearing all together at one site (see also Chapter 4). As Xishanping is located in the Hexi Corridor, the presence of these crops at the site suggests that this region was already a pivot of intensive interactions between different cultures in the third millennium BC.

The Majiayao culture has gained the honor of being the source of the earliest bronze object found in China – a tin alloyed bronze knife was unearthed at Linjia in Dongxiang, Gansu (ca. 2900–2700 BC). More copper and bronze items also have been found at sites in Gansu dating to the Machang period (2300–2000 BC) (Sun, S. and Han 1997). If bronze metallurgy was introduced from Central Asia, as many have believed (e.g., Mei 2000), this technology may have first arrived in the upper Yellow River region (more discussion on metallurgy in Chapter 9).

NORTHEAST CHINA

The Northeast, also called Manchuria in English, consists of Liaoning, Jilin, and Heilongjiang provinces. Whereas agriculture flourished over the inlands of the Yellow River, a hunting-gathering subsistence economy persisted in varies degrees in coastal areas and more arid regions farther north. In the Liaodong peninsulas, tool assemblages are predominantly of hunting, fishing, and gathering equipment, but reaping knives, a typical type of harvesting tool, and millet remains appeared around 3000 BC at the Xiaozhushan site. The population of the Liaodong peninsula appears to have been in frequent contact with the Longshan culture in Shandong, as suggested by the eggshell pottery and jade objects unearthed in Liaodong, which resemble their counterparts in

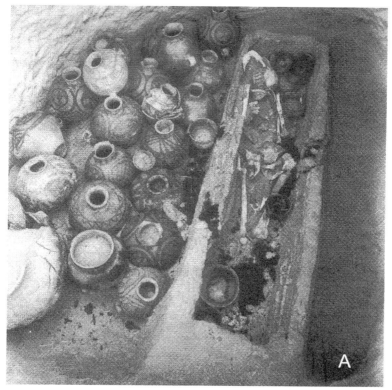

Figure 7.10. Majiayao culture remains. (A) Burial M895 from Liuwan in Qinghai, Machang phase. (B) Human figure in X-ray style on a pottery jar, from Shizhaocun, Banshan phase. (C) Human figure with bisexual features on a *hu* jar, from Liuwan, Machang phase (A and C: after color plate 2 and plate 14 of Qinghaisheng and Zhongguo 1984; B: after color plate 2 of Zhongguo Shehui Kexueyuan 1999a).

Shandong (Liu, L. 1996a). Liaodong is also a cultural pivot point that links the Central Plain with the Korean peninsula, and many shared material traits can be found in the two regions (Nelson 1993).

In the western part of the Liao River Valley, the Hongshan culture was succeeded by the Xiaoheyan culture, which shows a marked decline in population density and in the level of social complexity. The subsistence economy was primarily hunting-gathering, indicated by the absence of reaping knives and the presence of hunting-gathering tools, such as arrowheads and microblades (Li, X. 2008: 117–31). Similar to the Northern Zone, the western Liao River region is also sensitive to climatic change. The shift from Hongshan to Xiaoheyan represents a cyclic alternation between agriculture and the hunting-gathering way of life, which has later been repeated throughout history.

Farther north in the floodplains and mountainous regions – including the Jichang region, Songnen Plains, and Changbai Mountains – hunting, fishing, and gathering continued throughout the third millennium BC. Agriculture was not introduced into this region until some time after 2000 BC (Jia, W. 2007). It is interesting to note that many shell midden sites in the Liaodong peninsula, such as Xiaozhushan and Guojiacun, have grinding stones, presumably used for processing nuts and other wild foodstuffs (Liu, L. 2008); in addition, flotation has also revealed small amounts of millet at Xiaozhushan and Wujiacun (Jin, Y. and Jia 2008). These phenomena suggest that the broad-spectrum subsistence economy continued much longer in the Northeast than in neighboring southern regions.

THE YANGZI RIVER REGION

The Yangzi River region used to be regarded as of little importance for the development of Chinese civilization, but many discoveries made in recent decades indicate otherwise. Similar to their counterparts in the Yellow River region, many regional centers here were built with walled enclosures, social hierarchy was clearly expressed in mortuary practice, craft specialization was highly developed, and elite groups engaged in exchange of prestige items. The Liangzhu, late Qujialing-Shijiahe, and Baodun cultures are among the most complex Neolithic societies in the third millennium BC (Figure 7.1).

The Liangzhu Culture

The Liangzhu culture (3300–2000 BC) is distributed in northern Zhejiang and southern Jiangsu, primarily around the Lake Tai area (Figure 7.1). Its remains, characterized by black pottery, were first discovered at Liangzhu near Hangzhou in 1936 and thought to represent a diffusion of the Longshan culture from the Yellow River region (Shi, X. 1938; Xia, N. 1960). Not until the 1970s was the Liangzhu culture recognized as a local development, which was

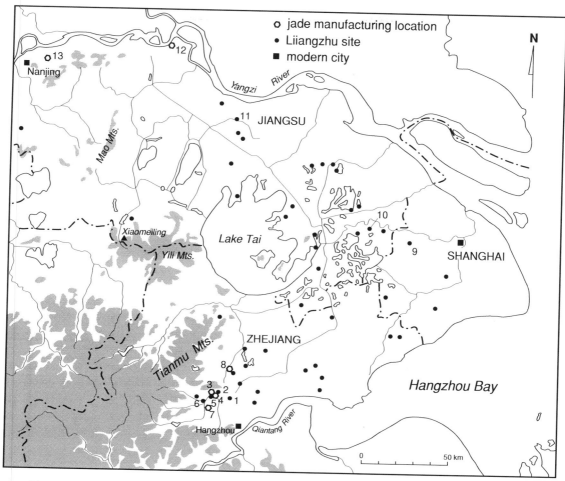

Figure 7.11. Location of major Liangzhu sites that yielded jade artifacts. 1: Liangzhu;
2: Yaoshan; 3: Lucun; 4: Anxi; 5: Mojiaoshan, Fanshan; 6: Huiguanshan; 7: Wenjiashan;
8: Yangdun; 9: Fuquanshan; 10: Zhaolingshan; 11: Sidun; 12: Mopandun; 13: Dingshadi (modified from Xu, Huping 1996: Liangzhu sites map).

contemporary with, and even started slightly earlier than, the Longshan culture
(Xia, N. 1977). To date, more than 200 Liangzhu sites have been recorded,
and many of them are burials that often contained jade artifacts. Numerous
studies have been devoted to Liangzhu remains, particularly its jades (e.g., Xu,
H. 1996; Zhejiangsheng 1999).

Liangzhu sites tend to occur in clusters, each of which seems to have a central
place identified by either large public architecture or elaborate burials. These
centers include Mojiaoshan in Yuhang, Zhaolingshan in Kunshan, Sidun in
Wujin, and Fuquanshan in Qingpu (Zhang, C. 2003; Zhang, Z. 1996) (Figure
7.11).

The Mojiaoshan site cluster has been investigated extensively, revealing
a complex settlement system. Archaeological surveys and excavations have

located 135 sites/locales in an area of 34 km² on the alluvial plains between
the northern and southern ranges of the Tianmu Mountains. Most sites are
small, around 1–2 ha in area, and may have been residential in character; but
several large sites apparently assumed special functions. The major center is
located at Mojiaoshan, which is a man-made terrace, about 10 m high and
30 ha in area. Several rammed-earth architectural foundations, up to 3 ha in
size, have been found on top of the terrace. This locale is most likely to have
been the political center of the site cluster. To the northwest of Mojiaoshan
is a high ranking elite burial site, Fanshan. This is an artificial mount, about
2,700 m² in area and 5 m above the surrounding land, on which 11 tombs
associated with 1,100 jade objects have been found. Mojiaoshan and Fanshan,
together with several smaller sites, are surrounded by a large rammed-earth
enclosure (290 ha). Farther away from the enclosure, there are two sacrificial
altars at Yaoshan and Huiguanshan; both are situated near mountains. These
are rammed-earth terraces built on top of natural mounts, and elite tombs were
dug into the terraces. Several locales may have been craft production centers
for making jade or pottery. Jade raw materials, semifinished jade products,
and manufacturing tools have been found at Lucun and Wenjiashan, and large
quantities of pottery waste products have been unearthed at Changfen and
Hengxuli. To the north of the site cluster is a long wall, 5 km long and 20–50 m
wide, constructed partially with rammed earth and partially with piled-up sand
and pebbles. This wall was built parallel to the Tianmu Mountain ranges, and
no site has been found in the area between the wall and the mountains. Some
archaeologists believe that the main function of this wall was for flood control
(Figure 7.12). These sites are not all contemporary; most datable sites belong
to the middle and late phases (3000–2100 BC), and the wall enclosure dates
to the late phase. A layer of silt has been found on top of the late Liangzhu
culture deposits in many areas around the Mojiaoshan enclosure, suggesting
that the abandonment of these sites may have been related to floods (Liu, B.
2008; Zhejiangsheng 2005a).

Social hierarchy is clearly shown in the mortuary practice. Whereas many
of the small tombs had no grave offerings, the large ones contained up to a
few hundred jade and ceramic objects. At Fuquanshan, four human skeletons,
which were buried in nonceremonial fashion, have been identified as sacrificial
victims (Huang, X. 2000). Numerous jade items have been unearthed from
elite burials at many sites (Huang, T.-m. 1992; Mou, Y. and Yun 1992). Most
jade artifacts are geometrical in form, but some were carved in anthropomorphic and zoomorphic shapes. The typical jade forms are *cong* tubes, which
are square outside and round inside, and *bi* discs. A typical motif, referred to
as human-beast motif, is a recurrent image incised on different types of jade
objects, but more often on *cong* tubes (Figure 7.13) (Wang, M. 1988). Such a
motif depicts a creature with a half human and half animal body; the upper part
is human-like, wearing a large feathered headdress and showing human arms

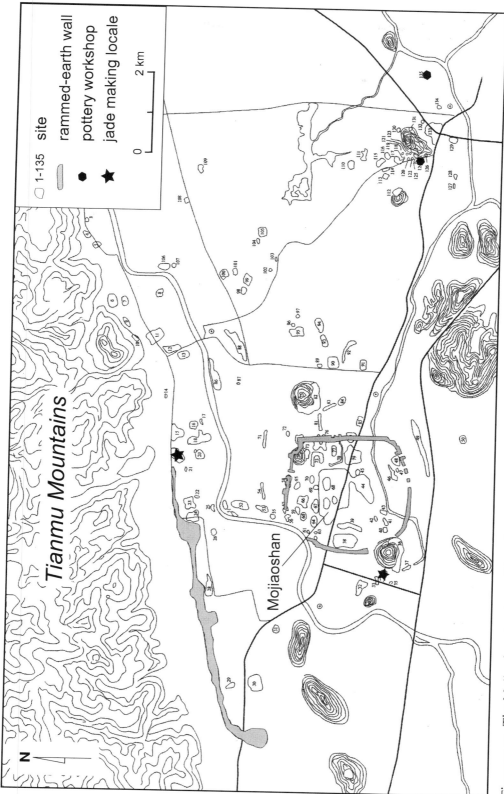

Figure 7.12. The Mojiaoshan site cluster, Liangzhu culture (redrawn from figure 10 of Zhejiangsheng 2005a and figure 1 of Liu, B. 2008).

and hands, and the lower part is animal-like, with large round eyes and sharp claws. Numerous opinions on the meaning of *cong* tubes and associated motifs have been proposed (Li, X. 2004), and the most widely accepted interpretation is to view the man-beast motif as a shamanistic alter-ego image and the *cong* tubes as symbolic expressions of a heaven-earth connection (Chang 1989).

The jade raw materials are most likely to have come from local sources in the mountains and rivers, such as Mt. Xiaomeiling (Jing, Z. and Wen 1996; Wen, G. and Jing 1993). Jade manufacture evidently took place at some Liangzhu sites, as jade-working tools and semifinished products have been found at several sites, including Lucun, Wenjiashan, and Anxi in Yuhang, Yangdun in Deqing, Dingshadi in Jurong, and Mopandun in Dantu (Jiang, W. 1999; Nanjing 2001). Most of these sites are distributed around the Yuhang area, suggesting that the jade objects found in the elite burials were produced locally in the Liangzhu region, and the development of the Mojiaoshan cluster was also related to jade production (Figure 7.11).

Some elite individuals may have been involved in jade manufacturing. In several elite burials, large quantities of particular forms of unfinished jade/stone artifacts were found, such as *bi* discs, *cong* tubes, or *yue* axes (Jiang, W. 1999; Liu, L. 2003). At Fuquanshan, stone drills have been uncovered from an elite burial (M60) (Huang, X. 2000). At Wenjiashan, twenty stone cores from making perforated *yue* axes were found; correspondingly, thirty-four *yue* axes were unearthed from an elite tomb (M1) at the site (Liu, B. 2008). These phenomena suggest not only that these high-status individuals may have been the artisans engaged in jade manufacturing, but also that making particular forms of jade items may have become a highly specialized class of activity among the elite artisans. Liangzhu jade, together with its symbolic meanings, had great influence on many Neolithic cultures in other regions.

Pictographic symbols have been found on Liangzhu jade and pottery artifacts. A recurrent motif is composed of a bird standing on an altar; the altars are decorated with symbols, two of which may be identified as the sun and moon (Figure 7.4) (Ren, S. 1996; Yang, X. 2000). This theme seems to echo the sun-bird motif first seen at Hemudu (Wu, H. 1985). Most scholars agree that these signs are pictographic and schematic, as a form of clan emblems or insignia that later further developed in the Shang inscriptions; but they are unlikely to have intended to write the name of the clan, and it is difficult to assess their phonetic values, which by definition are required for writing. Therefore, like those symbols on *dakouzun* vessels from the Dawenkou culture, these pictograms are not a part of a writing system (Boltz 1986; Keightley 2006). Inscriptions consisting of multiple symbols also have been found on several Liangzhu pottery vessels (Yang, X. 2000: 72–3). All these symbols could have been used for communication and may be regarded as proto-writing, but none of them can be seen as a writing system.

Figure 7.13. Jade objects from the Liangzhu culture. 1: *Cong* tube; 2: man–beast motif carved on jade; 3: *bi* discs found in burial M23 at Fanshan (after figure 38 and color plates 137 and 1076 of Zhejiangsheng 2005b).

Evidently, Liangzhu society was hierarchically organized. Some archaeologists have suggested that the Liangzhu culture was a state level society (Su, B. 1997; Zhang, Z. 2000); thus, the Mojiaoshan site cluster may have been the state capital, and the burial sites at Fanshan and Yaoshan could have been kings' tombs (Yan, W. 1996). Because there are a number of site clusters coexisting with Mojiaoshan in the region, more studies of settlement patterns are needed to determine whether Mojiaoshan was the primary center that controlled the entire Liangzhu region.

The Liangzhu culture came to its end in the late third millennium BC. Although some pottery and tools in Liangzhu styles continued in the following Maqiao culture, the ritual goods (especially jade), elite tombs, and large earth mounds entirely vanished (Huang, X. and Sun 1983; Li, B. 1989; Zhu,

G. 1996). Liangzhu's disappearance has roused many speculations about the collapse of this highly developed complex society. Some archaeologists believe that internal social crises implicit in excessive energy expenditure for the production of jade and the construction of large burial mounds were responsible (Zhao, H. 1999); others suggest that invasion from the Longshan culture was one of the major factors for the Liangzhu collapse (Song, J. 2004). Also, some scholars argue that natural disasters, such as flood and marine transgression, were the major causes (Stanley et al. 1999; Wang, F. et al. 1996; Wu, J. 1988; Yu, W. 1993). All these factors may have contributed to the collapse of this cultural system. The construction of the flood-control wall parallel to the Tianmu Mountains and a layer of silt found on top of the Liangzhu deposits in the Mojiaoshan site cluster, as mentioned earlier in text, seem to particularly support the flood hypothesis.

While the Liangzhu culture disappeared around the Lake Tai region, some sites dating to the end of the third millennium BC and outside of the Liangzhu core area have revealed strong Liangzhu material characteristics. For example, many jade and pottery artifacts nearly identical to those from Liangzhu culture sites were found in burials at the Haochuan site in Suichang, southwestern Zhejiang (Lu, W. 1996). As the resemblance of the Haochuan material remains (not only prestige goods but also utilitarian items) to the Liangzhu culture is so prominent, some scholars believe that the Haochuan cemetery indicates the southward migration of population at the time of the Liangzhu collapse (Wang, M. 2004).

Qujialing (3400–2500 BC) and Shijiahe (2500–2000 BC)

These two cultures are distributed on the Jianghan Plains in the middle Yangzi River region; east to the Dabie Mountains, south to Lake Dongting, west to the Three Gorges, and north to the Nanyang Basin. Nearly 1,000 Qujialing sites and about an equal number of Shijiahe sites have been identified, and many show evidence of continuous occupation at the same location. This region was covered by large areas of water in ancient times, and sites are normally located on high ground. These sites tend to be grouped into several clusters, and some central places were encircled by earth walls. At least nine such walled sites have been found (Figure 7.2).

These walled sites were constructed in a similar way: They were located at the juncture between a high mount and flat alluvial land near rivers or lakes. Wide moats were dug first, and the soil removed from the moats was piled up to build walls. As a result, land inside the enclosure was sloping, and residential areas were always situated on the high ground. Most walls were built in the late Qujialing era, and the sites were abandoned after the middle stages of the Shijiahe period. They vary in size, ranging from 7.8 ha to 120 ha; the largest one is at Shijiahe in Tianmen, Hubei (Ma, S. 2003).

The Shijiahe site cluster consists of more than forty sites on small or large terraces in an area of 8 km² between two rivers (East and West). It was first populated as a small village during the Daxi period, became a large walled settlement in the late Qujialing period, and was finally abandoned in the late Shijiahe period. The core of the site cluster, measuring about 120 ha in area, is surrounded by sections of earth walls, within which a smaller walled enclosure with a moat (up to 100 m wide) is located in the northeast part. The entire site area is higher in the northwestern part and lower in the southeast, where there used to be an ancient lake, according to the *County Chronicle* (Wang, H. 2003; Zhang, C. 2003) (Figure 7.14).

These enormous constructions appear to have been related to flood control. Wang Hongxing (2003) has pointed out that threats of flooding have normally come from the Han River in the northwest. In the 1935 flood, water burst from the Han River, and an area of 1,570 km² in Tianmen County was inundated. The two rivers on the east and west sides of the site also have been the source of flooding during the rainy seasons in recent years. The fact that ancient geographical conditions of the region may have been similar to those at present would explain why the walls were built to protect the northwest, southwest, and east, whereas the unwalled southeast lowland may have functioned as an exit for water.

Several locations at the site seem to have assumed different functions: Some were craft production locales. At Dengjiawan and Tanjialing, residential houses, pits, ritual activity areas, and more than 100 tombs have been found. In addition, two pits yielded several thousand small clay figurines, including birds, fish, chickens, dogs, sheep, turtles, pigs, elephants, tigers, and humans holding fish (Figure 7.15). Most of the figurines are evidently waste products, found together with large amounts of slag, suggesting it was all the refuse of a production area. Tens of thousands of red pottery cups also have been found at Sanfangwan (Shijiahe 2003; Zhang, C. 2003; Zhang, X. 1991). Several hundred spindle-whirls and architectural remains characteristic of a jade/stone workshop have been found at Luojiabailing, and large numbers of semifinished stone tools have been unearthed near this site on the other side of the East River (Hubeisheng and Zhongguo 1994) (Figure 7.14). In addition, at Xiaojiawuji in the southern part of the Shijiahe site cluster, the residents seem to have specialized in pottery production. Some burials of the early Shijiahe phase contain more than 100 pottery vessels of identical types, suggesting that the tomb occupants were probably potters (Shijiahe 1999).

During the late Shijiahe phase (ca. 2200–2000 BC), people used burial urns for the dead and jade artifacts as grave goods. At Xiaojiawuji, the numbers of jade vary among burials, ranging from none to several dozen. The most wealthy urn burial (W6) contained fifty-six jade items. These jade objects appear to be made of similar raw material, and many are semifinished products, suggesting they were made at the site (Shijiahe 1999; Zhang, C. 2003).

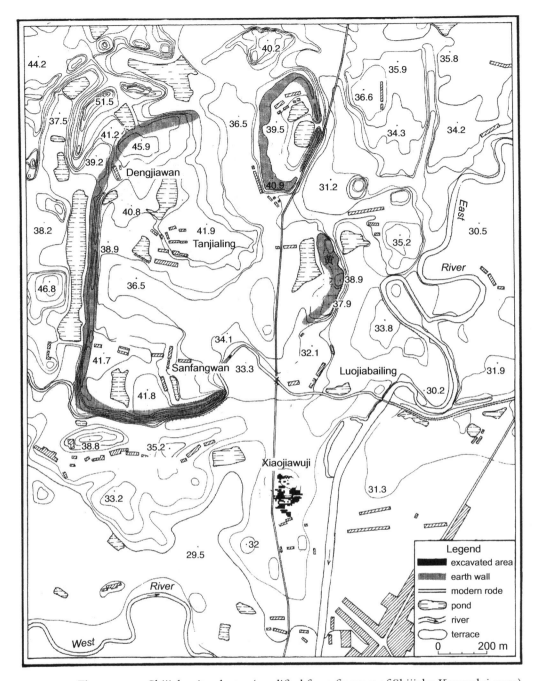

Figure 7.14. Shijiahe site cluster (modified from figure 2 of Shijiahe Kaogudui 1999).

Most Shijiahe jade artifacts have been uncovered from several late Shijiahe culture sites. The jade forms include anthropomorphic heads, *cong* tubes, birds, eagles, dragons, cicadas, and phoenix. Most of them have parallels in the Liangzhu culture, suggesting a strong cultural influence from the east (Wang, J. 1996). The Shijiahe site cluster is also similar in many ways to the Mojiaoshan

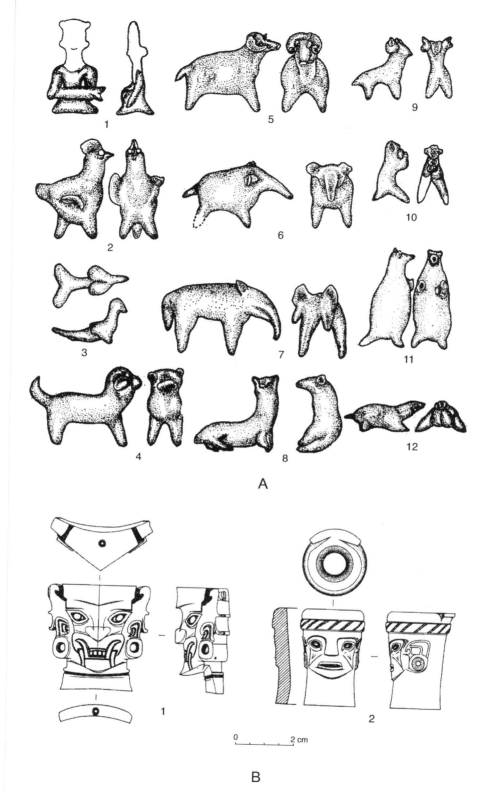

Figure 7.15. Shijiahe art representations. **(A)** Clay figurines. 1: Man holding fish; 2: chicken; 3: bird; 4 and 8: dogs; 5 and 9: sheep; 6 and 7: elephants; 10: monkey; 11: unidentified animal; 12: turtle (not to scale). **(B)** Jade human heads from Xiaojiawuji (A: modified from Zhang, X. 1991: 56; B: after Shijiahe 1999: 316).

site cluster. They both had outer walls, probably built for flood control, and a small inner enclosure was constructed at the center; various specialized crafts were produced at different locations in the cluster, and jade items, many made locally, were used as status symbols in mortuary rituals.

The Shijiahe culture ended around 2000 BC. All the large earth enclosures were abandoned, and settlements became much smaller in size and fewer in number. Different from the complete disappearance of the Liangzhu culture, the Shijiahe culture seems to have experienced a considerable decrease in population level. Some sites also show characteristics of the Longshan material culture from the Central Plain. Some scholars believe that the Shijiahe population decline is attributable to the southward expansion of the Longshan culture, leading to warfare between different populations (Zhang, C. 2003).

In any event, the entire middle and lower Yangzi River region became sparsely populated by the end of the Neolithic period. Such a large scale of decline is unlikely to have been caused by a single incidence of natural disaster; rather, multiple causes, probably consisting of both natural and social factors, may have been responsible for bringing down these early complex societies.

The Baodun culture (2500–1700 BC) is a newly defined archaeological entity, distributed in the Chengdu Basin and nearby low hills. The sites were mostly found in recent decades. Several walled settlements along the Min River formed the core area of this culture (Figure 7.2). These walled sites vary in size, ranging from 10 ha to 60 ha (Chen, J. 2005; Li, S. 2010; Ma, S. 2003). The enclosures were built on terraces, rectangular or irregular in shape, and the orientations are aligned with nearby rivers. Such settlement planning also may have been related to flood control, which has been a constant concern of urban planning in the Chengdu Plain throughout history. Excavations at two walled sites, Baodun and Guchengcun, have revealed large public architectural foundations at the center of each site. The subsistence economy was characterized by agriculture as well as hunting and fishing, judging from the tool assemblages (Jiang, Z. et al. 2001). The construction of large walled enclosures and public buildings at many settlements indicates the existence of a complex social organization; however, there is little sign of social inequality in the intrasettlement material remains. Ongoing regional surveys and excavations will certainly provide more information for reconstruction of social organization in this area.

SOUTH AND WEST CHINA

Our knowledge about Neolithic cultural development in South and West China is less comprehensive than that in the Yellow and Yangzi River regions because of the lack of research focus on these regions. This situation has begun

to change in recent years, thanks to the rapid development of local archaeological institutions and the promotion of Su Bingqi's *quxi leixing* theory, which
emphasizes multiregional development of Chinese civilization. In addition,
scholarly interactions among archaeologists from Taiwan and mainland China,
as well as international collaborations, also have led to many breakthroughs in
our understanding of cultural developments in these regions, in particular, the
expansion of proto-Austronesian populations. These ancient southern frontier
regions are not only important for reconstruction of the multiregional origins of early civilizations within China, but are also crucial for understanding
broader interregional interactions in Southeast Asia.

Southeast China

In this geographically highly diverse region, ancient people developed various
subsistence strategies to adapt to different ecosystems, and the late Neolithic
cultures are represented by different types of settlements. Agricultural village
sites are distributed in the inland areas, where traces of rice farming are evident. In contrast, sand dune and shell midden sites are scattered over the coastal
areas, where people relied primarily on aquatic resources. These subsistence
economies can be exemplified by the Shixia culture in northern Guangdong,
the Yonglang culture in the Pearl River Delta, and the Tanshishan and Huangguashan cultures in Fujian (Figure 7.1). In this region the Neolithic cultures
continued for several hundred years, during the second millennium BC, after
northern China had entered the Bronze Age.

The Shixia culture (ca. 3000–2000 BC) was evidently an agricultural society. At its type site, Shixia, rice grains, husks and stems, along with agricultural tools, were uncovered from burials. Many jade objects have been found,
including *cong* tubes and *bi* discs, some identical to the examples from the
Liangzhu culture. Shixia culture sites have their own distinctive characteristics,
in terms of burial patterns and pottery forms; but the material assemblages
apparently show strong connections with Neolithic cultures in Jiangxi and the
lower Yangzi River region, where agriculture already had been established
for several thousand years (Shixia 1978; Su, B. 1978b). These connections
seem to suggest southward population movement from those heavily populated agricultural areas, a phenomenon that occurred throughout the Neolithic
period.

The Yonglang culture (ca. 3000–2000 BC) is distributed in the Pearl
River Delta and Hong Kong areas, characterized by sand dunes. When people
resided in these coastal areas, the sea level was lower and the extent of land
between ocean and hills was much broader than at present. The dwellings were
built on the lower part of the hills. The rising sea level afterward inundated
much of those sites, forming the dune sites. At the Yonglang site in Hong

Kong, for example, the lithics are predominantly stone axes, adzes, arrow-heads, and net weights; ceramics are simple in form, mostly jars and caul-drons; ceramic decorations include cord-mark and various stamped patterns. A few burials have been found, and some houses appear to have been pile-dwellings. Some material cultural traits from Yonglang are similar to the Shixia culture (agricultural society), based on stylistic comparison of stone and ceramic artifacts, indicating contacts between them through exchange and/or migration. The Yonglang subsistence economy, however, apparently relied on hunting-gathering and fishing, with little evidence for agriculture (An, Z. 1997; Hong Kong 1997). There are two possible explanations for this phe-nomenon: First, the Yonglang culture adapted well to the coastal environment with no need to develop farming, despite their contact with the agricultural population; second, the agricultural people may have given up the practice of farming when they migrated to a marine ecosystem.

The **Tanshishan** (ca. 3000–2000 BC) and **Huangguashan** (ca. 2300–1500 BC) cultures are distributed along the southeast coastal region in Fujian, char-acterized by shell middens. People seem to have relied primarily on marine resources as well as on hunting terrestrial animals. No evidence for agricultural activity is present in the Tanshishan culture sites, but carbonized seeds and phy-toliths from rice, wheat, and barley have been uncovered at the Huangguashan site in Xiapu County. This change seems to suggest that agriculture was added to a maritime economy by the end of the third millennium BC in the coastal areas. Adzes were the main stone tools, and many of the adzes had angled tangs. This typological characteristic continued for more than 1,500 years, suggesting a well-developed and long-lasting exchange network. Many adzes from Tan-shishan culture sites were made of nonlocal volcanic rocks, and the analysis of chemical elements of stone adzes from the Damaoshan site (ca. 3000–2300 BC) in Dongshan County, Fujian, suggests that people may have procured the raw materials from places as far removed as the Penghu Archipelago in the middle of the Taiwan Strait. In addition, many Damaoshan pottery sherds and stone tools stylistically resemble those of contemporaneous sites in Penghu and west-ern Taiwan, suggesting a close cultural connection among the three locations. Such long-distance voyages across the Taiwan Strait may have constituted part of a mechanism for the proto-Austronesian expansion (Jiao 2007).

There are many theories regarding the dynamics of southward migration by proto-Austronesian populations from the mainland to Taiwan and then Southeast Asia. Bellwood (1997) suggests that population pressure induced by the adoption of rice agriculture was the main reason for the migration. Chang and Goodenough (1996) argue that the southward population expansion was in response to a demand for valued marine and tropical forest products. Kirch (2000) believes that the division of family and the founder lineage ideology led ancient Austronesians to expand into the Pacific. Tsang (1992) points out the importance of maritime adaptation, which played a decisive role (summarized by Jiao 2007). Jiao (2007: 258–9) argues for multiple causes in different time periods; whereas maritime adaptation served as a major factor favoring exploration of the ocean, the motivations may have shifted from the search for new resources in the early Neolithic to the need for more agricultural land when rice farming became more fully developed in the late Neolithic.

Southwest and West China

The third millennium BC witnessed the further development of various Neolithic cultures in Southwest China, including Tibet, Yunnan, and Guizhou. Because of the mountainous topography, there are many regional variations in material cultural assemblages in this region, many of which have been recognized only in recent decades. In general, our knowledge about the overall development of ancient societies in this region is still limited.

Neolithic development also reached the Tibetan Plateau, represented by the Karuo culture distributed in the northeastern part of Tibet. The type site, Karuo (1 ha) in Changdu, is located on the second terrace of the west bank of the Lancang River, at an elevation of 3,100 m above sea level. The cultural deposits were up to 2 m thick, and radio carbon dates place this settlement to ca. 3300–2300 BC. People lived in dwellings, used pottery, and made chipped and ground stone tools, including microliths. The material culture appears to be more similar to that in Sichuan than to findings from the Gansu-Qinghai region. The subsistence economy was reportedly characterized by hunting, gathering, millet farming, and pig domestication (Aldenderfer and Zhang 2004; Xizang and Sichuan 1985).

In Yunnan, Neolithic remains before 3000 BC are rare, but sites dating to the third millennium BC have been found in three geographic settings, including river terraces, caves near rivers, and shell middens near lakes. The Shizhaishan culture is the earliest Neolithic assemblage reported. The sites are shell middens distributed near lakes. Shell deposits are often extensive, as thick as 4–6 m. Stone tools are mainly axes and adzes, and ceramics include various forms of plates, jars, and cups. Some pottery paste contained rice husks and spikelets, suggesting that rice was exploited (Huang, Z. and Zhao 1959; Xiao, M. 2001). Recent excavations at Haimenkou in Jianchuan have revealed a water-logged pile-dwelling settlement near Lake Jian. Its Neolithic deposits (ca. 3000–1900 BC) contained extremely rich material remains, including rice and millet. Rice may have been introduced from the Yangzi River region, whereas millet apparently came from northwestern regions. Some stone knives from Haimenkou show characteristics similar to those from Karuo in Tibet, pointing to Haimenkou's cultural connections (Min, R. 2009). Yunnan has been a pivotal point for cultural/ethnic interactions from the surrounding regions, as several great rivers running from northwest to southeast through this region formed the major communication routes between China and Southeast Asia, which later developed into the Southwest Silk Road. Human migration and trade along these routes are likely to have begun during the Neolithic period.

In Xinjiang, archaeological assemblages prior to the Bronze Age, around 2000 BC, appear to be characterized by microliths, which are nevertheless not well dated. There are no material remains in this region that can be assigned to the Neolithic.

To summarize, in South and Southwest China, the full development of the Neolithic was a relatively late phenomenon as compared to that in the north. These late arrivals are often viewed as the result of southward dispersal of populations with agricultural technologies. There appear to have been several waves of such migration, originating from the middle and lower Yangzi River region, during the fourth and third millennia BC (Zhang, C. and Hung 2008) and eventually spreading over the Southeast Asian mainland during the third millennium BC (Bellwood 2005; Higham 2009). This hypothesis can be supported by close similarities in material assemblages shared by Neolithic communities in a broad region of Southeast Asia. Several cultural traits occurred first in the Yangzi River region and subsequently appeared in South China and then Southeast Asia. These traits include mortuary practices, rice cultivation, animal husbandry, polished stone and shell industry, and ceramic types and decorations, particularly the incised and impressed pottery style (Rispoli 2007). Such a dispersal in material culture is likely to have been accompanied by the movement of populations and their languages (Bellwood 2006; Higham 2002).

CONCLUSIONS

Cultural development during the late Neolithic period was diverse. Whereas complex agricultural societies flourished along the great river systems, particularly the Yellow and Yangzi Rivers, many small communities in the surrounding regions continued to practice a broad-spectrum subsistence economy with simpler social organization. From an evolutionary perspective, the third millennium BC was the transitional period during which the Neolithic complex societies developed to the first state-level societies, and many cultures show traits that later became essential characteristics of civilizations, such as bronze metallurgy, proto-writing, pronounced social hierarchy, and nucleated regional settlement patterns. Whether these Neolithic cultures (e.g., Taosi, Liangchengzhen, and Liangzhu) can be categorized as states is a matter of debate, and increasing numbers of Chinese archaeologists believe that they were. This issue will be discussed in the next chapter. In our view, however, it is not so crucial to decide which Neolithic cultures qualify as states; the argument depends on how one defines a state. Instead, it is more important, as archaeologists, to provide understanding of how these complex societies developed, operated, and changed.

Despite many regional variations, there were commonalities shared by many of these complex societies: Agricultural surplus was essential to form the economic foundation for the emergence of social complexity; as the elite created and maintained their political authority by controlling ritual power, production and exchange of prestige ritual items were crucial for the formation of social status and elite networks. Not all regional cultures that manifested advanced degrees of social complexity evolved further into state-level social organizations. Taosi and Liangzhu, for example, represent the most developed complex societies during the third millennium BC in China. They both formed highly stratified political systems. The elite groups were able to obtain and maintain political status through their ritual power. Remarkably, however, they both disappeared from the archaeological record around the end of the third millennium BC.

Taosi and Liangzhu are not the only cultures that vanished at this time. The decline of site number and abandonment of regional centers were common phenomena across the landscape along the Yellow and Yangzi River Valleys. By the beginning of the second millennium BC, many well-developed complex societies disappeared from the archaeological record. Given that the Mid-Holocene Climatic Optimum was waning and many regions experienced climatic fluctuation, environmental change often has been viewed as a major factor contributing to the decline of some complex societies. Many archaeologists have suggested that this change coincided with the time of the Great Flood as recorded in ancient texts. Traditionally, the flood was believed to have been controlled by Yu the Great, the legendary founding king of the Xia dynasty, about 4,000 years ago. Although the historical background for the formation of the flood myth needs to be studied in its own right (Lewis 2006), several scientific investigations have indeed shown an episode of climatic deterioration around 2200–2000 BC in China (Wu, W. and Ge 2005; Wu, W. and Liu 2004; Xia, Z. and Yang 2003). Some Neolithic sites also show evidence of flooding at the end of the third millennium BC, such as Mengzhuang in Huixian, Henan (Henansheng Wenwu Kaogu 2003), and Mojiaoshan in Zhejiang, as discussed earlier in text. Therefore, although the stories about Yu's controlling floodwaters may have been fabrications, it is possible that frequent devastating floods in many river valleys indeed destroyed many settlements in prehistory, and these events became a collective memory of ancient people that was passed down through oral traditions.

In summary, the rise and fall of these Neolithic complex societies manifested diverse relationships between different social groups as well as between natural forces and human societies. The cycles of rise and fall of these social systems often parallel the climatic fluctuations, and such parallels may be plausible to explain the end of many Neolithic cultures around 2000 BC in the archaeological record. Nevertheless, climatic changes cannot be used as a simplistic explanation, and in many cases it is the social responses and leadership strategies that defined the ultimate social changes. A particular challenge for archaeologists is to explain why the early state, the Erlitou culture, evolved successfully, whereas most comparable complex societies collapsed at this time. This topic will be addressed in the next chapter.

CHAPTER 8

FORMATION OF EARLY STATES IN THE CENTRAL PLAIN: ERLITOU AND ERLIGANG (1900/1800–1250 BC)

> The great affairs of a state are sacrifices [both to ancestors] and [in] war. At sacrifices [in the ancestral temple], [the officers] receive the roasted flesh; in war they receive that [raw flesh] offered at the altar of the land: – these are the great ceremonies in worshipping the Spirits.
>
> Chapter, "Duke Cheng's Thirteenth Year [577 BC]," in *Zuozhuan* (compiled within 475–221 BC); translated by James Legge, modified

国之大事, 在祀与戎, 祀有执膰, 戎有受脤, 神之大节也。〈〈左传〉〉成公十三年

China is one of a few regions in the world where the earliest state-level civilizations developed, independently of determining external influence. Questions about the origins of the state may be approached both historically and archaeologically. China has a long tradition of recording historical events, a legacy that provides rich quantities of information concerning its early dynasties and offers important sources for study of the origins of dynastic civilization. The archaeological record also reveals abundant data for investigation of social, political, and technological changes in locales wherein these early dynasties developed, and excavations have primarily focused on large sites that presumably correspond to dynastic capital cities. Therefore, the origins of early states in China involve four intertwined issues: state formation, development of urbanism, emergence of civilization, and beginning of dynastic history.

State formation is also one of the most controversial research topics in Chinese archaeology today, owing to the fact that such study constitutes a juncture at which the divergent claims of tradition and modernity meet in Chinese intellectual discourse. Scholars struggle in various ways to integrate and mutually accommodate these two realms of thought, and the problems involved in doing so are both conceptual and practical. First, the early dynastic period prior to the late Shang dynasty at Yinxu (ca. 1250–1046 BC) is, properly speaking, prehistoric, being without a writing system. Therefore, the study of early state formation is often pursued based on events recorded in texts that were undoubtedly composed a thousand years, more or less, after those events supposedly happened. Thus, scholarly debates as to the applicability of these textual records to archaeological investigations have been ongoing. Second, lack of consensus regarding the definition of state, and use of various criteria for the concept of state in scholarly research, has led to confusion in some cases. Third, the term "state" has been used interchangeably with the word "civilization" in Chinese archaeological literature, in which "civilization" occurs more frequently than "state." Because civilization is often used in a more general way than state is, and different scholars usually use different definitions for these two concepts, many interpretations are ambiguous (Chang 2004; Chen, X. 1987).

Furthermore, the study of state formation involves many disciplines, including archaeology, history, and anthropology; scholars from these fields often use different approaches and address different issues. As a result, there is a lack of agreement about where, when, and how the first state emerged in China. To understand the process of state formation in China we must begin by comprehending the different intellectual traditions involved in such study. In this chapter we will first review some of the main methodological approaches to research on early states, and then we will discuss the archaeological evidence for reconstructing the emergence of archaic states during the early part of the second millennium BC in China.

APPROACHES AND DEFINITIONS

Studies of state formation can be described in terms of four general approaches, which may be traced back to different preferences toward defining the state, as held by particular scholarly traditions.

Xia Nai's Classic Evolutionary Approach

The interchangeable usage of civilization and state was first explicitly used by Xia Nai (Xia, N. 1985: 81) who wrote that "civilization refers to a society in which the clan system has disintegrated and a state organization with class differentiation has formed." Influenced by Gordon Childe's concept of urban revolution, Xia identified four essential and archaeologically detectable criteria for defining civilization/state: (1) state-level political organization (characterized by class differentiation), (2) urban center of political, economic, and cultural/religious activity, (3) writing, and (4) metallurgy. He further suggested that civilization in China had emerged in the Erlitou culture (1900–1500 BC), centered in the Yiluo region in Henan, at least in its late phase (Xia, N. 1985: 79–106).

Xia (1985: 96) regarded himself as a conservative archaeologist. When his article on the origins of Chinese civilization was published in the 1980s, Erlitou was the only site revealing archaeological evidence that largely met his criteria for a state. The current archaeological record shows that the level of social complexity observable at Erlitou has not been surpassed by any archaeological cultures prior to or contemporary with it (see further discussion later in this chapter). Xia's approach, which emphasizes hard archaeological evidence and is less concerned with textual information, has not been popular in China. Most publications relating to the Erlitou culture attempt to provide it with dynastic affiliations (See Du, J. and Xu 2006; Zhongguo Shehui Kexueyuan 2003b). Some new research has shown, however, that Xia Nai's principle needs to be reconsidered; archaeological information and historical records relating to prehistoric societies should be dealt with independently before each set of data is systematically studied in its own right (Liu, L. 2004: 9–10; Liu, L. and Chen 2003; Liu, L. and Xu 2007).

Su Bingqi's Neolithic Civilization Approach

Su Bingqi (1999) took a more radical approach than did Xia Nai, using the term civilization loosely and without a clear definition. He traced the early development of some cultural traits back to the Neolithic period more than 5,000 years ago and described these traits as signifying the dawn of civilization, manifest in archaic states. These characteristics include walled settlements, jade objects with dragon designs, large public architecture, and burial differentiation. Because such traits could be found in many regions, Su (1999) described this situation as *mantian xingdou* ("the sky full of stars") at the dawn of civilization. He further suggested that there were many regional trajectories toward civilization and that such processes started more than 5,000 years ago (Su, B. 1999: 119–27). The examples he used highlight changes in artifactual styles and archaeological features found in different sites over several thousand years; therefore, Su's models seem to be related more to general cultural evolution than to the process of state formation.

Su's view has been shared by many archaeologists and historians in China, who believe that the origins of civilization/state should be traced back to Neolithic times (e.g., Li, X. 1997a; Yan, W. 2000; Zhang, Z. 2000). Examples of these early civilizations include many archaeological cultures, such as late Yangshao, Hongshan, Dawenkou, Qujialing, Liangzhu, and Longshan, dating to the fifth through third millennia BC (Zhang, Z. 2000). In these studies, the presence of hierarchical society and construction of public buildings and settlement fortifications are most frequently cited as marking the emergence of early states (e.g., Li, X. 1997a: 7–10). Although opposing views have appeared (e.g., An, Z. 1993a; Chen, X. 1987), this approach seems to have gained more momentum in recent years, as new discoveries from several late Neolithic cultures have shown construction of large-scale public architecture, such as rammed-earth enclosures, and evolution of rather advanced social organization during the third millennium BC. These discoveries of complex

Neolithic societies are particularly exemplified by the Taosi, Wangchenggang, and Liangzhu sites, which all show large, rammed-earth enclosures, as discussed in the previous chapter. Current archaeological data from these sites are not sufficient, however, for determining their political organizations as states.

Historiographical Approach

Before the development of modern archaeology, historical texts were the only sources for the interpretation of social development, and they traced the origins of Chinese civilization to legendary sages, kings, and dynasties. Modern archaeology conducted by Chinese archaeologists began in the 1920s and was the result of interplay among the Chinese tradition of historiography, the introduction of Western scientific methodology, and rising nationalism. The primary objective was to reconstruct national history (Falkenhausen 1993; Liu, L. and Chen 2001a; see also Chapter 1). Early historical dynasties, namely the retrospectively named, pre-imperial "Three Dynasties" (Xia, Shang, and Zhou; collectively, ca. 2100–200 BC), developed in the middle Yellow River Valley, a region known during most of the last two millennia as the Central Plain; searching for capitals of these dynasties has always been a primary goal of modern archaeology. Investigations in the past century have brought to light a number of large sites, some of which indeed generally coincide in time and space with early dynastic capitals mentioned in historical records. These sites include Xinzhai, Erlitou, Zhengzhou, Yanshi, Xiaoshuangqiao, Huanbei, and Yinxu, all located in the Central Plain (Figure 8.1) and showing characteristics of political centers (more discussion later in this chapter). These discoveries have inspired much enthusiasm for reconstructing the early dynastic history of China, and numerous interpretations have been put forward to link these sites to various capitals of the Xia and Shang dynasties mentioned in ancient texts. As a general trend, the historiographic approach has become the mainstream in China.

The historiographical approach is problematic in practice. References in ancient texts are often brief and ambiguous, and the early Bronze Age sites before the late Shang have revealed no writing that identifies the site. The result of this situation is that each archaeological site may be matched to multiple ancient cities or places, by citing various putative textual authorities. Therefore, there is little consensus among scholars regarding which ancient capitals may correspond to which sites, leading to endless debate in archaeological circles. The only exception is Yixu in Anyang: Owing to the oracle-bone inscriptions unearthed at the site, its identity as the last capital of the Shang dynasty has been generally regarded as effectively indisputable.

The historiographical approach is highly controversial in terms of its methodology. Because these texts were written in much later times, many scholars believe that place names mentioned in these texts should not be used

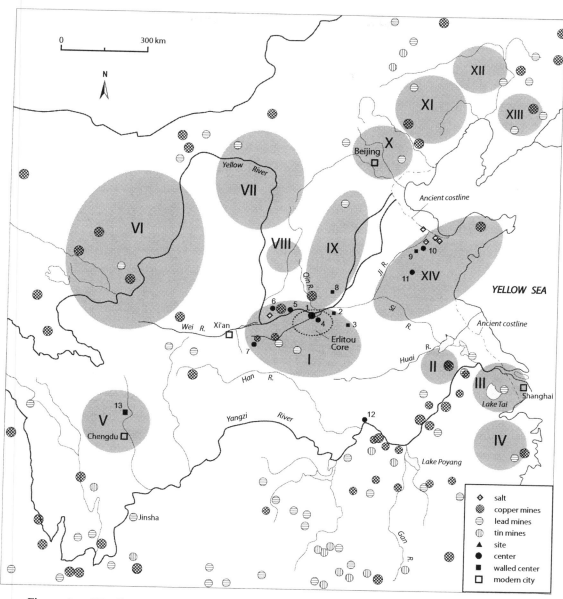

Figure 8.1. Distribution of contemporary cultures during the Erlitou period and distribution of natural resources (metals and salt). Cultures – I: Erlitou; II: Doujitai; III: Maqiao; IV: Lower Dianjiangtai; V: Sanxingdui; VI: Qijia; VII: Zhukaigou; VIII: Guangshe; IX: Xiaqiyuan; X: Datuotou; XI: Lower Xiajiadian; XII: Gaotaishan; XIII: Miaohoushan; XIV: Yueshi. Sites – 1: Erlitou; 2: Dashigu; 3: Wangjinglou; 4: Nanwa; 5: Nanguan; 6: Dongxiafeng; 7: Donglongshan; 8: Mengzhuang; 9: Chengziya; 10: Shijia; 11: Yinjiacheng; 12: Panlongcheng; 13: Sanxingdui (areas of cultural distribution based on description in Zhongguo Shehui Kexueyuan 2003).

to anachronistically project back into prehistory the identities of archaeological sites defined by modern research. The debate is particularly focused on the interpretation of the Erlitou culture, of which at least a part is commonly interpreted as remnants from the first dynasty, the Xia. Contrary and critical views, in contrast, question such a link for the lack of hard supporting evidence, such as writing from the site. The debate over the Erlitou–Xia relationship highlights the weakness of historiographical orientation in Chinese archaeology, suggesting that alternative approaches are needed for study of prehistoric complex societies (for a summary, see Liu, L. and Xu 2007).

Social Archaeological Approach

This approach uses anthropological theory and interdisciplinary methods developed in the West, which have been introduced to China in recent decades through a number of Sino-foreign collaborative projects and have become increasingly popular in Chinese archaeology.

Two Sino-foreign projects in southeast Shandong and the Yiluo Basin (Henan) are particularly concerned with issues of state formation. These projects, involving full-coverage regional survey and excavation, use the methodology of settlement archaeology to study social change from a regional perspective (e.g., Adams and Jones 1981; Fish and Kowalewski 1990; Kowalewski 1989; Wright 1984). For this approach, a state is defined as a society with a minimum of two social strata: a professional ruling class and a commoner class. The ruling class is characterized by a centralized decision-making process, which is both externally specialized, with regard to the local processes it regulates, and internally specialized in that the central process is divisible into separate activities, which can be performed in different places at different times (Marcus and Feinman 1998: 4; Wright 1977: 383). Furthermore, a state-level social organization often develops at minimum a four-tiered regional settlement hierarchy, equivalent to three or more levels of political hierarchy (Earle 1991: 3; Flannery 1998: 16–21; Wright 1977: 389; Wright and Johnson 1975). This definition is used by the authors of this book.

In both regions – southeastern Shandong and the Yiluo Basin – settlement patterns show a long period of population development during the Neolithic. In southeastern Shandong, two large, late Neolithic settlements emerged as regional centers at Liangchengzhen and Yaowangcheng, each dominating a settlement system with three tiers of political hierarchy. They disappeared, however, by the beginning of the second millennium BC. There is also a lack of sufficient data to assert the nature of the local political organization before more excavations are carried out at these sites (Underhill et al. 2008).

The situation in the Yiluo region seems to be unique. Whereas most regions experienced a decline in population density and level of social complexity around 2000 BC, settlement patterns in the Yiluo Basin show a rapid process of population nucleation during the Erlitou period, when a large urban center developed at the Erlitou site (300 ha), and the settlement system in the survey region (860 km²) shows three tiers of political hierarchy (Liu, L. et al. 2002–2004; Xu, H. et al. 2005). A process of state formation is clearly manifested in the archaeological record from the Yiluo region (more discussion later in this chapter).

In addition, two recent studies have attempted to clarify the relationship between the concepts of state and civilization. Sarah Allan (2007) argues that a common elite culture, which was associated with a particular set of religious practices, was first crystallized in the region centered at Erlitou. Erlitou thus represents the highest form of political organization (a state) at the early part of the second millennium BC, and the common elite culture associated with Erlitou may be called civilization. A similar treatment of the two concepts is also given by Yoffee and Li (2009), who suggest that early states as the governmental centers of a society were created in cities, and a set of cultural values as a civilization was shared by several early microstates. The separation of these two concepts will help to untangle some ambiguous interpretations between material cultural sphere and political entity.

The social archaeological approach, which is favored by the present authors, shows great potential in the study of early states, providing objective criteria for evaluating the levels of social complexity of archaeological cultures. This approach does not use historical records as blueprints for interpretations; however, the results arising from independent archaeological inquiry eventually may be compared with textual information.

In this chapter, we will focus on the earliest Bronze Age states, Erlitou and Erligang, as well as their close neighbors in the surrounding regions. We do not correlate Erlitou with the Xia dynasty; in this way, we acknowledge the controversial character of debates regarding Erlitou's cultural identity. We are not ruling out the possibility, however, that Xia, either as a people or as a dynasty so named, may have existed in antiquity and that, if so, its material remains may be eventually recognized in the archaeological record in the future.

SEARCH FOR THE XIA DYNASTY

The Erlitou culture was named after the discovery of a large Bronze Age site at Erlitou in Yanshi County, western Henan, in 1959. The discovery was made by Xu Xusheng, who intended to find a capital of the Xia dynasty that was recorded in ancient texts as being situated in the Yiluo River Valley (Xu, X. 1959). To date, more than 300 sites sharing similar material characteristics, referred to as Erlitou culture sites, have been found over a large region in the middle Yellow River Valley (Figure 8.1).

The Erlitou culture dates to ca.1900–1500 BC, an era that partially overlaps with the dates traditionally ascribed to the Xia dynasty (ca. 2070–1600 BC)

(Xia Shang Zhou 2000). Because the spatial and temporal distributions of this archaeological culture largely coincide with the late part of the Xia dynasty as described in ancient texts, most Chinese archaeologists strongly believe that there is a direct link between Erlitou and late Xia (Du, J. and Xu 2006) and that the earlier phase of Xia should be found in archaeological cultures prior to Erlitou. This belief led to the investigation of the Xinzhai phase, which appears to be an intermediate period between the Neolithic Longshan culture and the Erlitou culture in this region. Consequently, Xinzhai and Erlitou have become the primary foci for pursuing the archaeological remains of the Xia dynasty.

The Xinzhai Phase

The Xinzhai phase was first named in the 1980s, to describe a distinctive ceramic assemblage that appears to be earlier than Erlitou but later than Longshan in western Henan. To date, Xinzhai assemblages have been found at about fifteen sites, which are mostly multicomponent. It is possible that more sites also contain Xinzhai assemblages, which may be so identified in the future. These known Xinzhai sites are mainly distributed in the region surrounding the Song Mountains, with two medium-sized regional centers, Xinzhai in Xinmi and Huadizui in Gongyi (Pang, X. and Gao 2008) (Figure 8.2).

Xinzhai is situated on the floodplain east of the Song Mountains, lying on the north bank of the Shuangji River (Figure 8.2A). The site was first occupied during the late Longshan period, and fortified walls were built, suggesting its important position in the region. The subsequent Xinzhai phase witnessed the full development of the settlement; it was surrounded by two concentric outer ditches and an inner ring of rammed-earth walls with moats. The occupied area within the walls measured 70 ha, but the entire site within the outer ditches is nearly 100 ha in size. Xinzhai's high sociopolitical status is indicated by the presence of goods not found in ordinary settlements, including a copper object, jade objects, and elaborate pottery vessels. A large semisubterranean structure (ca. 1,400 m² in area) has been found; it was probably dedicated to ritual activities, according to the excavators (Figure 8.2B). The site was continuously occupied during the early Erlitou period, but deposits are rather scattered, suggesting a considerably lower population density (for a summary, see Zhao, C. 2009).

Huadizui is located on loess terrace, east of the Yiluo River. The site is about 30 ha in area, surrounded by four concentric ditches. House foundations, kilns, and pits have been found. Some pits appear to have been sacrificial in nature, revealing large numbers of artifacts, including jade ritual objects (e.g., *yue* axe, spade, *zhang* blade, and *cong* tube) and pottery vessels containing grains and animal bones. Two pottery urns decorated with elaborate patterns are among the exceptional finds (Gu and Zhang 2005; Gu and Zhang 2006).

Recently, a series of carbon 14 AMS (Accelerator Mass Spectrometry) dates from the Xinzhai and Erlitou sites provided a sequence of chronology from

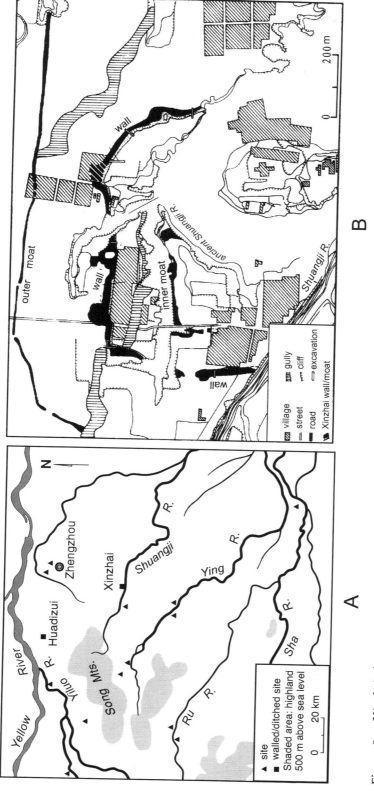

Figure 8.2. Xinzhai phase sites. (A) Distribution of major Xinzhai phase sites (modified from figure 1 of Pang and Gao 2008). (B) Plan of the Xinzhai site (modified from figure 1 of Zhao, C. 2009).

the late Longshan (ca. 2200–1855 BC), through Xinzhai (ca. 1870–1720 BC), to Erlitou period (ca. 1750–1530 BC) (Zhang, X. et al. 2007). These dates place these cultures in a temporal sequence that is considerably later than that previously published, particularly for the beginning of the Erlitou culture. In the future, these new results should be tested with more samples from more sites.

The discovery of impressive remains at Xinzhai has promoted a new wave of speculations regarding the historical identity of this walled site. It has been suggested that the site was the capital either of King Qi, who is traditionally named as the second king of the Xia dynasty (Xu, S. 2004; Zhao, C. 2004), or of Houyi and Hanzhuo, who are said to have come from the East and to have taken power in the Xia dynasty (Gu 2002). These interpretations assume that the Xia was a unified and powerful dynasty occupying the region where Xinzhai sites are distributed, and that the Xinzhai site was the primary center occupied by a linear succession of kings.

Nevertheless, we know little about the settlement pattern of the Xinzhai phase at a regional level, as only a few Xinzhai sites have been found and their sizes are mostly unknown. The relationship between Xinzhai and Huadizui is also unclear. The linear distance between these two sites is about 50 km, but the actual distance in travel is much greater, as they are separated by the Song Mountains. Given the long distance between them, the two sites may have been competing regional centers, each dominating some small settlements in the surrounding areas on either side of the Song Mountains. It is interesting to note that the area where Xinzhai is situated was characterized by a multicentered settlement system during the late Longshan period, and these regional centers (Wangchenggang, Wadian, Guchengzhai, and Xinzhai) were also fortified by walls or ditches (see Chapter 7 and Figure 7.2). The Xinzhai walled settlement of the Xinzhai phase appears not much different from those Longshan regional centers, in terms of scale and material remains. This situation suggests that the social formation of the Xinzhai phase may have been rather similar to that of the Longshan period in the same region, characterized by multiple medium-sized polities competing for power and domination. This scenario apparently contradicts the traditional interpretation of the Xia dynasty as a large and powerful political entity.

THE ERLITOU CULTURE AND ERLITOU STATE

Erlitou culture sites have been found over an area much larger than that of Xinzhai. They are mostly concentrated in the middle Yellow River region, including central and western Henan and southern Shanxi. These sites have been divided into two variants, Erlitou in Henan and Dongxiafeng in Shanxi. A few sites with Erlitou components also have been found near the middle Yangzi River to the south and the Dan River to the southwest, representing Erlitou's southward expansion. The Yiluo Basin and its adjacent region around the Song Mountains appear to define the core area of the Erlitou culture, where the Erlitou site (300 ha), as the primary center, and more than 200 smaller sites are distributed on the alluvial plains and loess tablelands, forming a settlement system with a three-tiered political hierarchy. Erlitou is situated in the alluvial plains on the southern bank of the modern Luo River today, but it was on the northern bank of the ancient Luo River, which changed its course in antiquity. The site location was chosen not only for its importance to transportation through the Yiluo River system, but also because the basin was surrounded by mountain ranges that formed natural protective barriers (Beijing Daxue and Henanshang 2007: 665–775; Liu, L. et al. 2002–2004; Qiao, Y. 2007; Xu, H. et al. 2005) (Figure 8.3).

Outside the Yiluo Basin, two walled settlements have been found within the area of the Erlitou culture horizon. One of them is the Dashigu site (51 ha) in Xingyang, 70 km northeast of Erlitou. Discovery of some bronze (tool) and jade (e.g., *cong* tube) objects at this site indicates the existence of high-status individuals there. The second walled site is located at Wangjinglou in Xinzheng, about 100 km southeast of Erlitou (Figure 8.1). Both sites have been interpreted either as military strongholds to guard the Xia against enemies or as satellite states of the Xia (Zhang, S. and Wu 2010; Zhengzhoushi 2004). In any event, the fact that the Erlitou primary center was not fortified, whereas the secondary center in the periphery was walled, reveals a political landscape differing from that of the previous Longshan culture. Whereas Longshan is characterized by multiple competing polities, each occupying a relatively small territory, Erlitou, in contrast, shows a monocentered political system spread over a large region.

The Erlitou Urban Center

Erlitou was first occupied during the Neolithic period by three small late Yangshao culture (ca. 3500–3000 BC) settlements and subsequently by one small early Longshan culture (ca. 3000–2600 BC) settlement. There was a gap of about 500–600 years between the abandonment of the Longshan settlement and the arrival of new groups of people who were the carriers of the Erlitou culture. This settlement rapidly developed into the largest urban center in the region. The archaeological record shows pronounced social differentiation, as indicated by the sharp contrast between the commoners' small and semisubterranean houses and poor burials, on the one hand, and the elite's large, rammed-earth palatial structures and rich tombs containing artifacts made of bronze, jade, turquoise, cowry shell, ivory, and kaolinic clay (white pottery), on the other hand. More than forty glyphs, some of which are similar in form to later oracle-bone inscriptions, have been found on pottery vessels at Erlitou. Although some scholars believe that these glyphs are remains of putative Xia writing (Cai, D. 2004), others do not regard them as representing a writing system (Figure 8.4).

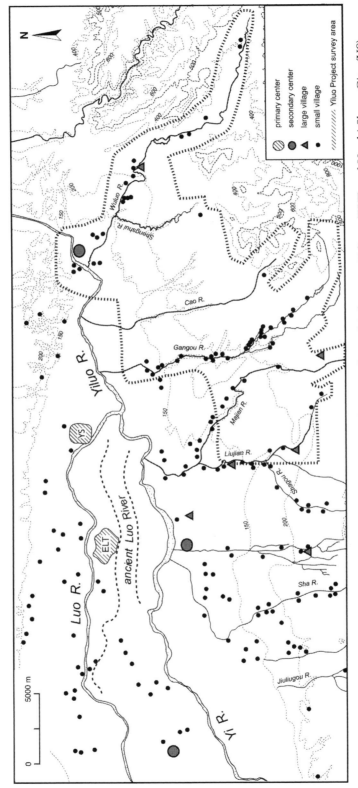

Figure 8.3. Distribution of Erlitou culture sites in the Yiluo region; showing relationship between Erlitou (ELT) and Yanshi Shang City (YS).

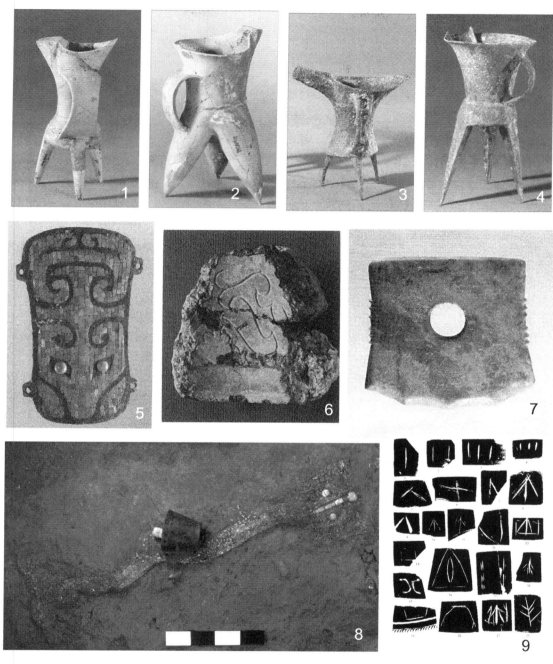

Figure 8.4. Artifacts discovered at Erlitou. 1 and 2: White pottery *jue* and *gui* vessels made of kaolinic clay; 3 and 4: bronze *jue* and *jia* vessels; 5: bronze plate inlaid with turquoise; 6: clay mold with animal design for casting bronze vessel; 7: jade *yue* axe; 8: turquoise dragon and bronze bell found in burial; 9: pottery marks (1 and 2 after plates 5 and 54 of Zhongguo Shehui Kexueyuan 1995; 3 and 4 after figures 63 and 82 of Ma 1996; 5–8 after plates 5; 6.3, 4; 7.1 of Du and Xu 2005; 9 after figure 128 of Zhongguo Shehui Kexueyuan 1999b).

The temporal dimension of the Erlitou culture is a matter of ongoing investigation. Several dozens of carbon 14 dates taken from Erlitou before the year 2000 gave a range of 1900–1500 BC, but recent AMS dates obtained from organic remains at Xinzhai and Erlitou provide a range of 1750–1530 BC (Zhang, X. et al. 2007). Another series of AMS dates obtained from carbonized seeds at the Huizui site, 15 km south of Erlitou, supports the former range (authors' data, publication in preparation). It is possible that the AMS dates from Xinzhai and Erlitou do not cover the entire temporal span of the Erlitou culture, and that more sites need to be dated. Therefore, we use the dates of ca. 1900–1500 BC for the Erlitou culture in this book.

The Erlitou culture is divided into four phases based on ceramic typology, but the exact duration of each phase is difficult to determine. Our understanding of the development of the Erlitou urban center, as described later in this chapter, is based on more than forty years of excavations and research (Du, J. and Xu 2005, 2006; Zhongguo Shehui Kexueyuan 1999b, 2003b) (Figure 8.5).

Erlitou Phase I: The site measures more than 100 ha in area and appears to have grown into the largest center within and beyond the Yiluo region. Such rapid population nucleation can be explained only by migration from surrounding areas. Artifacts unearthed from this phase include many elite items, such as white pottery, ivory and turquoise artifacts, and bronze tools, but the settlement layout is unclear because of severe disturbance of the Phase I deposits by later occupations (Liu, L. and Xu 2007).

Several types of craft goods were produced on site, including small bronze objects, pottery, and bone artifacts. Bronze casting, suggested by the presence of slag, was probably limited to small objects, as only knives have been found. Tool assemblages also include various types of agricultural and hunting-fishing implements (Liu, Li 2006). Erlitou was first developed as a large settlement with a number of craft workshops, producing both elite and utilitarian goods, and the population was most likely engaged in both craft making and agricultural activities. This character is continuously reflected in the Erlitou site throughout the greater part of its occupation.

Erlitou Phase II: At this time, Erlitou witnessed the beginning of full-fledged prosperity, and the primary urban development was completed.

The site expanded to its maximal size, 300 ha, and a complex of rammed-earth buildings (12 ha) emerged in the southeastern area, demarcated by four intercrossing roads, about 20 m wide. These buildings, similar to palaces in the later Shang period, are large in size and complex in layout. A number of medium-sized, rammed-earth foundations and burials were spread over the northeastern and northwestern areas outside the palatial complex. Within the complex, there were two rammed-earth foundations situated side by side, a drainage system made of wooden structures, and a large area of rammed-earth to the south of a palace. Two groups of elite burials associated with

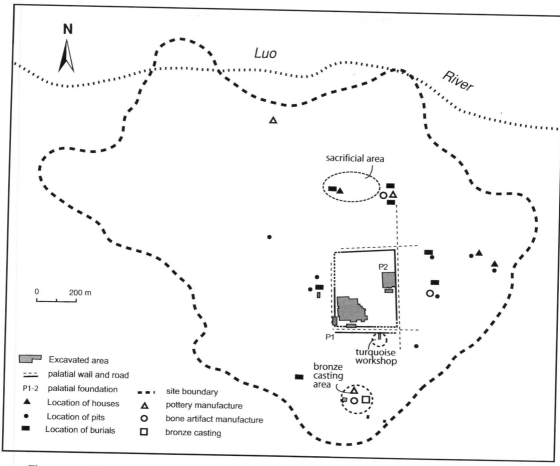

Figure 8.5. Plan of the Erlitou site and location of archaeological features, Erlitou Phase III.

rich grave goods were unearthed from the courtyards of a palace. One burial (no. 3) contained a skeleton of an adult male, 30–35 years of age, which was accompanied by bronzes, jades, lacquer, ceramics, and cowries. A dragon-shaped artifact made of about 2,000 pieces of turquoise and jade was placed on top of the skeleton, signifying his high social status (Figure 8.4.8) (Liu, Li 2006; Liu, L. and Xu 2007).

Pottery and bone artifacts continued to be made on site. A bronze casting foundry, surrounded by a rammed-earth enclosure, was established in the southeast part of the site, about 300 m south of the palace complex's southern road. Other types of craft production, such as turquoise workshops, also may have been located within this enclosure. Houses and burials of children and adults were found in close proximity within the foundry, indicating that this locale was densely populated by craftsmen and their families. Craft production, focused on prestige items and situated in such constrained areas closely associated with the palatial zone, may have been carried out by attached specialists under the control of the state. Attached specialists, as defined by Costin (2001), generally produce high-prestige goods for a patron, either a social elite or a governing institution, in complex societies, particularly states. If this were the case, Phase II of Erlitou would have witnessed the emergence of attached craft specialization, in which bronze metallurgy and precious stone production were dominant (Liu, Li 2006; Liu, L. and Xu 2007).

Among all tool types, agricultural tools make up the highest proportion (42%) of the tool assemblages. This finding suggests development of intensive agricultural activities to cope with the growing population (Liu, Li 2006).

Erlitou Phase III: The Erlitou urban center continued to prosper, with rapid growth in population density and craft production, as indicated by thick cultural deposits and markedly increased numbers of pits, houses, burials, and kilns (Figure 8.5) (Liu, Li 2006).

Several new developments are noteworthy regarding the urban center. First, rammed-earth walls, about 2 m in width, were constructed around the palatial complex (10.8 ha), forming a palatial town. Second, palaces of Phase II were abandoned, and six new structures were built in a more regulated pattern. Third, in contrast to the increased construction of palaces, domestic features, such as water wells and storage pits, were dramatically reduced in number within the palatial town. These changes point to the interpretation that the palatial area became a more privileged and exclusive locale, occupied by small groups of elite residents for conducting particular activities. Fourth, within the workshop enclosure, an area of some 1,000 m² in the northern section appears to have been devoted to the production of turquoise artifacts, indicated by the distribution of turquoise wasters in the area. This development echoes the finding of a number of turquoise inlaid bronze plaques from contemporary elite burials at Erlitou. In addition, the bronze foundry began to produce ritual vessels, mainly *jue* and *jia* drinking vessels (Figure 8.4), which have been found primarily in elite burials and residential areas at Erlitou (Liu, L. and Xu 2007).

Agricultural tools decreased in proportion to craft goods, compared with findings from previous phases. This change suggests that the Erlitou population may have become increasingly dependent on tribute or exchange for food, as the level of craft specialization increased. Phase III also experienced the greatest growth in number of arrowheads (377), which is more than 10 times that in Phase II (35) (Liu, Li 2006). This situation is likely to be attributable to the expansion of the Erlitou territories toward the peripheral regions, driven by the need for procurement of key resources, particularly metals and salt (Liu, L. and Chen 2003: 57–84).

The centralized placement of bronze-casting workshops near the palatial complex at the urban center suggests an increased state monopoly in producing high status symbols. In contrast, bone and ceramic workshops spread over more extended areas at the site, indicating a continuous development of independent craft productions (Liu, Li 2006).

Erlitou Phase IV and Lower Erligang: Cultural deposits of this stage are both concentrated in the central area and scattered in the periphery of the site. The settlement size, however, remains the same as during the previous phase (300 ha). All the palatial structures, with the four intercrossing roads, built in Phase III remained continuously in use. In addition, in Phase IV at least three new edifices were constructed. All the craft workshops were also in production. Bronze vessels unearthed from burials increase in number, type, and quality as compared to previous phases (Liu, L. and Xu 2007). The quantities of tools in all categories increased, except for those, such as needles and awls, used in domestic craft production. Arrowhead production increased dramatically, probably indicating military conflict in the region (Liu, Li 2006). Evidently, Erlitou maintained its position as the largest urban center in the Yiluo region then.

During the late part of Phase IV, another large settlement emerged at Yanshi, about 6 km northeast of Erlitou, known to archaeologists as "Yanshi Shang City," It was started with the construction of a small area of palatial buildings, and then expanded to a large fortified city (200 ha). The material remains are characterized by the Erligang (or early Shang) style. The rise of Yanshi City apparently coincided with the final phase of Erlitou, a scenario that has led to heated debates about the relationship between the two sites. The dominant view in recent years is that Yanshi's emergence in the heartland of the Erlitou culture represents the historical development in which Shang conquered Xia (Du, J. and Wang 2004; Zhongguo Shehui Kexueyuan 2003b).

At Erlitou few remains are datable to the early phase of the Lower Erligang period. Since the dates of Erlitou Phase IV (ca. 1560–1520 BC) and the Lower Erligang period (ca. 1600–1415 BC) (Zhang, X. et al. 2007) are partially overlapping, it is possible that the Erlitou residents continued to produce and use pottery of Erlitou Phase IV style, whereas its close neighbors at Yanshi were making Erligang style pottery. If this were the situation, it would have some important implications relating to ceramic production and sociopolitical organization. More analyses of ceramic provenances need to be conducted to understand the production and relative distribution of pottery types at these two sites.

Upper Erligang phase: Elite-goods production, particularly of bronzes, completely stopped at Erlitou after Phase IV. Cultural remains of the Upper Erligang phase (ca. 1450–1300 BC) at the Erlitou site include small houses, ash pits, and burials, which are concentrated in the area of the previous palatial town, measuring about 30 ha in area. This urban center seems to have been reduced to an ordinary village by then.

The decline of Erlitou coincided not only with the emergence of Yanshi, but also with the rise of an even larger walled city at Zhengzhou, some 85 km east of Erlitou, where the production of bronze tools, weapons, and ritual vessels was a major urban component (Henansheng Wenwu Kaogu 2001). The metallurgical technology and bronze styles found at Zhengzhou show strong continuities from those of Erlitou, suggesting a close relationship between the two centers. Erlitou's decline may have been a strategic decision, involving migration of the Erlitou urban population, including craftsmen, to the Zhengzhou area.

Erlitou Urban Planning and Population

Erlitou shows some regular patterns in its urban planning that clearly indicate a hierarchical structure. The palatial complex was located almost in the center of the site, and residences mixed with burials belonging to the minor elite were concentrated in the east and southeast areas adjacent to the palatial complex. This general area, inhabited by elite groups of different ranks, witnessed the longest occupation at the site, forming the core of the urban expansion. A ceremonial area appears to have been situated to the north of the palatial complex, as indicated by special forms of buildings and attached burials. Enclosed bronze and turquoise workshops were situated immediately south of the palatial complex, suggesting close controls over the production of these prestige goods by the high elite. Commoners' residential areas mixed with burials were situated in the western and northern periphery of the site (Figure 8.5).

The population size at Erlitou is difficult to determine. One study estimates the maximum population size during its peak period (Phase III) as 18,000–30,000 persons, with a mean of 24,000. The Erlitou population included not only the elite and craftsmen, but also farmers, as indicated by large numbers of agricultural tools (Liu, Li 2006). There is a lack of regular burial areas designated for the dead at the site, as tombs and houses often are superimposed on each other. If a formal bounded disposal area, used exclusively for the dead, is indicative of a society with a corporate group structure in the form of a lineal descent system (Goldstein 1981: 61), Erlitou has shown little evidence for such a society. This situation is in sharp contrast to many Neolithic sites (Liu, L. 1996a, 2000a) and the late Shang capital at Anyang (Tang, J. 2004), which have revealed well-defined lineage cemeteries as important components of settlements.

The recurrent alternation between burials and houses in the same areas at Erlitou may also suggest frequent movement of the population. This scenario seems to echo a general settlement pattern of the Erlitou culture region, meaning that rapid territorial expansion was accompanied by movement of the population, who were the carriers of Erlitou's material culture, to the resource-rich peripheries (Liu, L. and Chen 2003: 69–84).

Given that Erlitou was most likely first formed by populations that came from the surrounding areas, it is possible that these first migrants came as many different small kin groups, with no overarching kinship tie connecting all members of the urban community. The initial formative process of the Erlitou population may be better described as discrete groups of people being bound together by a common urban setting, rather than as occupation by a preexisting ethnic group from Xia or Shang. Apparently, future study of the emergence of the Erlitou state and urbanism needs to be decoupled from the traditional concept of early dynasty, which often implies a homogenous ethnicity.

Erlitou Bronze Metallurgy and Ritual Power

The Erlitou site has revealed more than a hundred metal items, including copper, lead, and the alloys consisting of tin-copper, lead-copper, tin-lead-copper, and arsenic-copper. Lead and tin were intentionally added to make alloys, although their proportions show no clear pattern in the bronze (Jin, Z. 2000; Liang, H. and Sun 2006). Arsenic bronze is rare (one item), but it points to Erlitou's connection with some remote cultures in the northwestern region, such as Siba in Gansu (Mei 2006). Despite the lack of standardization in the composition of alloys, and the relatively simple form of the artifacts, Erlitou bronze metallurgy was clearly beyond the formative stage of this technology, and it was the largest production site in China at the time.

The major innovative achievement of Erlitou bronze metallurgy is the use of piece-mold techniques to make ritual vessels as prestige-goods production. Ritual vessels for drinking and cooking, which first appeared in Erlitou Phase III, were the most important medium used in ancestral cult ceremonies for enhancing the political legitimacy of the ruling elite. This tradition was continuously practiced by the dynastic rulers throughout the Bronze Age of China (Chang 1983).

The clay molds recovered from the bronze foundry include those used for casting ritual vessels, weapons, and small woodworking tools (Zhongguo Shehui Kexueyuan 1999b) (Figure 8.4). No mold for making agricultural implements has been identified. The metal products were closely associated with state political affairs, which centered on ritual and warfare rather than agriculture.

Among its contemporary sites, Erlitou is the only locale that has yielded evidence for the manufacture of bronze ritual vessels with piece-mold techniques. This technology, therefore, may have been specially controlled by a particular group of craftsmen attached to the Erlitou high elite in the primary center. Bronze casting was also carried out at several sites in the periphery, such as Dongxiafeng and Nanguan near the copper-rich Zhongtiao Mountains, but, in contrast, only tools and weapons were produced there, with less sophisticated bivalve stone molds (Liu, L. and Chen 2003: 69–73).

The piece-mold technique seems to have been either invented or significantly improved specifically for making bronze ritual vessels, which became the most important symbols of political, religious, and economic power throughout the Bronze Age of China (Chang 1983). This method also marked the divergence of metallurgy at Erlitou from the contemporary surrounding regions, as well as the rest of the world, where bronze products were often nonritual ornamental or utilitarian items.

Erlitou bronze vessels seem to have been distributed predominantly at the Erlitou site, suggesting that the Erlitou rulers monopolized not only production but also distribution of bronze ritual vessels. These vessels were the most prestige items and were exclusively processed by elite members with the highest social status.

The earliest bronze vessels, *jue, jia,* and *he,* appear to be drinking utensils, which resemble their white pottery counterparts found in elite burials predating the appearance of bronze vessels (Figure 8.4). The forms of these drinking vessels inherited a ceramic tradition associated with ritual feasting as a part of the ancestral cult ceremony, and this tradition can be traced back to the Neolithic period (Fung 2000; Keightley 1985). The stylistic continuity of these vessels as ritual paraphernalia from the Neolithic to Bronze Ages suggests a continuous practice of similar forms of ritual observances. The new metallurgical material was integrated into the existing prestige-goods system only when the new products were meaningful and usable within the traditional ritual framework. This achievement was made in the Erlitou period, when the craftsmen developed new technology capable of rendering sophisticated bronze vessels to imitate traditional ceramic vessels (Liu, L. 2003).

Piece-mold bronze production, using multiple inner and outer clay molds, requires high levels of division of labor, great control of material resources, and high degrees of technical and managerial complexity (Bagley 1987; Barnard 1961, 1993; Chase 1983). These requirements could be met only within a highly stratified social organization and, in turn, may have further stimulated the development of social complexity (Franklin 1983, 1992).

Erlitou Hinterland and Periphery

Erlitou was surrounded by fertile alluvial land, an ideal location for agriculture, in the Luoyang Basin. This floodplain, however, offered few nonagricultural natural resources that were crucial for the development of urbanism. These resources include timber for building palatial structures; lithic materials for making stone tools; kaolinic clay for manufacturing white pottery; turquoise for making prestige objects; copper, tin, and lead for making bronzes; fuel for casting bronze alloys and firing pottery; and salt for daily consumption by the entire population of the region. Many prestige goods found at Erlitou, such as proto-porcelain and jade artifacts, appear to have their origins elsewhere. Most of these items were available from the surrounding regions within a radius of 20–200 km from Erlitou, but some may have been derived from the middle Yangzi River Valley, more than 500 km southeast of Erlitou. Erlitou's relationships with its hinterland and periphery demonstrate a complex political-economic system, in which the primary center exercised hegemonic power, whereas the lesser elite in local centers also may have formed their social networks for negotiating power and social status.

Erlitou hinterland: Recent systematic regional surveys and excavations in the Erlitou core area have identified a number of secondary regional centers (Figure 8.3); some of them were developed for manufacturing particular material goods, both prestigious and utilitarian. For example, Huizui in Yanshi was a stone-tool production center which made spades for export (Chen, Xingcan et al. 2010a, b; Owen 2007; Webb et al. 2007), and Nanwa in Dengfeng was one of the locations where white pottery vessels were made (Han, G. et al. 2006, 2007; Li, B. et al. 2008). Stone spades were distributed mainly in the Yiluo region, whereas white pottery vessels have been found over a much larger region. It is notable that, although Erlitou received products from these manufacturing locales, the production and distribution of these items do not seem to have been controlled by Erlitou. Instead, these regional centers are likely to have exchanged their products, such as white pottery and stone tools, directly with each other (Liu, L. et al. 2007a).

This situation suggests that, although Erlitou was the most dominant political center in the region, there was also a heterarchical dimension in the power structure. Independent craftsmen making both elite and nonelite artifacts in the hinterland did not just play a subordinate role in support of the urban elite, but actively pursued status and wealth through their craft skills. There were many competing interests from agents at all levels of society during state formation in the Erlitou core area, and nonstate craft specialization seems to have played a significant role in this power structure (Liu, L. et al. 2007a).

Erlitou periphery: The Erlitou polity expanded rapidly toward the northwest, west, and south, by setting up outposts in its periphery. These outposts include Dongxiafeng and Nanguan in the Zhongtiao Mountains, and Donglongshan in the Qinling Mountains. Erlitou material assemblages also have been found at Panlongcheng in the middle Yangzi River, representing some attempts to explore more distant regions. All of these sites were locations close to important natural resources (Figure 8.1).

Salt, for example, could have been obtained from the Hedong Salt Lake near the Zhongtiao Mountains, which was the only major salt source for the Erlitou culture. Yunxian in northwestern Hubei is known to have rich turquoise deposits, but the sources of the turquoise pieces from Erlitou have not been identified. Copper deposits occurred in abundance in the Zhongtiao Mountains, Qinling Mountains, and the middle Yangzi River. Archaeological evidence indicates that metallurgy was present in regional centers at Nanguan, Dongxiafeng, and Donglongshan, pointing to the motivations for Erlitou's expansion (Liu, L. and X. Chen 2001b, 2003). Compositional and lead isotope analyses on bronze objects unearthed from the Erlitou site show, however, that the metal alloys for Erlitou Phases II and III belong to a single source, which is still unidentifiable. There was a switch of metal sources between Phase III and IV, and most bronzes from Phase IV may have used alloys derived from Shandong in the east (Jin, Z. 2000).

To summarize, Erlitou was evidently a highly stratified society and an urban center with political, ritual, and economic importance in the region. It was occupied by a dense and stratified population, who were involved in agricultural production and various types of specialized craft manufacturing, including both elite goods and utilitarian items. The Erlitou state may be described as a territorial state (Liu, L. and Chen 2003: 79–84), which by definition refers to a political entity with a single ruler who controls a large area through a hierarchy of provincial and local administrators and administrative centers (Trigger 2003: 92–4).

THE NEIGHBORS OF THE ERLITOU STATE

Beyond the sphere of the Erlitou material assemblage, many archaeological cultures have been identified (Zhongguo Shehui Kexueyuan 2003b: 440–658). Each culture may have consisted of a number of independent polities, which interacted with one another, as well as with the Erlitou state. These interactions took place in various ways, such as exchange, trade, warfare, and population migration. The contemporary cultures peripheral to the early state included Yueshi in the east, Xiaqiyuan in the north, Lower Xiajiadian in the farther northeast, Qijia in the west, Sanxingdui in the southwest, and Maqiao in the southeast (Figure 8.1). In this chapter we focus on the most immediate neighbors of Erlitou, namely, Xiaqiyuan and Yueshi.

Xiaqiyuan

The Xiaqiyuan culture (ca. 1800–1500 BC), distributed in northern Henan and southern Hebei, appears to have originated from several Longshan cultural traditions in the region, and developed into a number of variants based on ceramic styles. There is no agreement about the names of these Xiaqiyuan variants, but in general they are named Yuegezhuang, Zhanghe, and Huiwei, from north to south. Archaeologists have identified more than eighty Xiaqiyuan culture sites, primarily distributed along the alluvial region between the Tai-hang Mountain ranges and the ancient courses of Yellow River (Zhongguo Shehui Kexueyuan 2003b: 140–64).

Most Xiaqiyuan sites are small. For instance, all fourteen sites found along the Huan River are less than 5 ha in size (Jing, Z. et al. 2002). There were, however, several medium-sized regional centers, among which Mengzhuang in Huixian was a walled settlement (12.7 ha in the occupied area) (Figure 8.1). Warfare and violence seem to have been present, suggested by three human skulls associated with a rammed-earth feature (Henansheng Wenwu Kaogu 2003).

This walled settlement may have partially functioned as protection for populations residing in the surrounding areas.

A boundary line between the Erlitou and Xiaqiyuan cultures lies in the Qin River and a part of the Yellow River, dividing Erlitou sites on the south from Xiaqiyuan sites on the north (Figure 8.1). Relations between these two cultural groups seem to have been characterized by conflict and violence. A walled Erlitou site is located at Dashigu in Xingyang, about 13 km south of the Yellow River (Wang, W. et al. 2004), and two skeletons with traits of scalping have been unearthed at Dasima in Wuzhi, about 5 km south of the Qin River (Chen, X. 2000; Yang, G. et al. 1994). These two sites are located in the northeast frontiers of the Erlitou culture.

The Xiaqiyuan culture received rather diverse influences from the surrounding regions. Ceramics from Mengzhuang show some strong influence from the Erlitou culture (Henansheng Wenwu Kaogu 2003), whereas some bronze items unearthed from Hebei are of typical Northern Zone styles, including knife with ring-shaped handle, arrowhead with socketed stem, and earring with flared end (Zhongguo Shehui Kexueyuan 2003b: 154–5).

Many archaeologists have attempted to match the cultural variants with names of predynastic states mentioned in ancient texts, such as by equating the Zhanghe variant with the proto-Shang culture and the Huiwei variant with the Wei ethnic group (Henansheng Wenwu Kaogu 2003; Zhongguo Shehui Kexueyuan 2003b: 140–64). Because a ceramic variant may not necessarily correlate to a political entity, it is unclear how many polities existed in the distribution area of Xiaqiyuan culture. In any event, settlement patterns and material remains show that the Xiaqiyuan culture is most likely to have consisted of multiple polities, which were competing with one another and were in conflict with the Erlitou state. The level of social complexity in the Xiaqiyuan polities was much lower than that in the Erlitou state.

Yueshi

The Yueshi culture (ca. 1900–1500 BC) is distributed mainly in Shandong, eastern Henan, and north Jiangsu (Figure 8.1). It was contemporary with the Erlitou and part of the Erligang cultures. Its core area is around the Taiyi Mountains region; when the Erligang culture expanded to the east, the Yueshi culture went into decline and retreated eastward to the Jiaodong Peninsula. Some late Yueshi sites continued to exist after 1500 BC (Shandongsheng 2005: 280–325).

The Yueshi culture was formed partly by direct succession from the Shandong Longshan tradition and partly by derivation from the cultures in surrounding areas. More than 340 Yueshi sites have been identified in Shandong (Shandongsheng 2005: 284). Compared to the total number of Shandong Longshan sites (1,492) identified (Guojia 2007), there was a marked decline in population density from the Longshan to Yueshi periods. This trend is more observable in eastern than in western Shandong. In the east coast region, for example, Yueshi period sites are extremely sparse, as revealed by the full-coverage regional survey (Underhill et al. 2008). In contrast, the Yueshi culture in northern Shandong may have maintained a level of social complexity similar to that of the Longshan period. At Chengziya in Zhangqiu, rammed-earth walls continued to be rebuilt. At Shijia in Zibo, a ritual pit containing 355 items was found, including pottery vessels, tools, ornaments, and oracle-bones incised with glyphs. The glyphs, read as characters *liu* (six) and *bu* (divination), are similar in structure to the oracle-bone inscriptions of the late Shang dynasty (Shandongsheng 2005: 280–325; Zhang, G. et al. 1997).

Yueshi ceramics are less elaborate than those of the Longshan period; among them, brown-colored sandy wares and gray fine wares predominate. These thick, heavy pottery types were once interpreted as evidence of cultural degeneration. Nevertheless, other material remains seem to suggest improvements in agricultural production. The major Yueshi agricultural implements include spades, sickles, knives, and *jue* hoes (Figure 8.6). Agricultural tools also increased proportionately in tool assemblages at many sites dated from Longshan to Yueshi, suggesting growing significance of agriculture in the subsistence economy (Shandongsheng 2005: 320).

Metal objects, mainly small tools and ornaments, including arrowheads, chisels, knives, awls, drills, and rings, have been unearthed from several Yueshi sites (Figure 8.6) (Luan 1996a: 319–22). Analyses of nine metal objects from Yinjiacheng suggest that they belong to five types of alloys: copper, tin bronze, lead bronze, tin–lead bronze, and arsenic bronze; the metallurgical methods are primarily single-mold casting, but some items were further worked with cold or hot hammering on the edges after casting. A few copper and lead deposits exist in Sishui, Xintai, Laiwu, and Mengyin Counties at present, and one mine at Licheng holds copper compounded with arsenic. Some of these mines appear to have been exploited in ancient times. Therefore, it is likely that the Yueshi copper and bronze objects were produced locally. The diverse techniques and metal alloy components observed in the Yinjiacheng metal remains suggest an early stage of metallurgy in this area (Sun, S. 1990).

No luxury items from long-distance exchange, such as jade objects or elaborate burial goods, have been found in Yueshi culture sites. The Yueshi people seem to have engaged in frequent interactions with polities in the surrounding areas, especially the early states centered at Erlitou and Zhengzhou. The most recognizable Yueshi items in other regions are its ceramics, stone knives, and stone *jue* hoes, many found at Erlitou and Erligang sites in Henan (Luan 1996a: 330–2). The highest concentration of Yueshi material found outside of the Yueshi culture area is from Xiaoshuangqiao near Zhengzhou, which was a major political center of the middle Shang period. Nearly forty stone *jue* hoes were uncovered, mainly from a ritual area for human and animal sacrifice

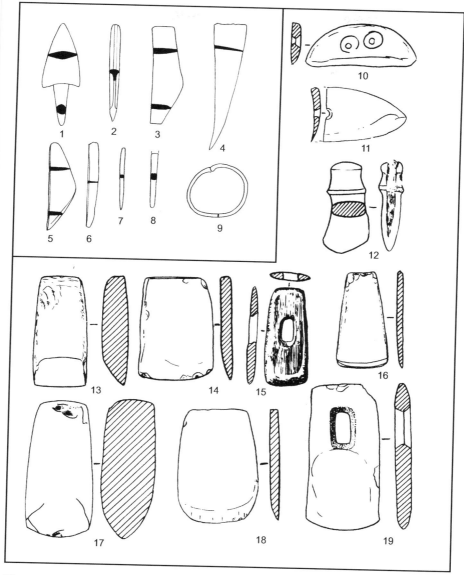

Figure 8.6. Artifacts from the Yueshi culture (1–9 bronze; 10–19 stone). 1: Arrowhead; 2, 7, and 8: awls; 3–6: knives; 9: ring; 10 and 11: knives; 12: axe; 13: adze; 14, 16, and 18: spades; 15: stone tool with a rectangular hole; 17: axe; 19: *jue* hoe (after figures 96 and 97 of Shandongsheng 2005).

(Song, G. et al. 1996). The *jue* hoe is a distinctively Yueshi artifact, rectangular or square in shape with a square-shaped perforation and sharp edges on two or three sides (Figure 8.6.19). Some archaeologists have argued that these hoes were the trophies of warfare between the Shang and Yueshi cultures (Ren, X. 1997). These Yueshi artifacts from different sites reflect various kinds of relationships between Yueshi and other cultures, which may include trade, warfare, and population movement.

In the late Shang oracle-bone inscriptions the name "Renfang" was used to refer to the region, in south Shandong and north Jiangsu, of alien people against whom the Shang kings waged wars (Chang 1980: 252). It is also commonly believed that the characters "Ren" in the late Shang inscriptions and "Yi" in Zhou and Han documents both refer to the same people, who resided in the east. Accordingly, peoples identified by the Zhou as residing to the east were also commonly called Dongyi (Eastern Barbarian). Many Chinese archaeologists often use the term Dongyi to represent the Yueshi culture (Luan 1996a; Yan, W. 1989a). Apparently, these Yi peoples did not belong to a single ethnic group. Archaeologically, the Yueshi culture has been divided into several variants based on ceramic typology, but it is not possible to connect a ceramic type with the ethnic identity of a social group (Cohen 2001).

THE ERLIGANG CULTURE AND ERLIGANG STATE

During the Erlitou Phase IV period, two other walled settlements at Yanshi and Zhengzhou emerged, associated with material remains known as the Erligang culture (ca. 1600–1400 BC). Zhengzhou, which was more than four times the size of Erlitou, became the primary center in the middle Yellow River region, and Yanshi appears to have been a secondary center of Zhengzhou. At least three tiers of political hierarchy are observable in the core area of the Erligang culture, the material remains of which spread over a much greater region than that of Erlitou. Most Erligang regional centers, unlike those of the Erlitou period, became fortified, suggesting an intensification of warfare. These changes redefined the political landscape, forming a more complex and militarized state-level society in north China (Figure 8.7).

Zhengzhou and Yanshi are often regarded by Chinese archaeologists as Shang capitals, with Yanshi in particular demarcating the dynastic transition from Xia to Shang (Gao, W. et al. 1998). This view, nevertheless, is controversial. We prefer the term "Erligang state" when referring to the political dimension of Erligang culture, but follow the conventional use of "early Shang" in the Chinese archaeological literature when describing relevant material remains.

The Erligang Core Area

Central Henan and the Yiluo Basin comprise the core area of the Erligang culture, where two large walled sites, Zhengzhou and Yanshi, appear to have been the primary and secondary centers.

Yanshi Shang City: During the late part of Erlitou Phase IV, a group of large palaces surrounded by a rammed-earth enclosure (4 ha) were built at Yanshi, 6 km northeast of Erlitou, referred to as "the Palace town." A second rammed-earth circumvallation (80 ha) was then added, enclosing an area referred to by archaeologists as "the small town." Finally, a third, outer-most walled enclosure (17–21 m in thickness) was subsequently constructed,

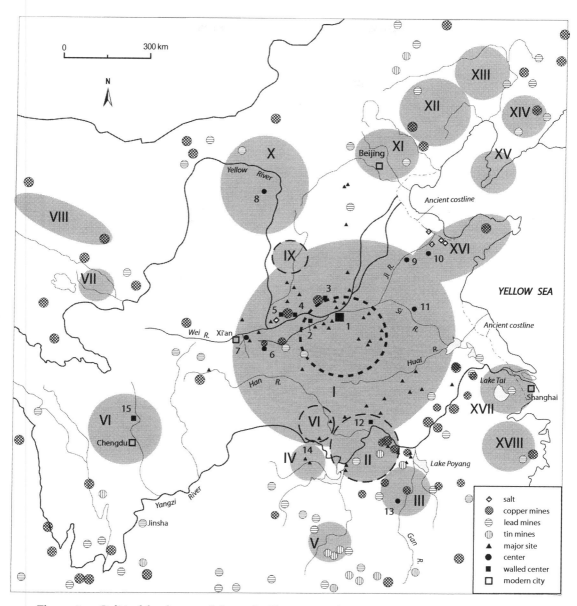

Figure 8.7. Political landscape of the early Shang period. Archaeological cultures –
I: Erligang; II: Panlongcheng; III: Wucheng; IV: Baota; V: Xiang River region
press-marked ceramics; VI: Sanxingdui; VII: Kayue; VIII: Siba; IX: Guangshe;
X: Zhukaigou; XI: Datuotou; XII: Lower Xiajiadian; XIII: Gaotaishan; XIV: Miaohoushan; XV: Shuangtuozi II; XVI: Yueshi; XVII: Maqiao; XVIII: Hushu (distribution of sites and cultures based on Zhongguo Shehui Kexueyuan 2003b). Sites
1: Zhengzhou; 2: Yanshi; 3: Fucheng; 4: Nanguan; 5: Dongxiafeng; 6: Donglongshan; 7: Laoniupo; 8: Zhukaigou; 9: Daxinzhuang; 10: Shijia; 11: Qianzhangda;
12: Panlongcheng; 13: Wucheng; 14: Zaoshi; 15: Sanxingdui.

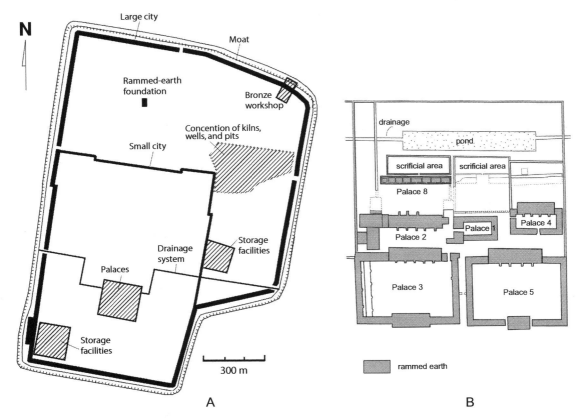

Figure 8.8. Yanshi Shang City. (A) Plan of Yanshi Shang City. (B) Major features and buildings in the palatial area (redrawn from figures 4 and 5 of Zhongguo Shehui Kexueyan 2003b and figure 2 of Du, J. 2006).

enclosing an area known to archaeologists as "the large town," making the entire site a large, fortified city (200 ha). The material assemblages from the lowest strata at Yanshi show a mixture of Erlitou and a transitional form, which is a stylistic stage between the Xiaqiyuan (or proto-Shang) and Erligang (or early Shang) types, and later deposits are predominantly of the Erligang culture. Within the city there were large storage facilities, a pottery workshop, a bronze foundry, residential areas, and burials. The Palace town was partitioned into three areas: in the south there was the palatial area, consisting of at least six large buildings; in the center there were areas (ca. 3,000 m²) dedicated to ritual sacrifices, where large numbers of plants and skeletal remains identifiable as human, pig, cattle, sheep/goat, dog, deer, and fish have been revealed; and in the north there was an artificial pond with drainage systems connecting to water sources outside of the city (Figure 8.8) (Du, J. 2003, 2006; Wang, X. 2002). The Yanshi city appears to have been particularly military and ceremonial in nature, judging from its massive construction of fortifications and the large scale of sacrificial activities.

Zhengzhou Shang City: Zhengzhou is surrounded on the north by the Yellow River, on the southwest by foothills of the Song Mountains, and on

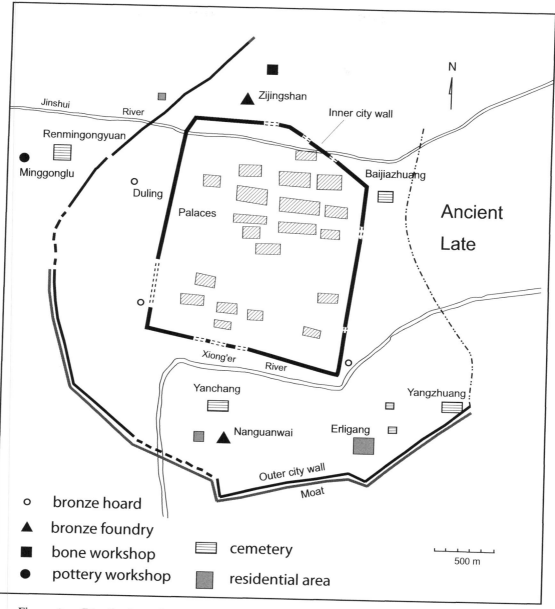

Figure 8.9. Distribution of major archaeological remains at Zhengzhou Shang City, Erligang period (redrawn from Liu, Y. et al. 2010: 98 and figure 1 of Yuan, G. and Zeng 2004).

the southeast by massive alluvial plains; lakes covered the eastern area of the site in antiquity. The entire site covers an area of around 25 km², centered on two concentric rammed-earth walls: a rectangular inner city (300 ha) and a nearly round outer city (ca. 18 km²). A few dozen rammed-earth house foundations, ranging from 100 m² to 2,000 m² in size, have been found within the inner city, especially concentrated in the northeastern part. These foundations were probably the remains of royal palaces and temples (Figure 8.9).

The northeastern area near the northern wall may have been used as a ritual locale, associated with large erected rocks and sacrificial pits containing humans and animals. Some 100 human skullcaps, many with saw marks, have been unearthed in a ditch near an architectural foundation (Liu, Y. et al. 2010; Yuan, G. and Zeng 2004). These skullcaps may have been the remains of human sacrifices that took place near a temple (Henansheng Wenwu Kaogu 2001).

Cemeteries, residential areas, and craft production workshops were mostly distributed within the outer city and a few in areas outside the enclosure. These workshops manufactured bronze, ceramic, and bone objects used for both prestige and utilitarian purposes. Some workshops became highly specialized in making certain types of products. A pottery workshop at Minggonglu yielded mainly two types of vessel products, fine-paste basins and steamers. One bronze foundry at Nanguanwai, about 700 m south of the southern inner city wall, mainly produced ritual vessels, tools, and weapons (Figure 8.10). The other bronze foundry at Zijingshan, some 300 m north of the northern inner-city wall, manufactured weapons and small tools, as well as small numbers of chariot fittings and ritual vessels (An, J. et al. 1989; Henansheng Wenwu Kaogu 2001: 307–83). These two bronze foundries are the only locations that have yielded hard evidence for casting of ritual vessels in the Erligang culture. As at Erlitou, the production of bronze ritual objects appears to have been monopolized by the highest ruling groups in the primary center of the Erligang state (Liu, L. and Chen 2003: 92–9).

Two pieces of animal bone bearing inscriptions have been found at Erligang in Zhengzhou; one piece was incised with twelve characters and the other with one. These characters are similar in style to the oracle-bone inscriptions found at Yinxu of the late Shang (Henansheng Wenhuaju 1959: 38) (Figure 8.10).

Population size at Zhengzhou is difficult to estimate. Given its large site size, presence of various craft workshops, and numerous construction projects involved, Zhengzhou must have had a much larger population than Erlitou. If we use the population density range derived from Erlitou (60–100 persons/ha), as discussed earlier in text, Zhengzhou's population would have been 78,000–130,000 with a mean of 104,000 persons. A large proportion of the population may have been involved in construction works; based on one estimate, at least 10,000 people had to work for ten years to build the city walls at Zhengzhou (Henansheng Wenwu Kaogu 2001: 1020–1).

The population of Zhengzhou was clearly segregated by the inner walls, with mainly the elites and their close associates occupying the inner city, while commoners engaged in various types of craft production lived mainly in the outer city. As at Erlitou, the early Shang bronzes were used for ritual and warfare, rather than for agricultural production. In contrast, tools made of stone, bone, and shell have been found in many areas at Zhengzhou (Henansheng Wenwu Kaogu 2001: 154–60). Therefore, also as at Erlitou, the urban population at Zhengzhou included elite, craftsmen, and farmers.

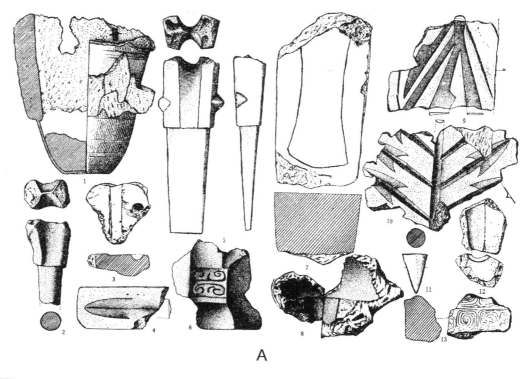

A

B

C

Figure 8.10. Artifacts from Zhengzhou Shang City, Erligang culture. (A) Clay molds from Nanguanwai bronze foundry, indicating that ritual vessels, weapons, and tools were cast at the primary center (not to scale; after figure 6 of An, J. et al. 1989). (B) Bronze assemblage from the Nanshunchengjie Hoard, including two *jue* vessels, two *jia* vessels, two *ge* daggers, one *yue* axe, one *gui* vessel, and four *fangding* tetrapods (after color plate 2 of Henansheng Wenwu Kaogu 1999b). (C) Animal bone bearing twelve inscriptions unearthed from Erligang in Zhengzhou (after figure 12 of Henansheng Wenhuaju 1959).

The society was evidently highly stratified, and warfare was common. The military nature is indicated by the construction of defensive walls and the practice of human sacrifice, as well as the fact that raw materials in the bone workshop include a large proportion of human bones (Henansheng Wenwu Kaogu 2001: 460–82).

Many bronze ritual vessels from Zhengzhou are similar in style to those from Erlitou, whereas others are new, such as large *fangding* tetrapod (Figure 8.10B). The largest tetrapod from Zhengzhou measures 100 cm in height and weighs 86.4 kg (Henansheng Wenwu Kaogu 1999b). Vessels of this new type appear to have been owned, as status symbols, by the highest ranking royals during the Shang period (Yang, B. and Liu 1991). The scale of bronze production at Zhengzhou was much greater than at Erlitou. This situation can be inferred from three hoards of bronze objects discovered in the outer city, which contained twenty-eight bronzes with a total weight of more than 500 kg (Henansheng Wenwu Kaogu 1999b). These objects were probably only a small fraction of the bronze products manufactured at Zhengzhou, as no large tombs, which normally contain many bronzes, have been discovered.

Numerous articles have been published in China debating the nature of Zhengzhou and addressing its affiliation with the capital cities of the Shang named explicitly in the traditional texts. This debate has been complicated by continuous discoveries of archaeological remains in the region and by ongoing refinement of ceramic typology and periodization. Still, no consensus has been reached among Chinese archaeologists, and Zhengzhou is generally regarded as either capital Ao (e.g., Henansheng Wenwu Kaogu 2001:1026–7) or capital Bo (Zou, H. 1998).

Erligang Expansion

The Erligang state expanded its power by setting up outposts in the periphery, a political strategy first used by the Erlitou state. Many of these outposts were already occupied by the Erlitou culture as regional centers, but now they became fortified. Such outposts have been found at Panlongcheng in the south; Dongxiafeng, Nanguan, and Donglongshan in the west; and Daxinzhuang in the east (Figure 8.7). This expansion, like Erlitou's earlier, appears to have been driven by the procurement of key resources and prestige items, such as metal alloys, salt, jade, and proto-porcelain. The interactions between the core and periphery may have created interdependent relationships. The regional centers in the periphery provided raw materials and exotic goods as tribute to the core area to support urban growth and craft production in the major center and to contribute to the formation of hierarchical sociopolitical structures. In return, the major center redistributed the products (mainly prestige goods, including bronze ritual vessels) of its restricted and sacred crafts, as well as exotic or scarce goods extracted from surrounding areas, such as salt and proto-porcelain (which likely contained prestigious items), to the regional elites as rewards (Liu, L. and Chen 2003: 102–30).

Westward expansion: Erligang's expansion toward the west is manifested by its construction of fortifications at two preexisting Erlitou regional centers: Dongxiafeng in Xiaxian and Nanguan in Yuanqu, both in southern Shanxi. Continuing on from the Erlitou period, these sites were functionally designed for extracting and transporting the most valuable local resources, particularly copper in the Zhongtiao Mountains; Dongxiafeng also produced salt from the Hedong Salt Lake (Liu, L. and Chen 2001b, 2003). A group of storage facilities at Dongxiafeng appears to resemble in form the salt storage illustrated in ancient texts (Figure 8.11). Chemical analysis of the soil samples from the storage floor has confirmed that these structures were used for storing large quantities of salt, which may have been transported to other regions in the Erligang state (Chen, Xingcan et al. 2010).

Eastward expansion: Daxinzhuang in Jinan and Qianzhangda in Tengzhou were the first Erligang regional centers established in Shandong. Each was associated with a number of smaller sites that were set up as colonies in the local Yueshi culture area. The elite groups appear to have been exclusively Erligang in origin. Material remains show that local Yueshi cultural components coexisted with Erligang elements in the beginning, but gradually diminished, as a result of Erligang political domination. The early state's interest was apparently drawn to this region for its rich natural resources, including marine products (e.g., pearls and shells), agricultural products (e.g., grains), and metals (Fang, H. 2009). Whether salt was also exploited by the Erligang people is unclear, but given that intensified salt production by the late Shang state is clearly evident in northern Shandong (Li, S. et al. 2009; Wang, Q. 2006b), it is possible that this resource also attracted the attention of the Erligang state, although hard evidence is still lacking.

Southward expansion: The Erligang culture reached the middle Yangzi region, represented by Panlongcheng in Hubei, Wucheng in Jiangxi, and Zaoshi in Hunan (Liu, L. and Chen 2003: 116–30).

Panlongcheng, situated near Lake Panlong in Huangpi County near Wuhan, Hubei, was the largest outpost established by early states in the middle Yangzi River area. It was initially occupied by the Erlitou people, and is likely to have been used for exploring the rich copper deposits and other resources in the region. The site location was apparently chosen as a focal point for transportation. It has easy access to several major water communication routes: the Yangzi River to the southeast, the Han River to the southwest, as well as a number of small rivers originating in the Dabie Mountains to the north and leading directly to the Henan region (Figure 8.7) (Liu, L. and Chen 2003: 75–9, 116–19).

During the Erlitou period, Panlongcheng (ca. 20 ha) was occupied by several small settlements, which may have engaged in pottery manufacturing

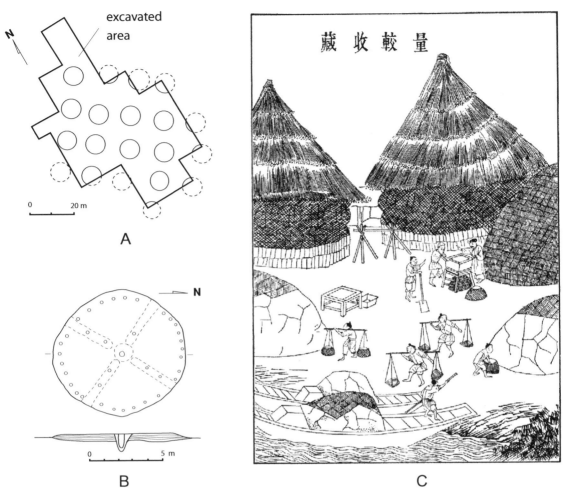

Figure 8.11. Salt storage facilities at Dongxiafeng in Xiaxian, Erligang culture, and salt storage recorded in ancient texts. (**A**) A group of salt storage facilities at Dongxiafeng. (**B**) An example of the Dongxiafeng storage structural remains (redrawn from figures 138 and 139 of Zhongguo Shehui Kexueyuan et al. 1988). (**C**) Salt storage facilities depicted in *Tiangong kaiwu* (*T'ien-kung k'ai-wu*), originally printed in AD 1637 (after Sung 1966: 113).

and bronze metallurgy, indicated by finds of kilns and crucibles (Figure 8.12). Proto-porcelain vessels also have been unearthed at the site. It is not clear, based on available information, to what extent Erlitou directly controlled the copper mines in this region, and whether the metal was actually transported to the north (Hubeisheng 2001a; Liu, L. and Chen 2003: 75–9).

Rapid development occurred during the upper Erligang period, when the site became surrounded by two concentric rammed-earth walls. The outer walls, which were discovered recently, embrace an area of about 290 ha (Liu, S. 2002). The inner walls (7.5 ha) enclose the center of the site, forming a palatial town within which a large structure was built. Between the inner and outer

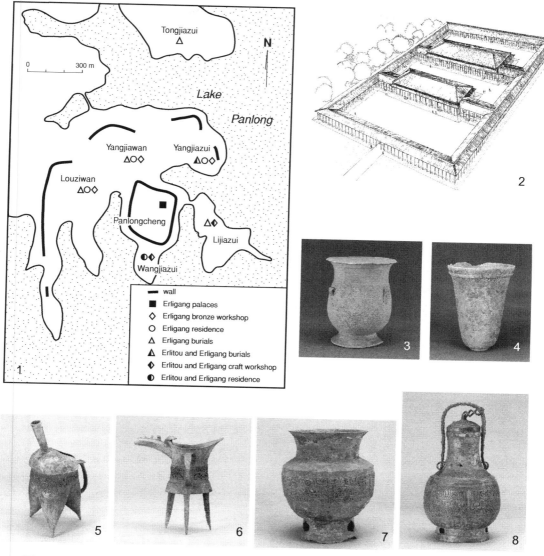

Figure 8.12. Panlongcheng. 1: The Panlongcheng site, showing spatial distribution of palaces, craft production centers, residential areas, and tombs (redrawn from figure 4 of Hubeisheng 2001a); 2: reconstruction of palatial structures; 3: proto-porcelain vessel; 4: crucible; 5–8: bronze ritual vessels (*he, jue, zun,* and *tiliangyou*) from elite burials (after color plates 9–1, 10–1, 11–1, 13–1, 2, 24 of Hubeisheng 2001a: 644).

walls archaeologists have found burials, residential areas, and bronze workshops. Crucibles, slag, and malachite have been uncovered at five locations, which all may have been involved in bronze metallurgy (Hubeisheng 2001a). The concentric, double-ringed design of the city walls at Panlongcheng is remarkably similar to that seen at Yanshi and Zhengzhou, and definitive characteristics of material remains from Panlongcheng resemble those found at early Shang cities in the Central Plain. Such traits include the styles and types of bronze artifacts, techniques used in the construction of building foundations and town walls, and the layout of palatial structures, all showing Panlongcheng's close affiliation to the north (e.g., Bagley 1999; Hubeisheng 2001a: 493). Several elite tombs contained large numbers of bronze vessels along with crucibles, suggesting that the Panlongcheng elite groups were closely associated with control of metal resources (Figure 8.12) (Hubeisheng 2001a).

Bronze metallurgy was present at Panlongcheng, as judged from the finding of crucibles and slag. Many people have argued that the bronze artifacts unearthed at the site were produced locally, given the rich copper deposits available in the region. There is a lack of hard evidence (e.g., casting molds) for casting of ritual vessels at the site, however. Experts have not been able to pinpoint source locations of metallic ores used to produce the Panlongcheng bronzes. Although the copper and tin appear to have come from the same sources, the lead was not from local deposits (Hubeisheng 2001a: 517–73). Considering the stylistic similarities between bronzes from major Erligang sites in the north and those found at Panlongcheng, it may be that the latter were also cast at Zhengzhou and then imported to Panlongcheng.[1] The same situation seems to have occurred at other regional centers, such as Dongxiafeng and Yuanqu. This phenomenon is consistent with organizational characteristics of bronze production also evident in the Erlitou culture, demonstrating a continued political strategy aimed at monopolizing production and distribution of ritual vessels by the state rulers.

South of Panlongcheng was the walled site (61 ha) at Wucheng in Jiangxi (Jiangxisheng and Zhangshushi 2005). As at Panlongcheng, material remains at Wucheng show a predominant Erligang component combined with local traditions. In contrast to Panlongcheng, which went into decline after the Erligang period, Wucheng began to flourish during the late Shang and became a regional center with intensified local characteristics. This development will be discussed in Chapter 10.

Erligang's focus on the middle Yangzi region was expressed in a continuous effort to exploit the rich metal deposits in this area, demonstrating the most important political strategy for controlling and manipulating ritual power by the ruling elite of early states. The Erligang leadership targeted at least two major copper-mining sites – Tongling in Ruichang, Jiangxi (Liu, S. and Lu 1998) and Tonglüshan in Daye, Hubei (Huangshi 1999), as suggested by the discovery of Erligang material remains associated with evidence of mining and smelting in these locations (Liu, L. and Chen 2003: 116–23).

To facilitate transporting valuable southern resources to the north, Panlongcheng and Wucheng apparently functioned as communication nodes. In

---

[1] A recent study of clay residues from bronze vessels unearthed from burials at Panlongcheng shows that the clay resembles the local soil rather than that from north China, and therefore infers local production of Panlongcheng bronze vessels (Nan, P. et al. 2008). This result, however, is controversial (Jin, Zhengyao 2009, personal communication).

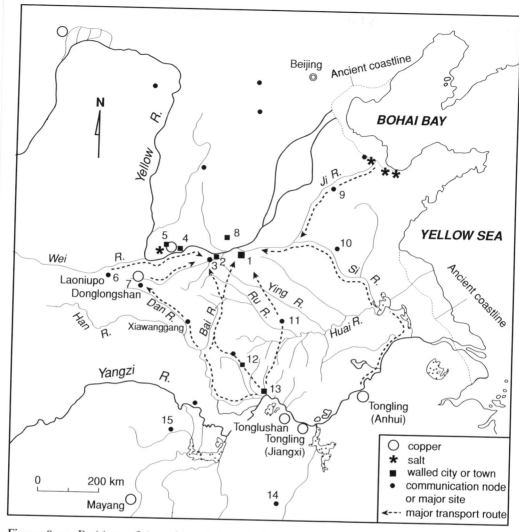

Figure 8.13. Positions of river channels in early dynastic times, locations of key natural resources, and four major transportation routes with communication nodes linking primary centers in the core area with the middle and lower Yangzi River Valley in the south, the Wei River in the west, and the coastal region in the east. 1: Zhengzhou; 2: Yanshi; 3: Erlitou; 4: Yuanqu; 5: Dongxiafeng; 6: Laoniupo; 7: Donglongshan; 8: Fudian; 9: Daxinzhuang; 10: Qianzhangda; 11: Fantang;12: Wangjiashan; 13: Panlongcheng; 14: Wucheng (modified from figure 10 of Liu and Chen 2003 and figure 8 of Jiang, G. 2008).

addition, at least four routes, either on land or by river, appear to have been used by early states for conveying critical resources and prestige items. Along these routes the Erligang state established more regional centers and small fortifications, to further exploit local resources and to ensure effective transfer of luxury and strategic goods (Figure 8.13) (Jiang, G. 2008; Liu, L. and Chen 2003: 50–4).

Summary

The Erligang state's appetite for material resources was enormous. Materials procured include salt from the Hedong Salt Lake, marine products from the east, proto-porcelain from the Yangzi region, and metal from all surrounding regions. Given that frequent ritual sacrifice of animals and food offerings were conducted by the ruling elite, grains and livestock must also have been important parts of the state's regular procurement.

The Erligang state's cultural expansion was extraordinary. Erligang cultural assemblages consist not only of prestigious items, such as bronzes and jades, but also of pottery types, house structures, burial customs, and urban planning. The appearance of Erligang ceramics as a coherent assemblage in many regions outside the Erligang core is particularly interesting. As ordinary pottery was normally made locally for daily use, and pottery styles were associated with craftsmen's technical traditions, it is most likely that the Erligang pottery in the periphery was made by migrant Erligang craftsmen. The widespread Erligang cultural traits, therefore, are likely to have resulted directly from the Erligang populations who were sent to colonize new lands. Such a state-organized migration scenario is consistent with the later textual record that shows that craftsmen, including potters, were sent with ruling clans to resettle in new territory during the Western Zhou dynasty (Hsu and Linduff 1988: 153–4). This tradition appears to have had much deeper roots in prehistory.

Many scholars have argued that Erligang culture and the later Shang culture seen at Yinxu manifest a continuous development (through middle Shang) within the same archaeologically defined tradition. Furthermore, if Yinxu has been more precisely confirmed by the oracle-bone inscriptions as the late Shang, then Erligang should be understood as the early Shang. Accordingly, the Erligang expansion into the surrounding regions changed the political landscape of the Erlitou culture. It altered the Erlitou state's relatively balanced relationship with Xiaqiyuan and Yueshi to the north and east, linked up transportation routes with the Yangzi region to the south, and further secured colonization in the west. Although not all the Erligang cultural areas can be seen as falling within the early Shang's domain, it is fair to say that the political power of the Erligang state, as expressed through the growth of the early Shang dynasty, reached its peak during the middle of the second millennium BC (Sun, H. 2009).

AFTERMATH OF THE ERLIGANG EXPANSION: THE MIDDLE SHANG DECENTRALIZATION

The Erligang expansion ceased around 1400 BC, when Zhengzhou and many of its regional centers in the core and periphery were abandoned, marking the end of this highly centralized system of political economy. The causes of this transition are unclear, but it may have occurred because of sociopolitical conflict and the sudden outbreak of destabilizing turmoil. In three cases, precious ritual bronzes were buried with great haste in a dry well or in pits at Zhengzhou, and all of these bronze hoards date to the end of the Upper Erligang phase (Figure 8.9 for location of the hoards, Figure 8.10B for bronzes). These bronzes may have been intentionally buried for safe-keeping during a time of turmoil, with the owners expecting to return in the near future (Chen, X. 1986; Henansheng Wenwu Kaogu 1999b). This situation resembles that of the bronze hoards found at Zhouyuan, believed to have been hidden away by Western Zhou elite families as they escaped from the capital under enemy attack (Zhongguo Shehui Kexueyaun, 2004: 62).

Following the collapse of Zhengzhou, nearly all the Erligang centers in and near the core disappeared from the archaeological record, and several large and medium centers emerged in other locations, represented by Xiaoshuangqiao near Zhengzhou and Huanbei in Anyang, which were much smaller than Zhengzhou. Regional centers in the periphery continued to flourish. The Shang material culture appears to have been shared by a broad region (Figure 8.14), but mixed with increased proportions of local characteristics. These changes mark a new cultural phase, referred to as the middle Shang (ca. 1400–1250 BC) (Tang, J. 2001). In general, the middle Shang is a period characterized by political instability, weakened dynastic centralization probably involving factional competition, and the rise of regional powers.

Xiaoshuangqiao (150 ha), 20 km northwest of Zhengzhou (Figure 8.14), has revealed large rammed-earth palatial foundations, sacrificial pits, and bronze casting remains. Sacrificial pits were located near palaces and contained large quantities of human and animal (mainly cattle and dogs) skeletons. Some ceramic urns from bovine sacrificial pits bear glyphs written with brushstrokes in red pigment. These glyphs can be categorized as numbers and pictograms, among other types. They are similar in form to the oracle-bone inscriptions from Anyang dating to 100 years later (Figure 8.15). The function of this site has been a matter of debate among Chinese archaeologists, who regard Xiaoshuangqiao either as a Shang capital named Ao in traditional texts or as a ceremonial locale associated with Zhengzhou (Song, G. 2003; Zhongguo Shehui Kexueyuan 2003b: 274–5).

Huanbei: Recent investigations north of the Huan River, opposite Yinxu on the south bank, have shown that a walled city, known to archaeologists as Huanbei Shang City, was built on the north bank during the late middle Shang period (see Chapter 10; Figure 10.4). The size of the city enclosure (470 ha) exceeds that of the inner city at Zhengzhou. Several sectors with rammed-earth foundations formed a palatial area inside the city, and two of the surviving foundations (F1 and F2) have been excavated (He, Y. and Tang 2010; Tang, J. et al. 2003a; Tang, J. et al. 2010a; Tang, J. et al. 2003b; Tang, J. et al. 2010c). F1 (1.5 ha) was a large-scale quadrangle with east and

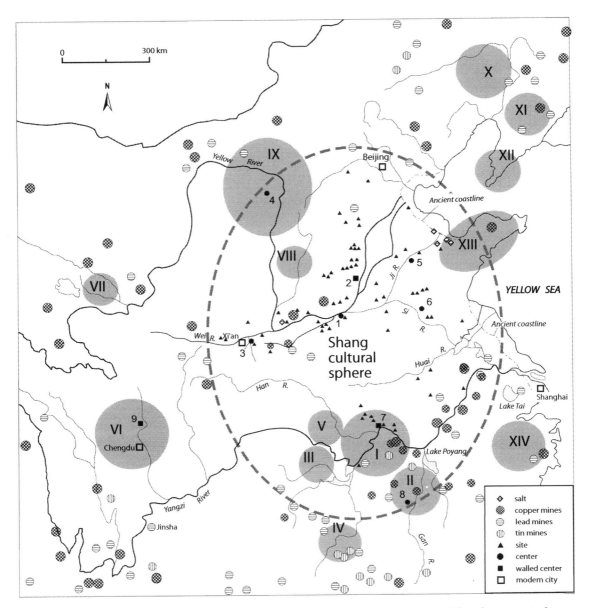

Figure 8.14. Distribution of archaeological cultures in the middle Shang period. Archaeological cultures – I: Panlongcheng; II: Wucheng; III: Baota; IV: Xiang River region press-marked ceramics; V: Jingnansi; VI: Sanxingdui; VII: Kayue; VIII: Guang-she; IX: Zhukaigou; X: Gaotaishan; XI: Miaohoushan; XII: Shuangtuozi III; XIII: Yueshi; XIV: Hushu (distribution of sites and cultures based on Zhongguo Shehui Kexueyuan 2003b). Sites – 1: Xiaoshuangqiao; 2: Huanbei; 3: Laoniupo; 4: Zhukaigou; 5: Daxinzhuang; 6: Qianzhangda; 7: Panlongcheng; 8: Wucheng; 9: Sanxingdui.

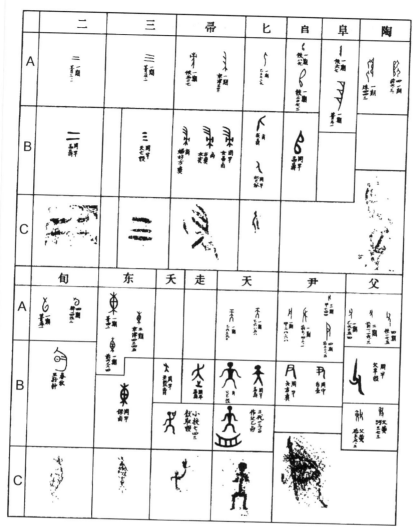

Figure 8.15. Selective Xiaoshuangqiao glyphs compared with corresponding oracle-bone and bronze inscriptions. (**A**) Oracle-bone inscription; (**B**) bronze inscription; (**C**) Xiaoshuangqiao glyphs (after table 1 of Song, G. 2003).

west wings. The main hall had ten bays on the façade, a porch with a colonnade, and small annexes on both sides. This structure appears to have functioned as an ancestral temple, as judged from its layout and more than forty locales of human and animal sacrifices. F2 (0.6 ha) was a smaller architectural complex, situated 29 m north of F1. Its main hall had four bays on the façade and was surrounded by porches on all sides. F2 may have functioned as a residential area for the Shang elite, as few sacrificial pits have been found in the courtyard (Du, J. 2004; Tang, J. et al. 2010b).

The discovery of Huanbei was crucial for understanding fully the development of the last capital of Shang, named Yin by traditional texts, and partially known archaeologically for the last eight decades through excavation of Yinxu

(Remains of Yin) on the southern bank of the Huan River. This recent northern find at Huanbei has also generated a wave of debate aimed at confirming
the historical identity of the new site. Chronologically, Huanbei is intermediate between Xiaoshuangqiao and Yinxu. The sequential occurrence of these
political centers has been interpreted as indicating Shang's repeated transfer of
its capital, but there is no consensus on how the textually known historical
capitals and the archaeological sites are to be correlated. Huanbei has been
identified either as Xiang, where the Shang King Hedanjia resided, or as Yin,
established by King Pangeng (Zhongguo Shehui Kexueyuan 2003b: 276–7).

The effort to match archaeological sites with recorded capital cities has a
major conceptual flaw. It assumes that the Shang royal history was a continuous
lineal succession, as portrayed in ancient texts, and that all the capitals were
duly recorded in the texts. It is possible, however, that the received royal
genealogy, which was reconstructed by later historians, did not fully record
all components of Shang history, including the existence of some political
centers. For example, in cases of factional competition for political power,
some losing factions may have been regarded as illegitimate by the dominant
ruling groups who later wrote the transmitted historical texts. In such cases,
it would be inherently impossible to match the data from archaeology with
existing textual records.

CONCLUSIONS

When the first states, Erlitou and Erligang, emerged in the Central Plain,
their levels of social complexity were considerably higher than in contemporary neighboring regions, where state structures did not yet exist. We have
no intention to assert a Central Plain-centric perspective toward the development of Chinese civilization, but it is difficult to deny that a core area of
sociopolitical complexity first emerged in the Central Plain. The interactions
between the core and peripheries cannot be simply interpreted as trade or
reciprocity between equal partners, because the material items involved were
predominantly strategic and prestigious goods demanded by the ruling elite in
the state-core area. We have interpreted these interactions as material manifestations of a tributary system under the hegemony of a territorial state (Liu,
L. and Chen 2003: 131–48). This is not simply to throw a Western typology
onto Chinese data, but to generalize about the nature of early states in China,
to facilitate cross-cultural comparison with other civilizations in the world (cf.
Feinman and Marcus 1998; Trigger 2003; Yoffee 2004). The political domination of the Erlitou-Erligang core areas and their unprecedented cultural
expansion provide excellent examples for understanding the formation of state
and civilization in China, as defined by Allan (2007) and Yoffee and Li (2009).

Whether these early states developed a writing system is still unclear. The
inscriptions found on pottery vessels and animal bones from Erlitou, Erligang,

and Xiaoshuangqiao, however, share strong similarities with the writing shown in the oracle-bone inscriptions of the late Shang, suggesting a long prehistoric process in the development of a true writing system in China.

Early states' territorial expansion started during the Erlitou period and reached a peak during the Erligang period. A general trend in some peripheral areas is that the Central Plain's cultural assemblages were predominant at the beginning of colonization, then became integrated with local traditions, and eventually the local cultural characteristics prevailed. Such a process coincided with increased political localization, leading to a multicentered political landscape in the late Shang. From a long-term historical perspective, the period from Erlitou to middle Shang manifests the first cycle of political centralization and decentralization, which was later repeated many times in Chinese dynastic history.

More than a quarter-century ago, Kwang-chih Chang argued that early civilization in China differed in fundamental ways from those developed in the Near East and Europe. Chang regarded the emergence of civilization in China as a political accomplishment expressed through concentration of material wealth, rather than as a technological achievement manifested in improvement of productive means. He also pointed out, on the basis of archaeological data available then, that the early Chinese city was a hierarchically organized political center composed of palace citadel, cemeteries, residential areas, and workshops, rather than being a dense agglomeration of buildings (Chang 1983: 124–5; 1986a: 362–4). A similar view was held by Wheatley, who described early urban centers in China as ceremonial complexes. Exemplified by Zhengzhou and Anyang, each city was composed of a centrally situated ceremonial and administrative enclave occupied primarily by royalty, priests, and a few selected craftsmen, whereas the peasantry and the majority of the artisans lived in villages dispersed through the surrounding countryside (Wheatley 1971: 30–47). Falkenhausen has further pointed out that, in the formative stage of urbanism in China, cities were nodes of sociopolitical organization and centers of religious activity, lacking some common features that characterized the ancient Greek polis and medieval European cities, and also noted that these early Chinese cities were not culturally differentiated from the surrounding rural areas (Falkenhausen 2008). As contributions to general cross-cultural comparison, all these observations are enlightening, and point toward unique pathways through which early states/civilizations emerged in China.

Some modifications of these remarks may be made, based on new archaeological data. Early urban centers in China clearly show hierarchical planning, in terms of urban layout and population allocation. This planning is manifested particularly by the palatial or inner city walls, which segregated different population groups. Although the political-religious elite was the central focus, various types of craft production were also a significant part of urban development. Thus, craft workshops, some quite large in scale, made both elite goods and utilitarian items for the urban center as well as for the surrounding hinterland. Therefore, economic functions were also an important part of early urbanism in China. Population level in the city was much greater than in the hinterland, so the urban–rural differentiation is shown primarily in settlement patterns (e.g., site size) and material remains (e.g., concentration of elite items and residences), as documented in the archaeological record. The urban population included not only ruling elite and craftsmen, but also farmers. A considerable proportion of people in the city may have been engaged in urban construction, including building rammed-earth palaces and walls, which appear to have been constantly rebuilt throughout the life span of cities.

Marked differences of design are also evident between urban centers in the core area and those in the periphery, due to their differing functional roles within the overall political system. Whereas cities in the core areas show fuller development of urbanism, peripheral towns appear to be copies of the core cities (e.g., construction of palatial structures and fortification) with a primary emphasis on specific functional components (e.g., salt storage and bronze workshops) appropriate to each case. Therefore, the functional roles of early cities are diverse, and the characteristics of early urbanism are determined by the nature of the early states as they evolved.

One of the major cultural developments that made early Chinese civilization unique is the elite's obsession with bronze ritual vessels. Such a passion is inseparable from the ruling elite's desire for ritual power believed to be embedded in bronze vessels, which were used as a necessary component in various religious ceremonies (Chang 1983). The acquisition of this ritual power by elites, through performance of religious ceremonies directed at royal lineage ancestors and natural deities, helped state rulers to obtain and maintain political legitimacy, whereas military expansion aimed at controlling vital resources and agricultural surplus promoted the material manifestation of related political goals. From this perspective, it all becomes understandable, why monopolizing production and distribution of ritual vessels was the priority of the high ruling elite, why bronze metallurgy was almost exclusively reserved for ritual and military purposes and did not play any significant role in agricultural production during most of the Bronze Age in China, and why the earliest cities were primarily ritual and political centers with lesser emphasis on economic functions. As cited at the beginning of this chapter, the text *Zuozhuan* (*Tso Chuan*), more than two thousand years ago, recorded that "the great affairs of a state are sacrifices and war." This politicized ritual orientation of statecraft seems to have been present from the beginning of state formation in ancient China.

CHAPTER 9

BRONZE CULTURES OF THE NORTHERN FRONTIERS AND BEYOND DURING THE EARLY SECOND MILLENNIUM BC

> South of the West Sea, at the edge of shifting sands, beyond the Red River and before the Black River is a mountainous massif, called the Kunlun Promontory.... Someone there wears a jade headdress, a mouthful of tiger teeth and a leopard's tail, and lives in a cave. Her name is Queen Mother of the West. At this mountain all manner of things are found.
>
> Chapter, "Dahuangxi jing," in *Shanhaijing*, compiled around late first millennium BC or later

> 西海之南, 流沙之滨, 赤水之后, 黑水之前, 有大山, 名曰昆仑之丘。...有人戴胜, 虎齿, 有豹尾, 穴处, 名曰西王母。此山万物尽有。〈〈山海经 · 大荒西经〉〉

Most regions in contemporary China north of the Great Wall are marginal for farming, and have historically been part of a transitional zone wherein southern agriculturalists met northern steppe pastoralists. During the Mid-Holocene Climatic Optimum, long before the Great Wall was built, these northern regions were largely occupied by farmers, but starting from the end of the third, and continuing in the early second millennium BC, some of these northern regions experienced the initial transformation from predominantly agricultural to mixed agropastoral economy, before the emergence of full pastoral nomadism. Several characteristic archaeological cultures have been identified, known as Lower Xiajiadian, Zhukaigou, Qijia, Siba, and Tianshanbeilu, stretching from Northeast to Northwest China, including western Liaoning, northern Hebei, Inner Mongolia, northern Shanxi, northern Shaanxi, Ningxia, Gansu, Qinghai, and eastern Xinjiang (Figure 9.1).

These cultures, which are usually referred to as situated on the northern frontiers of the Central Plain, are characterized by bronze metallurgy and an increased pastoralist economy, with strong influences from contemporary Bronze Age cultures in Central Asia and the Eurasian steppe, including those of the Afanasievo and Okunevo cultures in the Minusinsk Basin and the Altai, the Andronovo culture distributed over a large area from the Urals to the Yenisey (Mallory 1989: 223–7), the Seima-Turbino transcultural phenomenon

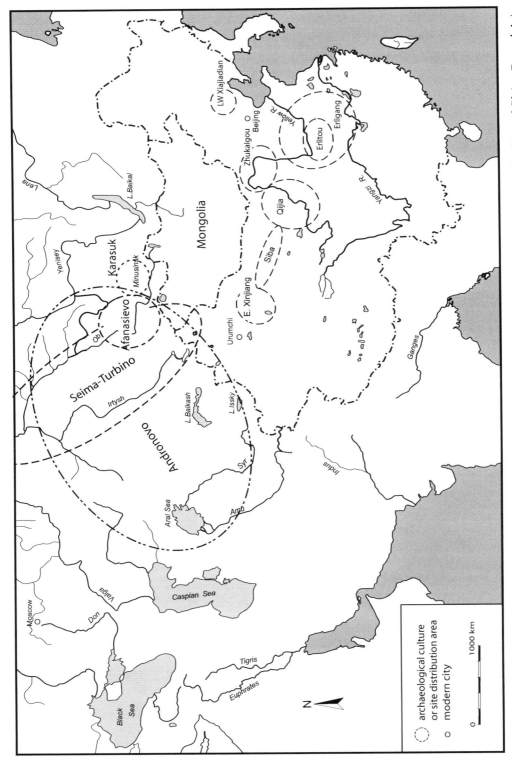

Figure 9.1. Distribution of northern frontier cultures in northern China, in relation to Bronze Age cultures in the Central Plain, Central Asia, and the Eurasian steppe during the late third and early second millennia BC (distribution of the Bronze Age cultures in the Eurasian steppe based on figures 67 and 90 of Chernykh 1992).

TABLE 9.1. *Chronology of cultures in North China and the steppe mentioned in Chapter 9*

Cultures	Dates (ca. BC)
Lower Xiajiadian	2000–1400
Zhukaigou	2000–1400
Qijia	2200–1600
Siba	1900–1500
Tianshanbeilu	2000–1550
Afanasievo	3300/3200–2600/2400
Okunevo	2500–1600
Andronovo/Seima–Turbino	2100–1500
Karasuk	1600–700

in the Eurasian steppe, and the Karasuk culture centered in the Minusinsk Basin on the middle Yenisey (Chernykh et al. 2004; Chernykh 1992: 215–33, 264–71) (Figure 9.1; Table 9.1). The most notable finds from the Central Plain's northern frontier cultures comparable with typical material remains of those steppe communities are metal weapons, tools, and ornaments with unique steppe styles (Kuz'mina 2004; Mei 2000), often collectively referred to in Chinese archaeological literature as the Northern Zone bronze cultural complex.

The northern frontier cultures were contemporaries of the Erlitou and Erligang states, and show various levels of interaction with people in the Central Plain. Some of the Northern Zone bronze items also found their way to the core areas of early dynasties in the Yellow River region. Cultural interactions seem to have occurred continuously between East and West across Eurasia. Considered within this broader perspective, the northern frontier cultures functioned as intermediaries, facilitating interregional interactions between the agricultural states in the Central Plain and pastoral communities in Central Asia and the Eurasian steppe.

To what extent early Chinese civilization was influenced by cultures in Central Asia and the Eurasian steppe has been a question of recurrent interest among archaeologists. Bronze metallurgy, in particular, has drawn considerable attention. There has been a long debate between the holders of two opinions on this subject: independent invention in China and diffusion from the Eurasian steppe (Kuz'mina 2004; Linduff 2004; Linduff and Mei 2009). The northern frontier cultures may hold the key to resolving this issue.

Social formation of the northern frontiers during the second and first millennia BC also has received a great deal of attention from archaeologists and historians. Whereas some scholars focus primarily on the reconstruction of regional history (e.g., Tian, G. and Guo 2005; Yang, J. 2004), others tend to explore the dynamics behind the rise of frontier bronze cultures (e.g., Di Cosmo 1999, 2002; Linduff 1998; Mei 2009; Shelach 1999, 2009a, b).

The emergence of the northern frontier societies and the formation of their particular cultural characteristics involved many environmental, social, and technological factors. These factors include the changing climatic conditions in the post-Holocene optimum era, the emergence of mobile pastoralism in the Eurasian steppe and Central Asia, the spread of copper-based bronze metallurgy, the political expansion of early states in the Central Plain, and the internal development of social complexity within all regional cultures in the northern frontier region. This chapter mainly focuses on the first half of the second millennium BC. We will review archaeological data and discuss some of the underlying factors leading to socioeconomic changes in these cultures, in terms of cultural interactions between East and West. The major sites and locations mentioned in this chapter are shown in Figure 9.2.

ENVIRONMENTAL CONDITIONS AND CULTURAL BACKGROUND

The northern frontier regions are situated along the northern extremity of the East Asian monsoon belt; therefore, they often have been affected by the fluctuation of the monsoon systems. During the Mid-Holocene Climatic Optimum, Neolithic settlements expanded toward the north and northwest to the extent that almost all the northern frontier regions were occupied by agricultural villages, as represented by the Hongshan, Yangshao, and Majiayao cultures (see Chapter 6). This situation changed when the climatic optimum came to an end in the third millennium BC.

Several studies on pollen remains and lake core from the Ordos (Guo, L. et al. 2007; Li, Xiaoqiang et al. 2003) and Daihai (Xiao, J. et al. 2006; Xiao, J. et al. 2004) regions, both in central Inner Mongolia, show fine-grained climatic change during the Holocene. They all detected a transition from the Mid-Holocene Climatic Optimum (ca. 8100–3300 cal. BP) to the late Holocene deteriorated climate (ca. 3300–0 cal. BP) with several episodes of fluctuations. Xiao J. et al. (2004), for example, demonstrate a cold and dry event around 4450–3950 cal. BP, followed by a warm and slightly humid interval at about 3950–3500 cal. BP and a mild, slightly dry episode ca. 3500–2900 cal. BP. The ecological systems in this region were fragile and changeable, forcing the human population to adapt to the environments with new strategies. Thus the change in the subsistence economy, from agriculture to agropastoralism, reflected such adaptations.

The Eurasian steppe is a massive landmass most suitable for pastoralism, but large-scale herding activities characterized by great mobility did not develop until the beginning of the second millennium BC. This new way of life was a result of three fundamental factors in the socioeconomic progress of the region; all of these factors had undergone long periods of development farther

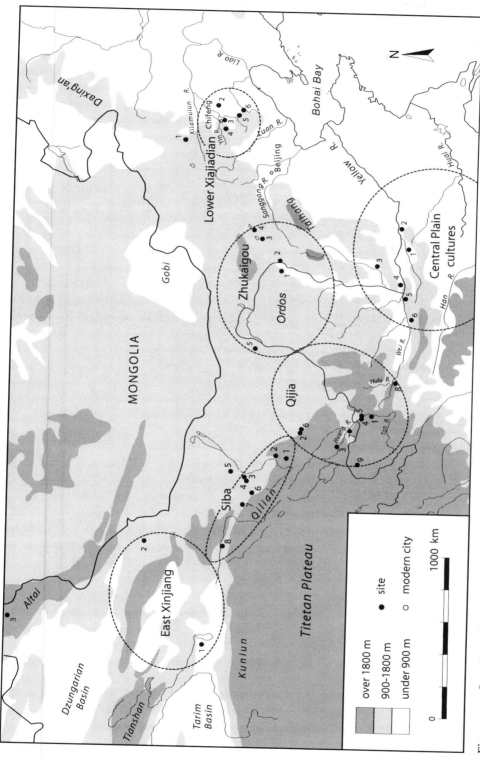

Figure 9.2. Location of major sites mentioned in Chapter 9. Lower Xiajiadian culture: 1: Dajing; 2: Dadianzi; 3: Erdaojingzi; 4: surveyed sites on the Banzhijian River region; 5: Niuheliang; 6: Dongshanzui. Zhukaigou culture: 1: Zhukaigou; 2: Xicha; 3: Shihushan; 4: Miaozigou; 5: Huogeqi. Qijia culture: 1: Qijiaping; 2: Huangniangniangtai; 3: Liuwan; 4: Qinweijia; 5: Dahezhuang; 6: Haicangsi; 7: Lajia; 8: Shizhaocun; 9: Gamatai. Siba culture: 1: Donghuishan; 2: Sibatan; 3: Huoshiliang; 4: Ganggangwa; 5: Baishantang copper mine; 6: Ganguya; 7: Huoshaogou; 8: Yingwoshu. Xinjiang: 1: Qäwrighul, Xiaohe; 2: Tainshanbeilu; 3: Qiemurqiek. Central Plain cultures: 1: Erlitou; 2: Zhengzhou; 3: Xiajin; 4: Qingliangsi; 5: Hengzhen; 6: Laoniupo.

301

west. These are, first, the introduction of domesticated grazing stock – sheep and cattle; second, the introduction of horseback riding and wheeled vehicles; and third, the development of metallurgy. These innovations dramatically stimulated the growth of pastoralism and increased human mobility and social hierarchy based on differential accumulation of precious metals and livestock. In this new type of social formation, the search for new pasturage and quarries, trade in utilitarian and elite goods, and military competition for prestige may have provided dynamics for spreading certain styles of material culture and ritual practice over a broad region (Anthony 1998). Movements of the steppe people and their material cultures and technologies during the early second millennium BC unquestionably made great impacts on the formation of the northern frontier cultures in China, where we see an increase in use of metallic objects, herding of grazing animals, and cultivation of crops that originated in the West, such as wheat and barley.

From the south, the formation of early states in the Central Plain also strongly influenced the development of neighboring northern cultures. The search for deposits of metallic ores and other resources, such as jade, may have been the primary motivation for the elites of early states to expand political power toward remote regions, as exemplified in other peripheral regions (see Chapter 8).

These multidirectional interactions certainly affected the formation of the northern frontier cultures, but, as will be demonstrated throughout this chapter, it was the internal dynamics of these societies that were most crucial in determining the trajectories of their development and decline.

THE LOWER XIAJIADIAN CULTURE

The Lower Xiajiadian culture was named after an excavation site at Xiajiadian in Chifeng, Inner Mongolia, revealing a stratigraphic sequence of two distinctive Bronze Age cultures, namely Lower Xiajiadian and Upper Xiajiadian (Zhongguo Kexueyuan 1974). The Lower Xiajiadian culture (ca. 2000–1400 BC) was distributed over a vast area, centered in the western Liao River Valley in southeastern Inner Mongolia. This cultural region is mainly defined by the Laoha, Daling, and Xiaoling Rivers, with its southern boundary drawn along the Luan River, separating it from the Datuotou culture (Zhongguo Shehui Kexueyuan 2003b: 593–605) (Figure 9.2).

Subsistence and Settlement Patterns

The western Liao River region is a semiarid and arid region at present, dominated by mountains, tablelands, and river systems. About a dozen Lower Xiajiadian sites have been excavated, providing important information about subsistence economies. Lower Xiajiadian houses were round or square-shaped and were built on either subterranean level or ground level. Walls were made of rammed earth, mud bricks, or stone. Houses varied considerably in size, ranging from 1.5 to 23 m², based on one observation (Shelach 1999: 99). Houses were often surrounded by storage pits. Ceramics, dominated by *li* tripods, *yan* tripods, *pen* basins, and *guan* jars, were made by coiling, molding, and fast-wheel techniques. Stone tool assemblages included primarily hoes, knives, and axes (Zhongguo Shehui Kexueyuan 2003b: 595–600). Faunal remains from the Dashanqian site in Kelaqin Banner revealed that the people's main source of protein was domestic animals, predominantly pigs (48.2%), cattle (24.3%), sheep/goats (15.3%), and dogs (10.9%) (Wang, L. 2004: 256). It is commonly agreed among archaeologists that the subsistence economy was primarily agricultural, although pastoralism had already played an important role.

Several archaeological survey projects have been conducted in this region, and a few hundred, if not a thousand, Lower Xiajiadian culture sites have been found (Chifeng 2002; Linduff et al. 2002–2004; Shelach 1997; Xu, G. 1986). There seems to have been a dramatic increase in site density from the previous Xiaoheyan culture (ca. 3000–2200 BC) to the Lower Xiajiadian culture in this region. Within a survey area of 221 km² in the middle Banzhijian River Valley, for instance, archaeologists have identified only six Xiaoheyan sites but 155 Lower Xiajiadian sites. Most sites are distributed on the bluffs above the main rivers, but some are located on mountaintops between rivers. There may have been functional differences between these two types of site location. The sites near the river valleys, which were apparently chosen for their easy access to arable land and water resources, seem grouped into clusters and densely populated, judging from densities of surface ceramics. The site groupings tend to be situated on the low bluffs near the prime agricultural lands. In some areas a three-tiered settlement hierarchy is observable, and the largest site found so far is 23 ha in area. In contrast, the sites distributed on mountaintops appear to have been less populated, but were often constructed with massive walls and gateways, with foundations of circular construction, and with large, artificially leveled areas (Chifeng 2002). Such walled settlements are best exemplified by the newly discovered site (3 ha) at Erdaojingzi in Chifeng, where excavations have revealed well-preserved ditches, walls, dwellings, storage pits, burials, roads, and numerous artifacts (Figure 9.3) (Cao, J. and Sun 2009).

Archaeologists believe that these hilltop sites were political centers, ritual locations, and/or defensive refuges for people from villages near the valley floor (Linduff et al. 2002–2004; Shelach 1999; Xu, G. 1986). The sites with defensive features, such as stone walls, vary significantly in proportion to different regional settlement systems. In an area of 200 km² along the Yin River, about 73 percent of Lower Xiajiadian sites (51 of 70) were built with stone walls or dug-out ditches (Shelach 1999: 91). In contrast, in the middle Banzhijian River region (221 km²), only 8 percent (12 of 155) of Lower Xiajiadian sites appear to have been associated with either stone walls or stone

Figure 9.3. A walled Lower Xiajiadian site at Erdaojingzi in Chifeng, Inner Mongolia (Cao and Sun 2009).

features, all of which are located on the highlands more than 800 m in elevation (Chifeng 2002).

In the Banzhijian area, 145 sites have been found. The sites tend to be clustered into many small groups distributed on mountain ranges and alluvial plains, and sites with stone walls/features are located in most clusters (Figure 9.4). There are 3 large sites (10–20 ha), along with 12 medium sites (4–6 ha), and some 130 small sites (<4 ha), forming a three-tiered settlement hierarchy (Figure 9.5). The largest site (KX8) is situated on the mountain area, overlooking the lowlands and in close proximity to two stone-walled sites (Figure 9.4). The location of site KX8 seems to suggest its special position and function as a regional center. The rank-size curve, however, shows a moderately convex

Figure 9.4. Distribution of Lower Xiajiadian sites in the Banzhijian survey area (redrawn from figure 3 of Chifeng 2002).

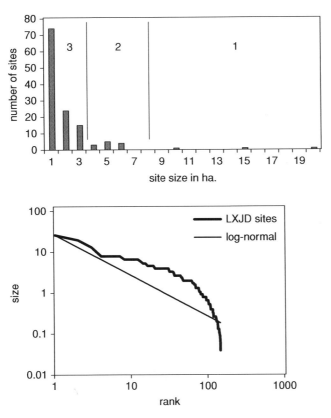

Figure 9.5. Three-tiered settlement hierarchy and convex curve of rank-size distribution observed in the Banzhijian survey area, Lower Xiajiadian culture.

distribution (Figure 9.5), suggesting a competitive relationship between centers. Such settlement groups have been documented in other areas of Chifeng and in the Yuncheng Basin of Shanxi. It has been suggested that the size and nature of these settlement groups reflect the scale of political integration and the degree of regional centralization. Accordingly, the Lower Xiajiadian communities appear to have been much less integrated politically than those of the late Longshan and Erlitou cultures in the Central Plain (Drennan and Dai 2010).

The settlement pattern in the Banzhijian area conforms to the pattern of conflict in the Lower Xiajiadian societies. In sharp contrast to the centrally organized Erlitou settlement pattern, the Lower Xiajiadian is characterized by multiple medium-sized local centers, perhaps competing with one another or with outside rivals. There is no evidence of a single, large, primary center as a supravillage/supradistrict political authority dominating the entire region.

Mortuary Pattern and Social Relations

One of the most thoroughly excavated and reported sites is Dadianzi in Chifeng, which provides important information about the organization of

Figure 9.6. The Dadianzi cemetery, showing distribution of burials with bronze objects and Erlitou-style *jue* and *gui* vessels (redrawn from figure 22 of Zhongguo Shehui Kexueyuan 1996).

Xiajiadian society. The Dadianzi site consists of a residential area (7 ha) surrounded by rammed-earth walls and a cemetery (1 ha) containing 804 rectangular shaft burials. The cemetery appears to have been partitioned into three sections, each of which can be further divided into several subsections (Figure 9.6). Most tombs are single interments, and many were furnished with wooden chambers. Grave goods include tools, pottery vessels, cowries, jade ornaments, and a small number of metal objects. Some ceramics were painted with elaborate designs after firing, perhaps intended as funeral offerings (Figure 9.7) (Zhongguo Shehui Kexueyuan 1996).

Archaeologists classified the tombs into large, medium, and small categories, with more than half belonging to the medium category. The observed spatial patterns of burials and accompanying artifacts suggest that society was kinship-based, with social differentiation existing among kin groups. Furthermore, the society seems to have practiced a clear division of labor based on gender, as indicated by the nearly exclusive association between females with ceramic spindle whorls and males with stone axes (Zhongguo Shehui Kexueyuan 1996: 214–21). Gender differentiation is also revealed by burial orientations, as all females were positioned with their heads toward the northeast, and all males toward the southwest. Females appear to have had much higher rates of tooth cavities than do males, suggesting that women may have consumed more carbohydrate food than did men (Pan 1996).

More elaborate statistical analyses of tomb structure and grave goods indicate that the status of individuals may have been ascribed at birth and that males tended to hold higher social positions in the society than did females. There was no specific artifact type possessed exclusively by the elite, however (Shelach 2001a). The focus of ritual practice may have varied during the 200 years of occupation of the Dadianzi cemetery. In the early period, stress seems to have been placed on the ceremonial phase of the funeral rite, but during the late period emphasis may have shifted toward the elaboration of grave goods used as status symbols for deceased individuals (Flad 2001). Furthermore, the spatial distribution of bronze items and the two types of elite pottery vessels, *jue* and *gui*, which imitated their counterparts from Erlitou, appears to be concentrated in the northern section of the cemetery (Figure 9.6), suggesting that social stratification already may have emerged within the community.

Metallurgy

Metal objects have been found at about ten Lower Xiajiadian sites (Shelach 1999: 106), among which Dadianzi is the most metal-rich site, yielding about sixty items, mostly rings. The metallic remains from Dadianzi also include bronze and lead mace heads and protective caps originally mounted on wooden axe handles that disintegrated long ago, as well as gold and bronze earrings and bronze fingerings (Figure 9.7). The bronze artifacts were made with both casting and hammering techniques (Zhongguo Shehui Kexueyuan 1996). The metal objects from Lower Xiajiadian sites are similar to those from northwest China, southern Siberia, and Central Asia. This similarity is particularly exemplified by the earrings with flared or trumpet-shaped ends, which have been found at sites in Lower Xiajiadian and in several contemporary cultures in northwest China, as well as in the Seima-Turbino and Andronovo cultures in the Eurasian steppe (Bunker 1998; Lin, Y. 1994; Linduff 2000: 11–13). The Dadianzi bronze objects are primarily made of tin-copper and tin-lead-copper alloys (Li, Y. et al. 2003), a metallurgical technology consistent with other bronze cultures in the eastern part of Eurasia (Mei 2003).

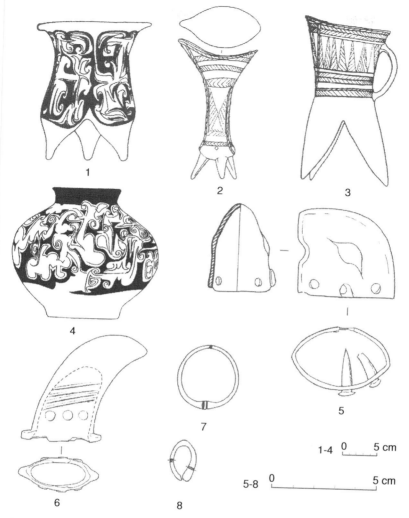

Figure 9.7. Artifacts from Dadianzi cemetery, Lower Xiajiadian culture. 1 and 4: painted pottery; 2 and 3: pottery *jue* and *gui* vessels, Erlitou style; 5: lead cap on axe handle; 6: bronze mace head; 7: bronze finger ring: 8: gold earring (modified from figures 86 and 95 of Zhongguo Shehui Kexueyuan 1996).

The Xiajiadian culture area is rich in metal deposits. Gold, copper, tin, and lead mines have been found in the Aohan Banner where Dadianzi is located. Farther north, there are concentrations of copper and tin deposits over an area of 100,000 km^2 between the Xilamulun River and the Tao'er River, in the south of the Daxing'an Mountains. Some of these deposits appear to have been mined in antiquity (Li, Y. et al. 2003). Ancient mining and smelting sites have been found at a number of locations in the upper Xilamulun River Valley, centered in Dajing in Linxi (Figure 9.2). These sites date from the Upper Xiajiadian culture in the first millennium BC (Li, Y. and Han 1990; Li, Y. et al. 2006a, b). It is possible that mining activities in this region started during the second millennium BC, but archaeologists are still waiting to find evidence of this.

In contrast, archaeologists have discovered evidence of bronze production. Furnace remains were unearthed from two locations (Zhuanshanzi and Xiaofushan) at Niuheliang in Lingyuan County, Liaoning. Chemical analysis suggests that they were used for smelting oxidized copper ores, and a single thermoluminescence (TL) date places the remains at a range between 3494 ± 340 and 3100 ± 310 BP (2300–800 BC), which corresponds to the Lower Xiajiadian period (Li, Y. et al. 1999). In addition, a clay mold for casting bead-shaped ornaments was reported from a Lower Xiajiadian pit at Dongshanzui in Chifeng (Li, G. 1983).

These lines of evidence point to the conclusion that the bronze and gold artifacts from Lower Xiajiadian sites were most likely produced locally. It is worth noting that these metal items are all ornaments; no tools or vessels have been found in clear association with Lower Xiajiadian cultural assemblages. Several bronze vessels showing the Central Plain style have been unearthed, but these are isolated finds in the Lower Xiajiadian culture area and probably reflect interactions with the Shang culture rather than local production.

Cultural Interactions

The Lower Xiajiadian people were in contact with their neighbors as well as with more remote cultures. At the Dadianzi cemetery, more than twenty Erlitou-style ceramic vessels, *jue* and *gui* (Figure 9.7), have been unearthed from thirteen relatively elaborate burials, mostly located in the northern section of the cemetery (Figure 9.6). These vessels appear to have been used for a long period before being buried, as indicated by traces of smoke on their exterior surfaces (Zhongguo Shehui Kexueyuan 1996: 219). In the Erlitou culture *jue* and *gui* were typical drinking vessels with ritual functions, and the Dadianzi examples marked the northeasternmost extent of the Erlitou-style ceramic distribution. These vessels were likely made locally, because their surface decorations (combed geometrical patterns) show local characteristics that may have been related to cultures situated both farther eastward, in the Nenjiang Plain of northeastern China, as well as westward, in particular, the Andronovo culture of the Eurasian steppe (Lin, Y. 1994; Wang, L. and Bu 1998). The presence of such a stylistic mixture in Dadianzi points to cultural amalgamation of various influences.

Such a material cultural complex seems to correlate with a mixed population at Dadianzi. On the basis of physical anthropological investigations, we know that the Dadianzi population represents two groups of people who are morphologically distinguishable. Group I is close to the populations distributed in the Yellow River region, whereas Group II is similar to those of east and north Asian types of Mongoloid. The Dadianzi settlement, therefore, may have been a melting pot, combining populations from both southern and northern regions. It is also interesting to note that the Group I individuals, of Yellow River type, were relatively concentrated in two burial clusters in the north and center of the cemetery, and most Erlitou-style vessels were also excavated from burials in the north cluster (Figure 9.6). Three skeletons associated with these vessels were preserved well enough for measurements: Two were males belonging to Group I, and the other was a female belonging to Group II (Pan 1996). Despite the small sample size, the Dadianzi remains suggest a clear correlation between the presence of males affiliated with the Central Plain and the use of Erlitou-style ceramics. This correlation suggests that some people from the Erlitou culture region, particularly males, may have migrated to the Liao River region.

The presence of Erlitou population elements in this metal-rich eastern periphery, such as Dadianzi, may be more than coincidental, and similar inferences are also evident in the cases of southern Shanxi and the middle Yangzi River (see Chapter 8; Liu, L. and Chen 2003). The abundant resources of copper, tin, and lead found in the Lower Xiajiadian culture area may have attracted Erlitou elites who were searching for precious metal alloys in outlying lands. This proposition, however, needs to be tested by more evidence in the future.

The Lower Xiajiadian people's interest in exotic materials extends to a long list, including objects made of jade, marble, turquoise, and agate, as revealed in Dadianzi burials, and none of these materials was locally available. A total of 659 cowry shells uncovered from Dadianzi were used mostly as part of the decorations on heads and cloths (Zhongguo Shehui Kexueyuan 1996). Cowry shells discovered at Neolithic and Bronze Age sites in China most likely derived from the Indian Ocean by transmission through Central Asia, although the exact routes and mechanisms of such long-distance trade are unclear (Peng, K. and Zhu 1999).

Interactions between Lower Xiajiadian and its neighboring cultures were multidirectional. A distinctive type of pottery, which was elaborately painted after firing and perhaps made exclusively as funeral goods, shows designs similar to the *toatie* motifs on Shang bronzes (Figure 9.7), although the meaning of this similarity is still elusive. Lower Xiajiadian has yielded material elements, similar to characteristic finds at Datuotou (situated south of the Yan Mountains), such as bronze finger rings and earrings (Zhongguo Shehui Kexueyuan 2003b: 605–8) that are ultimately attributable to influence from the steppe.

All these observations suggest that Lower Xiajiadian polities were organized hierarchically, that interpolity conflict was intensive, and that elite individuals competed for power through long-distance exchange of prestige items. Rapid population growth and increased agricultural production may have led to overexploitation of natural resources, generating stress on communities in the region and resulting in interpolity conflict. As a whole, Lower Xiajiadian polities were relatively small in scale and did not form a unified political organization on a large regional level. Their contacts with state-level societies in the Central Plain are evident, but this region appears never to have been under the direct political control of the Central Plain states.

THE ZHUKAIGOU CULTURE

The Zhukaigou culture (ca. 2000–1400 BC) refers to a material complex distributed mainly in central southern Inner Mongolia. More than forty Zhukaigou culture sites have been surveyed or excavated. They are centered in the Ordos and are spread over a large region, extending eastward to Daihai or beyond, westward to the Helan Mountains, northward to the Yin Mountains, and southward to the Yan River Valley and the Lüliang Mountains (Zhongguo Shehui Kexueyuan 2003b: 575–84). The Ordos is situated within the bend of the Yellow River, dominated by desert, hills, and alluvial lands. To the east of the Ordos is a hilly landscape dotted with a series of lakes and basins (Figure 9.2). This region is a mosaic of diverse geographical configurations, providing many different environmental niches for a variety of subsistence economies, including agriculture, pastoralism, hunting, and fishing (Tian, G. and Shi 2004).

Subsistence

When the first agricultural communities arrived in this Ordos-centered region during the Yangshao period, its wild flora and fauna were richly abundant, and hunting-gathering was an important dimension of their subsistence strategy. After two thousand years of intensive exploitation of the environment, natural resources were dramatically depleted (see Chapter 7). By the beginning of the second millennium BC, people had become heavily reliant on domestic animals and crops, and pastoralism developed. At the Huoshiliang site (ca. 2000 BC) in northern Shaanxi, sheep/goats (59%) and cattle (9%) account for 68 percent of the total number of identified specimens (NISP) of the faunal assemblage. A similar situation is also seen in the faunal remains from Zhukaigou (ca. 2000–1400 BC) in the Yijinhuoluo Banner (ca. 2000–1500 BC), where sheep/goats account for 41 percent and cattle account for 24 percent of the total NISP. At these sites, wild animals account for only 19 and 8 percent, respectively (Hu, S. et al. 2008; Huang, Y. 1996).

During the process of ecological change in this region, the Zhukaigou culture underwent the transition from Neolithic farming villages to an early Bronze Age agropastoral society, and generated some of the earliest characteristics of the Northern Zone bronze cultures. The material remains found in this area show a mixture of different traditions from neighboring cultures, reflecting complex relationships between various ethnic groups.

TABLE 9.2. *Proportion of Qijia culture elements in Phases III and IV graves, Zhukaigou*

Phase	Zhukaigou graves	Graves with Qijia pottery/burials	Bronze	Total graves
III	138 (85%)	24 (15%)	6 (4%)	162
IV	64 (84%)	12 (16%)	3 (4%)	76

The Zhukaigou Site

The best-excavated and studied site is Zhukaigou in the Yijinhuoluo Banner, Inner Mongolia (Neimenggu and Ordos 2000; Tian, G. 1988). This site is located at the eastern part of the Ordos plateau, about 1,400 m above sea level (Figure 9.2). Near the site, the Zhoukaigou River runs from northeast to southwest and joins the Yellow River's tributary system. As a result of deforestation and soil erosion, the landscape today is predominantly slopes and terraces divided by gullies, with little natural coverage of vegetation. Archaeological features are distributed over an area extending about 2 km long and 1 km wide along the slopes. The residential areas appear to be grouped into three clusters on the lower slopes, whereas most burials are located on higher ground outside residential areas. The material remains at Zhukaigou are divided into five phases, dating to the late Longshan (Phases I and II), Erlitou (Phases III and IV), and early Shang (Phase V) periods. The Longshan remains at the site show the formation of local traditions, with strong influences from the Wei River Valley and southern Shanxi. Some distinctive ceramic styles, particularly snake pattern *li* tripods, developed locally and later became diagnostic features of the Northern Zone complex (Tian, G. and Guo 1988) (Figure 9.8).

During the Erlitou period (Phases III and IV) local traditions continued, whereas some ceramics and burial costumes show strong characteristics of the Qijia culture, which was centered in the upper Yellow River Valley to the southwest. The most typical cultural elements of Qijia include double-handled and high-collared *guan* jars, as well as collective burials centered on a male, with female and/or juvenile remains beside him. It is notable that these Qijia-style ceramics always coexisted with Zhukaigou-style pottery in graves. Copper and bronze objects also appeared, but were limited to a small number of tools and ornaments, which are stylistically similar to the Northern Zone examples (Figure 9.9). The appearance of Qijia ceramics and burials is generally interpreted as the result of migration of the Qijia population (Linduff 1995; Neimenggu and Ordos 2000: 280).

Among the burials of Phases III and IV, small proportions of Qijia-style pottery (15–16%) and bronze objects (4%) have been found in the grave offering assemblages (Table 9.2). Qijia-style pottery and burial customs appear to

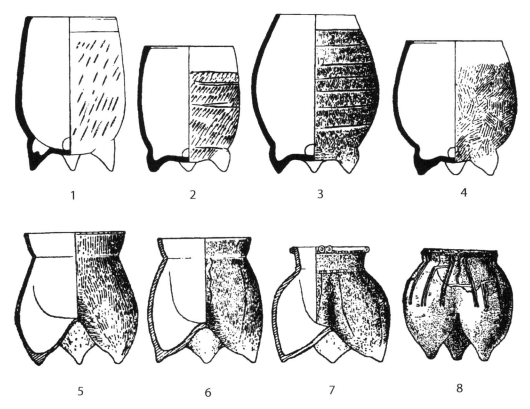

Figure 9.8. Zhukaigou ceramics. 1–4: Tripod *weng* urns, dated to Phases II–V, regional traditions; 5–7: snake-pattern *li* tripods developed in the Zhukaigou culture, dated to Phases II–V; 8: snake-pattern *li* tripod from Transbaikal (modified from figures 6 and 7 of Tian, G. and Guo 1988).

be spread over almost the entire Zhukaigou site, whereas bronzes tend to be concentrated in the southern and eastern parts of the settlement and to be associated with both Qijia and non-Qijia burials (Figure 9.10). If we assume that continued preference for certain types of pottery and certain burial customs has more to do with ethnicity than with social status in this village, these patterns of ceramic interment seem to suggest that, although the Qijia migrants became well integrated with the Zhukaigou locals, they nevertheless maintained their own traditions of pottery production and burial customs for a few hundred years. In contrast, the more limited spatial distribution of bronze items suggests that metal objects may have become associated with an emergent social status that crossed ethnic boundaries in the community.

Zhukaigou Phase V was a contemporary of the Erligang culture. Local pottery forms – such as the snake pattern *li* tripods and flower-pattern-rimmed *guan* jars – are continuously predominant in the Phase V ceramic assemblage. In addition, many bronze objects show unmistakable Northern Zone characteristics, exemplified by knives with ring handles, short daggers, and earrings (Figure 9.9).

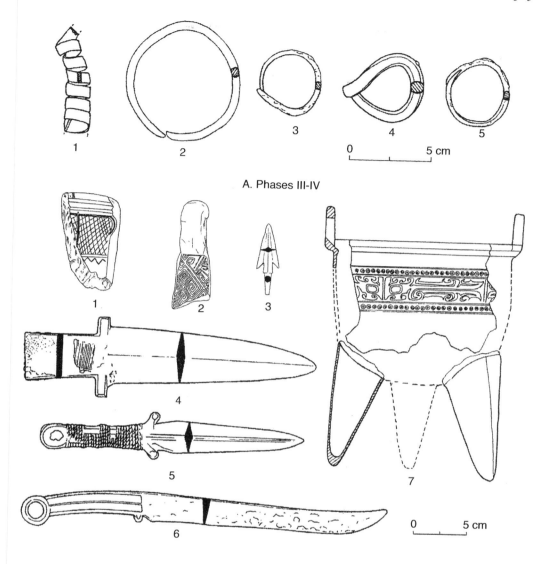

A. Phases III-IV

B. Phase V

Figure 9.9. Bronze artifacts and craft tools from Zhukaigou. A. Phases III and IV bronzes: 1: ornament; 2: ring; 3 and 4: finger rings; 5: earring. B. Phase V craft tools and bronzes: 1: stone mold for making axes; 2: potter's tool with spiral patterns; 3: arrowhead; 4: *ge* dagger; 5: short dagger; 6: ring-handled knife; 7: *ding* tripod (modified from figures 61, 87, 192, and 215 of Neimenggu and Ordos 2000 and figure 31 of Tian, G. 1988).

At the same time, Phase V also seems to show a new wave of cultural intrusion from the Erligang culture in the Central Plain, as indicated by the presence of Erligang-style ceramics and bronzes. Fragments of Shang bronze *ding* and *jue* vessels have been unearthed from an ash pit in the residential area of Zhukaigou's Section V, and *ge* daggers were found in several burials

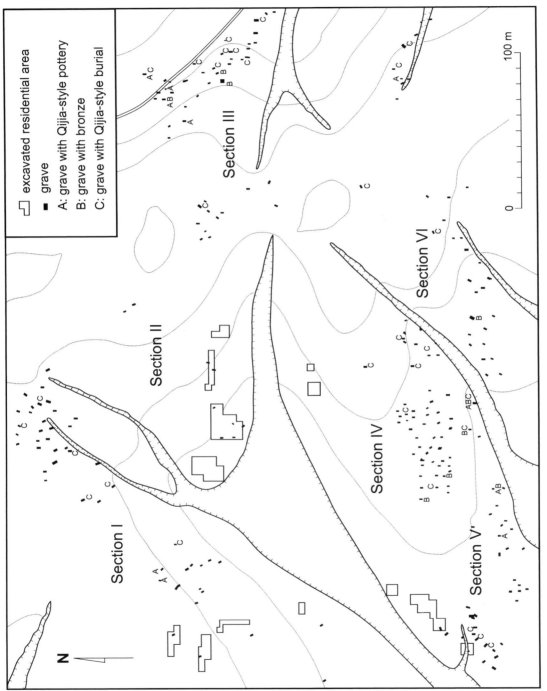

Figure 9.10. Zhukaigou site showing spatial distribution of graves associated with bronzes and Qijia-style pottery and burials, Phases III and IV (redrawn from figure 2 of Neimenggu and Ordos 2000).

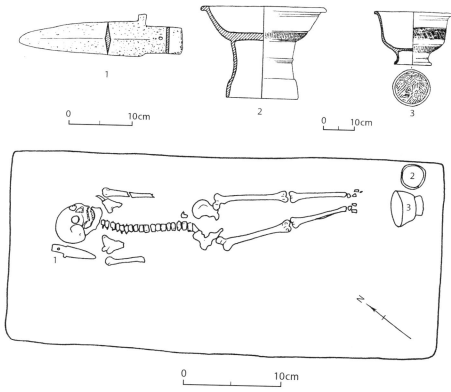

Figure 9.11. Burial M1052 at Zhukaigou, containing Shang style bronze dagger and ceramics. Phase V. 1: Bronze *ge* dagger; 2: *dou* pedestal plate; 3: *gui* vessel (after figure 182 of Neimenggu and Ordos 2000).

(Figure 9.9). In one case, a *ge* dagger associated with Erligang-style ceramics was found in burial M1052 (Figure 9.11). Erligang-style ceramics were found in both residential areas and burials, and were likely manufactured at Zhukaigou. This inference is suggested by finds of potter's tools, including two clay molds bearing spiral patterns (*yunleiwen*) (Figure 9.9), which was a common Erligang style decoration on pottery.

Among the forty burials dating to Phase V, nineteen (48%) contained grave goods, most of which were utilitarian materials. Only six burials (15%) had bronzes, including Shang-style *ge* daggers and a Northern Zone–style knife, short dagger, earring, plaque, and beads (Figure 9.9). All the burials associated with bronze weapons belong to adult males, so these items were probably status markers representing personal achievements. Some bronzes may have been produced locally, as is suggested by the find of a stone mold for casting axes (Figure 9.9).

Only fifteen graves' cultural affiliations can be identified based on the ceramic and bronze typology. They can be divided into three categories:

TABLE 9.3. *Ceramics and bronzes, showing cultural affiliation, in Phase V graves at the Zhukaigou site (total graves: 15)*

Grave #	Grave goods	Cultural affiliation
1070	ZKG pottery & NZ bronze	
4020	ZKG pottery & NZ bronze	
1019	ZKG pottery	
1027	ZKG pottery	
1064	ZKG pottery	Type A
1084	ZKG pottery	(*N* = 10; 67%)
2006	ZKG pottery	ZKG only
3016	ZKG pottery	
4005	ZKG pottery	
5020	ZKG pottery	
1083	ZKG pottery & NZ bronze, Shang bronze	Type B
2012	ZKG pottery & NZ bronze, Shang bronze	(*N* = 3; 20%)
1040	NZ & Shang bronzes	ZKG–Shang mixed
1052	Shang pottery & bronze	Type C
2003	Shang pottery & bronze	(*N* = 2; 13%)
		Shang only

ZKG = Zhukaigou; NZ = Northern Zone.

> A: ZKG type (ten graves; 67%) – only Zhukaigou pottery or Northern Zone bronzes are present. These graves are clearly the majority, likely representing the local population.
>
> B: Mixed type (three graves; 20%) – Zhukaigou pottery/Northern Zone bronze and Shang bronze are present. These graves probably belong to the local population who obtained Shang-style bronzes as status symbols.
>
> C: Shang type (two graves; 13%) – only Shang pottery/bronze are present, probably representing the Shang population (Table 9.3).

The spatial distribution of Phase V burials shows that Type A graves are spread over the entire site, whereas Types B and C graves appear to be relatively concentrated in the central area of the site (Figure 9.12). It is interesting to note that finds of Zhukaigou pottery and of Shang pottery, as grave goods, are mutually exclusive at the site. Also, in two graves Zhukaigou pottery was found with a Shang bronze *ge* dagger, but none of the graves with Shang pottery also contained Northern Zone bronzes.

It is useful to examine the distribution of bronze items in residential areas. For Phase V, four house foundations and sixty-one ash pits were found, spread over all residential areas at the site, but nearly half of the entire bronze assemblage (13 of 27 items) from this phase was retrieved from only one house (F5001) and two pits (H5003 and H5028) in Section V. Among these bronzes, three fragmentary ritual vessels (two *ding* tripods and one *jue* vessel) and four

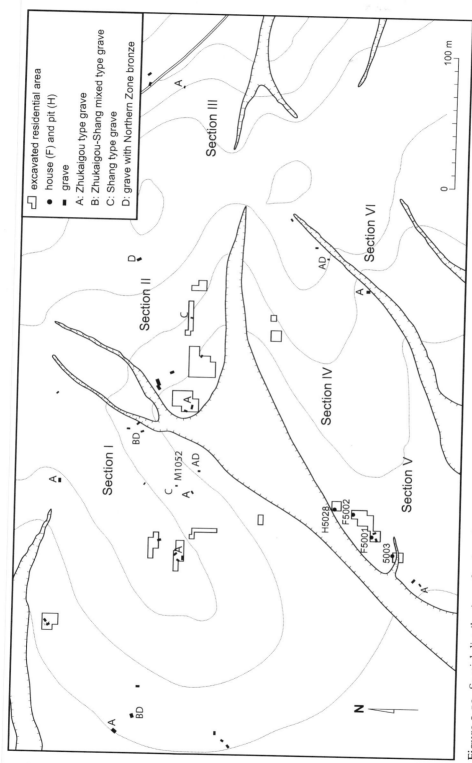

Figure 9.12. Spatial distribution of archaeological features at Zhukaigou, showing graves, houses, and pits associated with Zhukaigou or Shang style artifacts, Phase V (redrawn from figure 2 of Neimenggu and Ordos 2000).

arrowheads are clearly Shang in style, and one of the knives is of the Northern Zone type (Guo, S. 1993). It is also noteworthy that a house (F5002) in Section V was constructed using a method characteristic of the Central Plain, comparable to a house at Erlitou (Neimenggu and Ordos 2000: 285) (Figure 9.12). These phenomena seem to suggest that part of the population residing in Section V at Zhukaigou had close connections with the Central Plain states and had exclusive access to Shang bronze ritual vessels.

As shown by archaeological remains from burials and residential areas, Shang materials were spread over a large part of the site. If the presence of Shang pottery in burials (Type C graves) and the construction of Central Plain–style houses imply affiliations with the Shang population, it may be inferred that a small number of residents at Zhukaigou maintained their heritage of Shang cultural identity. In contrast, Shang bronze weapons (*ge* daggers), as well as Northern Zone bronzes, may have been used by a wider range of individuals in the community; however, Shang ritual bronzes appear to have been used only by an exclusive group of people, affiliated with the Central Plain, who continued to practice hierarchical forms defined by the Erligang state. This last phenomenon suggests a clear segregation, not only of status, but also of culture and ethnicity, existing in the Zhukaigou community.

Taken as a whole, the Zhukaigou settlement represents a multiethnic community, with little sign of internal conflict. Nevertheless, people with different ethnic backgrounds were not completely integrated, especially at the elite level, as indicated by the restricted distribution of ritual bronzes. The Shang elite seem to have maintained a distinctive identity exclusive from the rest of the community. This pattern seen in the Shang period is rather different from that of the Qijia materials found in the earlier phases.

Zhukaigou may have functioned as a trade center through which goods from the Central Plain were exchanged with communities on the northern frontiers (Linduff 1995, 1998). More importantly, as we have argued earlier in text, Zhukaigou is likely to have been actively cultivated by the Shang state as an outpost for resource procurement, particularly of metals, from this remote region (Liu, L. and Chen 2003: 106–9). The Shang's expeditionary presence at Zhukaigou was nevertheless short-lived, and the Ordos region later (during the late Shang) became dominated by regional bronze cultures with strong characteristics of steppe culture (see Chapter 10).

Metallurgy and the Formation of the Northern Zone Tradition

A copper-mining site of the Bronze Age, covering an area of 25 km^2, has been found at Huogeqi in Wulatehou Banner (Figure 9.2), revealing furnaces, ore-processing implements, mining tunnels, and a large amount of slag (Guojia 2003: 618). This mining site may have been one of the metal resources that provided alloys for metal-producing sites. Considering its distance from Zhukaigou (more than 300 km), however, it is likely that Zhukaigou exploited other metal resources available in its adjacent areas, which remain undiscovered.

Thirty-three metal objects from Zhukaigou have been analyzed. Metallic products unearthed from Phases III and IV (thirteen items analyzed) resemble in form those of the Qijia metal assemblage, and most of them are composed of pure copper (38.5%) and tin bronze (39.5%) (Li, X. and Han 2000). This compositional pattern is also manifest in metal artifacts from the Qijia culture (Sun, S. and Han 1997). Therefore, the Qijia people may have brought the metallurgy techniques into the Ordos.

All metal items from Phase V at Zhukaigou are of bronze (copper-tin-lead and copper-tin alloys), but the composition of alloys varies greatly. All three Shang-style ritual vessels and four of six arrowheads from the assemblage contain high lead levels (20.4–37.5%) and low tin levels (8.7–16.5%). These seven samples share rather similar compositions of tin and lead. In contrast, all other samples have low lead levels (0–12.7%), and their tin levels vary greatly (5.4–35.9%) (Li, X. and Han 2000).

Bronze alloys with high lead content are not a Northern Zone tradition, but have been identified in weapons, tools, and vessels from Erlitou, Zhengzhou, and Panlongcheng (Hao, X. and Sun 2001; table 4 of Li, Z. et al. 1986; Zhongguo Shehui Kexueyuan 1999b: 399), dated slightly earlier than, or contemporary with, Zhukaigou Phase V. It is possible that the Shang-style ritual vessels and some arrowheads unearthed from Zhukaigou were produced in the Central Plain. Their consistent ratios of alloy composition also suggest a high level of craft specialization. In contrast, the other items from Zhukaigou were probably cast in different places, including Zhukaigou itself, using raw materials derived from various sources. It is noteworthy that the bronze composition of Shang-style *ge* daggers found here is consistent with the range typical of the Northern Zone, suggesting that they may have been made locally. The fact that *ge* daggers were distributed in a scattered pattern at Zhukaigou, similar to the spatial pattern of the Northern Zone bronzes, seems to support the conclusion that they were manufactured locally.

The diverse designs of bronze weapons and ornaments at Zhukaigou may also imply broad cultural interaction between the Ordos and the Eurasian steppe. Single-edged knives with ring handles, double-edged short daggers with metal hilts, plaques, and an axe mold from Zhukaigou are among the earliest known examples of the Northern Zone bronze tradition (Guo, S. 1993; Tian, G. and Guo 1988). Knives with ring handles have been found in the Qijia and Siba cultures at the Tianshanbeilu cemetery in eastern Xinjiang (see later in this chapter) and in the Seima-Turbino and Karasuk cultures (figures 73–76 of Chernykh 1992; figures 3–6 of Mei 2003). The short dagger from Zhukaigou particularly resembles the examples commonly found in the

Karasuk culture in the Minusinsk region (figures 91 and 92 of Chernykh 1992). Both Seima–Turbino and Karasuk cultures represent mobile pastoral communities in the Eurasian steppe, and chronologically overlap with Zhukaigou Phase V around the sixteenth or fifteenth centuries BC (Chernykh 1992: 215–34, 264–9). Given that these steppe populations were mobile pastoralists and metallurgists, some of the Zhukaigou bronzes may have originated from the steppe regions and been brought to Zhukaigou as trade items. It remains unclear, however, how the Zhukaigou and Karasuk/Seima–Turbino cultures interacted, because we know little about the intermediary area in Mongolia.

The Zhukaigou culture disappeared from the landscape after ca. 1500 BC, but some of its material elements continued to thrive in the steppe. The diagnostic pottery form is the snake pattern *li* tripod, which has been unearthed in several sites in Inner Mongolia and Transbaikal (Figure 9.8). The Northern Zone bronze complex, sharing similarities with the Zhukaigou assemblages, spread over the vast steppe region and northern China beginning from the late second millennium BC (Tian, G. and Guo 1988). Production of Northern Zone–style bronzes continued after Zhukaigou in the Ordos. A large site at Xicha (120 ha) in Qingshuihe County, Inner Mongolia, has revealed a long human occupation extending from the Yangshao, through late Longshan and Zhukaigou cultures, to the late Shang-Zhou period. The site is about 100 km east of Zhukaigou (Figure 9.2), and its last phase has yielded not only Northern Zone bronze objects (shaft-hole axes, knives, earrings, etc.), but also clay molds for making Northern Zone–style bronzes (Cao, J. and Sun 2004). The evidence of metallurgy at Zhukaigou and Xicha suggests that the Ordos region, as a center of the Northern Zone bronze complex, developed its own metallurgical industry with a style similar to that of the steppe traditions.

Osteological examination of human remains from Zhukaigou suggests that there is minimal differentiation within the Zhukaigou population through time, and these people show more similarities with the agricultural populations in the Yellow River region than with the northern Mongoloid nomadic groups (Pan 2000). Mitochondrial DNA (mtDNA) analysis of seven Zhukaigou individuals shows that the matrilineal genetic structure of the Zhukaigou people is close to that of the later population in the same area in Inner Mongolia, and also shares similarities with modern populations in Mongolia and the Central Plain (Wang, H. et al. 2007). Both studies indicate that the Zhukaigou population maintained local continuity, while interacting with or migrating to other regions in the north and south. This scenario is largely consistent with the distribution of Zhukaigou material assemblages in the archaeological record.

THE QIJIA CULTURE

The Qijia culture was first discovered by J. G. Andersson at Qijiaping in Guanghe County, Gansu, in the 1920s, when he searched for the Western origins of Yangshao painted pottery. Anderson believed that, due to its monochrome pottery and the lack of metal objects, the Qijia culture represented the earliest among the archaeological assemblages that he found in the Hexi corridor (Andersson 1925, 1943). Since Andersson's initial work, archaeologists have identified more than 1,000 Qijia culture sites, excavated about 20, and established detailed chronologies and typologies. We now understand that Qijia was a Bronze Age culture, dating to a period of ca. 2200–1600 BC. The region that the Qijia people inhabited is the loess area, drained by a number of tributaries of the upper Yellow River, with the Tenggeli Desert in the north and the Qilian Mountains in the south. Qijia sites are centered in the upper Wei River Valley, middle and lower Tao River, and middle and lower Huang River, but the entire distribution of the Qijia culture was spread over a much larger area, about 700 km east-west and 600 km north-south, including western Shaanxi, Gansu, Ningxia, eastern Qinghai, and central-southern Inner Mongolia (Figure 9.2). (Zhang, T. and Xiao 2003; Zhongguo Shehui Kexueyuan 2003b: 535–7).

Settlement Patterns and Subsistence

The upper Yellow River Valley is the marginal area of the East Asian monsoon zone and is sensitive to climatic changes. The flourishing of the Qijia culture coincided with a cold-dry period in 4300–3700 cal. BP (Wu, W. and Liu 2004: 157). This condition no doubt affected the Qijia people's way of life.

An archaeological survey of Neolithic and Bronze Age sites in the Hulu River region, upper Wei River Valley, revealed changing regional settlement patterns through time. From the Neolithic Lower Changshan culture (ca. 2800–2200 BC) to the Qijia culture, the number of sites increased by 370 percent (from 80 to 376), whereas the average site size and average thickness of site deposit decreased by 61 percent (from 10 to 3.9 ha) and 38 percent (from 1.6 to 1 m), respectively. These data seem to suggest that the population as a whole was growing, but that communities became smaller in size and mobility became greater from the pre-Qijia to Qijia period in this region. The increased mobility of agricultural settlements may have been attributable to climatic deterioration coupled with the overexploitation of land, leading to a rapid decline in soil fertility and the frequent abandonment of settlements (Li, F. et al. 1993).

Qijia settlements are usually found near rivers, and site sizes range between less than 1 ha to 20 ha; most are 5–7 ha in area. Settlement layouts vary considerably. At some sites, residential structures and burials are intermingled (e.g., Dahezhuang and Shizhaocun), whereas at other sites the residential areas and cemeteries are separate (e.g., burials at Liuwan in Ledu and Qinweijia in Yongjing) (Zhongguo Shehui Kexueyuan 2003b: 535–48) (Figure 9.2).

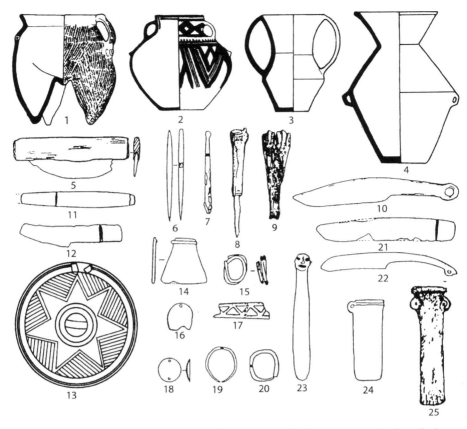

Figure 9.13. Qijia culture pottery and bronzes. 1: *Li* tripod; 2: double-handled *guan* jar; 3: large, double-handled *guan* jar; 4: high-collar *guan* jar; 5: knife mounted in bone handle; 6, 8, and 9: awls; 7: drill; 10–12, 21, and 22: knives; 13: mirror; 14: axe; 15: finger ring; 16: plaque; 17: knife handle; 18: button; 19: bracelet; 20: earring; 23: dagger; 24 and 25: axes (modified from figures 8–27: 1, 15, 38, 44 of Zhongguo Shehui Kexueyuan 2003b and figure 2 of Li, S. 2005).

The Qijia ceramic assemblage is characterized by many types of jars, mostly reddish in color, rendered with two or three handles, or with high necks, some painted with simple geometric patterns (Figure 9.13). The subsistence economy was based on cereal cultivation and domesticated animals (particularly pigs), increasingly supplemented by grazing animal husbandry and hunting. Dahezhuang in Yongjing, for example, consisted of semisubterranean and rectangular houses, paved with lime plaster on the floors, and surrounded by pits and burials (Figure 9.14). Various types of tools, pottery vessels, animal bones, and millet remains have been uncovered at the site. A large number of pig and sheep/goat mandibles were buried with the dead as grave goods. Among the total number of faunal remains (256 minimum number of individuals [MNI]), which were largely from sacrificed animals in burials, the ratios for pigs, sheep/goats, and cattle are 76, 22, and 2 percent, respectively (Zhongguo Shehui Kexueyuan Gansu 1974). Starch analysis of three human

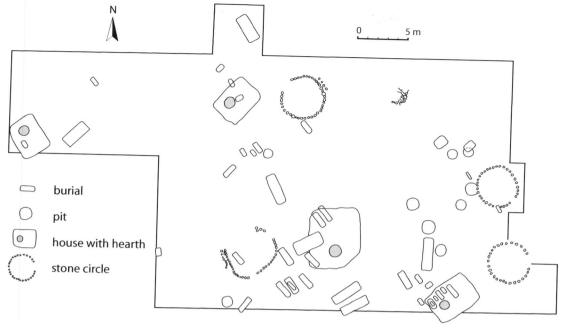

Figure 9.14. Excavated western section of the Dahezhuang site, Qijia culture (redrawn from figure 4 of Zhongguo Shehui Kexueyuan Gansu 1974).

teeth from Mogou in Lintan has revealed direct evidence that plants were consumed by humans, predominantly cereals (millet and wheat/barley), followed by beans and other possible plants (Li, M. et al. 2010). Microliths have been found at many sites, especially along the Hexi corridor. Huangniangniangtai in Wuwei yielded nearly 900 microlithic tools (such as arrowheads and scrapers), 200 microcores, and 2,000 microflakes (Guo, D. 1960). The higher rate of settlement abandonment and the growing importance of pastoralism and hunting suggest that a transition from agriculture to agropastoralism began to take place in the Qijia culture.

A peculiar feature – stone circles, each measuring about 4 m in diameter and with a gap suggestive of an entrance – has been found at two Qijia culture sites at Dahezhuang and Qinweijia (Xie, D. 1975b; Zhongguo Shehui Kexueyuan Gansu 1974). At Dahezhaung, five such stone circles are spread over the site, and animal skeletons and oracle bones were also found near some of these structures (Figure 9.14). These stone circles are commonly explained as ritual features, and the animal remains as sacrificial offerings. This interpretation, however, has been challenged by Fitzgerald-Huber (1995: 39), who argues that these structures are comparable to remains of similar stone arrangements in some nomadic cultures, in which stone circles functioned as weights to anchor down the wall edges of tents (cf. Cribb 1991: 171). These stone circles, therefore, may have been the remains of tents used by nomads from the steppe who were searching for pastoral land and metal sources (Fitzgerald–Huber 1995: 52).

Based on the published report, several phenomena suggest that these stone circles were probably residential structures rather than ritual features. First, similar to other rectangular semisubterranean houses, the stone circles appear to have been surrounded by pits and burials. Second, also similar to the houses, the stone circles were built in various orientations, a phenomenon different from cult structures with a fixed orientation found in many nomadic cultures (Steven Rosen 2005, personal communication). Third, their association with three oracle bones is not unique, as eleven such bones have been found in other parts of the site. Fourth, a headless cattle skeleton said to be associated with the stone circle F1 is 7 m away from the structure, and in fact is situated in a rather empty area at a similar distance from two stone circles and one house (Figure 9.14). Fifth, the animals found near the stone circles were cattle and sheep/goats, rather than pigs, suggesting a close relationship between these structures and grazing animals. Nevertheless, the Dahezhuang stone circles are much simpler in form than the stone structures used by pastoralists in the archaeological record from other parts of the world (cf. Rosen, S. 1987, 1993). Further investigation is needed to determine the functions of the Dahezhuang stone structures.

Burial Patterns

The mortuary practice of the Qijia culture shows clear evidence of social hierarchy, and individuals of different social status belonging to the same kin group were buried together in a well-arranged pattern in the same cemetery. Most burials are in rectangular pits, but some are in cave-chamber tombs (*dongshimu*). Social differentiation is evident in the varying quantity and quality of grave goods: Whereas poor burials contained no grave goods, some rich burials contained a few dozen items, such as pottery, jade, precious stone, and animal mandibles.

The majority of burials contain a single interment, but some sites have revealed multiple-interment tombs (Mao, R. et al. 2009). The most striking characteristic of mortuary practice is the widespread incidence of multiple-interment burials across the Qijia culture region. In each of these cases, a male was accompanied by one or two females, commonly arranged with the male lying in an extended supine posture and females positioned on his side(s). The females were usually placed in a flexed posture and facing the male, and in some cases grave goods appear to have been associated only with the male (Figure 9.15).

There are several interpretations of this mortuary custom. It was first interpreted as women being sacrificed for their husbands in a patriarchal society (Wei, H. 1978; Zhang, Z. 1987). Fitzgerald–Huber, in contrast, proposed a provocative explanation, that this burial type resembled the distinctive Indo-European practice of suttee (Fitzgerald-Huber 1995: 38). She compared the Qijia burial patterns with Gryaznov's study of the Eurasian steppe, where the practice of suttee arose due to the economic change from hunting to agropastoralism, leading to greater social dominance by males, who might capture wives from other clans. Having lost the protection of their own clans, these wives could have been made to accompany their spouses in death (Gryaznov 1969). Fitzgerald-Huber (1995: 48) further pointed out that the Qijia-style of suttee, shown in the way the deceased were arranged in the tombs, finds a close parallel in the suttee burials of the eastern branch of the Seima-Turbino people in the Ob valley of the Eurasian steppe, as described by Gryaznov (1969: 94).

A recent study of Qijia burials, however, suggests that some skeletons in these tombs were incomplete, indicating that these were secondary burials for members of the same family, who died at different times (Ye 1997). Nevertheless, not all multiple-interment skeletons appear to be secondary burials, so this argument may be applicable to only some cases.

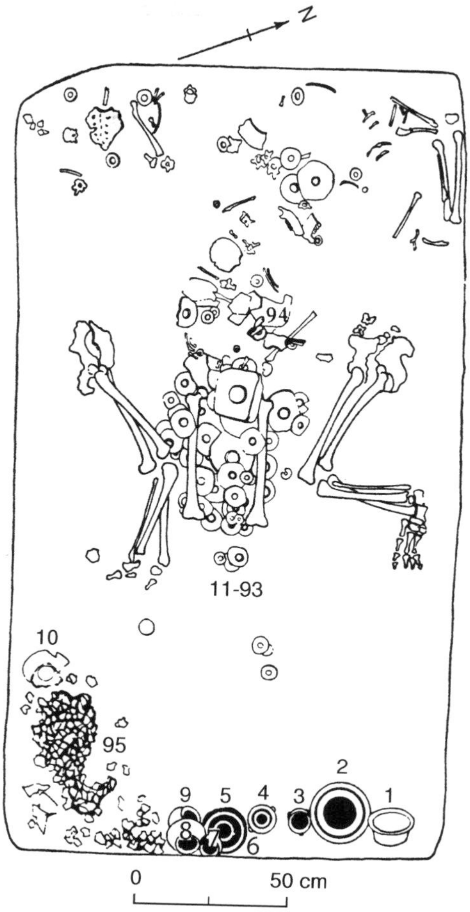

If some Qijia burials do indeed reflect the adoption of suttee, archaeologists have

Figure 9.15. Burial M48 from Huangniang-niangtai, Qijia culture, showing a male in the center associated with grave goods and two females on both sides. 1–10: Ceramics; 11–93: stone *bi* discs; 94: jade ornament; 95: stone wasters (after figure 17 of Wei, H. 1978).

not found evidence that foreign populations appeared in Qijia cemeteries. Human skeletons in the 291 burials at Liuwan in Ledu, Qinghai, have been analyzed. The results show clear continuity in the physical features of the population at this site (ca. 2500–1900 BC) from Banshan and Machang to Qijia. The population was racially Mongoloid, most similar to the East Asian types (Pan and Han 1998). This result may be interpreted in two ways. First, the new type of mortuary practice, suttee, may have been a result of cultural adaptation rather than population migration, although we cannot explain why some Qijia communities accepted such a custom. Second, the populations in the Eurasian steppe included both Europoids and Mongoloids, and it may have been the latter group who were in contact with the Qijia people. If the steppe population was similar to the Qijia people in race and their contacts were infrequent, the morphology of skeletons may not show obvious changes. Nevertheless, the argument for Qijia's contacts with remote cultures in Eurasia seems to be supported by other lines of evidence. As mentioned in Chapter 4, the Qijia culture has revealed the earliest remains of domesticated equines in China, often occurring together with sheep and cattle as grave offerings (Flad et al. 2007). This mortuary tradition was different from those of the Central Plain regions, but resembled those in the steppe. A more notable influence from the Eurasian steppe is evidenced in metallurgy, which will be discussed later in this chapter.

Jade and Stone Ritual Objects

Many Qijia culture sites have yielded jade and stone ritual objects, often in burials, and the best examples are the sites of Huangniangniangtai in Wuwei (Wei, H. 1978), Shizhaocun in Tianshui (Zhongguo Shehui Kexueyuan 1999a: 174, 213), and Lajia in Minhe (Ren, X. et al. 2002). Among the stone/jade objects, *bi* discs are the most common form, followed by *cong* tubes and *huan* rings (Figure 9.16).

At Huangniangniangtai, for example, 260 jade/stone ritual objects (primarily *bi* discs) and production debitage were found in one third of the 62 burials. The best-furnished tomb (M48), which contained an adult male in the center accompanied by two females on the sides, was associated with a large quantity of grave goods, including 83 stone *bi* discs, 1 jade pendant, 304 small pieces of jade and stone wasters, and 10 pottery vessels. All the *bi* discs were placed near the male skeleton, and the females were buried in flexed positions facing the male (Figure 9.15). These jade/stone objects were most likely made locally, as suggested by the find of a jade manufacturing site at Haicangsi, about 1.5 km from Huangniangniangtai (Ye 1997).

The Lajia site in Minhe, Qinghai, is the largest Qijia site (20 ha), surrounded by a moat and located near the Yellow River. In a house (F4), four pieces of raw jade material were found; two of them were on the floor with two finished jade *bi* discs, whereas the two other pieces were stored in a pottery jar. The jade material appears to have been quarried, rather than obtained from river cobbles. Some stray finds from Lajia include jade *bi* discs, axes, an adze, and a knife (Figure 9.16). Lajia also may have been a jade-manufacturing locale (Ye and He 2002).

Jade *bi* discs and *cong* tubes were characteristic of the Liangzhu culture in the lower Yangzi River region. Compared to those from Liangzhu, Qijia jades are less elaborate in form, fewer in type, and later in time. Close parallels to them can be found at Longshan culture sites in south Shanxi (see section on cultural interactions later in this chapter), suggesting an east–west direction of cultural influence. The fact that these jade/stone ritual objects appeared as prestige

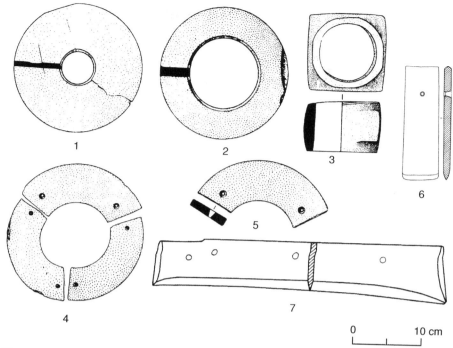

Figure 9.16. Qijia culture jade objects (1–5: from Shizhaocun; 6 and 7: from Lajia).
1: *Bi* disc; 2: *huan* ring; 3: *cong* tube; 4: segmental *bi* disc; 5: *huang* pendant; 6: adze;
7: knife (modified from figure 8-29 of Zhongguo Shehui Kexueyuan 2003b and figure
1 of Ye, M. and He K. 2002).

items in Qijia mortuary contexts suggests that the Qijia people adopted a
symbolic tradition from the east to express their status within an interregional
system of social hierarchy.

Although the evidence for local manufacturing of finished Qijia jades is
clear, the provenance of those jade materials has not been confirmed. Based
on Wen Guang's (1998) analyses, however, jades from Qijia and Longshan
culture sites in the middle and upper Yellow River region are characterized
by yellowish and neutral gray remnants of sedimentary structures, typically
showing traits of pudding stone and rhythmic banding. Such jades appear to
be similar to raw materials available in Lintao, Gansu. Yang Boda (1997), in
contrast, examined thirty-five Qijia jades, among which he identified those
found at eighteen sites as Hetian jade from Xinjiang. It is possible that the raw
materials of Qijia jade products were derived from multiple sources, including
local procurement and long-distance trade.

Metallurgy

The upper Yellow River Valley witnessed the earliest development of copper and bronze metallurgy during the third millennium BC in China

(see Chapter 7). Metallurgical technology flourished in the Qijia culture, and more than 100 copper and bronze objects have been unearthed from at least ten Qijia sites. This number is in sharp contrast to a find of only a few metal objects from the previous Majiayao and Machang cultures during the third millennium BC in the same region. Qijia metal objects are mainly small implements and ornaments, including knives, awls, rings, axes, mirrors, plaques, and a spearhead. The majority of them are pure copper, especially from the early period, but lead–bronze, tin–bronze, lead–tin–bronze, and arsenical copper are also found. Both hammering and casting methods were used in manufacturing (Mei 2003; Ren, S. 2003; Sun, S. and Han 2000b).

Metal deposits are available in a number of locations in the Qilian Mountains, and ores are diverse in composition, including various proportions of copper, tin, lead, and arsenic. Even today, Gansu alone has more than 200 mines containing about a dozen nonferrous metals. Sites associated with early metalwork appear to be located along the Hexi corridor in close proximity to raw material sources in the nearby mountain range (figure 11 of Sun, S. and Han 1997; Sun, S. and Han 2000a, b). Some of the Qijia metal products are likely to have been manufactured locally, as indicated by slag found at Huangniangniangtai (Guo, D. 1960). These phenomena suggest that metalworkers used local metal sources, resulting in the diverse alloy compositions of the products. Given that Qijia metal objects are small, were used mainly for utilitarian purposes, and were scattered throughout the region, it seems probable that metal manufacturing was organized as small-scale, independent production.

Cultural Interactions

The Qijia culture appears to have had broad interactions with populations in all directions. There is unmistakable evidence of cultural contacts with the eastern regions. Some diagnostic Qijia cultural elements have been found at various sites of the Laoniupo type, a cultural assemblage in eastern Shaanxi that was contemporary with Erlitou and Qijia. Such elements include a male-female double burial at Hengzhen in Huayin, the custom of placing stone *bi* discs on top of skeletons in burials at Laoniupo in Xi'an, and the presence of pottery jars with two or three handles at many Laoniupo-type sites (Zhang, T. 2000; Zhang, T. and Xiao 2003). Given that Laoniupo was located between Qijia and Erlitou, it may have played an intermediate role in the interactions between these two cultures.

The prototypes of some Qijia jades, particularly *cong* tubes, *huan* rings, and segmental *bi* discs, may be traced back to corresponding jade forms excavated from Longshan sites in south Shanxi, including Qingliangsi in Ruicheng (Shanxisheng 2002), as well as Taosi (Gao, W. and Li 1983) and Xiajin (Song, J.

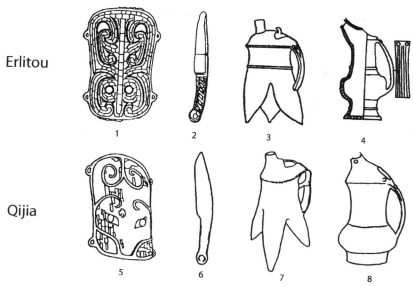

Erlitou

Qijia

Figure 9.17. Comparison of bronze plaques inlaid with turquoise, ring-handled bronze knives, and pottery *he* vessels from Erlitou (1–4) and Qijia sites (5–8) (modified from figure 17 of Li, S. 2005).

and Xue 1998) in Xiangfen. Chronologically, these sites are either earlier than or overlap with the Qijia culture.

In addition, two types of peculiar Erlitou artifacts, pottery *he* vessels and bronze plaques inlaid with turquoise, have been found in Qijia sites (Fitzgerald-Huber 2003: 65–70; Li, S. 2005: 266; Zhang, T. 2002) (Figure 9.17). The *he* vessels were probably associated with drinking rituals in the Erlitou culture. The occurrence of this vessel type at Qijia sites suggests that Erlitou's ritual influence reached its western neighbors. A bronze plaque found in Tianshui, Gansu, is nearly identical in form to its Erlitou counterparts, and was most likely manufactured at Erlitou (see Chapter 8). A jade knife of the Qijia culture type unearthed at Lajia is 41.2 cm long, with four small holes (Figure 9.16.7) (Ye and He 2002), and similar examples can be found at Erlitou (Zhongguo Shehui Kexueyuan 1999b: 250, 342). There is no evidence of jade manufacturing at the Erlitou site, so it is possible that some of the Erlitou jades were derived from Qijia.

As the current data show, Qijia's eastern connections appear to have been two-way interactions, perhaps involving both population migration and material transmission. With regard to the use and production of prestige goods as status symbols, Qijia appears to have been influenced by the eastern cultural traditions.

The most intriguing cultural interactions of the Qijia are their contacts with the northwest, which may have resulted in a wider use of metals and an increased practice of pastoralism in the Qijia culture. There have traditionally been two opinions among Chinese archaeologists regarding the origins of Qijia metallurgy. Whereas some favor the view that Qijia metals indicate an independent innovation and an indigenous development from copper to bronze metallurgy (Sun, S. and Han 1997; Zhang, Z. 1987), others believe that the sudden flourishing of Qijia metallurgy is attributable to influence from the West (e.g., An, Z. 1993b). The latter opinion has been further elaborated on lately by more scholars, based on comparative study with material remains from Eurasian steppe cultures. Fitzgerald-Huber (1995: 40–52) and Mei (2003), for example, have pointed out that most Qijia metal forms – including socketed axes and spearheads, back-curved knives, and bone-mounted awls and knives – resemble those from the Okunev culture, the Minusinsk and the Altai, and the eastern part of the Seima-Turbino complex, particularly at Rostovka and Sopka in the upper Ob River Valley. The Seima-Turbino complex was derived from two cultural groups, the Altai metallurgists and horsemen, and the mobile hunters of the eastern Siberian taiga, who formed a population of warriors, nomads, and metallurgists (Chernykh et al. 2004; Chernykh 1992: 215–33). These general cultural characteristics of the Seima-Turbino complex seem to fit well with the material assemblages found in Qijia sites, including microliths, grazing animal husbandry, and metallurgy. Qijia apparently had close contacts with nomadic people from the Eurasian steppe who were skilled metallurgists (Fitzgerald-Huber 1995, 2003).

The discovery of a mirror decorated with a star and bordered by parallel sunken lines from Gamatai in Guinan, Qinghai (Figure 9.13.13), suggests possible contacts with cultures of Xinjiang and western Central Asia. A mirror with a similar style has been unearthed at Tianshanbeilu in eastern Xinjiang (Figure 9.2) (Mei 2003: 36–7), and the star motif can be found on bronze objects from the Andronovo culture in the Bactria-Margiana regions of Afghanistan and southern Turkmenistan (Fitzgerald-Huber 1995: 52–3).

The Qijia culture's connection with the Eurasian steppe has been a fascinating research topic. Some scholars hold that these contacts were indirect, and were likely to have been facilitated through a number of intermediary links between the Hexi corridor and the Eurasian steppe. Such connections have been identified at sites along the western part of the Hexi corridor, including the Siba culture in western Gansu and the Tianshanbeilu site in eastern Xinjiang. These sites date to the first half of the second millennium BC, largely overlapping with the Qijia culture (Li, S. 2003; Mei 2000, 2003). Recent mtDNA analysis of human remains from Tianshanbeilu has confirmed that the Qijia population indeed had close genetic affinity with the Tianshanbeilu people (Gao, S. 2009). In addition, there are likely to have been other routes for traveling between the Eurasian steppe and the Hexi corridor through Mongolia, but we are constrained by lack of knowledge regarding archaeological finds in Mongolia (cf. Fitzgerald-Huber 1995: 51; Mei 2003: 38).

The Qijia people appear to have acted as intermediates, transferring material items between the Central Plain and steppe regions. Their contacts with the steppe cultures, however, appear to have been different from those with their eastern neighbors. Although several scholars have argued that these were two-way interactions rather than a one-way diffusion between Qijia and steppe cultures (Li, S. 2003; Mei 2003), the fact is that no Qijia material has been found in the steppe region west of Xinjiang. The cultural influence from the steppe to Qijia appears to have been dominant.

It is also worth noting that, although metals were used by many Qijia communities, these artifacts were not incorporated into the prestige-goods system regularly expressed in their mortuary rituals. Instead, jade/stone ritual items, in addition to pottery, appear to have functioned as the primary status symbols among elite groups in this culture (e.g., Fitzgerald-Huber 2003: 65; Liu, L. 2003: 14). The Qijia people seem to have shown preference for cultural values originating locally and from the Central Plain.

THE SIBA CULTURE

The Siba culture was named after the discovery of an assemblage of pottery and stone tools at Sibatan in Shandan county, Gansu province, in 1948 (An, Z. 1959). This culture is distributed east-west along the narrow Hexi corridor for about 800 km, south to the Qilian Mountains, north to the Badanjilin Desert, west to the Shule River, and east to Wuwei in Gansu (Figure 9.2). Several carbon dates from Siba culture sites fall into the time period of 1900–1500 BC, largely contemporary with the Qijia culture. Only a few sites have been excavated, including Huoshaogou in Yumen, Donghuishan in Minle, and Ganguya in Jiuquan. These are all burial sites, and we know little about the residential settlement patterns of the Siba culture (Li, S. 1993; Zhongguo Shehui Kexueyuan 2003b: 558–62).

Subsistence and Settlement Distribution

Siba ceramic assemblage is dominated by reddish sandy jars, many painted with geometric patterns. The typological analysis of pottery suggests that the Siba culture was formed from a combination of sources. First, it was mainly derived from the Machang variant of the Majiayao culture through an intermediate phase distributed in the same region. Second, it received influence from the Qijia culture in the east. Third, it interacted with the Kayue culture (ca. 1600–700 BC) in the southeast.

Both ground and chipped stone tools were used, including axes, knives, hammer stones, disc-shaped implements, grinding slabs, pestles, mortars, hoes, and stone balls. Large numbers of microlithic tools were also found in burials, particularly at Huoshaogou and Shaguoliang, both in Yumen (Li, S. 1993).

The faunal assemblage from Donghuishan is dominated by pig and deer bones, followed by those of sheep and dogs (Qi, G. 1998). A variety of crops were unearthed, including millet, wheat, barley, and rye (Li, F. et al. 1989).

Siba culture sites can be divided into two types based on their ecological adaptation. Sites of the first type, including Shaguoliang and Huoshaogou in Yumen, are distributed on grasslands in the northern part of the western Hexi Corridor. People in these settlements mainly practiced pastoralism and hunting, as suggested by the high frequencies of grazing animal bones and microlithic tools shown in the archaeological record. Sites of the second type, such as Ganguya in Jiuquan, are located on the northern piedmont of the Qilian Mountains. This piedmont region is characterized by fertile soil and abundant water resources, and traditionally has been exploited as an agricultural zone. These settlements appear to have been occupied primarily by agriculturalists, as revealed by their high density of site distribution and thickness of cultural deposits, but low frequencies of grazing animal bones and microliths (Li, S. 1993: 116–17).

It is noteworthy that, although Siba cemeteries appear to have been revisited and reused over many generations, no residential remains have been found. This situation may indicate that Siba communities were relatively mobile, so that no substantial residues of their dwellings have survived as archaeologically visible vestiges. This settlement pattern seems to resemble some of the Eurasian steppe cultures that became increasingly mobile and relied on pastoralism, such as Yamnaya in the west of the Caspian Sea (Anthony 1998: 102–3).

Physical anthropological studies of human remains from Donghuishan and Huoshaogou suggest a Mongoloid population closest to the East Asian types, a situation consistent with the Qijia culture (Zhu, H. 1998). Many archaeologists compare the Siba culture with the Qiang people, who are mentioned in ancient texts (see Li, S. 1993: 119–20). According to "Xi Qiang Zhuan" in *Hou Hanshu* (written in the fifth century AD), the Qiang people in the Hexi corridor were pastoral nomads, who herded grazing stock and constantly migrated in search of water and pasture. The characteristics of the archaeological Siba culture seem to match quite well with the historical Qiang described in textual records.

Burial Patterns

Siba burials were all laid with locally consistent arrangements in cemeteries near residential areas, but such cemeteries in different locales show rather varying mortuary patterns. The Huoshaogou cemetery contains mostly single burials constructed as side-tunnel pits or vertical pits; the Ganguya cemetery is mainly characterized by cists with multiple interments; the Donghuishan cemetery is predominated by rectangular pits with secondary burials and male-female double burials; and at Yingwoshu in Anxi, no skeletons have been found in burials, perhaps suggesting a practice of cremation (Li, S. 1993: 106).

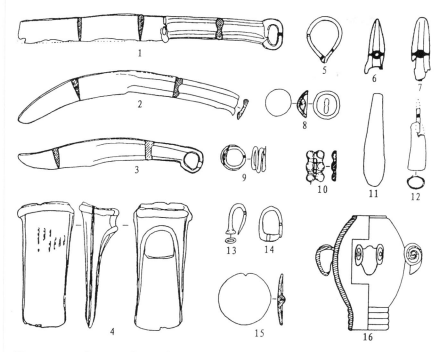

Figure 9.18. Bronze objects from the Siba culture. 1–3: knives; 4: socketed axe; 5, 13, and 14: earrings; 6 and 7: arrowheads; 8: button; 9: finger ring; 10, 15: ornaments; 11: dagger; 12: awl with bone handle; 16: mace head (1–10, 12–15 from Ganguya; 11 and 16 from Huoshaogou; not to scale) (after figure 3 of Li, S. 2005).

The majority of burials are associated with grave goods of various quantity and quality, including animal sacrifices, stone tools, ceramics, metal objects, jades, and cowry shells. At Donghuishan, two-thirds of the 249 burials held grave goods, ranging from 1 to 20 items per burial. At Huoshaogou, more than one-third of the 312 burials are associated with metal objects, some of which may have symbolized power and authority, such as mace heads (Gansusheng 1998). These differences in mortuary rites suggest the emergence of social differentiation in Siba communities.

Metallurgy and Cultural Interactions

Metal objects – including those made of copper, bronze, silver, and/or gold – are common in burials. More than 270 copper and bronze objects have been discovered in Siba sites, comprising a wide range of types, such as knives, axes, awls, bracelets, plaques, earrings, nose rings, buttons, arrowheads, spearheads, and a mace head (Figure 9.18). These objects clearly resemble their stylistic counterparts found in the Eurasian steppe and Central Asia. The bronze mace head has close correlations in Central Asia and the Near East. Gold earrings and a silver nose ring, which are the earliest examples of their kind in China, can find parallels only in Central Asia and further west. Despite similarities in style with those from the West, some Siba metal items show local innovations in technology. Unlike its western counterparts, which were made of lost-wax techniques, the Huoshaogou mace head was made with piece-mold casting techniques (Bunker 1998; Li, S. 2003; Li, S. and Shui 2000; Mei 2003).

Both casting and hammering techniques were used. The find of a stone-casting mold for arrowheads at the Huoshaogou site suggests that metal objects were manufactured locally (figure 8 of Sun, S. and Han 1997). Interestingly, Siba metal objects are largely made of tin bronze and arsenical copper/bronze; these are different from the Qijia metals, which are mainly pure copper and tin bronze, but are similar to those found at Tianshanbeilu in eastern Xinjiang. The arsenic component points to a metallurgical tradition from the West. Arsenical copper was a metallurgical technology that flourished in the Urals, whereas tin bronze was common in the Altai and eastern Kazakhstan around the beginning of the second millennium BC. The Siba culture and contemporary sites in eastern Xinjiang may have played intermediate roles connecting the Eurasian steppe with the Qijia culture (Mei 2003: 37–8). It is also possible that the difference in alloy components might be attributed to the variability of locally available metal-bearing ores near individual metalware production sites (Li, S. 2005: 262).

Two bronze production sites, indicated by the presence of slag, copper ore, and charcoal, have been identified at Huoshiliang and Ganggangwa in northwestern Gansu. Bronze production began at the sites perhaps as early as 2135 BC and lasted until ca. AD 70. The bronze artifacts from the sites are arsenic bronze, and the major sources of ore were the nearby Baishantang mine site (Figure 9.2), as well as other unidentified sites. The Bronze Age people there were farmers who planted cereals such as wheat and millet (Dodson et al. 2009). These sites' affiliation with archaeological culture is unclear, as no ceramic study has been carried out; but they are located within the Siba culture region. These discoveries confirm that bronze production indeed took place locally.

The Siba culture's material assemblages suggest that it played an intermediary role between cultures to the east and west. The fact that two types of Siba sites coexisted in different ecological zones and shared a similar ceramic assemblage suggests close interaction and exchange between agricultural and pastoral-hunting communities. Such interactions were apparently not limited to an intraregional level, but may have extended to a much greater geographic horizon in the Eurasian steppe, as testified by the metal objects with Eurasian and Central Asian styles found at Siba sites. It is also interesting to note that the Huoshaogou site, which represents a hunting/pastoralist community located in the western part of the Siba culture zone, yielded many more metal objects (more than 200 metal items) than the total number of metal items from all other Siba sites combined. This finding seems to indicate that the hunting/pastoralist communities may have played the most important role in the east–west communication through production and trade of metal products.

THE EARLY BRONZE AGE IN EAST XINJIANG

Xinjiang Uygur Autonomous Region, in the northwest of modern China, geographically and demographically belongs to the eastern part of Central Asia, separated from western Central Asia by the Pamir and Hindu Kush Mountains. Many valleys in these mountains form traversable passes, facilitating communications between these two regions. Xinjiang is characterized by three high mountain ranges (Kunlun, Tian, and Altai) embracing two desert basins, the Tarim (Talimu) in the south and Dzungaria (Zhunge'er) in the north (Figure 9.2). Along the edges of the desert basins are isolated oases, allowing intensive sedentary occupation and agropastoral activities. This type of economy appears to have developed around 2000 BC, as a result of new migrations by groups of metal-using people from the West into Xinjiang, thus replacing the local Paleolithic and Microlithic traditions (Chen, K. and Hiebert 1995). Because of extremely dry conditions in the desert areas, many cemeteries of these newcomers have yielded well-preserved organic remains, including human mummies, providing unusual information about their cultures.

During the first half of the second millennium BC, Xinjiang, particularly its eastern part, appears to have played a pivotal role in east-west interactions. Eastern Xinjiang, lying at the eastern end of the Tian Mountains, connects to the Hexi corridor to the east, and extends to the Tarim Basin to the west. Three sites are particularly important: (1) Qäwrighul (Gumugou) and (2) Xiaohe in the Könchi (Kongque) River Valley of the Tarim Basin's eastern rim, and (3) Tianshanbeilu (also named Yalinban, Yamansukuang, and Lin-ya in different publications) in the Hami Basin.

Qäwrighul and Tieban River Cemeteries

Qäwrighul cemetery is situated west of Lake Lop Nur, on the bank of the Könchi River. Eight radiocarbon dates show a wide range of time differences, but mostly concentrate around ca. 2100–1500 BC (An, Z. 1998: 56–7; Zhongguo Shehui Kexueyuan 1991: 303–4). A total of forty-two excavated graves can be divided into two types. The first type, which is earlier than the second type, consists of thirty-six shaft-pit burials, furnished with coffins and covered with sheep/goat skins or grass cloth. The bodies, placed in an extended position, wore felt hats and were wrapped with woolen blankets. The second type of grave includes six shaft-pits, each surrounded by upright wooden poles forming seven concentric circles and then multiple lines radiating outward (Figure 9.19). Funerary goods from both sets of graves are similar, including artifacts made of grass, wood, bone, horn, stone, and metal. A small bag

containing broken ephedra twigs was attached to the chest area of clothing. Wheat grains and bones from sheep/goat, ox, camel, deer, moufflon, and
birds are the remains of sacrificial offerings (Figure 9.19). The metal objects are
small pure copper fragments, but the excavators believe that the Qäwrighul
people may have had bronze cutting tools, as judged from tool marks on
wooden objects. Funerary remains indicate that the Qäwrighul people cultivated crops, hunted wild mammals and birds, and fished in nearby rivers.
Their crafts include leatherworking, weaving of woolen fabrics, felt-making,
and jade-/stoneworking (Barber 1999; Kuz'mina 1998; Mallory and Mair 2000;
Wang, B. 1983, 2001a: 29–48).

A similar burial site was excavated near the Tieban River in Lop Nur,
revealing a well-preserved female mummy dated to 3,800 years ago (Figure
9.19). Examinations of the corpse indicate that she was about 40–45 years
of age, and 155.8 cm in height. There is a huge quantity of black, granular
sediment in her lungs, suggesting that she lived in an atmosphere containing
a large amount of carbon dust and wind-blown sand. This factor may reflect
domestic working conditions typical for women and in the desert environment
in Lopnur (Wang, B. 2001a: 29–48).

Because ceramics are absent from the graves, it is difficult to determine
the cultural association of the people from the Qäwrighul and Tieban River
cemeteries. Physical appearances of all corpses are Caucasoid, however, and no
scholars dispute their affiliation with the proto-Europoid complex. MtDNA
analysis on ten Qäwrighul human individuals confirmed that these people
were indeed close to the European population (Cui et al. 2004). Han Kangxin
also suggested that, on the basis of physical morphology, people in the first type
of graves at Qäwrighul are similar to the Afanasievo population, whereas people in the second type of graves are comparable to the Andronovo population
(Han, K. 1986). Afanasievo was the first bronze culture (third/second millennium BC) found in the steppe region of eastern Kazakhstan and southwestern
Siberia, whereas the subsequent Andronovo culture (second millennium BC)
is distributed over a large area from the Caspian Sea to Mongolia (Chen, K. and
Hiebert 1995: 249) (Figure 9.1). Both groups were Europoid, and it is difficult
to differentiate Afanasievo and Andronovo skulls (Kuz'mina 1998: 68).

Many elements in mortuary rites and material remains at Qäwrighul show
parallels to those of Eurasian steppe cultures. Pure copper artifacts are particularly similar to those of Afanasievo in style and material, and the Qäwrighul
faunal assemblage also shows correspondence with that of Afanasievo. The
clothing complex in burials and the structure of graves resemble those found
in the Afanasievo and Andronovo cultures (Kuz'mina 1998: 68–9). The
Qäwrighul cemetery, therefore, provides concrete evidence that Afanasievo
and/or Andronovo people arrived in eastern Xinjiang by the early part of the
second millennium BC. It is unknown if these people had direct contact with
Mongoloid populations from the east, as the archaeological evidence for such
contacts remains unclear at this site.

Figure 9.19. Archaeological finds from Qäwrighul, Xinjiang. 1: Stone female figurine; 2: basket woven of grass containing grains of wheat; 3: female mummy from the Tieban River; 4: excavation at the Qäwrighul cemetery (after Wang, B. 2001b: 30, 33, 35, 45).

Xiaohe

The Xiaohe site near the lower reach of the Könchi River in Lop Nur (Figure 9.2) was first found by a local hunter in the early twentieth century, and later partially excavated by Bergman, a Swedish archaeologist, in 1934 (Bergman 1939). These early explorations revealed a large prehistoric cemetery with well-preserved human and material remains belonging to previously unknown cultures. Archaeologists have recently excavated the entire site, providing new information about the material culture of this lost society in Xinjiang.

The Xiaohe site (2,500 m²) was a sandy mount, about 7 m in height, formed by many layers of graves, indicating a long period of occupation (Figure 9.20). Because of severe disturbance, however, the remaining site is only a half of the original cemetery. From 2002 through 2005, archaeologists excavated 167 graves, and collected several thousand artifacts and some thirty well-preserved mummies. These burials can be divided into five phases based on stratigraphy and burial patterns, although only the upper two strata (1–2) (1690–1420 BC) have been published in relatively detailed reports (Xiaohe 2005; Yidilisi et al. 2004, 2007).

All burials were furnished with wooden coffins, and a standing wooden ensign was erected in front of each coffin. These wooden insignia differ in shape between female and male burials, in that a phallus is associated with female, and a wide paddle with male coffins. Grasses, ox heads, and small metal rings or plaques were attached on the postlike insignia. More than 80 percent of the tomb occupants are adults, who were buried in extended supine position with heads toward the east. The corpses wore woolen capes, leather boots, and felt hats decorated with feathers, fur, and woolen strings. Small bags attached to clothing contained wheat, millet, and broken ephedra twigs. Many wooden masks or figurines, ox skulls, and sheep/goat skulls were buried as grave goods (Figure 9.20).

One of the tombs was constructed in the form of a house, showing higher social status than other tombs in the cemetery. In this tomb two piles of ox skulls, stacked up in seven layers, were placed on the sides of the burial chamber; a stone mace head, a bell-shaped copper/bronze object, and a copper/bronze mirror decorated with gold rings were unearthed from the bottom of the burial chamber; and numerous human masks made of bone and wood, painted wooden plaques, and more than 100 ox and sheep/goat skulls were also found in the area immediately surrounding this burial.

The mummies from graves show clear Caucasoid features; but, because no pottery is present in the burials, the Xiaohe people's cultural affiliation is unclear. The burial customs in the upper strata at Xiaohe appear to have been similar to those in the second type of Qäwrighul graves, which were surrounded by large numbers of upright short wooden poles. This similarity indicates that the late Xiaohe burials were contemporary with the Qäwrighul cemetery, which dates to the early second millennium BC, and the early

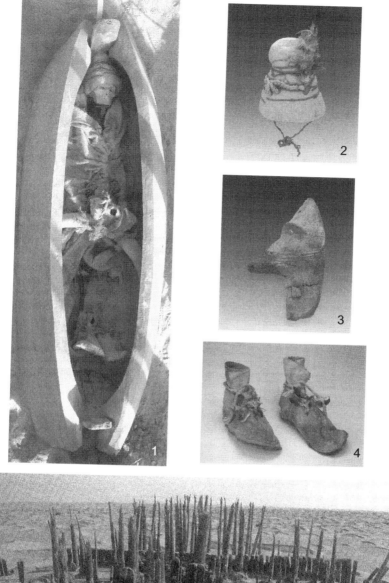

Figure 9.20. Xiaohe cemetery and artifacts unearthed, Xinjiang. 1: Female mummy in wooden coffin; 2: felt hat; 3: wooden mask; 4; boots (all from Burial M13); 5: Xiaohe cemetery (after figures 2, 14, 20, 24, and 27 of Yidilisi et al. 2007).

Xiaohe burials were earlier than Qäwrighul. It is possible that, similar to the Qäwrighul population, the Xiaohe people were also related to Afanasievo or/and Andronovo. MtDNA analysis of seventeen individuals from Xiaohe shows that their genetic structure was complex, consisting of European and Central Asian elements, with the closest genetic relationships being to modern populations of Uzbekistan and Turkmenistan (Xie, C. 2007).

Xiaohe people were apparently agropastoralists. They grew wheat and millet, raised sheep/goats and cattle, and hunted wild animals. The millet grains unearthed from the site appear to have been the earliest millet remains found in Xinjiang. The people practiced some unique customs, which have not been seen in other parts of Central Asia. The Xiaohe people may represent one of the earliest Bronze Age populations in the oases of Xinjiang; further research will help us to understand their origins and their interactions with people in the surrounding regions.

Tianshanbeilu

The Tianshanbeilu site is located near Hami city. Since 1988 more than 700 graves have been excavated, revealing a large Bronze Age cemetery that was continuously used for a few hundred years (ca. 2000–1550 BC) (Hami 1990; Li, S. 2002). Two kinds of graves have been found: shaft pits and mud-brick shaft pits. The dead were placed in flexed position, with females oriented to the northeast and males to the southwest. Grave goods include objects made of pottery, bronze, silver, bone, and/or stone. Pottery vessels are handmade and red and gray in color. Some of them are painted with triangles, zigzag lines, wavy lines, dots, and plant patterns. Tianshanbeilu pottery can be divided into two groups. Group A includes jars with single or double handles and basins with two handles, which are comparable to those of the Siba culture. Group B includes jars with a deep belly or ball-shaped body, and with two lugs on the rim. The latter group of vessels finds a close correlation in remains from the Qiemurqiek (Ke'ermuqi) cemetery in the Altai, northwest Xinjiang; furthermore, the material assemblage from Qiemurqiek also shows links with Bronze Age cultures in southern Siberia and western Mongolia (Li, S. 2002), which are probably related to the Andronovo and Karasuk cultures (Shui 1993) (Figure 9.21).

Many copper and bronze artifacts have been found at Tianshanbeilu, including small implements and ornaments made of copper and bronze, and hairpins made of silver. Their typological connections with the Eurasian steppe cultures to the west and with the Siba and Qijia cultures to the east are shown in the cases of ring-handled knives with curved backs, knives with two protrusions on the back, socketed axes, daggers, sickles, mirrors with or without decoration on the back, ring-shaped earrings, buttons, and awls with bone handles (Li, S. 2005: 249–50; Mei 2000, 2003: 36–7) (Figure 9.22). The use

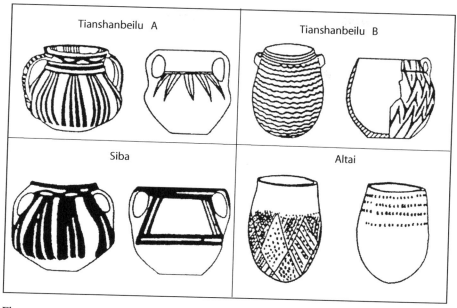

Figure 9.21. Tianshanbeilu ceramics compared with Siba and Qiemurqiek in Altai (modified from figure 8 of Li, S. 2005).

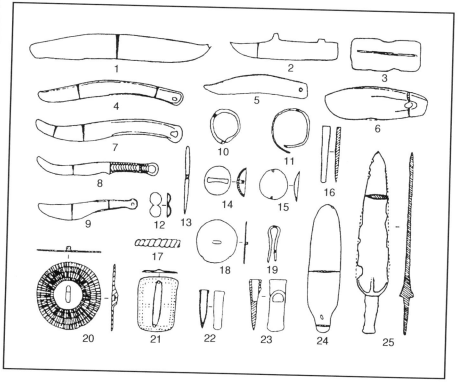

Figure 9.22. Metal objects from Tianshanbeilu, eastern Xinjiang. 1, 2, 4, 7–9: Knives; 3 and 21: plaques; 5 and 6: sickles; 10 and 11: earrings; 12: ornament; 13: awl; 14 and 15: buttons; 16: chisel; 17: tube; 18 and 20: mirrors; 19: pin; 22 and 23: socketed axes; 24: spear; 25: short dagger (after figure 7 of Li, S. 2005; not to scale).

of silver ornaments also points to a custom widespread in the Eurasian steppe and northern frontier cultures in China (Bunker 1998).

Among the nineteen metal samples examined, fifteen are tin bronzes, one is copper, and three are tin bronzes containing a small amount of arsenic or lead. Metallurgical technologies include casting, forging, annealing, and cold working. The predominant use of tin bronze and arsenical bronze also points to connections with cultures farther to the west and north in the Eurasian steppe, such as Seima–Turbino and Andronovo (Mei 2000: 38–9, 2003: 36–7).

Such mixed characteristics of material culture, as revealed in the Tianshanbeilu cemetery, are highly consistent with the local mtDNA data. The demographic analysis of haplogroups suggests that peoples from northwest China, Siberia, and Central Asia all contributed to the mtDNA gene pool of the Tianshanbeilu population. Of East Asian populations, the Lajia group of the Qijia culture had close affinity with the Tianshanbeilu people (Gao, S. 2009).

In addition to the fertile oasis environments suitable for supporting agropastoral communities, metal deposits in Xinjiang also probably attracted Bronze Age populations from other regions. Metallic ores, containing copper, tin, and lead, are extensive in distribution but small in quantity in Xinjiang. A study of a mining and smelting site of the first millennium BC at Nulasai in Nileke County, western Xinjiang, demonstrates that arsenic copper may have been produced there. This discovery raises the hope of finding missing links in Xinjiang that might indicate the progress of metallurgy from west to east; but because the Nulasai mining site is rather late, it is unclear whether these deposits were explored by the Bronze Age populations who migrated to Xinjiang during the first part of the second millennium BC (Mei 2000: 50–7; Mei and Shell 1998).

These early metal-using sites in Xinjiang show clear evidence for interactions between populations from different regions in both east and west, exemplified by Caucasoid human remains, metallurgy, and domestic wheat from the west, as well as pottery from the east. Eastern Xinjiang, therefore, was likely the pivotal point for the earliest contacts between the Eurasian steppe and western China in the late third and early second millennia BC. The Tianshanbeilu site is particularly important, in that not only does its material culture indicate interregional influences, but its mtDNA also confirms gene flow in both directions along an east-west axis. Nevertheless, current data do not support the proposition that Xinjiang was a springboard for the diffusion of metallurgical technology from the steppe area to western China in the third millennium BC, because the earliest metal in Xinjiang (ca. 2000 BC) is still later than its counterpart in the Longshan and Qijia cultures in north China during the late third millennium BC.

CONCLUSIONS

The northern frontier cultures assumed a distinctive intermediating role at a time of numerous changes in China and the Eurasian steppe and of unprecedented interregional activity. The material items exchanged between the northern frontier cultures and their neighbors were predominantly prestige goods. Such activity was probably associated with elite strategies for creating and maintaining social status, forming alliances, and seeking wealth and symbolic power from distant lands, all of which are common elite behaviors observable in many parts of the world, including Bronze Age cultures in the steppe (Hanks and Linduff 2009).

Three major factors may have encouraged such interactions. First, the Central Asian and Eurasian steppe cultures' exploration of the east; second, the Erlitou and Erligang states' expansion toward the north and northwest; and third, the northern frontier cultures' own growing social complexity, accompanied by the competition for power and prestige among various polities.

Eastward Exploration by Central Asian and Eurasian Steppe Cultures

From the steppe and desert zones of Central Eurasia, vegetational records show a shift toward adaptation to a more arid climate around 2200 BC, in reaction to climatic change. The reduction of deciduous forests in valleys, and the corresponding increase of steppe landscapes near settlements, led to a new subsistence strategy, with greater emphasis on pastoralism. In particular, environmental change stimulated the adaptive use of horses, carts, and metal implements, giving rise to Bronze Age mobility and wide-ranging pastoralism. The period from 2000 to 1800 BC witnessed expanded exploration of the Eurasian steppe by pastoral groups. Underlying factors included continuing steppification, discovery of new metal resources east of the Urals in the Kazakhstan steppe, spread of mobile pastoral adaptation toward the east, and contacts between mobile pastoralists and the oasis dwellers of Central Asia (Anthony 2007; Hiebert 2000).

In the steppe region of eastern Eurasia, the development of metallurgical technology, in association with increased mobile pastoralism, was apparently driven by both economic and political motivations. During the second millennium BC, production of metalwares gave new focus to their symbolic significance, so metallurgical activity grew beyond mere utilitarian tool-making and became a medium of negotiation for power among social groups and individuals. As metal resources were scarce and distribution was uneven, control over important sources and trade routes became a matter of crucial concern for metallurgically interested pastoralist groups. Therefore, growth of metal production encouraged more intensive exploitation of new metal resources and expansion of social networks and interactions, resulting in even greater mobility of human populations on a transregional level (Frachetti 2002).

Increased mobility of pastoral cultures in the Eurasian steppe enabled these groups to travel great distances to the south and southeast, searching for new sources of metal ores, and making direct and indirect contacts with the cultures of northern China. Within these broad environmental, economic, and sociopolitical contexts, the northern frontier communities became intensively involved with networks of steppe cultures. Therefore, it is not surprising that these frontier cultures were generally situated in regions boasting an abundance of both metal resources and pastures.

The emergence of fully specialized pastoralism required coexistence with farming communities for agricultural products to supplement the limited pastoral diet (Cribb 1991). In contrast, the farming communities, and especially their elites, also may have sought pastoral products for both utilitarian and symbolic value. Such mutual needs therefore would have encouraged contacts between pastoralists and agriculturalists in north China. These contacts may have also stimulated the transition from agriculture to agropastoralism in these frontier cultures.

Interactions with the steppe are best indicated by the presence in Northern Zone communities of three types of cultural traits, which originated in places farther northwest. These include the following: first, widespread use of bronze artifacts with steppe styles (certain types of tools, weapons, and ornaments); second, increased husbandry of grazing animals (cattle, sheep, and occasionally horse), which were often used for mortuary sacrifices; and third, cultivation of wheat and barley. These cultural traits, however, did not appear as a consistently packaged set throughout the Northern Zone, but rather occurred selectively in various combinations in different regions. This phenomenon may indicate that these influences were derived from multiple origins over the vast steppe, a region that is still not fully understood by archaeologists.

Political Expansion of the Central Plain States

As discussed in Chapter 8, the early states of Erlitou and Erligang are characterized by ever-greater scales of political centralization, urbanization, and territorial expansion toward the peripheries, including the northern frontiers. One of the primary motivations of such expansion was to procure raw materials for making prestige goods, such as bronzes and jades. The desire for such items stimulated extensive interactions between early states and culturally remote regions where relevant natural resources were available. Prestige goods found in the frontier cultures, which were either imported from the Central Plain, or imitations of Central Plain styles made by local artisans, particularly reflect the outbound movements. This point is attested by the Shang ritual bronzes found at Zhukaigou in the Ordos, and ceramic *jue* and *jia* vessels of the Erlitou style, which appeared at Dadianzi in the Liao River Valley and at several Qijia sites in the upper Yellow River Valley. All three locales were situated near rich metal resources. In contrast, bronze objects of steppe styles also found their way to Erlitou, indicating inbound movements of prestige goods. The interactions between early states and these peripheries likely involved migration of populations as well as long-distance trade in goods.

Influences exerted by the Erlitou and Erligang states toward the northern frontiers were limited and did not exceed the vicinities of the Lower Xiajiadian, Zhukaigou, and Qijia cultures. Traveling westward from the core area of the Erlitou and Erligang states, characteristics of the Central Plain gradually diminish, whereas cultural connections with the steppe regions correspondingly increase. The northward expansion of the two early Central Plain states appears to have been short-lived. After the Erligang period, during the middle and late Shang, phases of decentralization and regeneration occurred in the Central Plain (see Chapters 8 and 10), and interactions there with the northern cultures changed to predominantly military competition.

Development of Social Complexity in the Northern Frontier Cultures

Many recent studies have focused on the dynamics relating to the development of social complexity and to the changing economies of the northern frontier cultures. Two competing approaches have been taken by archaeologists. The first approach emphasizes the interrelationship between the external environment and human societies, believing that climatic change and human-induced environmental deterioration led to new economic adaptations, which increasingly relied on mobile pastoralism (e.g., Jin, G. 2004; Li, F. et al. 1993; Shui 2001a,b; Song, Y. 2002; Tian, G. and Shi 2004). The second approach focuses on internal factors, arguing that political systems, leadership strategies, and interregional interaction determined the transition from agricultural production to pastoralist adaptation (e.g., Linduff 1998; Shelach 1999: 193–4, 232; 2009a: 68–70). In our view, however, these two arguments address different aspects of the same social phenomenon, and are complementary to one another for understanding socioeconomic changes in the northern frontier cultures.

As mentioned earlier in this chapter, climatic fluctuations indeed occurred more frequently after the Mid-Holocene Climatic Optimum era. Recent research on paleoenvironment suggests that an abrupt climatic change occurred around 4000 cal. BP on a global scale, including China (Wu, W. and Liu 2004). The climatic change, however, did not affect all of China uniformly, nor lead to the same level of ecological deterioration cross-regionally. Colder and drier conditions seem to have occurred in Northwest China earlier than in North and Northeast China, probably because of the changing patterns of the monsoon systems and variable microenvironments in different regions. In the archaeological record, at a phase when the Lower Xiajiadian and Zhukaigou cultures still practiced a predominantly agricultural economy, the Qijia and Siba cultures had begun agropastoralism (Shui 2001b; Tian, G. and Shi 1997).

In all these regions, however, environmental deterioration occurred periodically, probably because of both climatic fluctuation and human overexploitation. In the Liao River region, for example, agricultural societies underwent cycles of development and decline during the Holocene. Agriculture in these cultures shows progressively increased productive intensity but ever-shorter duration, as exemplified by the Hongshan period (ca. 1000 years), the Lower Xiajiadian period (ca. 500 years), the Liao dynasty (ca. 200 years), and the late Qing dynasty (a few decades). Agricultural cycles were often disrupted suddenly, likely as a result of human-induced ecological deterioration, such as desertification. These cycles were intermediated by either pastoralism or depopulation that would allow regeneration of the natural habitat (Song, Y. 2002: 31–54).

Climatic deterioration coupled with overexploitation of the environment would have led to depletion of natural resources available for traditional farming communities. This in turn might hypothetically result in three situations: increased competition among social groups, population migration to other regions, and change in economic strategies. All these scenarios are observable in the archaeological record from the northern frontier cultures. These archaeological traces include the widespread construction of stone walls for defensive purposes in the Lower Xiajiadian culture, the Qijia population's move to Zhukaigou for better agricultural land, and some Siba communities' transformation to a pastoral economy when the environment became favorable for herding.

Political agencies evidently played crucial roles in social change. In all northern frontier cultures, elite behavior was characterized by long-distance exchange of prestige items, especially jades, semiprecious stones, metal objects, and cowry shells. Similar forms of jade/stone objects, particularly *bi* discs and *cong* tubes, have been found in many sites across a broad region, suggesting a formative process of some shared belief systems and the emergence of ancient elite networks at a supraregional level (Liu, L. 2003).

In most cases we do not know exactly how local elite members were involved in controlling the resource acquisition, productive processes, and profitable distribution of valuables, but the presence of such prestige goods in a small number of burials at Dadianzi, Zhukaigou, and Huangniangniangtai suggests that not all members of these communities had equal access to resources. Archaeological evidence also indicates that artisans who made prestige items may have enjoyed high social status in a community.

The production and circulation of metal objects also contributed to the emergence of social complexity. Metal ornaments, tools, and weapons were apparently much valued in Bronze Age cultures, and desire for these objects by elite individuals would have led to heightened control over relevant resources and trade routes, further encouraging cross-regional interactions. There is no evidence, however, for any centralized or vertical control of metal resourcing, production, and distribution in the northern frontier regions; therefore, metal production may have operated on a small scale at a local level. This situation sharply contrasts with that observed in urban centers of the Central Plain states: Erlitou and Zhengzhou.

Settlement data from the northern frontier regions also show multicentered patterns, with relatively small regional centers (25 ha for the largest Lower Xiajiadian site and 20 ha for Qijia). In the Lower Xiajiadian culture, the construction of fortifications particularly points to interpolity conflict and a decentralized political system. This situation is also different from the centralized Erlitou and Erligang states in the Central Plain.

All of these phenomena lead us to conclude that, during the first half of the second millennium BC, the northern frontier cultures emerged as polities with high levels of social complexity. The growth of their cultural and social sophistication derived from their adaptation to changing climatic conditions, from competition for prestige and power among local elite groups, and from interactions with surrounding cultures. These Bronze Age frontier cultures enhanced their economic strategies by increased reliance on pastoralism and formed social and cultural networks with particularly close connections to populations in the steppe. They were politically independent of the contemporary Erlitou and Erligang states, although interactions among them are clearly evident.

CHAPTER 10

THE LATE SHANG DYNASTY AND
ITS NEIGHBORS (1250–1046 BC)

Heaven commissioned the swallow,
To descend and give birth to [the father of our] Shang.
[His descendants] dwelt in the land of Yin, and became great.......

The royal domain of a thousand li,
Is where the people rest;
But there commence the boundaries that reach to the four seas.

> Chapter, "Xuan Niao" in *Book of Poetry* (written in 1000–600 BC);
> translated by James Legge (1892)

天命玄鸟、降而生商、宅殷土芒芒。...邦畿千里、维民所止、肇域彼四海。

〈〈诗经 · 玄鸟〉〉

The later half of the second millennium BC witnessed many changes in the political landscape of China. In the Central Plain, there was a period of political instability and decentralization during the middle Shang (ca. 1400–1250 BC), reflected in remains of multiple regional centers, including Huanbei Shang City to the north of the Huan River at Anyang (see Chapter 8). Then the Shang dynasty established its last capital city in the area south of the Huan River, which initiated the era known as the late Shang period (ca. 1250–1046 BC) (Tang, J. 2001). The Shang regained political and military superiority over its surrounding neighbors, while many regional cultures in the peripheries rapidly developed into state-level societies, and their relationships with the Shang core varied according to circumstances. Interactions between agropastoralist communities in the Eurasian steppe and agricultural societies in China intensified. These interactions were multidirectional, manifested by the spread of Northern Zone bronze artifacts southward into a large region (as far as Yunnan), the introduction of horses and chariots to the Shang, and the dispersal of Shang-style bronzes and jades into outer regions far from the Shang core area.

In this chapter we will primarily focus on the late Shang period. Our discussion is organized according to the distribution of archaeological cultures, shown in Figure 10.1.

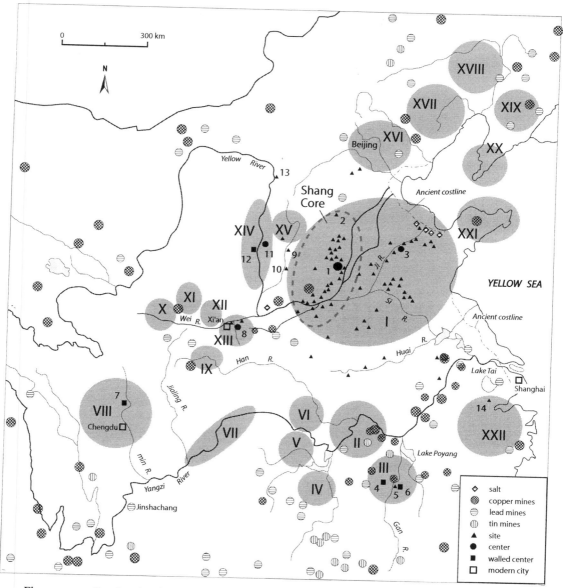

Figure 10.1. Regional cultures and major sites of the late Shang period. Archaeological cultures – I: Shang; II: Panlongcheng; III: Wucheng; IV: Duimenshan-Feijiahe; V: Baota; VI: Zhouliangyuqiao; VII: Lujiahe; VIII: Sanxingdui; IX: Baoshan (Chengyang Bronze Assemblage); X: Liujia; XI: Proto-Zhou; XII: Zhengjiapo; XIII: Laoniupo; XIV: Lijiaya; XV: Guangshe; XVI: Weifang III; XVII: Weiyingzi; XVIII: Gaotaishan; XIX: Miaohoushan; XX: Shuangtuozi III; XXI: Zhenzhumen; XXII: Hushu. Sites – 1: Yinxu; 2: Taixi; 3: Daxinzhuang; 4: Wucheng; 5: Dayangzhou; 6 Niucheng; 7: Sanxingdui; 8: Laoniupo; 9: Jingjie; 10: Qiaobei; 11: Gaohong; 12: Lijiaya; 13: Xicha; 14: ceramic kilns in the Dongtiaoxi River region (distribution of cultures and Shang sites based on Zhongguo Shehui Kexueyuan 2003).

RESEARCH QUESTIONS

The late Shang period has long been a center of attention in the study of early Chinese civilization, ever since modern archaeology was established in China in the 1920s. Numerous studies, in both Chinese and Western languages, have been devoted to the reconstruction of Shang society and ideology, using data derived from archaeological remains, inscriptions on bronzes and oracle-bones, as well as ancient texts. The wealth of archaeological remains discovered from many regions shows a fully developed historical dynasty, attested by the presence of a large urban center at Anyang, and characterized by pronounced social stratification, high levels of craft specialization, use of a writing system, a hegemonic domination of many polities in its surrounding areas, and constant waging of wars against its enemies.

The late Shang has in recent years attracted lively discussion with regard to the nature and processes of state formation in early China. The debate has focused on the extent of Shang power, the constitutional character of the state, and its relations with other polities in the surrounding regions. Some scholars argue for a large territorial state (Trigger, B. 1999), whereas others suggest a rather small city-state or segmentary state (Keightley 1999; Lin, Y. 1998b; Yates 1997). Some archaeologists have endeavored to determine the Shang's political boundaries and, based on the verified distribution of ceramic and bronze styles, and have tended to claim a relatively large territory, including the entire middle and lower Yellow River valley and the region southward to the north bank of the Yangzi River (e.g., Song, X. 1991). In contrast, Wheatley (1971: 97) has regarded only the Shang's core area as its proper territory, covering a small region based around the middle Yellow River. Scholars do not always reach the same conclusions about the extent of Shang territories even when using the same type of information. Li Boqian (2009), for example, has studied emblems in bronze and inscriptions in oracle-bones and has argued that the political power of the late Shang extended over a large region basically congruent with the distribution of Shang material culture. It covered, says Li, an area reaching north to northern Hebei, south to southern Henan, west to central Shaanxi, and east to eastern Shandong. In contrast, on the basis of oracle-bone inscriptions, Keightley (1979–80: 26) has described the Shang state as "*gruyere*, filled with non-Shang holes, rather than *tou-fu*, solidly Shang throughout." Keightley's notion about the Shang territory is shared by several Chinese historians. For instance, Song Zhenhao (1994) points out that Shang and non-Shang territories formed a jagged, interlocking pattern. Similarly, Wang Zhenzhong (2007) argues that Shang's territory was formed by the core area of the capital together with surrounding outposts and subordinate states, and that these outposts and subordinate states were interspersed among polities that were hostile to the Shang.

In sum, conceptually speaking, we should not apply the modern concept of territorial boundary to the Shang. As Keightley (1983) has observed, the Shang's ruling strategies did not rely extensively on centralized bureaucratic control. Furthermore, methodologically speaking, it is a challenge to determine the territories of the Shang state through archaeology alone. For example, although inscriptions from oracle bones and bronzes, made for ritual purposes, are valuable sources of information about the activities of Shang rulers, it is also true that such information, taken by itself, is biased and incomplete. Therefore, it would be more fruitful to combine this source with other forms of archaeological evidence and with traditional documentary records, to cast the greatest possible light on relationships between the Shang and its neighboring polities over a broad region. For this purpose, we will adopt a two-part conceptual scheme that distinguishes core from periphery; thus, we will first review the archaeology of the Shang core area, as discovered at the Yinxu site in Anyang, and then focus on interactions between the Shang core and its peripheries, viewing this second topic from the perspective of the procurement of resources and information. The reason for taking this core-periphery approach is not because sociocultural developments outside the Central Plain are any less important than those of the Shang itself, but because this is an effective way to understand the nature of their interregional relations and, especially, the reasons why certain goods spread cross-regionally.

THE SHANG WORLD

The spatial relationship between the Shang and its neighboring polities has attracted considerable interest as a major research topic in archaeology. Oracle-bone inscriptions depict three categories of polities in the late Shang world: (1) Shang or *dayishang*, including the last and greatest Shang capital, Yin (called Yinxu, the ruins of Yin, after its demise), and its immediate surrounding areas, which can be regarded as the Shang core; (2) *tu* (the Lands) or *situ* (the Four Lands), referred to as *dongtu* (the Eastern Land), *beitu* (the Northern Land), *xitu* (the Western Land), and *nantu* (the Southern Land), which can be considered as the territories occupied by many subordinate polities within the Shang domain; and (3) *fang* (the Regions) or *sifang* (the Four Regions), which often meant the non-Shang polities outside the Shang territories, such as Tufang, Qiangfang, and Guifang. Numerous studies have been devoted to identifying the locations of these subordinate states and non-Shang polities according to inscriptions on bronzes and oracle bones (e.g., Chang 1980; Keightley 1983; Li, X. 1959; Shima 1958; Song, X. 1991; Song, Z. 1994; Wang, Z. 2007).

The concepts of *dayishang*, *situ*, and *sifang* have been schematically illustrated as several concentric bands, representing layered domains extending outward from the capital to the farthest periphery (see summary in Wang, Z. 2007).

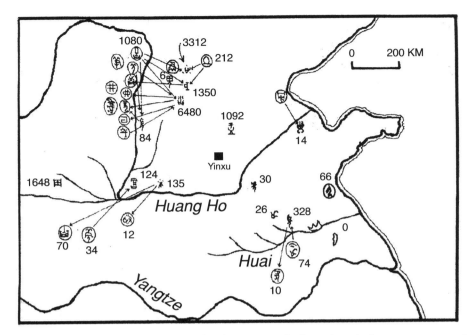

Figure 10.2. Distribution of named polities in oracle-bone inscriptions reconstructed by Shima Kunio (numbers are state scores indicating the degree of interaction with the Shang as calculated by Keightley (1983), noting the highest scores in the northwest region (after Keightley 1983: map 17.2).

This idealized territorial pattern can be misleading, as it gives an impression that the Shang established well-defined state boundaries and had hegemonic control over all the subordinate polities. This is unlikely to have been the case, as discussed earlier in this chapter. The most frequently cited reference to the Shang political landscape is found in Shima Kunio's (1958) research, based on oracle-bone inscriptions, in which Shima plotted locations of Shang's major allies and enemies on maps, showing several clusters of polities in all directions surrounding Yinxu. The densest distribution of such polities appears to have been along the Yellow River to the northwest of Yinxu, and it was the polities in that sector which had the most intensive interactions with the Shang state, as recorded in oracle-bone inscriptions (Keightley 1983) (Figure 10.2). When comparing this map of named polities with the distribution of archeological cultures in Figure 10.1, it is clear that the two diagrams show fundamentally different types of information, which may be supplementary to each other and thus instructive for research. There are apparently fewer archaeological cultures than the number of polities in the Shang written record. An archaeological culture, as defined by material assemblages, may reflect a common or similar pattern of economic subsistence adopted by people in the region, whereas the presence of differently named groups or polities within the same region, as identified in the Shang inscriptions, suggests that political organization in this region was decentralized.

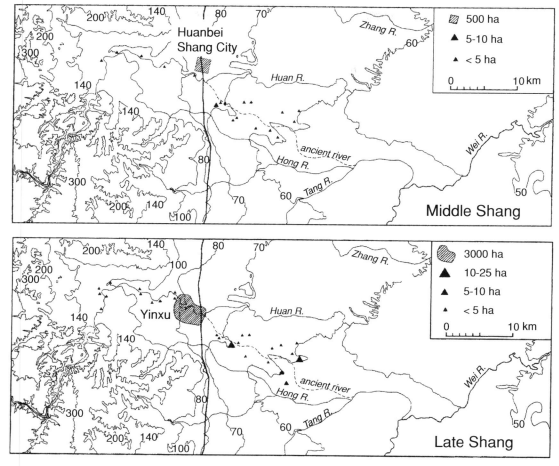

Figure 10.3. Site distribution along the Huan River Valley in the middle and late Shang periods (after figures 1 and 2 of Tang and Jing 2009).

YINXU: SITE OF THE LATE SHANG CAPITAL CITY

The late Shang dynasty was centered at its new capital city, Yin (or Yinxu), in modern Anyang, Henan. Yin was developed mainly on the south bank of the Huan River after the Huanbei walled site was abandoned for unknown reasons. Regional surveys along the Huan River Valley have revealed marked population growth from the middle Shang to the late Shang, indicated by a significant increase in site number (from around 20 to 30) and site size, particularly the size of the major centers (from 500 to 3,000 ha) (Figure 10.3) (Tang, J. and Jing 1998, 2009).

Yinxu was discovered as the result of the deciphering of Shang inscriptions on oracle bones. Excavations at the site, beginning in 1928, were conducted by the first generation of Chinese archaeologists, led by Li Chi (1977). This site provided opportunities for archaeologists and historians not only to study the material culture and social system of an early dynasty in China, but also to test the archaeological record against ancient texts. After more than eighty years of excavation by several generations of Chinese archaeologists, enormous amounts of data are now available to help us understand the basic layout of this urban site, although we are still unable to appreciate its full magnitude.

The size of Yinxu is roughly estimated as 24 sq. km, within which the Shang remains are distributed rather densely. If scattered finds in the periphery of the site are included, the ancient city underlying Yinxu measured nearly 30 sq. km during its heyday. Representing the largest political center of its time in China, Yinxu contains various features that distinguish it from other contemporary settlements. A large palatial complex, estimated to have been about 70 ha in size, was situated near Xiaotun to the south of the Huan River. Within this complex, fifty-three rammed-earth foundations have been found concentrated in an area of 3.5 ha; some of these foundations are from royal residences, whereas others, associated with sacrificial pits containing humans and animals, are from royal ancestral temples. Elite burials (including the well-known tomb of Fuhao) and craft workshops also have been found within the palatial zone. A royal cemetery, consisting not only of royal burials but also of many human and animal sacrificial pits, was located at Xibeigang, north of the Huan River. Many craft production workshops, used for making bronze, pottery, stone/jade, and bone artifacts, were spread over the site. Residences and burials of lesser elites and of commoners were distributed in many clusters (Figure 10.4) (Zhongguo Shehui Kexueyuan 1994b). Yinxu appears to have been composed of a few dozen small residential clusters, called *yi*, which may be translated as "district." Each *yi* appears to have been normally associated with houses, storage pits, water wells, roads, drainages, and water storage systems (Tang, J. and Jing 2009). As shown by mortuary data and oracle-bone inscriptions, the Shang society revealed at Yinxu was organized by lineage groups (Tang, J. 2004; Zhu, F. 2004).

In addition to the discovery of numerous objects made of bronze, jade/stone, ivory, ceramics, and bone, a writing system, reflected through inscriptions carved on oracle bones and cast on bronzes, has been found, marking the inception of written historical records in China (Chang 1980; Keightley 1978b; Li, C. 1977; Zhongguo Shehui Kexueyuan 1994b) (Figure 10.5). A great wealth of information has been extracted from oracle-bone inscriptions and other material remains at Yinxu, which enables scholars to date this late Shang site to four phases, and to interpret the political, social, economic, and ideological systems of the Shang society (e.g., Bagley 1999; Chang 1980; Childs-Johnson 1998; Keightley 1999, 2000). Most interestingly, the oracle-bone inscriptions generally support the dynastic genealogy of the late Shang, as recorded in the ancient texts (Chang 1980). This finding further confirms the late Shang as a distinct era of dynastic history.

The society of the late Shang was highly stratified. Mortuary patterns show at least six social classes in the population identified at Yinxu (Tang, J. 2004).

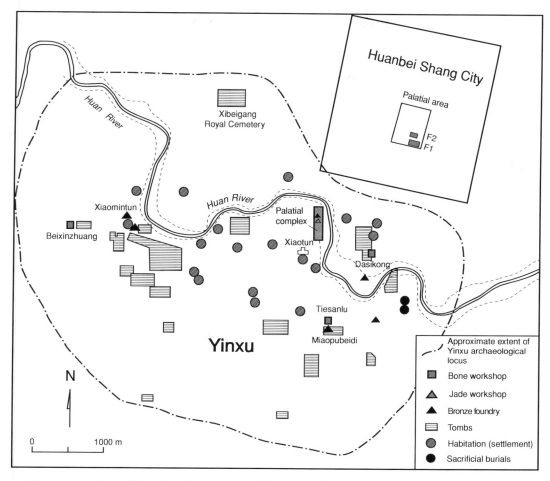

Figure 10.4. Plan of Huanbei Shang city and Yinxu (middle and late Shang) (redrawn from figure 1 of Tang, J. 2001 and figures 1 and 2 of Yue and Wang 2007).

Although most of the royal tombs were looted long ago, a few remaining intact burials excavated by archaeologists have indeed revealed spectacular material assemblages presided over by members of the Shang royal elite. The Fuhao tomb, for instance, contained 1,928 items of grave goods, including bronzes, jades, ceramics, and objects made of stone, shell, and ivory, as well as nearly 7,000 cowry shells (Zhongguo Shehui Kexueyuan 1980). The recently discovered tomb M56 at Huayuanzhuang, which belonged to a member of the military elite, has also revealed more than 1,600 pieces of grave goods, predominantly bronzes and jades (Zhongguo Shehui Kexueyuan 2007).

Like the major cities of the Erlitou and Erligang periods, in addition to being a political center, Yinxu was also a craft production center, and its degree of craft specialization reached a higher level than ever before. Its main products included bronzes, bone artifacts, stone/jade ritual objects, and ceramics. Three bone workshops have been discovered. Excavation at the Tiesanlu workshop has yielded thirty-two tons of animal bones (Li, Z. et al. 2010), showing the magnitude of this craft production. Bone workshops at Beixinzhuang and Dasikong appear to have produced mainly hairpins. A pottery workshop at the south of Huayuanzhuang yielded mostly *dou* pedestal plates (Zhongguo Shehui Kexueyuan 1994b: 93–6, 439–41).

Some craft production, such as that of jade and bronze, is likely to have been under the direct control of the royal court. Archaeologists have identified two structures, located within the palatial complex, which seem to have played specialized roles mainly associated with grinding and polishing jade and stone *zhang* ritual blades (Zhongguo Shehui Kexueyuan 1987, 1994b). Six bronze foundry sites have been discovered at Yinxu, although not all of them were contemporaneous. The number of foundries increased through time, probably to meet a growing demand for bronze products. Judging by the shapes of molds, these foundries appear to have made a wide variety of bronze products, including ritual vessels, weapons, and tools. The Miaopubeidi bronze foundry (1 ha), about 700 m south of the palatial complex, was in operation during almost the entire period revealed at Yinxu (Li, Y.-t. 2003; Zhongguo Shehui Kexueyuan 1994b: 42–96). The largest bronze production area found at Yinxu, however, is near the modern locale Xiaomintun. It consisted of two foundries, 200 m apart and measuring 4 ha and 1 ha in area, respectively (Figure 10.4). Products include various types of ritual vessels, tools, and weapons, including some of the largest vessel molds ever found at Yinxu (Figure 10.5). The main production activities date to Phases III and IV (Yue, Z. and Wang 2007).

Chinese archaeologists have suggested that both the Miaopubeidi and the Xiaomintun bronze foundries were under the royal court's direct control (Yue, Z. and X. Wang 2007; Zhongguo Shehui Kexueyuan 1994b: 83–93). Notably, the Miaopubeidi foundry, one of the earliest bronze production locales at Yinxu, was situated in close proximity of the palatial complex, to its south. This spatial pattern is consistent with those seen at Erlitou and Zhengzhou. The foundries established later near Xiaomintun were located much farther from the palatial zone, and were also larger in size than the Miaopubeidi foundry, a situation that may imply gradual decentralization of bronze production at Yinxu.

The demand for bronze alloys during the Late Shang was enormous. For example, the Fuhao tomb yielded 468 bronze objects weighing 1,625 kg (Zhongguo Shehui Kexueyuan 1980: 15). This figure is about three times the total weight of bronzes from three hoards in Zhengzhou (around 510 kg), dating to the early Shang (Henansheng Wenwu Kaogu 1999b). Fuhao was a royal consort of King Wuding, and her tomb was only a medium-sized burial (22 m²), much smaller than the burials of the eleven kings (107–192 m²) in the royal cemetery at Xibeigang. Considering these finds, it is not difficult to imagine the magnitude of bronze production at Yinxu (Chang 1991).

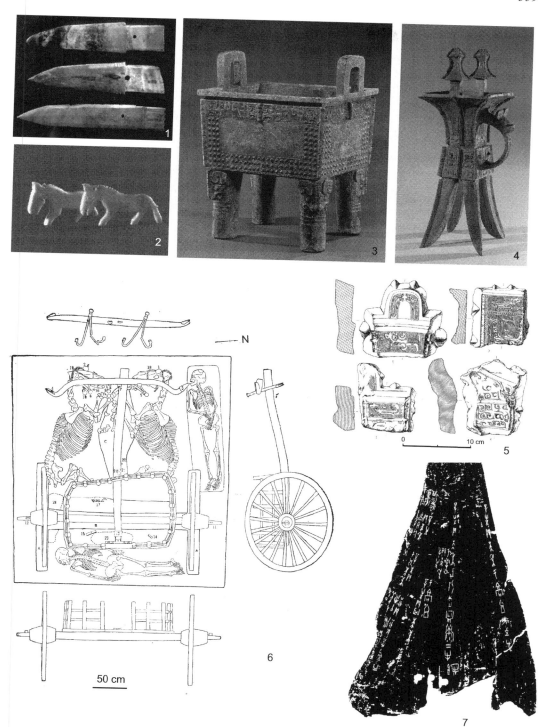

Figure 10.5. Archaeological remains from Yinxu, late Shang. 1: Jade *ge* blades; 2: pair of jade horse; 3: bronze *ding* tetrapod; 4: bronze *jia* drinking vessel; 5: clay molds for casting bronze ritual vessels; 6: sacrificial horses, chariot, and charioteers; 7: oracle-bone inscriptions (1–4: after color plates 1, 10.1, 18.1, 30.2 of Zhongguo Shehui Kexueyuan 1980; 6: after figures 6 of Yue and Wang 2007; 7: after figure 9 of Keightley 2000).

As in the early Shang, a large part of the raw metal ores (copper, tin, and lead) used at Yinxu for making bronzes was likely obtained from the Yangzi River region. Archaeological evidence for the mining of copper deposits by the late Shang has been discovered in Tongling, Jiangxi (Jiangxisheng and Ruichangshi 1997), and Tonglushan, Hubei (Huangshi 1999), both situated in the Middle Yangzi River Basin. Furthermore, results of lead isotopic analysis on 178 bronzes from Yinxu show that many of them consist of an unusual type of lead, high-radiogenic lead (HRL). Bronzes with HRL constitute the majority of the tested items in Yinxu Phases I and II (78% and 81%), but they markedly decline in proportion during Phase III (38%), and nearly disappear during Phase IV (Jin, Z. et al. 1998). Because of the rarity of this HRL in China, its provenance is most likely to have been in areas near Jinshachang in Yongshan, northeastern Yunnan, a region rich in lead, tin, and copper (Figure 10.1) (Jin, Z. 2003; Jin, Z. et al. 1995).

Metal is not the only item at Yinxu acquired from other regions. The inventory of prestige goods and key resources sought by the Shang elite from remote places includes cowry shells, jades and other precious stones, salt, proto-porcelain, turtle shells for divination, and large numbers of animals (cattle, sheep/goats, dogs, horses, etc.) and humans for ritual sacrifice. The question is how the Shang obtained these goods.

The state's control of territories appears to have been much more restricted during the Late Shang than during the Early Shang period (Tang, J. 2001: fig. 5), suggesting a weakened Shang court. Concurrent with the prosperous era of the capital city that left Yinxu's remains, several large regional centers independently emerged outside the Shang domains, and stylistic variations of bronze vessels, along with evidence for the local casting of sophisticated ritual objects, also occurred in some of these regions. The new situation, of a weakened core surrounded by a stronger periphery, redefined power relations at that time, and the Late Shang court was no longer able to establish outposts in remote regions to extract resources, as the Early Shang had done. Therefore, different mechanisms for resource procurement had to be developed.

SHANG AND ITS NEIGHBORS

As indicated in Shang inscriptions, the relationships between Yinxu and other regional polities were constantly changing in accord with new circumstances. To serve their needs, the Shang kings used various methods for dealing with their neighbors, including trade, granting gifts, exacting tribute, marriage, forming alliances, and waging wars (Chang 1980: 248–59; Keightley 1979–80; Li, B. 2009). These relationships may have left traces in the archaeological record. We can examine material assemblages in peripheral regions and investigate the types of goods flowing between center and periphery, to understand the nature of their interactions. Here we focus on six areas, which are Taixi

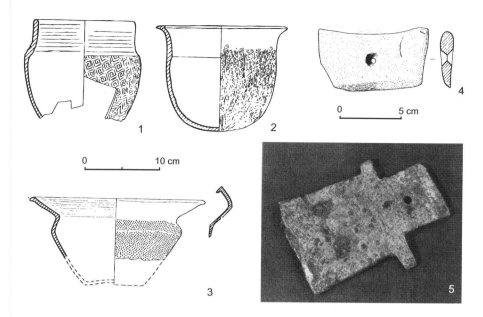

Figure 10.6. Artifacts from Taixi in Gaocheng, Hebei. 1 and 2: Stamp-pattern hard ware *zun* and *guan* vessels; 3: proto-porcelain *zun* vessel; 4: stone saddle-back knife; 5: *yue* axe with iron blade (length 11.1 cm) (after figures 42–5; 44–1, 2; 46–1; and color plate 1 of Hebeisheng 1985).

in the north, Shandong in the east, Wucheng in the south, Sanxingdui in the southwest, Laoniupo in the west, and the Loess Plateau (particularly the Ordos) in the northwest.

Taixi in the North

To the north of Yinxu, Shang sites are distributed over a large part of Hebei province, and more than 100 Shang sites have been identified along the Hai River system. Site distribution in the Shijiazhuang area is particularly dense, revealing many Shang ritual bronzes bearing lineage emblems. This region was probably a part of the Shang core. One of the most important sites in this area is Taixi in Gaocheng, dating from the middle Shang to the early part of the Yinxu period. It has revealed houses, water wells, and burials, as well as large numbers of ceramics, tools, and bronzes (Hebeisheng 1985).

A total of 172 pieces of proto-porcelain and 106 pieces of stamp-pattern hard wares, similar in form to examples from southern China (e.g., Wucheng in Jiangxi), have been unearthed (Figure 10.6). These are high-quality ceramics, made of special types of clay and fired at high temperatures, which were technologies developed in southern China (Peng, S. 1987). Only small numbers of these types of ceramics have been found in northern China, often in elite burials and in large regional centers. The number of ceramics found at Taixi is unusually high for a nonurban site in northern China.

The provenance of proto-porcelain during the Shang period has been a topic of debate among archaeologists for decades. On the basis of trace element analysis, some argue for a southern Chinese provenance (Luo, H. et al. 1996), whereas others believe there were multiple centers of production in both the south and north (Zhu, J. et al. 2008). Recent surveys and excavations in the middle Dongtiaoxi River Valley, Zhejiang province, have revealed more than thirty kiln sites that produced proto-porcelain and stamp-pattern hard wares, dating to the Shang period. Many proto-porcelain products made here are nearly identical to their counterparts found in the Shang core area, mainly at Yinxu. These discoveries strongly support the southern Chinese provenance of these ceramics (Zheng, J. et al. 2011). In contrast, the presence of waste products of proto-porcelain at several Shang sites in the north (e.g., Zhengzhou, Xiaoshuangqiao, and Anyang) has been used as evidence for northern Chinese production (An, J. 1960; Sun, X. and Sun 2008). The view of the multiple centers of production is also supported by recent trace-element analysis of proto-porcelain from Daxinzhuang in Shandong, which shows a composition clearly different from that from Wucheng in Jiangxi (Zhu, J. et al. 2008).

The proto-porcelain and stamp-pattern hard wares from Taixi were all uncovered from residential areas rather than from burials, suggesting that these vessels were used as ordinary items by the residents, a scenario consistent with the location of production. One proto-porcelain sherd appears to be a waste product, also suggesting local manufacture. In addition, Taixi has revealed saddle-shaped stone knives (Figure 10.6). Their forms resemble the stone and ceramic knives used as potter's tools at Wucheng in Jiangxi (see section on Wucheng later in this chapter), which was a production center for proto-porcelain and hard wares during the Shang period (Jiangxisheng and Zhangshushi 2005).

Although strong evidence exists showing that major production centers of these precious ceramics were located in southern China, we cannot rule out the possibility that the Shang people in the north attempted to imitate the southern-style proto-porcelain (Chen, T. et al. 1999). Taixi may have been one such place where Shang craftsmen experimented with this technology, following the southern tradition, to meet increased demand for such vessels.

Taixi seems to have assumed some military importance in the region. Among nineteen bronze-bearing burials, fourteen contained weapons, including a bronze *yue* axe inserted with a meteoric iron blade, which is a rare find in this period (Figure 10.6). Taixi apparently had contacts with the Northern Zone cultures, which were distributed in areas to its north and are represented by the Weifang III and Weijiangzi cultures (Figure 10.1). This contact is indicated by the presence at Taixi of tools and weapons in the Northern Zone style, including socketed arrowheads, socketed spearheads, and daggers with ram pommel (Hebeisheng 1985: 81–3). It has been suggested that Taixi was situated in a key position, of strategic importance for the Shang (Song, X. 1991: 72–5).

Shandong in the East

The entire Shandong region was occupied by the indigenous Yueshi culture during the Erlitou and Lower Erligang periods. In the beginning of the Upper Erligang phase, however, a settlement with typical Erligang assemblage appeared at Daxinzhuang in Jinan, northern Shandong. This site represents the first known intrusion of early Shang people into the Shandong region. During the middle Shang period, when the Henan region underwent instability and decentralization, Shang settlements in Shandong increased rapidly in number, particularly clustered in two areas: the Daxinzhuang cluster along the Ji River Valley and the Qianzhangda cluster along the Xue River Valley in Tengzhou. The elite material assemblages unearthed from these new settlements are bronzes and jades in the typical Shang style, whereas the indigenous status symbols of the Yueshi culture – painted pottery – disappeared completely. These phenomena suggest that the Shang colonization in these areas was achieved by replacing the local authorities with the Shang elite (Chen, X. 2007; Fang, H. 2009).

During the Yinxu period, the Shang population spread over most of Shandong. The indigenous peoples were pushed farther east to the Jiaodong peninsula, represented by the Zhenzhumen culture in the archaeological record (Figure 10.1). Several Shang settlement clusters with large centers were distributed around the Taiyi Mountains and coastal areas (Figure 10.7). Some of these large sites may have been the political centers of states. These polities seem to have maintained strong ties with the Shang core, as indicated by the close resemblance of their material culture to that of Yinxu. Many scholars believe that Shandong was part of the Shang domain, referred to as *dongtu*, the eastern land (Chen, X. 2007; Fang, H. 2009).

Shang's expansion to the east was apparently directed at both acquiring the rich natural resources of the region, including metal, salt, and products of the freshwater and marine environments, and controlling the transportation routes. Daxinzhuang in Jinan, for example, was situated to the south of the ancient Ji River, which connected the Bohai Bay region to the Yellow River. This regional center was thus placed at a strategic location on a main communication route, along which materials obtained from north Shandong could be transported to the Shang core. Likewise, the Qianzhangda cluster was situated near the ancient Si River, which linked the Huai River to the Central Plain; the Shang's expansion into this area could have facilitated the flow of material

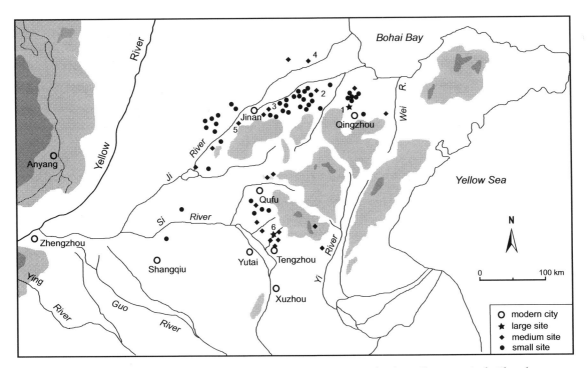

Figure 10.7. Distribution of settlement clusters in the late Shang period. Shandong (shown are ancient river systems). Sites: 1: Subutun; 2: Shijia; 3: Daxinzhuang; 4: Lanjia; 5: Xiaotun; 6: Qianzhangda (site locations based on figures 4 and 5 of Chen, X. 2007).

goods from the southeast to the Shang capital (Fang, H. 2009; Liu, L. and Chen 2003: 113–16).

Archaeological evidence relating to salt production has been abundantly confirmed in Shandong's coastal regions. So-called helmet-shaped pottery jars, *kuixingqi*, have been uncovered at more than eighty sites in northern Shandong. These vessels are distributed in particularly great concentrations near the coastal areas around the Bohai Bay, coinciding with the distribution belt of underground brine. Chemical analysis of the residues on *kuixingqi* confirms that they were used for making salt. Salt production appears to have been a seasonal operation, organized by people residing in the inland areas. *Kuixingqi* were produced inland and transported to salt-making sites; in return, salt and marine products were brought back (Figure 10.8). These sites all date to the late Shang and Zhou, suggesting that large-scale salt production began here in the Yinxu period (Li, S. et al. 2009; Wang, Q. 2006a, b). *Kuixingqi* jars can be classified into several types; those belonging to the same type appear to be similar in size, suggesting that these jars were also used as standard units of measurement in the trade and distribution of salt (Fang, H. 2004).

In oracle-bone inscriptions from Yinxu, certain functionaries at the Shang court were titled *luxiaochen*, meaning "petty officer for salt," suggesting a supervisory role in the production and distribution of salt. Interestingly, a

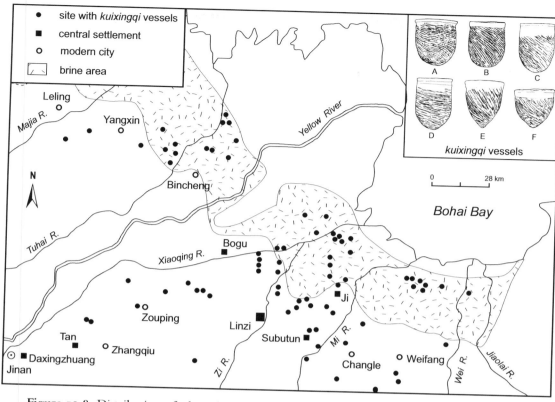

Figure 10.8. Distribution of salt-making vessel, *kuixingqi*, in relation to underground brine area in north Shandong. *Kuixingqi* vessels: A and B: Late Shang; C: Shang–Zhou; D–F: Western Zhou (redrawn from figure 9 of Wang, Q. 2006a and figure 7 of Li, S. et al. 2009).

bronze vessel with two *lu* glyphs (Figure 10.9), meaning "salt," has been unearthed, together with a group of ritual objects, from a Shang tomb in Binzhou, north Shandong. This site belongs to the Lanjia settlement cluster situated in the salt production area. It is likely that this tomb belonged to a salt official, *luxiaochen*, who was sent by the Shang court to manage salt production there. It is also possible that the regional centers, around which settlement clusters arose in north Shandong, functioned partially as depots for collecting and distributing salt (Fang, H. 2004, 2009).

Shell-inlaid lacquer wares have been found at royal tombs in Anyang as well as in elite burials at Qianzhangda (Figure 10.9). Qianzhangda is located in a region generally referred to as Xuzhou (comprising southern Shandong and northern Jiangsu) in the ancient text *Yugong*, which records tributary goods flowing from different regions to early dynastic centers in the Central Plain. According to this text, major tributary goods received from Xuzhou include pearls, shells, and wood of the genus *Calophyllum*, the last two of which could be used as materials for making ornamented lacquer wares. Indeed a large quantity of shells identifiable with seven species of freshwater shellfish, which all produce pearls, has been recovered from a Shang site at Tongshan, Qiuwan, northern Jiangsu, supporting the *Yugong* documentary tradition (Fang, H. 2009). *Yugong* was compiled in much later times (from the fifth century BC, during the Warring States phase of the late Eastern Zhou period) but reports a well-established ancient tributary system as having existed around a millennium earlier. Although *Yugong* cannot be used as an accurate blueprint for reconstructing the economic system of the Shang, many archaeological findings do corroborate *Yugong's* records, suggesting that this text possesses considerable heuristic value for comprehending the availability of natural resources in particular regions of ancient China (Shao 1989).

Shandong also had copper and lead deposits (Sun, S. 1990). The Shijia settlement cluster in northern Shandong is situated near the Changbaishan copper deposits, which now make up the largest copper mine in Shandong. A clay mold for making metal tools has been uncovered at the site of Langjun in Zouping County, indicating the existence of local metallurgy (Fang, H. 2009: 78). Bronze ritual vessels in Shandong are highly homogeneous in style with the Yinxu bronzes (Figure 10.9), however, and there is no reliable evidence for the production of bronze vessels in Shandong. It is likely that most, if not all, ritual bronzes in Shandong were derived from Yinxu.

The Shang's attempt to control its eastern frontier was a long process, and interactions between the Shang and the indigenous Yueshi people varied in different locales. In the Daxinzhuang cluster, the early Shang and Yueshi pottery traditions coexisted in the same archaeological contexts, suggesting that two distinct populations lived side by side in the same area for some time. In contrast, in the Qianzhangda cluster, when the early Shang intruded into this region, the material assemblage appears to be purely Shang. This phenomenon is best exemplified by mortuary practices at Qianzhangda, such as use of bronze assemblages and horse-chariot sacrifice in typical Shang style (Figure 10.9). In addition, the Shang influence in Shandong became more dominant during the late Shang period. Objects bearing the names of Shang lineages have been found in Shandong, suggesting that this region was more or less under the direct control of elite individuals from Yinxu. The states in this region did not always maintain subordinate affiliations with the Shang core, however. The Shang sometimes waged war against states there, such as Xue in southern Shandong, as recorded in the oracle-bone inscriptions (Fang, H. 2009). The process of a given locality's "becoming Shang" may be conceptualized as a resolution of ongoing tensions between the Shang state's claim to overall supremacy and the diversity of local circumstances (Li, M. 2008).

Nevertheless, the material culture in Shandong largely resembles that of the Shang core, including pottery, bronzes, jades, oracle-bone inscriptions, and burial patterns (Figure 10.9). Thus, it is likely that much of the Shandong region was a part of the Shang domain.

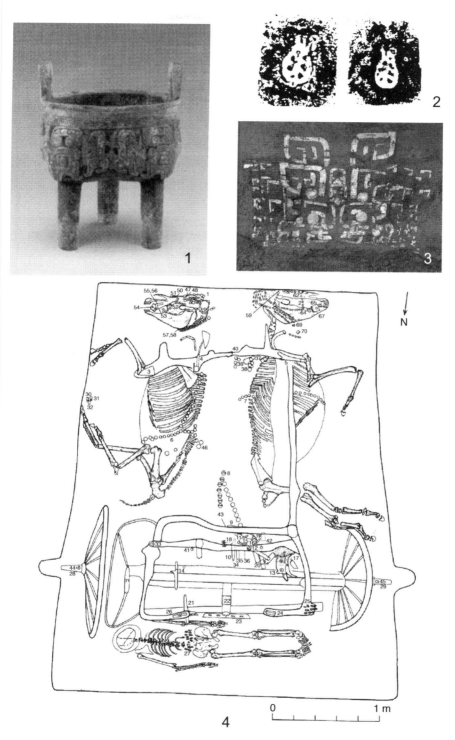

Figure 10.9. Archaeological remains from Shandong, late Shang period. 1: Bronze *ding* tripod typical of the Shang style; 2: glyphs of *lu* for salt on bronze from Lanjiacun in Binzhou, north Shandong; 3: shell inlaid artifact; 4: sacrificial horses, chariot, and charioteer from M40, Qianzhangda burial site (1, 3, and 4: after color plates 5 and 33 and figure 95 of Zhongguo Shehui Kexueyuan 2005; 2: after figure 7 of Fang 2004).

Wucheng in the South

In the middle Yangzi River region, Panlongcheng, the most important early Shang outpost, disappeared by the late Shang period. Instead, Wucheng in Zhangshu, Jiangxi, became a regional center. The site is located to the south of the Xiao River, a tributary of the Gan River, and is close to rich copper deposits (Figure 10.1). The first presence in this region of cultural materials from the Central Plain began in the Erligang period. At Wucheng, cultural deposits can be divided into three phases that, in terms of a Central Plain–based chronology, are equivalent to the Upper Erligang, early Yinxu, and late Yinxu periods. A rammed-earth enclosure (61 ha) was built during the Upper Erligang phase, and the site grew to an area of 400 ha during the Yinxu phase. The material assemblages show strong influence from the Central Plain, mixed with local cultural traditions (Jiangxisheng and Zhangshushi 2005).

Inside the enclosure were found four clusters of residential areas on high terraces, revealing houses, water wells, pits, and storage. A ceremonial precinct has been identified in the center of the enclosure, consisting of a red-soil platform, well-constructed roads, the foundation of a large building, and a group of postholes (more than 100), some of which may have been related to architectural construction. Several groups of kilns for making high-quality ceramics, including stamp-pattern hard ware and proto-porcelain, have been found in the northwest area, and bronze workshops for casting tools and weapons in the northeastern area. Numerous artifacts have been unearthed, including bronze tools, weapons and ritual vessels, proto-porcelain, and hard wares. Many potter's tools have been found at the site, including lithic and ceramic knives with the saddle-shaped back. Stone molds for making tools and weapons were also uncovered; however, there is no evidence that ritual vessels were cast on site. One hundred twenty inscriptions have been found on ceramics and stone molds, many resembling the Shang inscriptions. Most of them occur as single or double glyphs, but some inscriptions consist of as many as twelve characters (Figure 10.10) (Jiangxisheng and Zhangshushi 2005). The similarity between the Wucheng inscriptions and the Shang writing system indicates that part of the Wucheng population, particularly some of the literate craftsmen who were probably employed on managerial levels, were migrants from the Central Plain.

Wucheng's function appears to have been predominantly related to the production of metal and proto-porcelain, both of which were greatly desired by elites in the Shang's core region. Jiangxi has rich copper deposits, of which the best known are the mines at Tongling, which have been exploited since the Erligang period (Jiangxisheng and Zhangshushi 2005). Bronze metallurgy was carried out in many locations across the region, as attested by the discovery of stone molds for casting tools and weapons at twelve localities in Jiangxi (Peng, M. 2005: 123, 129–31).

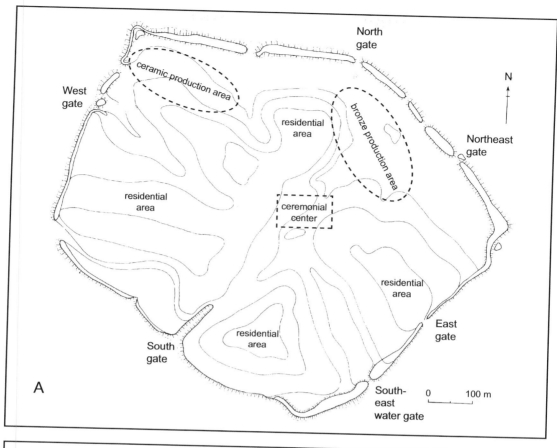

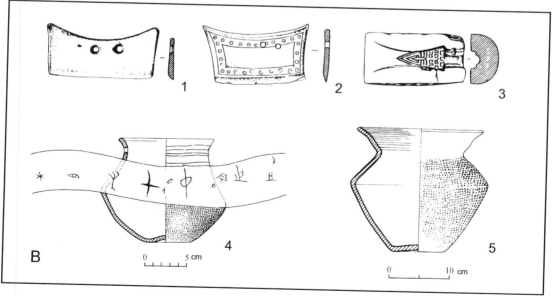

Figure 10.10. Wucheng in Jiangxi. (**A**) Plan of walled site at Wucheng; (**B**) artifacts discovered. 1 and 2: Potter's tools (saddle-shaped stone and pottery knives); 3: stone mold for making bronze adze; 4: proto-porcelain guan jar incised with twelve inscriptions; 5: hard-ware *zun* vessel (modified from figures 20, 69–9, 137–1, 150B–1, 210–4 of Jiangxisheng and Zhangshushi 2005).

Wucheng's proto-porcelain and hard ceramic wares are stylistically similar to those unearthed in the Central Plain. One provenance study of proto-porcelain wares from several Shang sites, including Wucheng, Panlongcheng, Zhengzhou, Jingnansi in Hubei, and Tonggushan in Hunan, suggests that Wucheng was a proto-porcelain production center during the Shang dynasty, and that proto-porcelain vessels found at other sites were imported (Chen, T. et al. 1999). Other studies, however, show that trace elements contained in proto-porcelain samples from sites in north China are not always consistent with those from Wucheng, suggesting multiple production centers in both south and north China (Zhu, J. et al. 2008; Zhu, J. et al. 2005). This suggestion is also supported by the finding of many kiln sites in Zhejiang, as discussed early in this chapter. In any event, given the large scale of ceramic production on site, Wucheng was evidently one of the major centers of proto-porcelain manufacture, and some of its products are likely to have been transported to the north.

Wucheng was probably an outpost of the early Shang state, established for procurement of resources and later developed to a powerful regional force (Liu, L. and Chen 2003: 119–23). The rapid development of Wucheng during the late Shang period was unquestionably related to stimulus received from the Central Plain, but an equally important factor was the rise of local political powers. By the late Shang, some sixty-seven sites were distributed across the Jiangxi region, including at least two walled sites: Wucheng and Niucheng. Niucheng (50 ha) emerged to the east of the Gan River, about 23 km from Wucheng (Figure 10.1). The coexistence of these two walled centers indicates a competitive political landscape, which probably also accounts for the fall of Wucheng (Jiangxisheng and Zhangshushi 2005: 422; Peng, M. 2005: 22–3).

The nature of local polities in the Wucheng area may be understood from a large tomb at Dayangzhou in Xin'gan, about 20 km east of Wucheng and a few kilometers from Niucheng (Figure 10.1). It contained about 480 bronze objects and is dated to the late Shang (Jiangxisheng 1997). It is not clear whether the Dayangzhou tomb is more closely associated with Wucheng or Niucheng. Its bronzes are similar to those from Phase II at Wucheng (Jiangxisheng and Zhangshushi 2005); Niucheng has not been excavated.

The bronzes from this tomb consist of ritual objects, weapons, and tools. They fall into four categories: the traditional Shang style, an indigenous style, a mixture of the two, and the proto-Zhou style (Figure 10.11) (Jiangxisheng and Zhangshushi 2005). The grave goods include an adze mold made of kaolin clay, indicating that the local elite was involved in some bronze manufacture. Although molds for casting bronze ritual vessels have not been found at Wucheng, the presence of indigenous-style bronze tools and vessels often has been regarded as evidence of local manufacture.

The bronze objects of indigenous style seem to express ideology and cultural values quite different from the spiritual outlook symbolized in the traditional

Shang style   mixed style   indigenous style

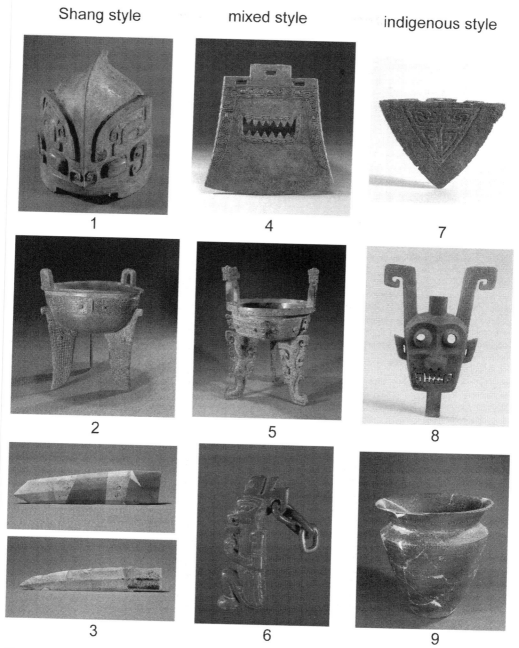

Figure 10.11. Artifacts unearthed from the Dayangzhou tomb in Xin'gan, Jiangxi, showing different cultural traditions (all bronzes except 3, 6, and 9). 1–3: Shang-style helmet, *ding* tripod, and jade *ge* blades; 4–6: mixed-style *yue* axe, *ding* tripod, and jade winged human figurine; 7–9: indigenous-style plow, human facemask, and proto-porcelain *zun* vessel (after color plates 6; 7–1; 30–1; 37; 45–1; 41–2,3; 46; 48–3 of Jiangxisheng 1997).

style of the Shang core region. For example, a human facemask made of bronze may have been used as ritual paraphernalia in the southern context. Several elaborately designed types of bronze agricultural tools were evidently used as ritual objects, a situation in sharp contrast to the metropolitan Shang tradition, in which agricultural tools were almost completely excluded from bronze industry (Chang 1980: 223–5). The Dayangzhou mortuary remains manifest a stage of cultural development displaying increased regional characteristics distinctive from those in the Central Plain. Jade objects from Dayangzhou, however, show remarkable similarities, in form and raw material, to the Shang jades from Anyang, particularly the *ge* blades, *cong* tubes, *yuan* rings, and *huang* pendants (Jiangxisheng and Zhangshushi 2005) (Figure 10.11). Jiangxi has no jade resources, and there is no evidence for jade manufacture at Wucheng. It is possible that these jades came from Yinxu. Southern copper, proto-porcelain, and other goods may have been exchanged for northern jade ritual objects in a reciprocal or tributary relationship between Wucheng and the Shang core.

Lead isotope analysis of eleven bronze objects from Dayangzhou shows that all the tested items consist of HRL, which may have derived from northeastern Yunnan (Jin, Z. et al. 1994). This situation is comparable to the case of the Yinxu bronzes (Jin, Z. et al. 1998), as discussed earlier in this chapter. Given that Jiangxi has rich copper deposits and that copper mining was evidently undertaken during the Shang period, it is unlikely that the copper used in the Dayangzhou bronzes came from Yunnan. It remains to be investigated whether lead and/or tin containing HRL were obtained, either directly or via the Shang core, from Yunnan. The latter scenario would involve a much larger and more complex sphere of interaction and a more centralized redistribution system.

There was apparently a close relationship between Wucheng and Shang. The earliest rulers of Wucheng may have come from the early Shang elite group. Later phases of the material remains at Wucheng, however, reveal increasing dominance of local characteristics, and it is unlikely that Wucheng was a proper part of the Shang territory then. Because it was an independent polity, its obligation to pay tribute to Anyang was less involuntary. As recorded in oracle-bone inscriptions, the Shang kings waged wars against many groups in the south (Jiang, H. 1976). These wars were probably intended to ensure the flow of tribute, including metal and precious ceramics, from Jiangxi.

Sanxingdui in the Southwest

To the southwest of Shang, the Sanxingdui culture in Sichuan represented the most powerful state-level polity during the Shang period. The topography of Sichuan forms a large basin with fertile land surrounded by high mountains and plateaus. It has been a land of plenty, but communication with the outside was difficult before modern times. River systems formed the transportation

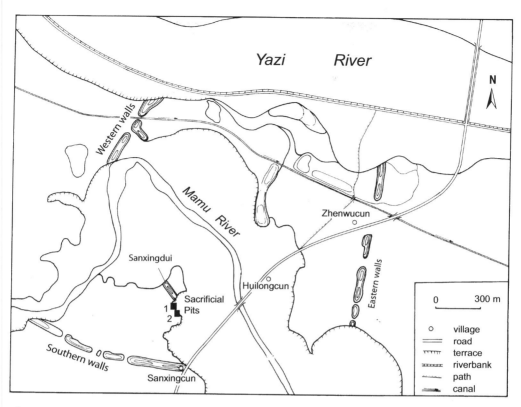

Figure 10.12. Plan of the Sanxingdui site in Guanghan, Sichuan (modified from figure 3 of Sichuansheng 1999).

channels, with the Jialing and Min Rivers connecting to the north and the Yangzi River to the east, west, and south (Figure 10.1). Archaeological cultures developed in such a geographically circumscribed region show strong local character and traditions, but they are by no means isolated from the outside.

Sanxingdui lies about 40 km north of Chengdu (Figure 10.12). It was the center of thirteen contemporary sites distributed along the Yazi and Mamu Rivers. Dating to 2800–1000 BC, Sanxingdui can be divided into four phases, equivalent to a time span from Longshan, Erlitou, and Erligang to Yinxu in north China. A walled enclosure (260 ha) was built at Sanxingdui during the phase contemporary with Erlitou (1700–1500 BC) and was abandoned about 1000 BC. Inside the enclosure, large building foundations, dating to 2000–1400 BC, have been found. Some of them were rebuilt many times; the largest one covers an area of 200 m² and contains several rooms. These foundations may have been palatial or temple structures (Sichuansheng 1999; Wang, Y. et al. 1987; Xu, J. 2001b; Zhao, D. 1996).

Closely packed buildings indicate a high population density in a flourishing metropolis. Craft workshops, kilns, and numerous finds of jade, stone, bronze, and gold suggest a high level of craft specialization. The presence of ritual objects suggests that the site may have been a ritual center, possibly even a city of pilgrimage. More than six sacrificial pits have been discovered both inside and outside the town since the 1930s. These pits have yielded a few thousand items, including ivory tusks, gold and bronze objects, jade/stone artifacts, and cowry shells. The most impressive discoveries are the two sacrificial pits (no. 1 and no. 2), excavated in 1986, revealing a highly developed bronze culture (Sichuansheng 1999; Xu, J. 2001b).

The bronze objects were for the most part locally made with indigenous styles, characterized by life-size bronze figures and heads, bronze face masks in human form, diamond- and hook-shaped fittings, and bronze trees decorated with birds. Some ritual vessels (*zun* and *lei*) show typical Shang style, however (Figure 10.13). Bronze techniques used are a combination of piece-mold technique, which was likely a Central Plain influence, and soldering/brazing, which was a local development. The sheer quantity of bronze items is extraordinary, but the metalworking skills involved show less refinement in these pieces than in artifacts from the Yellow River region (Sichuansheng 1999; Xu, J. 2001a).

As in Dayangzhou, the jade/stone ritual objects found at Sanxingdui show a strong influence from the Central Plain, although these artifacts were made mainly of local stone material with a small number of jade (nephrite) objects being imported. The forms are predominately *ge* and *zhang* blades, *bi* disks, and *huan* and *yuan* rings. Some of them may have either come from the Central Plain or been made locally as exact imitations of the Central Plain style; but the majority clearly show local variations (So 2001). For example, nearly 100 stone/jade *ge* blades were unearthed from two sacrificial pits; they can be classified into seven types based on stylistic variation, of which Types A and B resemble those found in the Central Plain, and Types C–G are local variations. Among these *ge* blades, only three have been identified as nephrite, all belonging to Types A and B. The ritual objects with Central Plain styles seem to have been incorporated into local ceremonial events, as illustrated by two bronze human sculptures. One sculpture portrays a kneeling person holding a *zhang* blade, and the other shows a kneeling person supporting a *zun* vessel on his head (Figure 10.13) (Sichuansheng 1999).

Sanxingdui's contacts with the Central Plain can be traced back to the Erlitou period, as suggested by the presence of ceramic *he* vessels, jade/stone *ge* and *zhang* blades, and turquois-inlaid bronze plaques at Sanxingdui, which resemble corresponding items found at Erlitou. It is likely that Sanxingdui's bronze metallurgy was first inspired by the Central Plain cultures.

Sanxingdui during the Shang period was a political and religious center of an independent polity, most likely a state. Two ancient peoples (Ba and Shu) were the principal ethnic groups residing in Sichuan, according to ancient texts. Both names appear in the Shang oracle-bone inscriptions, but the Shu seem to have had more frequent contacts with the Shang (Tong, E. 2004).

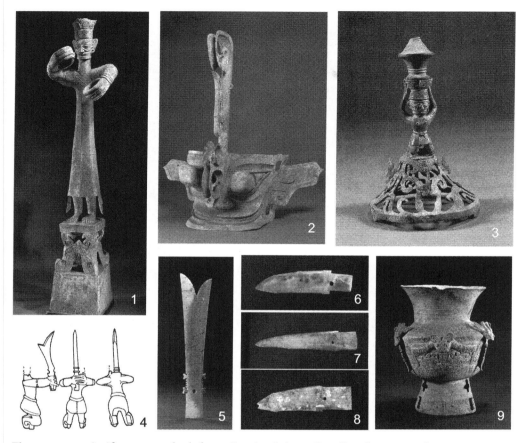

Figure 10.13. Artifacts unearthed from Sanxingdui. 1: Standing human sculpture (height 260.8 cm); 2: bronze mask (height 82.5 cm); 3: bronze stand depicting a human holding a *zun* vessel (height 15.6 cm); 4: bronze human figure holding a *zhang* blade (height 4.7 cm); 5: stone *zhang* blade (height 30.5 cm); 6–8: stone *ge* blades, types B, C, and D (length 24.3, 35.8, 29.5 cm); 9: bronze *zun* vessel (height 43.3 cm) (after plates 8–1, 58, 60, 70, 140–3, 157–4; color plates 27,102; and figure 133 of Sichuansheng 1999).

Many scholars believe that Sanxingdui was the political center of the ancient Shu state (Lin, X. 1989; Sichuansheng 1999; Xu, J. 2001a).

Lead isotope analysis of fifty-three Sanxingdui bronzes shows that most items contain HRL, probably derived from ores in northeastern Yunnan. Given that Sanxingdui has revealed evidence of bronze metallurgy on a large scale, it must have had easy access to metal resources in the region, including nearby parts of Yunnan (Jin, Z. et al. 1995).

The presence of HRL in both Sanxingdui and Shang (Zhengzhou and Yinxu) bronzes also suggests the possibility that Sanxingdui supplied metal to the Shang (Jin, Z. et al. 1995), although it remains unclear what alloys – copper, lead, or/and tin – would have been involved. In any event, Sanxingdui's development of greater social complexity may have been closely related to its intermediary position between the advanced bronze-working states to the north and the rich metal deposits easily accessible in the southwest.

If Sanxingdui had been involved in metal ware procurement networks, the ores and products may have been transported through the north–south river systems that connect the Yangzi River with the Hanzhong Plain, in southern Shaanxi, and the Central Plain. This hypothesis is supported by the discovery of 710 bronzes from 19 localities along the Han River and its tributary, the Xu River, in Chenggu and Yangxian, southern Shaanxi. These bronzes, referred to as the Chengyang bronze assemblages, date to middle and late Shang and include ritual objects, weapons, tools, and armor. All these items are isolated finds discovered in farmlands by local residents. Morphologically they can be classified into three styles: Shang, Sanxingdui/Sichuan, and local. Most ritual vessels are clearly of the Shang tradition and likely have been made in the Shang core region. They are predominantly storage vessels, including *zun* and *lei* (Figure 10.14), which also appear at Sanxingdui (Zhao, Congcang 2006). Lead isotope analysis of thirty-one bronzes, including all three styles from five localities, shows that all but three items contain the distinctive HRL (Jin, Z. et al. 2006). It is interesting to note that the occurrence of the HRL bronzes in the Shang core area at Zhengzhou and Yinxu (Phases I–III) was contemporaneous with the Chengyang bronzes, which date from Upper Erligang to Yinxu Phase III, indicating the existence of an exchange network for bronze objects between the two regions.

Settlements contemporary with the Chengyang bronze assemblages also have been found in the Hanzhong basin, referred to as the Baoshan culture (Figure 10.1). Excavation at the Baoshan site in Chenggu has revealed a material assemblage with strong local tradition (e.g., roasting pits) and influence from the Sichuan basin and Xiajiang area (e.g., pottery and bronzes), further confirming that the people in Hanzhong had frequent interactions with the Yangzi River region (Xibei 2002).

The coexistence of three cultural traditions in the Chengyang bronze assemblage suggests that the Hanzhong area played an intermediary role in facilitating interactions between Sichuan and the Central Plain. These interactions were apparently two-way traffic through which ideology and artifacts were moved between north and south. The adoption of Shang-style ritual objects (bronze vessels and jades) in local ceremonies at Baoshan and Sanxingdui suggests that the Shang influence was primarily reflected at an ideological level. In contrast, the presence of HRL in bronze objects found at Yinxu, Chengyang, and Sanxingdui indicates close connections among these regions; such links most likely were related to their common procurement of metallic ores from Yunnan in the far southwest (Jin, Z. et al. 2006). This pattern of exchange between information/technology and raw materials seems to have characterized the relationships between the Shang and contemporary bronze-using centers to the south, including Sanxingdui and Wucheng.

Figure 10.14. Bronze artifacts from Chenggu and Yangxian, southern Shaanxi. 1: *Zun* vessel (height 46 cm); 2: *zhang*-shaped object (length 21.1 cam); 3: triangle-shaped *ge* dagger with snake pattern (length 24.1 cm); 4: human mask (height 16.1 cm); 5: buffalo mask (height 19.1 cm); 6: *yue* axe with frog design (length 14.5 cm) (after plates 27, 98, 114, 129, 167, 261 of Zhao, C. 2006).

Laoniupo in the West

Laoniupo is situated by the northern bank of the Ba River, which is a tributary of the Wei River. The site (50 ha in total area) was occupied from the Neolithic Yangshao culture to the Shang, the remains of which make up the main part of the occupation. During the Erligang period, the site was rather small, and its material assemblages closely resemble those from Zhengzhou. Bronze arrowheads and awls, clay molds, and slag have been found in deposits of the Upper Erligang phase, suggesting that bronze metallurgy was carried out at the site (Liu, S. 2001). During the late Shang period, it became a large regional center surrounded by a cluster of small sites (Figure 10.15) (Guojia 1999: 57).

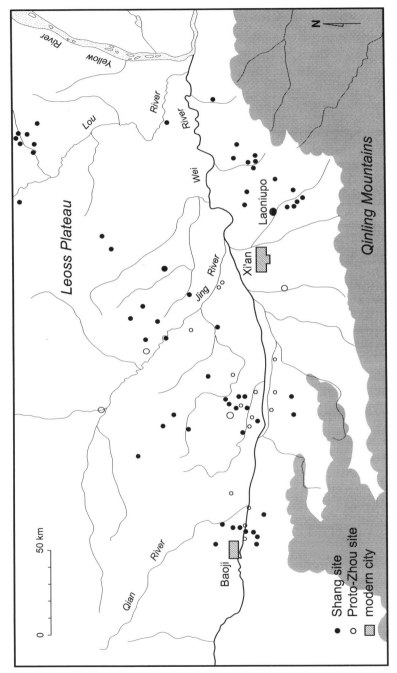

Figure 10.15. Distribution of Shang and proto-Zhou sites in the Wei River region (redrawn from Guojia 1999: 57).

Figure 10.16. Bronze and jade artifacts from Laoniupo in Xi'an. 1: Bronze *jia* vessel (height 23 cm); 2: bronze human mask (height 6.5 cm); 3: bronze buffalo mask (height 16 cm); 4: clay mold for casting Shang-style ritual vessel; 5: jade *ge* blade (after color plates 5, 8, 10–1, 2 and plate 111 of Liu, S. 2001).

Most material remains found at the site are dated to the late Shang, including pottery kilns, copper smelting and bronze casting workshops, large-sized tombs associated with bronze ritual objects, chariot-and-horse sacrificial pits, houses, and large, rammed-earth foundations (Liu, S. 2001).

Laoniupo is located at an important strategic juncture of the routes connecting the Wei River in the north with the Dan and Han Rivers in the south. Historically, the Qinling Mountains in Luonan possessed rich copper deposits (Huo 1993), and a copper smelting site of the Erligang period has been discovered at Huaizhenfang, 14 km south of Laoniupo (Xi'an 1981). Laoniupo was first established probably as an outpost by the Erligang state to exploit metal and other resources in this region (Liu, L. and Chen 2003: 110–13).

Laoniupo became a powerful regional state in the Wei River Valley during the late Shang, and had a close relationship with Yinxu. The bronze ritual vessels from Laoniupo stylistically resemble those from Yinxu, and many of these vessels may have been made at Anyang. Some bronze objects are similar to those from the Chengyang assemblages (human and buffalo masks), but they were made at Laoniupo, as shown by the presence there of the corresponding clay molds. Laoniupo began to produce Shang-style bronze ritual vessels by its Phase IV (Yinxu Phase IV), as suggested by the discovery of clay molds for making *li*, *yan*, and other types of vessels (Figure 10.16) (Liu, S. 2001). This bronze foundry is the only location that shows hard evidence, based on the current archaeological record, for manufacture of authentic Shang-style ritual vessels outside Yinxu. This phenomenon supports the inference that bronze production became decentralized during the Yinxu period, as discussed earlier in this chapter.

Laoniupo also has revealed jade objects identical in style to those from Yinxu, particularly the *ge* blades (Figure 10.16). It is unclear where these jades were made, as no evidence of jade production has been found at Laoniupo. Like Wucheng, Laoniupo may have obtained jades from Yinxu.

Numerous human sacrifices were found in the late Shang burials at Laoniupo (Phase IV). Among thirty-eight medium and small tombs, twenty tombs contained ninety-seven human sacrificial victims, ranging from one to twelve individuals per tomb (Liu, S. 2001). Such a large number of human sacrifices is comparable with the elite burials at Yinxu. According to oracle-bone inscriptions, Shang kings used at least 14,197 persons for sacrifice, among which 7,426 belonged to the Qiang people (Hu, H. 1974). The Shang obtained the Qiang in two capacities: as war captives and as tribute offered from other states (Keightley 1979–80). Many scholars believe that the Qiang were tribes or peoples inhabiting regions to the west of the Shang; although their exact locations are disputable, these localities ranged from southern Shanxi and western Henan (Li, X. 1959; Shelach 1996) to various areas along the Wei River Valley (Chen, M. 1956: 281–2; Niu, S. 2006; Wang, M.-k. 2001: 227–32; Zhang, T. 2004: 277–343). Archaeological surveys have shown a few late Shang sites distributed in areas of southern Shanxi and western Henan (Liu, L. et al. 2002–2004; Zhang, D. et al. 1989); therefore, the Qiang are more likely to have been peoples living in the vicinity of the Wei River. Settlement patterns in this region show several clusters of sites during the late Shang period, including the Laoniupo site cluster and proto-Zhou sites (Guojia 1999: 57), probably representing several competitive polities. These polities show diverse cultural traditions, and it is not possible to determine their ethnic affiliations based on archaeological remains. The name Qiang may have been a general term used by the Shang to refer to all the non-Shang peoples in the general area of the Wei River Valley.

Some archaeologists have identified Laoniupo as Chong, which was a tributary state of the Shang, according to ancient documents (Liu, S. 2001). The question is, then, what kinds of tribute did Chong pay to Shang? The practice of human sacrifice at Laoniupo reflects its hostile relationship with some of the regional polities. Whether the sacrificial victims at Laoniupo were of the Qiang type is difficult to determine; but, given that Laoniupo's location was near the Qiang, that its ritual practice, particularly the human sacrifice, resembled the Shang's traditional usages, and that it was closely affiliated with the Shang core, it is therefore possible that Laoniupo was one of the regional states that brought Qiang captives as tribute to Yinxu for ceremonial sacrifice. This proposition, nevertheless, needs to be tested with more evidence in the future.

Although Laoniupo had close associations with Yinxu, particularly at the level of elite culture, its pottery types and some burial customs show indigenous styles. It also had connections with surrounding regional cultures, as suggested by the presence of Northern Zone bronzes (socketed axe and hole-handle *ge* blade) and Chengyang-style bronzes (human and buffalo masks) (Figure 10.16) (Liu, S. 2001). Laoniupo seems to have gradually become more independent of the Shang core over the course of time, as suggested by its evident capability, in the late Yinxu period, of manufacturing ritual vessels. This development signifies a change in the political relationship between the Shang and its affiliated states, reflecting the growing power of regional polities in the Shang's periphery. Laoniupo's rise to regional power, however, was short lived, as indicated by its sudden decline after Phase IV, which was most likely caused by the intervention of the Zhou, who finally conquered Shang (Liu, S. 2001).

The Loess Plateau in the Northwest

In oracle-bone inscriptions and early textual records, the Shang's northwest frontier is depicted as being occupied by hostile peoples, most frequently referred to as Qiongfang (or Gongfang) and Guifang (Figure 10.2). They often raided Shang settlements and, in response, the Shang kings waged wars against them (Hu, H. 2002; Keightley 2000: 66–7; Li, Y. 1985). These records indicate that Shang and non-Shang groups/polities lived in close proximity in this region. It is not easy to determine the territorial scale of these polities. As Chang (1980: 219–22) pointed out, when the locations of these non-Shang groups and Shang subordinate polities are plotted on a map, based on data recorded in oracle-bone inscriptions, some of them overlap with others. This phenomenon, according to Chang, indicates that the extent of Shang's control in this region varied through time.

Sites dating to the late Shang period have been found in areas to the east and west of the Yellow River's north-south section, including parts of northern Shaanxi, western Shanxi, and central-southern Inner Mongolia. This general region is also referred to as the Ordos. The material remains from these sites show characteristics both similar to and different from the Shang, represented by the burial sites at Jingjie (in Lingshi, Shanxi) and Qiaobei (in Fushan, Shanxi), the Lijiaya culture, and the Xicha culture (although the spatial distribution of the Xicha culture has not been determined) (Figures 10.1 and 10.17).

The Jingjie site is located in the middle reaches of the Fen River Valley, and consists of three elite burials of the Shang type. The burials were furnished with wooden chambers and coffins, human and animal sacrifices, and large quantities of grave objects, including bronzes, jade and shell ornaments, pottery vessels, stone tools, and an alligator drum (Figure 10.18). The metal objects consist of two types: Shang-style objects and Northern Zone artifacts. Forty-two bronzes bear lineage emblems, among which thirty-four contain the same character, which has been deciphered as Bing (Shanxisheng 2006). The Bing lineage emblem also occurs on more than 100 bronzes from other places, some

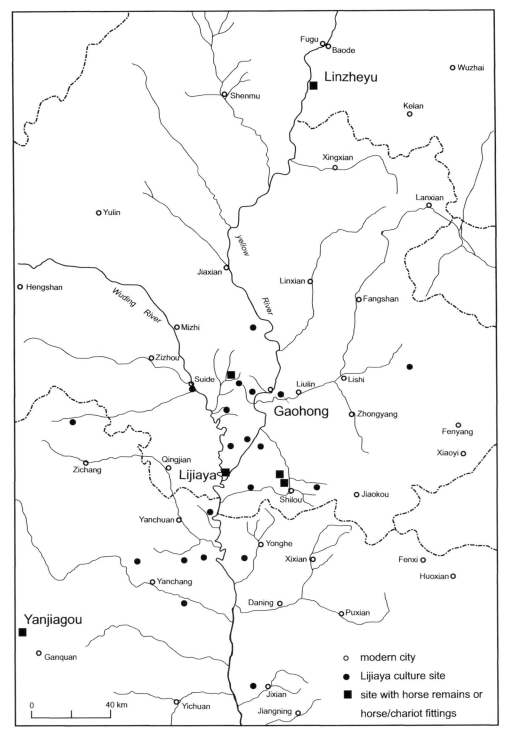

Figure 10.17. Major sites of the Lijiaya culture in northern Shaanxi and western Shanxi, late Shang period (site locations partially based on figure 1 of Dai, Y. 1993).

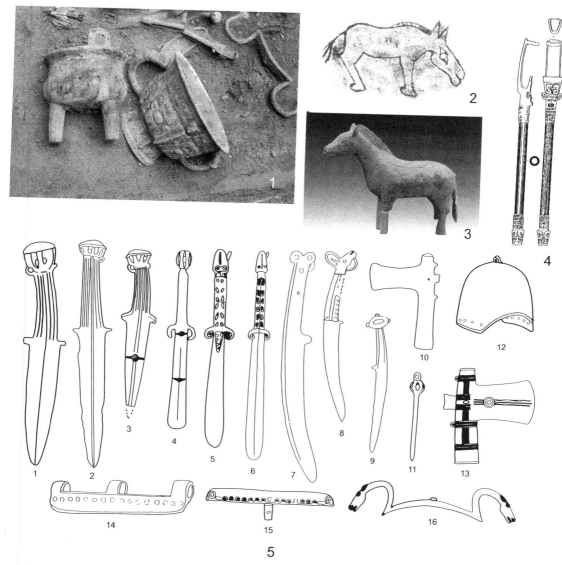

Figure 10.18. Artifacts from the Loess Plateau region, late Shang period. 1: Bronze remains, including a crop and a rein hook, from Jingjie Tomb M1; 2: horse glyph on bronze vessel from Jingjie; 3: horse sculpture from Yanjiagou; 4: bronze crops from Jingjie; 5: Northern Zone style bronze objects unearthed from the Ordos region (1, 2, and 4: after figures 11, 32, and 93 of Shanxisheng 2006; 3: after figure 20 of Wang, Y. et al. 2007; 5: after figure 68 of Wu'en 2007).

with inscriptions documenting that the Bing people assisted the Shang king in military campaigns and received rewards from the king. Apparently the Jingjie burials contain elite individuals of a polity allied with the Shang and located in the middle Fen River region (Li, B. 1988).

The Qiaobei site is situated in the eastern margin of the Linfen Basin. It consists of more than thirty burials dating from late Shang to Eastern Zhou.

The site has been badly looted, but several tombs appear to be typical of Shang style, indicated by congruence among the remaining bronze and jade artifacts, and the grave structures, with Shang elite mortuary practice. Horses and chariots made up part of the system of status symbols in this society. Tomb M1, for example, contained a chariot with two horses and one charioteer, along with a range of bronze artifacts, including chariot fittings. Some bronzes from the site bear the inscription Xian, which may have been the lineage emblem of this polity (Guojia 2005a). This burial site, like that at Jingjie, belonged to a polity allied with the Shang.

The Lijiaya culture refers to more than forty sites located in northern Shaanxi and western Shanxi, most of them being densely distributed in a narrow strip about 300 kg from north to south along the Yellow River (Figure 10.17). The more than 500 bronze objects were retrieved from various contexts, including burials, hoards, and isolated finds. The bronzes can be classified into three types: Type A consists of typical Shang bronzes, mainly ritual vessels, with some bearing inscriptions. Type B is a mixed style, combining Shang and local characteristics. Type C is a local style, resembling the Northern Zone tradition (e.g., knives with animal–head or bell pommel, shaft–hole axes, shaft-hole *ge* daggers, and gold ornaments) (Lü, Z. 1987) (Figure 10.18). Most sites consisted of a combination of different types. For example, fully two-thirds of the twenty-one Lijiaya culture sites inventoried by Wu'en (2007: 142–4) revealed a varied repertory: Fourteen held bronzes belonging to Shang, mixed and indigenous styles, whereas only two sites contained solely Shang bronzes, and five others had only Northern Zone artifact.

Of the few Lijiaya culture sites excavated, the one at Lijiaya in Qingjian, northern Shaanxi, provides the most detailed data. It was a walled settlement (6.7 ha in area within the walls) on high terraces to the east of the Wuding River and 4.5 kg west of the Yellow River. The site was protected on the east and west by walls made of stones and rammed earth, and the other two sides faced natural cliffs. Archaeologists have excavated houses, storage pits, and burials. Artifacts uncovered are mostly pottery and tools made of stone and bone. A group of three buildings with a large courtyard was surrounded by rammed–earth walls on the highest spot of the Lijiaya site, and a stone carved with skeleton-style human images was unearthed from a pit in the courtyard. These structures may have housed ritual functions, and the human sculpture represents a local ritual tradition, which was apparently different from the Shang's, at least in this respect. A thick layer of millet grains was discovered in a storage pit, and animal bones were identifiable as remains of horses, cattle, sheep/goats, pigs, dogs, boars, and deer (Lü, Z. 1993, 1998; Zhang, Y. and Lü 1988). Apparently the Lijiaya people practiced agriculture with a certain degree of pastoralism, including horse breeding.

The level of social complexity in the Lijiaya culture is manifested at the Gaohong site in Liulin, Shanxi, about 5 km east of the Yellow River

TABLE 10.1. *Faunal remains from Xicha in Qingshuihe, Inner Mongolia (NISP)*

Chronology (BC)	Pigs	Dogs	Cattle	Sheep/Goats	Horses	Wild animals	Total
Longshan 2500–2000	17 (46%)	4 (11%)	2 (5%)	6 (16%)	4 (11%)	4 (11%)	37
Zhukaigou 1600–1300	1 (10%)	4 (40%)	4 (40%)	–	–	1 (10%)	10
Shang-Zhou 1300–1000	2,509 (43%)	457 (8%)	712 (12%)	1,410 (24%)	531 (9%)	216 (4%)	5,835

(Figure 10.17). More than twenty locations at this site have revealed rammed-earth platforms, covering a total area of 4,000 m², with the largest one measuring 46.8 m in length and 11 m in width. These remains are of large architectural foundations, indicating the existence of a highly developed social organization in the region. Among the artifacts unearthed are proto-porcelain sherds (Guojia 2005b). The population here, as at other Lijiaya sites, also seems to have participated in the elite exchange system of the Shang. The location of Gaohong strongly suggests that it was the center of a regional polity within the Lijiaya culture area.

The Xicha culture: Recent excavations and survey work at Xicha and Duijiugou in Qingshuihe County, Inner Mongolia, have revealed settlements containing agricultural tools and bronzes of the Northern Zone style (e.g., shaft-hole axes and earrings), dating to the Late Shang (Cao, J. 2001; Cao, J. and Hu 2001). Xicha (120 ha) was occupied for a long time, from the Neolithic to the Bronze Age; a majority of its material deposits date to a phase called the Xicha culture, which is contemporary with the late Shang and early Western Zhou periods. Large numbers of houses, pits, and burials were unearthed, indicating a sedentary village. The faunal remains include both domesticated (5,619 number of identified specimens [NISP]) and wild (216 NISP) animals; the former category consists of pigs, dogs, sheep, goats, cattle, and horses. Grazing animals (2,653 NISP) account for 45 percent of the total bones, slightly higher than pig bones (43%; 2,509 NISP) (Table 10.1). Evidently, Xicha's subsistence economy was characterized by agropastoralism, supplemented with hunting activities. Xicha also yielded clay molds used for making the Northern Zone bronzes (e.g., dagger and shaft-hole axe); the forms of artifacts cast from these molds match the corresponding items found in the area. Apparently the Northern Zone bronze objects could have been made locally (Cao, J. and Sun 2004).

Bronze metallurgy: The bronzes discovered in the Loess Plateau region have attracted much interest, particularly concerning their locations of manufacture. Many people believe that most of the Shang style bronzes were made at Yinxu and that the mixed and indigenous types were made locally. The discovery of clay molds at Xicha confirms that at least some of the Northern Zone bronze weapons and tools were locally made, but no hard evidence yet confirms local production of those elaborate vessels, in either the Shang or the mixed style. A recent metallurgical analysis of fourteen bronzes from the Jingjie burials demonstrates that the metallurgical technology is consistent with the Shang tradition. Most items are made of copper-tin or copper-tin-lead alloy, but one item is pure copper. These bronzes in general contain low levels of tin and lead, reflecting a regional characteristic that distinguishes them from the Yinxu products. It is suggested that the Jingjie bronzes may have come from multiple sources (Chen, K. and Mei 2006); however, this analysis has not resolved the issue of identifying the specific provenances of these bronzes.

Horses and chariots: The Loess Plateau region, particularly the vicinity of the Ordos, experienced a long history of horse exploitation from the Paleolithic to the Bronze Age (see Chapter 4). During the late Shang, people in this region may have been responsible for the introduction of horses and chariots to the Shang, as suggested by the higher frequency of domesticated horses and chariots found in the Ordos, as compared to other regions of China, except for Yinxu. This proposition draws support from several lines of evidence, including artifacts, writing, and faunal remains.

Artifactual evidence: Two nearly identical solid bronze horse sculptures, along with fifty-five other bronze items (in both Shang and Northern Zone styles), were discovered from a burial at Yanjiagou in Xiasiwan, Ganquan County, north Shaanxi. The horses are configured with a short body and legs, a sturdy neck, a stand-up mane, and a long, straight dorsal delineation, perhaps indicating a dark line on the horse's back. These are the morphological characteristics of the indigenous wild horse, *Equus przewalskii*, of northwest China. Each horse is also rendered, however, with an oval-shaped object on the back, most likely a saddle, indicating that the illustrations represent a domesticated form of Przewalski's horse (Figure 10.18). This bronze assemblage dates to Yinxu Phase II, and forms the earliest examples of bronze horse sculpture in China (Wang, Y. et al. 2007). They are comparable with a pair of jade horses unearthed from the Fuhao Tomb, which also show characteristics of Przewalski's horse (Figure 10.5).

Nineteen horse-chariot fittings, along with seven Shang-style ritual vessels and five Northern Zone tools and weapons, have been recovered from a burial at Linzheyu in Baode County, north Shanxi. Besides a horse bell and a chariot bell, nine other artifacts were rendered with bells, manifesting characteristics associated with a horse-chariot culture. The grave goods also included 112 cowry shells and 109 bronze imitations of cowry shells, which were unearthed together with the horse-chariot fittings. It is suggested that these shells were probably ornaments on the horse gear (Wu, Z. 1972).

At least seven sites of the Lijiaya culture (Figure 10.17) have yielded *tongpao* (bronze buttons) as part of grave offerings (Wu'en 2007: 142–4). Such objects often have been found as parts of horse fittings at Yinxu and Qianzhangda. For example, they have been found in an arrangement resembling the shape of an equine headstall, together with other horse fittings, in the Fuhao Tomb (Zhongguo Shehui Kexueyuan 1980: 9–11). The presence of such horse fittings in burials suggests that the occupants of these tombs were during their lifetime closely affiliated, whether functionally or symbolically, with horses.

Two burials (M1 and M2) from Jingjie contained *gongxingqi* (bow-shaped objects) and *guanzhuangqi* (tubular-shaped objects) (Shanxisheng 2006). *Gongxingqi* often have been found in association with chariots and were used as rein hooks (*guajianggou*) (Lin, Y. 1998a), whereas *guanzhuangqi* were riding crops (Wu'en 2007: 129). In addition, a bronze *gui* vessel from burial M1 bears the image of a horse, the features of which resemble *E. przewalskii* (Linduff 2003) (Figure 10.18). Given that the chariot fittings are present in the tomb, this equine image most likely depicts a domesticated form of Przewalski's horse. Apparently the Bing lineage, represented at the Jingjie burials, held a special relationship with horses and chariots.

Inscription evidence: The glyph for horse, *ma*, occurs repeatedly in oracle-bone inscriptions (Mair, V. 2003). The form of this glyph is highly representational, depicting an animal with erect mane and short legs, resembling the wild *E. przewalskii* (Linduff 2003). Because there may not be obvious morphological differences between wild and domesticated Przewalski horses (as discussed in Chapter 4), it is therefore equally possible that the horse glyph depicts a domesticated form of *E. przewalskii*, which was familiar to the Shang people at Yinxu. Because horses known at Yinxu were derived from elsewhere, those locales with high concentrations of horse-related remains would have been probable sources of the Yinxu horses. The current archaeological record points to the Loess Plateau as one of those sources.

Ma was often used together with *fang* (land), referring to a polity or people outside the Shang domain, such as Mafang (the country/land of horses). According to Shaughnessy (1988), Mafang consisted of various groupings of peoples, who were closely affiliated with horses; they are generally assumed to have resided in western Shanxi, east of the Yellow River. Likewise, based on ancient inscriptions and texts, Lin Huan (2003) has argued that a number of tribes or polities that specialized in horse tending and breeding, including Mafang and the Bing lineage, were distributed in the area west of the Fen River. The recently discovered Qiaobei site also may represent one of such polities distributed along the Fen River Valley.

Zooarchaeological evidence: The most important evidence is derived from faunal remains. As discussed in Chapter 4, the northwestern region, particularly the Ordos, has revealed the most densely distributed horse-bearing sites in ancient China, dating from the Palaeolithic to the early Bronze Age. The equine remains from late Yangshao sites (Miaozigou and Dabagou) have been identified as *E. przewalskii* (Huang, Y. 2003), suggesting that horses present in later sites also belong to this species. The high representation of grazing animals, including horses, cattle, and sheep/goats, in the Xicha fauna is especially noteworthy. Horses were used here for food, as ceremonial offerings, and as raw material for making tools. Evidently, the horse was a part of the agropastoralist economy.

In short, whenever taxonomic identification has been attempted, horse remains from Neolithic and Bronze Age sites in China have been assigned to *E. przewalskii*. All artistic representations and written pictographs of horses seem to depict the characteristics of *E. przewalskii*. In a number of cases, the artifacts (horse and chariot fittings) clearly indicate an association with domesticated horses. Northwest China, particularly the Ordos, was a part of a broad region of the Eurasian steppe where domestication of the Asian wild horse may have taken place in prehistory. In the northwest region, horses were an important part of the subsistence economy, and horses and chariots served as status symbols in the local hierarchical system, as demonstrated by bronze artifacts in burials. The Ordos region apparently played an intermediating role between the agropastoralist and seminomadic cultures of the steppe, on the one hand, and the Shang civilization in the Central Plain, on the other. The Ordos people's cultural and technical aptitudes relating to horses and chariots were especially valued at the Shang capital.

Ethnicity: Archaeological sites distributed in the Loess Plateau region generally overlap with the presumed locales of polities, both allied and hostile, lying to the northwest of Yinxu, as recorded in the oracle-bone inscriptions (Figure 10.2). Many archaeologists believe that Jingjie and Qiaobei belong to states allied with the Shang, whereas the Lijiaya and Xicha cultures represent non-Shang polities (Li, B. 1988; Lü, Z. 1990). An inscription on pottery from Lijiaya has been deciphered as the word *gui*, and is interpreted as indicating the ethnic identity of this archaeological culture; this view, however, has not been accepted by all scholars (Wu'en 2007: 168). There were probably multiple polities or tribes that used similar styles of artifacts, particularly bronze objects, and practiced similar agropastoralism on the Loess Plateau. It is difficult, however, to pinpoint their ethnic identities based on oracle-bone inscriptions.

Summary: The Loess Plateau region's strong connections with horses and chariots, in both subsistence economy and elite culture, were unparalleled among other contemporary archaeological cultures in China. Considering its metallurgical tradition and overall agropastoralist economy, the culture of the Loess Plateau strongly resembles the Karasuk culture (ca. 1400–1000 BC), in the Minusinsk Basin of the south Siberian steppe, which featured sedentary habitations; raising of sheep, cattle, and horses; and hunting of deer and wild boar (Legrand 2004). It is possible that the Loess Plateau was one of the regions through which the horse-chariot complex developed in the steppe was introduced to the Shang.

Shang's intensive interactions with polities to its northwest, as recorded in the oracle-bone inscriptions, may have been partially motivated by the intent to procure horses, chariots, and related technology. This purpose was probably pursued through alliances with nearer polities, such as Jingjie and Qiaobei in central Shanxi, which were situated between the Shang core and the more northerly Lijiaya and Xicha cultures. The elite of the non-Shang polities in the Ordos may have obtained Shang-style bronze vessels and proto-porcelains through their immediate Shang-allied neighbors by various means, such as trade, gift exchange, and warfare. All these phenomena suggest that both the Shang cultural values and the pastoralist heritage derived from the Eurasian steppe were well integrated into the local cultural traditions, particularly at the elite level. Analogous sorts of cultural mixing repeatedly occurred in other peripheral regions, as discussed earlier in this chapter.

DISCUSSION AND CONCLUSIONS

The change from early Shang to late Shang can be described as a gradual paradigm shift, from a more centralized political-economic system to a more decentralized one. When the Erlitou and Erligang states were established, their neighbors were in much weaker positions politically, allowing the early Central Plain states to expand quickly and colonize large neighboring regions. One result of this political and cultural expansion was to stimulate development of regional political powers in the outer peripheries. Starting from the middle Shang, the political landscape became multicentered, and the late Shang was unable to restore its political domination to the level enjoyed by the Erligang/early Shang state.

Archaeological evidence clearly suggests a close link between territorial expansion and attempts to control resources, as undertaken by the Erlitou and early Shang state rulers. These purposes were accomplished mainly by military means and colonization (see Chapter 8). During the late Shang period, as regional polities became more powerful, Shang's procurement of resources could not be achieved by military force alone. Instead, various forms of interaction arose between the Shang and its neighbors, as discussed throughout this chapter, which reflect the Shang state's strategies for resource procurement.

Viewed from the Shang core's perspective, a consistent pattern of center-periphery interactions is evident. On the one hand, what the Shang exported to the peripheries were mainly ceremonial paraphernalia, including finished jades and bronze ritual objects. Shang was able to use its superiority in bronze metallurgy and jade craftsmanship to gain influence with neighboring polities. These objects, symbolizing wealth and power, formed part of a hierarchical system among regional polities. It has been pointed out by several scholars that the late Shang material remains represent a cultural sphere rather than a politically controlled territory (Xu, L. 1998). It can be described as the Shang civilization sphere, representing shared cultural values.

On the other hand, the Shang imported raw materials, exotic goods, and other types of resources from the peripheries. These imports include metal alloys, jade raw material, proto-porcelain, salt, horses and chariots, humans and animals for sacrifice, and so forth. Agricultural products, such as grains and animals, also may have been among the goods imported to Yinxu. These items functioned either as status symbols to help the Shang elite maintain political superiority and legitimacy or as subsistence necessities for rapid urban growth. These goods were primarily obtained through tribute, exchange, and/or force. The Shang state may have indeed been full of holes (like Swiss cheese), as Keightley (1979–80: 26) suggested, because the Shang preferred to procure the resources through any of various means, rather than to occupy the land.

Viewed from the perspective of the periphery, the regional archaeological cultures that show characteristically Shang-style materials were by no means all under the direct political control of the Shang court. They range from parts of the Shang domain to autonomous polities, and show different degrees of cultural influence from the Shang. The nature and balance of the two-way interaction between regional polities and the Shang were defined variously, according to local resource availability and demand from the Shang, but it was also up to these regional polities to decide to what extent they would incorporate Shang elements into their indigenous cultural systems. In many cases, the Shang ritual system was only superficially adopted by local elites, as symbolic of high social status, but their original ritual concepts may have been lost, or they were used in different ways from Shang symbolic elements. For example, the Shang-style bronze assemblage, found in elite burials of the Lijiaya culture, consisted mainly of food vessels, a pattern contrasting the commonly seen assemblage of the Shang, in which drinking vessels predominated (Wang, Y. et al. 2007). Likewise, the attendant circumstances of the human figurine supporting a *zun* vessel, as recovered from Sanxingdui (Figure 10.13), indicate that this Shang-style food container was not used as a receptacle for display in the ancestral temple, as customary Shang practice would require. The Shang objects were incorporated into local ritual systems of social hierarchy, but it is unclear whether the original religious meanings connoted by the objects were maintained.

The political weakness of the Shang during the Yinxu period is also manifested in the bronze production. Control of the manufacturing and distribution of ritual bronze vessels was a political strategy of early states. As demonstrated in Chapter 8, only the major political centers at Erlitou and Zhengzhou show evidence of the manufacturing of vessels during the Erlitou and Erligang periods. This situation changed during the late Shang, when several regional centers began to make their own vessels and other type of bronzes, thus enhancing an established hierarchical system, as exemplified by Sanxingdui, Laoniupo, and probably Dayangzhou and the Ordos region.

Nevertheless, the quality and quantity of bronze metallurgy at Yinxu were not surpassed by those of other regional polities. The Shang bronze technology influenced the surrounding regions in a centrifugal pattern. Elaborate bronze objects with mixed characteristics of Shang and local tradition have been discovered as isolated finds from fields in Ningxiang, Hunan, and were thought to belong to a southern bronze tradition of the late Shang. Recent excavation at Tanheli in Ningxiang, however, has revealed a large Western Zhou city with evidence of bronze metallurgy. These Shang-style bronzes from Ningxiang and adjacent regions were apparently made at Tanheli during the Western Zhou period, probably by Shang craftsmen who migrated from the north when the Shang was conquered by the Zhou (Xiang 2008).

The sociopolitical landscape of the late Shang period in China may be depicted as multiple overlapping regional systems, forming a mosaic pattern of many center-periphery relationships. Shang civilization was defined by the extended dispersal of Shang elite cultural values, incorporated and amalgamated with traditions from all the surrounding regions by the introduction of foreign materials and technologies.

CHAPTER 11

CHINESE CIVILIZATION IN COMPARATIVE PERSPECTIVE

> We are in the midst of a Golden Age of Chinese archaeology, because we
> have the opportunity to witness the creation of a completely new body of
> knowledge concerning the prehistory of a quarter of all humanity.
>
> Kwang-chih Chang 1986a: 412

Throughout this book we have noted marked diversities among regional cultural traditions in China. If viewed from a global perspective, however, are there any unique characteristics that distinguish early Chinese cultures from those in other regions? In this final chapter we will broaden our scope, while attempting to understand ancient Chinese civilization in comparison with civilizations in other parts of the world.

INTERPRETING CHINESENESS

Scholars from various intellectual backgrounds have been fascinated by questions like the following: How was Chinese civilization different from other civilizations in the world? What made Chinese "Chinese"? What held Chinese society together for so many centuries? These broad issues have been addressed by anthropologists, archaeologists, and historians, who often have used various analytical methods and reached different conclusions.

It is commonly acknowledged that some features characteristic of many civilizations in the world were also developed in ancient China by the second millennium BC. These features include urbanization, palatial structures, temples, metallurgy, a writing system, and institutionalized social stratification. Some of these traits, however, are only superficially similar among civilizations. When investigating each attribute in detail, marked differences are observable. As outlined by K. C. Chang (1983, 1984, 1986a) in several publications, in ancient China bronze metallurgy was applied to politics, in the form of ritual vessels and weapons, rather than to food production, whereas stone tools for agriculture remained the same from the Neolithic to the Bronze Age; the earliest surviving Chinese written records, dated to the late Shang, appear in oracle-bone inscriptions and are mainly concerned with divination; and the earliest cities were built as political centers rather than as economic foci. These traits are in sharp contrast to those of ancient Mesopotamian civilization. That civilization was marked by economic and technological developments, such as the construction of irrigation systems and the use of metal tools in agriculture, initial use of writing to facilitate economic transactions, and urban growth with emphasis on marketplaces. Chang (1984) further stated that politics, rather than technology and trade, was the prime mover of the major societal transformations that resulted in the formation of Chinese civilization, particularly as manifested in the Shang dynasty. In this context, he argued, a crucial factor in the rise of civilization in ancient China was the political leaders' close relationship with shamanism, a religious tradition that can be traced back to Neolithic times. Shamans, in Chang's discussion, were religious practitioners who possessed the power of communication between humans and the supernatural; such persons were identified in ancient texts as *wu* (shamaness) and *xi* (shaman) (Chang 1983: 44–55). Through shamanism the rulers communicated with the spirit world and gained access to the wisdom of the dead. Therefore, Chang wrote, the central role of shamanism was the most remarkable trait that distinguishes early Chinese civilization from counterparts in Mesopotamia. In contrast, shamanism was a feature of Mayan culture in Mesoamerica, and Chang believed that a China–Maya cultural continuum in ideology has roots in the Upper Paleolithic substratum of the Old World, with the further implication that it was the Near East civilization that broke out of this earlier primitive pattern (Chang 1984).

Chang's essay provoked a series of discussions on the topics of putative China–Maya continuum and Near Eastern breakout among anthropologists at Harvard University (Lamberg-Karlovsky, C. C. 2000; Maybury-Lewis 2000; Willey 2000). These discussions, which emphasize the role that ideology played in the origins of civilization, reflect a general theoretical departure from the ecological and material interpretations emphasized by the New Archaeology in the 1980s (Lamberg-Karlovsky, M. 2000: xi). These studies also share a common analytical method, adopting a neoevolutionary approach and looking for a universal explanation or a prime mover that shaped the past.

Chang's thesis, focusing the role of *wu*-shamanism in ancient China, particularly his argument about the shamanistic implications of the Shang bronze decorations, has also generated much debate among Sinologists. Whereas some scholars, like Chang, believe that the decorations are directly related to mythology and represent the religious ideology of Shang people (e.g., Allan 1993; Childs-Johnson 1998), others insist that the design of ritual utensils is purely ornamental and cannot be traced back to Shang religion (e.g., Bagley 1993).

Different from the anthropological approach (focused on conceptual gen-
eralizations) discussed earlier in this chapter, David Keightley has used an
alternative view of history by exploiting particular events and situations without attempting to develop broader, explanatory meanings. He has attempted to
identify particular features that reveal prehistoric natural conditions and habits
of human thought and behavior corresponding to strategic factors in the genesis of Shang culture. These features range from environmental circumstances,
manufacture of artifacts, ritual practice, to human mentality (Keightley 1978a,
1987, 2004). For example, Keightley pointed out that the geography of ancient
China can help to explain the cultural forms that developed there. The agrarian
basis of the culture bears on what appears to have been the relative unimpor-
tance of markets in early China. In addition, the major rivers flowed from west
to east, a natural condition that did not greatly encourage interregional trade,
because they flowed through latitudes where the natural environments were
similar. The lack of extensive trading networks in China may also be explained
by the widespread natural availability of resources needed for daily life. These
geographic features stand in clear contrast to those of ancient Mesopotamia,
where metal ores, hard stone, and good timber were all lacking and an extensive network of trade routes was crucial for social development (Keightley
2004). For Keightley, the underdevelopment of markets in early Chinese civilization is apparently unrelated to religious practice or political decisions, but
was determined by China's physical configuration.

As Keightley has stated, nobody can fully know what made the Chinese
Chinese, but by trying to understand the social mechanisms, cultural decisions, and ecological choices that people made, we can come closer to an
understanding of the factors that would have been involved in the process
leading to that distinctive outcome (Keightley 2004).

ANCIENT CHINA WITH OTHER PARTS OF THE WORLD

What makes Chinese culture different from that of other parts of the world
does, indeed, have much to do with China's geography. As discussed in Chapter
2, it traditionally has been suggested that Chinese culture and the Chinese state
arose largely in isolation, because other major centers of early civilization in the
Indus Valley and Mesopotamia were far away and difficult to reach, and their
interchange with China was minimal (Murphey 1972). Throughout this book
we have demonstrated that interactions between China and other parts of the
world occurred in prehistory, long before the Han dynasty established China's
first historically recorded regular trade routes through the western and southwestern frontiers. Communication through the northern routes apparently
existed in late Paleolithic times, evidenced by the wide dispersal of microlithic
technologies over the Eurasian steppe and northern China. Therefore, there

is probably no reason for similar interactions through the northern routes to have stopped in later times.

Archaeological data have shown that Chinese civilization could not have achieved such a high level of sophistication without adoption of many techno-logical innovations introduced from regions outside China. The most notable inventions include bronze metallurgy, chariots, and domesticated wheat, bar-ley, horses, cattle, and sheep/goats, all of which came to China from Central Asia (see Chapters 4 and 10). China's interactions with the Eurasian steppe may have taken place through multiple routes over the vast regions in the north and northwest, but the direct contacts are most likely to have been made with populations in the northern frontier who played an intermediate role between the two regions.

Southwestern China was also connected to South Asia in ancient times through a less well known communication route, which can be traced back at least to the second half of the first millennium BC. This ancient trade route linked Sichuan, via Yunnan and Burma, to India, also connecting farther to Central Asia and Europe. Material goods traded along this route probably included textiles, bamboo products, and salt from Sichuan and Yunnan, and cowry shells, glass beads, carnelian beads, and other valuables from South and Central Asia (Jiang, Y. 1995; Zhang, X. 1995). Such communications already may have developed in prehistory, exemplified by the large quantity of cowry shells found at Sanxingdui in Sichuan (Sichuansheng 1999).

Communication along the coastline, by seafaring technology, evidently developed during the Neolithic period. This capability enabled Neolithic people of the southeast coast to cross the Taiwan Strait, as revealed in the Dabenkeng culture, dated to as early as 4500 BC (Chang and Goodenough 1996). Ceramic objects resembling the Liangzhu style (3300–2000 BC) of the lower Yangzi River have been found at sites in the coastal areas of Shandong (Luan 1996: 57). Seeds of wheat (ca. 2000 BC), a northern crop, have been found in the southeast coastal site of Huangguashan in Fujian (Jiao 2007). How far the seafaring voyages may have reached is currently unclear, but it would not be surprising if communications between China and Japan had been facilitated by boat in prehistory. As demonstrated by An Zhimin (1984, 1990), material remains with characteristics of the Neolithic Yangzi River (e.g., *jue* earrings, pile-dwellings, and certain tools associated with rice cultivation) have been unearthed in Japan.

It is important to note that interactions with the outside world stimulated new social and technological development in China. Received foreign tech-nologies, however, were adapted innovatively by the Central Plain people to integrate them into existing indigenous sociopolitical and ideological systems. Therefore, relevant questions for future inquiry concern not only what partic-ular cultural elements were passed on from the steppe to China, but also how they were accepted and what role they played in the formation of Chinese civilization.

Whether newly introduced technologies entered China as a package or independently of one another is unclear. Once adopted in China, they seem to have spread slowly across a larger horizon. By the time of state formation, from Erlitou to Shang, almost all such technologies were used at heightened levels of concentration and intensification. The introduced domesticates, wheat, barley, sheep/goats, and cattle, first appeared in the late Neolithic and gradually became regular elements of Erlitou and Shang settlements, providing additional sources of food, allowing rapid population growth in urban centers, and facilitating territorial expansion of the early states. From this perspective, we would argue that the dynamic role of these improved agricultural technologies, during the formative period of civilization in China, was exerted not by heightened efficiency of tool materials (metal vs. stone) but by access to increased sources of nutritive energy.

Other introduced technologies, namely metallurgy, horses, and chariots, seem to have served a different function: creating and reinforcing social hierarchy. This function was not crystallized, however, until the formation of states. Small bronze tools (e.g., knives) and ornaments were used in many areas of north China in several late Neolithic cultures without being incorporated into their regular symbolic system to express social hierarchy. Only at Erlitou did bronze ritual vessels begin to be made. By imitating the forms of white pottery drinking vessels, bronze objects became integrated with the already established ritual systems. Similarly, horses as a form of protein were consumed by the Qijia culture people several hundred years before the late Shang; but only the royal elite at Yinxu seized the opportunity to create a new status symbol with horses and chariots. During the process of adoption and reformulation, these technologies helped to inspire new types of cultural value and new phases of social development in early Chinese civilization.

FORMATION OF CHINESE CIVILIZATION AND CULTURAL IDENTITY

As many scholars have pointed out, unlike the Mesopotamian civilization, in which external trade for obtaining both subsistence necessities and prestige goods was essential for its economy as well as for the formation of its political systems (e.g., Pollock 1999), ancient people in China largely relied on rich local resources for subsistence needs. Such relatively self-sufficient regional economic modes, nevertheless, were accompanied by active, long-distance exchange of luxuries and scarce raw materials, during prehistory as well as in early historical times. These activities were closely related to ritual practices involving certain types of prestige items, particularly those made of jade and bronze. Such ceremonial patterns would have helped to shape common belief systems, ritual behaviors, and symbolic assemblages over a broad region during the formative period of Chinese civilization.

In the Neolithic period, intercommunal relations, involving ritual activities and expressed through certain religious paraphernalia, were apparently decentralized, while also showing a trend of amalgamation among different local traditions. These processes helped to form some common values expressed in art forms. With the establishment of early dynastic capital cities in the Central Plain, however, a marked shift is observable, in which prestige goods and resources were extracted as tribute from the periphery to political centers. These developments may have helped to create the concept of *Zhongguo*, the Central State, suggesting that people in the Central Plain regarded their land as the center of the known world. This term first occurred in the inscription on an early Western Zhou bronze, the *hezun* vessel, recording that King Cheng of Zhou built the capital Chengzhou in *Zhongguo*, referring to the Yiluo region; but the underlying conception of such political geography may have already existed during the Shang dynasty (Hsu and Linduff 1988: 96–101). This privileged notion may not have been acknowledged by all regional polities outside the Central Plain, but it is difficult for us to evaluate their views without a written record from these contemporary cultures.

The formation of new ethnic self-consciousness during the early dynastic period, particularly the Shang and Western Zhou, may have to do with increased contacts between the Central Plain's population and people from remote regions, particularly the pastoralists in the northern frontiers and beyond (Chen, L. 1989; Fei, X. 1989; Wang, M.-k. 2001).

RISE AND FALL OF COMPLEX SOCIETIES

Although much has been said about the rise of civilization in past decades, a new research topic, concerned with the collapse of complex society and civilization, has gained greater interest in recent years (e.g., Diamond 2005; McAnany and Yoffee 2010; Tainter 1988; Yoffee and Cowgill 1991). Two general approaches are commonly taken. One approach (climatic explanation) identifies spatial and temporal correlations between climatic changes and drastic transformations of complex social systems, and regards environmental catastrophes as a major factor in the fall of civilizations (e.g., Diamond 2005; Weiss and Raymond 2001; Wu, W. and Liu 2004). The other approach highlights human resilience (resilience theory), viewing societies as mechanisms with an inbuilt capability for dealing with external challenges; accordingly, changes are episodic, with periods of slow accumulation of natural capital punctuated by sudden releases and reorganizations of these legacies (Redman 2005; Redman and Kinzig 2003). Supporting the latter view, a number of case studies have shown that societies often modify their practices successfully in response to perceived crises, but it is possible that responses to recurrent short-term crises might not solve some of the more persistent and severe problems (McAnany and Yoffee 2010; Rosen 2007b). We believe that both approaches have their merits for understanding past human-environment relationships. We need to understand the levels of environmental impact and to evaluate social strategies (that may or may not have been successful) in response to the external challenges.

Collapse is recurrent in human history, but it is important to distinguish the collapse of a state (a political organization) from the collapse of civilization (a great cultural tradition). As Yoffee (1991) has discussed them, these two terms represent different concepts, and the processes of their collapse manifest separate trajectories of social change. The collapse of a civilization is rare, represented only by the Mesopotamian example. In contrast, the collapse of a state, referring to the fragmentation of a large, centralized political system, is more common. Examples can be found in Maya and Harappa civilizations.

As demonstrated in previous chapters, there were several episodes of rise and fall of early complex societies in different parts of China during the Neolithic times, such as the Hongshan, Liangzhu, and Shijiahe cultures. In these cases it seems to have been a total collapse of political organization along with a great cultural tradition, as indicated by the disappearance of material culture together with depopulation at a regional level. The causal factors for these collapses have often been attributed to climatic change, ecological catastrophe, and human failure to overcome external pressures.

Bronze Age China also witnessed episodes of environmental deterioration, which nevertheless did not always lead to collapse. The Erlitou state, for instance, emerged as a regional superpower during a period of climatic fluctuation when population in many other regions declined. The rise of Erlitou seems to serve as a good example to support the resilience theory, but the underlying mechanism of this transition is still elusive. Wang Wei (2004) has suggested environmental and economic factors to explain the rise of early states. First, the Erlitou culture is found at relatively high altitude in sites distributed around the Song Mountains; this strategic placement no doubt helped to prevent destruction by large-scale flooding, which may have indeed destroyed Neolithic settlements in many low-altitude regions, particularly in the Yangzi River Valley. Second, the practice of multicropping, used in the middle Yellow River region, which included mainly millets, soybeans, rice, and wheat, may have helped to sustain the society better than did the agricultural systems of those regions where only rice was the main staple because, as Wang suggested, millets are more resilient than rice to climatic fluctuations, and a diversified agricultural regime would also have helped to buffer crop failure.

This argument seems to explain the cultural continuity evident around the Song Mountains region from the Longshan to the Erlitou culture, but it does not address why the state-level organization developed at this time. It is also unclear how effective the multicropping system was in the Erlitou culture, as soybeans, rice, and wheat only account for small percentages of plant remains in archaeobotanical assemblages (Lee, G. and Bestel 2007; Lee, G. et al. 2007; Zhao, Zhijun 2009). Previous studies have demonstrated a rapid population increase in the Erlitou core area (Liu, L. 2006: 182–6; Liu, L. et al. 2002–2004; Xu, H. et al. 2005). Therefore, it remains to be explained why population growth, which was an important component of state formation, took place in the Yiluo Basin during a period of unstable climate.

Based on the results of geographic information system (GIS) modeling, the Erlitou population in the Yiluo Basin, at 78 percent of maximum carrying capacity, exceeded the optimum ratio (Qiao 2007). The Erlitou population appears to have produced more food than ever before, using agricultural technology similar to that used in the previous late Longshan period. A crucial social factor in this scenario is leadership strategy, in that rulers of the Erlitou state were able to make more people work harder, either by force or by persuasion. This situation would have entailed the elite's manipulation of ritual and political power, a topic that still needs further research.

There were also events of decline and regeneration during the transitional period from Zhengzhou to Anyang, known as the middle Shang, when the primary center at Zhengzhou disappeared and multiple smaller centers emerged over the landscape. A traditional explanation for these changes is relocation of the capital city; but the situation apparently involved multiple coexisting "capitals," rather than a unilineal succession within a single royal lineage, as described in ancient texts. This situation is particularly clear in the Shandong area, where regional centers increased in number and continuously flourished from early Shang to late Shang (Fang, H. 2009). This development may be explained as the collapse of one kind of social organization (monocentered Erligang state) and its replacement by another one (a multicentered state system), leading later to a new phase of recentralization (late Shang centered in Anyang). During this transition the great cultural tradition, which is archaeologically recognizable as Shang, persisted. Thus, early Bronze Age Shang culture exhibits an example of regeneration of civilization, in which the political system collapsed but the cultural tradition continued. A similar scenario can be found in the Han dynasty, more than a thousand years later, in which the collapse of a political system by no means presupposes a similar breakdown of existing civilizational values (Hsu 1991).

CONCLUSIONS

Chinese history often has been described as the long and enduring record of a civilization that held together a large but diverse population for millennia. It is not the political systems that have persisted; rather, it is the civilizational values, evidently deeply rooted in ancient times, that have facilitated the longevity of Chinese culture.

As we have attempted to illustrate in this book, the pathways to Chinese civilization were long, bumpy, and multidirectional. This civilization has experienced great environmental challenges, episodic rise and fall of complex societies, social conflict and political controversy, unintended social transformations, and foreign influences. We may never be able to demonstrate how Chineseness was formed or to fully understand what Chineseness was in ancient times. In addition, there are always more research questions than answers. We hope that this book may help to open a window that allows us to see more clearly the long social progress of more than 8,000 years, during which small villages were transformed into a great civilization in the land that we call China today.

APPENDIX

HORSE BONES IN FAUNAL ASSEMBLAGES FROM NEOLITHIC AND EARLY BRONZE AGE SITES IN NORTH CHINA

Site	Culture Chronology (BC)	Horse NISP (% of total)	Total Fauna (NISP)	References
Neolithic				
Banpo, Xi'an, Shaanxi	Yangshao 5000–3000	4 *E.* cf. *przewalskii*	Unknown	(Li, Y. and Han 1963)
Gaodui, Linfen, Shanxi	Yangshao 5000–3000	Present	Unknown	(Zhang, D. 1956)
Guantaoyuan, Baoji, Shaanxi	Late Yangshao 3500–3000	1 (1.4%) *E. przewalskii*	70	(Hu, S. 2007)
Miaozigou, Chayouqian Banner, Inner Mongolia	Late Yangshao 3800–3000	12 (5.13%) *E.* cf. *przewalskii*	234	(Huang, Y. 2003)
Dabagou, Chayouqianqi, Inner Mongolia	Late Yangshao 3800–3000	2 (0.88%) cf. *E. przewalskii*	227	(Huang, Y. 2003)
Zhuanlongcang, Baotou, Inner Mongolia	Microlithic	Present	Unknown	(Wang, Y. 1957)
Wuzhuangguoliang, Jingbian, Shaanxi	Late Yangshao 3500–3000	2 NISP 1 MNI *Equus* sp.	Unknown 149 MNI	(Hu, S. and Sun 2005)
Majiawan, Yongjing, Gansu	Majiayao 3000–2500	Present	–	(Xie, D. 1975a)
Xicha, Qingshuihe, Inner Mongolia	Longshan 3000–2000	4 (10.81%) *Equus* sp.	37	(Yang, C. 2007)
Shizhaocun, Tianshui, Gansu	Majiayao 3000–2500	1 (0.08%)	1,202	(Zhou, B. 1999)
Xishanping, Tianshui, Gansu	Majiayao 3000–2500	1 (0.4%)	245	(Zhou, B. 1999)
Huoshiliang and Yuanxihaizi, Yulin, Shaanxi	Longshan-Erligou 2100–1900	3 (0.2%) *Equus* sp.	1,111	(Hu, S. et al. 2008)

(*continued*)

Site	Culture Chronology (BC)	Horse NISP (% of total)	Total Fauna (NISP)	References
Beiwutun, Dalian, Shandong	Xiaozhushan 4500–3500	1	–	(Fu, R. 1994)
Chengziya, Licheng, Shandong	Longshan 2500–2000	Present	–	(Liang, S. 1934)
Bronze Age				
Dahezhuang, Yongjing, Gansu	Qijia 2300–1900	5	–	(Zhongguo Shehui Kexueyuan 1974)
Qinweijia, Yongjing, Gansu	Qijia 2300–1900	Present	–	(Xie, D. 1975b)
Jijiachuan, Yongjing, Gansu	Xindian 1600–600	Present	–	(Xie, D. 1980)
Zhangjiazui, Yongjing, Gansu	Qijia 2300–1900	3	–	(Xie, D. 1980)
Xicha, Qingshuihe, Inner Mongolia	Late Shang – early W. Zhou	531 (9.1%) *Equus* sp.	5,835	(Yang, C. 2007)
Lijiaya, Qingjian, Shaanxi	Late Shang – early W. Zhou	Present	Unknown	(Zhang, Y. and Lü 1988)
Qiaobei, Fushan, Shanxi	Late Shang	2 complete skeletons with a chariot	–	(Guojia 2005a)
Laoniupo, Xi'an, Shaanxi	Late Shang	5 complete skeletons, incl. 2 horses with a chariot	–	(Liu, S. 2001)
Nanshacun, Huaxian, Shaanxi	Possible Shang	2 complete skeletons in a pit	–	(Wang, Z. and Song 2001)
Yinxu, Anyang, Henan	Late Shang	2 teeth: *E. prvewalskii*; More than 300 sacrificial horses	–	(Teilhard de Chardin and Young 1936; table 11.2 of Linduff 2003)
Qianzhangda, Tengzhou, Shandong	Late Shang	5 horse-chariots with 10 horses; 4 pits with 5 horses;	–	(Zhongguo Shehui Kexueyuan 2005)
Guantaoyuan, Baoji, Shaaxni	Western Zhou 1045–710	9 (32.1%) *E. przewalskii*	28	(Hu, S. 2007)
Huoshaogou, Yumen, Gansu	Siba 2000–1600	Present	–	(Gansusheng Bowuguan 1979)
Ganggangwa and Huoshiliang, Gansu	2000 BC – AD 700	Present	–	(Dodson et al. 2009)

GLOSSARY

Altai/A'ertai (Mountains)	阿尔泰 (山)	Beiwutun	北吴屯
Anban	案板	Beixin	北辛
Antu	安图	Beixinzhuang	北辛庄
Anxi (in Gansu)	安西	Beiyinyangying	北阴阳营
Anxi (in Zhejiang)	安溪	*bi*	璧
Anyang	安阳	Bianbiandong	扁扁洞
Ao	敖	Bianxianwang	边线王
Aohan	敖汉	Bing	丙
Ba	巴	Binzhou	滨州
Ba (River)	灞 (河)	Bo	亳
Badanjilin	巴丹吉林	*bo*	钵
Baijia	白家	Bo'ai	博爱
Baishantang	白山堂	*bu*	卜
Baiyangdian	白洋淀	*cai*	采
Baiyinchanghan	白音长汗	Cangyuan	沧源
Baiying	白营	Caoxieshan	草鞋山
Bancun	班村	Chahai	查海
Banpo	半坡	*chan*	铲
Banshan	半山	Changbai (Mountains)	长白 (山)
Banzhijian (River)	半支箭 (河)	Changbaishan (in Shandong)	长白山
Baode	保德	Changdu	昌都
Baodun	宝墩	Changfen	长坟
Baoji	宝鸡	Changguogou	昌果沟
Baoshan (in Yunnan)	保山	Changshan	常山
Baoshan (in Shaanxi)	宝山	Chayouqian	察右前
Baota	宝塔	Cheng	成
Baotou	包头	Chengbeixi	城背溪
Baozitou	豹子头	Chenggu	城固
Bashidang	八十垱	Chenghu	澄湖
bei	杯	Chengtoushan	城头山
Beifudi	北福地	Chengzhou	成周
Beiniantou	北埝头	Chengzi	呈子
Beishouling	北首岭	Chengziya	城子崖
beitu	北土	Chifeng	赤峰

403

Chong (Mountains)	崇 (山)	Diaolongbei	雕龙碑
Chunban (River)	椿板 (河)	Diaotonghuan	吊桶环
Chuodun	绰墩	*ding*	鼎
cigu	慈姑	Dingcun	丁村
Cishan	磁山	Dinggong	丁公
cong	琮	Dingshadi	丁沙地
Dabagou	大坝沟	Dingsishan	顶蛳山
Dabenkeng	大坌坑	Donghuishan	东灰山
Dabie (Mountains)	大别 (山)	Donghulin	东胡林
Dadai Liji	大戴礼记	Donglongshan	东龙山
Dadianzi	大甸子	Dongshan	东山
Dadiwan	大地湾	Dongshancun	东山村
Dagudui	大固堆	Dongshanzui	东山嘴
Dahaimeng	大海猛	dongshimu	洞室墓
Dahecun	大河村	Dongtiaoxi (River)	东苕溪
Dahezhuang	大何庄	Dongting (Lake)	洞庭 (湖)
Daihai (Lake)	岱海	dongtu	东土
Dajing	大井	Dongxiafeng	东下冯
Dakou	大口	Dongxiang	东乡
dakouzun	大口尊	Dongyi	东夷
Dali	大荔	Dongzhai	东寨
Daling (River)	大凌 (河)	*dou*	豆
Dalongtan	大龙潭	Doujitai	斗鸡台
Damaoshan	大帽山	Duijiugou	碓臼沟
Damudantun	大牡丹屯	Duimenshan	对门山
Dan (River)	丹 (江)	*duoyuan yiti*	多元一体
Dantu (in Jiangsu)	丹徒	Dzungaria/Zhunge'er	准格尔
Dantu (in Shandong)	丹土	Egou	莪沟
dao	刀	Elunchun	鄂伦春
Daoxian	道县	ercengtai	二层台
Daqing	大青	Erdaojingzi	二道井子
Dashanqian	大山前	Erdaoliang	二道梁
Dashigu	大师姑	Erligang	二里岗
Dasikong	大司空	Erlitou	二里头
Dasima	大司马	Ewenke	鄂温克
Datuotou	大坨头	*fang*	方
Daundong	多雪洞	Fangcheng	方城
Dawenkou	大汶口	*fangding*	方鼎
Daxi	大溪	Fangshan	房山
Daxing'an (Mountains)	大兴安 (岭)	Fanshan	反山
Daxinzhuang	大辛庄	Fantang	繁汤
Dayan	大岩	Feijiahe	费家河
Dayangzhou	大洋洲	Fenghuangshan	凤凰山
Daye	大冶	Fengtai	丰台
dayishang	大邑商	Fengzhai	冯寨
Dengfeng	登封	*fu* (axe)	斧
Dengjiawan	邓家湾	*fu* (cauldron)	釜
Deqing	德清	Fucheng	府城
Dianjiangtai	点将台	Fudian	府店

Fufeng	扶风	Haicangsi	海藏寺
Fuguodun	富国墩	Haidai	海岱
Fuhao	妇好	Haimenkou	海门口
Fuquanshan	福泉山	Hami	哈密
Fushan	浮山	Han (people)	汉
Fuxin	阜新	Han (River)	汉 (江)
Gacha	嘎查	Hanshan	含山
Gamatai	尕马台	Hanzhong	汉中
Gan (River)	赣 (江)	Hanzhuo	寒浞
Ganggangwa	缸缸洼	Haochuan	好川
Ganguya	干骨崖	Haojiatai	郝家台
Ganquan	甘泉	*he*	盉
gaobingbei	高柄杯	Hedanjia	河亶甲
Gaocheng	藁城	Hedong (Salt Lake)	河东 (盐池)
Gaodui	高堆	Helan (Mountains)	贺兰 (山)
Gaohong	高红	Hemudu	河姆渡
Gaomiao	高庙	Hengshan	横山
Gaoshan	高山	Hengxuli	横圩里
Gaotaishan	高台山	Hengzhen	横镇
Gaotousi	高头寺	Hetian	和田
Gaoyou	高邮	Hexi	河西
ge	戈	Hezhe	赫哲
gegen	葛根	*hezun*	何尊
gongxingqi	弓形器	Hong (River)	红 (河)
Gongyi	巩义	Honghuatao	红花套
Gu (Mountains)	鼓 (山)	Hongshan	红山
guajianggou	挂缰钩	Hongshanhou	红山后
guan	罐	*Hou Hanshu*	后汉书
Guanghe	广河	Hougang	后冈
Guangrao	广饶	Houli	后李
Guangshe	光社	Houtaizi	后台子
Guanhugada	关胡疙瘩	Houyi	后羿
Guanmiaoshan	关庙山	Houzhaizimao	后寨子峁
Guantaoyuan	关桃园	*hu*	壶
guanzhuangqi	管状器	Huadizui	花地嘴
Guanzi	管子	Huai (River)	淮 (河)
Guchengcun	古城村	Huairou	怀柔
Guchengzhai	古城寨	Huaizhenfang	怀珍坊
gui (pitcher)	鬶	*huan*	环
gui (vessel)	簋	Huan (Duke)	桓 (公)
Guifang	鬼方	Huanbei	洹北
Guilin	桂林	*huang*	璜
Guilongyan	桂龙岩	Huang (Yellow River)	黄 (河)
Guinan	贵南	Huang (River, in Qinghai)	湟 (水)
Gumugou/Qäwrighul	古墓沟	Huangdi	黄帝
Gun	鲧	Huangguashan	黄瓜山
Guojiacun	郭家村	Huanghuai	黄淮
Guoyu	国语	Huangniangniangtai	皇娘娘台
Hai (River)	海 (河)	Huangpi	黄陂

Huangqihai (Lake)	黄旗海	Jinzishan	金子山
Huaxia	华夏	Jiuquan	酒泉
Huaxian	华县	Jixian	吉县
Huayin	华阴	*jue* (earring)	玦
Huayuanzhuang	花园庄	*jue* (hoe)	镢
Huiguanshan	汇观山	*jue* (vessel)	爵
Huiluogou	惠落沟	Jurong	句容
Huiwei	辉卫	Juxian	莒县
Huixian	辉县	Kalaqin	喀喇沁
Huizui	灰嘴	Kangjia	康家
Hujiawuchang	胡家屋场	*Kaogu*	考古
Hulu (River)	葫芦 (河)	*Kaogu Xuebao*	考古学报
huo	获	Karuo	卡若
Huogeqi	霍各乞	Kayue	卡约
Huoshaogou	火烧沟	Kazuo	喀左
Huoshiliang	火石梁	Keqiutou	壳丘头
Hushu	湖熟	Könchi/Kongque (River)	孔雀 (河)
Hutougou	虎头沟	Kuahuqiao	跨湖桥
Hutouliang	虎头梁	*kuixingqi*	盔形器
Huzhu	互助	Kunlun (Mountains)	昆仑 (山)
Ji (River)	济 (水)	Kunshan	昆山
jia	斝	Laiwu	莱芜
Jiahu	贾湖	Lajia	喇家
Jialing (River)	嘉陵 (江)	Lancang (River)	澜沧 (江)
Jian (Lake)	剑 (湖)	Langjun	郎君
Jianchuan	剑川	Lanjia	兰家
jiandiping	尖底瓶	Lantian	蓝田
Jianghan	江汉	Laoguantai	老官台
Jiangxian	绛县	Laoha (River)	老哈 (河)
Jiangzhai	姜寨	Laohushan	老虎山
Jianping	建平	Laoniupo	老牛坡
Jiaochangpu	教场铺	Laoshan	老山
Jiaodong	胶东	Ledu	乐都
Jiaxian	佳县	*lei*	罍
Jichang	吉长	*leixing*	类型
Jiepian	戒篇	*li*	鬲
Jijiachuan	姬家川	Li (Mountains)	骊 (山)
Jijiaocheng	鸡叫城	Liangcheng	凉城
Jimingcheng	鸡鸣城	Liangchengzhen	两城镇
Jinan	济南	Liangzhu	良渚
Jingbian	靖边	*lian'ou*	莲藕
Jingjie	旌介	Liao (River)	辽 (河)
Jingnansi	荆南寺	Liaodong	辽东
Jinguishan	金龟山	Liaoxi	辽西
Jingyanggang	景阳岗	Licheng	历城
Jinmen	金门	Lijiacun	李家村
Jinniushan	金牛山	Lijiagou	李家沟
Jinshachang	金沙厂	Lijiang (River)	漓 (江)
Jinyu	晋语	Lijiaya	李家崖

Lin (River)	临 (河)
Linfen	临汾
Lingbao	灵宝
Lingjiatan	凌家滩
Lingnan	岭南
Lingshi	灵石
Lingui	临桂
Lingyanghe	凌阳河
Lingyuan	凌源
Linjia	林家
Linli	临澧
Lintan	临潭
Lintao	临洮
Lintong	临潼
Linxi	林西
Linzheyu	林遮峪
Linzi	临淄
Lishui (River)	澧 (水)
liu	六
Liujia	刘家
Liulin	柳林
Liuwan	柳湾
Lixian	澧县
Liyang	澧阳
Longgangsi	龙岗寺
longgu	龙骨
Longqiuzhuang	龙虬庄
Longshan	龙山
Longwangchan	龙王辿
lu	卤
Luan (River)	滦 (河)
Lucun	卢村
Luo (River)	洛 (河)
Luojiabailing	罗家柏岭
Lujiahe	路家河
Luojiajiao	罗家角
Luonan	洛南
Luoyang	洛阳
Luoyang Xijiao	洛阳西郊
Lushanmao	芦山峁
luxiachen	卤小臣
Lüliang (Mountains)	吕梁 (山)
ma	马
Ma'an	马安
Machang	马厂
Mafang	马方
Majiabang	马家浜
Majiawan	马家湾
Majiayao	马家窑
Majiayuan	马家塬
Mamu (River)	马牧 (河)
Mangcheng	芒城
Manhan	蛮汗
mantian xingdou	满天星斗
Maoqinggou	毛庆沟
Maqiao	马桥
Mawangdui	马王堆
Menbanwan	门板湾
Mengchang	蒙城
Menggezhuang	孟各庄
Mengyin	蒙阴
Mengzhuang	孟庄
Mentougou	门头沟
Mianchi	渑池
Miaodigou	庙底沟
Miaohoushan	庙后山
Miaopubeidi	苗圃北地
Miaoyan	庙岩
Miaozigou	庙子沟
Min (River)	岷 (江)
Ming (River)	洺 (河)
Minggonglu	铭功路
Minhe	民和
Minle	民乐
mobang	磨棒
Mogou	磨沟
Mojiaoshan	莫角山
mopan	磨盘
Mopandun	磨盘墩
Nanguan	南关
Nanguanwai	南关外
Nanjiaokou	南交口
Nanling	南岭
Nanning	南宁
Nanshacun	南沙村
Nanshunchengjie	南顺城街
Nantaizi	南台子
nantu	南土
Nanwa	南洼
Nanyang	南阳
Nanzhuangtou	南庄头
Nenjiang	嫩江
Nihewan	泥河湾
Nileke	尼勒克
Ningshao	宁绍
Ningxiang	宁乡
Niuchang	牛场
Niucheng	牛城

Niucun Gucheng	牛村古城	Qujialing	屈家岭
Niuheliang	牛河梁	*quxi leixing*	区系类型
Nu (River)	怒 (江)	Ren	人
Nulasai	奴拉赛	Renfang	人方
Ordos/E'erduosi	鄂尔多斯	renshu	荏菽
pan	盘	rongshu	戎菽
Pangeng	盘庚	Ruichang	瑞昌
Panlong (lake)	盘龙 (湖)	Ruicheng	芮城
Panlongcheng	盘龙城	Saidun	塞墩
Peiligang	裴李岗	Salawusu	萨拉乌苏
pen	盆	Sanfangwan	三房湾
Penghu	澎湖	Sanggan (River)	桑干 (河)
Pengtoushan	彭头山	Sanxingcun	三星村
ping	瓶	Sanxingdui	三星堆
Pinghu	平湖	Sanyuangong	三元宫
Pingliangtai	平粮台	Shaguoliang	沙锅梁
Pingtan	平潭	Shajing	沙井
Pishan	毗山	Shawoli	沙窝李
Pujiang	浦江	Shandan	山丹
Pupiao	蒲缥	Shangqiu	商丘
Puyang (River)	浦阳 (江)	Shangshan	上山
Qi (state)	齐	Shangzhai	上宅
Qi	启	Shanrong	山戎
Qianbuxia	前埠下	Shantaisi	山台寺
Qiang	羌	Shanxian	陕县
Qiangfang	羌方	*shanyao*	山药
Qianshanyang	钱山漾	Shawoli	沙窝李
Qiantang (River)	钱塘 (江)	Shazui	沙嘴
Qianzhangda	前掌大	Shengzhou	嵊州
Qiaobei	桥北	Shenmu	神木
Qiemurqiek/Ke'ermuqi	克尔木齐	Shigu	石固
Qijia	齐家	Shihushan	石虎山
Qijiaping	齐家坪	Shijia	史家
Qilian (Mountains)	祁连 (山)	Shijiahe	石家河
Qin (River)	沁 (河)	*Shijing*	诗经
Qin'an	秦安	Shilingxia	石岭下
Qingjian	清涧	Shiluoluoshan	石摞摞山
Qingliangsi	清凉寺	Shimao	石峁
Qinglongshan	青龙山	Shixia	石峡
Qingpu	青浦	Shiyu	峙峪
Qingshantou	青山头	Shizhaishan	石寨山
Qingshui (River)	清水 (河)	Shizhaocun	师赵村
Qingshuihe	清水河	Shizitan	柿子滩
Qingyang	庆阳	Shu	蜀
Qinling (Mountains)	秦岭	*shu* (broomcorn millet)	黍
Qinweijia	秦魏家	*shu* (soybean)	菽
Qiongfang (or Gongfang)	舌方	Shuanghe	双河
Qiuwan	丘湾	Shuangji (River)	双洎 (河)
quan Han	全汉	Shuangtuozi	双砣子

Shuiquan	水泉	Tianshui	天水
Shule (River)	疏勒 (河)	Tianwang	田旺
Shun	舜	*tianxia*	天下
Si (River)	泗 (水)	Tieban (River)	铁板 (河)
Siba	四坝	Tiesanlu	铁三路
Sibatan	四坝滩	Tieshenggou	铁生沟
Sidun	寺墩	tiliangyou	提梁卣
sifang	四方	Tonggushan	铜鼓山
Sihailongwan (Lake)	四海龙湾 (湖)	Tonglin	桐林
situ	四土	Tongling	铜岭
Siwa	寺洼	Tonglüshan	铜绿山
Song (Mountains)	嵩 (山)	*tongpao*	铜泡
Songnen	松嫩	Tongshan	铜山
Songze	崧泽	*tu*	土
su	粟	Tufang	土方
Subutun	苏埠屯	Wadian	瓦店
Suichang	遂昌	*wan*	碗
Sun Yat-sen	孙逸仙 (孙中山)	Wangchenggang	王城岗
Suzhou	苏州	Wangdong	王洞
Tarbagatai (Mountains)	塔尔巴哈台 (山)	*Wanghuijie*	王会解
Ta'er (Mountains)	塔儿 (山)	Wangjiashan	王家山
Tai (Lake)	太 (湖)	Wangjiazui	王家嘴
Tai'an	泰安	Wangjinglou	望京楼
Taihang (Mountains)	太行 (山)	Wangzhuang	王庄
Taihu (Mountains)	太湖 (山)	Wannian	万年
Taixi	台西	Wayaozui	瓦窑嘴
Taiyi (Mountains)	泰沂 (山)	Wei (River)	渭 (河)
Tanghu	唐户	Weidun	圩墩
Tangjiagang	汤家岗	Weifang (in Hebei)	围坊
Tangye	唐冶	Weifang (in Shandong)	潍坊
Tangzi	塘子	Weiyingzi	魏营子
Tanheli	炭河里	*wen yi*	文邑
Tanjialing	谭家岭	*weng*	瓮
Tanshishan	昙石山	Wenjiashan	文家山
Tao (River)	洮 (河)	*Wenwu*	文物
Tao'er (River)	洮儿 (河)	*wu*	巫
Taojiahu	陶家湖	Wubu	吴堡
Taosi	陶寺	Wucheng	吴城
Tarim/Talimu	塔里木	Wucun	五村
Tenggeli	腾格里	Wudi	五帝
Tenghualuo	藤花落	Wuding	武丁
Tengxian	滕县	Wuding (River)	无定 (河)
Tengzhou	滕州	Wuerji	乌尔吉
Tian (Mountains)	天 (山)	Wujiacun	吴家村
Tianluoshan	田螺山	Wujin	武进
Tianmen	天门	Wulajie	乌拉街
Tianmu (Mountains)	天目 (山)	Wulatehou	乌拉特后
Tianposhuiku	天坡水库	Wulian	五莲
Tianshanbeilu	天山北路	Wuluo (River)	坞罗 (河)

Wuluoxipo	坞罗西坡	Xilamulun (River)	西拉木伦 (河)
Wushan	巫山	Xindian	辛店
Wuwei	武威	Xin'gan	新干
Wuxian	吴县	Xing'an (Mountains)	兴安 (岭)
Wuyang	舞阳	Xinglonggou	兴隆沟
Wuzhi	武陟	Xinglongwa	兴隆洼
Wuzhuangguoliang	五庄果墚	Xingyang	荥阳
wuzu gonghe	五族共和	Xinhua	新华
xi	觋	Xinmi	新密
Xi (River)	西 (河)	Xintai	新泰
Xi Qiang Zhuan	西羌传	Xinzhai	新砦
Xiachuan	卜川	Xinzheng	新郑
Xiajiadian	夏家店	Xipo	西坡
Xiajiang	峡江	Xishan	西山
Xiajin	卜靳	Xishanping	西山坪
Xian	先	Xishuipo	西水坡
Xi'an	西安	Xishuiquan	西水泉
Xiang (place)	相	*xitu*	西土
Xiang (River)	湘 (江)	Xiuyan	岫岩
Xiangfen	襄汾	Xizhai	西寨
Xianrendong	仙人洞	Xu (River)	滑 (河)
Xiantouling	咸头岭	Xubaocun	徐堡村
Xiao (River)	萧 (河)	Xue (River)	薛 (河)
Xiaofushan	小福山	Xue (state)	薛
Xiaogushan	小孤山	Xuegucheng	薛故城
Xiaohe	小河	Xuejiagang	薛家岗
Xiaoheyan	小河沿	Xujiayao	许家窑
Xiaohuangshan	小黄山	Xushui	徐水
Xiaojiawuji	肖家屋脊	Xuzhou	徐州
Xiaojin	晓锦	Yalinban	雅林办
Xiaojingshan	小荆山	Yalu (River)	鸭绿 (江)
Xiaoling (River)	小凌 (河)	Yamansukuang	雅满苏矿
Xiaomeiling (Mountains)	小梅岭	*yan*	甗
Xiaomintun	孝民屯	Yan (Mountains)	燕 (山)
Xiaoshan	萧山	Yan (River)	延 (河)
Xiaoshuangqiao	小双桥	Yan'an	延安
Xiaotun	小屯	Yandian	盐店
Xiaozhushan	小珠山	Yangcheng	阳城
Xiapu	霞浦	Yangdun	杨墩
Xiaqiyuan	下七垣	Yangguanzhai	杨官寨
Xia–Shang–Zhou	夏商周	Yangshan	阳山
Xiasiwan	下寺湾	Yangshao	仰韶
Xiaxian	夏县	Yangxian	洋县
Xiaxiaozheng	夏小正	Yangzi (River)	扬子 (长江)
Xibeigang	西北冈	Yanjiagang	阎家岗
Xicha	西岔	Yanjiagou	阎家沟
Xihe	西河	Yanjinggou	盐井沟
Xijincheng	西金城	Yanshi	偃师
Xikangliu	西康留	Yao	尧

Yao (River)	姚 (江)
Yaoshan	姚山
Yaowangcheng	尧王城
yazhang	牙璋
Yazi (River)	鸭子 (河)
Yi (people)	夷
yi (residential cluster)	邑
yi (vessel)	匜
yigupai	疑古派
Yi Zhou Shu	逸周书
Yijinhuoluo	伊金霍洛
Yiluo (River)	伊洛 (河)
Yin (River)	阴 (河)
Yingwoshu	鹰窝树
Yinjiacheng	尹家城
Yinxiangcheng	阴湘城
Yinxu	殷墟
Yiyuan	沂源
Yong (River)	邕 (江)
Yongji	永吉
Yongjing	永靖
Yonglang	涌浪
Yongning	邕宁
Yongshan	永善
You (River)	右 (江)
Yu (the Great)	禹
yu (taro)	芋
yu (vessel)	盂
yuan	瑗
Yuan (River)	沅 (江)
Yuanmou	元谋
Yuanqu	垣曲
Yuanshan	圆山
Yuanxihaizi	园西海子
Yuchanyan	玉蟾岩
Yuchisi	尉迟寺
yue	钺
Yuegezhuang	岳各庄
Yueshi	岳石
Yuezhuang	月庄
Yufucheng	鱼凫城
Yugong	禹贡
Yuhang	余杭
Yujiagou	于家沟
Yulin	榆林
Yumen	玉门
yunleiwen	云雷纹
Yunxian	郧县
Yuxi (River)	裕溪 (河)

yuxingqi	盂形器
Yuyao	余姚
zao	灶
Zaojiaoshu	皂角树
Zaoshi	皂市
Zengpiyan	甑皮岩
Zhaimao	寨峁
zhang (ritual blades)	璋
Zhang (River)	漳 (河)
Zhangjiagang	张家港
Zhangjiazui	张家咀
Zhangqiu	章丘
Zhangshu	樟树
Zhaobaogou	赵宝沟
Zhaojiazhuang	赵家庄
Zhaolingshan	赵陵山
Zhecheng	柘城
Zhen (River)	溱 (河)
Zhengzhou	郑州
Zhenzhumen	珍珠门
Zhichengbei	枝城北
zhijia	支架
zhijiao	支脚
zhizuo	支座
zhongguo	中国
Zhongtiao (Mountain)	中条 (山)
Zhongyi (River)	中易 (水)
Zhongyuan	中原
Zhoujiazhuang	周家庄
Zhoukoudian	周口店
Zhouliangyuqiao	周梁玉桥
Zhouyuan	周原
Zhu (River)	珠 (江)
Zhuanglixi	庄里西
Zhuangqiaofen	庄桥坟
Zhuanlongcang	转龙藏
Zhuannian	转年
Zhuanshanzi	转山子
Zhucheng	诸城
Zhudingyuan	铸鼎原
Zhukaigou	朱开沟
Zibo	淄博
Zijingshan	紫荆山
Zizhou	子洲
Zizhucun	紫竹村
Zoumaling	走马岭
Zouping	邹平
zun	尊
Zuo (River)	左 (江)

REFERENCES

Adams, R. E. W. and Richard C. Jones, 1981,
Spatial patterns and regional growth among
Classic Maya cities. *American Antiquity* 46(2):
301–22.

Aikens, C. Melvin and Takeru Akazawa, 1996,
The Pleistocene-Holocene transition in Japan
and adjacent northeast Asia. In *Humans at
the End of the Ice Age: The Archaeology of
the Pleistocene-Holocene Transition*, edited by
Lawrence G. Straus, Berit V. Eriksen, Jon M.
Erlandson, and David R. Yesner, pp. 215–27.
Plenum Press, New York.

Albarella, Umberto, Keith Dobney, and Peter
Rowley-Conway, 2006, The domestication
of the pig (*Sus scrofa*): New challenges and
approaches. In *Documenting Domestication: New
Genetic and Archaeological Paradigms*, edited by
M. A. Zeder, D. G. Bradley, E. Emshwiller,
and B. D. Smith, pp. 209–27. University of
California Press, Berkeley.

Aldenderfer, Mark and Yinong Zhang, 2004,
The prehistory of the Tibetan Plateau to
the seventh century A.D.: Perspectives and
research from China and the west since 1950.
Journal of World Prehistory 18(1):1–55.

Allan, Sarah, 1993, Art and meaning. In *The
Problem of Meaning in Early Chinese Ritual Bronzes*, edited by Roderick Whitfield,
pp. 9–33. University of London, London.

———, 2007, Erlitou and the formation of
Chinese civilization: Toward a new paradigm.
The Journal of Asian Studies 66:461–96.

Allard, Francis, 2001, Mortuary ceramics and
social organization in the Dawenkou and
Majiayao cultures. *Journal of East Asian Archaeology* 3(3–4):1–22.

An, Cheng-Bang, Zhao-Dong Feng, and Loukas
Barton, 2006, Dry or humid? Mid-Holocene
humidity changes in arid and semi-arid
China. *Quaternary Science Reviews* 25:351–
61.

An, Jinhuai 安金槐, 1960, Tantan Zhengzhou
Shangdai jihe yinwen yingtao 谈谈郑州商代
几何印纹硬陶. *Kaogu* 8:26–8.

An, Jinhuai 安金槐, Pei Mingxiang 裴明相, Zhao
Shigang 赵世纲, and Yang Yubin 杨育彬, 1989,
Zhengzhou Shangdai Erligangqi zhutong jizhi
郑州商代二里岗期铸铜基址. *Kaoguxue Jikan*
6:100–22.

An, Zhimin, 1989, Prehistoric agriculture in
China. In *Foraging and Farming: The Evolu-
tion of Plant Exploitation*, edited by David R.
Harris and Gordon C. Hillman, pp. 643–50.
Unwin Hyman, London.

———, 1998, Cultural complexes of the Bronze
Age in the Tarim basin and surrounding areas.
In *The Bronze Age and Early Iron Age Peo-
ples of Eastern Central Asia*, edited by Victor
Mair, pp. 45–62. The University of Pennsyl-
vania Museum, Philadelphia.

An, Zhimin 安志敏, 1959, Gansu Shandan
Sibatan xinshiqi shidai yizhi 甘肃山丹四坝滩
新石器时代遗址. *Kaogu Xuebao* 3:7–16.

———, 1984, Changjiang xiayou shiqian wenhua dui haidong de yingxiang 长江下游史前文
化对海东的影响. *Kaogu* 5:439–48.

———, 1990, Jiangnan wenhua he gudai
de Riben 江南文化和古代的日本. *Kaogu* 4:375–
80.

———, 1993a, Lun huan Bohai de shiqian wenhua – jianping "quxi" guandian 论环渤海的史
前文化 – 兼评 "区系" 观点. *Kaogu* 7:609–15.

————, 1993b, Shilun Zhongguo de zaoqi tongqi 试论中国的早期铜器. *Kaogu* 12:1110–19.

————, 1997, Hong Kong kaogu de huigu yu zhanwang 香港考古的回顾与展望. *Kaogu* 6:1–10.

An, Zhisheng, Stephen C. Porter, John E. Kutzbach, Wu Xihao, Wang Suming, Liu Xiaodong, Li Xiaoqiang, and Zhou Weijian, 2000, Asynchronous Holocene optimum of the East Asian monsoon. *Quaternary Science Reviews* 19:743–62.

Andersson, J. Gunnar, 1925, Preliminary report on archaeological research in Kansu. *Memoirs of the Geological Survey of China Series* A(5).

————, 1943, Researches into the prehistory of the Chinese. *The Museum of Far Eastern Antiquities* 15.

————, 1973 [orig. 1934], *Children of the Yellow Earth*. The MIT Press, Cambridge, MA.

————, 1923, An early Chinese culture. *Bulletin of the Geological Survey of China* 5:1–68.

Anhuisheng (Anhuisheng Wenwu Kaogu Yanjiusuo 安徽省文物考古研究所) (editor), 2000, *Lingjiatan Yuqi* 凌家滩玉器. Wenwu Chubanshe, Beijing.

————, 2006, *Lingjiatan* 凌家滩. Wenwu Chubanshe, Beijing.

Anonymous, 1975, Xiangzi de caiji yu Chucang 橡子的采集与储藏. *Shengming Shijie* 3:31.

Anthony, David W., 1998, The opening of the Eurasian steppe at 2000 BCE. In *The Bronze Age and Early Iron Age Peoples of Eastern Central Asia*, edited by Victor Mair, pp. 94–113. The University of Pennsylvania Museum, Philadelphia.

————, 2007, *The Horse, the Wheel and Language: How Bronze-Age Riders from the Eurasian Steppes Shaped the Modern World*. Princeton University Press, Princeton.

Arnold, Philip J., 1999, *Tecomates*, residential mobility, and Early Formative occupation in coastal lowland Mesoamerica. In *Pottery and People*, edited by James M. Skibo and Gary M. Feinman, pp. 157–70. The University of Utah Press, Salt Lake City.

Atahan, P., F. Itzstein-Davey, D. Taylor, J. Dodson, J. Qin, H. Zheng, and A. Brooks, 2008, Holocene-aged sedimentary records of environmental changes and early agriculture in the lower Yangtze, China. *Quaternary Science Reviews* 27:556–70.

Bagley, Robert W., 1987, *Shang ritual bronzes in the Arthur M. Sackler collections*. Harvard University Press, Cambridge, MA.

————, 1993, Meaning and explanation. In *The Problem of Meaning in Early Chinese Ritual Bronzes*, edited by Roderick Whitfield. University of London, London.

————, 1999, Shang archaeology. In *The Cambridge History of Ancient China*, edited by Michael Loewe and Edward Shaughnessy, pp. 124–231. Cambridge University Press, Cambridge.

Bai, Kun 白坤, Zhao Zhixing 赵智星, and Jing Xiaohui 景晓辉, 2000, Xiangzi ziyuan de kaifa he chanpin jiagong jishu 橡子资源的开发和产品加工技术. *Zhongguo Shangban Gongye* 5:50–1.

Ban, Gu 班固, 1962, *Han Shu* 汉书. Zhonghua Shuju, Beijing.

Bar-Yosef, Ofer, 2002, The role of the Younger Dryas in the origin of agriculture in West Asia. In *The Origins of Pottery and Agriculture*, edited by Yoshinori Yasuda, pp. 39–54. Roli Books, New Delhi.

Barber, Elizabeth, 1999, *The Mummies of Urumchi*. Norton, New York.

Barnard, Noel, 1961, *Bronze Casting and Bronze Alloys in Ancient China*. Australia National University and Monumenta Serica, Canberra.

————, 1993, Thoughts on the emergence of metallurgy in pre-Shang and early Shang China, and a technical appraisal of relevant bronze artifacts of the time. *Bulletin of the Metals Museum* 19:3–48.

Barnes, Gina, and Dashun Guo, 1996, The ritual landscape of "Boar Mountain" basin: The Niuheliang site complex of northeastern China. *World Archaeology* 28(2):209–19.

Barton, Loukas, Seth D. Newsome, Fa-Hu Chen, Hui Wang, Thomas P. Guilderson, and Robert L. Bettinger, 2009, Agricultural origins and the isotopic identity of domestication in northern China. *Proceedings of the National Academy of Sciences USA* 106(14):5523–8.

Beijing Daxue and Henansheng (Beijing Daxue Kaogu Wenboxueyuan 北京大学考古文博学院 and Henanshang Wenwu Kaogu Yanjiu suo 河南省文物考古研究所) (editors), 2007, *Dengfeng Wangchenggang Kaogu Faxian yu Yanjiu (2002–2005)* 登封王城岗考古发现与研究 (2002–2005). Daxiang Chubanshe, Zhengzhou.

Belfer-Cohen, Anna, and Ofer Bar-Yosef, 2000, Early sedentism in the Near East: A bumpy ride to village life. In *Life in Neolithic Farming Communities: Social Organization, Identity, and Differentiation*, edited by Ian Kuijt, pp. 19–37. Kluwer Academic/Plenum Publishers, New York.

Bellwood, Peter, 1995, Austronesian prehistory in Southeast Asia: Homeland, expansion and transformation. In *The Austronesians: Historical and Comparative Perspectives*, edited by Peter Bellwood, James J. Fox, and Darrel Tryon, pp. 96–111. Australian National University, Canberra.

———, 1997, *Prehistory of the Indo-Malaysian Archipelago*. University of Hawai'i Press, Honolulu.

———, 2005, *First Farmers: The Origins of Agricultural Societies*. Blackwell Publishing, Oxford.

———, 2006, Asian farming diasporas? Agriculture, languages, and genes in China and Southeast Asia. In *Archaeology of Asia*, edited by Miriam Stark, pp. 96–118. Blackwell Publishing, Malden, Oxford, Carlton.

Bender, B., 1978, Gatherer-hunter to farmer: A social perspective. *World Archaeology* 10:204–22.

Bennett, Gwen, 2001, *Longshan Period Lithic Production in Southeastern Shandong*. Paper presented at SAA Symposium on Early State Formation in East Asia, New Orland, April 20, 2001.

Bergman, Folke, 1939, *Archaeological Research in Sinkiang, Especially the Lop-nor Region*. Bokforlags Aktiebolaget Thule, Stockholm.

Bettinger, Robert L., 2001, Holocene hunter-gatherers. In *Archaeology at the Millennium: A Sourcebook*, edited by Gary M. Feinman and T. Douglas Price, pp. 137–95. Kluwer Academic/Plenum Publishers, New York.

Bettinger, Robert L., David B. Madsen, and Robert G. Elston, 1994, Prehistoric settlement categories and settlement systems in the Alashan Desert of Inner Mongolia, P.R.C. *Journal of Anthropological Archaeology* 13:74–101.

Bettinger, Robert L., R. Malhi, and H. McCarthy, 1997, Central Place Models of acorn and mussel processing. *Journal of Archaeological Science* 24:887–99.

Binford, Lewis R., 1980, Willow smoke and dogs' tails: Hunter-gatherer settlement systems and archaeological site formation. *American Antiquity* 45:4–20.

Binford, Lewis R. and Chuan Kun Ho, 1985, Taphonomy at a distance: Zhoukoudian, "the cave home of Beijing Man"? *Curr Anthropol* 26(4):413–42.

Boaretto, Elisabetta, Xiaohong Wu, Jiarong Yuan, Ofer Bar-Yosef, Vikki Chu, Yan Pan, Kexin Liu, David Cohen, Tianlong Jiao, Shuicheng Li, Haibin Gu, Paul Goldberg, and Steve Weiner, 2009, Radiocarbon dating of charcoal and bone collagen associated with early pottery at Yuchanyan Cave, Hunan Province, China. *Proceedings of the National Academy of Sciences USA* 106(24):9595–600.

Boltz, William G., 1986, Early Chinese writing. *World Archaeology* 17(3):420–36.

Bond, Gerard, William Showers, Maziet Cheseby, Rusty Lotti, Peter Almasi, Peter deMenocal, Paul Priore, Heidi Cullen, Irka Hajdas, and Georges Bonani, 1997, A pervasive millennial-scale cycle in north Atlantic Holocene and glacial climates. *Science* 278(14):1257–66.

Boyd, Brian, 2006, On "sedentism" in the later Epipalaeolithic (Natufian) Levant. *World Archaeology* 38(2):164–78.

Bradley, Daniel G. and David A. Magee, 2006, Genetics and the origins of domestic cattle. In *Documenting Domestication: New Genetic and Archaeological Paradigms*, edited by Melinda A. Zeder, Daniel G. Bradley, Eve Emshwiller, and Bruce D. Smith. University of California Press, Berkeley.

Brunson, Katherine, 2008, *Shifting animal exploitation strategies in Late Neolithic China: A zooarchaeological analysis of the Longshan culture site of Taosi, Shanxi Province*. BA thesis, Harvard University, Cambridge, MA.

Brysac, Shareen B., 1997, Last of the "Foreign Devils." *Archaeology* (November/December): 53–9.

Bu, Gong 卜工, 1999, Huan Zhujiangkou xingshiqi shidai wanqi kaoguxue yicun de biannian yu puxi 环珠江口新石器时代晚期考古学遗存的编年与谱系. *Wenwu* 11:48–56.

Bunker, Emma, 1998, Cultural diversity in the Tarim basin vicinity and its impact on ancient Chinese culture. In *The Bronze Age and Early Iron Age Peoples of Eastern Central Asia*, edited by Victor Mair, pp. 604–18. The University of Pennsylvania Museum, Philadelphia.

Butler, Ann, 1989, Cryptic anatomical characters as evidence of early cultivation in the grain legumes (pulses). In *Foraging and Farming: The Evolution of Plant Exploitation*, edited by D. R. Harris and G. C. Hillman, pp. 390–405. Unwin Hyman, London.

Cai, Baoquan 蔡保全, 2006, Hemudu wenhua "sigeng nongye" shuo zhiyi 河姆渡文化"耜耕农业"说质疑. *Xiamen Daxue Xuebao* 1:49–55.

Cai, Da-Wei, Lu Han, Xiao-Lei Zhang, Hui Zhou, and Hong Zhu, 2007, DNA analysis of archaeological sheep remains from China. *Journal of Archaeological Science* 34:1347–55.

Cai, Dawei, Zhuowei Tang, Lu Han, Camilla F. Speller, Dongya Y. Yang, Xiaolin Ma, Jian'en Cao, Hong Zhu, and Hui Zhou, 2009, Ancient DNA provides new insights into the origin of the Chinese domestic horse. *Journal of Archaeological Science* 36:835–42.

Cai, Dawei, Zhuowei Tang, Huixin Yu, Lu Han, Xiaoyan Ren, Xingbo Zhao, Hong Zhu, and Hui Zhou, 2011, Early history of Chinese domestic sheep indicated by ancient DNA analysis of Bronze Age individuals. *Journal of Archaeological Science* 38:896–902.

Cai, Xin, Hong Chen, Chuzhao Lei, Shan Wang, Kai Xue, and Bao Zhang, 2007, MtDNA diversity and genetic lineages of eighteen cattle breeds from *Bos taurus* and *Bos indicus* in China. *Genetica* 131:175–83.

Cao, Dingyun 曹定云, 2004, Xiadai wenzi qiuzheng – Erlitou wenhua taowen 夏代文字求证－二里头文化陶文. *Kaogu* 12:76–83.

Cao, Jianen 曹建恩, 2001, Qingshuihexian Duijiugou yizhi diaocha jianbao 清水河县碓臼沟遗址调查简报. In *Wanjiazhai Shuili Shuniu Gongcheng Kaogu Baogaoji* 万家寨水利枢纽工程考古报告集, edited by Cao Jianen 曹建恩, pp. 81–7. Yuanfang Chubanshe, Huhehaote.

Cao, Jianen 曹建恩 and Hu Xiaonong 胡晓农, 2001, Qingshuihexian Xicha yizhi fajue jianbao 清水河县西岔遗址发掘简报. In *Wanjiazhai Shuili Shuniu Gongcheng Kaogu Baogaoji* 万家寨水利枢纽工程考古报告集, edited by Cao Jianen 曹建恩, pp. 60–78. Yuanfang Chubanshe, Huhehaote.

Cao, Jianen 曹建恩 and Sun Jinsong 孙金松, 2004, Neimenggu Qingshuihe xian Xicha yizhi fajue qude zhongyao chengguo 内蒙古清水河县西岔遗址发掘取得重要成果. *Zhongguo Wenwubao*. 19 Nov.:1. Beijing.

———, 2009, Chifengshi Erdaojingzi Xiajiadian xiaceng wenhua juluo yizhi kaogu huo zhongda faxian 赤峰市二道井子夏家店下层文化聚落遗址获重大发现. *Zhongguo Wenwubao*. 25 Dec.:5. Beijing.

Chang, Kwang-chih, 1963, *Archaeology of Ancient China*. Yale University Press, New Haven.

———, 1964, Prehistoric and early historic culture horizons and traditions in South China. *Current Anthropology* 5(5):359–75.

———, 1969, *Fengpitou, Tapenkeng and the Prehistory of Taiwan*. Yale University Press, New Haven.

———, 1977, Chinese archaeology since 1949. *Journal of Asian Studies* 36(4):623–46.

———, 1980, *Shang Civilization*. Yale University Press, New Haven.

———, 1981a, The affluent foragers in the coastal areas of China: Extrapolation from evidence on the transition to agriculture. In *Senri Ethnological Studies*, pp. 177–86. National Museum of Ethnology, Suita, Osaka.

———, 1981b, Archaeology and Chinese historiography. *World Archaeology* 13(2):156–69.

———, 1983, *Art, Myth, and Ritual*. Harvard University Press, Cambridge, MA.

———, 1984, Ancient China and its anthropological significance. *Symbols* Spring/Fall: 2–4, 20–2.

———, 1986a, *Archaeology of Ancient China*. Yale University Press, New Haven.

———, 1986b, Xia Nai (1910–1985). *American Anthropologist* 88:442–44.

———, 1989, An essay on cong. *Orientations* 20(6):37–43.

———, 1991, Introduction: The importance of bronzes in ancient China. In *Ancient Chinese Bronze Art: Casting the Precious Sacral Vessel*, edited by W. Thomas Chase, pp. 15–18. China House Gallery, China Institute America, New York.

———, 1995, Ritual and power. In *China: Ancient Culture, Modern Land*, edited by Robert Murowchick, pp. 61–9. University of Oklahoma Press, Norman.

Chang, Kwang-chih and Ward H. Goodenough, 1996, Archaeology of southeastern China and its bearing on the Austronesian homeland. In *Prehistoric Settlement of the Pacific*, edited by Ward H. Goodenough, pp. 36–56. American Philosophical Society, Philadelphia.

Chang, Kwang-chih 张光直, 1988, Puyang sanqiao yu Zhongguo gudai meishu shang de ren shou muti 濮阳三蹻与中国古代美术上的人兽母题. *Wenwu* 11:36–9.

————, 1998, Ershi shiji houbande zhongguo kaoguxue 二十世纪后半的中国考古学. *Gujin Lunheng* 1:40–1.

————, 1999, Kaoguxue yu "ruhe jianshe juyou Zhongguo tese de renleixue" 考古学与 "如何建设具有中国特色的人类学". In *Zhongguo Kaoguxue Lunwenji* 中国考古学论文集, edited by Chang Kwang-chih 张光直, pp. 1–9. Sanlian Shudian, Beijing.

————, 2004, Lun "Zhongguo wenming de qiyuan" 论 "中国文明的起源". *Wenwu* 1:73–82.

Chang, Te-tzu, 1976, The origin, evolution, cultivation, dissemination, and diversification of Asian and African rice. *Euphytica* 25:431–41.

Chase, Thomas W., 1983, Bronze casting in China: A short technical history. In *The Great Bronze Age of China: A Symposium*, edited by George Kuwayama, pp. 100–23. Los Angeles County Museum of Art, Los Angeles.

Chen, Gongrou 陈公柔, 1995, "Zengbo Qi fu" ming zhong de "Jindao xihang" ji xiangguan wenti "曾伯霖簠" 铭中的 "金道锡行" 及相关问题. In *Zhongguo kaoguxue luncong* 中国考古学论丛, edited by Zhongguo Shehui kexueyuan kaogu yanjiusuo 中国社会科学院考古研究所, pp. 331–8. Kexue Chubanshe, Beijing.

Chen, Hongbo 陈洪波, 2007, Lu Yu Wan guwenhuaqu de juluo fenbu yu huanjing bianqian 鲁豫皖古文化区的聚落分布与环境变迁. *Kaogu* 2:48–60.

Chen, Jian 陈剑, 2005, Dayixian Yandian he Gaoshan xinshiqi shidai gucheng yizhi 大邑县盐店和高山新石器时代古城遗址. In *Zhongguo Kaoguxue Nianjian (2004)* 中国考古学年鉴 (2004), edited by Zhongguo Kaogu Xuehui 中国考古学会, pp. 353–4. Wenwu Chubanshe, Beijing.

Chen, Jiuheng 陈久恒 and Ye Xiaoyan 叶小燕, 1963, Luoyang Xijiao Hanmu fajue baogao 洛阳西郊汉墓发掘报告. *Kaogu Xuebao* 2:1–58.

Chen, Kunlong 陈坤龙 and Mei Jianjun 梅建军, 2006, Shanxi Lingshixian Jingjiecun Shangmu chutu tongqi de kexue fenxi 山西灵石县旌介村出土铜器的科学分析. In *Lingshi Jingjie Shangmu* 灵石旌介商墓, edited by Shanxisheng Kaogu Yanjiusuo 山西省考古研究所, pp. 209–28. Kenue Chubanshe, Beijing.

Chen, Kwang-tzuu and Fredrik Hiebert, 1995, The late prehistory of Xinjiang in relation to its neighbors. *Journal of World Prehistory* 9(2):243–300.

Chen, Liankai 陈连开, 1989, Zhongguo, hua yi, fan han, Zhonghua, Zhonghua minzu 中国、华夷、蕃汉、中华、中华民族. In *Zhonghua Minzu Duoyuan Yiti Geju* 中华民族多元一体格局, edited by Fei Xiaotong 费孝通, pp. 72–113. Zhongyang Minzu Xueyuan Chubanshe, Beijing.

Chen, Mengjia 陈梦家, 1956, *Yinxu Buci Zongshu* 殷墟卜辞综述. Kexue Chubanshe, Beijing.

Chen, Shan-Yuan, Yan-Hua Su, Shi-Fang Wu, Tao Sha, and Ya-Ping Zhang, 2005, Mitochondrial diversity and phylogeographic structure of Chinese domestic goats. *Molecular Phylogenetics and Evolution* 37(3):804–14.

Chen, Shilong 谌世龙, 1999, Guilin Miaoyan dongxue yizhi de fajue yu yanjiu 桂林庙岩洞穴遗址的发掘与研究. In *Zhongshiqi Wenhua ji Youguan Wenti Yantaohui Lunwenji* 中石器文化及有关问题研讨会论文集. Guangdong Renmin Chubanshe, Guangzhou.

Chen, Tiemei, George Rapp, and Zhichun Jing, 1999, Provenance studies of the earliest Chinese protoporcelain using instrumental neutron activation analysis. *Journal of Archaeological Science* 26:1003–15.

Chen, Wenhua 陈文华, 1991, *Zhongguo Gudai Nongye Kejishi Tupu* 中国古代农业科技史图谱. Nongye Chubanshe, Beijing.

————, 1994, *Zhongguo Nongye Kaogu Tulu* 中国农业考古图录. Jiangxi Kexue Jishu Chubanshe, Nanchang.

Chen, Xingcan, Li Liu, and Chunyan Zhao, 2010, Salt from southern Shanxi and the development of early states in China. In *Salt Production in China in a Comparative Perspective, Salt Archaeology in China, vol. 2*, edited by Shuicheng Li and Lothar von Falkenhausen, pp. 42–65. Kexue Chubanshe, Beijing.

Chen, Xingcan 陈星灿, 1987, Wenming zhuyinsu de qiyuan yu wenming shidai 文明诸因素的起源与文明时代. *Kaogu* 5:458–61, 437.

————, 1990, Fengchan wushu yu zuxian chongbai – Hongshan wenhua chutu nuxing suxiang shitan 丰产巫术与祖先崇拜 — 红山文化出土女性塑像试探. *Huaxia Kaogu* 3:92–8.

————, 1997, *Zhongguo Shiqian Kaoguxueshi Yanjiu (1895–1949)* 中国史前考古学史研究 (1895–1949) Sanlian Shudian, Beijing.

————, 2000, Zhongguo gudai de botoupi fengsu ji qita 中国古代的剥头皮风俗及其它. *Wenwu* 1:48–55.

————, 2009, *Zhongguo Kaoguxueshi Yanjiu Luncong* 中国考古学史研究论丛 Wenwu Chubanshe, Beijing.

————, Forthcoming, Cong "Longshan xingchengqi" dao "xianghu zuoyongquan" – Chang Kwang-chih xiansheng dui Zhongguo wenming qiyuan yanjiu de renshi he gongxian 從 "龍山形成期" 到 "相互作用圈" – 張光直先生對中國文明起源研究的認識和貢獻. In *Chang Kwang-chih Xiansheng Shishi Shi Zhounian Jinian Zhuankan* 張光直先生逝世十週年紀念專刊, edited by Chen Kwang-tzuu 陳光祖. Academia Sinica, Taipei.

Chen, Xingcan 陈星灿 and Lee Yun Kuen 李润权, 2004, Shelun zhongguo shiqian de guijia xiangqi 申论中国史前的龟甲响器. In *Taoli Chengxi Ji – Qingzhu An Zhimin Xiansheng Bashi Shouchen* 桃李成蹊集 – 庆祝安志敏先生八十寿辰, edited by Tang Chung 邓聪 and Chen Xingcan 陈星灿, pp. 72–97. Hong Kong Chinese University Press, Hong Kong.

Chen, Xingcan 陈星灿, Li Yongqiang 李永强, and Liu Li 刘莉, 2010a, 2002–2003 nian Henan Yanshi Huizui yizhi de fajue 2002–2003 年河南偃师灰嘴遗址的发掘. *Kaogu Xuebao* 3:393–422.

————, 2010b, Henan Yanshishi Huizui yizhi xizhi 2004 nian fajue jianbao 河南偃师市灰嘴遗址西址 2004 年发掘简报. *Kaogu* 2:36–46.

Chen, Xu 陈旭, 1986, Zhengzhou Duling he Huimin shipinchang chutu qingtongqi de fenxi 郑州杜岭和回民食品厂出土青铜器的分析. *Zhongyuan wenwu* 4:65–71.

Chen, Xuexiang 陈雪香, 2007, Shandong diqu Shang wenhua juluo xingtai yanbian chutan 山东地区商文化聚落形态演变初探. *Huaxia Kaogu* 1:102–12, 139.

Chen, Xuexiang 陈雪香 and Fang Hui 方辉, 2008, Cong Jinan Daxinzhuang yizhi fuxuan jieguo kan Shangdai nongye jingji 从济南大辛庄遗址浮选结果看商代农业经济. In *Dongfang Kaogu (Di 4 Ji)* 东方考古(第4集), edited by Shandong Daxue Dongfa Kaogu Yanjiu Zhongxin 山东大学东方考古研究中心, pp. 43–64. Kexue Chubanshe, Beijing.

Chen, Xuexiang 陈雪香, Wang Liangzhi 王良智, and Wang Qing 王青, 2010, Henan Boaixian Xijincheng yizhi 2006–2007 nian fuxuan jieguo fenxi 河南博爱县西金城遗址 2006–2007 年浮选结果分析. *Huaxia Kaogu* 3:67–76.

Chen, Y. S. and X. H. Li, 1989, New evidence of the origin and domestication of the Chinese swamp buffalo (*Bubalus bubalis*). *Buffalo Journal* 5(1):51–5.

Chen, Yeu-Gau and Tsung-Kwei Liu, 1996, Sea-level changes in the last several thousand years, Penghu Islands, Taiwan Strait. *Quaternary Research* 45:254–62.

Chen, Yuanzhang 陈远璋, 2003, Guangxi kaogu de shiji huigu yu zhanwang 广西考古的世纪回顾与展望. *Kaogu* 10:7–21.

Chen, Zheying 陈哲英, 1996, Xiachuan yizhi de xincailiao 下川遗址的新材料. *Zhongyuan Wenwu* 4:1–22.

Chernykh, Evgenii, Evgenii V. Kuz'minykh, and L. B. Orlovskaia, 2004, Ancient metallurgy of northeast Asia: From the Urals to the Saiano-Altai. In *Metallurgy in Ancient Eastern Eurasia from the Urals to the Yellow River*, edited by Katheryn M. Linduff, pp. 15–36. Edwin Mellen Press, Lewiston.

Chernykh, Evgenii Nikolaevich, 1992, *Ancient Metallurgy in the USSR: The Early Metal Age*. Cambridge University Press, New York.

Chiang, Kai-shek, 1947, *China's Destiny and Chinese Economic Theory*. Dennis Dobson Ltd., London.

The Chifeng International Collaborative Archaeological Research Project (editor), 2003, *Regional Archeology in Eastern Inner Mongolia: A Methodological Exploration*. Science Press, Beijing.

Chifeng Kaogudui, 赤峰考古队, 2002, *Banzhijianhe Zhongyou Xian Qin Shiqi Yizhi* 半支箭河中游先秦时期遗址. Kexue Chubanshe, Beijing.

Childs-Johnson, Elizabeth, 1998, The metamorphic image: A predominant theme in the ritual art of Shang China. *Bulletin of the Museum of Far Eastern Antiquities* 70:5–171.

Choi, Duk-Hyang 崔德卿, 2004, Dadou zaipei de qiyuan he Chaoxian bandao (The origins of cultivated soybean and Korean Peninsola) 大豆栽培的起源和朝鲜半岛. *Nongye Kaogu* 3:225–40, 285.

Clark, John E. and Michael Blake, 1994, The power of prestige: Competitive generosity and the emergence of rank societies in lowland Mesoamerica. In *Factional Competition and Political Development in the New World*, edited by Elizabeth M. Brumfiel and John Fox, pp. 17–30. Cambridge University Press, Cambridge.

Cockrill, W. Ross, 1981, The water buffalo: A review. *British Veterinary* 137:8–16.

Cohen, David J., 2001, *The Yueshi culture, the Dong Yi, and the archaeology of ethnicity in early Bronze Age China.* PhD dissertation, Harvard University, Cambridge, MA.

————, 2002, New perspectives on the transition to agriculture in China. In *The Origins of Pottery and Agriculture*, edited by Yoshinori Yasuda, pp. 217–27. Roli Books, New Delhi.

Costin, Cathy L., 2001, Craft production systems. In *Archaeology at the Millennium: A Sourcebook*, edited by Gary M. Feinman and T. Douglas Price, pp. 273–328. Kluwer Academic/Plenum Publishers, New York.

Crawford, Gary W., 1997, Anthropogenesis in prehistoric northeastern Japan. In *People, Plants, and Landscapes*, edited by Kristen Gremillion, pp. 86–103. The University of Alabama Press, Tuscaloosa and London.

————, 2006, East Asian plant domestication. In *Archaeology of Asia*, edited by Miriam Stark, pp. 77–95. Blackwell Publishing, Malden, Oxford, Carlton.

————, 2008, The Jomon in early agriculture discourse: Issues arising from Matsui, Kanehara and Pearson. *World Archaeology* 40(4):445–65.

————, 2011, Early rice exploitation in the lower Yangzi valley: What are we missing? *The Holocene.* DOI: 10.1177/0959683611424177. Available online http://hol.sagepub.com/content/early/2011/11/18/0959683611424177.

Crawford, Gary W. and Gyoung-Ah Lee, 2003, Agricultural origins in the Korean Peninsula. *Antiquity* 77(295):87–95.

Crawford, Gary W. and Chen Shen, 1998, The origins of rice agriculture: Recent progress in East Asia. *Antiquity* 72:858–66.

Crawford, Gary W., Anne Underhill, Zhijun Zhao, Gyoung-Ah Lee, Gary Feinman, Linda Nicholas, Fengshi Luan, Haiguang Yu, Hui Fang, and Fengshu Cai, 2005, Late Neolithic plant remains from northern China: Preliminary results from Liangchengzhen, Shandong. *Current Anthropology* 46(2):309–17.

Crawford, Gary W., Chen Xuexiang 陈雪香, and Wang Jianhua 王建华, 2006, Shandong Jinan Changqingqu Yuezhuang faxian Houli wenhua shiqi de tanhuadao 山东济南长清区月庄遗址发现后李文化时期的炭化稻. In *Dongfang Kaogu (Di 3 Ji)* 东方考古(第 3 集), edited by Shandong Daxue Dongfa Kaogu Yanjiu Zhongxin 山东大学东方考古研究中心, pp. 247–51. Kexue Chubanshe, Beijing.

Cribb, Roger, 1991, *Nomads in Archaeology.* Cambridge University Press, Cambridge.

Cui, Yanqin 崔岩勤, 2006, Hongshan wenhua yuqi zaoxing chuxi 红山文化玉器造型初析. In *Hongshan Wenhua Yanjiu* 红山文化研究, edited by Xi Yongjie 席永杰 and Liu Guoxiang 刘国祥, pp. 274–89. Wenwu Chubanshe, Beijing.

Cui, Yinqiu 崔银秋, Xu Yue 许月, Yang Yidai 杨亦代, Xie Chengzhi 谢承志, Zhu Hong 朱泓, and Zhou Hui 周慧, 2004, Xinjiang Lopnur diqu tongqi shidai gudai jumin mtDNA duotaixing fenxi 新疆罗布诺尔地区铜器时代居民 mtDNA 多样态性分析. *Jilin Daxue Xuebao (Yixueban)* 4:650–52.

Cunnar, Geoffrey, 2007, *The production and use of stone tools at the Longshan period site of Liangchengzhen, China*, PhD dissertation, Yale University, New Haven.

Dai, Xiangming 戴向明, 1998, Huanghe liuyu xinshiqi shidai wenhua geju zhi yanbian 黄河流域新石器时代文化格局之演变. *Kaogu Xuebao* 4:389–418.

Dai, Xiangming 戴向明, Wang Yueqain 王月前, and Zhuang Lina 庄丽娜, 2009, 2007–2008 nian Shanxi Jiangxian Zhoujiazhuang yizhi zuantan yu fajue 2007–2008 年山西绛县周家庄遗址钻探与发掘. In *2008 Zhongguo Zhongyao Kaogu Faxian 2008* 中国重要考古发现, edited by Guojia Wenwuju 国家文物局, pp. 6–11. Wenwu Chubanshe, Beijing.

Dai, Yingxin 戴应新, 1993, Shanbei he Jinbei Huanghe liangan chutu de Yinshang tongqi jiqi youguan wenti de tansuo 陕北和晋北黄河两岸出土的殷商铜器及其有关问题的探索. In *Kaoguxue Yanjiu*, edited by Kaoguxue Yanjiu Bianweihui 〈〈考古学研究〉〉编委会, pp. 219–35. Sanqin Chubanshe, Xi'an.

Daniel, Glyn, 1981, *A Short History of Archaeology.* Thames and Hudson, London.

Davis, Simon L. M., 1987, *The Archaeology of Animals.* Yale University Press, New Haven and London.

Denham, Tim, 2004, The roots of agriculture and arboriculture in New Guinea: Looking beyond Austronesian expansion, Neolithic package and indigenous origins. *World Archaeology* 36(4):610–20.

Di Cosmo, Nicola, 1999, The northern frontier in pre-imperial China. In *The Cambridge History of Ancient China: From the Origins of Civilization to 221 B.C.*, edited by Michael Loewe and Edward L. Shaughnessy, pp. 885–966. Cambridge University Press, Cambridge.

————, 2002, *Ancient China and Its Enemies*. Cambridge University Press, Cambridge.

Diamond, Jared, 2005, *Collapse: How Societies Choose to Fail or Succeed*. Viking, New York.

Diaz-Andreu, Margarita, 2001, Nationalism and archaeology. *Nations and Nationalism* 7(4):429–40.

Dietler, Michael and Brian Hayden (editors), 2001, *Feasts: Archaeological and Ethnographic Perspectives on Food, Politics, and Power*. Smithsonian Institution Press, Washington.

Dikotter, Frank, 1992, *The Discourse of Race in Modern China*. Stanford University Press, Stanford.

Ding, Jinlong 丁金龙 and Zhang Tiejun 张铁军, 2004, Chenghu yizhi faxian Songze shiqi shuidaotian 澄湖遗址发现崧泽时期水稻田. *Zhongguo Wenhua Yichan* 1:70–1.

Ding, Qingxian 丁清贤 and Zhang Xiangmei 张相梅, 1989, 1988 nian Henan Puyang Xishuipo yizhi fajue jianbao 1988 年河南濮阳西水坡遗址发掘简报. *Kaogu* 12:1057–66.

Dobney, Keith, Yuan Jing 袁靖, Anton Ervynck, Umberto Albarella, Peter Rowley-Conwy, Yang Mengfei 杨梦菲, and Luo Yunbing 罗运兵, 2006, Jiazhu qiyuan yanjiu de xinshijiao 家猪起源研究的新视角. *Kaogu* 11:74–80.

Dodson, John, Xiaoqiang Li, Ming Ji, Keliang Zhao, Xinying Zhou, and Vladimir Levchenko, 2009, Early bronze in two Holocene archaeological sites in Gansu, NW China. *Quaternary Research* 72:309–14.

Drennan, Robert D. and Xiangming Dai, 2010, Chiefdoms and states in the Yuncheng Basin and the Chifeng region: A comparative analysis of settlement systems in North China. *Journal of Anthropological Archaeology* 29:455–68.

Driver, Harold, 1961, *Indians of North America*. The University of Chicago Press, Chicago & London.

Du, Jinpeng 杜金鹏, 2003, *Yanshi Shangcheng Chutan* 偃师商城初探. Zhongguo Shehui Kexue Chubanshe, Beijing.

————, 2004, Huanbei Shangcheng yihao gongdian jizhi chubu yanjiu 洹北商城一号宫殿基址初步研究. *Wenwu* 5:50–64.

————, 2006, Yanshi Shangcheng dibahao gongdian jizhi chubu yanjiu 偃师商城第八号宫殿基址初步研究. *Kaogu* 6:43–52.

Du, Jinpeng 杜金鹏 and Wang Xuerong 王学荣 (editors), 2004, *Yanshi Shangcheng Yizhi Yanjiu* 偃师商城遗址研究. Kexue Chubanshe, Beijing.

Du, Jinpeng 杜金鹏 and Xu Hong 许宏 (editors), 2005, *Yanshi Erlitou Yizhi Yanjiu* 偃师二里头遗址研究. Kexue Chubanshe, Beijing.

————, 2006, *Erlitou Yizhi yu Erlitou Wenhua Yanjiu* 二里头遗址与二里头文化研究. Kexue Chubanshe, Beijing.

Du, Zaizhong 杜在忠, 1980, Shandong Zhucheng Chengzi yizhi fajue baogao 山东诸城呈子遗址发掘报告. *Kaogu Xuebao* 3:329–85.

Duan, Hongzhen 段宏振 (editor) 2007, *Beifudi* 北福地. Wenwu Chubanshe, Beijing.

Duanmu, Xin 端木炘, 1995, Woguo qinggangshu ziyuan de zonghe liyong 我国青冈属资源的综合利用. *Beijing Linye Daxue Xuebao* 17(2):109–10.

————, 1997, Zhongguo shili ziyuan zonghe liyong 中国石栎资源综合利用. *Linchan Huagong Tongxun* 6:33–5.

Earle, Timothy K., 1991, The evolution of chiefdom. In *Chiefdoms: Power, Economy, and Ideology*, edited by Timothy Earle, pp. 1–15. Cambridge University Press, Cambridge.

Engels, Friedrich, 1972 [orig. 1884], *The Origin of the Family, Private Property and the State*. International Publishers, New York.

Fagan, Brian M., 2000, *Ancient North America: The Archaeology of a Continent*. Thames & Hudson, New York.

Falkenhausen, Lothar von, 1992, Serials on Chinese archaeology published in the People's Republic of China. *Early China* 17:247–96.

————, 1993, On the historiographical orientation of Chinese archaeology. *Antiquity* 67(257):39–849.

————, 1995, The regionalist paradigm in Chinese archaeology. In *Nationalism, Politics, and the Practice of Archaeology*, edited by Philip L. Kohl and Clare Fawcett, pp. 198–217. Cambridge University Press, Cambridge.

————, 1999a, Su Bingqi. In *Encyclopedia of Archaeology: The Great Archaeologists*, edited by Tim Murray, pp. 601–13. ABC-CLIO, Santa Barbara.

————, 1999b, Xia Nai. In *Encyclopedia of Archaeology: The Great Archaeologists*, edited by Tim Murray, pp. 601–14. ABC-CLIO, Santa Barbara.

————, 2006, *Chinese Society in the Age of Confucius (1000–250 BC): The Archaeological Evidence*.

Cotsen Institute of Archaeology, University of California, Los Angeles.

———, 2008, Stages in the development of "cities" in pre-imperial China. In *The Ancient City: New Perspectives on Urbanism in the Old and New World*, edited by Joyce Marcus and Jeremy A. Sablof, pp. 209–28. A School for Advanced Research Resident Scholar Book, Santa Fe.

Fang, Dianchun 方殿春 and Wei Fan 魏凡, 1986, Liaoning Niuheliang Hongshan wenhua "nushenmiao" yu jishizhongqun fajue jianbao 辽宁牛河梁红山文化'女神庙'与积石冢群发掘简报. *Wenwu* 8:1–17.

Fang, Hui 方辉, 2004, Shang Zhou shiqi Lubei diqu haiyanye de kaoguxue yanjiu 商周时期鲁北地区海盐业的考古学研究. *Kaogu* 4:53–67.

———, 2009, Shangwangchao jinglue dongfang de kaoguxue guancha 商王朝经略东方的考古学观察. In *Duowei Shiyu – Shang Wangchao yu Zhongguo Zaoqi Wenming Yanjiu* 多维视域 一商王朝与中国早期文明研究, edited by Jing Zhichun 荆志淳, Tang Jigen 唐际根, and Takashima Ken-ichi 高嶋谦一, pp. 70–84. Kexue Chubanshe, Beijing.

Fei, Xiaotong 费孝通, 1989, Zhonghua minzu de duoyuan yiti geju 中华民族多元一体格局. In *Zhonghua Minzu Duoyuan Yiti Geju* 中华民族多元一体格局, edited by Fei Xiaotong 费孝通, pp. 1–36. Zhongyang Minzu Xueyuan Chubanshe, Beijing.

Feinman, Gary and Joyce Marcus (editors), 1998, *Archaic States*. School of American Research Press, Santa Fe, NM.

Feng, Shi 冯时, 1990, Henan Puyang Xishuipo 45 hao mu de tianwenxue yanjiu 河南濮阳西水坡45号墓的天文学研究. *Wenwu* 3:52–60.

———, 1994, Shandong Dinggong Longshan shidai wenzi jiedu 山东丁公龙山时代文字解读. *Kaogu* 1:37–54.

———, 2008, "Wen yi" kao "文邑" 考. *Kaogu Xuebao* 3:273–90.

Feng, Z.-D., C. B. An, L. Y. Tang, and A. J. T. Jull, 2004, Stratigraphic evidence of a Megahumid climate between 10,000 and 4000 years B.P. in the western part of the Chinese Loess Plateau. *Global and Planetary Change* 43:145–55.

Feng, Z.-D., C. B. An, and H. B. Wang, 2006, Holocene climatic and environmental changes in the arid and semi-arid areas of China: A review. *The Holocene* 16(1):119–30.

Feng, Zuojian 冯祚建, Cai Guiquan 蔡桂全, and Zheng Changlin 郑昌琳, 1986, *Xizang Burulei* 西藏哺乳类. Kexue Chubanshe, Beijing.

Fish, Suzanne K. and Stephen A. Kowalewski (editors), 1990, *The Archaeology of Regions: A Case for Full-Coverage Survey*. Smithsonian Institution Press, Washington, DC.

Fiskesjö, Magnus and Xingcan Chen, 2004, *China Before China*. Museum of Far Eastern Antiquities monograph series, No. 15, Stockholm.

Fitzgerald, John, 1996, The nationless state: The search for a nation in modern Chinese nationalism. In *Chinese Nationalism*, edited by Jonathan Unger, pp. 56–85. M.E. Sharpe, Armonk, NY.

Fitzgerald-Huber, Louisa, 1995, Qijia and Erlitou: The question of contacts with distant cultures. *Early China* 20:17–68.

———, 2003, The Qijia culture: Paths East and West. *The Museum of Far Eastern Antiquities* 75:55–78.

Flad, Rowan, 2001, Ritual or structure? Analysis of burial elaboration at Dadianzi, Inner Mongolia. *Journal of East Asian Archaeology* 3(3–4):23–51.

Flad, Rowan, Jing Yuan, and Shuicheng Li, 2007, Zooarcheological evidence of animal domestication in northwest China. In *Late Quaternary Climate Change and Human Adaptation in Arid China*, edited by David B. Madsen, Fa-Hu Chen, and Xing Gao, pp. 167–203. Elsevier, Amsterdam.

Flannery, Kent V., 1998, The ground plans of archaic states. In *Archaic States*, edited by Gary M. Feinman and Joyce Marcus, pp. 15–58. School of American Research Press, Santa Fe, NM.

Frachetti, Michael, 2002, Bronze Age exploitation and political dynamics of the eastern Eurasian steppe zone. In *Ancient Interactions: East and West in Eurasia*, edited by Katie Boyle, Colin Renfrew, and Marsha Levine, pp. 161–70. McDonald Institute for Archaeological Research, Cambridge, UK.

Franklin, Ursula M., 1983, The beginnings of metallurgy in China: A comparative approach. In *The Great Bronze Age of China*, edited by G. Kuwayama. Los Angeles County Museum, Los Angeles.

———, 1992, *The Real World of Technology*. Anansi, Ontario.

Fu, Renyi 傅仁义, 1994, Dalianshi Beiwutun yizhi chutu shougu de jianding 大连市北吴屯遗址出土兽骨的鉴定. *Kaogu Xuebao* 3:377–79.

Fu, Sinian 傅斯年, 1934, Xu yi 序一. In *Cheng-tzu-yai* 城子崖, edited by Li Chi 李济, pp. 293–96. Zhongyang Yanjiuyuan Lishi Yuyan Yanjiusuo 中央研究院历史语言研究所, Nanjing.

———, 1996, Kaoguxue de Xinfangfa 考古学的新方法. In *Fu Sinian Xuanji* 傅斯年选集, edited by Yue Yuxi 岳玉玺, Li Quan 李泉, and Ma Liangkuan 马亮宽, pp. 184–91. Tianjin Renmin Chubanshe, Tianjin. Reprinted from *Shixue* 1930.1.

Fu, Xianguo 傅宪国, He Zhanwu 贺战武, Xiong Zhaoming 熊昭明, and Wang Haotian 王浩天, 2001, Guilin diqu shiqiang wenhua mianmao lunkuo chuxian 桂林地区史前文化面貌轮廓初现. *Zhongguo Wenwubao*. 4 April:page 1. Beijing.

Fu, Xianguo 傅宪国, Li Xinwei 李新伟, Li Zhen 李珍, Zhang Long 张龙, and Chen Chao 陈超, 1998, Guangxi Yongningxian Dingsishan yizhi de fajue 广西邕宁县顶蛳山遗址的发掘. *Kaogu* 考古 11:11–33.

Fu, Yongkui 傅永魁, 1980, Gongxian Tieshenggou faxian Peiligang wenhua yizhi 巩县铁生沟发现裴李岗文化遗址. *Henan Wenbo Tongxun* 2:28–9.

Fullagar, Richard, Li Liu, Xingcan Chen, and Xiaolin Ma, in preparation, Functional analysis of stone sickles from the early Neolithic Peiligang culture, China.

Fuller, Dorian, Emma Harvey, and Ling Qin, 2007, Presumed domestication? Evidence for wild rice cultivation and domestication in the 5th millennium BC of the lower Yangtze region. *Antiquity* 81:316–31.

Fuller, Dorian Q, Ling Qin, Yunfei Zheng, Zhijun Zhao, Xugao Chen, Leo Aoi Hosoya, and Guo-Ping Sun, 2009, The domestication process and domestication rate in rice: spikelet bases from the Lower Yangtze. *Science* 323(5921):1607–1610.

Fuller, Dorian Q., and Ling Qin, 2009, Water management and labour in the origins and dispersal of Asian rice. *World Archaeology* 41:88–111.

Fung, Christopher, 2000, The drinks are on us: Ritual, social status, and practice in Dawenkou burials, North China. *Journal of East Asian Archaeology* 2(1–2):67–92.

Gansusheng (Gansusheng Wenwu Kaogu Yanjiusuo) 甘肃省文物考古研究所) (editor) 1998, *Minle Donghuishan Kaogu* 民乐东灰山考古. Kexue Chubanshe, Beijing.

———, 2006, *Qin'an Dadiwan* 秦安大地湾. Wenwu Chubanshe, Beijing.

Gansusheng Bowuguan, 甘肃省博物馆, 1979, Gansusheng wenwu kaogu gongzuo sanshinian 甘肃省文物考古工作三十年. In *Wenwu Kaogu Gongzuo Sanshinian* 文物考古工作三十年, edited by Wenwu Bianji Weiyuanhui 文物编辑委员会, pp. 139–53. Wenwu Chubanshe, Beijing.

Gao, Guangren 高广仁, 2000, Dawenkou wenhua de zangsu 大汶口文化的葬俗. In *Haidai Diqu Xian Qin Kaogu Lunji* 海岱地区先秦考古论集, edited by Gao Guangren 高广仁, pp. 125–43. Kexue Chubanshe, Beijing.

Gao, Guangren 高广仁 and Shao Wangping 邵望平, 1986, Zhongguo shiqian shidai de guiling yu quansheng 中国史前时代的龟灵与犬牲. In *Zhongguo Kaoguxue Yanjiu* 中国考古学研究, edited by Zhongguo Kaoguxue Yanjiu Bianweihui 中国考古学研究编委会, pp. 57–70. Wenwu Chubanshe, Beijing.

Gao, Ming-jun and Jiaju Chen, 1988, Isozymic studies on the origin of cultivated foxtail millet. *ACTA Agronomica Sinica* 14(2):131–6.

Gao, Qiang and Yun Kuen Lee, 1993, A biological perspective on Yangshao kinship. *Journal of Anthropological Archaeology* 12:266–98.

Gao, Shizhu 高诗珠, 2009, *Zhongguo xibei diqu sange gudai renqun de xianliti DNA yanjiu* 中国西北地区三个古代人群的线粒体 DNA 研究. PhD dissertation, Jilin University, Changchun.

Gao, Wei 高炜 and Li Jianmin 李健民, 1983, 1978–1980 nian Shanxi Xiangfen Taosi mudi fajue jianbao1978–1980 年山西襄汾陶寺墓地发掘简报. *Kaogu* 1:30–42.

Gao, Wei 高炜, Yang Xizhang 杨锡璋, Wang Wei 王巍, and Du Jinpeng 杜金鹏, 1998, Yanshi Shangcheng yu Xia Shang wenhua fenjie 偃师商城与夏商文化分界. *Kaogu* 10:66–79.

Gao, Xing, 2010, Revisiting the origin of modern humans in China and its implications for global human evolution. *Science China: Earth Sciences* 53(12):1927–40.

Gao, Xing, and Chunxue Wang, 2010, In search of the ancestors of Chinese people. *Paleoanthropology* 24(2):111–14.

Gao, Xing 高星, and Hou Yamei 侯亚梅 (editors), 2002, *Ershi Shiji Jiushiqi Shidai kaogu Yanjiu*

二十世纪旧石器时代考古研究. Kexue Chubanshe, Beijing.

Gardner, Paul S., 1997, The ecological structure and behavioral implications of mast exploitation strategies. In *People, Plants, and Landscapes: Studies in Paleoethnobotany*, edited by Kristen J. Gremillion, pp. 161–78. The University of Alabama Press, Tuscaloosa and London.

Ge, Sangben 格桑本, 1979, Qinghai Minhe Hetaozhuang majiayao leixing diyihao muzang 青海民和核桃庄马家窑类型第一号墓葬. *Wenwu* 9:29–32.

Ge, Wei 葛威, 2010, *The application of starch analysis in archaeology* 淀粉粒分析在考古学中的应用. PhD dissertation, University of Science and Technology of China, Hefei.

Germonpré, Mietje, Mikhail V. Sablin, Rhiannon E. Stevens, Robert E.M. Hedges, Michael Hofreiter, Mathias Stiller, and Viviane R. Després, 2009, Fossil dogs and wolves from Palaeolithic sites in Belgium, the Ukraine and Russia: osteometry, ancient DNA and stable isotopes. *Journal of Archaeological Science* 36(2):473–90.

Goldstein, Lynne G., 1981, One-dimensional archaeology and multi-dimensional people: Spatial organisation and mortuary analysis. In *The Archaeology of Death*, edited by Robert Chapman, Ian Kinnes, and Klavs Randsborg, pp. 53–69. Cambridge University Press, Cambridge.

Gong, Shengsheng 龚胜生, 1994, Yugong zhong de Qinling Huaihe dili jiexian 〈〈禹贡〉〉中的秦岭淮河地理界限. *Hubei Daxue Xuebao (Zhexue Shehui Kexueban)* 6:93–7.

Goodenough, Ward H. (editor), 1996, *Prehistoric Settlement of the Pacific*. American Philosophical Society, Philadelphia.

Gryaznov, Mikhail P., 1969, *The Ancient Civilization of Southern Siberia, translated from the Russian by James Hogarth.* Cowles Book Co., New York.

Gu, Wanfa 顾万发 and Zhang Songlin 张松林, 2005, Henan Gongyishi Huadizui yizhi "Xinzhaiqi" yicun 河南巩义市花地嘴遗址"新砦期"遗存. *Kaogu* 6:3–6.

Gu, Wen 顾问, 2002, "Xinzhaiqi" yanjiu 新砦期研究. *Yindu Xuekan* 4:26–40.

Gu, Wen 顾问 and Zhang Songlin 张松林, 2006, Huadizui yizhi suochu "Xinzhaiqi" zhushahui taoweng yanjiu 花地嘴遗址所出"新砦期"朱砂绘陶瓮研究. *Zhongguo Lishi Yanjiu* 1:19–37.

Guo, Dashun 郭大顺, 1997, Zhonghua wuqiannian wenming de xiangzheng – Niuheliang Hongshan wenhua tan miao zhong 中华五千年文明的象征 — 牛河梁红山文化坛庙冢. In *Niuheliang Hongshan Wenhua Yizhi yu Yuqi Jingcui* 牛河梁红山文化遗址与玉器精粹, edited by Liaoningsheng Wenwu Kaogu Yanjiusuo 辽宁省文物考古研究所, pp. 1–48. Wenwu Chubanshe, Beijing.

Guo, Dashun 郭大顺 and Zhang Keju 张克举, 1984, Liaoning Kazuoxian Dongshanzui Hongshan wenhua jianzhuqunzhi fajue jianbao 辽宁喀左东山嘴红山文化建筑群址发掘简报. *Wenwu* 11:1–11.

Guo, Deyong 郭德勇, 1960, Gansu Wuwei Huangniangniangtai yizhi fajue baogao 甘肃武威皇娘娘台遗址发掘报告. *Kaogu Xuebao* 2:53–71.

Guo, Deyong 郭德勇 and Meng Li 孟力, 1984, Gansu Dongxiang Linjia yizhi fajue baogao 甘肃东乡林家遗址发掘报告. In *Kaoguxue Jikan (4)* 考古学集刊 (4), edited by Kaogu Bianjibu 考古编辑部, pp. 111–61. Zhongguo Shehui Kexue Chubanshe, Beijing.

Guo, J., L.-X. Du, Y.-H. Ma, W.-J. Guan, H.-B. Li, Q.-J. Zhao, X. Li, and S.-Q. Rao, 2005, A novel maternal lineage revealed in sheep (*Ovis aries*). *Animal Genetics* 36(4):331–6.

Guo, Lanlan, Zaodong Feng, Xinqing Li, Lianyou Liu, and Lixia Wang, 2007, Holocene climatic and environmental changes recorded in Baahar Nuur Lake core in the Ordos Plateau, Inner Mongolia of China. *Chinese Science Bulletin* 52(7):959–66.

Guo, Moruo 郭沫若, 1930, *Zhongguo Gudai Shehui Yanjiu* 中国古代社会研究. Lianhe Shudian, Shanghai.

Guo, Ruihai and Jun Li, 2002, The Nanzhuangtou and Hutouliang sites: Exploring the beginnings of agriculture and pottery in North China. In *The Origins of Pottery and Agriculture*, edited by Yoshinori Yasuda. Roli Boods, New Delhi.

Guo, Suxin 郭素新, 1993, Zailun Eerduosi shi qingtongqi de yuanyuan 再论鄂尔多斯式青铜器的渊源. *Neimenggu Wenwu Kaogu* 1–2: 89–96.

Guo, Wentao 郭文韬, 1996, Shilun Zhongguo zaipei dadou qiyuan wenti 试论中国栽培大豆起源问题. *Ziran Kexueshi Yanjiu* 15(4):326–33.

———, 2004, Luelun Zhongguo zaipei dadou de qiyuan 略论中国栽培大豆的起源. *Nanjing*

Nongye Daxue Xuebao (Shehui Kexueban) 4:60–9.

Guo, Yuanwei 郭远谓 and Li Jiahe 李家和, 1963, Jiangxi Wannian Dayuan Xianrendong dongxue yizhi shijue 江西万年大源仙人洞洞穴遗址试掘. *kaogu Xuebao* 1:1–16.

Guojia Wenwuju, 国家文物局 (editor), 1991, *Zhongguo Wenwu Dituji Henan Fence* 中国文物地图集河南分册. Wenwu Chubanshe, Beijing.

———, 1992, Zhonghua renmin gongheguo kaogu shewai gongzuo guanli banfa 中国人民共和国考古涉外工作管理办法. In *Zhonghua Renmin Gongheguo Wenwu Fagui Xuanbian* 中华人民共和国文物法规选编, edited by National Bureau of Cultural Relics, pp. 337–41. Wenwu Chubanshe, Beijing.

———, 1999, *Zhongguo Wenwu Dituji Shaanxi Fence* 中国文物地图集陕西分册. Wenwu Chubanshe, Beijing.

———, 2002, Shanxi Xiangfen Taosi wenhua chengzhi 山西襄汾陶寺文化城址. In *2001 Zhongguo Zhongyao Kaogu Faxian, 2001* 中国重要考古发现, edited by Guojia Wenwujiu 国家文物局, pp. 24–7. Wenwu Chubanshe, Beijing.

———, 2003, *Zhongguo Wenwu Dituji Neimenggu Zizhiqu Fence* 中国文物地图集内蒙古自治区分册. Xi'an Ditu Chubanshe, Xi'an.

———, 2004a, Shanxi Jixian Shizitan Jiushiqi shidai yizhiqun 山西吉县柿子滩旧石器时代遗址群. In *Zhongguo Zhongyao Kaogu Faxian* 中国重要考古发现, edited by Guojia Wenwuju 国家文物局, pp. 5–9. Wenwu Chubanshe, Beijing.

———, 2004b, Niuheliang Hongshan wenhua yizhiqun 牛河梁红山文化遗址群. In *2003 Zhongguo Zhongyao Kaogu Faxian, 2003* 中国重要考古发现, edited by Guojia Wenwuju 国家文物局, pp. 17–22. Wenwu Chubanshe, Beijing.

———, 2005a, Shanxi Fushan Qiaobei Shang Zhou mu 山西浮山桥北商周墓. In *2004 Zhongguo Zhongyao Kaogu Faxian 2004* 中国重要考古发现, edited by Guojia Wenwuju 国家文物局, pp. 61–4. Wenwu Chubanshe, Beijing.

———, 2005b, Shanxi Liulin Gaohong Shangdai hangtu jizhi 山西柳林高红商代夯土基址. In *2004 Zhongguo Zhongyao Kaogu Faxian 2004* 中国重要考古发现, edited by Guojia Wenwuju 国家文物局, pp. 57–60. Wenwu Chubanshe, Beijing.

———, 2006, *Zhongguo Wenwu Dituji Shanxi Fence* 中国文物地图集山西分册. Zhongguo Ditu Chubanshe, Beijing.

———, 2007, *Zhongguo Wenwu Dituji Shandong Fence* 中国文物地图集山东分册. Zhongguo Ditu Chubanshe, Beijing.

Habu, Junko, 2004, *Ancient Jomon of Japan*. Cambridge University Press, Cambridge.

Hami Mudi Fajuezu, 哈密墓地发掘组, 1990, Hami Linchang banshichu, Yamansukuang caigouzan mudi 哈密林场办事处、雅满苏矿采购站墓地. In *Zhongguo Kaoguxue Nianjian* 中国考古学年鉴, edited by Zhongguo Kaogu Xuehui 中国考古学会, pp. 330–1. Wenwu Chubanshe, Beijing.

Han, Defen, 1988, The fauna from the Neolithic site of Hemudu, Zhejiang. In *The Palaeoenvironment of East Asia from the Mid-Tertiary: Proceedings of the Second Conference*, edited by Pauline Whyte, pp. 868–72. Centre of Asian Studies, University of Hong Kong, Hong Kong.

Han, Guohe 韩国河, Zhang Jihua 张继华, and Xu Junping 许俊平, 2006, Henan Dengfeng Nanwa yizhi 2004 nian chun fajue jianbao 河南登封南洼遗址 2004 年春发掘简报. *Zhongyuan Wenwu* 3:4–12, 22.

Han, Guohe 韩国河, Zhao Weijuan 赵维娟, Zhang Jihua 张继华, and Zhu Junxiao 朱君孝, 2007, Yong zhonzi huohua fenxi yanjiu Nanwa baitao de yuanliao chandi 用中子活化分析研究南洼白陶的原料产地. *Zhongyuan Wenwu* 6:83–6.

Han, Jianye 韩建业, 2003, *Zhongguo Beifang Diqu Xinshiqi Shidai Wenhua Yanjiu* 中国北方地区新石器时代文化研究. Wenwu Chubanshe, Beijing.

Han, Kangxin 韩康信, 1986, Xinjiang Kongquehe Gumugou mudi rengu yanjiu 新疆孔雀河古墓沟墓地人骨研究. *Kaogu Xuebao* 3:361–84.

Hancock, James F., 1992, *Plant Evolution and the Origin of Crop Species*. Prentice Hall, Englewood Cliffs, NJ.

Hanks, Bryan K. and Katheryn M. Linduff (editors), 2009, *Social Complexity in Prehistoric Eurasia*. Cambridge University Press, Cambridge.

Hao, Shougang 郝守刚, Xue Jinzhuang 薛进庄, and Cui Haiting 崔海亭, 2008, Donghulin sihaoren muzangzhong de guohe 东胡林四号人墓葬中的果核. *Renleixue Xuebao* 27(3):249–55.

Hao, Shougang 郝守刚, Ma Xueping 马学平, Xia Zhengkai 夏正楷, Zhao Chaohong 赵朝洪, Yuan Sixun 原思训, and Yu Jincheng 郁金城,

2002, Beijing Zhaitang Donghulin Quanxinshi zaoqi yizhi de huangtu poumian 北京斋堂东胡林全新世早期遗址的黄土剖面. *Dizhi Xuebao* 3:420–8.

Hao, Xin 郝欣 and Sun Shuyun 孙淑云, 2001, Panlongcheng Shangdai qingtongqi de jianyan yu chubu yanjiu 盘龙城商代青铜器的检验与初步研究. In *Panlongcheng* 盘龙城, edited by Hubeisheng kaogu yanjiusuo 湖北省考古研究所, pp. 517–38. Wenwu Chubanshe, Beijing.

Hardy-Smith, T. and P. C. Edwards, 2004, The garbage crisis in prehistory: Artefact discard patterns at the Early Natufian site of Wadi Hammeh 27 and the origins of household refuse disposal strategies. *Journal of Anthropological Archaeology* 23:253–89.

Harris, David, 2010, *Origins of Agriculture in Western Central Asia: An Environmental-Archaeological Study*. University of Pennsylvania Museum of Archaeology and Anthropology, Philadelphia.

Harrison, Richard J., 1996, Arboriculture in Southwest Europe: *Dehesas* as managed woodlands. In *The Origins and Spread of Agriculture and Pastoralism in Eurasia*, edited by David R. Harris, pp. 363–7. UCL Press, London.

Hayden, Brian, 1995, A new overview of domestication. In *Last Hunters-First Farmers*, edited by T. Douglas Price and Anne B. Gebauer, pp. 273–99. School of American Research Press, Santa Fe, NM.

———, 2003, Were luxury foods the first domesticates? Ethnoarchaeological perspectives from Southeast Asia. *World Archaeology* 34(3):458–69.

———, 2011, Rice: The first Asian luxury food? In *Why Cultivate? Anthropological and Archaeological Approaches to Foraging-Farming Transitions in Southeast Asia*, edited by Graeme Barker and Monica Janowski, pp. 73–91. McDonald Institute Monographs, Cambridge, UK.

He, Jiejun 何介均, 1996, Huan Zhujiangkou de shiqian caitao yu Daxi wenhua 环珠江口的史前彩陶与大溪文化. In *Hunan Xianqin Kaoguxue Yanjiu* 湖南先秦考古学研究, edited by He Jiejun 何介均, pp. 79–84. Yuelu Shushe, Changsha.

———, 1999, Lixian Chengtoushan guchengzhi 1997–1998 niandu fajue jianbao 澧县城头山古城址 1997－1998 年度发掘简报. *Wenwu* 6:4–17.

He, Nu 何驽, 2004, Shanxi Xiangfenxian Taosi chengzhi faxian Taosi wenhua daxing jianzhu jizhi 山西襄汾县陶寺 城址发现陶寺文化大型建筑基址. *Kaogu* 2:3–6.

———, 2007a, Shanxi Xiangfenxian Taosi zhongqi chengzhi daxing jianzhu IIFJT1 jizhi 2004–2005 nian fajue jianbao 山西襄汾县陶寺中期城址大型建筑 IIFJT1 基址 2004－2005 年发掘简报. *Kaogu* 4:3–25.

———, 2007b, Taosi yizhi bianhu zhushu "wenzi" xintan 陶寺遗址扁壶朱书"文字"新探. In *Xiangfen Taosi Yizhi Yanjiu* 襄汾陶寺遗址研究, edited by Xie Xigong 解希恭, pp. 633–6. Kexue Chubanshe, Beijing.

———, 2009, Shanxi Xiangfen Taosi chengzhi zhongqi wangji damu IM22 chutu qigan "guichi" gongneng shitan 山西襄汾陶寺城址中期王级大墓 IM22 出土漆杆"圭尺"功能试探. *Ziran Kexueshi Yanjiu* 28(3):261–76.

He, Nu 何驽, Gao Jiangtao 高江涛, and Wang Xiaoyi 王晓毅, 2008, Shanxi Xiangfenxian Taosi chengzhi faxian Taosi wenhua zhongqi daxing hangtu jianzhu jizhi 山西襄汾县陶寺城址发现陶寺文化中期大型夯土建筑基址. *Kaogu* 3:3–6.

He, Y., W. H. Theakstone, Zhonglin Zhang, Dian Zhang, Tandong Yao, Tuo Chen, Yongping Shen, and Hongxi Pang, 2004, Asynchronous Holocene climate change across China. *Quaternary Research* 61:52–63.

He, Yuling 何毓灵 and Tang Jigen 唐际根, 2010, Henan Anyangshi Huanbei Shangcheng gongdianqu erhao jizhi fajue jianbao 河南安阳市洹北商城宫殿区二号基址发掘简报. *Kaogu* 1:9–18.

Hebeisheng Wenwu Yanjiusuo 河北省文物研究所 (editor), 1985, *Gaocheng Taixi Shangdai Yizhi* 藁城台西商代遗址. Wenwu Chubanshe, Beijing.

Henansheng Wenhuaju (Henansheng Wenhuaju Wenwu Gongzuodui 河南省文化局文物工作队) (editor), 1959, *Zhengzhou Erligang* 郑州二里岗. Kexue Chubanshe, Beijing.

Henansheng Wenwu Kaogu (Henansheng Wenwu Kaogu Yanjiusuo) 河南省文物考古研究所) (editor), 1999a, *Wuyang Jiahu* 舞阳贾湖. Kexue Chubanshe, Beijing.

———, 1999b, *Zhengzhou Shangdai tongqi jiaocang* 郑州商代铜器窖藏. Kexue Chubanshe, Beijing.

———, 2001, *Zhengzhou Shangcheng* 郑州商城. Wenwu Chubanshe, Beijing.

———, 2003, *Huixian Mengzhuang* 辉县孟庄. Zhongzhou Guji Chubanshe, Zhengzhou.

Henansheng Wenwu Yanjiusuo 河南省文物研究 所 (editor), 1992, *Dengfeng Wangchenggang yu Yangcheng* 登封王城岗与阳城. Wenwu Chubanshe, Beijing.

Hiebert, Fredrik, 2000, Bronze Age Central Eurasian cultures in their steppe and desert environments. In *Environmental Disaster and the Archaeology of Human Response*, edited by Garth Bawden and Richard Reycraft, pp. 51–62. Maxwell Museum of Anthropology, Albuquerque, NM.

Higham, Charles, 1995, The transition to rice cultivation in Southeast Asia. In *Last Hunters – First Farmers: New Perspectives on the Prehistoric Transition to Agriculture*, edited by Douglas T. Price and Anne B. Gebauer, pp. 127–55. School of American Research Press, Santa Fe, NM.

———, 2002, Languages and farming dispersals: Austroasiatic languages and rice cultivation. In *Examining the Farming/Language Dispersal Hypothesis*, edited by Peter Bellwood and Colin Renfrew, pp. 223–32. McDonald Institute for Archaeological Research, University of Cambridge, Cambridge.

———, 2009, A new chronological framework for prehistoric Southeast Asia, based on a Bayesian model from Ban Non Wat. *Antiquity* 83:125–44.

Higham, Charles and Tracey L.-D. Lu, 1998, The origins and dispersal of rice cultivation. *Antiquity* 72:867–77.

Higham, Charles, B. Manly, A. Kihingam, and S. J. E. Moore, 1981, The Bovid third phalanx and prehistoric ploughing. *Journal of Archaeological Science* 8(4):353–65.

Hillman, Gordon C. and M. Stuart Davies, 1999, Domestication rate in wild wheats and barley under primitive cultivation. In *Prehistory of Agriculture*, edited by Patricia C. Anderson, pp. 70–102. The Institute of Archaeology, University of California, Los Angeles.

Hitchcock, Robert K., 1987, Sedentism and site structure: Organizational changes in Kalahari Basarwa residential locations. In *Method and Theory for Activity Area Research: An Ethnoarchaeological Approach*, edited by Susan Kent, pp. 374–423. Columbia University Press, New York.

Ho, Ping-ti, 1975, *The Cradle of the East*. The Chinese University of Hong Kong, Hong Kong.

Hong Kong Guwu Guji Banshichu 香港古物古迹 办事处, 1997, Hong Kong Yonglang xinshiqi shidai yizhi fajue jianbao 香港涌浪新石器时代遗址发掘简报. *Kaogu* 6:35–53.

Hongo, Hitomi and Richard Meadow, 1998, Pig exploitation at Neolithic Cayonu Tepesi (Southeastern Anatolia). In *Ancestors for the Pigs in Prehistory*, edited by Sarah Nelson, pp. 77–88. University of Pennsylvania Museum of Archaeology & Anthropology, Philadelphia.

Hopkerk, Peter, 1980, *Foreign Devils on the Silk Road: The Search for the Lost Cities and Treasures of Chinese Central Asia*. John Murray, London.

Hsu, Cho-yun, 1991, The roles of the literati and of regionalism in the fall of the Han dynasty. In *The Collapse of Ancient States and Civilizations*, edited by Norman Yoffee and George L. Cowgill, pp. 176–95. The University of Arizona Press, Tucson.

Hsu, Cho-yun and Katheryn Linduff, 1988, *Western Chou Civilization*. Yale University Press, New Haven.

Hu, Houxuan 胡厚宣, 1974, Zhongguo nuli shehui de renxun he renji 中国奴隶社会的人殉和人祭. *Wenwu* 8:56–72.

———, 2002, Yindai Gongfankao 殷代工方考. In *Jiaguxue Shangshi Luncong Chuji* 甲骨学商史论丛初集, edited by Hu Houxuan 胡厚宣, pp. 158–205. Hebei Jiaoyu Chubanshe, Shijiazhuang.

Hu, Songmei 胡松梅, 2007, Yizhi chutu dongwu yicun 遗址出土动物遗存. In *Baoji Guantaoyuan* 宝鸡关桃园, edited by Shaanxisheng Kaogu Yanjiusuo 陕西省考古研究所 and Baojishi Kaogu Gongzuodui 宝鸡市考古工作队, pp. 283–318. Wenwu Chubanshe, Beijing.

Hu, Songmei 胡松梅 and Sun Zhouyong 孙周勇, 2005, Shaanbei Jingbian Wuzhuangguoliang dongwu yicun ji guhuanjing fenxi 陕北靖边五庄果墚动物遗存及古环境分析. *Kaogu yu Wenwu* 6:72–84.

Hu, Songmei 胡松梅, Zhang Pengcheng 张鹏程, and Yuan Ming 袁明, 2008, Yulin Huoshiliang yizhi dongwu yicun yanjiu 榆林火石梁遗址动物遗存研究. *Renleixue Xuebao* 3:232–48.

Hu, Yaowu, Stanley H. Ambrose, and Changsui Wang, 2006, Stable isotopic analysis of human bones from Jiahu site, Henan, China: Implications for the transition to agriculture. *Journal of Archaeological Science* 33:1319–30.

Huang, Cuimei 黄翠梅 and Ye Guiyu 叶贵玉, 2006, Ziran huanjing yu yukuang ziyuan 自

然环境与玉矿资源. In *Xinshiji de Kaoguxue* 新世纪的考古学, edited by Hsu Choyun 许倬云 and Zhang Zhongpei 张忠培, pp. 442–70. Zijincheng Chubanshe, Beijing.

Huang, Qixu 黄其煦, 1982, "Huixiangfa" zai kaoguxue zhong de yunyong "灰像法" 在考古学中的运用. *Kaogu* 4:418–20.

Huang, Tsui-mei, 1992, Liangzhu – a late Neolithic jade-yielding culture in southeastern coastal China. *Antiquity* 66:75–83.

Huang, Wei-wen and Ya-mei Hou, 1998, A perspective on the archaeology of the Pleistocene-Holocene transition in north China and the Qinghai-Tibetan Plateau. *Quaternary International* 49/50:117–27.

Huang, Weijin 黄渭金, 1998, Hemudu daozuo nongye pouxi 河姆渡稻作农业剖析. *Nongye Kaogu* 1:124–30.

Huang, Xuanpei 黄宣佩 (editor), 2000, *Fuquanshan* 福泉山. Wenwu Chubanshe, Beijing.

Huang, Yunping 黄蕴平, 1996, Neimenggu Zhukaigou yizhi shougu de jianding yu yanjiu 内蒙古朱开沟遗址兽骨的鉴定与研究. *Kaogu Xuebao* 4:515–36.

———, 2001, Shihushan I yizhi dongwu guge jianding yu yanjiu 石虎山I遗址动物骨骼鉴定与研究. In *Daihai Kaogu (2)* 岱海考古(二), edited by Tian Guangjin 田广金 and Akiyama Shinko 秋山进午, pp. 489–513. Kexue Chubanshe, Beijing.

———, 2003, Miaozigou yu Dabagou yizhi dongwu yihai jianding baogao 庙子沟与大坝沟遗址动物遗骸鉴定报告. In *Miaozigou yu Dabagou* 庙子沟与大坝沟, edited by Neimenggu Wenwu Kaogu Yanjiusuo 内蒙古文物考古研究所, pp. 599–611. Zhongguo Dabaikequanshu Chubanshe, Beijing.

Huang, Zhanyue 黄展岳 and Zhao Xueqian 赵学谦, 1959, Yunnan Dianchi dong 'an xinshiqi shidai yizhi diaochaji 云南滇池东岸新石器时代遗址调查记. *Kaogu* 4:173–5, 184.

Huang, Xuanpei 黄宣佩, and Sun Weichang 孙维昌, 1983, Maqiao liexing wenhua fenxi 马桥类型文化分析. *Kaogu yu Wenwu* 3:58–61.

Huangshi Bowuguan 黄石市博物馆 (editor), 1999, *Tonglüshan Gu Kuangye Yizhi* 铜绿山古矿冶遗址. Wenwu Chubanshe, Beijing.

Hubeisheng Wenwu Kaogu Yanjiusuo 湖北省文物考古研究所 (editor), 2001a, *Panlongcheng* 盘龙城. Wenwu Chubanshe, Beijing.

———, 2001b, *Yidu Chengbeixi* 宜都城背溪. Wenwu Chubanshe, Beijing.

Hubeisheng and Zhongguo (Hubeisheng wenwu kaogu yanjiusuo 湖北省文物考古研究所 and Zhongguo Shehui kexueyuan kaogu yanjiusuo 中国社会科学院考古研究所), 1994, Hubei Shijiahe Luojiabailing xinshiqi shidai yizhi 湖北石家河罗家柏岭新石器时代遗址. *Kaogu Xuebao* 2:191–229.

Hunansheng Wenwu Kaogu Yanjiusuo 湖南省文物考古研究所 (editor), 1999, *Hunan kaogu manbu* 湖南考古漫步. Hunan Meishu Chubanshe, Changsha.

———, 2006, *Pengtoushan yu Bashidang* 彭头山与八十垱. Kexue Chubanshe, Beijing.

———, 2007, *Lixian Chengtoushan: Xinshiqi Shidai Yizhi Fajue Baogao* 澧县城头山：新石器时代遗址发掘报告. Wenwu Chubanshe, Beijing.

Hunansheng and Guoji (Hunansheng Wenwu Kaogu Yanjiusuo 湖南省文物考古研究所 and Guoji Riben Wenhua Yanjiu Zhongxin 国际日本文化研究中心) (editors), 2007, *Lixian Chengtoushan: Zhongri Hezuo Liyang Pingyuan Huanjing Kaogu yu Youguan Zonghe Yanjiu* 澧县城头山：中日合作澧阳平原环境考古与有关综合研究. Wenwu Chubanshe, Beijing.

Hung, Hsiao-chun, 2008, *Migration and cultural Interaction in southern coastal China, Taiwan and the northern Philippines, 3000 BC to AD 1: The early history of the Austronesian-speaking populations*. PhD dissertation, The Australian National University, Canberra.

Huo, Youguang 霍有光, 1993, Shitan Luonan Hongyashan gutongkuang caiyedi 试探洛南红崖山古铜矿采冶地. *Kaogu yu Wenwu* 1:94–7.

Hymowitz, T., 1970, On the domestication of the soybean. *Economic Botany* 24:408–21.

Hymowitz, T. and R. J. Singh, 1986, Taxonomy and speciation. In *Soybeans: Improvement, Production, and Uses*, edited by J. R. Wilcox, pp. 23–48. American Society of Agronomy, Madison, WI.

Ikawa-Smith, Fumiko, 1986, Late Pleistocene and early Holocene technologies. In *Windows on the Japanese Past: Studies in Archaeology and Prehistory*, edited by Richard J. Pearson, Gina L. Barnes, and Karl L. Hutterer, pp. 199–216. Center for Japanese Studies, The University of Michigan, Ann Arbor.

Jansen, T., P. Forster, M. A. Levine, H. Oelke, M. Hurles, C. Renfrew, J. Weber, and K. Olek, 2002, Mitochondrial DNA and the origins of the domestic horse. *Proceedings of the National Academy of Sciences USA* 99:10905–10.

Jia, Henglong 荚恒龙 and Zhou Ruifang 周瑞芳, 1991, Xiangzi Dianfen de Kaifa he liyong 橡子淀粉的开发和利用. *Zhengzhou Liangshi Xueyuan Xuebao* 2:74–8.

Jia, Lanpo and Weiwen Huang, 1990, *The Story of Peking Man*. Foreign Language Press, Beijing.

Jia, Lanpo 贾兰坡, 1991, Guanyu Zhoukoudian Beijingren yizhi de ruogan wenti 关于周口店北京人遗址的若干问题. *Kaogu* 1:62, 77–84.

Jia, Lanpo 贾兰坡, Gai Pei 盖培, and You Yuzhu 尤玉柱, 1972, Shanxi Shiyu Jiushiqi shidai yizhi fajue baogao 山西峙峪旧石器时代遗址发掘报告. *Kaogu Xuebao* 1:39–58.

Jia, Weiming, 2007, *Transition from Foraging to Farming in Northeast China*. BAR International Series, Oxford.

Jiang, Gang 蒋刚, 2008, Panlongcheng yizhiqun chutu Shangdai yicun de jige wenti 盘龙城遗址群出土商代遗存的几个问题. *Kaogu yu Wenwu* 1:35–46.

Jiang, Hong 江鸿, 1976, Panlongcheng yu Shangchao de nantu 盘龙城与商朝的南土. *Wenwu* 2:42–6.

Jiang, Leping and Li Liu, 2005, The discovery of an 8000-year old dugout canoe at Kuahuqiao in the Lower Yangzi River, China. *Antiquity* 79(305):(Project Gallery) http://antiquity.ac.uk/projgall/liu/index.html.

Jiang, Leping and Li Liu, 2006, New evidence for the origins of sedentism and rice domestication in the Lower Yangzi River, China. *Antiquity* 80:1–7.

Jiang, Leping 蒋乐平, 2007, Zhejiang Pujiangxian Shangshan yizhi fajue jianbao 浙江浦江县上山遗址发掘简报. *Kaogu* 9:7–18.

———, 2008, Kuahuqiao yizhi "jiedu" de ruogan wenti 跨湖桥遗址 "解读" 的若干问题. *Zhongguo Wenwubao*. 18 January:7. Beijing.

Jiang, Qinhua and Dolores R. Piperno, 1999, Environmental and archaeological implications of a late Quaternary palynological sequence, Poyang Lake, southern China. *Quaternary Research* 52(2):250–8.

Jiang, Weidong 蒋卫东, 1999, Liangzhu yuqi de yuanliao he zhizuo 良渚玉器的原料和制作. In *Liangzhu Wenhua Yanjiu* 良渚文化研究, edited by Zhejiangsheng wenwu kaogu yanjiusuo 浙江省文物考古研究所, pp. 177–86. Kexue Chubanshe, Beijing.

Jiang, Yuxiang 江玉祥, 1995, Gudai Zhongguo xinan sichou zhilu 古代中国西南丝绸之路. In *Gudai Xinan Sichou Zhilu Yanjiu* 古代西南丝绸之路研究, edited by Jiang Yuxiang 江玉祥, pp. 42–63. Sichuan Daxue Chubanshe, Chengdu.

Jiang, Zhanghua 江章华, Wang Yi 王毅, and Zhang Qing 张擎, 2001, Chengdu pingyuan zaoqi chengzhi jiqi kaoguxue wenhua chulun 成都平原早期城址及其考古学文化初论. In *Su Bingqi yu Dangdai Zhongguo Kaoguxue* 苏秉琦与当代中国考古学, edited by Su Bai 宿白, pp. 699–721. Kexue Chubanshe, Beijing.

Jiang, Zudi 蒋祖棣, 2002, Xizhou niandai yanjiu zhi yiwen – dui "Xia Shang Zhou duandai gongcheng" fangfalun de piping 西周年代研究之疑问 – 对 "夏商周断代工程" 方法论的批评. In *Su Bai Xiansheng Bashi Huadan Jinian Wenji* 宿白先生八十华诞纪念文集, edited by "Su Bai Xiansheng Bashi Huadan Jinian Wenji" Bianji Weiyuanhui 《〈宿白先生八十华诞纪念文集〉》编辑委员会, pp. 89–108. Wenwu Chubanshe, Beijing.

Jiangxisheng Wenwu Kaogu Yanjiusuo, 江西省文物考古研究所 (editor), 1997, *Xingan Shangdai Damu* 新干商代大墓. Wenwu Chubanshe, Beijing.

Jiangxisheng and Ruichangshi (Jiangxisheng Wenwu Kaogu Yanjiusuo 江西省文物考古研究所 and Ruichangshi Bowuguan 瑞昌市博物馆) (editors), 1997, *Tongling Gutongkuang Yizhi Faxian yu Yanjiu* 铜岭古铜矿遗址发现与研究. Jiangxi Kexue Jishu Chubanshe, Nanchang.

Jingxisheng and Zhangshushi (Jiangxisheng Wenwu Kaogu Yanjiusuo 江西省文物考古研究所 and Zhangshushi Bowuguan 樟树市博物馆) (editors), 2005, *Wucheng: 1973–2002 Nian Kaogu Fajue Baogao* 吴城: 1973–2002 年发掘报告. Kexue Chubanshe, Beijing.

Jiao, Tianlong, 2007, *The Neolithic of Southeast China*. Cambria Press, Youngstown, NY.

Jiao, Tianlong 焦天龙, 1994, Gengxinshimo zhi quanxinshichu Lingnan diqu de shiqian wenhua 更新世末至全新世初岭南地区的史前文化. *Kaogu Xuebao* 1:1–24.

———, 2006, Lun Kuahuqiao wenhua de laiyuan 论跨湖桥文化的来源. In *Zhejiangsheng Wenwu Kaogu Yanjiusuo Xuekan* 浙江省文物考古研究所学刊, edited by Zhejiangsheng Wenwu Kaogu Yanjiusuo 浙江省文物考古研究所, pp. 372–9. Kexue Chubanshe, Beijing.

Jin, ChangZhu, Pan WenShi, Zhang YingQi, Cai YanJun, Xu QinQi, Tang ZhiLu, Wang Wei, Wang Yuan, Liu JinYi, Qin DaGong, R. Lawrence Edwards, and Cheng Hai, 2009, The Homo sapiens Cave hominin site of Mulan Mountain, Jiangzhou District,

Chongzuo, Guangxi with emphasis on its age. *Chinese Science Bulletin* 54(21):3848–56.

Jin, Guiyun 靳桂云, 2004, Yanshan nanbei changcheng didai zhong quanxinshi qihou huanjing de yanhua ji yingxiang 燕山南北长城地带中全新世气候环境的演化及影响. *Kaogu Xuebao* 4:485–505.

———, 2007, Zhongguo zaoqi xiaomai de kaogu faxian yu yanjiu 中国早期小麦的考古发现与研究. *Nongye Kaogu* 4:11–20.

Jin, Li and Bing Su, 2000, Native or immigrants: Modern human origin in East Asia. *Nature Reviews* 1:126–33.

Jin, Yingxi 金英熙 and Jia Xiaobing 贾笑冰, 2008, Liaoningsheng Dalianshi Changhaixian Guangludao Xiaozhushan yizhi he Wujiacun yizhi de fajue 辽宁省大连市长海县广鹿岛小珠山遗址和吴家村遗址发掘. *Zhongguo Shehui Kexueyuan Gudai Wenming Yanjiu Zhongxin Tongxun* 16:38–45.

Jin, Zhengyao 金正耀, 2000, Erlitou qingtongqi de ziran kexue yanjiu yu Xia wenming tansuo 二里头青铜器的自然科学研究与夏文明探索. *Wenwu* 1:56–64.

———, 2003, Qian tongweisu shizong fangfa yingyong yu kaogu yanjiu de jinzhan 铅同位素示踪方法应用于考古研究的进展. *Diqiu Xuebao* 24(6):548–51.

Jin, Zhengyao 金正耀, W. T. Chase 齐思, Yoshimitsu Hirao 平尾良光, Hisao Mabuchi 马渊久夫, Yang Xizhang 杨锡璋, and Karoku Miwa 三轮嘉六, 1998, Zhongguo lianghe liuyu qingtong wenming zhijian de lianxi 中国两河流域青铜文明之间的联系. In *Zhongguo Shang wenhua guoji xueshu taolunhui lunwenji* 中国商文化国际学术讨论会论文集, edited by Zhongguo Shehui kexueyuan kaogu yanjiusuo 中国社会科学院考古研究所, pp. 425–33. Zhongguo Dabaikequanshu Chubanshe, Beijing.

Jin, Zhengyao 金正耀, W. T. Chase, Yoshimitsu Hirao 平尾良光, Peng Shifan 彭适凡, Hisao Mabuchi 马渊久夫, Karoku Miwa 三轮嘉六, and Zhan Kaixun 詹开逊, 1994, Jiangxi Xingan Dayangzhou Shang mu qingtongqi de qian tongweisu bizhi yanjiu 江西新干大洋洲商墓青铜器的铅同位素比值研究. *Kaogu* 8:744–7.

Jin, Zhengyao 金正耀, Zhao Congcang 赵丛苍, Chen Fukun 陈福坤, Zhu Bingquan 朱炳泉, Chang Xiangyang 常向阳, and Wang Xiuli 王秀丽, 2006, Baoshan yizhi he Chengyang bufen tongqi de qiantongweisu zucheng yu xiangguan wenti 宝山遗址和城洋部分铜器的铅同位素组成与相关问题. In *Chengyang Qingtongqi* 城洋青铜器, edited by Zhao Congcang 赵丛苍, pp. 250–9. Kexue Chubanshe, Beijing.

Jin, Zhengyao 金正耀, Hisao Mabuchi 马渊久夫, Tom Chase, Chen De'an 陈得安, Karoku Miwa 三轮嘉六, Yoshimitsu Hirao 平尾良光, and Zhao Dianzeng 赵殿增, 1995, Guanghan Sanxingdui yiwukeng qingtongqi de qian tongweisu bizhi yanjiu 广汉三星堆遗物坑青铜器的铅同位素比值研究. *Wenwu* 2:80–5.

Jinancheng Fenghuangshan Yiliuba Hao Hanmu Fajue Zhenglizu, 纪南城凤凰山一六八号汉墓发掘整理组, 1975, Jinancheng Fenghuangshan yiliuba hao Hanmu fajue jianbao 纪南城凤凰山一六八号汉墓发掘简报. *Wenwu* 9:1–8, 22.

Jing, Ke 景可, Lu Jinfa 卢金发, and Liang Jiyang 梁季阳, 1997, *Huanghe Zhongyou Qinshi Huanjing Tezheng he Bianhua Qushi* 黄河中游侵蚀环境特征和变化趋势. Huanghe Shuili Chubanshe, Zhengzhou.

Jing, Zhichun and Guang Wen, 1996, Mineralogical inquiries into Chinese Neolithic jade. In *The Chinese Journal of Jade*, edited by Sam Bernstein, pp. 135–51. S. Bernstein and Co., San Francisco, CA.

Jing, Zhichun, Jigen Tang, George (Rip) Rapp, and James Stoltman, 2002, Co-Evolution of Human Societies and Landscapes in the Core Territory of Late Shang State – An Interdisciplinary Regional Archaeological Investigation in Anyang, China. Unpublished Interim Report submitted to the National Science Foundation, National Geographic Society, Malcom H. Wiener Foundation, University of Minnesota Foundation, and The Henry Luce Foundation.

Karega-Munene, 2003, The East African Neolithic: A historical perspective. In *East African Archaeology: Foragers, Potters, Smiths, and Traders*, edited by Chapurukha Kusimba and Sibel Kusimba, pp. 17–32. University of Pennsylvania Museum of Archaeology and Anthropology, Philadelphia.

Ke, Yuehai, Bing Su, Xiufeng Song, Daru Lu, Lifeng Chen, Hongyu Li, Chunjian Qi, Sangkot Marzuki, Ranjan Deka, Peter Underhill, Chunjie Xiao, Mark Shriver, Jeff Lell, Douglas Wallace, R Spencer Wells, Mark Seielstad, Peter Oefner, Dingliang Zhu, Jianzhong Jin, Wei Huang, Ranajit Chakraborty, Zhu Chen, and Li Jin, 2001, *African Origin of Modern Humans in East Asia: A Tale of 12,000 Y Chromosomes*. *Science* 292:1151–3.

Keally, Charles T., Y. Taniguchi, and Y. V. Kuzmin, 2003, Understanding the beginnings of pottery technology in Japan and neighboring East Asia. *The Review of Archaeology* 24(2):3–14.

Keightley, David N., 1978a, The religious commitment: Shang theology and the genesis of Chinese political culture. *History of Religion* 17:212–14.

———, 1978b, *Sources of Shang History: The Oracle-Bone Inscriptions of Bronze Age China*. University California Press, Berkeley.

———, 1979–80, The Shang state as seen in the oracle-bone inscriptions. *Early China* 5:25–34.

———, 1983, The late Shang state: When, where, and what? In *The Origins of Chinese Civilization*, edited by David Keightley, pp. 523–64. University of California Press, Berkeley.

———, 1985, *Dead but not Gone: Cultural Implications of Mortuary Practice in Neolithic and Early Bronze Age China ca.8000 to 1000 B.C.* Paper presented at the Ritual and Social Significance of Death in Chinese Society, Oracle, Arizona.

———, 1987, Archaeology and mentality: The making of China. *Representations* 18:91–128.

———, 1999, The Shang: China's first historical dynasty. In *The Cambridge History of Ancient China: From the Origins of Civilization to 221 B.C.*, edited by Michael Loewe and Edward L. Shaughnessy. Cambridge University Press, Cambridge.

———, 2000, *The Ancestral Landscape: Time, Space, and Community in Late Shang China (ca. 1200–1045 B.C.)*. Institute of East Asian Studies, Berkeley.

———, 2004, What Did Make the Chinese "Chinese"? Some Geographical Perspectives. *Education About Asia* 9(2):17–23.

———, 2006, Marks and Labels: Early Writing in Neolithic and Shang China. In *Archaeology of Asia*, edited by Miriam T. Stark, pp. 177–201. Blackwell, Malden, MA.

Kelly, Robert L., 1992, Mobility/sedentism: Concepts, archaeological measures, and effects. *Annual Review of Anthropology* 21:43–66.

Kidder, Edward, 1957, *The Jomon Pottery of Japan*. Switzerland Artibus Asiae, Ascona.

Kirch, Patrick V., 2000, *On the Road of the Wind: An Archaeological History of the Pacific Islands before European Contact*. University of California Press, Berkeley and Los Angeles.

Kobayashi, Tatsou, 2004, *Jomon Reflections*. Oxbow Books, Oxford.

Kohl, Philip L. and Clare Fawcett (editors), 1995, *Nationalism, Politics, and the Practice of Archaeology*. Cambridge University Press, Cambridge.

Kong, Zhaochen 孔昭宸 and Du Naiqiu 杜乃秋, 1985, Neimenggu Aohanqi Xinglongwa yizhi zhiwu de chubu baogao 内蒙古敖汉旗兴隆洼遗址植物的初步报告. *Kaogu* 10:873–4.

Kong, Zhaochen 孔昭宸, Liu Changjiang 刘长江, and He Deliang 何德亮, 1999a, Shandong Tengzhoushi Zhuanglixi yizhi zhiwu yicun jiqi zai huanjing kaoguxue shang de yiyi 山东滕州市庄里西遗址植物遗存及其在环境考古学上的意义. *Kaogu* 7:59–62.

Kong, Zhaochen 孔昭宸, Liu Changjiang 刘长江, and Zhang Juzhong 张居中, 1999b, Mianchi Bancun xinshiqi qizhi zhiwu yicun jiqi zai renlei huanjingxue shang de yiyi 渑池班村新石器遗址植物遗存及其在人类环境学上的意义. *Renleixue Xuebao* 18(4):291–5.

Kong, Zhaochen 孔昭宸, Liu Changjiang 刘长江, and Zhao Fusheng 赵福生, 2011, Beijing Laoshan Hanmu zhiwu yicun ji xiangguan wenti 北京老山汉墓植物遗存及相关问题. *Zhongyuan Wenwu* 3:103–8.

Kong, Zhaochen 孔昭宸, Du Naiqiu 杜乃秋, Xu Qinghai 许清海, and Tong Guobang 童国榜, 1992, Zhongguo beifang quanxinshi danuanqi zhiwuqun de guqihou bodong 中国北方全新世大暖期植物群的古气候波动. In *Zhongguo Quanxinshi Danuanqi Qihou yu Huanjing* 中国全新世大暖期气候与环境, edited by Shi Yafeng 施雅风 and Kong Zhaochen 孔昭宸, pp. 48–65. Haiyang Chubanshe, Beijing.

Kowalewski, Stephen A., 1989, *Prehispanic Settlement Patterns in Tlacolula, Etla, and Ocotlan, the Valley of Oaxaca, Mexico*. Regents of the University of Michigan, Museum of Anthropology, Ann Arbor.

Kumar, S., M. Nagarajan, J. S. Sandhu, N. Kumar, V. Behl, and G. Nishanth, 2007, Mitochondrial DNA analyses of Indian water buffalo support a distinct genetic origin of river and swamp buffalo. *Animal Genetics* 38(3):227–32.

Kuz'mina, Elena E., 1998, Cultural connections of the Tarim basin people and pastoralists of the Asian steppes in the Bronze Age. In *The Bronze Age and Early Iron Age Peoples of Eastern*

Central Asia, edited by Victor Mair, pp. 63–93. The University of Pennsylvania Museum, Philadelphia.

————, 2004, Historical perspectives on the Andronovo and metal use in Eastern Asia. In *Metallurgy in Ancient Eastern Eurasia from the Urals to the Yellow River*, edited by Katheryn M. Linduff, pp. 37–84. Edwin Mellen Press, Lewiston, NY.

Kuzmin, Yaroslav, 2003a, Introduction: Changing the paradigm. *The Review of Archaeology* 24(2):1–3.

————, 2003b, The Paleolithic-to-Neolithic transition and the origin of pottery production in the Russian Far East: A geoarchaeological approach. *Archaeology, Ethnology & Anthropology of Eurasia* 3(15):16–26.

Kuzmin, Yaroslav and Lyubov Orlova, 2000, The Neolithization of Siberia and Russian Far East: Radiocarbon evidence. *Antiquity* 74:356–64.

Lai, Yin 来茵, Zhang Juzhong 张居中, and Yin Ruochun 尹若春, 2009, Wuyang Jiahu yizhi shengchan gongju jiqi suofanying de jingji xingtai fenxi 舞阳贾湖遗址生产工具及其所反映的经济形态分析. *Zhongyuan Wenwu* 2:22–8.

Lamberg-Karlovsky, Martha (editor), 2000, *The Breakout: The Origins of Civilization*. Peabody Museum Monographs, Cambridge, MA.

Lamberg-Karlovsky, C. C., 2000, The Near Eastern "breakout" and the Mesopotamian social contract. In *The Breakout: The Origins of Cvilization*, edited by Martha Lamberg-Karlovsky, pp. 13–23. Peabody Museum Monographs, Cambridge, MA.

Lang, Shude 郎树德, 1986, Gansu Qin'an Dadiwan 901 hao fangzhi fajue jianbao 甘肃秦安大地湾 901 号房址发掘简报. *Wenwu* 2:1–12.

Lang, Shude 郎树德, Xu Yongjie 许永杰, and Shui Tao 水涛, 1983, Qin'an Dadiwan di jiu qu fajue jianbao 甘肃秦安大地湾第九区发掘简报. *Wenwu* 11:1–14.

Larson, Greger, Keith Dobney, Umberto Albarella, Meiying Fang, Elizabeth Matisoo-Smith, Judith Robins, Stewart Lowden, Heather Finlayson, Tina Brand, Eske Willerslev, Peter Rowley-Conwy, Leif Andersson, and Alan Cooper, 2005, Worldwide phylogeography of wild boar reveals multiple centers of pig domestication. *Science* 307(5715):1618–22.

Lee, Gyoung-Ah, 2003, *Changes in subsistence systems in southern Korea from the Chulmun to Mumun periods: Archaeobotanical investigation*. PhD dissertation, University of Toronto, Toronto.

Lee, Gyoung-Ah and Sheahan Bestel, 2007, Contextual analysis of plant remains at the Erlitou-period Huizui site, Henan, China. *Bulletin of the Indo-Pacific Prehistory Association* 27:49–60.

Lee, Gyoung-Ah, Gary W. Crawford, Li Liu, and Xingcan Chen, 2007, Plants and people from the early Neolithic to Shang periods in North China. *Proceedings of the National Academy of Sciences USA* 104(3):1087–92.

Lee, Gyoung-Ah, Gary W. Crawford, Li Liu, Yuka Sasaki, and Xuexiang Chen, 2011, Archaeological Soybean (*Glycine max*) in East Asia: Does size matter? *PLoS ONE* 6(11) e26720. Available online at: http://dx.plos.org/10.1371/journal.pone.0026720.

Lee, Yun Kuen, 1993, *Spatial Expression of Segmentary Organization: A Case Study of a Yangshao Settlement Site*. Paper presented at the 58th Annual Meeting of Society of American Archaeology, Saint Louis, April 14–18.

————, 2002, Building the chronology of early Chinese history. *Asian Perspectives* 41(1):15–42.

Lee, Yun Kuen and Naicheng Zhu, 2002, Social integration of religion and ritual in prehistoric China. *Antiquity* (76):715–23.

Legge, James, 1879, *The Sacred Books of China: The Yi King*. The Clarendon Press, Oxford.

————, 1891, *The Sacred Books of China: The Texts of Taoism*. The Clarendon Press, Oxford.

————, 1892, *The She King (The Chinese Classics, v.4)*. Oxford University Press, Oxford.

————, 1960a, *Chinese Classics: The Chun Tsew with The Tso Chuen*. Hong Kong University Press, Hong Kong.

————, 1960b, *Chinese Classics: The Shoo King*. Hong Kong University Press, Hong Kong.

Legrand, Sophie, 2004, Karasuk metallurgy: Technological development and regional influence. In *Metallurgy in Ancient Eastern Eurasia from the Urals to the Yellow River*, edited by Katheryn M. Linduff, pp. 139–55. Edwin Mellen Press, Lewiston, NY.

Lei, C. Z., X. B. Wang, M. A. Bower, C. J. Edwards, R. Su, S. Weining, L. Liu, W. M. Xie, F. Li, R. Y. Liu, Y. S. Zhang, C. M.

Zhang, and H. Chen, 2009, Multiple maternal origins of Chinese modern horse and ancient horse. *Animal Genetics* 4:933–44.

Lei, C. Z., W. Zhang, H. Chen, F. Lu, R. Y. Liu, X. Y. Yang, H. C. Zhang, Z. G. Liu, L. B. Yao, Z. F. Lu, and Z. L. Zhao, 2007, Independent maternal origin of Chinese swamp buffalo (*Bubalus bubalis*). *Animal Genetics* 38(2):97–102.

Leibold, James, 2006, Competing narratives of racial unity in Republican China: From the Yellow Emperor to Peking Man. *Modern China* 32:181–220.

Levine, Marsha, 2006, MtDNA and horse domestication: The archaeologist's cut. In *Equids in Time and Space*, edited by Marjan Mashkour, pp. 192–201. Oxbow Books, Oxford.

Levine, Marsha, Colin Renfrew, and Katie Boyle (editors), 2003, *Prehistoric Steppe Adaptation and the Horse*. McDonald Institute for Archaeological Research, Cambridge, UK.

Lewis, Mark E., 2006, *The Flood Myths of Early China*. State University of New York Press, New York.

Li, Baoping, Li Liu, Jianxin Zhao, Xingcan Chen, Yuexing Feng, Guohe Han, and Junxiao Zhu, 2008, Chemical fingerprinting of whitewares from Nanwa site of the Chinese Erlitou state: Comparison with Gongxian and Ding kilns. *Nuclear Instruments and Methods in Physics Research B* 266:2614–22.

Li, Boqian 李伯谦, 1988, Cong Lingshi Jingjie Shangmu de faxian kan Jin Shaan gaoyuan qingtongqi wenhua de guishu 从灵石旌介商墓的发现看晋陕高原青铜器文化的归属. *Beijing Daxue Xuebao* 2:17–31.

———, 1989, Maqiao wenhua de yuanliu 马桥文化的源流. In *Zhongguo Yuanshi Wenhua Lunji* 中国原始文化论集, edited by Tian Changwu 田昌五 and Shi Xingbang 石兴邦, pp. 222–8. Wenwu Chubanshe, Beijing.

———, 2009, Cong Yinxu qingtongqi zuhui suo daibiao zushi de dili fenbu kan Shangwangchao de tongxia fanwei yu tongxia cuoshi 从殷墟青铜器族徽所代表族氏的地理分布看商王朝的统辖范围与统辖措施. In *Duowei Shiyu – Shang Wangchao yu Zhongguo Zaoqi Wenming Yanjiu* 多维视域—商王朝与中国早期文明研究, edited by Zhichun Jing 荆志淳, Jigen Tang 唐际根, and Ken-ichi Takashima 高嶋谦一, pp. 139–51. Kexue Chubanshe, Beijing.

Li, Chi, 1977, *Anyang*. University of Washington Press, Seattle.

Li, Chi 李济, 1990 [orig. 1934], Chengziya fajue baogao xu 城子崖发掘报告序. In *Li Chi Kaoguxue Lunwenji* 李济考古论文集, edited by Chang Kwang-Chih and Li Guangmo, pp. 189–93. Wenwu Chubanshe, Beijing.

———, 1990 [orig. 1968], Anyang fajue yu Zhongguo gushi wenti 安阳发掘与中国古史问题. In *Li Chi Kaoguxue Lunwenji* 李济考古学论文集, edited by Chang Kwang-Chih 张光直 and Li Guangmo 李光谟, pp. 796–822. Wenwu Chubanshe, Beijing.

Li, Chun-Hai, Gang-Ya Zhang, Lin-Zhang Yang, Xian-Gui Lin, Zheng-Yi Hu, Yuan-Hua Dong, Zhi-Hong Cao, Yun-Gei Zheng, and Jin-Long Ding, 2007, Pollen and phytolith analyses of ancient paddy fields at Chuodun site, the Yangtze River Delta. *Pedosphere* 17(2):209–18.

Li, Fan 李璠, 2001, Dahecun yizhi chutu liangshi biaoben de jianding 大河村遗址出土粮食标本的鉴定. In *Zhengzhou Dahecun* 郑州大河村, edited by Zhengzhoushi Wenwu Kaogu Yanjiusuo 郑州市文物考古研究所, pp. 671. Kexue Chubanshe, Beijing.

Li, Fan 李璠, Li Jingyi 李敬仪, Lu Ye 卢晔, Bai Pin 白品, and Cheng Huafang 程华芳, 1989, Gansusheng Minlexian Donghuishan xinshiqi yizhi gunongye yicun xinfaxian 甘肃省民乐县东灰山新石器遗址古农业遗存新发现. *Nongye Kaogu* 1:56–69, 73–4.

Li, Fei 李非, Li Shuicheng 李水成, and Shui Tao 水涛, 1993, Hulu he liuyu de guwenhua yu guhuanjing 葫芦河流域的古文化与古环境. *Kaogu* 9:822–42.

Li, Feng, 2006, *Landscape and Power in Early China: The Crisis and Fall of the Western Zhou 1045–771 BC*. Cambridge University Press, Cambridge.

———, 2008, *Bureaucracy and the State in Early China: Governing the Western Zhou*. Cambridge University Press, Cambridge.

Li, Gongdu 李恭笃, 1983, Neimenggu Chifengxian Sifendi Dongshanzui yizhi shijue jianbao 内蒙古赤峰县四分地东山咀遗址试掘简报. *Kaogu* 5:420–9.

Li, Jiahe 李家和, 1976, Jiangxisheng Wannian Dayuan Xianrendong yizhi dierci fajue 江西省万年大源仙人洞遗址第二次发掘. *Wenwu* 12:23–35.

Li, Jun 李珺, Qiao Qian 乔倩, and Ren Xueyan 任雪岩, 2010, 1997 nian Hebei Xushui

Nanzhuangtou yizhi fajue baogao 1997 年河北
徐水南庄头遗址发掘报告. *Kaogu Xuebao* 3:361–
85.

Li, Min, 2008, *Conquest, concord, and consumption: Becoming Shang in eastern China.* PhD dissertation, The University of Michigan, Ann
Arbor.

Li, Mingqi, Yang Xiaoyan, Wang Hui, Wang
Qiang, Jia Xin, and Ge Quansheng, 2010,
Starch grains from dental calculus reveal
ancient plant foodstuffs at Chenqimogou site,
Gansu Province. *Science China: Earth Sciences*
53(5):694–9.

Li, Shuicheng, 2002, The interaction between
northwest China and Central Asia during the
second millennium BC: An archaeological
perspective. In *Ancient Interactions: East and
West in Eurasia*, edited by Katie Boyle and
Colin Renfrew, pp. 171–82. McDonald Institute for Archaeological Research, Cambridge,
UK.

———, 2003, Ancient interactions in Eurasia
and northwest China: Revisiting J.G. Andersson's legacy. *Bulletin of The Museum of Far
Eastern Antiquities* 75:9–30.

Li, Shuicheng 李水城, 1993, Siba wenhua yanjiu
四坝文化研究. In *Kaoguxue Wenhua Lunji* 考古学
文化论集, edited by Su Bingqi 苏秉琦. Wenwu
Chubanshe, Beijing.

———, 1998, *Banshan yu Machang Caitao Yanjiu*
半山与马厂彩陶研究. Beijing Daxue Chuban-
she, Beijing.

———, 2005, Xibei yu Zhongyuan zaoqi
yetongye de quyu tezheng ji jiaohu zuoyong
西北与中原早期冶铜业的区域特征及交互作用.
Kaogu Xuebao 3:239–78.

———, 2010, Chengdu pingyuan shehui fuza-
hua jincheng quyu diaocha 成都平原社会复
杂化进程区域调查. In *Zhongguo Juluo Kaogu
de Lilun yu Shijian (Di yi Ji)* 中国聚落考古
的理论与实践(第一辑), edited by Zhonguo
Shehui Kexueyuan Kaogu Yanjiusuo 中国
社会科学院考古研究所 and Zhengzhoushi
Wenwu Kaogu Yanjiuyuan 郑州市文物考
古研究院, pp. 95–101. Kexue Chubanshe,
Beijing.

Li, Shuicheng 李水成 and Shui Tao 水涛, 2000,
Siba wenhua tongqi yanjiu 四坝文化铜器研究.
Wenwu 3:36–43.

Li, Shuicheng 李水成, Lan Yufu 兰玉富, and Wang
Hui 王辉, 2009, Lubei – Jiaodong yanye kaogu
diaochaji 鲁北—胶东盐业考古调查记. *Huaxia
Kaogu* 1:11–25.

Li, Xiaoqiang, John Dodson, Xinying Zhou,
Hongbin Zhang, and Ryo Masutomoto, 2007,
Early cultivated wheat and broadening of
agriculture in Neolithic China. *The Holocene*
17(5):555–60.

Li, Xiaoqiang, Zhou Weijian, An Zhisheng, and
John Dodson, 2003, The vegetation and monsoon variations at the desert-loess transition
belt at Midiwan in northern China for the last
13 ka. *The Holocene* 13(5):779–84.

Li, Xinwei, 2008, *Development of Social Com-
plexity in the Liaoxi Area, Northeast China.*
BAR International Series 1821, Archaeopress,
Oxford.

Li, Xinwei 李新伟, 2004, Zhongguo shiqian yuqi
fanying de yuzhouguan 中国史前玉器反映的宇
宙观. *Dongnan Wenhua* 3:66–71.

Li, Xiuhui 李秀辉 and Han Rubin 韩汝玢,
2000, Zhukaigou yizhi chutu tongqi de jinx-
iangxue yanjiu 朱开沟遗址出土铜器的金相学研
究. In *Zhukaigou* 朱开沟, edited by Neimenggu
wenwu kaogu yanjiusuo 内蒙古文物考古研究所,
pp. 422–46. Wenwu Chubanshe, Beijing.

Li, Xueqin, Garman Harbottle, Juzhong Zhang,
and Changsui Wang, 2003, The earliest writing ? Sign use in the seventh millennium BC
at Jiahu, Henan Province, China. *Antiquity*
77(295):31–44.

Li, Xueqin 李学勤, 1959, *Yindai Dili Jianlun* 殷代
地理简论. Kexue Chubanshe, Beijing.

———, 1997a, *Zhongguo Gudai Wenming yu
Guojia Xingcheng Yanjiu* 中国古代文明与国家形成
研究. Yunnan Renmin Chubanshe, Kunming.

———, 1997b, *Zouchu Yigu Shidai* 走出疑古时代.
Liaoning Daxue Chubanshe, Shenyang.

Li, Yanxiang 李延祥, and Han Rubin 韩汝玢,
1990, Linxixian Dajing gutongkuang yizhi
yelian jishu yanjiu 林西县大井古铜矿冶遗址
冶炼技术研究. *Ziran Kexueshi Yanjiu* 2:151–
60.

Li, Yanxiang 李延祥, Zhu Yanping 朱延平, Jia
Haixin 贾海新, Han Rubin 韩汝玢, Bao Wenbo
宝文博, and Chen Tiemei 陈铁梅, 2006a, Xiliaohe liuyu de zaoqi yejin jishu 西辽河流域的
早期冶金技术. In *Zhongguo Yejinshi Lunwenji
(4)* 中国冶金史论文集(第四辑), edited by Beijing Keji Daxue Yejin yu Cailiaoshi Yanjiusuo
北京科技大学冶金与材料史研究所 and Beijing
Keji Daxue Kexue Jishu yu Wenming Yanjiu
Zhongxin 北京科技大学科学技术与文明研究中
心, pp. 39–52. Kexue Chubanshe, Beijing.

Li, Yanxiang 李延祥, Jia Haixin 贾海新, and Zhu
Yanping 朱延平, 2003, Dadianzi mudi chutu

tongqi chubu yanjiu 大甸子墓地出土铜器初步研究. *Wenwu* 7:78–84.

Li, Yanxiang 李延祥, Chen Jianli 陈建立, and Zhu Yanping 朱延平, 2006b, Xilamulunhe shangyou diqu 2005 niandu gukuangye yizhi kaocha baogao 西拉木伦河上游地区 2005 年度古矿冶遗址考察报告. In *Zhongguo Yejinshi Lunwenji (4) 中国冶金史论文集(第四辑)*, edited by Beijing Keji Daxue Yejin yu Cailiaoshi Yanjiusuo 北京科技大学冶金与材料史研究所 and Beijing Keji Daxue Kexue Jishu yu Wenming Yanjiu Zhongxin 北京科技大学科学技术与文明研究中心, pp. 335–46. Kexue Chubanshe, Beijing.

Li, Yanxiang 李延祥, Han Rubin 韩汝玢, Bao Wenbo 宝文博, and Chen Tiemei 陈铁梅, 1999, Niuheliang yetong lubi canpian yanjiu 牛河梁冶铜炉壁残片研究. *Wenwu* 12:44–51.

Li, Yifu 李毅夫, 1985, Guifang Gongfang kao 鬼方工方考. *Qi Lu Xuekan* 6:12–15, 47.

Li, Youheng 李有恒 and Han Defen 韩德芬, 1963, Banpo xinshiqi shidai yizhi zhong zhi shoulei guge 半坡新石器时代遗址中之兽类骨骼. In *Xi'an Banpo 西安半坡*, edited by Zhongguo Kexueyuan Kaogu Yanjiusuo 中国科学院考古研究所, pp. 255–69. Wenwu Chubanshe, Beijing.

———, 1978, Guangxi Guilin Zengpiyan yizhi dongwuqun 广西桂林甑皮岩遗址动物群. *Gujizhui Dongwu yu Gurenlei* 16(4):244–54.

Li, Youmou 李友谋, 1980, Henan Gongxian Tieshenggou xinshiqi zaoqi yizhi shijue jianbao 河南巩县铁生沟新石器早期遗址试掘简报. *Wenwu* 5:16–19.

Li, Yuecong 李月从, Wang Kaifa 王开发, and Zhang Yulan 张玉兰, 2000, Nanzhuangtou yizhi de guzhibei he guhuanjing yanbian yu renlei de guanxi 南庄头遗址的古植被和古环境演变与人类的关系. *Haiyang Dizhi yu Disiji Dizhi* 20(3):23–30.

Li, Yung-ti, 2003, *The Anyang bronze foundries: Archaeological remains, casting technology, and production organization.* PhD dissertation, Harvard University, Cambridge, MA.

Li, Zhipeng 李志鹏, Roderick Campbell 江雨德, He Yuling 何毓灵, and Yuan Jing 袁靖, 2010, Yixu Teishanlu zhigu zuofang yizhi chutu zhigu yicun fenxi yu chubu renshi 殷墟铁三路制骨作坊遗址出土制骨遗存的分析与初步认识. *Zhongguo Wenwubao.* 17 Sept.:7. Beijing.

Li, Zhongda 李仲达, Hua Jueming 华觉明, and Zhang Hongli 张宏礼, 1986, Shang Zhou qingtongqi rongqi hejin chengfen de kaocha 商周青铜器容器合金成分的考察. In *Zhongguo Yezhushi Lunji 中国冶铸史论集*, edited by Hua Jueming 华觉明, pp. 149–65. Wenwu Chubanshe, Beijing.

Liang, Honggang 梁宏刚 and Sun Shuyun 孙淑云, 2006, Erlitou yizhi chutu tongqi yanjiu zongshu 二里头遗址出土铜器研究综述. In *Zhongguo Yejinshi Lunwenji (4) 中国冶金史论文集(第四辑)*, edited by Beijing Keji Daxue Yejin yu Cailiaoshi Yanjiusuo 北京科技大学冶金与材料史研究所 and Beijing Keji Daxue Kexue Jishu yu Wenming Yanjiu Zhongxin 北京科技大学科学技术与文明研究中心, pp. 99–116. Kexue Chubanshe, Beijing.

Liang, Qichao 梁启超, 1992, Zhongguo jiruo suyuan lun 中国积弱溯源论. In *Liang Qichao Wenxuan (Vol.1) 梁启超文选 (上集)*, edited by Xia Xiaohong 夏晓虹, pp. 64–90. Zhongguo Guangbo Dianshi Chubanshe. Reprinted from Zhongguo jiruo suyuan lun, *Qingyibao* (1901), pp. 77–80, Beijing.

Liang, Ssu-yung 梁思永, 1934, Shoulei niaolei yigu ji jielei yike 兽类鸟类遗骨及介类遗壳. In *Chengziya 城子崖*, edited by Li Chi 李济, pp. 90–1. Guoli Zhongyang Yanjiuyuan Lishi Yuyan Yanjiusuo, Nanking.

Liao, Yongmin 廖永民 and Liu Hongmiao 刘洪淼, 1997, Wayaozui Peiligang wenhua yicun shixi 瓦窑嘴裴李岗文化遗存试析. *Zhongyuan Wenwu* 1:53–7.

Liaoningsheng Wenwu Kaogu Yanjiuso, 辽宁省文物考古研究所 (editor), 1997, *Niuheliang Hongshan Wenhua Yizhi yu Yuqi Jingsui 牛河梁红山文化遗址与玉器精髓*. Wenwu Chubanshe, Beijing.

Lin, Huan 林欢, 2003, Xia Shang shiqi Jinnan diqu kaoguxue wenhua yu Fen Tao jian gu Taizu 夏商时期晋南地区考古学文化与汾洮间古骀族. In *Shang Chengzuo Jiaoshou Bainian Danchen Jinian Wenji 商承祚教授百年诞辰纪念文集*, edited by Zhongguo Wenwu Xuehui 中国文物学会, pp. 189–96. Wenwu Chubanshe, Beijing.

Lin, Xiang 林向, 1989, Sanxingdui yizhi yu Yinshang de xitu 三星堆遗址与殷商的西土. *Sichuang Wenwu* 1:23–30.

Lin, Yun 林沄, 1994, Zaoqi beifangxi qingtongqi de jige niandai wenti 早期北方系青铜器的几个年代问题. In *Neimenggu Wensu Kaogu Wenji 内蒙古文物考古文集*, edited by Li Yiyou 李逸友 and Wei Jian 魏坚, pp. 291–5. Zhongguo Dabaike Quanshu Chubanshe, Beijing.

———, 1998a, Guanyu qingtong gongxingqi de ruogan wenti 关于青铜弓形器的若干

问题. In *Lin YunXueshu Wenji* 林沄学术文集, edited by Lin Yun 林沄, pp. 251–61. Zhongguo Dabaike Quanshu Chubanshe, Beijing.

———, 1998b, Jiaguwen zhong de Shangdai fangguo lianmeng 甲骨文中的商代方国联盟. In *Lin Yun Xueshu Wenji* 林沄学术文集, edited by Lin Yun 林沄, pp. 69–84. Zhongguo Dabaike Quanshu Chubanshe, Beijing.

Linduff, Katheryn M., 1995, Zhukaigou, steppe culture and the rise of Chinese civilization. *Antiquity* 69(262):133–45.

———, 1998, The emergence and demise of bronze-producing cultures outside the Central Plain of China. In *The Bronze Age and Early Iron Age Peoples of Eastern Central Asia*, edited by Victor H. Mair, pp. 619–46. Institute for the Study of Man Inc., Washington DC.

———, 2000, Introduction. Metallurgists in ancient East Asia: The Chinese and who else? In *The Beginnings of Metallurgy in China*, edited by Katheryn M. Linduff, Rubin Han, and Shuyun Sun, pp. 1–28. The Edwin Mellen Press, Lewiston, NY.

———, 2003, A walk on the wild side: Late Shang appropriation of horses in China. In *Prehistoric Steppe Adaptation and the Horse*, edited by Marcha Levine, Colin Renfrew, and Katie Boyle, pp. 139–62. McDonald Institute Monographs, Cambridge.

———, 2004, How far does the Eurasian metallurgical tradition extend? In *Metallurgy in Ancient Eastern Eurasia from the Urals to the Yellow River*, edited by Katheryn M. Linduff, pp. 1–14. Edwin Mellen Press, Lewiston, NY.

Linduff, Katheryn M., Robert Drennan, and Gideon Shelach, 2002–2004, Early complex societies in NE China: The Chifeng international collaborative archaeological research project. *Journal of Field Archaeology* 29(1–2):45–74.

Linduff, Katheryn M., and Jianjun Mei, 2009, Metallurgy in Ancient Eastern Asia: Retrospect and prospects. *Journal of World Prehistory* 22:265–81.

Ling, Chunsheng 凌纯声, 1934, *Songhuajiang Xiayou de Hezhezu* 松花江下游的赫哲族. Zhongyang Yanjiuyuan Lishi Yuyan Yanjiusuo 中央研究院历史语言研究所, Nanjing.

Lippold, Sebastian, Michael Knapp, Tatyana Kuznetsova, Jennifer A. Leonard, Norbert Benecke, Arne Ludwig, Morten Rasmussen, Alan Cooper, Jaco Weinstock, Eske Willerslev, Beth Shapiro, and Michael Hofreiter, 2011, Discovery of lost diversity of paternal horse lineages using ancient DNA. *Nature Communications* 23 Aug. Available online at: DOI: 10.1038/ncomms1447.

Liu, Bin 刘斌, 2008, Hangzhoushi Yuhangqu Liangzhu gucheng yizhi 2006–2007 nian de fajue 杭州市余杭区良渚古城遗址 2006–2007 年的发掘. *Kaogu* 7:3–10.

Liu, Changjiang 刘长江, 2006, Dadiwan yizhi zhiwu yicun jianding baogao 大地湾遗址植物遗存鉴定报告. In *Qin'an Dadiwan* 秦安大地湾, edited by Gansusheng Wenwu Kaogu Yanjiusuo 甘肃省文物考古研究所, pp. 914–16. Wenwu Chubanshe, Beijing.

Liu, Chang 刘昶, and Fang Yanming 方燕明, 2010, Henan Yuzhou Wadian yizhi chutu zhiwu yicun fenxi 河南禹州瓦店遗址出土植物遗存分析. *Nanfang Wenwu* 4:55–64.

Liu, Ciyuan 刘次沅, 2009, Taosi guanxiangtai yizhi de tianwenxue fenxi 陶寺观象台遗址的天文学分析. *Tianwen Xuebao* 50(1):1–10.

Liu, Guoxiang 刘国祥, 2001, Xinglongwa wenhua juluo xingtai chutan 兴隆洼文化聚落形态初探. *Kaogu yu Wenwu* 6:58–67.

———, 2004, Zhaobaogou wenhua jingji xingtai ji xiangguan wenti taolun 赵宝沟文化经济形态及相关问题讨论. In *Dongbei Wenwu Kaogu Lunji* 东北文物考古论集, edited by Liu Guoxiang 刘国祥, pp. 87–109. Kexue Chubanshe, Beijing.

———, 2006, Hongshan wenhua yu Xiliaohe liuyu wenming qiyuan tansuo 红山文化与西辽河流域文明起源探索. In *Hongshan Wenhua Yanjiu* 红山文化研究, edited by Xi Yongjie 席永杰 and Liu Guoxiang 刘国祥, pp. 62–104. Wenwu Chubanshe, Beijing.

Liu, Kam-biu, 1988, Quaternary history of the temperate forests of China. *Quaternary Science Reviews* 7:1–20.

Liu, Li, 1996a, Mortuary ritual and social hierarchy in the Longshan culture. *Early China* 21:1–46.

———, 1996b, Settlement patterns, chiefdom variability, and the development of early states in north China. *Journal of Anthropological Archaeology* 15:237–88.

———, 1999, Who were the ancestors? The origins of Chinese ancestral cult and racial myths. *Antiquity* 73:602–13.

———, 2000a, Ancestor worship: An archaeological investigation of ritual activities in

Neolithic North China. *Journal of East Asian Archaeology* 2(1–2):129–64.

———, 2000b, The development and decline of social complexity in China: Some environmental and social factors. *Indo-Pacific Prehistory Association Bulletin (Maelaka Papers)* 20(4):14–33.

———, 2003, "The products of minds as well as of hands": Production of prestige goods in the Neolithic and early state periods of China. *Asian Perspectives* 42(1):1–40.

———, 2004, *The Chinese Neolithic: Trajectories to Early States.* Cambridge University Press, Cambridge.

———, 2006, Urbanization in China: Erlitou and its hinterland. In *Urbanism in the Preindustrial World: Cross-Cultural Approaches*, edited by Glenn Storey, pp. 161–89. University of Alabama Press, Tuscaloosa.

———, 2007, Early figurations in China: Ideological, social and ecological implications. In *Image and Imagination: A Global Prehistory of Figurative Representation*, edited by C. Renfrew and I. Morley, pp. 271–86. The McDonald Institute for Archaeological Research, Cambridge University, Cambridge, UK.

Liu, Li and Xingcan Chen, 2001a, China. In *Encyclopedia of Archaeology: History and Discoveries*, edited by Tim Murray, pp. 315–33. ABC-CLIO, Santa Barbara.

———, 2001b, Cities and towns: The control of natural resources in early states, China. *Bulletin of the Museum of Far Eastern Antiquities* 73:5–47.

———, 2001c, Settlement archaeology and the study of social complexity in China. *The Review of Archaeology* 22(2):4–21.

———, 2003, *State Formation in Early China.* Duckworth, London.

———, 2011, Were Neolithic rice paddies ploughed? – Usewear analysis of plough-shaped tools from Pishan (4000–3300 BC), Zhejiang. Poster presented at *The International Symposium, Rice and Language Across Asia: Crops, Movement, and Social Change*, Cornell University, ILR, September 22–25.

Liu, Li, Xingcan Chen, and Leping Jiang, 2004, A study of Neolithic water buffalo remains from Zhejiang, China. *Bulletin of the Indo-Pacific Prehistory Association: The Taipei Papers* 24(2):113–20.

Liu, Li, Xingcan Chen, Yun Kuen Lee, Henry Wright, and Arlene Rosen, 2002–2004, Settlement patterns and development of social complexity in the Yiluo region, north China. *Journal of Field Archaeology* 29(1–2):75–100.

Liu, Li, Xingcan Chen, and Baoping Li, 2007a, Non-state crafts in the early Chinese state: An archaeological view from the Erlitou hinterland. *Bulletin of the Indo-Pacific Prehistory Association* 27:93–102.

Liu, Li, Judith Field, Richard Fullagar, Sheahan Bestel, Xiaolin Ma, and Xingcan Chen, 2010a, What did grinding stones grind? New light on Early Neolithic subsistence economy in the Middle Yellow River Valley, China. *Antiquity* 84:816–33.

Liu, Li, Judith Field, Richard Fullagar, Chaohong Zhao, Xingcan Chen, and Jincheng Yu, 2010b, A functional analysis of grinding stones from an early Holocene site at Donghulin, north China. *Journal of Archaeological Science* 37:2630–9.

Liu, Li, Judith Field, Alison Weisskopf, John Webb, Leping Jiang, Haiming Wang, and Xingcan Chen, 2010c, The exploitation of acorn and rice in early Holocene Lower Yangzi River, China. *Acta Anthropologica Sinica* 29:317–36.

Liu, Li, Wei Ge, Sheahan Bestel, Duncan Jones, Jingming Shi, Yanhua Song, and Xingcan Chen, 2011, Plant exploitation of the last foragers at Shizitan in the Middle Yellow River Valley China: evidence from grinding stones. *Journal of Archaeological Science* 38:3524–32.

Liu, Li, Gyoung-Ah Lee, Leping Jiang, and Juzhong Zhang, 2007b, Evidence for the early beginning (c. 9000 cal. BP) of rice domestication in China: A response. *The Holocene* 17(8):1059–68.

Liu, Li and Hong Xu, 2007, Rethinking Erlitou: Legend, history and Chinese archaeology. *Antiquity* 81:886–901.

Liu, Li 刘莉, 2006, Zhiwuzhi taoqi, shizhufa ji taoqi de qiyuan: kuawenhua de bijiao 植物质陶器、石煮法及陶器的起源：跨文化的比较. In *Xibu Kaogu: Jinian Xibei Daxue Kaoguxue Zhuanye Chengli Wushi Zhounian Zhuankan* 西部考古：纪念西北大学考古专业成立五十周年专刊, edited by Xiebei Daxue Kaoguxi 西北大学考古系, pp. 32–42. Sanqin Chubanshe, Xi'an.

———, 2008, Zhongguo shiqian de nianmo shiqi, jianguo caiji, dingju ji nongye qiyuan 中国史前的碾磨石器，坚果采集，定居及农业起源. In *Ho Ping-ti Xiansheng Jiushi Huadan*

Wenji 何炳棣先生九十华诞文集, edited by Ho Ping-ti Xiansheng Jiushi Huadan Wenji Bianji Wenyuanhui 《〈何炳棣先生九十华诞文集〉》编辑委员会, pp. 105–32. Sanqin Chubanshe, Xi'an.

Liu, Li 刘莉, Gary Crawford, Gyoung-Ah Lee, Chen Xingcan 陈星灿, Ma Xiaolin 马萧林, Li Jianhe 李建和, and Zhang Jianhua 张建华, 2012, Zhengzhou Dahecun Yangshao Wenhua "gaoliang" yicun de zai yanjiu 郑州大河村仰韶文化"高粱"遗存的再研究. *Kaogu* 1:91–96.

Liu, Li 刘莉, Chen Xingcan 陈星灿, and Liu Guoxiang 刘国祥, in preparation, Xinglonggou yizhi chutu nianmo shiqi canliuwu ji weihen fenxi 兴隆沟遗址出土碾磨石器的残留物及微痕分析. In *Aohan Xinglonggou – 2001–2003 Niandu Xinshiqi Shidai Juluo Kaogu Fajue Baogao* 放汉兴隆沟–2001–2003年度新石器时代聚落考古发掘报告, edited by Zhongguo Shehui Kexueyuan Kaogu Yanjiusuo 中国社会科学院考古研究所. Wenwu Chubanshe, Beijing.

Liu, Li 刘莉, Yang Dongya 杨东亚, and Chen Xingcan 陈星灿, 2006, Zhongguo jiayang shuiniu de qiyuan 中国家养水牛的起源. *Kaogu Xuebao* 2:141–78.

Liu, Li 刘莉, Yan Yumin 阎毓民, and Qin Xiaoli 秦小丽, 2001, Shaanxi Lintong Kangjia Longshan wenhua yizhi 1990 nian fajue dongwu yicun 陕西临潼康家龙山文化遗址1990年发掘动物遗存. *Huaxia Kaogu* 1:3–24.

Liu, Qingzhu 刘庆柱 (editor), 2010, *Zhongguo kaogu faxian yu yanjiu (1949–2009)* 中国考古发现与研究 (1949–2009). Renmin Chubanshe, Beijing.

Liu, Qiyu 刘起釪, 2003, Gushibian yu Engesi de weiwushiguan 古史辨与恩格斯的唯物史观. In *Kaoguxue Yanjiu (5)* 考古学研究 (5), edited by Beijing Daxue Kaogu Wenboxueyuan 北京大学考古文博学院, pp. 820–50. Kexue Chubanshe, Beijing.

Liu, Senmiao 刘森森, 2002, Panlongcheng waiyuan daizhuang hangtu yiji de chubu renshi 盘龙城外缘带状夯土遗迹的初步认识. *Wuhan Wenbo* 1:12–15.

Liu, Shi'e 刘士莪 (editor), 2001, *Laoniupo* 老牛坡. Shaanxi Renmin Chubanshe, Xi'an.

Liu, Shimin 刘世民, Shu Shizhen 舒世珍, and Li Fushan 李福山, 1987, Jilin Yongji chutu dadou tanhua zhongzi de chubu jianding 吉林永吉出土大豆炭化种子的初步鉴定. *Kaogu* 4:365–9.

Liu, Shizhong 刘诗中 and Lu Benshan 卢本珊, 1998, Jiangxi Tongling tongkuang yizhi de fajue yu yanjiu 江西铜岭铜矿遗址的发掘与研究. *Kaogu Xuebao* 4:465–96.

Liu, Xu 刘绪, 2001, Youguan Xiadai niandai he Xia wenhua cenian de jidian kanfa 有关夏代年代和夏文化测年的几点看法. *Zhongyuan Wenwu* 2:32–3.

Liu, Yanfeng 刘彦锋, Wu Qian 吴倩, and Xue Bing 薛冰, 2010, Zhengzhou Shangcheng buju ji waiguocheng zouxiang xintan 郑州商城布局及外廓城走向新探. *Zhengzhou Daxue Xuebao* 3:164–8.

Liu, Yi-Ping, Gui-Sheng Wu, Yong-Gang Yao, Yong-Wang Miao, Gordon Luikart, Mumtaz Baig, Albano Beja-Pereira, Zhao-Li Ding, Malliya Gounder Palanichamy, and Ya-Ping Zhang, 2006, Multiple maternal origins of chickens: Out of the Asian jungles. *Molecular Phylogenetics and Evolution* 38:12–19.

Loewe, Michael, 1993, Shih ching. In *Early Chinese Texts: A Bibliographical Guide*, edited by Michael Loewe, pp. 415–23. The Society for the Study of Early China, Berkeley.

Longqiuzhuang Yizhi Kaogudui, 龙虬庄遗址考古队 (editor), 1999, *Longqiuzhuang* 龙虬庄. Kexue Chubanshe, Beijing.

Lu, Houyuan, Jianping Zhang, Kam-biu Liu, Naiqin Wu, Yumei Li, Kunshu Zhou, Maolin Ye, Tianyu Zhang, Haijiang Zhang, Xiaoyan Yang, Licheng Shen, Deke Xu, and Quan Li, 2009, Earliest domestication of common millet (*Panicum miliaceum*) in East Asia extended to 10,000 years ago. *Proceedings of the National Academy of Sciences USA* 106:6425–6.

Lu, Tracey L.-D., 1998, Some botanical characteristics of green foxtail (*Setaria viridis*) and harvesting experiments on the grass. *Antiquity* 72:902–7.

——, 1999, *The transition from foraging to farming and the origin of agriculture in China*. British Archaeological Report International Series 774. Hadrian Books, Oxford.

——, 2002, A green foxtail (*Setaria viridis*) cultivation experiment in the middle Yellow River valley and some related issues. *Asian Perspectives* 41(1):1–14.

——, 2006, The occurrence of cereal cultivation in China. *Asian Perspectives* 45(2):129–58.

——, 2010, Early pottery in South China. *Asian Perspectives* 49(1):1–42.

Lu, Wenbao 陆文宝, 1996, Zhejiang Yuhang Hengshan Liangzhu wenhua muzang qingli jianbao 浙江余杭横山良渚文化墓葬清理简报. In *Dongfang Wenming Zhiguang* 东方文明之光, edited by Xu Huping 徐湖平, pp. 69–77. Hainan Guoji Xinwen Chubanshe, Haikou.

Lü, Peng 吕鹏, 2010, Shilun Zhongguo jiayang huangniu de qiyuan 试论中国家养黄牛的起源. In *Dongwu Kaogu (Di 1 Ji)* 动物考古(第1辑), edited by Henansheng Wenwu Kaogu Yanjiusuo 河南省文物考古研究所, pp. 152–76. Wenwu Chubanshe, Beijing.

Lü, Zhirong 吕智荣, 1987, Shilun Shaan Jin beibu Huanghe liang 'an diqu chutu de Shangdai qingtongqi ji youguan wenti 试论陕晋北部黄河两岸地区出土商代青铜器及有关问题. In *Zhongguo Kaoguxue Yanjiu Lunji* 中国考古学研究论集, edited by Zhongguo Kaoguxue Yanjiu Lunji Bianweihui 中国考古学研究论集编委会, pp. 214–25. Sanqin Chubanshe, Xi'an.

———, 1990, Guifang wenhua ji xiangguan wenti chutan 鬼方文化及相关问题初探. *Wenbo* 1:32–7.

———, 1993, Lijiaya wenhua de shehui jingji xingtai ji fazhan 李家崖文化社会经济形态及发展. In *Kaoguxue Yanjiu* 考古学研究, edited by Shi Xingbang 石兴邦, pp. 117, 356–9. Sanqin Chubanshe, Xi'an.

———, 1998, Lijiaya guchengzhi AF1 jianzhu yizhi chutan 李家崖古城址AF1建筑遗址初探. In *Zhou Qin Wenhua Yanjiu* 周秦文化研究, edited by Shi Xingbang 石兴邦, Guan Donggui 管东贵, Zhang Yusheng 张豫生, Wang Wenqing 王文清, and Jiang Yunfei 蒋云飞, pp. 116–23. Shaanxi Renmin Chubanshe, Xi'an.

Lü, Zun'e 吕遵谔, 2004a, 20 shiji Zhongguo jiushiqi shidai kaogu de huigu yu zhanwang 20世纪中国旧石器时代考古的回顾与展望. In *Zhongguo Kaoguxue Yanjiu de Shiji Huigu* 中国考古学研究的世纪回顾, edited by Lü Zun'e 吕遵谔, pp. 3–26. Kexue Chubanshe, Beijing.

———, (editor), 2004b, *Zhongguo Kaoguxue Yanjiu de Shiji Huigu* 中国考古学研究的世纪回顾. Kexue Chubanshe, Beijing.

Luan, Fengshi 栾丰实, 1996a, *Dongyi Kaogu* 东夷考古. Shandong Daxue Chubanshe, Jinan.

———, 1996b, Liangzhu wenhua de beijian 良渚文化的北渐. *Zhongyuan Wenwu* 3:31, 51–8.

———, 1997, *Haidai Diqu Kaogu Yanjiu* 海岱地区考古研究. Shangdong Daxue Chubanshe, Jinan.

———, 2006, Guanyu Haidai diqu shiqian chengzhi de jige wenti 关于海岱地区史前城址的几个问题. In *Dongfang Kaogu* 东方考古, edited by Shandong Daxue Dongfang Kaogu Yanjiu Zhongxin 山东大学东方考古研究中心, pp. 66–78. Kexue Chubanshe, Beijing.

Luo, Chengzheng 骆承政 and Le Jiaxiang 乐嘉祥, 1996, *Zhongguo Dahongshui – Zaihaixing Hongshui Shuyao* 中国大洪水——灾害性洪水述要. Zhongguo Shudian, Beijing.

Luo, Hongjie 罗宏杰, Li Jiazhi 李家治, and Gao Liming 高力明, 1996, Beifang chutu yuanshici shaozao diqu de yanjiu 北方地区原始瓷烧造地区的研究. *Guisuanyan Xuebao* 24(3):297–302.

Luo, Yunbing 罗运兵, 2007, *Zhongguo gudai jiazhu yanjiu* 中国古代家猪研究. PhD dissertation, Chinese Academy of Social Sciences, Beijing.

Luoyangshi Wenwu Gongzuodui 洛阳市文物工作队 (editor), 2002, *Luoyang Zaojiaoshu* 洛阳皂角树. Kexue Chubanshe, Beijing.

Ma, Chengyuan 马承源 (editor) 1996, *Zhongguo Qingtongqi Quanji: Xia Shang* 中国青铜器全集: 夏商. Wenwu Chubanshe, Beijing.

Ma, Shizhi 马世之, 2003, *Zhongguo Shiqian Gucheng* 中国史前古城. Hubei Jiaoyu Chubanshe, Wuhan.

Ma, Xiaolin, 2005, *Emergent Social Complexity in the Yangshao Culture: Analyses of Settlement Patterns and Faunal Remains from Lingbao, Western Henan, China (c. 4900–3000 BC)*. BAR International Series, Oxford.

Ma, Xiaolin 马萧林, Chen Xingcan 陈星灿, Yang Zhaoqing 杨肇清, Zhang Juzhong 张居中, Zhang Huaiyin 张怀银, Li Xinwei 李新伟, and Huang Weidong 黄卫东, 1999, Henan Lingbao Zhudingyuan jiqi zhouwei kaogu diaocha baogao 河南灵宝铸鼎塬及其周围考古调查报告. *Huaxia kaogu* 3:19–42.

MacNeish, Richard S., and Jane G. Libby (editors), 1995, *Origins of Rice Agriculture: The Preliminary Report of the Sino-American Jiangxi (PRC) Project (SAJOR)*. The University of Texas, El Paso.

MacNeish, Richard. S., Geoffrey Cunnar, Zhijun Zhao, and Jane Libby, 1998, *Revised Second Annual Report of the Sino-American Jiangxi (PRC) Origin of Rice Project (SAJOR)*. Andover Foundation, Amherst, MA.

Madsen, David B., Robert G. Elston, Robert L. Bettinger, Xu Cheng, and Zhong Kan, 1996, Settlement patterns reflected in assemblages from the Pleistocene/Holocene transition of North Central China. *Journal of Archaeological Science* 23(2):217–31.

Mair, Victor, 2003, The horse in late Prehistoric China: Wresting culture and control from the "Barbarians." In *Prehistoric Steppe Adaptation and the Horse*, edited by Marsha Levine,

Colin Renfrew, and Katie Boyle, pp. 163–87. McDonald Institute for Archaeological Research, Cambridge, UK.

Mallory, J. P., 1989, *In Search of the Indo-Europeans: Language, Archaeology and Myth*. Thames and Hudson, London.

Mallory, J. P. and Victor Mair, 2000, *The Tarim Mummies: Ancient China and the Mystery of the Earliest Peoples from the West*. Thames & Hudson, London.

Mao, Longjiang, Duowen Mo, Leping Jiang, Yaofeng Jia, Xiaoyan Liu, Minglin Li, Kunshu Zhou, and Chenxi Shi, 2008, Environmental change since mid-Pleistocene recorded in Shangshan archaeological site of Zhejiang. *Journal of Geographical Science* 18:247–56.

Mao, Ruilin 毛瑞林, Qian Yaopeng 钱耀鹏, Xie Yan 谢焱, Zhu Yunyun 朱芸芸, and Zhou Jing 周静, 2009, Gansu Lintan Mogou Qijia wenhua mudi fajue jianbao 甘肃临潭磨沟齐家文化墓地发掘简报. *Wenwu* 10:4–24.

Marcus, Joyce and Gary Feinman, 1998, Introduction. In *Archaic States*, edited by Gary Feinman and Joyce Marcus, pp. 3–14. School of American Research Press, Santa Fe, NM.

Marshall, Yvonne, 2006, Introduction: Adopting a sedentary lifeway. *World Archaeology* 38(2):153–63.

Mashkour, M., 2006, *Equids in Time and Space: Papers in Honour of Véra Eisenmann*. Oxbow, Oxford.

Mashkour, Marjan, 2003, Equids in the northern part of the Iranian central plateau from the Neolithic to Iron Age: New zoogeographic evidence. In *Prehistoric Steppe Adaptation and the Horse*, edited by Marcha Levine, Colin Renfrew, and Katie Boyle, pp. 129–38. McDonald Institute Monographs, Cambridge, UK.

Mason, Sarah L. R., 1992, *Acorns in Human Subsistence*. Unpublished PhD thesis, University College London.

———, 1996, Acornutopia? Determining the role of acorns in past human subsistence. In *Food in Antiquity*, edited by John Wilkins, David Harvey, and Mike Dobson, pp. 12–24. University of Exeter Press, Exeter.

Maybury-Lewis, David H., 2000, On theories of order and justice in the development of civilization. In *The Breakout: The Origins of Civilization*, edited by Martha lanberg-Karlovsky, pp. 39–43. Peabody Museum Monographs, Cambridge, MA.

McAnany, Patricia A. and Norman Yoffee (editors), 2010, *Questioning Collapse: Human Resilience, Ecological Vulnerability, and the Aftermath of Empire*. Cambridge University Press, Cambridge.

McGahern, A., M. A. M. Bower, C. J. Edwards, P. O. Brophy, G. Sulimova, I. Zakharov, M. Vizuete-Forster, M. Levine, S. Li, D. E. MacHugh, and E. W. Hill, 2006, Evidence for biogeographic patterning of mitochondrial DNA sequences in Eastern horse populations. *Animal Genetics* 37:494–7.

McGovern, Patrick, Anne Underhill, Hui Fang, Fengshi Luan, Gretchen Hall, Haiguang Yu, Chen-shan Wang, Fengshu Cai, Zhijun Zhao, and Gary Feinman, 2005, Chemical identification and cultural implications of a mixed fermented beverage from late prehistoric China. *Asian Perspectives* 44(2):249–75.

McGovern, Patrick, Juzhong Zhang, Jigen Tang, Zhiqing Zhang, Gretchen Hall, Robert Moreau, Alberto Nunez, Eric Butrym, Michael Richards, Chen-shan Wang, Guangsheng Cheng, and Zhijun Zhao, 2004, Fermented beverages of pre- and proto-historic China. *Proceedings of the National Academy of Sciences USA* 101(51):17593–8.

Mei, Jianjun, 2000, *Copper and Bronze Metallurgy in Late Prehistoric Xinjiang*. BAR, Oxford.

———, 2003, Qijia and Seima-Turbino: The question of early contacts between northwest China and the Eurasian steppe. *Bulletin of the Museum of Far Eastern Antiquities* 75:31–54.

Mei, Jianjun and Colin Shell, 1998, Copper and bronze metallurgy in the prehistoric Xinjiang. In *The Bronze Age and Early Iron Age Peoples of Eastern Central Asia*, edited by Victor Mair, pp. 581–603. Institute for the Study of Man in Collaboration with the University of Pennsylvania Museum Publications, Washington, DC.

Mei, Jianjun 梅建军, 2006, Guanyu Zhongguo yejin qiyuan ji zaoqi tongqi yanjiu de jige wenti 关于中国冶金起源暨早期铜器研究的几个问题. In *Zhongguo Yejinshi Lunwenji (4)* 中国冶金史论文集 (第四辑), edited by Beijing Keji Daxue Yejin yu Cailiaoshi Yanjiusuo 北京科技大学冶金与材料史研究所 and Beijing Keji Daxue Kexue Jishu yu Wenming Yanjiu Zhongxin 北京科技大学科学技术与文明研究中心, pp. 11–23. Kexue Chubanshe, Beijing.

————, 2009, Early metallurgy and socio-cultural complexity: Archaeological discoveries in Northwest China. In *Social Complexity in Prehistoric Eurasia*, edited by Bryan K. Hanks and Katheryn M. Linduff, pp. 215–32. Cambridge University Press, Cambridge.

Min, Rui 闵锐, 2009, Yunnan Jianchuanxian Haimenkou yizhi disanci fajue 云南剑川县海门口遗址第三次发掘. *Kaogu* 8:3–22.

Mou, Yongkang 牟永抗, and Yun Xizheng 云希正 (editors), 1992, *Zhongguo Yuqi Quanji* 中国玉器全集. Hebei Meishu Chubanshe, Shijiazhuang.

Mudar, Karen and Douglas Anderson, 2007, New evidence for Southeast Asian Pleistocene foraging economies: Faunal remains from the early levels of Lang Rongrien rockshelter, Krabi, Thailand. *Asian Perspectives* 46(2):298–334.

Murowchick, Robert and David Cohen, 2001, Searching for Shang's beginnings: Great City Shang, city Song, and collaborative archaeology in Shangqiu, Henan. *The Review of Archaeology* 22(2):47–60.

Murphey, Rhoads, 1972, A geographical view of China. In *An Introduction to Chinese Civilization*, edited by J. Meskill, pp. 515–50. D.C. Heath, Lexington, MA.

Nan, Puheng 南濮恒, Qin Ying 秦颖, Li Taoyuan 李桃元, and Dong Yawei 董亚巍, 2008, Hubei Panglongcheng chutu bufen Shangdai qingtongqi zhuzaodi de fenxi 湖北盘龙城出土部分商代青铜器铸造地的分析. *Wenwu* 8:77–82.

Nanjing Bowuyuan Kaogu Yanjiusuo, 南京博物院考古研究所, 2001, Jiangsu Jurong Dingshadi yizhi di erci fajue jianbao 江苏句容丁沙地遗址第二次发掘简报. *Wenwu* 5:22–36.

Neimenggu and Ordos (Neimenggu Wenwu Kaogu Yanjiusuo 内蒙古文物考古研究所 and Ordos Bowuguan 鄂尔多斯博物馆) (editors), 2000, *Zhukaigou: Qingtong Shidai Zaoqi Yizhi Fajue Baogao* 朱开沟：青铜时代早期遗址发掘报告. Wenwu Chubanshe, Beijing.

Nelson, Sarah M., 1993, *The Archaeology of Korea*. Cambridge University Press, Cambridge.

————, 1995, Ritualized pigs and the origins of complex society: Hypotheses regarding the Hongshan culture. *Early China* 20:1–16.

Ning, Yintang 宁荫堂 and Wang Fang 王方, 1994, Shandong Zhangqiuxian Xiaojingshan yizhi diaocha jianbao 山东章丘县小荆山遗址调查简报. *Kaogu* 6:490–4.

Niu, Shishan 牛世山, 2006, Shangdai de Qiangfang 商代的羌方. In *Sandai Kaogu* 三代考古, edited by Zhongguo Shehui Kexueyuan Kaogu Yanjiusuo 中国社会科学院考古研究所, pp. 459–71. Kexue Chubanshe, Beijing.

Oka, Hiko-ichi and Hiroko Morishima, 1971, The dynamics of plant domestication: Cultivation experiments with *Oryza perennis* and its hybrid with *O. sativa*. *Evolution* 25:356–64.

Olsen, Sandra L., 2006, Early horse domestication: Weighing the evidence. In *Horses and Humans: The Evolution of Human-Equine Relationships*, edited by Sandra L. Olsen, Susan Grant, Alice M. Choyke, and Laszlo Bartosiewicz, pp. 81–113. BAR International Series 1560, Oxford.

Olsen, Stanley J., 1988, The horse in ancient China and its cultural influence in some other areas. *Proceedings of the Academy of Natural Sciences of Philadelphia* 140:151–89.

Olsen, Stanley J. and John W. Olsen, 1977, The Chinese wolf, ancestor of New World dogs. *Science* 197:533–5.

————, 1980, Zhongguo zhulei de xunyang 中国猪类的驯养. *Vertebrata PalAsiatica* 18:169–75.

Ortiz, Beverly R., 1991, *It Will Live Forever: Traditional Yosemite Indian Acorn Preparation*. Heyday Books, Berkeley.

Ovodov, Nikolai D., Susan J. Crockford, Yaroslav V. Kuzmin, Thomas F. G. Higham, Gregory W. L. Hodgins, and Johannes van der Plicht, 2011, A 33,000-Year-Old Incipient Dog from the Altai Mountains of Siberia: Evidence of the Earliest Domestication Disrupted by the Last Glacial Maximum. *PLoS ONE* 6(7):e22821. doi:10.1371/journal.pone.0022821.

Owen, Dale, 2007, An Exercise in Experimental Archaeology on Chinese Stone Spades. *Bulletin of the Indo-Pacific Prehistory Association* 27:87–92.

Pan, Qifeng 潘其风, 1996, Dadianzi muzang chutu rengu de yanjiu 大甸子墓葬出土人骨的研究. In *Dadianzi* 大甸子, edited by Zhongguo Shehui Kexueyuan Kaogu Yanjiusuo 中国社会科学院考古研究所, pp. 224–322. Kexue Chubanshse, Beijing.

————, 2000, Zhukaigou mudi rengu de yanjiu 朱开沟墓地人骨的研究. In *Zhukaigou* 朱开沟, edited by Neimenggu Wenwu Kaogu Yanjiusu 内蒙古文物考古研究所 and Ordos

Bowuguan 鄂尔多斯博物馆, pp. 340–99. Wenwu Chubanshe, Beijing.

Pan, Qifeng 潘其风 and Han Kangxin 韩康信, 1998, Liuwan mudi de rengu yanjiu 柳湾墓地的人骨研究. In *Qinghai Liuwan* 青海柳湾, edited by Qinghaisheng Wenwu Guanlichu Kaogudui 青海省文物管理处考古队 and Zhongguo Shehui Kexueyuan Kaogu Yanjiusuo 中国社会科学院考古研究所, pp. 261–303. Wenwu Chubanshe, Beijing.

Pang, Xiaoxia 庞小霞 and Gao Jiangtao 高江涛, 2008, Guanyu Xinzhaiqi yicun yanjiu de jige wenti 关于新砦期遗存的几个问题. *Huaxia Kaogu* 1:73–80.

Patel, Ajita, 1997, The pastoral economy of Dholavira: A first look at animals and urban life in third millennium Kutch. In *South Asian Archaeology 1995: Proceedings of the 13th Conference of the European Association of South Asian Archaeologists*, edited by Raymond Allchin and Bridget Allchin, pp. 101–13. Science Publishers, New Delhi.

Patel, Ajita and Richard Meadow, 1998, The exploitation of wild and domestic water buffalo in prehistoric northwestern South Asia. In *Archaeozoology of the Near East III*, edited by H. Buitenhuis, L. Bartosiewicz, and A. M. Choyke, pp. 180–98. ARC – Publicaties 18, Groningen.

Payne, Sebastian and Gail Bull, 1988, Components of variation in measurements of pig bones and teeth, and the use of measurements to distinguish wild from domestic pig remains. *Archaeozoologia* II(1,2):27–66.

Pearson, Richard J., 1988, Chinese Neolithic burial patterns: Problems of method and interpretation. *Early China* 13:1–45.

———, 2006, Jomon hot spot: Increasing sedentism in south-western Japan in the Incipient Jomon (14,000–9250 ca. bc) and Earliest Jomon (9250–5300 cal. bc) periods. *World Archaeology* 38(2):239–58.

Pechenkina, Ekaterina, Stanley H. Ambrose, Ma Xiaolin, and Robert A. Benfer Jr., 2005, Reconstructing northern Chinese Neolithic subsistence practices by isotopic analysis. *Journal of Archaeological Science* 32:1176–89.

Pedley, Helen, 1992, *Aboriginal Life in the Rainforest*. Ron Bastow Printing, Cairns, Queensland, Australia.

Pei, Anping, 1998, Notes on new advancements and revelations in the agricultural archaeology of early rice domestication in the Dongting Lake region. *Antiquity* 72:878–85.

———, 2002, Rice paddy agriculture and pottery from the middle reaches of the Yangtze River. In *The Origins of Pottery and Agriculture*, edited by Yoshinori Yasuda, pp. 167–84. Roli Books, New Delhi.

Pei, Anping 裴安平, 1996, Pengtoushan wenhua chulun 彭头山文化初论. In *Changjiang Zhongyou Shiqian Wenhua ji Dierjie Yazhou Wenming Xueshu Taolunhui Lunwenji* 长江中游史前文化暨第二届亚洲文明学术讨论会论文集, edited by Hunansheng Wenwu Kaogu Yanjiusuo 湖南省文物考古研究所, pp. 81–104. Yuelu Shushe, Changsha.

———, 2004, Liyang pingyuan shiqian juluo xingtai de yanjiu yu sikao 澧阳平原史前聚落形态的研究与思考. In *Qingzhu Zhang Zhongpei Xiansheng Qishisui Lunwenji* 庆祝张忠培先生七十岁论文集, edited by Jilin Daxue Bianjiang Kaogu Yanjiu Zhongxin 吉林大学边疆考古研究中心, pp. 192–242. Kexue Chubanshe, Beijing.

Peng, Ke 彭柯 and Zhu Yanshi 朱岩石, 1999, Zhongguo gudai suoyong haibei laiyuan xintan 中国古代所用海贝来源新探. *Kaoguxue Jikan* 12:119–47.

Peng, Minghan 彭明瀚, 2005, *Wucheng Wenhua Yanjiu* 吴城文化研究. Wenwu Chubanshe, Beijing.

Peng, Quanmin 彭全民, Huang Wenming 黄文明, Huang Xiaohong 黄小宏, and Feng Yongqu 冯永驱, 1990, Shenzhenshi Dapeng Xantouling shaqiu yizhi fajue jianbao 深圳市大鹏咸头岭沙丘遗址发掘简报. *Wenwu* 11:1–11.

Peng, Shifan 彭适凡, 1987, *Zhongguo nanfang gudai yinwentao* 中国南方古代印纹陶. Wenwu Chubanshe, Beijing.

Pollock, Susan, 1999, *Ancient Mesopotamia*. Cambridge University Press, Cambridge.

Price, Douglas T. and Anne B. Gebauer, 1995, *Last Hunters-First Farmers*. School of American Research Press, Santa Fe, NM.

Qi, Guoqin 祁国琴, 1988, Jiangzhai xinshiqi shidai yizhi dongwuqun de fenxi 姜寨新石器时代遗址动物群的分析. In *jiangzhai* 姜寨, edited by Xi'an Banpo Museum 西安半坡博物馆, Shaanxi Archaeological Institute 陕西省考古研究所, and Lintong County Museum 临潼县博物馆, pp. 504–39. Wenwu Chubanhse, Beijing.

———, 1989, Zhongguo beifang disiji buru dongwuqun jianlun yuanshi renlei shenghuo huanjing 中国北方第四纪哺乳动物群兼论原始

人类生活环境. In *Zhongguo Yuangu Renlei* 中国远古人类, edited by Wu Rukang 吴汝康, Wu Xinzhi 吴新智, and Zhang Senshui 张森水, pp. 277–308. Kexue Chubanshe, Beijing.

———, 1998, Donghuishan mudi shougu jianding baogao 东灰山墓地兽骨鉴定报告. In *Minle Donghuishan Kaogu* 民乐东灰山考古, edited by Gansusheng wenwu kaogu yanjiusuo 甘肃省文物考古研究所 and Jilin daxue Beifang kaogu yanjiushi 吉林大学北方考古研究室, pp. 184–5. Kexue Chubanshe, Beijing.

Qi, Guoqin 祁国琴 Lin Zhongyu 林钟雨, and An Jiayuan 安家瑗, 2006, Dadiwan yizhi dongwu yicun jianding baogao 大地湾遗址动物遗存鉴定报告. In *Qin'an Dadiwan* 秦安大地湾, edited by Gansusheng Wenwu Kaogu Yanjiusuo 甘肃省文物考古研究所. Wenwu Chubanshe, Beijing

Qian, Xiaokang 钱小康, 2002a, Li 犁. *Nongye Kaogu* 1:170–81.

———, 2002b, Li (Xu) 犁 (续). *Nongye Kaogu* 3:183–206.

Qiao, Yu, 2007, Development of complex societies in the Yiluo region: A GIS based population and agricultural area analysis. *Indo-Pacific Prehistory Association Bulletin* 27:61–75.

Qinghaisheng and Zhongguo (Qinghaisheng Wenwu Guanlichu Kaogudui, 青海省文物管理处考古队 and Zhongguo Shehui Kexueyuan Kaogu Yanjiusuo 中国社会科学院考古研究所) (editors), 1984, *Qinghai Liuwan* 青海柳湾. Wenwu Chubanshe, Beijing.

Qinghaisheng Wenwu Guanlichu (Qinghaisheng Wenwu Guanlichu Kaogudui, 青海省文物管理处考古队), 1978, Qinghai Datongxian Shangsunjiazhai chutu de wudaowen caitaopen 青海大通县上孙家寨出土的舞蹈纹彩陶盆. *Wenwu* 3:48–9.

Qinghaisheng Wenwu Kaogu (Qinghaisheng Wenwu Kaogu Yanjiusuo, 青海省文物考古研究所) (editor), 1990, *Minhe Yangshan* 民和阳山. Wenwu Chubanshe, Beijing.

Quine, T. A., D. Walling, and X. Zhang, 1999, Slope and gully response to agricultural activity in the rolling loess plateau, China. In *Fluvial Processes and Environmental Change*, edited by A. G. Brown and T. A. Quine, pp. 71–90. Wiley & Sons, New York.

Redman, Charles L., 2005, Resilience theory in archaeology. *American Anthropologist* 107(1):70–7.

Redman, Charles L. and Ann P. Kinzig, 2003, Resilience of past landscapes: Resilience theory, society, and the longue durée.

Conservation Ecology 7(1):14. Also available online at: http://www.consecol.org/vol7/iss1/art14.

Reid, Kenneth C., 1989, A materials science perspective on hunter-gatherer pottery. In *Pottery Technology: Ideas and Approaches*, edited by Gordon Bronitsky, pp. 167–80. Westview Press, Boulder, San Francisco, and London.

Ren, Guoyu and Hans-Juergen Beug, 2002, Mapping Holocene pollen data and vegetation of China. *Quaternary Science Reviews* 21:1395–422.

Ren, Shinan 任式楠, 1996, Liangzhu wenhua tuxiang yubi de tantao 良渚文化图像玉璧的探讨. In *Dongfang Wenming Zhiguang* 东方文明之光, edited by Xu Huping 徐湖平, pp. 324–30. Hainan Guoji Xinwen Chuban Zhongxin, Hainan.

———, 2003, Zhongguo shiqian tongqi zongshu 中国史前铜器综述. In *Zhongguo Shiqian Kaoguxue Yanjiu* 中国史前考古学研究, edited by Shaanxisheng Wenwuju 陕西省文物局, Shaanxisheng Kaogu Yanjiusuo 陕西省考古研究所, and Xi'an Banpo Bowuguan 西安半坡博物馆, pp. 384–93. Sanqin Chubanshe, Xi'an.

Ren, Shinan 任式楠 and Wu Yaoli 吴耀利, 1999, Zhongguo xinshiqi shidai kaoguxue wushi nian 中国新石器时代考古学五十年. *Kaogu* 9:11–22.

Ren, Xianghong 任相宏, 1997, Zhengzhou Xiaoshuangqiao chutu de Yueshi wenhua shiqi yu Zhongding zheng Lanyi 郑州小双桥出土的岳石文化石器与仲丁征蓝夷. *Zhongyuan Wenwu* 3:111–15.

Ren, Xiaoyan 任晓燕, Wang Guodao 王国道, Cai Linhai 蔡林海, He Kezhou 何克洲, and Ye Maolin 叶茂林, 2002, Qinghai Minhexian Lajia yizhi 2000 nian fajue jianbao 青海民和县喇家遗址 2000 年发掘简报. *Kaogu* 12:12–28.

Rhode, David, Haiying Zhang, David B. Madsen, Xing Gao, P. Jeffrey Brantingham, Haizhou Ma, and John W. Olsen, 2007, Epipaleolithic/early Neolithic settlements at Qinghai Lake, western China. *Journal of Archaeological Science* 34:600–12.

Rice, Prudence M., 1999, On the origins of pottery. *Journal of Archaeological Method and Theory* 6(1):1–51.

Rickett, W. Allyn, 1993, Kuan tzu. In *Early Chinese Texts: A Bibliographical Guide*, edited by Michael Loewe, pp. 244–51. The Society for the Study of Early China, Berkeley.

Riegel, Jeffrey K., 1993, Ta Tai Li chi. In *Early Chinese Texts: A Bibliographical Guide*, edited by Michael Loewe, pp. 456–9. The Society for the Study of Early China, Berkeley.

Rind, D., D. Peteet, W. Broecker, A. McIntyre, and W. Ruddiman, 1986, The impact of cold North Atlantic sea surface temperatures on climate: Implications for the Younger Dryas cooling (11–10K). *Climate Dynamics* 1:3–33.

Rindos, David, 1980, Symbiosis, instability, and the origins and spread of agriculture: A new model. *Current Anthropology* 21(6):751–72.

———, 1984, *The Origins of Agriculture: An Evolutionary Perspective*. Academic Press, Orlando, FL.

———, 1989, Domestication. In *Foraging and Farming: The Evolution of Plant Exploitation*, edited by D. R. Harris and G. C. Hillman, pp. 27–41. Unwin Hyman, London.

Rispoli, Fiorella, 2007, The incised & impressed pottery style of Mainland Southeast Asia: Following the paths of Neolithization. *East and West* 57(1–4):235–304.

Rolett, Barry V., Tianlong Jiao, and Gongwu Lin, 2002, Early seafaring in the Taiwan Strait. *Journal of East Asian Archaeology* 4(1–4):307–20.

Rosen, Arlene M., 2007a, The role of environmental change in the development of complex societies in China: A study from the Huizui site. *Bulletin of the Indo-Pacific Prehistory Association* 27:39–48.

———, 2007b, *Civilizing Climate: Social Responses to Climate Change in the Ancient Near East*. Rowman & Littlefield Publishers, Lanham, MD.

Rosen, Steven, 1987, Byzantine nomadism in the Negev: Results from the emergency survey. *Journal of Field Archaeology* 14(1):29–42.

———, 1993, A Roman-Period pastoral tent camp in the Negev, Israel. *Journal of Field Archaeology* 20(4):441–51.

Rosenswig, Robert M., 2006, Sedentism and food production in early complex societies of the Soconusco, Mexico. *World Archaeology* 38(2):330–55.

Ryder, Oliver A., 1993, Przewalski's horse: Prospects for reintroduction into the wild. *International Conservation News* 7(1):13–15.

Sassaman, Kenneth, 1993, *Early Pottery in the Southeast: Tradition and Innovation in Cooking Technology*. The University of Alabama Press, Tuscaloosa and London.

Sato, Yoichiro 佐藤洋一郎, 2002, Origin of rice cultivation in the Yangtze River Basin. In *The Origins of Pottery and Agriculture*, edited by Yoshinori Yasuda, pp. 143–50. Roli Books Pvt. Ltd, New Delhi.

Schettler, G., Qiang Liu, Jens Mingram, Martina Stebich, and Peter Dulski, 2006, East-Asian monsoon variability between 15000 and 2000 cal. yr BP recorded in varved sediments of Lake Sihailongwan (northeastern China, Long Gang volcanic field). *The Holocene* 16(8):1043–57.

Schiffer, Michael B., 1976, *Behavioral Archaeology*. Academic Press, New York.

Schiffer, Michael B. and James M. Skibo, 1987, Theory and experiment in the study of technological change. *Current Anthropology* 28(5):595–622.

Schneider, Laurence A., 1971, *Ku Chieh-kang and China's New History: Nationalism and the Quest for Alternative Traditions*. University of California Press, Berkeley.

Shaanxisheng (Shaanxisheng kaogu yanjiusuo 陕西省考古研究所) (editor), 2005, *Kaogu Nianbao 考古年报*. Shaanxisheng Kaogu Yanjiusuo, Xi'an.

Shaanxisheng and Shaanxisheng (Shaanxisheng Kaogu Yanjiusuo 陕西省考古研究所 and Shaanxisheng Ankang Shuidianzhan Kuqu Kaogudui 陕西省安康水电站库区考古队) (editors), 1994, *Shaannan Kaogu Baogaoji 陕南考古报告集*. Sanqin Chubanshe, Xi'an.

Shaanxisheng and Yulinshi (Shaanxisheng Kaogu Yanjiusuo 陕西省考古研究所 and Yulinshi Wenwu Baohu Yanjiusuo 榆林市文物保护研究所) (editors), 2005, *Shenmu Xinhua 神木新华*. Kexue Chubanshe, Beijing.

Shandongsheng Wenwu Kaogu Yanjiusuo 山东省文物考古研究所 (editor), 2005, *Shandong 20 Shiji de Kaogu Faxian he Yanjiu 山东 20 世纪的考古发现和研究*. Kexue Chubanshe, Beijing.

Shang, Hong, Haowen Tong, Shuangquan Zhang, Fuyou Chen, and Erik Trinkaus, 2007, An early modern human from Tianyuan Cave, Zhoukoudian, China. *Proceedings of the National Academy of Sciences USA* 104:6573–8.

Shanxisheng Kaogu Yanjiusuo 山西省考古研究所, 2002, Shanxi Ruicheng Qingliangsi Mudi Yuqi 山西芮城清凉寺墓地玉器. *Kaogu yu Wenwu* 5:3–6.

———, 2006 (editor), *Lingshi Jingjie Shangmu 灵石旌介商墓*. Kexue Chubanshe, Beijing.

Shao, Wangping 邵望平, 1984, Xinfaxian de Dawenkou wenhua 新发现的大汶口文化. In *Xinzhongguo de Kaogu Faxian he Yanjiu* 新中国的考古发现和研究, edited by Zhongguo Shehui Kexueyaun Kaogu yanjiusuo 中国社会科学院考古研究所, pp. 86–96. Wenwu Chubanshe, Beijing.

———, 1989, Yugong jiuzhou de kaoguxue yanjiu 禹贡九州的考古学研究. In *Kaoguxue Wenhua Lunji* 考古学文化研究, edited by Su Bingqi 苏秉琦, pp. 11–30. Wenwu Chubanshe, Beijing.

Shaughnessy, Edward L., 1988, Historical perspectives on the introduction of the chariot in China. *Harvard Journal of Asiatic Studies* 48(1):189–237.

———, 1993, I Chou shu. In *Early Chinese Texts: A Bibliographical Guide*, edited by Michael Loewe, pp. 229–33. The Society for the Study of Early China, Berkeley, CA.

———, 2008, Chronologies of ancient China: A critique of the "Xia-Shang-Zhou Chronology Project." In *Windows on the Chinese World: Reflections by Five Historians*, edited by Clara Ho, pp. 15–28. Lexington Books, London.

Shelach, Gideon, 1996, The Qiang and the question of human sacrifice in the late Shang period. *Asian Perspectives* 35(1):1–26.

———, 1997, A settlement pattern study in northeast China: Results and potential contributions of western theory and methods to Chinese archaeology. *Antiquity* 71:114–27.

———, 1999, *Leadership Strategies, Economic Activity, and Interregional Interaction: Social Complexity in Northeast China*. Kluwer Academic/Plenum, New York.

———, 2001a, Apples and oranges? A cross-cultural comparison of burial bata from northeast China. *Journal of East Asian Archaeology* 3(3–4):53–90.

———, 2001b, Interaction spheres and the development of social complexity in northeast China. *The Review of Archaeology* 22(2):22–34.

———, 2006, Economic adaptation, community structure, and sharing strategies of households at early sedentary communities in northeast China. *Journal of Anthropological Archaeology* 25:318–45.

———, 2009a, *Prehistoric Societies on the Northern Frontiers of China: Archaeological Perspectives on Identity Formation and Economic Change during the First Millennium BCE*. Equinox, London, Oakville.

———, 2009b, Violence on the frontiers? Sources of power and socio-political change at the easternmost parts of the Eurasian steppe during the late second and early first millennia BCE. In *Social Complexity in Prehistoric Eurasia*, edited by Bryan K. Hanks and Katheryn M. Linduff, pp. 241–71. Cambridge University Press, Cambridge.

Shen, Junshan 沈军山, 1994, Hebei Luanpingxian Houtaizi yizhi fajue jianbao 河北省滦平县后台子遗址发掘简报. *Wenwu* 3:53–74.

Sherratt, Andrew, 1981, Plough and pastoralism: Aspects of the secondary products revolution. In *Pattern of the Past: Studies in Honour of David Clarke*, edited by Ian Hodder, Glynn Isaac, and Norman Hammond, pp. 261–305. Cambridge University Press, Cambridge.

Shi, Jinming 石金鸣 and Song Yanhua 宋艳花, 2010, Shanxi Jixian Shizitan yizhi dijiu didian fajue jianbao 山西吉县柿子滩第九地点发掘简报. *Kaogu* 10:7–17.

Shi, Xingbang, 1992, The discovery of the pre-Yangshao culture and its significance. In *Pacific Northeast Asia in Prehistory: Hunter-Fisher-Gatherers, Farmers, and Sociopolitical Elites*, edited by C. Melvin Aikens and Song Nai Rhee, pp. 125–32. Washington State University Press, Pullman.

Shi, Xingeng 施昕更, 1938, *Liangzhu* 良渚. Zhejiang Jiaoyuting Chubanshe, Hangzhou.

Shi, Y., Z. Kong, S. Wang, L. Tang, F. Wang, T. Yao, X. Zhao, P. Zhang, and S. Shi, 1993, Mid-Holocene climates and environments in China. *Global and Planetary Change* 7:219–33.

Shi, Yafeng 施雅风, Kong Zhaochen 孔昭宸, and Wang Sumin 王苏民, 1992, Zhongguo Quanxinshi danuanqi qihou yu huanjing de jiben tezheng 中国全新世大暖期气候与环境的基本特征. In *Zhongguo Quanxinshi Danuanqi Qihou yu Huanjing* 中国全新世大暖期气候与环境, edited by Shi Yanfeng 施雅风 and Kong Zhaochen 孔昭宸, pp. 1–18. Kexue Chubanshe, Beijing.

Shih, Chang-ju 石璋如, 1953, Henan Anyang Xiaotun mu zhong de dongwu yihai 河南安阳小屯殷墓中的动物遗骸. *Wenshizhe Xuebao* 5:1–14.

Shijiahe Kaogudui, 石家河考古队 (editor), 1999, *Xiaojiawuji* 肖家屋脊. Wenwu Chubanshe, Beijing.

————, 2003, *Dengjiawan* 邓家湾. Wenwu Chubanshe, Beijing.

Shima, Kunio 島邦男, 1958, *Inkyo Bokuji Kenkyu* 殷墟卜辞研究. Kyuko Shoin, Tokyo.

Shipek, Florence C., 1989, An example of intensive plant husbandry: The Kumeyaay of southern California. In *Foraging and Farming: The Evolution of Plant Exploitation*, edited by David R. Harris and Gordon C. Hillman, pp. 159–70. Unwin Hyman, London.

Shixia Fajue Xiaozu, 石峡发掘小组, 1978, Guangdong Qujiang Shixia muzang fajue jianbao 广东曲江石峡墓葬发掘简报. *Wenwu* 7:1–15.

Shui, Tao 水涛, 1993, Xinjiang qingtong shidai zhu wenhua de bijiao yanjiu 新疆青铜时代诸文化的比较研究. *Guoxue Yanjiu* 1:447–90.

————, 2001a, Ganqing diqu qingtong shidai de wenhua jiegou he jingji xingtai yanjiu 甘青地区青铜时代的文化结构和经济形态研究. In *Zhongguo Xibei Diqu Qingtong Shidai Kaogu Lunji* 中国西北地区青铜时代考古论集, edited by Shui Tao 水涛, pp. 193–327. Kexue Chubanshe, Beijing.

————, 2001b (editor), *Ganqing diqu zaoqi wenming xingshuai de rendi guanxi* 甘青地区早期文明兴衰的人地关系. Kexue Chubanshe, Beijing.

Sichuansheng Wenwu Kaogu Yanjiusuo, 四川省文物考古研究所 (editor), 1999, *Sanxingdui Jisikeng* 三星堆祭祀坑. Wenwu Chubanshe, Beijing.

Skibo, James M., Michael B. Schiffer, and Kenneth C. Reid, 1989, Organic tempered pottery: An experimental study. *American Antiquity* 54(1):122–46.

Smith, Anthony D., 2001, Authenticity, antiquity and archaeology. *Nations and Nationalism* 7(4):441–9.

Smith, Barbara L., 2005, *Diet, health, and lifestyle in Neolithic North China*. Unpublished PhD dissertation, Harvard University, Cambridge.

Smith, Bruce D., 1995, *The Emergence of Agriculture*. Scientific American Library, New York.

————, 1998, *The Emergence of Agriculture*. Scientific American Library, New York.

————, 2001a, Low-level food production. *Journal of Archaeological Research* 9(1):1–43.

————, 2001b, The transition to food production. In *Archaeology at the Millennium: A Sourcebook*, edited by Gary M. Feinman and T. Douglas Price, pp. 199–230. Kluwer Academic/Plenum Publishers, New York.

So, Jenny F., 2001, Jade and stone at Sanxingdui. In *Ancient Sichuan: Treasures From A Lost Civilization*, edited by Robert Bagley, pp. 153–75. Seattle Art Museum, Seattle.

Soffer, Olga, 1989, Storage, sedentism and the Eurasian Palaeolithic record. *Antiquity* 63:719–32.

Song, Guoding 宋国定, 2003, Zhengzhou Xiaoshuangqiao yizhi chutu taoqi shangde zhushu 郑州小双桥遗址出土陶器上的朱书. *Wenwu* 5:35–44.

Song, Guoding 宋国定, Chen Xu 陈旭, Li Suting 李素婷, Zhang Guoshuo 张国硕, Zeng Xiaomin 曾晓敏, Xie Wei 谢巍, and Li Feng 李锋, 1996, 1995 nian Zhengzhou Xiaoshuangqiao yizhi de fajue 1995 年郑州小双桥遗址的发掘. *Huaxia Kaogu* 3:1–56.

Song, Jianzhong 宋建忠 and Xue Xinmin 薛新民, 1998, Shanxi Linfen Xiajin mudi fajue jianbao 山西临汾下靳墓地发掘简报. *Wenwu* 12:4–13.

Song, Jian 宋建, 2004, Cong Guangfulin yicun kan huan Taihu diqu zaoqi wenming de shuaibian 从广福林遗存看环太湖地区早期文明的衰变. In *Changjiang Xiayou Diqu Wenminghua Jincheng Xueshu Yantaohui* 长江下游地区文明化进程研讨会, edited by Shanghai Bowuguan 上海博物馆, pp. 214–28. Shanghai Shuhua Chubanshe, Shanghai.

Song, Xinchao 宋新潮, 1991, *Yin Shang Wenhua Quyu Yanjiu* 殷商文化区域研究. Shaanxi Renmin Chubanshe, Xi'an.

Song, Yuqin 宋豫秦, 2002, *Zhongguo Wenming Qiyuan de Rendi Guanxi Jianlun* 中国文明起源的人地关系简论. Kexue Chubanshe, Beijing.

Song, Zhaolin 宋兆麟, 1998, Yuanshi de pengtiao jishu 原始的烹调技术. In *Shiqian Yanjiu* 史前研究, edited by Xi'an Banpo Bowuguan 西安半坡博物馆, pp. 107–14. Sanqin Chubanshe, Xi'an.

Song, Zhenhao 宋镇豪, 1994, Shangdai de wangji, situ yu sizhi 商代的王畿、土与四至. *Nanfang Wenwu* 1:48, 55–9.

Stanley, Daniel J. and Zhongyuan Chen, 1996, Neolithic settlement distributions as a function of sea level-controlled topography in the Yangtze delta, China. *Geology* 24:1083–6.

Stanley, Daniel J., Zhongyuan Chen, and Jian Song, 1999, Inundation, sea-level rise and transition from Neolithic to Bronze Age cultures, Yangtze delta, China. *Geoarchaeology* 14(1):15–26.

Su, Bingqi 苏秉琦, 1948, *Doujitai goudongqu muzang* 斗鸡台沟东区墓葬. Guoli Beiping Yanjiuyuan Shixue Yanjiusuo, Beiping.

————, 1978a, Luelun woguo dongnan yanhai diqu de xinshiqi shidai kaogu 略论我国

东南沿海地区的新石器时代考古. *Wenwu* 3:40–2.

———, 1978b, Shixia wenhua chulun 石峡文化初论. *Wenwu* 7:16–28.

———, 1988, Zhonghua wenming de xin shuguang 中华文明的新曙光. *Dongnan Wenhua* 5:1–7.

———, 1991, Guanyu chongjian Zhongguo shiqian shi de sikao 关于重建中国史前史的思考. *Kaogu* 12:1109–18.

———, 1994, *Huaren, Longde Chuanren, Zhongguoren – Kaogu Xungenji* 华人, 龙的传人, 中国人 — 考古寻根记. Liaoning Daxue Chubanshe, Shenyang.

———, 1997, *Zhongguo Wenming Qiyuan Xintan* 中国文明起源新探. Shangwu Yinshuguan, Hong Kong.

———, 1999, *Zhongguo Wenming Qiyuan Xintan* 中国文明起源新探. Sanlian Chubanshe, Beijing.

Su, Bingqi 苏秉琦, and Yin Weizhang 殷伟璋, 1981, Guanyu kaoguxue wenhua de quxi leixing wenti 关于考古学文化的区系类型问题. *Wenwu* 5:10–7.

Sun, Bo 孙波, 2006, Houli wenhu juluo de chubu fenxi 后李文化聚落的初步分析. In *Dongfang Kaogu (Di 3 Ji)* 东方考古 (第3集), edited by Shandong Daxue Dongfa Kaogu Yanjiu Zhongxin 山东大学东方考古研究中心, pp. 104–18. Kexue Chubanshe, Beijing.

Sun, Bo 孙波 and Cui Shengkuan 崔圣宽, 2008, Shilun Shandong diqu xinshiqi shidai zaoqi yicun 试论山东地区新石器早期遗存. *Zhongyuan Wenwu* 3:23–8.

Sun, Chuanqing 孙传清, Wang Xiangkun 王象坤, Cai Hongwei 才宏伟, Yoshimura Atsushi 吉村淳, Doi Kazuyuki 土井一行, and Iwata Nobuo 岩田伸夫, 1997, Zhongguo putong yeshengdao de yazhou zaipeidao hejiyinzu de yichuan fenhua 中国普通野生稻和亚洲栽培稻核基因组的遗传分化. *Zhongguo Nongye Daxue Xuebao* 2(5):65–71.

Sun, Dehai 孙德海, Liu Yong 刘勇, and Chen Guangtang 陈光唐, 1981, Hebei Wu'an Cishan yizhi 河北武安磁山遗址. *Kaogu Xuebao* 3:303–38.

Sun, Dexuan 孙德萱, Ding Qingxian 丁清贤, Zhao Liansheng 赵连生, and Zhang Xiangmei 张相梅, 1988, Henan Puyang Xishuipo yizhi fajue jianbao 河南濮阳西水坡遗址发掘简报. *Wenwu* 3:1–6.

Sun, Guoping 孙国平 and Huang Weijin 黄渭金, 2007, Zhejiang Yuyao Tianluoshan xinshiqi shidai yizhi 2004 nian fajue jianbao 浙江余姚田螺山新石器时代遗址 2004 年发掘简报. *Wenwu* 11:4–24.

Sun, Hua 孙华, 2009, Shangdai qianqi de guojia zhengti – cong Erligang wenhua chengzhi he gongshi jianzhu jizhi de jiaodu 商代前期的国家政体 — 从二里岗文化城址和宫室建筑基址的角度. In *Duowei Shiyu – Shang Wangchao yu Zhongguo Zaoqi Wenming Yanjiu* 多维视域 — 商王朝与中国早期文明研究, edited by Jing Zhichun 荆志淳, Tang Jigen 唐际根, and Takashima Kenichi 高嶋谦一, pp. 171–97. Kexue Chubanshe, Beijing.

Sun, Shuyun and Rubin Han, 2000a, A preliminary study of early Chinese copper and bronze artifacts. In *The Beginnings of Metallurgy in China*, edited by Katheryn Linduff, Han Rubin, and Sun Shuyun, pp. 129–53. The Edwin Mellen Press, Lewiston, NY.

———, 2000b, A study of casting and manufacturing techniques of early copper and bronze artifacts found in Gansu. In *The Beginnings of Metallurgy in China*, edited by Katheryn Linduff, Han Rubin, and Sun Shuyun, pp. 175–93. The Edwin Mellen Press, Lewiston, NY.

Sun, Shuyun 孙淑云, 1990, Shandong Sishuixian Yinjiacheng yizhi chutu Yueshi wenhua tongqi jianding baogao 山东泗水县尹家城遗址出土岳石文化铜器鉴定报告. In *Sishui Yinjiacheng* 泗水尹家城, edited by Shandong daxue 山东大学, pp. 353–9. Wenwu Chubanshe, Beijing.

Sun, Shuyun 孙淑云 and Han Rubin 韩汝玢, 1997, Gansu zaoqi tongqi de faxian yu yelian, zhizao jishu de yanjiu 甘肃早期铜器的发现与冶炼、制造技术的研究. *Wenwu* 7:75–84.

Sun, Xinmin 孙新民 and Sun Jin 孙锦, 2008, Henan diqu chutu yuanshici de chubu yanjiu 河南地区出土原始瓷的初步研究. *Dongfang Wenbo* 4:97–101.

Sun, Yat-sen, 1943, *San Min Chu I, The Three Principles of the People*. Ministry of Information (Frank W. Price, translator), Chungking.

Sung, Ying-hsing, 1966 (orig. 1637), *T'ien-kung k'ai-wu: Chinese Technology in the Seventeenth Century*. The Pennsylvania State University Press, University Park and London.

Tainter, Joseph A., 1988, *The Collapse of Complex Societies*. Cambridge University Press, Cambridge.

Tan, Qixiang 谭其骧, 1981, Xihan yiqian de Huanghe xiayou hedao 西汉以前的黄河下游河道. *Lishi Dili* 1:48–64.

Tang, Chung 邓聪, 2007, Cong Dongya kaoguxue tan Aomen Heisha yizhi 从东亚考古学谈澳门黑沙遗址. In *Dongya Kaogu (Vol. B)* 东亚考古 (B卷), edited by Nanjing Shifan Daxue Wenboxi 南京师范大学文博系, pp. 67–81. Wenwu Chubanshe, Beijing.

Tang, Jigen, 2001, The construction of an archaeological chronology for the history of the Shang dynasty of early Bronze Age China. *The Review of Archaeology* 22(2):35–47.

———, 2004, *The Social organization of Late Shang China: A mortuary perspective.* unpublished PhD dissertation, University of London.

Tang, Jigen 唐际根, Yue Hongbin 岳洪彬, He Yuling 何毓灵, and Yue Zhanwei 岳占伟, 2003a, Henan Anyangshi Huanbei Shangcheng gongdianqu 1 hao jizhi fajue jianbao 河南安阳市洹北商城宫殿区 1 号基址发掘简报. *Kaogu* 5:17–23.

Tang, Jigen 唐际根 and Jing Zhichun 荆志淳, 1998, Huanhe liuyu quyu kaogu yanjiu chubu baogao 洹河流域区域考古研究初步报告. *Kaogu* 10:13–22.

———, 2009, Anyang de "Shangyi" yu "dayi Shang" 安阳的"商邑"与"大邑商". *Kaogu* 9:70–80.

Tang, Jigen 唐际根, Jing Zhichun 荆志淳, and Mayke Wagner, 2010a, New discoveries in Yinsu/Anyang and their contribution to the chronology of Shang capitals in Bronze Age China. In *Bridging Eurasia*, edited by Mayke Wagner and Wang Wei, pp. 125–44. Verlag Philipp von Zabern, Mainz.

Tang, Jigen 唐际根, Jing Zhichun 荆志淳, and He Yuling 何毓灵, 2010b, Huanbei Shangcheng gongdianqu yi er hao hangtu jizhi jianzhu fuyuan yanjiu 洹北商城宫殿区一、二号基址建筑复原. *Kaogu* 1:23–35.

Tang, Jigen 唐际根, Jing Zhichun 荆志淳, and Liu Zhongfu 刘忠伏, 2010c, Henan Anyangshi Huanbei Shangcheng yizhi 2005–2007 nian kancha jianbao 河南安阳市洹北商城遗址 2005–2007 年勘察简报. *Kaogu* 1:3–8.

Tang, Jigen 唐际根, Jing Zhichun 荆志淳, Liu Zhongfu 刘忠伏, and Yue Zhanwei 岳占伟, 2003b, Henan Anyangshi Huanbei Shangcheng de kancha yu shijue 河南安阳市洹北商城的勘察与试掘. *Kaogu* 5:3–16.

Tang, Zhuowei 汤卓炜, Cao Jian'en 曹建恩, and Zhang Shuqin 张淑芹, 2004a, Neimenggu Qingshuihexian Xicha yizhi baofen fenxi 内蒙古清水河县西岔遗址孢粉分析. In *Bianjiang Kaogu Yanjiu (3)* 边疆考古研究 (3), edited by Zhu Hong 朱泓, pp. 274–83. Kexue Chubanshe, Beijing.

Tang, Zhuowei 汤卓炜, Guo Zhizhong 郭治中, and Suo Xiufen 索秀芬, 2004b, Baiyinchanghan yizhi chutu de dongwu yicun 白音长汗遗址出土的动物遗存. In *Baiyinchanghan* 白音长汗, edited by Neimenggu Zizhiqu Wenwu Kaogu Yanjiusuo 内蒙古自治区文物考古研究所, pp. 546–75. Kexue Chubanshe, Beijing.

Tao, Fuhai 陶富海, 1991, Shanxi Xiangfen xian Daguduishan shiqian shiqi zhizaochang xincailiao jiqi zai yanjiu 山西襄汾县大崮堆山史前石器制造场新材料及其再研究. *Kaogu* 1:1–7.

Teilhard de Chardin, Pierre and C. C. Young, 1936, On the mammalian remains from the archaeological site of Anyang. *Palaeontologia Sinica series C.* 12(fasc 1).

Testart, Alain, 1982, The significance of food storage among hunter-gatherers: Residence patterns, population densities, and social inequalities. *Current Anthropology* 23(5):523–37.

Thomas, Julian, 1999, *Understanding the Neolithic.* Routledge, London and New York.

Tian, Guangjin 田广金, 1988, Neimenggu Zhukaigou yizhi 内蒙古朱开沟遗址. *Kaogu Xuebao* 3:301–31.

———, 1991a, Neimenggu zhongnanbu Longshan shidai wenhua yicun yanjiu 内蒙古中南部龙山时代文化遗存研究. In *Neimenggu Zhongnanbu Yuanshi Wenhua Yanjiu Wenji* 内蒙古中南部原始文化研究文集, pp. 140–60. Haiyang Chubanshe, Beijing.

———, 1991b, Neimenggu zhongnanbu Yangshao shidai wenhua yicun yanjiu 内蒙古中南部仰韶时代文化遗存研究. In *Neimenggu Zhongnanbu Yuanshi Wenhua Yanjiu Wenji* 内蒙古中南部原始文化研究文集, pp. 55–85. Haiyang Chubanshe, Beijing.

———, 1993, Neimenggu changcheng didai shicheng juluozhi ji xiangguan zhuwenti 内蒙古长城地带石城聚落址及相关问题. In *Jinian Chengziya Fajue 60 Zhounian Guoji Xueshu Taolunhui Wenji* 纪念城子崖发掘 60 周年国际学术讨论会文集, edited by Zhang Xuehai 张学海, pp. 119–35. Qi Lu Shushe, Jinan.

Tian, Guangjin 田广金 and Akiyama Shinko 秋山进午 (editors), 2001, *Daihai Kaogu (2) 岱海考古 (二)*. Kexue Chubanshe, Beijing.

Tian, Guangjin 田广金 and Guo Suxin 郭素新, 1988, Eerduosi shi qingtongqi de yuanyuan 鄂尔多斯式青铜器的渊源. *Kaogu Xuebao* 3:257–75.

———, 2004, Huan Daihai shiqian juluo xingtai yanjiu 环岱海史前聚落形态研究. In *Beifang Kaogu Lunwenji 北方考古论文集*, edited by Tian Guangjin 田广金 and Guo Suxin 郭素新, pp. 287–327. Kexue Chubanshe, Beijing.

———, 2005, *Beifang Wenhua yu Xiongnu Wenming 北方文化与匈奴文明*. Jiangsu Jiaoyu Chubanshe, Nanjing.

Tian, Guangjin 田广金 and Shi Peijun 史培军, 1997, Zhongguo beifang changcheng didai huanjing kaoguxue de chubu yanjiu 中国北方长城地带环境考古学的初步研究. *Neimenggu Wenwu Kaogu* 2:44–51.

———, 2004, Neimenggu zhongnanbu yuanshi wenhua de huanjing kaogu yanjiu 内蒙古中南部原始文化的环境考古研究. In *Beifang Kaogu Lunwenji 北方考古论文集*, edited by Tian Guangjin 田广金 and Guo Suxin 郭素新, pp. 350–63. Kexue Chubanshe, Beijing.

Tian, Guangjin 田广金 and Tang Xiaofeng 唐晓峰, 2001, Daihai diqu jujin 7000–2000 nianjian rendi guanxi yanbian yanjiu 岱海地区距今7000–2000年间人地关系研究. In *Daihai Kaogu (II) 岱海考古 (II)*, edited by Tian Guangjin 田广金 and Akiyama Shinko 秋山进午, pp. 28–343. Kexue Chubanshe, Beijing.

Tao, Dawei, Yan Wu, Zhizhong Guo, David V. Hill, and Changsui Wang, 2011, Starch grain analysis for groundstone tools from Neolithic Baiyinchanghan site: implications for their function in Northeast China. *Journal of Archaeological Science* 38(12):3577–83.

Tong, Enzheng 童恩正, 1990, Shilun woguo cong dongbei dao xinan de biandi banyuexing wenhua chuanbodai 试论我国从东北到西南的边地半月形文化传播带. In *Zhongguo Xinan Minzu Kaogu Lunwenji 中国西南民族考古论文集*, edited by Tong Enzheng 童恩正, pp. 253–72. Wenwu Chubanshe, Beijing.

———, 1998, *Renlie yu Wenhua 人类与文化*. Chongqing Chubanshe, Chongqing.

———, 2004, *Gudai de Ba Shu 古代的巴蜀*. Chongqiang Chubanshe, Chongqiang.

Tong, Weihua 佟伟华, 1984, Cishan yizhi de yuanshi nongye yicun jiqi xiangguan de wenti 磁山遗址的原始农业遗存及其相关的问题. *Nongye Kaogu* 1:194–207.

Townsend, James, 1996, Chinese nationalism. In *Chinese Nationalism*, edited by Jonathan Unger, pp. 1–30. M.E. Sharpe, Armonk, NY.

Tregear, T. R., 1965, *A Geography of China*. University of London Press, London.

———, 1980, *China: A Geographical Survey*. Hodder and Stoughton, London.

Trigger, Bruce G., 1984, Alternative archaeologies: Nationalist, colonialist, imperialist. *Man New Series*, 19(3):335–70.

———, 1999, Shang political organization: A comparative approach. *Journal of East Asian Archaeology* 1(1–4):43–62.

———, 2003, *Understanding Early Civilizations – A Comparative Study*. Cambridge University Press, Cambridge.

Tsang, Cheng-hwa, 1992, *Archaeology of the Penghu Islands*. Academia Sinica Press, Taipei.

———, 2005, Recent discoveries at the Tapenkeng culture sites in Taiwan: Implications for the problem of Austronesian origins. In *The Peopling of East Asia*, edited by L. Sagart, R. Blench, and A. Sanchez-Mazas, pp. 63–73. Routledge Curzon, London.

Tsutsumi, Takashi, 2002, Origins of pottery and human strategies for adaptation during the Termination of the Last-glacial period in the Japanese Archipelago. In *The Origins of Pottery and Agriculture*, edited by Yoshinori Yasuda, pp. 241–62. Roli Books, New Delhi.

Underhill, Anne P., 1994, Variation in settlements during the Longshan period of northern China. *Asian Perspectives* 33(2):197–228.

———, 2000, An analysis of mortuary ritual at the Dawenkou site, Shandong, China. *Journal of East Asian Archaeology* 2(1–2):93–128.

———, 2002, *Craft Production and Social Change in Northern China*. Kluwer Academic/Plenum Publishers, New York.

Underhill, Anne P., Gary M. Feinman, Linda M. Nicholas, Hui Fang, Fengshi Luan, Haiguang Yu, and Fengshu Cai, 2008, Changes in regional settlement patterns and the development of complex societies in southeastern Shandong, China. *Journal of Anthropological Archaeology* 27:1–29.

Vila, Carles, Jennifer A. Leonard, Anders Götherström, Stefan Marklund, Kaj Sandberg, Kerstin Lidén, Robert K. Wayne, and

Hans Ellegren, 2001, Widespread origins of domestic horse lineages. *Science* 291:474–7.

Vila, Carles, Peter Savolainen, Jesu´s E. Maldonado, Isabel R. Amorim, John E. Rice, Rodney L. Honeycutt, Keith A. Crandall, Joakim Lundeberg, and Robert K. Wayne, 1997, Multiple and ancient origins of the domestic dog. *Science* 276(13):1687–9.

Wang, Anan 王安安, 2006, "Xiaxiaozheng" lifa kaoshi 《〈夏小正〉》历法考释. *Lanzhou Xuekan* 5:23–4.

Wang, Binghua 王炳华, 1983, Kongquehe Gumugou fajue jiqi chubu yanjiu 孔雀河古墓沟发掘及其初步研究. *Xinjiang Shehui Kexue* 1:117–30.

———, 2001a, The mummies of Lopnur. In *Xinjiang Gushi* 新疆古尸, edited by Wang Binghua 王炳华, pp. 28–48. Xinjiang Renmin Chubanshe, Urumchi.

———, 2001b (editor), *Xinjiang Gushi* 新疆古尸. Xinjiang Renmin Chubanshe, Urumchi.

Wang, Fubao 王富葆, Cao Qiongjing 曹琼英, Han Huiyou 韩辉友, Li Minchang 李民昌, and Gu Jianxiang 谷建祥, 1996, Taihu liuyu Liangzhu wenhua shiqi de ziran huanjing 太湖流域良渚文化时期的自然环境. In *Dongfang Wenming Zhiguang* 东方文明之光, edited by Xu Huping 徐湖平, pp. 300–5. Hainan Guoji Xinwen Chubanshe, Hainan.

Wang, Haijing 王海晶, Chang E 常娥, Cai Dawei 蔡大伟, Zhang Quanchao 张全超, Zhou Hui 周慧, and Zhu Hong 朱泓, 2007, Neimenggu Zhukaigou yizhi gudai jumin xianliti DNA fenxi 内蒙古朱开沟遗址古代居民线粒体 DNA 分析. *Jilin Daxue Xuebao (Yixueban)* 33(1):5–8.

Wang, Hongxing 王红星, 2003, Cong Menbanwan chenghao juluo kan Changjiang zhongyou diqu chenghao juluo de qiyuan yu gongyong 从门板湾城壕聚落看长江中游地区城壕聚落的起源与功用. *Kaogu* 9:61–75.

Wang, Huiming 王海明 and Liu Shuhua 刘淑华, 2005, Hemudu wenhua de kuosan yu chuanbo 河姆渡文化的扩散与传播. *Nanfang Wenwu* 3:113, 114–18.

Wang, Jian 王建, Wang Xiangqian 王向前, and Chen Zheying 陈哲英, 1978, Xiachuan wenhua – Shanxi Xiachuan yizhi diaocha baogao 下川文化 — 山西下川遗址调查报告. *Kaogu Xuebao* 3:259–88.

Wang, Jianhua 王建华, Lu Jianying 卢建英, Lan Yufu 兰玉富, and Guo Junfeng 郭俊峰, 2006, Shandong Jinan Changqingqu Yuezhuang yizhi 2003 nian fajue baogao 山东济南长清区月庄遗址 2003 年发掘报告. In *Dongfang Kaogu (Di 2 Ji)* 东方考古 (第2集), edited by Shandong Daxue Dongfang Kaogu Yanjiu Zhongxin 山东大学东方考古研究中心, pp. 365–456. Kexue Chubanshe, Beijing.

Wang, Jihuai 王吉怀, 1983, Henan Xinzheng Shawoli xinshiqi shidai yizhi 河南新郑沙窝李新石器时代遗址. *Kaogu* 12:1057–65.

Wang, Jin 王劲, 1996, Shijiahe wenhua yuqi yu Jiang Han wenming 石家河文化玉器与江汉文明. In *Changjiang Zhongyou Shiqian Wenhua* 长江中游史前文化, edited by Hunansheng Kaogu Xuehui 湖南省考古学会, pp. 231–42. Yuelu Shushe, Changsha.

Wang, Lixin 王立新, 2004, Liaoxiqu Xia zhi Zhanguo shiqi wenhua geju yu jingji xingtai de yanjin 辽西区夏至战国时期文化格局与经济形态的演进. *Kaogu Xuebao* 3:243–70.

Wang, Lixin 王立新 and Bu Jida 卜箕大, 1998, Dui Xiajiadian Xiaceng wenhua yuanliu ji yu qita wenhua guanxi de zairenshi 对夏家店下层文化源流及与其它文化关系的再认识. In *Qingguoji* 青果集, edited by Jilin Daxue 吉林大学, pp. 179–85. Zhishi Chubanshe, Beijing.

Wang, Ming-ke 王明珂, 2001, *Huaxia Bianyuan: Lishi Jiyi yu Zuqun Rentong* 华夏边缘：历史记忆与族群认同. Yunchen Congkan, Taipei.

Wang, Mingda 王明达, 1988, Zhejiang Yuhang Fanshan Liangzhu mudi fajue jianbao 浙江余杭反山良渚墓地发掘简报. *Wenwu* 1:1–31.

———, 2004, Liangzhu wenhua de quxiang 良渚文化的去向. In *Changjiang Xiayou Diqu Wenminghua Jincheng Xueshu Yantaohui* 长江下游地区文明化进程研讨会, edited by Shanghai Bowuguan 上海博物馆, pp. 205–13. Shanghai Shuhua Chubanshe, Shanghai.

Wang, Ningsheng, 1987, Yangshao burial customs and social organization: A comment on the theory of Yangshao Matrilineal Society and its methodology. In *Early China*, pp. 6–32.

Wang, Ningsheng 汪宁生, 1983, Zhongguo kaogu faxianzhong de "dafangzi" 中国考古发现中的 "大房子". *Kaogu Xuebao* 3:271–94.

———, 1985, *Yunnan Cangyuan Yanhua de Faxian yu Yanjiu* 云南沧源岩画的发现与研究. Wenwu Chubanshe, Beijing.

Wang, Qiang 王强, 2008, *Haidai diqu shiqian shiqi mopan, mobang yanjiu* 海岱地区史前时期磨盘、磨棒研究. PhD dissertation, Shandong University, Jinan.

Wang, Qing 王青, 1993, Shilun shiqian Huanghe xiayou de gaidao yu guwenhua de fazhan 试论史前黄河下游的改道与古文化的发展. *Zhongyuan Wenwu* 4:63–72.

———, 2006a, Shandong beibu Shang Zhou kuixingqi de yongtu yu chandi zailun 山东北部商周盔形器的用途与产地再论. *Kaogu* 4:61–8.

———, 2006b, Shandong beibu yanhai xian Qin shiqi hai'an bianqian yu juluo gongneng yanjiu 山东北部沿海先秦时期海岸变迁与聚落功能研究. In *Dongfang Kaogu (Di 3 Ji)* 东方考古 (第3集), edited by Shandong Daxue Dongfang Kaogu Yanjiu Zhongxin 山东大学东方考古研究中心, pp. 282–97. Kexue Chubanshe, Beijing.

Wang, Qing 王青 and Li Huizhu 李慧竹, 1992, Huan Bohai huanjing kaogu tantao 环渤海环境考古探讨. *Liaohai Wenwu Xuekan* 1:87–95, 146.

Wang, Shiqi 王时麒, Zhao Chaohong 赵朝洪, Yu Guang 于洸, Yuan Xuemei 员雪梅, and Duan Tiyu 段体玉, 2007, *Zhongguo Xiuyanyu* 中国岫岩玉. Kexue Chubanshe, Beijing.

Wang, Shougong 王守功 and Ning Yintang 宁荫堂, 1996, Shandong Zhangqiushi Xiaojingshan yizhi diaocha fajue baogao 山东章丘市小荆山遗址调查、发掘报告. *Huaxia Kaogu* 2:1–23.

———, 2003, Shandong Zhangqiushi Xiaojingshan Houli wenhua huanhao juluo kantan baogao 山东章丘市小荆山后李文化环壕聚落勘探报告. *Huaxia Kaogu* 3:3–11.

Wang, Shuming 王树明, 1987, Shandong Jüxian Lingyanghe Dawenkou Wenhua Muzang Fajue Jianbao 山东莒县陵阳河大汶口文化墓葬发掘简报. *Shiqian Yanjiu* 3:62–82.

Wang, Tao, 1997, The Chinese archaeological school: Su Bingqi and contemporary Chinese archaeology. *Antiquity* 71:31–9.

Wang, Weilin 王炜林 and Ma Mingzhi 马明志, 2006, Shaanbei xinshiqi shidai shicheng juluo de faxian yu chubu yanjiu 陕北新石器时代石城聚落的发现与初步研究. *Zhongguo Shehui Kexueyuan Gudai Wenming Yanjiu Zhongxin Tongxun* 中国社会科学院古代文明研究中心通讯 11:34–44.

Wang, Wei 王巍, 2004, Gongyuanqian 2000 nian qianhou woguo dafanwei wenhua bianhua yuanyin tantao 公元前 2000 年前后我国大范围文化变化原因探讨. *Kaogu* 1:67–77.

Wang, Wei 王巍 and Zhao Hui 赵辉, 2010, Zhonggua wenming tanyuan gongcheng de zhuyao shouhuo 中华文明探源工程的主要收获, 光明日报, 2010 年. *Guangming Ribao*. 23 February:12. Beijing.

Wang, Wenchu 王文楚, 1996, *Gudai Jiaotong Dili Congkao* 古代交通地理丛考. Zhonghua Shuju, Beijing.

Wang, Wenhua 王文华, Chen Ping 陈萍, and Ding Lanpo 丁兰坡, 2004, Henan Xingyang Dashigu yizhi 2002 niandu fajue jianbao 河南荥阳大师姑遗址 2002 年度发掘简报. *Wenwu* 11:1–18.

Wang, Wenjian 王文建 and Zhang Chunlong 张春龙, 1993, Hunan Linlixian Hujiawuchang xinshiqi shidai yizhi 湖南临澧县胡家屋场新石器时代遗址. *Kaogu Xuebao* 2:171–202.

Wang, Xiangqian 王向前, Li Zhanyang 李占扬, and Tao Fuhai 陶富海, 1987, Shanxi Xiangfen Dagudui shan shiqian shiqi zhizaochang chubu yanjiu 山西襄汾大崮堆山史前石器制造场初步研究. *Renleixue Xuebao* 6(2):87–95.

Wang, Xiaoqing 王小庆, 2008, *Shiqi Shiyong Henji Xianwei Guancha de Yanjiu* 石器使用痕迹显微观察的研究. Wenwu Chubanshe, Beijing.

Wang, Xuerong 王学荣, 2002, Henan Yanshi Shangcheng Shangdai zaoqi wangshi jisi yizhi 河南偃师商城商代早期王室祭祀遗址. *Kaogu* 7:6–8.

Wang, Yinfeng 王银峰, 1988, Qinling Huaihe xian zai Zhongguo zonghe ziran quhua zhong de diwei 秦岭淮河线在中国综合自然区划中的地位. *Henan Daxue Xuebao* 1:67–70.

Wang, Yonggang 王永刚, Cui Fengguang 崔风光, and Li Yanli 李延丽, 2007, Shaanxi Ganquanxian chutu wan Shang qingtongqi 陕西甘泉县出土晚商青铜器. *Kaogu yu Wenwu* 3:11–22.

Wang, Youpeng 王有鹏, Chen De'an 陈德安, Chen Xiandan 陈显丹, and Mo Honggui 莫洪贵, 1987, Guanghan Sanxingdui yizhi 广汉三星堆遗址. *Kaogu Xuebao* 2:227–54.

Wang, Youping 王幼平, 1997, *Gengxinshi Huanjing yu Zhongguo Nanfang Jiushiqi Wenhua Fazhan* 更新世环境与中国南方旧石器文化发展. Beijing Daxue Chubanshe, Bejing.

———, 2005, *Zhongguo Yuangu Renlei Wenhua de Yuanliu* 中国远古人类文化的源流. Kexue Chubanshe, Beijing.

Wang, Youping 王幼平, Zhang Songlin 张松林, He Jianing 何嘉宁, Wang Songzhi 王松枝, Zhao Jingfang 赵静芳, Qu Tongli 曲彤丽, Wang Jiayin 王佳音, and Gao Xiaoxu 高霄旭, 2011, Henan Xinmishi Lijiagou yizhi fajue jianbao 河南新密市李家沟遗址发掘简报. *Kaogu* 4:3–9.

Wang, Yuping 汪宇平, 1957, Neimenggu zizhiqu faxiande xishiqi wenhua yizhi 内蒙古自治区发现的细石器文化遗址. *Kaogu Xuebao* 1:9–19.

Wang, Zhenzhong 王震中, 2007, Shangdai de wangji yu situ 商代的王畿与四土. *Yindu Xuekan* 4:1–13.

Wang, Zhijun 王志俊 and Song Peng 宋澎, 2001, Zhongguo beifang jiama qiyuan wenti tantao 中国北方家马起源问题探讨. *Kaogu yu Wenwu* 2:26–30.

Wang, Zijin 王子今, 1994, *Qin Han Jiaotong Shigao* 秦汉交通史稿. Zhonggong Zhongyang Dangxiao Chubanshe, Beijing.

Watanabe, Hitoshi, 1986, Community habitation and food gathering in prehistoric Japan: An ethnographic interpretation of the archaeological evidence. In *Windows on the Japanese Past: Studies in Archaeology and Prehistory*, edited by Richard J. Pearson, Gina L. Barnes, and Karl L. Hutterer, pp. 229–53. Center for Japanese Studies, The University of Michigan, Ann Arbor.

Watson, Patty J., 1995, Explaining the transition to agriculture. In *Last Hunters – First Farmers: New Perspectives on the Prehistoric Transition to Agriculture*, edited by T. D. Price and A. B. Gebauer, pp. 21–37. School of American Research Press, Santa Fe, NM.

Wayne, Robert K., Jennifer A. Leonard, and Carles Vila, 2006, Genetic analysis of dog domestication. In *Documenting Domestication: New Genetic and Archaeological Paradigms*, edited by Melinda A. Zeder, Daniel G. Bradley, Eve Emshwiller, and Bruce D. Smith, pp. 279–93. University of California Press, Berkeley.

Webb, John, Anne Ford, and Justin Gorton, 2007, Influences on selection of lithic raw material sources at Huizui, a Neolithic/Early Bronze Age site in northern China. *Bulletin of the Indo-Pacific Prehistory Association* 27:76–86.

Wei, Feng 魏丰, Wu Weitang 吴维堂, Zhang Minghua 张明华, and Han Defen 韩德芬, 1990, *Zhejiang Yuyao Hemudu Xinshiqi Shidai Yizhi Dongwuqun* 浙江余姚河姆渡新石器时代遗址动物群. Haiyang Chubanshe, Beijing.

Wei, Huaiheng 魏怀珩, 1978, Wuwei Huangniangniangtai yizhi disici fajue 武威皇娘娘台遗址第四次发掘. *Kaogu Xuebao* 4:421–47.

Wei, Jian 魏坚 and Cao Jianen 曹建恩, 1999, Neimenggu zhongnanbu xinshiqi shidai shicheng chubu yanjiu 内蒙古中南部新石器时代石城初步研究. *Wenwu* 2:57–62.

Wei, Xingtao 魏兴涛 and Li Shengli 李胜利, 2003, Henan Lingbao Xipo yizhi 105 hao Yangshao wenhua fangzhi 河南灵宝西坡遗址 105 号仰韶文化房址. *Wenwu* 8:4–17.

Wei, Xingtao 魏兴涛, Kong Zhaochen 孔昭宸, and Liu Changjiang 刘长江, 2000, Sanmenxia Nanjiaokou yizhi Yangshao wenhua daozuo yicun de faxian jiqi yiyi 三门峡南交口遗址仰韶文化稻作遗存的发现及其意义. *Nongye Kaogu* 3:77–9.

Wei, Xingtao 魏兴涛, Ma Xiaolin 马萧林, Li Yongqiang 李永强, Shi Zhimin 史智民, Zhang Yingqiao 张应桥, Li Shengli 李胜利, and Chen Xingcan 陈星灿, 2002, Henan Lingbaoshi Xipo yizhi 2001 nain chun fajue jianbao 河南灵宝市西坡遗址 2001 年春发掘简报. *Huaxia Kaogu* 2:31–52, 92.

Weidenreich, Franz, 1943, The skull of Sinanthropus Pekinensis. In *Palaeontologia Sinica, New Series D, No. 10, Whole Series 127*. The Geological Survey of China, Chungking.

Weiss, Harvey, 2000, Beyond the Younger Dryas: Collapse as adaptation to abrupt climate change in ancient West Asia and the Eastern Mediterranean. In *Environmental Disaster and the Archaeology of Human Response*, edited by Garth Bawden and Richard M. Reycraft, pp. 75–98. Maxwell Museum of Anthropology, Albuquerque.

Weiss, Harvey, and Raymond S. Bradley, 2001, What drives societal collapse? *Science* 291:609–10.

Wen, Guang 闻广, 1998, Zhongguo dalu shiqian guyu ruogan tezheng 中国大陆史前古玉若干特征. In *Dongya Guyu* 东亚古玉 *Vol. II*, edited by Tang Chung 邓聪, pp. 217–21. Centre for Chinese Archaeology and Art, The Chinese University of Hong Kong, Hong Kong.

Wen, Guang 闻广 and Jing Zhichun 荆志淳, 1993, Fuquanshan yu Songze yuqi dizhi kaoguxue yanjiu 福泉山与松泽玉器地质考古学研究. *Kaogu* 7:627–44.

Wheatley, Paul, 1971, *The Pivot of the Four Quarters: A Preliminary Enquiry into the Origins and Character of the Ancient Chinese City*. Aldine Publishing Company, Chicago.

Willey, Gordon R., 2000, Ancient Chinese, New World, and Near Eastern ideological traditions: Some observations. In *The Breakout: The Origins of Civilization*, edited by Martha lanberg-Karlovsky, pp. 25–36.

Peabody Museum Monographs, Cambridge, MA.

Winkler, Minkler and Pao K. Wang, 1993, The Late-Quaternary vegetation and climate of China. In *Global Climates Since the Last Glacial Maximum*, edited by H. E. Wright, Jr., J. E. Kutzbach, T. Webb III, W. F. Ruddiman, F. A. Street-Perrott, and P. J. Bartlein, pp. 221–64. University of Minnesota Press, Minnesota.

Wright, Henry T., 1977, Recent research on the origin of the state. *Annual Review of Anthropology* 6:379–97.

———, 1984, Prestate political formations. In *On the Evolution of Complex Societies: Essays in Honor of Harry Hoijer*, edited by T. Earle, pp. 41–77. Undena Publication, Malibu.

Wright, Henry T. and Gregory Johnson, 1975, Population, exchange, and early state formation in southwestern Iran. *American Anthropologist* 77:267–89.

Wu, Chin-ting, 1938, *Prehistoric Pottery in China*. Kegan Paul, Trench, and Trubner, London.

Wu, Hung, 1985, Bird motif in Eastern Yi art. *Orientations* 16(10):30–41.

Wu, Jian'an 吴加安, 1989, Luelun Huanghe liuyu qian Yangshao wenhua shiqi nongye 略论黄河流域前仰韶文化时期农业. *Nongye Kaogu* 2:118–25.

Wu, Jiabi 武家璧, Chen Meidong 陈美东, and Liu Ciyuan 刘次沅, 2008, Taosi guanxiangtai yizhi de tianwen gongneng yu niandai 陶寺观象台遗址的天文功能与年代. *Zhongguo Kexue (G Ji: Wulixue, Lixue, Tianwenxue)* 9:1–8.

Wu, Jianmin 吴建民, 1988, Changjiang sanjiaozhou shiqian yizhi de fenbu yu huanjing bianqian 长江三角洲史前遗址的分布与环境变迁. *Dongnan Wenhua* 6:16–36.

———, 1990, Subei shiqian yizhi de fenbu yu hai'anxian bianqian 苏北史前遗址的分布与海岸线变迁. *Dongnan Wenhua* 5:239–51.

Wu, Rukang and Shenglong Lin, 1983, Peking Man. *Scientific American* 248(6):78–86.

Wu, Rukang and John W. Olsen (editors), 1985, *Palaeoanthropology and Palaeolithic Archaeology in the People's Republic of China*. Academic Press, New York.

Wu, Wenxiang and Tungsheng Liu, 2004, Possible role of the "Holocene Event 3" on the collapse of Neolithic cultures around the Central Plain of China. *Quaternary International* 117:53–166.

Wu, Wenxiang 吴文祥 and Ge Quansheng 葛全胜, 2005, Xiachao qianxi hongshui fasheng de kenengxing ji Da Yu zhishui zhenxiang 夏朝前夕洪水发生的可能性及大禹治水真相. *Disiji Yanjiu* 6:742–9.

Wu, Xiaohong and Chaohong Zhao, 2003, Chronology of the transition from Palaeolithic to Neolithic in China. *The Review of Archaeology* 24(2):15–20.

Wu, Xinzhi, 1997, On the descent of modern humans in East Asia. In *Conceptual Issues in Modern Human Origins Research*, edited by G. A. Clark and C. M. Willermet. Aldone De Gruyter, New York.

———, 2004, On the origin of modern humans in China. *Quaternary International* 117:131–40.

Wu, Xinzhi 吴新智, 1999, 20 shiji de zhongguo renlei gushengwuxue yanjiu yu zhanwang 20世纪的中国人类古生物学研究与展望. *Renliexue Xuebao* 18(3):165–75.

Wu, Zhenlu 吴振录, 1972, Baodexian xinfaxian de Yindai qingtongqi 保德县新发现的殷代青铜器. *Wenwu* 4:62–6.

Wu'en, Yuesitu 乌恩岳斯图, 2007, *Beifang Caoyuan Kaoguxue Wenhua Yanjiu* 北方草原考古学文化研究. Kexue Chubanshe, Beijing.

Xi'an Banpo Bowuguan, 西安半坡博物馆, 1981, Shaanxi Lantian Huaizhenfang Shangdai yizhi shijue jianbao 陕西蓝田怀珍坊商代遗址试掘简报. *Kaogu yu Wenwu* 3:48–53.

Xi'an Banpo Bowuguan, 西安半坡博物馆 Shaanxisheng Kaogu Yanjiusuo, 陕西省考古研究所, and Lintongxian Bowuguan 临潼县博物馆 (editors), 1988, *Jiangzhai – Xinshiqi Shidai Yizhi Fajue Baogao* 姜寨 – 新石器时代遗址发掘报告. Wenwu Chubanshe, Beijing.

Xi, Yongjie 席永杰 and Liu Guoxiang 刘国祥 (editors), 2006, *Hongshan Wenhua Yanjiu* 红山文化研究. Wenwu Chubanshe, Beijing.

Xia, Nai 夏鼐, 1959, Guanyu kaoguxue shang wenhua de dingming wenti 关于考古学上文化的定名问题. *Kaogu* 4:169–72.

———, 1960, Changjiang liuyu kaogu wenti 长江流域考古问题. *Kaogu* 2:1–3.

———, 1973, Paris London zhanchu de xinzhongguo chutu wenwu zhanlan xunli 巴黎伦敦展出的新中国出土文物展览巡礼. *Kaogu* 3:150, 171–7.

———, 1977, Tan-14 ceding niandai he zhongguo shiqian kaoguxue 碳 — 14 测定年代和中国史前考古学. *Kaogu* 4:217–32.

———, 1979, Wusi yundong he Zhongguo jindai kaoguxue de xingqi 五四运动和中国近代考古学的兴起. *Kaogu* 3:193–6.

———, 1985, *Zhongguo Wenming de Qiyuan* 中国文明的起源. Wenwu Chubanshe, Beijing.

———, 2000, Zailun kaoguxue shang wenhua de dingming wenti 再论考古学上文化的定名问题. In *Xia Nai Wenji* 夏鼐文集, edited by Zhongguo Shehui Kexueyuan Kaogu Yanjiusuo 中国社会科学院考古研究所, pp. 359–66. Shehui Kexue Wenxian Chubanshe, Beijing.

———, 2000 [orig. 1946], Qijiaqi muzang de xinfaxian jiqi niandai de gaiding 齐家期墓葬的新发现及其年代的改订. In *Xianian Wenji* 夏鼐文集, edited by Zhongguo Shehui Kexueyuan Kaogu Yanjiusuo 中国社会科学院考古研究所, pp. 257–68. Shehui Kexue Wenxian Chubanshe, Beijing.

Xia, Nai 夏鼐 and Wang Zhongshu 王仲殊, 1986, Kaoguxue. In *Zhongguo Dabaike Quanshu: Kaoguxue* 中国大百科全书：考古学, edited by Xia Nai 夏鼐, pp. 1–21. Zhongguo Dabaike Quanshu Chubanshe, Beijing.

Xia Shang Zhou Duandai Gongcheng Zhuanjiazu, 夏商周断代工程专家组 (editor), 2000, *Xia Shang Zhou Duandai Gongcheng 1996–2000 Nian Jieduan Chengguo Baogao* 夏商周断代工程 1996 − 2000 年阶段成果报告. Shijie Tushu Chubanshe, Beijing.

Xia, Zhengkai, Chen Ge, Zheng Gongwang, Chen Fuyou, and Han Junqing, 2002, Climate background of the evolution from Paleolithic to Neolithic cultural transition during the last deglaciation in the middle reaches of the Yellow River. *Chinese Science Bulletin* 47(1):71–5.

Xia, Zhengkai 夏正楷 and Yang Xiaoyan 杨小燕, 2003, Woguo beifang 4ka B.P. qianhou yichang hongshui shijian de chubu yanjiu 我国北方 4ka B.P. 前后异常洪水事件的初步研究. *Disiji Yanjiu* 6:84–91.

Xiang, Taochu 向桃初, 2008, *Xiangjiang Liuyu Shang Zhou Qingtong Wenhua Yanjiu* 湘江流域商周青铜文化研究. Xianzhuang Shuju, Beijing.

Xiao, Jule, Jintao Wu, Bin Si, Wendong Liang, Toshio Nakamura, Baolin Liu, and Yoshio Inouchi, 2006, Holocene climate changes in the monsoon/arid transition reflected by carbon concentration in Daihai Lake of Inner Mongolia. *The Holocene* 16(4):551–60.

Xiao, Jule, Qinghai Xu, Toshio Nakamura, Xiaolan Yang, and Wendong Liang, 2004, Holocene vegetation variation in the Daihai Lake region of north-central China: A direct indication of the Asian Monsoon climatic history. *Quaternary Science Reviews* 23:1669–79.

Xiao, Minghua 肖明华, 2001, Yunnan kaogu shulue 云南考古述略. *Kaogu* 12:3–15.

Xiaohe Kaogudui, 小河考古队, 2005, Xinjiang Luobupo Xiaohe mudi quanmian fajue yuanman jieshu 新疆罗布泊小河墓地全面发掘圆满结束. *Zhongguo Wenwubao*. 13 April:1–2. Beijing.

Xibei Daxue Wenbo Xueyuan, 西北大学文博学院 (editor), 2000, *Fufeng Anban Yizhi Fajue Baogao* 扶风案板遗址发掘报告. Keixue Chubanshe, Beijing.

———, 2002, *Chenggu Baoshan* 城固宝山. Wenwu Chubanshe, Beijing.

Xie, Chengzhi 谢承志, 2007, *Xinjiang Tarim pendi zhoubian diqu gudai renqun ji Shanxi Yuhong muzhuren DNA fenxi* 新疆塔里木盆地周边地区古代人群及山西虞弘墓主人 DNA 分析. PhD dissertation, Jilin University, Jilin.

Xie, Duanju 谢端琚, 1975a, Gansu Yongjing Majiawan xinshiqi shidai yizhi de fajue 甘肃永靖马家湾新石器时代遗址的发掘. *Kaogu* 2:90–6, 101.

———, 1975b, Gansu Yongjing Qinweijia Qijia wenhua mudi 甘肃永靖秦魏家齐家文化墓地. *Kaogu Xuebao* 2:57–95.

———, 1980, Gansu Yongjing Zhangjiazui yu Jijiachuan yizhi de fajue 甘肃永靖张家咀与姬家川遗址的发掘. *Kaogu Xuebao* 2:187–219.

———, 1986, Majiayao wenhua yuanyuan shitan 马家窑文化渊源试探. In *Zhongguo Kaoguxue Yanjiu − Xia Nai Xiansheng Kaogu Wushi Nian Jinian Lunwenji* 中国考古学研究 − 夏鼐先生考古五十年纪念论文集, edited by Zhongguo Kaoguxue Yanjiu Bianweihui 中国考古学研究编委会, pp. 19–32. Wenwu Chubanshe, Beijing.

Xie, Xigong 解希恭 (editor), 2007, *Xiangfen Taosi Yizhi Yanjiu* 襄汾陶寺遗址研究. Kexue Chubanshe, Beijing.

Xie, Xigong 解希恭, Yan Jinzhu 阎金铸, and Tao Fuhai 陶富海 1989, Shanxi Jixian Shizitan zhongshiqi wenhua yicun 山西吉县柿子滩中石器文化遗存. *Kaogu Xuebao* 3:305–23.

Xizang and Sichuan (Xizang Zizhiqu Wenwu Guanli Weiyuanhui, 西藏自治区文物管理委员会 and Sichuan Daxue Lishixi 四川大学历史系) (editors), 1985, *Changdu Karuo* 昌都卡若. Wenwu Chubanshe, Beijing.

Xu, Guangji 徐光冀, 1986, Chifeng YingJinhe, Yinhe liuyu de shicheng yizhi 赤峰英金河、阴

河流域石城遗址. In *Zhongguo Kaoguxue Yan-jiu* 中国考古学研究, edited by Zhongguo Kaoguxue Yanjiu bianweihui 中国考古学研究编委会, pp. 82–93. Wenwu Chubanshe, Beijing.

Xu, Haosheng 徐浩生, Jin Jiaguang 金家广, and Yang Yonghe 杨永贺, 1992, Hebei Xushuixian Nanzhuangtou yizhi shijue jianbao 河北徐水县南庄头遗址试掘简报. *Kaogu* 11:961–70.

Xu, Hong 许宏, Chen Guoliang 陈国梁, and Zhao Haitao 赵海涛, 2005, Henan Luoyang pendi 2001–2003 nian kaogu diaocha jian-bao 河南洛阳盆地 2001–2003 年考古调查简报. *Kaogu* 5:18–37.

Xu, Huping 徐湖平 (editor), 1996, *Dongfang Wen-ming Zhiguang* 东方文明之光. Hainan Guoji Xinwen Chuban Zhongxin, Hainan.

Xu, Jay, 2001a, Bronze at Sanxingdui. In *Ancient Sichuan: Treasures From A Lost Civilization*, edited by Robert Bagley, pp. 59–152. Seattle Art Museum, Seattle.

———, 2001b, Sichuan before the Warring States Period. In *Ancient Sichuan: Treasures From A Lost Civilization*, edited by Robert Bagley, pp. 21–37. Seattle Art Museum, Seattle.

Xu, Lianggao 徐良高, 1998, Wenhua yinsu dingxing fenxi yu Shangdai "qingtong liqi wenhua quan" yanjiu 文化因素定性分析与商代"青铜礼器文化圈"研究. In *Zhongguo Shang wenhua guoji xueshu taolunhui lunwenji* 中国商文化国际学术讨论会论文集, edited by Zhong-guo Shehui kexueyuan kaogu yanjiusuo 中国社会科学院考古研究所, pp. 227–36. Zhongguo Dabaike Quanshu Chubanshe, Beijing.

Xu, Shunzhan 许顺湛, 2004, Xunzhao Xia Qi zhiju 寻找夏启之居. *Zhongyuan Wenwu* 4:46–50.

Xu, Xinmin 徐新民 and Cheng Jie 程杰, 2005, Zhejiang Pinghushi Zhuangqiaofen Liangzhu wenhua yizhi ji mudi 浙江平湖市庄桥坟良渚文化遗址及墓地. *Kaogu* 7:10–14.

Xu, Xusheng 徐旭生, 1959, 1959 nian xia Yuxi diaocha "Xiaxu" de chubu baogao 1959 年夏豫西调查"夏墟"的初步报告. *Kaogu* 11:592–600.

Xue, Xiangxu 薛祥熙 and Li Xiaochen 李晓晨, 2000, Shaanxi shuiniu huashi ji Zhong-guo huashi shuiniu de dili fenbu he zhongxi fasheng 陕西水牛化石及中国化石水牛的地理分布和种系发生. *Gujizhui Dongwu Xuebao* 38(3):218–31.

Yan, Wenming, 1992, Origins of agriculture and animal husbandry in China. In *Pacific North-east Asia in Prehistory: Hunter-Fisher-Gatherers,* *Farmers, and Sociopolitical Elites*, edited by C. Melvin Aikens and Song Nai Rhee, pp. 113–24. Washington State University Press, Pull-man.

———, 2002, The origins of rice agriculture, pottery and cities. In *The Origins of Pottery and Agriculture*, edited by Yoshinori Yasuda, pp. 151–6. Roli Books, New Delhi.

Yan, Wenming 严文明, 1982, Zhongguo Dao-zuo nongye de qiyuan 中国稻作农业的起源. *Nongye kaogu* 1:19–31, 151.

———, 1984, Zuotan Dongshanzui yizhi 座谈东山嘴遗址. *Wenwu* 11:13–14.

———, 1987, Zhongguo shiqian wenhua de tongyixing yu duoyangxing 中国史前文化的统一性与多样性. *Wenwu* 3:38–50.

———, 1989a, Dongyi wenhua de tansuo 东夷文化的探索. *Wenwu* 9:1–12.

———, 1989b, Jiangzhai zaoqi de cunluo buju 姜寨早期的村落布局. In *Yangshao Wenhua Yanjiu* 仰韶文化研究, edited by Yan Wenming 严文明, pp. 166–79. Wenwu Chubanshe, Beijing.

———, 1989c, *Yangshao Wenhua Yanjiu* 仰韶文化研究. Wenwu Chubanshe, Beijing.

———, 1996, Liangzhu suibi 良渚随笔. *Wenwu* 3:28–35.

———, 2000, The origins of rice agriculture, pottery and cities. In *Daozuo Taoqi he Dushi de Qiyuan* 稻作陶器和都市的起源, edited by Wenming Yan and Yoshinori Yasuda, pp. 3–15. Wenwu Chubanshe, Beijing.

———, 2001, Xu 序. In *Yidu Chengbeixi* 宜都城背溪, edited by Hubeisheng Wenwu Kaogu Yan-jiusuo 湖北省文物考古研究所, pp. 1–2. Wenwu Chubanshe, Beijing.

Yan, Zhibin 严志斌 and He Nu 何驽, 2005, Shanxi Xiangfen Taosi chengzhi 2002 nian fajue baogao 山西襄汾陶寺城址 2002 年发掘报告. *Kaogu Xuebao* 3:307–46.

Yang, Baocheng 杨宝成 and Liu Senmiao 刘森淼, 1991, Shang Zhou fangding chulun 商周方鼎初论. *Kaogu* 6:533–45.

Yang, Boda 杨伯达, 1997, Gansu Qijia yuqi wen-hua chutan 甘肃齐家玉器文化初谈. *Longyou Wenbo* 1:10–18.

Yang, Chun 杨春, 2007, *Neimenggu Xicha yizhi dongwu yicun yanjiu* 内蒙古西岔遗址动物遗存研究. MA Thesis, Jilin University, Changchun.

Yang, Dongya, Li Liu, Xingcan Chen, and Camilla F. Speller, 2008, Wild or domesti-cated: Ancient DNA examination of water buffalo remains from north China. *Journal of Archaeological Science* 35:2778–85.

Yang, Guijin 杨贵金, Zhang Lidong 张立东, and Wu Jianzhuang 毋建庄, 1994, Henan Wuzhi Dasima yizhi diaocha jianbao 河南武陟大司马遗址调查简报. *Kaogu* 4:289–300.

Yang, Hu 杨虎 and Liu Guoxiang 刘国祥, 1997, Neimenggu Aohanqi Xinglongwa juluo yizhi 1992 nian fajue jianbao 内蒙古敖汉旗兴隆洼聚落遗址 1992 年发掘简报. *Kaogu* 1:1–26.

Yang, Hu 杨虎 and Zhu Yanping 朱延平, 1985, Neimenggu Aohanqi Xinglongwa yizhi fajue jianbao 内蒙古敖汉旗兴隆洼遗址发掘简报. *Kaogu* 10:865–72.

Yang, Jianhua 杨建华, 2004, *Chunqiu Zhanguo Shiqi Zhongguo Beifang Wenhuadai de Xingcheng* 春秋战国时期中国北方文化带的形成. Wenwu Chubanshe, Beijing.

Yang, Ping 杨萍, Zhang Chuanjun 张传军, and Deng Kaiye 邓开野, 2005, Xiangzi mijiu de shengchan gongyi yanjiu 橡子米酒的生产工艺研究. *Gongyi Jishu* 26(11):93–6.

Yang, Quanxi 杨权喜, 1991, Shilun Chengbeixi wenhua 试论城背溪文化. *Dongnan Wenhua* 5:206–12.

Yang, Xiaoneng, 2000, *Reflections of Early China: Decor, Pictographs, and Pictorial Inscriptions*. The Nelson-Atkins Museum of Art in Association with the University of Washington Press, Seattle and London.

Yang, Xiaoyan, Yu Jincheng, Lü Houyuan, Cui Tianxing, Guo Jingning, Diao Xianmin, Kong Zhaochen, Liu Changjiang, and Ge Quansheng, 2009, Starch grain analysis reveals function of grinding stone tools at Shangzhai site, Beijing. *Science in China Series D: Earth Sciences* 52(8):1039–222.

Yang, Xiaoyan, Jianping Zhang, Linda Perry, Zhikun Ma, Zhiwei Wan, Mingqi Li, Xianmin Diao, and Houyuan Lu, 2012, From the modern to the archaeological: starch grains from millets and their wild relatives in China. *Journal of Archaeological Science* 39:247–54.

Yang, Yachang 杨亚长, 2001, Shaanxi shiqian yuqi de faxian yu chubu yanjiu 陕西史前玉器的发现与初步研究. *Kaogu yu Wenwu* 6:46–52.

Yang, Zemeng 杨泽蒙, 2001, Shihushan yizhi fajue baogao 石虎山遗址发掘报告. In *Daihai Kaogu (2)* 岱海考古 (二), edited by Tian Guangjin 田广金 and Akiyama Shinko 秋山进午, pp. 18–145. Kexue Chubanshe, Beijing.

Yang, Zhimin 杨直民, 1995, Zhongguo de xuli li 中国的畜力犁. *Nongye Kaogu* 1:183–9.

Yao, Ling, 2009, Plant microfossils analysis of prehistoric milling tools from Xiaohuangshan archaeological site in Zhejiang, China. In *The 19th Congress of the Indo-Pacific Prehistory Association*, Hanoi, Vietnam.

Yasuda, Yoshinori, 2002, Origins of pottery and agriculture in East Asia. In *The Origins of Pottery and Agriculture*, edited by Yoshinori Yasuda, pp. 119–42. Roli Books, New Delhi.

Yates, Robin, 1997, The city-state in ancient China. In *The Archaeology of City-states: Cross-Cultural Approaches*, edited by Deborah Nichols and Thomas Charlton, pp. 71–90. Smithsonian Institution Press, Washington DC.

Ye, Maolin 叶茂林, 1997, Qijia wenhua de yushiqi 齐家文化的玉石器. In *Kaogu Qiuzhiji* 考古求知集, edited by Zhongguo Shehui kexueyuan kaogu yanjiusuo 中国社会科学院考古研究所, pp. 251–61. Kexue Chubanshe, Beijing.

Ye, Maolin 叶茂林 and He Kezhou 何克洲, 2002, Qinghai Minhexian Lajia yizhi chutu Qijia wenhua yuqi 青海民和县喇家遗址出土齐家文化玉器. *Kaogu* 12:89–90.

Yi, Sangheon, and Yoshiki Saito, 2004, Latest Pleistocene climate variation of the East Asian monsoon from pollen records of two East China regions. *Quaternary International* 121:75–87.

Yi, Sangheon, Yoshiki Saito, Hideaki Oshima, Yongqing Zhou, and Helong Wei, 2003a, Holocene environmental history inferred from pollen assemblages in the Huanghe delta, China: Climatic change and human impact. *Quaternary Science Reviews* 22:609–28.

Yi, Sangheon, Yoshiki Saito, Quanhong Zhao, and Pinxian Wang, 2003b, Vegetation and climate changes in the Changjiang (Yangtze River) Delta, China, during the past 13,000 years inferred from pollen records. *Quaternary Science Reviews* 22:1501–19.

Yidilisi, 伊弟利斯, Liu Guorui 刘国瑞, and Li Wenying 李文瑛, 2004, Xinjiang Luobupo Xiaohe mudi quanmian fajue huo jieduanxing zhongyao chengguo 新疆罗布泊小河墓地全面发掘获阶段性重要成果. *Zhongguo Wenwubao*. 17 Sept.:1–2. Beijing.

Yidilisi, 伊弟利斯, Li Wenying 李文瑛, and Hu Xingjun 胡兴军, 2007, Xinjiang Luobupo Xiaohe mudi 2003 nian fajue jianbao 新疆罗布泊小河墓地 2003 年发掘简报. *Wenwu* 10:4–42.

Yin, Jianshun 尹检顺, 1996, Qianxi Hunan Dongtinghu diqu Zaoshi xiaceng wenhua de fenqi jiqi wenhua shuxing 浅析湖南洞庭湖地区

皂市下层文化的分期及其文化属性. In *Changjiang Zhongyou Shiqian Wenhua ji Dierjie Yazhou Wenming Xueshu Taolunhui Lunwenji* 长江中游史前文化暨第二届亚洲文明学术讨论会论文集, edited by Hunansheng Wenwu Kaogu Yanjiusuo 湖南省文物考古研究所, pp. 105–25. Yulu Shushe, Changsha.

————, 1999, Xiang E liangsheng zaoqi xinshiqi wenhua yanjiu zhong de jige wenti 湘鄂两省早期新石器文化研究中的几个问题. In *Kaogu Kengyunlu* 考古耕耘录, edited by He Jiejun 何介均, pp. 11–26. Yuelu Shushe Changsha.

Yin, Shaoting 尹绍亭, 1996, *Yunnan Wuzhi Wenhua: Nonggeng Juan (Xia)* 云南物质文化：农耕卷 (下). Yunnan Jiaoyu Chubanshe, Kunming.

Yin, Shenping 尹申平, and Wang Xiaoqing 王小庆, 2007, Shaanxisheng Yichuanxian Longwangchan yizhi 陕西省宜川县龙王辿遗址. *Kaogu* 7:3–8.

Yoffee, Norman, 1991, Orienting collapse. In *The Collapse of Ancient States and Civilizations*, edited by Norman Yoffee and George L. Cowgill, pp. 1–19. The University of Arizona Press, Tucson.

————, 2004, *Myths of the Archaic State: Evolution of the Earliest Cities, States, and Civilizations*. Cambridge University Press, Cambridge.

Yoffee, Norman and George L. Cowgill (editors), 1991, *The Collapse of Ancient States and Civilizations*. The University of Arizona Press, Tucson.

Yoffee, Norman and Li Min 李旻, 2009, Wangquan, chengshi yu guojia: bijiao kaoguxue shiye zhongde zhongguo zaoqi chengshi 王权、城市与国际：比较考古学视野中的中国早期城市. In *Duowei Shiyu – Shang Wangchao yu Zhongguo Zaoqi Wenming Yanjiu* 多维视域 – 商王朝与中国早期文明研究, edited by Jing Zhichun 荆志淳, Tang Jigen 唐际根, and Takashima Ken-ichi 高嶋谦一, pp. 276–90. Kexue Chubanshe, Beijing.

Yu, Jincheng 郁金城, Li Chaorong 李超荣, Yang Xuelin 杨学林, and Li Jianhua 李建华, 1998, Beijing Zhuannian xinshiqi shidai zaoqi yizhi de faxian 北京转年新石器时代早期遗址的发现. *Beijing Wenbo* 3:color plates 2–4.

Yu, Weichao 俞伟超, 1993, Longshan wenhua yu Liangzhu wenhua shuaibian de aomi 龙山文化与良渚文化衰变的奥秘. In *Jinian Chengziya Yizhi Fajue 60 Zhounian Guoji Xueshu Taolunhui Wenji* 纪念城子崖遗址发掘 60 周年国际学术讨论会文集, edited by Zhang Xuehai 张学海, pp. 9–11. Qi Lu Shushe, Jinan.

Yu, Wei 于薇, 2010, Huai Han zhengzhi quyu de xingcheng yu Huaihe zuowei nanbei zhengzhi fenjiexian de qiyuan 淮汉政治区域的形成与淮河作为南北政治分界线的起源. *Gudai Wenming* 4(1):38–52.

Yuan, Guangkuo 袁广阔 and Zeng Xiaomin 曾晓敏, 2004, Lun Zhengzhou Shangcheng neicheng he waicheng de guanxi 论郑州商城内城和外城的关系. *Kaogu* 3:59–67.

Yuan, Jiarong, 2002, Rice and pottery 10,000 yrs. BP at Yuchanyan, Dao county, Hunan province. In *The Origins of Pottery and Agriculture*, edited by Yoshinori Yasuda, pp. 157–66. Roli Books, New Delhi.

Yuan, Jing, 2002, The formation and development of Chinese zooarchaeology: A preliminary review. *Archaeofauna* 11:205–12.

Yuan, Jing and Rod Campbell, 2008, Recent archaeometric research on "the origins of Chinese civilization." *Antiquity* 83:96–109.

Yuan, Jing and Rowan Flad, 2002, Pig domestication in ancient China. *Antiquity* 76:724–32.

————, 2003, Two issues concerning ancient domesticated horses in China. *Bulletin of the Museum of Far Eastern Antiquities* 75:110–26.

————, 2005, New zooarchaeological evidence for changes in Shang dynasty animal sacrifice. *Journal of Anthropological Archaeology* 24:252–70.

————, 2006, Research on early horse domestication in China. In *Equids in Time and Space*, edited by Marjan Mashkour, pp. 124–31. Oxbow Books, Oxford.

Yuan, Jing 袁靖 and Li Jun 李珺, 2010, Hebei Xushui Nanzhuangtou yizhi chutu dongwu yicun yanjiu baogao 河北徐水南庄头遗址出土动物遗存研究报告. *Kaogu Xuebao* 3:385–91.

Yuan, Jing 袁靖 and Yang Mengfei 杨梦菲, 2003, Shuilushang dongwu yicun yanjiu 水陆生动物遗存研究. In *Guilin Zengpiyan* 桂林甑皮岩, edited by Zhongguo Shehui Kexueyuan Kaogu Yuanjiusuo 中国社会科学院考古研究所, Guangxi Zhuangzu Zizhiqu Wenwu Gongzuodui 广西壮族自治区文物工作队, Guilin Zengpiyan Yizhi Bowuguan 桂林甑皮岩遗址博物馆, and Guilinshi Wenwu Gongzuodui 桂林市文物工作队, pp. 297–340. Wenwu Chubanshe, Beijing.

————, 2004, Dongwu yanjiu 动物研究. In *Kuahuqiao* 跨湖桥, edited by Zhejiangsheng Wenwu Kaogu Yanjiusuo 浙江省文物考古研究所 and Xiaoshan Bowuguan 萧山博物馆, pp. 241–69. Wenwu Chubanshe, Beijing.

————, in press, *Neimenggu Chifeng Xinglongwa yizhi chutu dongwu guge yanjiu baogao* 内蒙古赤峰兴隆洼遗址出土动物骨骼研究报告.

Yuan, Sixun 原思训, Chen Tiemei 陈铁梅, and Zhou Kunshu 周昆叔, 1992, Nanzhuangtou yizhi tan shisi niandai ceding yu wenhuaceng baofen fenxi 南庄头遗址炭十四年代测定与文化层孢粉分析. *Kaogu* 11:967–70.

Yue, Zhanwei 岳占伟 and Wang Xuerong 王学荣, 2007, Henan Anyangshi Xiaomintun Shangdai zhutong yizhi 2003–2004 nian de fajue 河南安阳市孝民屯商代铸铜遗址 2003－2004 年的发掘. *Kaogu* 1:14–25.

Zeder, Melinda A., Eve Emshwiller, Bruce D. Smith, and Daniel G. Bradley, 2006, Documenting domestication: The intersection of genetics and archaeology. *Trends in Genetics* 22(3):139–56.

Zhai, Shaodong, 2011, *Lithic production and early urbanism in China – A case study of the lithic production at the Neolithic Taosi site (C. 2500–1900 BCE)*. PhD dissertation, La Trobe University, Melbourne.

Zhang, Chi and Hsiao-chun Hung, 2008, The Neolithic of Southern China – Origin, development, and dispersal. *Asian Perspectives* 47(2):299–329.

Zhang, Chi 张驰, 2003, *Changjiang Zhongxiayou Diqu Shiqian Juluo Yanjiu* 长江中下游地区史前聚落研究. Wenwu Chubanshe, Beijing.

Zhang, Daihai 张岱海, 1984, Shanxi Xiangfen Taosi yizhi shouci faxian tongqi 山西襄汾陶寺遗址首次发现铜器. *Kaogu* 12:1069–71.

Zhang, Daihai 张岱海, Zhang Yanhuang 张彦煌, Gao Wei 高炜, and Xu Diankui 徐殿魁, 1989, Jinnan kaogu diaocha baogao 晋南考古调查报告. *Kaoguxue Jikan* 6:1–51.

Zhang, Deguang 张德光, 1956, Jinnan wu xian gudai renlei wenhua yizhi chubu diaocha jianbao 晋南五县古代人类文化遗址初步调查简报. *Wenwu Cankao Ziliao* 9:53–6.

Zhang, Guangming 张光明, Xu Longguo 徐龙国, Zhang Lianli 张连利, and Xu Zhiguang 许志光, 1997, Shandong Huantai xian Shijia yizhi Yueshi wenhua mugoujia jisi qiwukeng de fajue 山东桓台县史家遗址岳石文化木构架祭祀器物坑的发掘. *Kaogu* 11:1–18.

Zhang, H. C., Y. Z. Ma, B. Wunnemann, and H. J. Pachur, 2000, A Holocene climatic record from arid northwestern China. *Palaeogeography, Palaeoclimatology, Palaeoecology* 162:389–401.

Zhang, Heng 张恒 and Wang Haiming 王海明, 2005, Zhejiang Shengzhou Xiaohuangshan yizhi faxian xinshiqi shidai zaoqi yicun 浙江嵊州小黄山遗址发现新石器时代早期遗存. *Zhongguo Wenwubao*. 30 Sept.:1. Beijing.

Zhang, Jingguo 张敬国 (editor), 2006, *Lingjiatan Wenhua Yanjiu* 凌家滩文化研究. Wenwu Chubanshe, Beijing.

————, 2008, Anhuisheng Hanshanxian Lingjiatan yizhi diwuci fajue de xinfaxian 安徽省含山县凌家滩遗址第五次发掘的新发现. *Kaogu* 3:7–17.

Zhang, Juzhong, Xinghua Xiao, and Yun Kuen Lee, 2004, The early development of music: Analysis of the Jiahu bone flutes. *Antiquity* 78(302):769–78.

Zhang, Juzhong 张居中 and Wang Xiangkun 王象坤, 1998, Jiahu yu Pengtoushan daozuo wenhua bijiao yanjiu 贾湖彭头山稻作文化比较研究. *Nongye Kaogu* 农业考古 1:108–17.

Zhang, Juzhong 张居中 and Pan Weibin 潘伟彬, 2002, Henan Wuyang Jiahu yizhi 2001 nian chun fajue jianbao 河南舞阳贾湖遗址 2001 年春发掘简报. *Huaxia Kaogu* 2:14–30.

Zhang, Juzhong 张居中, Wang Xiangkun 王象坤, Cui Zongjun 崔宗钧, and Xu Wenhui 许文会, 1996, Yelun Zhongguo zaipeidao de qiyuan yu dongchuan 也论中国栽培稻的起源与东传. In *Zhongguo Zaipeidao Qiyuan yu Yanhua Yanjiu Zhuanji* 中国栽培稻起源与演化研究专集, edited by Wang Xiangkun 王象坤 and Sun Chuanqing 孙传清, pp. 14–21. Zhongguo Nongyedaxue Chubanshe, Beijing.

Zhang, Li 张莉 and Wang Jihuai 王吉怀, 2004, Anhui Mengchengxian Yuchisi yizhi 2003 niandu fajue de xinshouhuo 安徽蒙城县尉迟寺遗址 2003 年度发掘的新收获. *Kaogu* 3:3–6.

Zhang, Long 张龙, 2003, Guangxi Nanning Baozitou beiqiu yizhi de fajue 广西南宁豹子头贝丘遗址的发掘. *Kaogu* 10:22–34.

Zhang, Senshui, 2000, The Epipaleolithc in China. *Journal of East Asian Archaeology* 2(1–2):51–66.

Zhang, Senshui 张森水, 1990, Zhongguo beifang jiushiqi gongye de quyu jianjin yu wenhua jiaoliu 中国北方旧石器工业的区域渐进与文化交流. *Renleixue Xuebao* 9(4):322–33.

Zhang, Songlin 张松林 and Wu Qian 吴倩, 2010, Xinzheng Wangjinglou faxian: Erlitou wenhua he Erligang wenhua chengzhi 新郑望京楼发现:二里头文化和二里岗文化城址. *Zhongguo Wenwubao*. 28 Dec:4. Beijing.

Zhang, Songlin 张松林, Xin Yingjun 信应君, Hu Yayi 胡亚毅, and Yan Fuhai 闫付海, 2008,

Henan Xinzhengshi Tanghu yizhi Peiligang wenhua yicun fajue jianbao 河南新郑唐户遗址裴李岗文化遗存发掘简报. *Kaogu* 5:3–20.

Zhang, Tianen 张天恩, 2000, Guanzhong dongbu Xia shiqi wenhua yicun fenxi 关中东部夏时期文化遗存分析. *Wenbo* 3:3–10.

———, 2002, Tianshui chutu de shoumian tongpaishi ji youguan wenti 天水出土的兽面铜牌饰及有关问题. *Zhongyuan Wenwu* 1:43–6.

———, 2004, *Guanzhong Shangdai Wenhua Yanjiu* 关中商代文化研究. Wenwu Chubanshe, Beijing.

Zhang, Tianen 张天恩 and Xiao Qi 肖琦, 2003, Chuankouhe Qijia wenhua taoqi de xinshenshi 川口河齐家文化陶器的新审视. In *Zhongguo Shiqian Kaoguxue Yanjiu* 中国史前考古学研究, edited by Zhang Tinghao 张廷皓, pp. 361–7. Sanqin Chubanshe, Xi'an.

Zhang, Wenxu, 2002, The bi-peak-tubercle of rice, the character of ancient rice and the origin of cultivated rice. In *The Origins of Pottery and Agriculture*, edited by Yoshinori Yasuda, pp. 205–16. Roli Books, New Delhi.

Zhang, Wenxu 张文绪, 2000, Gansu Qingyang yizhi gu zaipeidao de yanjiu 甘肃庆阳遗址古栽培稻的研究. *Nongye Kaogu* 3:80–5.

Zhang, Xingyong 张兴永, 1987, Yunnan xinshiqi shidai de jiaxu 云南新石器时代的家畜. *Nongye Kaogu* 1:370–7.

Zhang, Xuqiu 张绪球, 1991, Shijiahe wenhua de taosupin 石家河文化的陶塑品. *Jianghan Kaogu* 3:55–60.

Zhang, Xuejun 张学君, 1995, Nanfang sichou zhilu shang de shiyan maoyi 南方丝绸之路上的食盐贸易. In *Gudai Xinan Sichou Zhilu Yanjiu* 古代西南丝绸之路研究, edited by Yuxiang 江玉祥 Jiang, pp. 140–50. Sichuan Daxue Chubanshe, Chengdu.

Zhang, Xuelian 张雪莲, Qiu Shihua 仇士华, Cai Lianzhen 蔡莲珍, Bo Guancheng 薄官成, Wang Jinxia 王金霞, and Zhong Jian 钟建, 2007, Xinzhai – Erlitou – Erligang wenhua kaogu niandai xulie de jianli yu wanshan 新砦 — 二里头 — 二里岗文化考古年代序列的建立与完善. *Kaogu* 8:74–89.

Zhang, Xuelian 张雪莲, Wang Jinxia 王金霞, Xian Ziqiang 冼自强, and Qiu Shihua 仇士华, 2003, Gurenlei shiwu jiegou yanjiu 古人类食物结构研究. *Kaogu* 2:62–75.

Zhang, Yingwen 张映文 and Lü Zhirong 吕智荣, 1988, Shaanxi Qingjianxian Lijiaya guchengzhi fajue jianbao 陕西清涧县李家崖古城址发掘简报. *Kaogu yu Wenwu* 1:47–56.

Zhang, Yushi 张玉石, Zhao Xinping 赵新平, and Qiao Liang 乔梁, 1999, Zhengzhou Xishan Yangshao shidai chengzhi de fajue 郑州西山仰韶时代城址的发掘. *Wenwu* 7:4–15.

Zhang, Zengqi 张增祺, 1998, *Jinning Shizhaishan* 晋宁石寨山. Yunnan Meishu Chubanshe, Kunming.

Zhang, Zhen 张震, 2009, Jiahu yizhi muzang chubu yanjiu – shilun Jiahu de shehui fengong yu fenhua 贾湖遗址墓葬初步研究—试论贾湖的社会分工与分化. *Huaxia Kaogu* 2:42–62.

Zhang, Zhiheng 张之恒, 1996, Liangzhu wenhua juluoqun yanjiu 良渚文化聚落群研究. In *Dongfang Wenming Zhiguang* 东方文明之光, edited by Xu Huping 徐湖平, pp. 238–44. Hainan Guoji Xinwen Chubanshe, Hainan.

Zhang, Zhongpei 张忠培, 1987, Qijia wenhua yanjiu (xia) 齐家文化研究（下）. *Kaogu Xuebao* 2:153–75.

———, 2000, Zhongguo gudai wenming xingcheng de kaoguxue yanjiu 中国古代文明形成的考古学研究. *Gugong Bowuyuan Yuankan* 2:5–27.

Zhao, Chaohong 赵朝洪, 2006, Beijingshi Mentougouqu Donghulin shiqian yizhi 北京市门头沟区东胡林史前遗址. *Kaogu* 7:3–8.

Zhao, Chunqing 赵春青, 1995, Jiangzhai yiqi mudi zaitan 姜寨一期墓地再谈. *Huaxia Kaogu* 4:26–46.

———, 1998, Yetan Jiangzhai yiqi cunluozhong de fangwu yu renkou 也谈姜寨一期村落的房屋与人口. *Kaogu yu Wenwu* 5:49–55.

———, 2004, Xinmi Xinzhai chengzhi yu Xia Qi zhi ju 新密新砦城址与夏启之居. *Zhongyuan Wenwu* 3:12–16.

———, 2009, Xinzhai juluo kaogu de shijian yu fangfa 新砦聚落考古的实践与方法. *Kaogu* 2:48–54.

Zhao, Congcang 赵丛苍 (editor), 2006, *Chengyang Qingtongqi* 城洋青铜器. Kexue Chubanshe, Beijing.

Zhao, Dianzeng, 1996, The sacrificial pits at Sanxingdui. In *Mysteries of Ancient China: New Discoveries from the Early Dynasties*, edited by Jessica Rawson, pp. 232–9. George Braziller, New York.

Zhao, Hui 赵辉, 1999, Liangzhu wenhua de ruogan teshuxing 良渚文化的若干特殊性. In *Liangzhu Wenhua Yanjiu* 良渚文化研究, edited by Zhejiangsheng Wenwu Kaogu Yanjiusuo 浙江省文物考古研究所, pp. 104–19. Kexue Chubanshe, Beijing.

Zhao, Jianlong 赵建龙, 1990, Cong Gaositou dafangji kan Dadiwan daxing fangji de hanyi 从高寺头大房基看大地湾大型房基的含义. *Xibei Shidi* 3:27, 64–8.

———, 2003, Gansu Qin'an Dadiwan yizhi Yangshao wenhua zaoqi juluo fajue jianbao 甘肃秦安大地湾遗址仰韶文化早期聚落发掘简报. *Kaogu* 6:19–31.

Zhao, Songqiao, 1994, *Geography of China: Environment, Resources, Population and Development*. John Wiley & Sons, New York.

Zhao, Tuanjie 赵团结, and Gai Junyi 盖钧镒, 2004, Zaipei dadou qiyuan yu yanhua yanjiu jinzhan 栽培大豆起源与演化研究进展. *Zhongguo Nongye Kexue* 37(7):945–62.

Zhao, Xitao, 1993, *Holocene Coastal Evolution and Sea-level Changes in China*. Haiyang Press, Beijing.

Zhao, Xitao 赵希涛, 1984, *Zhongguo Haiyang Yanbian Yanjiu* 中国海洋演变研究. Fujian Kexue Jishu Chubanshe, Fuzhou.

———, 1996 (editor), *Zhongguo Haimian Bianhua* 中国海面变化. Shandong Kexue Jishu Chubanshe, Jinan.

Zhao, Yu'an 赵玉安, 1992, Gongyi shi Wuluo he liuyu Peiligang wenhua yicun diaocha 巩义市坞罗河流域裴李岗文化遗存调查. *Zhongyuan Wenwu* 4:1–7.

Zhao, Zhijun, 1998, The middle Yangtze region in China is one place where rice was domesticated: Phytolith evidence from the Diaotonghuan cave, northern Jiangxi. *Antiquity* 72:885–97.

———, 2009a, Eastward spread of wheat into China – new data and new issues. *Chinese Archaeology* 9:1–9.

Zhao, Zhijun 赵志军, 2004a, Cong Xinglonggou yizhi fuxuan jieguo tan Zhongguo beifang hanzuo nongye qiyuan wenti 从兴隆沟遗址浮选结果谈中国北方旱作农业起源问题. In *Dongya Kaogu* 东亚考古, edited by Nanjing Shifan Daxue Wenboxi 南京师范大学文博系, pp. 188–99. Wenwu Chubanshe, Beijing.

———, 2004b, Liangchengzhen yu Jiaochangpu Longshan shidai nongye shengchan tedian de duibi 两城镇与教场铺龙山时代农业生产特点的对比分析. In *Dongfang Kaogu (Di 1 Ji)* 东方考古(第1集), edited by Shandong Daxue Dongfang Kaogu Yanjiu Zhongxin 山东大学东方考古研究中心, pp. 210–16. Kexue Chubanshe, Beijing.

———, 2004c, Qinghai Huzhu Fengtai Kayue wenhua yizhi fuxuan jieguo fenxi baogao 青海互助丰台卡约文化遗址浮选结果分析报告. *Kaogu yu Wenwu* 2(85–91).

———, 2004d, Zhiwu kaoguxue de tianye gongzuo fangfa – fuxuanfa 植物考古学的田野工作方法 — 浮选法. *Kaogu* 3:80–7.

———, 2005a, Youguan Zhongguo Nongye qiyuan de xinziliao he xinsikao 有关中国农业起源的新资料和新思考. In *Xinshiji de Zhongguo Kaoguxue – Wang Zhongshu Xiansheng Bashi Huadan Jinian Lunwenji* 新世纪的中国考古学 — 王仲殊先生八十华诞纪念论文集, edited by Zhongguo Shehui Kexueyuan Kaogu Yanjiusuo 中国社会科学院考古研究所, pp. 86–101. Kexue Chubanshe, Beijing.

———, 2005b, Zhiwu kaoguxue jiqi xinjinzhan 植物考古学及其新进展. *Kaogu* 7:42–9.

———, 2006, Haidai diqu nanbu xinshiqi shidai wanqi de daohan hunzuo nongye jingji 海岱地区南部新石器时代晚期的稻旱混作农业经济. In *Dongfang Kaogu (Di 3 Ji)* 东方考古(第3集), edited by Shandong Daxue Dongfa Kaogu Yanjiu Zhongxin 山东大学东方考古研究中心, pp. 253–8. Kexue Chubanshe, Beijing.

———, 2009b, Gonyuanqian 2500 – gongyuanqian 1500 nian zhongyuan diqu nongye jingji yanjiu 公元前 2500 — 公元前 1500 年中原地区农业经济研究. In *Zhonghua Wenming Tanyuan Gongcheng Wenji: Jishu yu Jingji Juan (1)* 中华文明探源工程文集: 技术与经济卷 (1), edited by Kejibu Shehui Fazhan Kejisi 科技部社会发展科技司 and Guojia Wenwujiu yu Shehui Wenwusi 国家文物局与社会文物司, pp. 123–35. Kexue Chubanshe, Beijing.

Zhao, Zhijun 赵志军, Lu Liedan 吕烈丹, and Fu Xianguo 傅宪国, 2005, Guangxi Yongningxian Dingsishan yizhi chutu zhiguishi de fenxi yu yanjiu 广西邕宁县顶蛳山遗址出土植硅石的分析与研究. *Kaogu* 11:76–84.

Zhao, Zhijun 赵志军 and Xu Lianggao 徐良高, 2004, Zhouyuan yizhi (Wangjiazui didian) changshixing fuxuan de jieguo ji chubu fenxi 周原遗址 (王家嘴地点) 尝试性浮选的结果及初步分析. *Wenwu* 10:89–96.

Zhao, Zhijun 赵志军 and Zhang Juzhong 张居中, 2009, Jiahu yizhi 2001 niandu fuxuan jieguo fenxi baogao 贾湖遗址 2001 年度浮选结果分析报告. *Kaogu* 8:84–93.

Zhejiangsheng Wenwu Kaogu Yanjiusuo, 浙江省文物考古研究所 (editor), 1999, *Liangzhu Wenhua Yanjiu – Jinian Liangzhu Wenhua Faxian Liushi Zhounian Guoji Xueshu Taolunhui Wenji* 良渚文化研究 — 纪念良渚文化发现六十周年国际学术讨论会文集. Kexue Chubanshe, Beijing.

————, 2003, *Hemudu* 河姆渡. Wenwu Chubanshe, Beijing.

————, 2005a, *Liangzhu Yizhiqun* 良渚遗址群. Wenwu Chubanshe, Beijing.

————, 2005b, *Fanshan* 反山. Wenwu Chubanshe, Beijing.

Zhejiangsheng and Xiaoshan (Zhejiangsheng Wenwu Kaogu Yanjiusuo 浙江省文物考古研究所 and Xiaoshan Bowuguan 萧山博物馆) (editors), 2004, *Kuahuqiao* 跨湖桥. Wenwu Chubanshe, Beijing

Zheng, Jianming 郑建明, Chen Yuanfu 陈元甫, Shen Yueming 沈岳明, Chen Yun 陈云, Zhu Jianming 朱建明, and Yu Youliang 俞友良, 2011, Zhejiang Dongtiaoxi zhongyou Shangdai yuanshici yaozhiqun 浙江东苕溪中游商代原始瓷窑址群. *Kaogu* 7:3–8.

Zheng, Naiwu 郑乃武, 1984, 1979 nian Peiligang yizhi fajue baogao 1979 年裴李岗遗址发掘报告. *Kaogu Xuebao* 1:23–51.

————, 1986, 1984 nian Henan Gongxian kaogu diaocha yu shijue 1984 年河南巩县考古调查与试掘. *Kaogu* 3:193–6.

Zheng, Yunfei, Sun Guoping, Qin Ling, Li Chunhai, Wu Xiaohong, and Chen Xugao, 2009, Rice fields and modes of rice cultivation between 5000 and 2500 BC in east China. *Journal of Archaeological Science* 36:2609–16.

Zheng, Yunfei 郑云飞, Sun Guoping 孙国平, and Chen Xugao 陈旭高, 2007, 7000 nian qian kaogu yizhi chutu daogu de xiaosuizhou tezheng 7000 年前考古遗址出土稻谷的小穗轴特征. *Kexue Tongbao* 52(9):1037–41.

Zheng, Yunfei 郑云飞 and Jiang Leping 蒋乐平, 2007, Shangshan yizhi chutu de gudao yicun jiqi yiyi 上山遗址出土的古稻遗存及其意义. *Kaogu* 9:19–25.

Zheng, Zhou and Qianyu Li, 2000, Vegetation, climate, and sea level in the past 55,000 years, Hanjiang Delta, Southeastern China. *Quaternary Research* 53:330–40.

Zhengzhoushi Wenwu Kaogu Yanjiusuo, 郑州市文物考古研究所 (editor), 2001, *Zhengzhou Dahecun* 郑州大河村. Kexue Chubanshe, Beijing.

————, 2004, *Zhengzhou Dashigu* 郑州大师姑. Kexue Chubanshe, Beijing.

Zhongguo Kexueyuan Kaogu Yanjiusuo, 中国科学院考古研究所 (editor), 1959, *Miaodigou yu Sunliqiao* 庙底沟与三里桥. Kexue Chubanshe, Beijing.

————, 1963, *Xi'an Banpo* 西安半坡. Wenwu Chubanshe, Beijing.

Zhongguo Kexueyuan Kaogu Yanjiusuo Neimenggu Gongzuodui 中国科学院考古研究所内蒙古工作队, 1974, Chifeng Yaowangmiao, Xiajiadian yizhi shijue baogao 赤峰药王庙、夏家店遗址试掘报告. *Kaogu Xuebao* 1:115–48, 198–211.

Zhongguo Shehui Kexueyuan Kaogu Yanjiusuo, 中国社会科学院考古研究所 (editor), 1980, *Yinxu Fuhaomu* 殷墟妇好墓. Wenwu Chubanshe, Beijing.

————, 1983, *Baoji Beishouling* 宝鸡北首岭. Wenwu Chubanshe, Beijing.

————, 1984, *Xinzhongguo de Kaogu Faxian he Yanjiu* 新中国的考古发现和研究. Wenwu Chubanshe, Beijing.

————, 1987, *Yinxu Fajue Baogao* 殷墟发掘报告. Wenwu Chubanshe, Beijing.

————, 1991, *Zhongguo Kaoguxue Zhong Tan Shisi Niandai Shujuji* 中国考古学中碳十四年代数据集. Wenwu Chubanshe, Beijing.

————, 1994a, *Lintong Baijiacun* 临潼白家村. Bashu Chubanshe, Chengdu.

————, 1994b, *Yinxu de faxian yu yanjiu* 殷墟的发现与研究. Kexue Chubanshe, Beijing.

————, 1995, *Erlitou Taoqi Jicui* 二里头陶器集粹. Zhongguo Shehui Kexue Chubanshe, Beijing.

————, 1996, *Dadianzi* 大甸子. Kexue Chubanshe, Beijing.

————, 1999a, *Shizhaocun yu Xishanping* 师赵村与西山坪. Zhongguo Dabaikequanshu Chubanshe, Beijing.

————, 1999b, *Yanshi Erlitou* 偃师二里头. Zhongguo Dabaikequanshu Chubanshe, Beijing.

————, 2001, *Mengcheng Yuchisi* 蒙城尉迟寺. Kexue Chubanshe, Beijing.

————, 2003a, *Guilin Zengpiyan* 桂林甑皮岩. Wenwu Chubanshe, Beijing.

————, 2003b, *Zhongguo Kaoguxue: Xia Shang Juan* 中国考古学: 夏商卷. Zhongguo Shehui Kexue Chubanshe, Beijing.

————, 2004, *Zhongguo Kaoguxue: Liang Zhou Juan* 中国考古学: 两周卷. Zhongguo Shehui Kexue Chubanshe, Beijing.

————, 2005, *Tengzhou Qianzhangda Mudi* 滕州前掌大墓地. Wenwu Chubanshe, Beijing.

————, 2007, *Anyang Yinxu Huayuanzhuang Dongdi Shangdai Muzang* 安阳殷墟花园庄东地商代墓葬. Kexue Chubanshe, Beijing.

————, 2010, *Zhongguo Kaoguxue: Xinshiqi Juan* 中国考古学: 新石器卷. Zhongguo Shehui Kexue Chubanshe, Beijing.

Zhongguo Shehui Kexueyuan Gansu (Zhongguo Shehui Kexueyuan Kaogu Yanjiusuo Gansu Gongzuodui, 中国社会科学院考古研究所甘肃工作队), 1974, Gansu Yongjing Dahezhuang yizhi fajue baogao 甘肃永靖大何庄遗址发掘报告. *Kaogu Xuebao* 2:29–61.

Zhongguo Shehui Kexueyuan and Henansheng (Zhongguo Shehui Kexueyuan Kaogu Yanjiusuo, 中国社会科学院考古研究所, and Henansheng Wenwu Kaogu Yanjiusuo 河南省文物考古研究所) (editors), 2010, *Lingbao Xipo Mudi 灵宝西坡墓地*. Wenwu Chubanshe, Beijing.

Zhongguo Shehui Kexueyuan Kaogu Yanjiusuo 中国社会科学院考古研究所, Zhongguo Lishi Bowuguan 中国历史博物馆, and Shanxisheng Wenwu Gongzuo Weiyuanhui 山西省文物工作委员会 (editors), 1988, *Xiaxian Dongxiafeng 夏县东下冯*. Wenwu Chubanshe, Beijing.

Zhongguo Zhupinzhongzhi Bianweihui, 中国猪品种志编委会 (editor), 1986, *Zhongguo Zhupinzhongzhi 中国猪品种志编委会*. Shanghai Keji Chubanshe, Shanghai.

Zhou, Benxiong 周本雄, 1981, Hebei Wu'an Cishan yizhi de dongwu guhai 河北武安磁山遗址的动物骨骸. *Kaogu Xuebao* 3:339–47.

————, 1984, Zhongguo xinshiqi shidai de jiaxu 中国新石器时代的家畜. In *Xin Zhongguo de Kaogu Faxian he Yanjiu 新中国的考古发现和研究*, edited by Zhongguo Shehui Kexueyuan Kaogu Yanjiusuo 中国社会科学院考古研究所, pp. 196–210. Wenwu Chubanshe, Beijing.

————, 1992, Hebeisheng Xushuixian Nanzhuangtou yizhi de dongwu yihai 河北省徐水现南庄头遗址的动物遗骸 *Kaogu* 11:966–7.

————, 1999, Shizhaocun yu Xishanping yizhi de dongwu yicun 师赵村与西山坪的动物遗存. In *Shizhaocun yu Xishanping 师赵村与西山坪*, edited by Zhongguo Shehui Kexueyuan kaogu yanjiusuo 中国社会科学院考古研究所, pp. 335–9. Zhongguo Dabaike Quanshu Chubanshe, Beijing.

Zhou, Guoxing 周国兴 and You Yuzhu 尤玉柱, 1972, Beijing Donghulincun de xinshiqi shidai muzang 北京东胡林的新石器时代墓葬. *Kaogu* 6:12–15.

Zhou, Runken 周润星, Qian Jun 钱埈, Xiao Xianggong 肖向红, and Zhang Yongquan 张永泉, 2010, Jiangsu Zhangjiagangshi Dongshancun xinshiqi shidai yizhi 江苏张家港市东山村新石器时代遗址. *Kaogu* 8:3–12.

Zhou, S. Z., F. H. Chen, B. T. Pan, J. X. Cao, J. J. Li, and Edward Derbyshire, 1991, Environmental change during the Holocene in western China on a millennial timescale. *The Holocene* 1(2):151–6.

Zhou, Weijian, Xuefeng Yu, Timothy Jull, G. Burr, J. Y. Xiao, Xuefeng Lu, and Feng Xian, 2004, High-resolution evidence from southern China of an early Holocene optimum and a mid-Holocene dry event during the past 18,000 years. *Quaternary Research* 62:39–48.

Zhu, Fenghan 朱凤瀚, 2004, *Shang Zhou Jiazu Xingtai Yanjiu 商周家族形态研究*. Tianjin Guji Chubanshe, Tianjin.

Zhu, Guoping 朱国平, 1996, Liangzhu wenhua quxiang fenxi 良渚文化去向分析. In *Dongfang Wenming Zhiguang 东方文明之光*, edited by Xu Huping 徐湖平, pp. 285–90. Hainan Guoji Xinwen Chubanshe, Hainan.

Zhu, Hong 朱泓, 1998, Donghuishan mudi rengu de yanjiu 东灰山墓地人骨的研究. In *Minle Donghuishan Kaogu 民乐东灰山考古*, edited by Gansusheng wenwu kaogu yanjiusuo 甘肃省文物考古研究所, pp. 172–83. Kexue Chubanshe, Beijing.

Zhu, Jian 朱剑, Fang Hui 方辉, Fan Changsheng 樊昌生, Zhou Guangming 周广明, and Wang Changsui 王昌燧, 2008, Daxinzhuang yizhi chutu yuanshici de INAA yanjiu 大辛庄遗址出土原始瓷的 INAA 研究. In *Dongfang Kaogu (Di 5 Ji) 东方考古 (第5集)*, edited by Shandong Daxue Dongfang Kaogu Yanjiu Zhongxin 山东大学东方考古研究中心, pp. 139–44. Kexue Chubanshe, Beijing.

Zhu, Jian 朱剑, Wang Changsui 王昌燧, Wang Yan 王妍, Mao Zhenwei 毛振伟, Zhou Guangming 周广明, Fan Changsheng 樊昌生, Zeng Xiaomin 曾晓敏, Shen Yueming 沈岳明, and Gong Xicheng 宫希成, 2005, Shang Zhou yuanshici chandi de zaifenxi 商周原始瓷产地的再分析. In *Wucheng: 1973–2002 Nian Kaogu Fajue Baogao 吴城: 1973–2002 年发掘报告*, edited by Jiangxisheng Wenwu Kaogu Yanjiusuo 江西省文物考古研究所 and Zhangshushi Bowuguan 樟树市博物馆, pp. 518–24. Kexue Chubanshe, Beijing.

Zhu, Yaolun 朱尧伦, 2003, "Xiaxiaozheng" fenju yuyi zhushi 〈〈夏小正〉〉分句语译注释. *Nongye Kaogu* 3:266–70.

Zhushchikhovskaya, Irina, 1997, On early pottery-making in the Russian Far East. *Asian Perspectives* 36(2):159–74.

————, 2005, *Prehistoric Pottery-Making of the Russian Far East*. BAR, Oxford.

Zong, Guanfu 宗冠福 and Huang Xueshi 黄学诗, 1985, Yunnan Baoshan Pupiao quanxinshi zaoqi wenhua yiwu ji buru dongwu de yicun 云南保山蒲缥全新世早期文化遗物及哺乳动物的遗存. *Shiqian Yanjiu* 4:46–50.

Zong, Y., Z. Chen, J. B. Innes, C. Chen, Z. Wang, and H. Wang, 2007, Fire and flood management of coastal swamp enabled first rice paddy cultivation in east China. *Nature* 449(27):459–62.

Zou, Heng 邹衡, 1998, Zongshu Zaoshang Bodu zhi diwang 综述早商亳都之地望. In *Zhongguo Shang Wenhua Guoji Xueshu Taolunhui Lunwenji* 中国商文化国际学术讨论会论文集, edited by Zhongguo Shehui Kexueyuan Kaogu Yanjiusuo 中国社会科学院考古研究所, pp. 85–7. Zhongguo Dabaikequanshu Chubanshe, Beijing.

Zou, Houben 邹厚本, Gu Jianxiang 谷建祥, Li Minchang 李民昌, Tang Linghua 汤陵华, Ding Jinlong 丁金龙, and Yao Qinde 姚勤德, 2000, Jiangsu Caoxieshan Majiabang wenhua shuitian de faxian 江苏草鞋山马家浜文化水田的发现. In *Daozuo Taoqi he Dushi de Qiyuan* 稻作陶器和都市的起源, edited by Yan Wenming 严文明 and Yasuda Yoshinori 安田喜宪, pp. 97–113. Wenwu Chubanshe, Beijing.

Zou, Yilin 邹逸麟, 1990, *Qiangu Huanghe* 千古黄河. Zhonghua Shuju, Hong Kong.

INDEX

Made in the USA
Lexington, KY
19 April 2018